the Unofficial Guide® to Golf Vacations in the Eastern U.S.

1st Edition

Also available from IDG Books Worldwide:

the Unofficial Guide® to Golf Vacations in the Eastern U.S.

1st Edition

Joseph Mark Passov
with C. H. Conroy

Every effort has been made to ensure the accuracy of information throughout this book. Bear in mind, however, that prices, schedules, etc., are constantly changing. Readers should always verify information before making final plans.

IDG Books Worldwide, Inc.
An International Data Group Company
919 E. Hillsdale Blvd., Suite 400
Foster City, CA 94404

Produced by Menasha Ridge Press

UNOFFICIAL GUIDE is a registered trademark of IDG Books Worldwide, Inc.

ISBN 0-02-863404-7

ISSN 1523-0619

Manufactured in the United States of America

10 9 8 7 6 5 4 3 2 1

Contents

List of Maps

Acknowledgments

This book would not have been possible without the tireless efforts of my research and writing partner, C. H. Conroy. In addition, I must thank several other individuals who lent their guidance and expertise. I am indebted to Dan Gleason, "America's guest," for his insightful contributions to the Charleston and Myrtle Beach chapters. A tip of the hat as well to Ron Crowley for sharing his thoughts on the New England section.

Special thanks go to Steve Eubanks for his often humorous reminiscences of golf travel in Alabama and Georgia and to Reid Nelson, the "PR superstar," for his lively anecdotes on Charleston and Mississippi. Also helping out in a big way on the Mississippi chapter was my brother-in-law of one month, Richard Edelman. And I would be remiss if I failed to acknowledge the support offered by Mark Brown, one of golf's great purists, for his assistance with the Hilton Head chapter. Finally, a giant thank-you to the gang at Golf Marketing Services, Dave Richards, and Kevin Frisch, and also to Michael Stewart, who have all forgotten more about golf in Michigan and Wisconsin than I'll ever know.

Last, but not least, I have to thank Bob Sehlinger, Molly Burns Merkle, and Georgia Goff for their inexhaustible patience and encouragement. Thanks as well to Laura Poole and Rachel Pearce Anderson for their copyediting and proofreading skills, respectively.

Introduction

About This Guide

HOW COME "UNOFFICIAL"?

Let's be frank: There are dozens of guidebooks available on where to play golf in the United States. Few (if any) however, tell you anything more than the nuts and bolts of each course—par, yardage, and so on—plus an overly simplistic description of the layout that could have been (and probably was) written by someone at the course's public relations department.

In this "unofficial" guide, the authors and researchers have provided not just the facts but also their opinions and analysis as to the merits (or lack thereof) of each course. We also provided recommendations on resort hotels, restaurants, 19th Holes, and nearby activities for non-golfers. None of the descriptions, comments, or insider tips contained in this book have been reviewed, edited, or in any way approved by the golf courses and resorts profiled.

In this book, we'll tell you which courses suffer from bloated egos, the ones that simply aren't worth the money they charge. By the same token, we'll reveal hidden gems, or uncover destinations that are treasure troves of value-oriented golf experiences. If a course is plagued by slow play, poor design, or sloppy conditioning, we'll say so. If there's a region blessed with golf but there's nowhere to eat and nothing else to do, we'll say that as well. But we'll also point out why certain courses that cost a hundred dollars or more to play are still worth your money and certain resorts that demand stiff tariffs are worth your time. There are thousands of golf vacation opportunities out there. Our job is to help you identify the very best—or at least the right ones for you and your budget.

CREATING A GUIDEBOOK

The problem with most golf or travel guidebooks is that they don't *guide*. Many give you all the requisite facts and figures, but leave you out in the cold when it comes to providing any real direction. You're given a phone number and an address and perhaps a brief description of what type of course it is, but there's no honest information that can actually influences your purchase decision. You may as well pick up a golf phone book for all the good these types of guides do you.

On the other hand, there are one or two more ambitious guides on the market that at least attempt to offer some opinions and subjectivity regarding the quality of a particular golf course. One such guide features comments by readers about courses in their region. The problem with this approach is that readers frequently disagree. Thus, the purchaser of the guidebook is back to square one—he or she doesn't know whether to believe reviewer A or reviewer B, and in fact, we don't even know the first thing about reviewers A and B. Are they well-traveled? Good golfers? Inherently stingy? We simply don't know, so it's hard to trust their opinions.

HOW UNOFFICIAL GUIDES ARE DIFFERENT

With any restaurant, movie, or wine review, there is a special bond between author and reader. The reader may take action based on what the author has to say, whether or not the reader agrees or disagrees with the reviewer's assessment. For this to happen, the reviewer must demonstrate some expertise on the subject. In other words, he ought to know his subject cold. With respect to a golf guide, he must be able to distill the dizzying array of golf vacation alternatives into some logical, easy-to-act-on choices.

The co-authors of *The Unofficial Guide to Golf Vacations in the Eastern U.S.* have played, separately or together, more than 1,000 courses in 43 states and 22 countries. They have played, evaluated, and reviewed some of the top-ranked, most exclusive private clubs in the world and also played some of the cheapest, most grass-poor municipal courses in America. They've also putted out at many of the courses in golf that fall somewhere in between. In addition, they've sampled the hospitality at more than half the world's top-ranked golf resorts but have also basked in the simple, unadorned comforts of dozens of Hampton, Days, Red Roof, La Quinta, and Quality Inns as well. Joe Passov has written for, contributed to, or edited nearly every major golf/travel publication in the United States and several in Europe.

In areas where we lacked sufficient expertise or in spots where we hadn't traveled recently, we consulted similarly independent, well-traveled experts, who were intimately acquainted with their particular regions. All of this "expert" advice in the form of evaluations and recommendations makes up the meatiest portion of the guide: What the best golf destinations are and why.

A Great Golf Vacation Includes Much, Much More Than Great Golf

Although there are some golfers—the golf/eat/sleep/golf type—whose only concern is how many holes they can pack into each day, the majority of golf travelers are looking for a vacation that is more multidimensional. We fall into the latter category. Sure, golf is still the cornerstone of our vacations, but we recognize that contrary to popular belief, there is more to life than golf. We may be golf fanatics, but we are well-rounded golf fanatics.

There are many factors to consider in planning a full golf vacation. First and foremost are the golf courses themselves. You'll no doubt want to pick a destination that offers a variety of quality golf courses to satisfy your "linksy" appetite. Taking a golf vacation composed of mediocre golf courses is like visiting Paris when the Louvre is closed—it's just not worth the trip. But once the last putt drops on the 18th hole and you've finished toasting your round at the 19th hole, you will encounter the factors that can readily separate a mundane golf vacation from one you will never forget. That is where this book comes into play.

Are you bringing the kids along or a spouse who doesn't play too well or too often? You probably want to avoid destinations or resorts that feature nothing but "championship" courses. Are outside activities and first-class resorts of equal magnitude with the golf experience? You may want to skip Alabama's Robert Trent Jones Golf Trail and head to Orlando, Hilton Head, or Myrtle Beach. Is playing exceptional golf courses for bargain-basement prices the clear number one on your list? The Robert Trent Jones Golf Trail is the way to go. You want nightlife, T-shirt shops, and a supermarket of golf? Try Myrtle Beach in South Carolina. You want upscale, low-key, and a gourmet shop of golf? Try Hilton Head in South Carolina.

Do you want a hotel or villa accommodations? Again, for some, this is a personal preference issue. However, if you're traveling with family and you want to buy groceries and eat in, it's probably more cost-effective to go with a villa or vacation home. Likewise, if you're with a group of three or more like-minded individuals and you want to maximize the "bonding" experience, the villa route may likewise be your best bet. If room-service pampering is more your style, opt for a hotel.

Is your final destination a specific resort or a general destination known for its golf? If you're looking for sheer variety of playing experiences, you probably don't want to be confined to just one resort. However, if you want to play a certain "trophy" course at a good price, you may find yourself opting for a package deal at a top resort, which lowers the price of your golf and increases the likelihood of not only getting to play the course at all but getting to play it when you want to.

If you do have the financial wherewithal to play a steady diet of "trophy" courses, then don't mess around with the second-tier courses. But if you're Joe Average who happens to be passionate about the game, perhaps limit your "trophy course" outings to one or two (consult the "must-play" selections in the "Once You're There" section in each "Overview"), then fill in your vacation by playing some Sampler courses, that is, the "best of the rest" that offer good value for your money.

This book strives to provide comprehensive assistance for planning your golf vacation—from soup to nuts, as they say. We have thus identified those areas east of the Mississippi that offer all the key elements integral to a well-rounded golf vacation. As you read, you may find that we omitted some areas that do offer fine golfing. While it may be true that these areas have fine *golf courses,* they also lack some critical aspect of a *golf vacation.* No doubt that there are isolated exceptions to the above statement, and we'll mention them here. In New Jersey, we recommend the Seaview Marriott Resort in Absecon, with its two vintage championship layouts, and the Great Gorge Golf Reserve in McAfee, which boasts no fewer than four fine courses.

In Pennsylvania, we like various resorts in the Poconos for a nice weekend getaway, along with the venerable Hershey Resort west of Philadelphia, with its three excellent courses. One of them, the West, hosted the 1940 PGA Championship, when Byron Nelson edged Sam Snead one-up to win the title. Nearby, the chocolate factory tour and amusement park are two of the region's top family attractions.

Several noteworthy resorts dot the New York landscape, especially in the Catskills and Adirondacks, including the famous "Monster" Course at the Concord and the Leatherstocking Course at the Otesaga, near the Baseball Hall of Fame in Cooperstown. Nevertheless, the best public-access course in the state is a municipal layout, the Black Course at Bethpage State Park on Long Island, which will host the 2002 U.S. Open. It's so busy that it's often as hard to get on as a private course, but there aren't many U.S. Open courses you can play for under $25.

Illinois, Ohio, and Indiana all have occasional wonderful resorts, notably Illinois's Eagle Ridge and Indiana's French Lick (home to Larry Bird), but for pure value and variety in public golf, Chicago and its surrounds are hard to beat. Now if they could just do something about the weather.

There is no doubt that the main focus of this book are the golf courses themselves. However, we have also attempted to provide you valuable information on all the other aspects we just touched on that round out your golf vacation.

Accommodations We have identified a smorgasbord of hotels and resorts, at a variety of price tags. The majority of our attention is directed to each area's premier resorts. As you peruse this guide, you will see that some resorts have much more detail than others. These are the resorts that warrant the most attention since they are the ones that have been consistently awarded the hospitality industry's top honors because the resort offers a great golf experience as well as superior rooms, amenities, beautiful settings, and dining options. Not all resorts have the same off-course activities, but the common denominator is that they have more than enough to keep you busy. Or not so busy—relaxing poolside or devouring novel upon novel is always an acceptable option.

Regardless of what peaks your interest, these resorts deserve the bulk of your focus, if you can afford the price tag, for while they offer the broadest range of vacation options, they also demand the highest entry fee and unfortunately, it is rare to find a bargain in resort accommodations. The rates are set in advance for the season, and you won't find many special rates for weekday travel. In fact, you're more likely to get a good deal if you stay for an entire week, since many resorts offer weekly rates that are more reasonable and offer some savings from the nightly rate. Vacationing during a shoulder season can also defray the costs of a resort stay. Just prior to and immediately following high season, when the weather is usually quite pleasant, if a little less predictable, rates can drop dramatically. Beginning on page 6, we offer a chart that gives a comprehensive star rating for the major resorts. For more details, see the individual resort listings within the area's chapter.

If budget is a concern, we have also included a number of moderately priced resorts and hotels that are more than respectable. You'll also note that we have included two to four examples in each chapter of "budget-oriented" properties. We selected these on the basis of recommendations locals and wherever we could we listed properties which were recently renovated.

For those looking for lodging that can accommodate a group or a family, we have also included information on villas, condos, and homes, when available. It should be noted that if you are looking for one of these group-type options, there are certain regions that offer more choices than others. For instance, Myrtle Beach is filled with so many high-rise hotels that it almost gives Manhattan a run for its money. At the same time, however, there are only a few villas available. On the other hand, Hilton Head is chock-full of these larger accommodations even though there are only a handful of quality resorts. The long and short of it is that each region offers variety, and once you decide the accommodation that best suites your travel style and budget, you can choose from a selection of options.

Dining In the dining section, we identified restaurants that serve up a wide array of culinary choices, at a wide array of prices. You will find some hole-in-the-wall, off-beat, paper napkin, down-home, thumb licking, plastic silverware-style restaurants alongside the four-star, cloth napkin, fine china, sterling and crystal, wine steward-style ones. The common demnominator is good food, and each of these restaurants has earned the regard of our taste buds with consistently high-quality menus. Along with our own experiences, we picked the brains of local experts to find the insider's favorites.

Activities Can you imagine traveling to Chicago and skipping a chance to see Wrigley Field or heading to Philadelphia and not seeing the Liberty Bell? And to be be fair, you may be traveling with folks who are not quite as fanatical about playing golf every waking minute as you are, so a typical golf vacation often needs to include side trips to swimming pools, running trails, or local museums. In the activity section, we list some non-golf entertainment, both at the resorts themselves and within about an hour's drive of base camp, that will enhance your stay in the area.

19th Holes In the 19th Holes sections, we selected those post-round spots that are ideal for toasting your day on the links. Some are located smack dab at the golf course itself, while others are farther afield—though no less inviting. No matter which one appeals to you, we included those that offer good drink selections, an inviting atmosphere, and a special touch or view that made them stand out. They are our picks for grabbing a cold one, double checking the scorecard, settling a bet, and most importantly, enjoying the camaraderie of your golfing buddies.

Resort Ratings

Pinehurst, North Carolina

Foxfire Resort & Country Club	Foxfire Village	★★★
Mid Pines Inn & Golf Club	Southern Pines	★★★★
Pine Needles Lodge & Golf Club	Southern Pines	★★★★½
Pinehurst Resort and Country Club	Village of Pinehurst	★★★★★

Western North Carolina

Eseeola Lodge	Linville	★★★★
Grove Park Inn Resort	Asheville	★★★★
High Hampton Inn	Cashiers	★★★½
Hound Ears Club	Blowing Rock	★★★½

Charleston, South Carolina

Kiawah Island Golf & Tennis Club	Kiawah Island	★★★★★
The Resort at Seabrook Island	Seabrook Island	★★★★
Wild Dunes	Isle of Palms	★★★★½

Hilton Head, South Carolina

Hilton Oceanfront Resort	Hilton Head	★★★½
Hyatt Regency Hilton Head	Hilton Head	★★★½

Resort Ratings (continued)

Palmetto Dunes Resort	Hilton Head	★★★★
Sea Pines	Hilton Head	★★★★
The Westin Resort	Hilton Head	★★★½

Myrtle Beach, South Carolina
Beach Cove Resort	North Myrtle Beach	★★★½
Embassy Suites Kingston Plantation	Myrtle Beach	★★★½
Wyndam Myrtle Beach Resort	Myrtle Beach	★★★

Georgia
Callaway Gardens Resort	Pine Mountain	★★★½
Chateau Elan	Braselton	★★★½
Jekyll Island Club Hotel	Jekyll Island	★★★★
King & Prince Beach & Golf Resort	St. Simons Island	★★★★
Sea Palms Golf & Tennis Resort	St. Simon's Island	★★★½
The Cloister	Sea Island	★★★★★

Mississippi's Gulf Coast
Beau Rivage	Biloxi	★★★
The Bridges Golf resort	Biloxi	★★★

Northern Florida
Amelia Island Plantation	Amelia Island	★★★★½
Ponte Vedra Beach Resorts	Ponte Vedra Beach	★★★★½
Ritz-Carlton Amelia Island	Amelia Island	★★★★½
Sawgrass Marriott Resort	Ponte Vedra Beach	★★★★

Central Florida
Bay Hill Club and Lodge	Orlando	★★★★
Grand Cypress Resort	Orlando	★★★★★
Grand Floridian Resort & Spa	Orlando	★★★★
Grenelefe	Haines City	★★★½
Mission Inn Golf &Tennis Resort	Howey-in-the-Hills	★★★★
Renaissance Vinoy Resort	St. Petersburg	★★★★
Longboat Key Resort	Longboat Key	★★★★
Saddlebrook resort	Wesley Chapel	★★★★
Westin Innisbrook Resort	Palm Harbor	★★★★

Southern Florida
Boca Raton Resort & Club	Boca Raton	★★★★½
Doral Golf Resort & Spa	Miami	★★★★½
Fontainbleau Hilton Resort	Miami	★★★½
PGA National Resort & Spa	Palm Beach Gardens	★★★★

Resort Ratings (continued)

Sonesta Beach Resort	Key Biscayne	★★★
The Breakers	Palm Beach	★★★★½
The Four Seasons	Palm Beach	★★★★
Turnberry Isle Resort & Club	Aventura	★★★★
Westin Resort Miami Beach	Miami	★★★

Maryland

Coconut Malorie Resort	Ocean City	★★★

Virginia

The Homestead	Hot Springs	★★★★★
Kingsmill Resort	Williamsburg	★★★★½
Williamsburg Inn	Williamsburg	★★★★½

West Virginia

Canaan Valley resort	Davis	★★★
The Greenbriar	White Sulphur Springs	★★★★★

Maine

Samoset Resort	Rockport	★★★★
Sugarloaf Inn Resort	Carrabasset	★★★★

New Hampshire

Mount Washington Hotel & Resort	Bretton Woods	★★★★
The Balsams Grand Resort & Hotel	Dixville Notch	★★★★

Massachusetts

Ocean Edge	Brewster	★★★½

EVALUATING THE GOLF EXPERIENCE

Comparing one golf course or golf resort to another is an inexact science, as is the case with art, literature, or food, because there is necessarily some subjectivity involved. Nevertheless, our concern at *The Unofficial Guide to Golf Vacations in the Eastern U.S.* is that you, the reader, obtain the optimum value for your money through informed choices. Therefore we've identified a number of characteristics that should be assessed and evaluated in helping you make your decision on where to take your golf vacation. We've also compiled an overall star rating for each of the Major Courses in the book to give you an easy starting point.

First of all, let's acknowledge that the single most important ingredient to a successful golf vacation—by far—is the quality of the golf experience. (We'll identify the factors that go into a quality golf experience in a moment.) When we evaluate a given resort or destination, we figure that the golf experience counts for 75 percent of the overall golf vacation experience. The other 25 percent is comprised of such factors as the quality and variety of lodging opportunities and attractions, together with location, scenery, weather, and cost of a stay. Make no mistake: A memorable dining experience or activities for the kids can be every bit as important for some people as a smooth putting green when it comes to a successful golf vacation.

Because the peak times to visit your favorite destinations may differ across North America, we'll evaluate a given golf course, resort, or region using a mythical average day in prime time—high season—when the weather for that area is at its best, the courses are groomed their finest, and regular golfer traffic is average.

By the same token, we'll inform you as to what the best deals are, when to make use of a resort's off-peak season, and what to watch out for in terms of crowds, course maintenance, and weather.

Personal opinion is bound to enter into any evaluation of a golf course, but we feel there are a number of objective criteria that can be used to determine what separates a fair golf course from a good one and a good one from a great one. Likewise, the same goes for the quality of an overall golf experience, of which the quality of the course itself is the most significant factor.

What, then, comprises a golf experience? For us, 75 percent is the quality of the course itself (we'll identify what factors determine excellence in a golf course in a moment), and the other 25 percent is divided into such qualities as service (pro shop, cart staging, bag drop, lessons offered, ranger, starter, and so on) and facilities (standard of locker rooms, golf school, restaurant/food and beverage service, pro shop, practice range, other golf courses, putting greens, rest rooms, drinking water availability, and so on).

Sometimes, these factors are counterbalanced. In other words, can you live with a grouchy ranger if the greens are smooth as glass? So, too, we wouldn't unfairly downgrade a course for having bus station–style bathrooms, provided the variety of golf holes and scenery is outstanding; but all the same, these are all variables that enter into the equation.

Finally, then, we've arrived at the core of this book—the golf course itself. Let us say at the outset that although nearly every course with flagsticks has at least something going for it, only a tiny handful have everything going right.

Minimally speaking, a golf course simply should satisfy the person playing it. It can achieve this objective by providing the potential for an enjoyable four- to five-hour experience for virtually anyone who plunks down a greens fee and tees it up. An ideal course should challenge strong players without overly frustrating average players. Wherever possible, each hole should offer a choice of routes in its journey from tee to green, so that no matter what your ability, you'll have options as to how to play the hole.

"The key to great golf is memorability," says golf course architect Ken Kavanaugh, "and the key to memorability is variety." The very best courses offer tremendous variety. A course's individual par-3s, par-4s, and par-5s should vary in distance to provide the player with a mix of clubs to hit. After a round, you should ask yourself, "Did I hit every club in my bag at least once?" Each hole within the group of par-3s, 4s, and 5s should vary in direction, so that whatever wind is present won't affect too many shots in a row in the same way.

Preferably, the holes should vary in the use of terrain: uphill holes, downhill, side sloping, straight, and doglegging. The collection of holes should offer variety in hazard placement as well. We may admire a handsome hole fronted by a pond and ringed with a horseshoe of sand traps, but it would be numbingly repetitive if every hole featured this same configuration. Ultimately, the golfer would lose interest, having the same look and same shot greeting him or her 18 consecutive times.

A characteristic of North America's superior golf courses is the feelings of enticement and anticipation they provide. So-called tough courses entice highly skilled and average players alike, so they can determine how their skills measure up when tested on a demanding course.

First and foremost, however, a course should provide a sufficient if not overly taxing test for all classes of players. Again, if the holes are too easy or if they lack strategic interest, the player will get bored and lose interest in a hurry. Likewise, if a course is overwhelmingly or relentlessly difficult or its hazards unfairly placed, golfers will soon get frustrated. Searching for and losing golf balls on every hole isn't much fun, and if a course is laid out or set up so that this occurs on a regular basis, you have a course that folks won't go back to.

Other layouts entice with setting, both on-course and off. The very best courses are blessed with agreeable terrain. Gently rolling is highly preferred, with allowances for the occasional sharp elevation change, which can make for spectacular play. Again, maximum variety in fairway widths and green shapes, sizes, and configurations leads to golf that is memorable and highly satisfying.

North America's greatest courses tend to be the most visually striking as well. They're often situated near mountains, oceans, lakes, deserts, or forests. On-course aesthetic considerations include tree and flower plantings, lawn mowing patterns, sand bunker etchings, and water hazard placements. Clearly, a course's beauty is a powerful draw for the golfer seeking the ultimate in a game of golf.

Course management is another relevant factor in evaluating a golf course, although it is not as significant as a memorable design. Nevertheless, it is important. Obviously, weather, time of day, time of year, and budget all can influence the condition of the course. The bottom line is this: It's a treat to play a course in flawless condition, one with firm, fast, true-running greens; shaved fairways; and clearly delineated roughs; at a minimum, the course should be maintained at a level whereby it doesn't detract from your enjoyment of the course design and setting.

A bonus that's applied to a course's memorability quotient are the intangibles, such as ambience and course history. You may feel a heightened sense of anticipation in playing the course knowing that a famous tournament was once or is currently held there. Though west of the Mississippi, and thus not covered in this book, The Tournament Players Club at Las Colinas in Irving, Texas, near Dallas, serves up a mildly interesting course in a setting that could hardly be called spectacular. However, the course plays host annually to the PGA Tour's GTE Byron Nelson Classic, where such legends as Tiger Woods, Phil Mickelson, and Jack Nicklaus have won tournaments. The thrill of following in famous footsteps adds immensely to the enjoyment of the round and to the enticement of the course. Plus, when the tournament comes on TV, you can gather the kids around and say, "See, that's the hole I birdied! Tiger only made a par!"

To sum up, the most important aspect of a golf vacation is the actual golf experience, and the foundation of a great golf experience is the quality of the golf course itself. We acknowledge that reasonable minds may disagree on which courses are best, but we're confident that we've outlined for you the chief component that experts use in assessing what separates a great course from the not-so-great. Ultimately, it's our job to steer you to the best golf courses and golf vacations possible—or at least the best values for your money.

Golf Course Ratings

Course	Overall	Challenge	Variety	Terrain
Pinehurst, North Carolina				
Pinehurst Resort, No. 1	★★★½	★★★	★★★	★★★½
Pinehurst Resort, No. 2	★★★★½	★★★★½	★★★★	★★★★½
Pinehurst Resort, No. 7	★★★½	★★★★½	★★★½	★★★★
Pinehurst Resort, No. 8	★★★★	★★★★	★★★★	★★★★
Pine Needles Lodge & Golf Club	★★★½	★★★½	★★★	★★★★★
The Pit Golf Links	★★★	★★★★	★★★	★★★½
Western North Carolina				
Etowah Valley Country Club	★★★	★★★	★★★½	★★★½
The Grove Park Inn Resort	★★★	★★½	★★★	★★★
Hound Ears Golf Club	★★★	★★	★★★½	★★★½
Linville Golf Course	★★★★	★★★★	★★★½	★★★★
Mount Mitchell Golf Club	★★★	★★½	★★½	★★★
Reems Creek Golf Course	★★★½	★★★	★★★★	★★★
Charleston, South Carolina				
Charleston National Country Club	★★★½	★★★★	★★★½	★★★★
Dunes West Golf Club	★★★½	★★★½	★★★	★★★½
Kiawah Island, Ocean Course	★★★★	★★★★★	★★★½	★★★★½
Kiawah Island, Osprey Point Course	★★★½	★★★	★★★★	★★★½
Kiawah Island, Turtle Point Course	★★★½	★★★★	★★★½	★★★½
Wild Dunes Resort, Links Course	★★★★	★★★½	★★★★	★★★★½
Hilton Head, South Carolina				
Daufuskie Island, Melrose Course	★★★★	★★★★	★★★★	★★★½
Harbour Town Golf Links	★★★★	★★★★	★★★★★	★★★★
Palmetto Dunes, Arthur Hills Course	★★★★	★★★	★★★★	★★★★
Palmetto Dunes, George Fazio Course	★★★	★★★★	★★★	★★★
Palmetto Dunes, Robert Trent Jones	★★★	★★½	★★★	★★½
Palmetto Hall, Arthur Hills Course	★★★½	★★★½	★★★★	★★★½
Palmetto Hall, Robert Cupp Course	★★★½	★★★★	★★★½	★★
Myrtle Beach, South Carolina				
Caledonia Golf and Fish Club	★★★★	★★★½	★★★★	★★★★
The Dunes Golf and Beach Club	★★★★	★★★★½	★★★★	★★★½
Heather Glen	★★★½	★★★½	★★★★	★★★½
The Heritage Club	★★★½	★★★★½	★★★	★★★★
The Legends, Heathland Course	★★★★	★★★½	★★★★	★★★½
Oyster Bay Golf Links	★★★★	★★★	★★★★½	★★★½
Pawleys Plantation	★★★★	★★★★	★★★½	★★★★
Pine Lakes International Country Club	★★★½	★★½	★★★	★★★
The TPC of Myrtle Beach	★★★★	★★★★	★★★★	★★★★
Tidewater	★★★★	★★★½	★★★★	★★★★

Golf Course Ratings (continued)

Beauty	Pace of Play	Facilities	14-Club Test	Intangibles	Value
★★★	★★★	★★★★★	★★½	★★★★	★★★
★★★★	★★★★★	★★★★★	★★★★	★★★★★	★★★★
★★★★	★★★½	★★★½	★★★★	★★★½	★★½
★★★★	★★½	★★★★½	★★★★★	★★★★	★★★
★★★½	★★★	★★★★½	★★★½	★★★★½	★★★
★★★	★★½	★★★	★★★	★★★	★★★★
★★★½	★★½	★★★	★★★	★★★	★★★★
★★★★	★★	★★	★★	★★★★	★★½
★★★★	★★★	★★★	★★	★★★½	★★★
★★★★	★★★½	★★★	★★★	★★★★½	★★★★
★★★★½	★★	★★	★★★	★★★	★★★
★★★★	★★★	★★★	★★★★	★★★	★★★
★★★★	★★★	★★★★	★★★★	★★★	★★★½
★★★★	★★★½	★★★★	★★★½	★★★½	★★★★
★★★★★	★★★½	★★★★½	★★★★	★★★★★	★★★½
★★★★	★★★	★★★★½	★★★★	★★★	★★★★
★★★★	★★★½	★★★	★★★½	★★★	★★★½
★★★★½	★★★½	★★★★	★★★★	★★★½	★★★★
★★★★½	★★★★	★★★½	★★★★	★★★★½	★★★½
★★★★★	★★★½	★★★★½	★★★½	★★★★★	★★★★
★★★★	★★★½	★★★★	★★★½	★★★★	★★★★
★★★	★★★	★★	★★★	★★★½	★★★½
★★★½	★★★	★★★½	★★★	★★★	★★★
★★★½	★★★½	★★★★	★★★★	★★★	★★★★
★★½	★★★	★★★★	★★★★	★★★★	★★★
★★★★	★★★½	★★★★	★★★	★★★★	★★★★
★★★★	★★★★	★★★½	★★★★½	★★★★	★★★½
★★★★	★★★½	★★★★	★★★½	★★★½	★★★½
★★★★	★★★	★★★★	★★★½	★★★½	★★★½
★★★★	★★★★	★★★★	★★★½	★★★★	★★★★
★★★★	★★★	★★★★	★★★½	★★★★	★★★★
★★★½	★★★★	★★★★	★★★½	★★★★	★★★½
★★★★	★★★★	★★★★	★★★	★★★★½	★★★★½
★★★½	★★★½	★★★★★	★★★½	★★★★	★★½
★★★★	★★★½	★★★★	★★★★	★★★	★★★★

Golf Course Ratings (continued)

Course	Overall	Challenge	Variety	Terrain
Alabama				
Cambrian Ridge Golf Course	★★★★	★★★★½	★★★★	★★★★½
Grand National, Lake Course	★★★★	★★★★	★★★½	★★★★★
Grand National, Links Course	★★★★	★★★★½	★★★★	★★★★
Hampton Cove, Highlands Course	★★★½	★★★½	★★★	★★★½
Hampton Cove, River Course	★★★	★★★★	★★½	★★½
Highland Oaks Golf Course	★★★★	★★★★½	★★★★	★★★½
Magnolia Grove, Crossings Course	★★★½	★★★½	★★★	★★★½
Magnolia Grove, Falls Course	★★★½	★★★★	★★★	★★★½
Oxmoor Valley, Ridge Course	★★★★	★★★★	★★★½	★★★½
Oxmoor Valley, Valley Course	★★★½	★★★★	★★★½	★★★½
Silver Lakes Golf Course	★★★★	★★★★½	★★★★	★★★★
Georgia				
Jekyll Island, Indian Mound Course	★★★	★★★	★★★	★★★
Jekyll Island, Oleander Course	★★★	★★★	★★★	★★
Jekyll Island, Pine Lakes Course	★★★	★★★	★★★	★★½
Sea Island, Plantation Course	★★★★	★★★½	★★★½	★★★½
St. Simons Island Club	★★★½	★★★	★★★½	★★★½
Callaway Gardens, Gardens View	★★½	★★	★★	★★★
Callaway Gardens, Lake View	★★½	★★	★★	★★★
Callaway Gardens, Mountain View	★★★½	★★★★	★★★	★★★★
Chateau Elan, Chateau Elan Course	★★★★	★★★★	★★★★	★★★★
Chateau Elan, Legends Course	★★★½	★★★½	★★★	★★★★
Chateau Elan, Woodlands Course	★★★★	★★★	★★★★½	★★★★
Reynolds Plantation, Great Waters	★★★★	★★★★	★★★★	★★★★½
Reynolds Plantation, National Course	★★★	★★★★½	★★★	★★★½
Reynolds Plantation, Plantation Course	★★★½	★★½	★★★	★★★½
Mississippi's Gulf Coast				
The Bridges at Casino Magic	★★★	★★★★	★★★	★★★
Diamondhead, Cardinal Course	★★★	★★★	★★★	★★★
Diamondhead, Pine Course	★★★	★★★	★★★	★★★
Mississippi National Course	★★★	★★★	★★½	★★½
The Oaks	★★★★	★★★	★★★★	★★★★
Timberton	★★★½	★★★½	★★★★	★★★★
Windance Country Club	★★★	★★★	★★★½	★★★
Northern Florida				
Amelia Island, Long Point Golf Club	★★★½	★★★	★★★½	★★★★
Amelia Island, Oak Marsh Course	★★★½	★★★	★★★	★★★
LPGA Int'l, Champions Course	★★★½	★★★★	★★★	★★★½
Palm Coast Resort, Grand Haven	★★★½	★★★½	★★★½	★★★½

Golf Course Ratings (continued)

Beauty	Pace of Play	Facilities	14-Club Test	Intangibles	Value
★★★½	★★★	★★★★	★★★★	★★★★	★★★★
★★★★½	★★★½	★★★★	★★★★	★★★★	★★★★½
★★★★	★★★½	★★★★	★★★★½	★★★★	★★★★½
★★★★	★★★½	★★★★	★★★½	★★★	★★★★½
★★★	★★★½	★★★★	★★★	★★★	★★★★
★★★★	★★★½	★★★★	★★★★	★★★½	★★★★½
★★★½	★★★½	★★★★	★★★½	★★★★	★★★★
★★★½	★★★½	★★★★	★★★½	★★★★	★★★★
★★★★	★★★	★★★★	★★★★	★★★½	★★★★
★★★½	★★★½	★★★★	★★★½	★★★½	★★★★
★★★★	★★★	★★★★	★★★★	★★★½	★★★★
★★★	★★★	★★★	★★★	★★★	★★★★
★★★★	★★★	★★★	★★★	★★★½	★★★★½
★★★	★★★½	★★★	★★★½	★★★½	★★★★
★★★★	★★★★	★★★★	★★★½	★★★★½	★★★½
★★★★	★★★½	★★★½	★★★½	★★★	★★★
★★★½	★★★	★★★	★★	★★★	★★½
★★★½	★★½	★★★	★★	★★½	★★½
★★★½	★★★	★★★	★★★★	★★★★	★★★★
★★★★	★★★½	★★★★	★★★½	★★★½	★★★
★★★★	★★★½	★★★★	★★★	★★★★	★★★
★★★★	★★★	★★★★	★★★★	★★★★	★★★★
★★★★½	★★★★½	★★★★	★★★★	★★★★	★★★★
★★★	★★★½	★★★½	★★★½	★★★	★★½
★★★	★★★★	★★★★	★★★½	★★★½	★★★★
★★★½	★★	★★★★½	★★★	★★★½	★★★
★★★	★★★	★★★	★★★	★★★½	★★★½
★★★	★★★	★★★	★★★	★★★	★★★
★★★	★★	★★★★	★★★	★★★	★★★
★★★★	★★★	★★★★½	★★★½	★★★★	★★★★
★★★★	★★★	★★★	★★★★	★★★½	★★★★
★★★	★★★	★★★	★★★	★★★½	★★★
★★★★	★★★	★★★★½	★★★★	★★★★	★★★
★★★★	★★★½	★★★½	★★★½	★★★½	★★★½
★★★½	★★½	★★★★½	★★★★	★★★★	★★★★
★★★½	★★★½	★★★½	★★★	★★★½	★★★½

Golf Course Ratings (continued)

Course	Overall	Challenge	Variety	Terrain
Northern Florida (cont'd.)				
Ponte Vedra Inn, Ocean Course	★★★½	★★★	★★★½	★★★
Sawgrass Country Club	★★★½	★★★★	★★★★	★★★★
TPC at Sawgrass, Stadium Course	★★★★½	★★★★★	★★★★	★★★★
TPC at Sawgrass, Valley Course	★★★★	★★★½	★★★	★★★½
World Golf Village,				
Slammer and Squire Course	★★★½	★★★½	★★★★	★★★★
Marriott's Bay Point Resort,				
Lagoon Legend	★★★½	★★★★★	★★★	★★★
Sandestin Resort, Burnt Pine	★★★★	★★★½	★★★★½	★★★★
Central Florida				
Bay Hill Club & Lodge	★★★½	★★★★	★★★½	★★★½
Grand Cypress, New Course	★★★½	★★★	★★★½	★★★★
Grand Cypress, North/East/South	★★★½	★★★½	★★★½	★★★★
Grenelefe, West Course	★★★½	★★★★	★★★½	★★★
Mission Inn, El Campeon Course	★★★½	★★★	★★★½	★★★★
Renaissance Vinoy Resort	★★★	★★	★★★	★★★
WDW, Eagle Pines Course	★★★½	★★★	★★★	★★★
WDW, Magnolia Course	★★★	★★★½	★★½	★★★
WDW, Osprey Ridge Course	★★★★	★★★½	★★★½	★★★★
WDW, Palm Course	★★★½	★★★★	★★★½	★★★½
Westin Innisbrook, Copperhead Course	★★★★	★★★★	★★★★	★★★★
Westin Innisbrook, Island Course	★★★½	★★★½	★★★½	★★★½
World Woods Golf Club,				
Pine Barrens Course	★★★★½	★★★★	★★★★	★★★★½
World Woods Golf Club,				
Rolling Oaks Course	★★★★	★★★½	★★★½	★★★½
Southern Florida				
Boca Raton	★★★	★★½	★★★	★★★
Champions Club at Summerfield	★★★½	★★★	★★★½	★★★½
Crandon Park at Key Biscayne	★★★	★★★★	★★½	★★★
Doral, Blue Course	★★★★	★★★★	★★★½	★★★½
Emerald Dunes Golf Course	★★★	★★★½	★★★½	★★★★
Marriott's Golf Club at Marco	★★★½	★★★½	★★★½	★★★½
Pelican's Nest Golf Club	★★★★	★★★★	★★★★	★★★★
PGA Golf Club at The Reserve,				
North and South Courses	★★★★	★★★★	★★★★	★★★½
PGA National Golf Club,				
Champion Course	★★★	★★★★½	★★★½	★★★
Turnberry Isle Resort & Club,				
South Course	★★★½	★★★½	★★★½	★★★

Golf Course Ratings (continued)

Beauty	Pace of Play	Facilities	14-Club Test	Intangibles	Value
★★★★	★★★½	★★★½	★★★½	★★★★	★★★½
★★★½	★★★	★★★	★★★★	★★★★	★★★½
★★★★½	★★★	★★★★★	★★★★½	★★★★★	★★★★
★★★½	★★★½	★★★★★	★★★★	★★★★	★★★½
★★★	★★★½	★★★½	★★★	★★★★	★★
★★★★	★★½	★★★★	★★★	★★★★	★★★★
★★★★	★★★★	★★★★	★★★★	★★★★	★★★½
★★★	★★★★	★★★★	★★★★	★★★★★	★★★
★★★½	★★★½	★★★★★	★★★½	★★★★	★★★
★★★★	★★★	★★★★★	★★★½	★★★★	★★★
★★★½	★★★	★★★½	★★★½	★★★	★★★½
★★★½	★★★	★★★★	★★★★	★★★	★★★★
★★★	★★★½	★★★	★★★	★★★	★★½
★★★	★★★½	★★★★½	★★★½	★★★½	★★★½
★★★½	★★★	★★★	★★★½	★★★½	★★½
★★★★	★★★	★★★★½	★★★★	★★★½	★★★½
★★★★	★★★½	★★★	★★★½	★★★★	★★★
★★★★	★★★	★★★★	★★★★½	★★★★	★★★
★★★½	★★★	★★★★	★★★½	★★★	★★★½
★★★★½	★★★★	★★★★★	★★★★	★★★★½	★★★★½
★★★★	★★★½	★★★★★	★★★½	★★★½	★★★★
★★★★	★★★½	★★★½	★★½	★★★½	★★★½
★★★½	★★★	★★★½	★★★½	★★★	★★★★
★★★★	★★	★★	★★★	★★★½	★★★★
★★★★	★★★½	★★★★½	★★★★	★★★★½	★★★½
★★★★	★★★	★★★★	★★★★	★★★★	★★★½
★★★½	★★★	★★★★	★★★½	★★★	★★★½
★★★★	★★★★	★★★★½	★★★★	★★★★	★★★★
★★★★	★★★	★★★★	★★★★	★★★★	★★★★½
★★★½	★★½	★★★	★★★★	★★★★	★★★
★★★½	★★★★	★★★★	★★★½	★★★	★★★½

Golf Course Ratings (continued)				
Course	Overall	Challenge	Variety	Terrain
Maryland				
Eagle's Landing	★★★½	★★★½	★★★½	★★★½
Virginia				
Golden Horseshoe, Gold Course	★★★½	★★★½	★★★★	★★★★
The Homestead, Cascades Course	★★★★	★★★½	★★★★½	★★★★½
Kingsmill Resort & Club, River Course	★★★★	★★★★	★★★★	★★★★
Royal New Kent Golf Club	★★★★	★★★★½	★★★½	★★★★
West Virginia				
The Greenbriar, Greenbriar Course	★★★★	★★★½	★★★★	★★★★
The Greenbriar, Old White Course	★★★★	★★★½	★★★★	★★★★
Maine				
The Samoset	★★★★	★★★	★★★★	★★★★
Sugarloaf, USA Golf Course	★★★★	★★★★½	★★★★½	★★★★½
Massachusetts				
Crumpin-Fox Club	★★★★	★★★★½	★★★★	★★★★★
Stow Acres, North Course	★★★½	★★★½	★★★★	★★★
Stow Acres, South Course	★★★	★★½	★★★★	★★★
Ocean Edge Resort & Golf Club	★★★	★★★	★★★½	★★★★
Connecticut				
Richter Park Golf Club	★★★	★★★★	★★★½	★★★
New Hampshire				
The Balsams Grand Resort, Panorama Course	★★★★	★★★★	★★★★	★★★★½
Country Club of New Hampshire	★★★★	★★★½	★★★★	★★★★
Vermont				
The Gleneagles Course	★★★½	★★★½	★★★½	★★★★

How to Use This Guidebook

Let's talk about the format of this book. Within each chapter, you will find an introduction to the region that is comprised of several sections. The "Overview" provides a look at the history of each region and a glimpse at what awaits you on your arrival. The "Where to Go and What It Will Cost" portion supplies information on the most and least desirable times of year to visit and just what's in store for you dollar-wise. As you might guess, often these two categories are closely linked—Mother Nature has some obvious influence on the best times to head to an area (for instance, you might want to avoid parts of Florida if you melt in humidity), but there are

Beach is heavenly, and the course magical. But the architect made use of the surroundings, creating a course that blends seamlessly with its landscape and takes full advantage of what Mother Nature offered up on a silver platter.

Pace of Play   Unless you are playing a private country club, you are looking at a four-hour-plus round. However, there are certain courses that play slower than others. This can be a result of difficult course conditions, often due to the design itself, where golfers have to search for numerous wayward balls. Other courses are simply too crowded, especially at lower-priced municipal-style courses in heavily populated areas where there's often a lack of quality courses. As a rule, resort and semi-private courses tend to flow better than public/municipal ones where inexperienced golfers typically tee it up.

Golf Facilities   It used to be that a course's golf facilities consisted of a small pro shop, an unremarkable putting green, and more likely than not a brown-grass driving range. Today, when designing a course, the facilities get almost as much attention as the actual course does. Magnificent pro shops that offer everything from clubs to clothes to crystal ware to books and videos are the rule rather than the exception. Who needs to shop anywhere else? Outside, golfers are often treated to facilities that actually make you want to practice. Spectacular driving ranges, challenging putting greens, and even warm-up holes get you primed for your golf match.

14-Club Test   For decades good players have measured the quality of a course by whether their golf skills are thoroughly tested throughout a round. One yardstick that is commonly used to determine whether a course offers a complete exam of a golfer's skill is whether that player was able to use each and every club in the bag. A course where you play driver/ nine iron on hole after hole will grow boring, whereas a course that is overly brutal, requiring a driver/three iron on every hole, is also neither enjoyable nor memorable.

Intangibles   This category measures those nongolfy factors that might not overtly contribute to the enjoyment of your golf game but still play a role. Among the factors considered are: if a renowned architect, such as Donald Ross, had a hand in the design; whether a famous celebrity or personality is associated with a course; or whether a significant tournament took place there. Or possibly, there is some other factor that in certain respects makes your round more unique or memorable, such as a one-of-a-kind design or setting. All of these contribute to the subtle and somewhat unconscious indulgence as you play your round.

Value   This final category gives you an indication if you are going to get your money's worth as you play a course. We are not measuring whether a course is inexpensive or not, but rather if your experience will be matched to the price tag. Contributing to this assessment is the course itself, its practice facilities, clubhouse, pro shop, and service.

After we leave the golf, you will find information on lodging, restaurants, activities, and the proverbial 19th hole. For the lodging, we tried to provide a variety of accommodations at a variety of price points. Although some guests want the full-resort atmosphere, others are seeking a more intimate, quiet offering. Still others, those traveling in groups of family members or friends, are looking for condominiums or homes to rent.

In the dining sections, you will find that we have outlined a full range of restaurants, attempting to identify something for every taste and wallet. For each restaurant, we have indicated the type of food that is served, the price range, information about reservations, and just what makes this restaurant merit inclusion in this book.

When you select a destination, make sure to block out some time to explore the area you are visiting. In Charleston, you could devote a full week to sight-seeing and still not see it all, whereas other areas are covered in a day. You will have to decide how much time you want to devote to nongolf activities, but the "Activities" section highlights the top attractions—some are off the wall (but that's half the fun) while others are old standbys.

A FEW FINAL THOUGHTS

If you are trying to save some money and effort, you should consider a golf package. Many of the resorts located within or near a prominent golf area, both expensive and moderate ones, have preexisting golf packages from which to choose. Often these packages can be customized for you, but the bottom line is that they are an ideal way to save some money, get preferred tee times, and avoid numerous phone calls.

Speaking of making tee times, in the past few years, a number of Internet booking services have sprung up. Some of these services have had to work out a number of bugs, but making your tee times from cyberspace is definitely catching on. Thus, in the near future, when you want to make a tee time, you will no longer need to pick up the phone but can instead log on and head to one of these Web sites, such as the soon-to-be-launched greens.com or linkstime.com, and electronically schedule your round.

We hope you find this guidebook informative, entertaining, and, most of all, useful. The whole idea behind this book is to help you get the most from your golf vacation experience. For avid golfers, there are few things in life more enjoyable and rejuvenating than great golf vacations. Here's to your next one!

Part One

Pinehurst, North Carolina

Overview

Pinehurst. To serious traveling golfers, the very name conjures up images of reverence and awe, commensurate with the very best in golf, such as St. Andrews and Pebble Beach. Located an hour's drive south from Raleigh-Durham, no resort destination in America is as rich in golf history and lore as Pinehurst, North Carolina. Nestled among the quaint villages and towns in the Pinehurst area are the traditions that epitomize golf's grandest era. Despite the understandable increase in crowds and traffic, in many ways, the mood and setting in Pinehurst proper is unchanged from the last 100 years. Thus, it's easy to imagine golf's heroes, from Bobby Jones to Ben Hogan to Jack Nicklaus to Tiger Woods, striding about the town's dogwood- and azalea-lined paths, breathing in the scent of longleaf pines on a breezy spring evening.

The gently rolling floor of these pine forests is composed of sandy subsoil, which gives rise to the descriptive term, "the Sandhills," a geographic label affixed to all of Pinehurst and surrounding communities. One hundred years ago, Pinehurst founder James Tufts recognized the region's soil: It compared favorably with the soil of coastal Scotland's, which meant it was perfect for golfing ground. It made for easy walking and drained quickly after a rain. By 1900, the Pinehurst area had its first golf course.

Pinehurst is now home to dozens of courses, some private, but mostly public access. Today, as it has been for the past century, it remains a marvelous place to spend a golf vacation provided you like to eat, sleep, and breathe golf. The Sandhills region offers numerous golf and lodging opportunities, but clearly the area's anchor is the Pinehurst Resort & Country Club. Nowhere else in North America does history and tradition run deeper than at Pinehurst.

Let's be fair, however. The Pinehurst Resort & Country Club is only the tip of the iceberg. If you picture the Village of Pinehurst as the hub of a

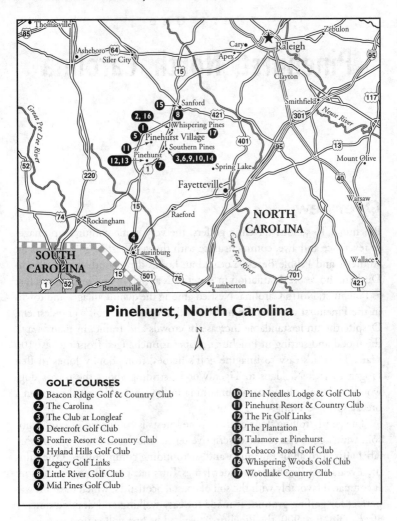

Pinehurst, North Carolina

N

GOLF COURSES

1. Beacon Ridge Golf & Country Club
2. The Carolina
3. The Club at Longleaf
4. Deercroft Golf Club
5. Foxfire Resort & Country Club
6. Hyland Hills Golf Club
7. Legacy Golf Links
8. Little River Golf Club
9. Mid Pines Golf Club
10. Pine Needles Lodge & Golf Club
11. Pinehurst Resort & Country Club
12. The Pit Golf Links
13. The Plantation
14. Talamore at Pinehurst
15. Tobacco Road Golf Club
16. Whispering Woods Golf Club
17. Woodlake Country Club

wheel, its spokes extend to such communities as Southern Pines, Aberdeen, Whispering Pines, and Carthage. Fan out for 15 minutes in any direction from Pinehurst and you'll encounter one good golf course after the next. Some are Donald Ross–designed classics that date to the 1920s, such as Pine Needles and Mid Pines, whereas others represent the most innovative in modern design, such as Talamore and the Carolina. Make no mistake: There's not much else to do in these parts, but few places in North America can touch Pinehurst and the Sandhills as a golf mecca. With the possible exception of Myrtle Beach, South Carolina, nowhere are there as many courses in a concentrated area where expert players can be truly tested, and beginner and intermediate players can tee up without being intimidated.

WHEN TO GO AND WHAT IT WILL COST

Ideally, spring is the season to experience Pinehurst. Daytime temperatures are usually heavenly, warm with gentle breezes, and pink and white dogwood trees are blossoming everywhere—especially in mid-April—turning normally staid pine forests into riots of color. Mid-April through mid-May is best, but of course, that's when courses are most crowded and prices are highest. Autumn is next best. Check before you book a stay, however, as much course maintenance takes place in early fall. You don't want to have your dream vacation ruined by having to putt bumpy greens that have just been aerated.

If you're on a budget, consider the shoulder season, summer. Even though the heat can be stifling, you can still play 36 holes a day for a semireasonable price, especially if you go the golf package route. For the very best deal, try the winter (off-season) packages, which typically extend from mid-November until the first week of March.

If you're willing to brave the elements a bit, several Pinehurst-area resorts offer a midwinter package, where conditions are at their least crowded and greens fees at their lowest, but prepare to bundle up. Average daytime highs range in the mid-50s for December, January, and February, but are up in the mid-60s for November and March. Average nighttime lows are in the mid-30s, and snow is rare. Perhaps the wisest choice (though it's still a roll of the dice) is to book your stay for mid- to late-November for your best chance at a temperate climate. Note that at many resorts, Thanksgiving stays are more expensive.

In the height of peak season, most of the area courses are booked to capacity seven days a week, but as is true nearly everywhere, it's easiest to find a tee time (and a slight break on greens fees) Monday through Thursday. Mornings are best during the summer, as midday heat and humidity can be stifling.

For fall, winter, and spring, I'd recommend a midmorning or early afternoon start. In winter, it's simply too cold most mornings to feel and play your best, whereas early morning starts in spring and fall feature moisture-laden fairways and dewy greens. The wet conditions inhibit roll, so your drives won't go as far and the greens don't roll as quickly. Plus, it's tough keeping the cuffs of your pants dry.

One advantage to playing early, especially on the region's more modestly maintained courses: The greens aren't spiked up as badly first thing in the morning. Then again, these days, with 65 percent of the nation's golfers using nonmetal spikes in their shoes, this isn't the problem it was a few years ago. A few area courses, following a national trend, now prohibit metal-spiked shoes. If you're still into heavy metal, definitely phone ahead to check the course policy.

Pinehurst in high season isn't for the faint of wallet, but there's enough variety in the golf experiences to find something to fit your budget. At courses such as Beacon Ridge and Deercroft, maximum fees top off at around $40, but the 1999 U.S. Open course, Pinehurst No. 2, will set you back a couple of Franklins. Most of the others are priced from $65 to $135.

Travel at nonpeak time, though, and prices come down, sometimes dramatically. If you're looking to stay and play a few days, golf packages can make your games even cheaper. So ingrained is the golf package in the Pinehurst area that even such properties as the Best Western, Comfort Inn, Days Inn, and Hampton Inn offer them.

WHAT TO BRING

Sweaters and windbreakers are a good idea for daytime play November through March, where daytime highs average in the mid-50s to mid-60s. In spring and fall, they're handy at night as well. For summer play, I'd recommend a combination insect repellent/sunblock; slather up early and often.

If you're playing the old Pinehurst favorites, you won't need too many golf balls. There are few water hazards on the old masterpieces, and the brown pine needles in the woods make it easy to spot a wayward white ball. More water hazards populate the newer breed of courses; you may need an extra sleeve of balls.

No special clubs are needed for the Pinehurst-area courses, nor is it especially windy. An umbrella is a good idea, but the region's sandy soil allows for outstanding drainage, so even if you have to stop play for a while, you'll be back on pretty quickly.

ONCE YOU'RE THERE

Pinehurst offers a multitude of courses from which to choose. Where you play and in what order is a function of how much time and money you have to spend. Obviously, if you can afford to stay at one of the Pinehurst Resort & Country Club hotels and you can handle (or at least cope with) the rigors of the famous Pinehurst No. 2 course, that's the one must-play course in the area. Its sister course, No. 8, is nearly its equal. It's more spectacular, but with less charm or history. Either one is memorable. Perhaps start with Pinehurst No. 1 as a warm-up. It's got the look, charm, and conditioning of No. 2 without being so demanding.

Away from Pinehurst proper, for pure pleasure, history, and quality, Pine Needles is what you want. It's challenging enough to have played host to the U.S. Women's Open in 1996 (and will again in 2001), but is pure fun. It's on the pricey side, but it says "Pinehurst" better than any course in the region outside of No. 2. Its sibling, the Mid Pines course, is nearly as good, though nearly as expensive, but also comes highly recommended.

If your budget won't allow for too many $100 rounds, you can still afford Pinehurst. I might start with a warm-up round at Whispering Woods, a nice value, with fees ranging from $22 to $32, then head to Little River Farm, a wonderful design by local legend Dan Maples, who grew up in Pinehurst when his father worked for master architect Donald Ross. This surprisingly hilly course peaks at $57 and is a true bargain. A good place for a third or fourth round is The Pit Golf Links, another fun Maples design, which was sculpted from a 230-acre sand quarry. Two other fine tracks comparably priced ($24–72) are the Legacy, designed by Jack Nicklaus II and Talamore, a Rees Jones design featuring llama caddies. (As Dave Barry would say, "I am not making this up.")

GATHERING INFORMATION

For more information on the Pinehurst area and Sandhills region, an excellent source is the *Play & Stay Golf Vacation Guide*, updated annually by the Convention & Visitors Bureau.

> Convention & Visitors Bureau
> P.O. Box 2270, Southern Pines, NC 28388
> Phone (800) 346-5362 or (910) 692-3330; fax (910) 692-0619
> email cvb4golf@mindspring.com; Web www.homeofgolf.com

Books to read may include *Pinehurst Stories* and *Sandhills Classics,* both by Lee Pace, which contain treasure troves of golf history. If you want to see how some area courses look, buy or rent videos of the 1999 U.S. Open or the U.S. Senior Open of 1994, both held at Pinehurst No. 2, or the U.S. Women's Open of 1996, held at Pine Needles. Another video for sale is the Shell's Wonderful World of Golf Match, which took place in 1994 at Pinehurst No. 2 between Arnold Palmer and Jack Nicklaus.

The Major Courses

PINEHURST RESORT & COUNTRY CLUB

If you're the kind of traveling golfer who appreciates an experience that whispers greatness rather than screams it, one who favors charming and subtle more than garish and bold, you should find Pinehurst Resort & Country Club to be a perfect spot. If you're a golf history, architecture, or major championship fanatic, Pinehurst is truly the place to pursue your passion. No golf resort in the United States is more steeped in golf history.

Mainly, Pinehurst's fame stems from its unparalleled golf facilities, where both quantity and quality reign supreme. The practice range at the Pinehurst Country Club is so famous it has its own name, Maniac Hill. Its on-site golf instruction school, Golf Advantage, has worked with thousands of students and has produced some of the nation's finest teachers. The Country Club boasts no less than eight golf courses. And its No. 2 course is as revered as perhaps any course in the nation. One of the few public-access courses in North American golf that has hosted major championships, Pinehurst No. 2 is a past site of the Ryder Cup, PGA Championship, more than two dozen PGA Tour events, and every significant amateur tournament. In 1999, this course capped its own list of notable events when it hosted the men's U.S. Open. Guests at the Pinehurst Hotel have access to all eight courses, the first five of which originate at the same clubhouse.

Most of the Pinehurst Country Club courses are traditional looking, even slightly old-fashioned in appearance. All are tree-lined, lay-of-the-land affairs. Only Tom Fazio's No. 8 course and the Rees Jones–designed No. 7 course feature a "modern" look in terms of hazard placement and landscape architecture.

How To Get On

You must be a guest of the Pinehurst Resort to play the golf courses at Pinehurst Country Club. This doesn't mean you have to stay in the excellent, if pricey, Pinehurst Hotel (now called The Carolina), however. Guests of the Manor Inn, a less-expensive property owned by the Pinehurst Resort, also have full access. So, too, do guests of the fairway villas and condominiums owned by the Pinehurst Resort. In 1999, refurbishment of the venerable Holly Inn, recently purchased by the Pinehurst Resort, began giving vacationers yet another option. If you fit into one of these categories, you can simply call the resort (phone (800) 487-4653) and ask to be connected with golf reservations. Starting times on all courses are taken six months in advance.

Note: Guests of the Pinehurst Resort properties may not entertain outside guests on the golf courses of Pinehurst Country Club. In addition, the club does not reciprocate with members of other private country clubs with respect to playing privileges on the Pinehurst courses. So, then, if you're looking to piggyback a game with a friend who happens to be staying at one of the Pinehurst Resort properties, you'll have to pull a little bit of a fast one and have him vouch for the fact that you're staying in the same room.

As a last resort: If you're desperate to play one of the Pinehurst Country Club courses but you cannot arrange for a stay at one of the resort's properties, we've got one more way of getting on. Outside play is accepted by calling that day, to see if there are any tee time vacancies that day. Or, you can simply show up that day, taking your chances on payment of a greens fee. The best chances you have are on hot summer days, when there's plenty of daylight and the high heat and humidity will dissuade many members and guests from heading out. Likewise, on less than balmy days, your odds of getting on increase dramatically. The only exception at Pinehurst is with its No. 2 course. Until the hoopla dies down (which may take years) with respect to its hosting the 1999 U.S. Open, it's going to be a tough ticket getting on unless you're a resort guest.

Pinehurst No. 1

One Carolina Vista, P.O. Box 4000, Village of Pinehurst, NC 28374; phone (800) ITS-GOLF or (910) 295-6811; www.pinehurst.com

Tees:

> Blue: 6,128 yards, par-70, USGA rating 69.4, slope 116
>
> White: 5,857 yards, par-70, USGA rating 68.0, slope 115
>
> Red: 5,297 yards, par-73, USGA rating 70.5, slope 117

Challenge: ★★★	Golf Facilities: ★★★★★
Variety: ★★★	14-Club Test: ★★½
Terrain: ★★★½	Intangibles: ★★★★
Beauty/Visual Appeal: ★★★	Value: ★★★
Pace of Play: ★★★	

Just the Facts Year Opened: 1898; Course Designer: Donald Ross; Walking: Yes (only with caddie—caddie fee is $35); Greens Fee: $72–$116; 9-Hole/Twilight Rate: No; Pull Carts: No; Practice Range: Yes; Club Rental: Yes.

Description and Comments No. 1 is Pinehurst's oldest course, parts of which date to 1898. As such, you're bound to feel a sense of history. The golf itself is quite pleasant, sufficiently challenging for the fair to good golfer, without being overly taxing. It's especially wonderful for intermediate-level women and seniors, maybe the best of all the Pinehurst courses in this department. Perfect golfing terrain awaits, gently rolling with the occasional large dip or swale. Actually, the amount of elevation change is surprising, as its more famous neighbor, No. 2, is significantly flatter. The greens were rebuilt in 1997 by master architect Rees Jones and are wonderful, large, fast, and true. They're mostly round and firm, with little internal contour, but many of them fall off sharply at the edges, in classic Donald Ross fashion. Stay below the hole, or risk a near-certain three putt. Number 11 is the best hole, a long, slightly uphill par-3, measuring 216 yards, which plays across a pond to a green sheltered in the pines and dogwoods.

Insider Tips This is truly a perfect warm-up course before you tackle famous No. 2. The greens are big, quick, and only mildly undulating. They don't boast the terrifying, bewildering contours that No. 2 does, but they're quite challenging in their own right.

Pinehurst No. 2

One Carolina Vista, P.O. Box 4000, Village of Pinehurst, NC 28374; phone (800) ITS-GOLF or (910) 295-6811; www.pinehurst.com

Tees:

> Gold: 7,252 yards, par-72, USGA rating 75.9, slope 138
>
> Blue: 6,869 yards, par-72, USGA rating 74.1, slope 133
>
> White: 6,337 yards, par-72, USGA rating 71.5, slope 129
>
> Red: 5,825 yards, par-74, USGA rating 74.6, slope 130

Challenge: ★★★★½	Golf Facilities: ★★★★★
Variety: ★★★★	14-Club Test: ★★★★
Terrain: ★★★★½	Intangibles: ★★★★★
Beauty/Visual Appeal: ★★★★	Value: ★★★★
Pace of Play: ★★★★★	

Just the Facts Year Opened: 1901; Course Designer: Donald Ross; Walking: Yes (only with caddie—caddie fee is $37.50–$75); Greens Fee: $150–$190; 9-Hole/Twilight Rate: No; Pull Carts: No; Practice Range: Yes; Club Rental: Yes.

Description and Comments Walking the halls of the vast, sprawling Pinehurst clubhouse, past the memorabilia and trophy cases, past the Donald Ross Grill, in anticipation of meeting your caddie and tackling ol' No. 2 is one of golf's singular thrills. Plenty of veteran caddies are still around to help you negotiate one of the fiercest tests of chipping and putting anywhere.

A smattering of holly, oak, and dogwood trees combines with row after row of tall longleaf pines (which yield pine cones as big and brown as footballs), to make every hole an attractive treat. Miss a fairway on No. 2 and sandy scrub, wisps of love grass, and scores of pine needles await. Miss one of the crowned (built-up, to a crest in the middle) greens and watch your ball carom wildly off a slope or funnel gently down a swale. In either case, getting up and down for par requires extraordinary talent and possibly a magician's wand. There are no island greens at No. 2 and no 15-foot-deep sand traps, just a succession of strong, playable holes.

At first blush, many players, as they do at the Old Course at St. Andrews, Scotland, may wonder what all the fuss is about. You practically ask yourself, "*This* is the course that every major golf publication ranks in the top 10 of *all* courses in the United States?" It's hard to discern No. 2's virtues at first glance. The topography is pretty tame—no soaring peaks or plunging valleys, nor any expansive water hazards. Even after you've played the course, try picturing in your mind's eye the individual holes. You can blink as often as you want and it's still tough to recall many of the holes. As the immortal Ben Hogan once said, "The trouble with Pinehurst is that when you try to think of one great hole, you can't. Nothing jumps into your mind."

Ah, but you have to delve a bit deeper. The course is amazing, a masterpiece of subtlety. It's one of the only courses in the nation that can accommodate a beginner, yet rigorously test the best. Regardless of what any "local" tries to tell you, No. 2 is neither terribly exciting nor challenging from tee to green. Therein lies it genius.

True, the fairways are amply wide, but master architect Donald Ross has angled and sloped each green so that it is receptive to an approach shot fired from only a certain side of the fairway. If you hit your drive to the wrong portion of the fairway, you'll still have a reasonable shot to the green, but it will be virtually impossible to hold the firm, speedy putting surface. From the correct position of the fairway, the task becomes more manageable, though still difficult. The genius of the design lies in the fact that good golfers are constantly challenged by the puzzles presented, while so-so golfers can enjoy the walk, the history, the scenery, and the lack of difficult forced carries off the tees and into the greens.

Insider Tips   For starters, do yourself a favor and take a caddie when you play this course, even with the extra $37.50 to $75 plus tip, depending on whether he's caddying single (one bag) or double (two bags). Not many resorts offer this service, and it remains the ultimate way to play golf. You get the benefit of companionship and support, plus help on yardages, club selection, reading putts on the greens, raking bunkers, and looking for balls that have found the woods, plus the main benefit of a wonderful walk—some actual exercise—without having to lug your bag around. Besides, if you do choose to take a cart, they force you to stay on the cart paths at all times, which are always routed along the tree lines in the rough. Thus, you never really get to see how the course unfolds, as you're always walking laterally to your ball—with several clubs in tow.

Second, you'll save money on golf balls when you play No. 2. Because there's just one measly pond on the whole course, in front of the 16th tee, and given the wide fairways and absence of heavy rough, you may get through your round with the same ball you started with. Even if you're prone to big hooks and slices, your caddie will probably track down most shots that find the trees. Allow for two balls if you take a caddie at No. 2, three or four if you play without one.

If you are truly atrocious at the fine art of chipping onto a putting green, I recommend skipping No. 2 entirely. So demanding are the unconventional, firm, smooth as glass, "crowned" (convex) greens, that if you're not at least somewhat proficient at this shot, you'll endure a nightmare of continually hitting it onto the green, then watching in horror as it either rolls straight back to your feet, or else catches a far slope and rolls off the other side. Frequently repeating this painful exercise will frustrate not only you but your playing partners and the folks playing behind you as well.

My favorite hole at No. 2 is the 5th, which ranks statistically as the hardest hole on the course. From the gold tee, this monster par-4 stretches to 485 yards. From the blue, it's 463, 435 from the whites, and 422 from the reds.

The teeing ground for the fifth is recessed in a chute of longleaf pines. The landing area for the tee shot looks awfully generous at first glance, but again, be on guard. Only the right side of the fairway will work because the fairway tilts from right to left. Thus, any tee shot hit left of center will hit the firm, sloping fairway and run away unchecked to the left side. From that spot, a brutally difficult approach awaits, to be played around trees from an awkward sidehill lie.

While a drive up the right side is the preferred shot, a tee shot that strays too far right may tangle with light rough, pine, dogwood, holly, and oak, or worse yet, out of bounds. The long second shot is played to a large green placed on a diagonal, which features a pronounced right-to-left slope. If the flag is set on the left side of the green, behind a large oval of sand, avoid the temptation of shooting right for it, because if you're short, you're in a bunker, and if you pull it slightly to the left, your ball will most likely cascade down a steep, hard embankment and wind up in the middle of the fourth fairway. Better to take your medicine and play safely up the right side for the length of the hole. Bogey at the fifth is not a bad score.

Pinehurst No. 7

One Carolina Vista, P.O. Box 4000, Village of Pinehurst, NC 28374, phone (800) ITS-GOLF or (910) 295-6811; www.pinehurst.com

Tees:

    Gold: 7,114 yards, par-72, USGA rating 75.6, slope 145

    Blue: 6,719 yards, par-72, USGA rating 73.7, slope 142

    White: 6,216 yards, par-72, USGA rating 70.4, slope 130

    Red: 4,924 yards, par-72, USGA rating 69.7, slope 124

Challenge: ★★★★½	Golf Facilities: ★★★½
Variety: ★★★½	14-Club Test: ★★★★
Terrain: ★★★★	Intangibles: ★★★½
Beauty/Visual Appeal: ★★★★	Value: ★★½
Pace of Play: ★★★½	

Just the Facts   Year Opened: 1986; Course Designer: Rees Jones; Walking: Unrestricted; Greens Fee: $120–165; 9-Hole/Twilight Rate: No; Pull Carts: No; Practice Range: Yes; Club Rental: Yes.

Description and Comments   Just ten years ago, all the buzz at Pinehurst was not over the famed No. 2 course nor any upcoming major championships, but rather on its three-year-old No. 7 course. Designed with high expectations by Rees Jones, the expectations were apparently met—and exceeded—at least according to one golf course critic: His Airness, former basketball superstar Michael Jordan, who at the time proclaimed No. 7 to be his favorite course in all of golf. Ten years later, No. 7 still stacks up awfully well in a neighborhood full of tough competition.

To be fair, there's not as much buzz about No. 7 these days. It's a bit like the Pirates of the Caribbean ride at Walt Disney World: It's still one of the best attractions, but there's just been a slew of new attention-grabbers lately to steal its thunder.

No. 7 is one of the three courses at Pinehurst (the others being Nos. 6 and 8) that is part of the "good news/bad news" scenario: The good news is that it sits off by itself, on the perimeter of the Village of Pinehurst, an isolated entity. The bad news is, well, the same thing. If you like the "bee-hive of golf activity" atmosphere that the main complex at Pinehurst provides, you'll feel a little out of it here. If it's solitude on a tremendously challenging course that you seek, you've come to the right place.

Jones designed No. 7 on terrain vastly different from the usual Pine-hurst sandhills. As opposed to "gently rolling," this property is quite hilly, with a ravine, wetlands, and a natural berm as natural components of the design. Most of the Pinehurst courses feature a dearth of hazards, with pri-mary strategic interest around the greens. At No. 7, there are eye-catching, fear-inducing hazards scattered throughout. You name it, and No. 7 has got it: huge sand bunkers, multiple grass bunkers, tall pines, forced carries over water, abrupt elevation change, contoured greens, plus walls of con-tainment mounds lining many of the fairways, making play seems as if it takes place in the bottom of a cereal bowl.

Rugged and beautiful, No. 7 features several all-star holes on a team with no weak links. The second hole typifies the brawn required to handle No. 7, and in many ways illustrates the course's virtues. It is both brutally long and intimidatingly narrow, yet is satisfying to play because it's not unfair. It simply requires everything a good golfer is capable of throughout the hole. As with many of the holes here, the golfer drives from an elevated tee to a valley fairway, then faces an uphill approach to a large, undulating green bunkered closely on the left.

The 16th is certainly the most memorable hole. Again, it reveals much about the character of No. 7, in that it is the shortest of the par-3s—at 196 yards! It's a striking hole of enormous scale, but one you will find tougher than old beef jerky. The 16th is graced with a fist of sand for a fairway that explodes in swirls of sandy fingers, all of which must be carried to reach the green. To the sides of the fairway are tree-covered tiny islands in the sandy, scrub-filled wasteland. This is big, bold golf at its finest—or its most frustrating, depending on your perspective.

Insider Tips   Let's just say this in advance: If you're not a particularly skilled player, or you're not wild about semiblind drives and approaches, skip this course. There are too many other appealing choices in and around Pinehurst where you can have pure fun. Moreover, if you're going to spend the money to beat yourself up, pick either the ancient "trophy" course, No. 2, or else the modern one, No. 8. If you can cope with long carries, multiple hazards, and uphill approaches, however, don't hesitate to sample the tasty, eye-pleasing difficulties that No. 7 presents. Play when conditions are at their firmest, preferably in the afternoon. The course plays so long, you're going to need all the fairway run you can get.

An advantage to trying No. 7 if you can handle its rigors is that you should move around pretty well. Since it's not the "in-demand star" that Nos. 2 and 8 are, it should be easy to access. And with its $183 price tag, there won't be a lot of curiosity-seekers slowing things down.

If it's serious golf atmosphere you're seeking, No. 7 may be lacking. The course was built as the centerpiece of a real estate development, called the Fairwoods on 7. Now that the property has been fully developed, with predictably huge, beautiful homes, you feel as if you could be playing golf in any fancy neighborhood, rather than in historic, sleepy, golf-rich Pinehurst. What saves No. 7 is simply that it such a marvelous, attractive test of golf. Those are hard to come by no matter where you are.

Pinehurst No. 8

One Carolina Vista, P.O. Box 4000, Village of Pinehurst, NC 28374; phone (800) ITS-GOLF or (910) 295-6811; www.pinehurst.com

Tees:

Championship: 7,092 yards, par-72, USGA rating 74.0, slope 135

Blue: 6,698 yards, par-72, USGA rating 71.7, slope 125

White: 6,302 yards, par-72, USGA rating 69.8, slope 121

Red: 5,177 yards, par-72, USGA rating 68.9, slope 112

Challenge: ★★★★	Golf Facilities: ★★★★½
Variety: ★★★★	14-Club Test: ★★★★★
Terrain: ★★★★	Intangibles: ★★★★
Beauty/Visual Appeal: ★★★★	Value: ★★★
Pace of Play: ★★½	

Just the Facts   Year Opened: 1996; Course Designer: Tom Fazio; Walking: Yes; Greens Fee: $130–180; 9-Hole/Twilight Rate: No; Pull Carts: No; Practice Range: Yes; Club Rental: Yes.

Description and Comments   It took nearly 90 years, but the folks at the Pinehurst Resort & Country Club finally built a golf course to compete with its legendary No. 2. In 1996, the premier modern-day architect, Tom Fazio completed "The Centennial," a course named for Pinehurst's celebration of 100 years as a resort. Today, nearly everyone refers to this anniversary present as "No. 8."

Tee to green, No. 8 blows No. 2 away in terms of drama, variety, and challenge. For that reason, there are plenty of folks who feel No. 8 is simply the better course, period. Purists and many course connoisseurs point to No. 2's subtleties, its history, and its playability for all classes of golfers, even if it's conquerable by only the best.

For our purposes, none of this is all that important, except for grill-room debates. If you're in the neighborhood and can afford to play both courses, do so. If you can only afford only one, you must play No. 2. It's history, it's brilliant, it's unique, it's the U.S. Open course. No. 8, if taken in a vacuum, is simply more interesting at every turn.

No. 8 shares certain characteristics with No. 2 and is markedly different in other respects. Fazio's course benefits from remarkable terrain, occupying grounds that formerly housed the Pinehurst Resort Gun Club, which once employed Annie Oakley as an instructor. Tall longleaf pines and rolling sandhills are parts of the equation—typical Pinehurst, if you will. Atypical, however, are such features as an abandoned sand pit, freshwater marshes, and a man-made dune ridge, all of which influence play. The hilly landscape and multiple hazards lends themselves perfectly to incredible variety in lies, stances, shot-making opportunities, and "looks." Some holes are open and play alongside vast marshes or other water hazards, others are locked in the trees. You get blind and semiblind shots, uphill and downhill drives and approaches, long forced carries over trouble, and Scottish-style bump-and-run shots into greens. Typically of Fazio's work, No. 8 has a tremendous mix of short and long holes, each with different appearance and hazard placement. In short, this is a textbook of modern design where variety is concerned.

Except in one area: the greens. The Pinehurst people by their own admission asked Fazio to give them a star-studded course, to add a true second "marquee" course, to help deflect traffic from the incredibly popular No. 2. Fazio succeeded, but his efforts at paying homage to No. 2 by creating firm, fast, crowned greens for No. 8 is the course's most controversial aspect. When the greens get a bit too firm and fast, the course becomes an exercise in frustration for most golfers. Unlike at No. 2, it's not always easy getting to the green at No. 8, and too often, your efforts go unrewarded at best, unfairly punished at worst.

The reason for this is simple: Fazio designed huge, very firm, smoothly rolling greens, which unfortunately tend to funnel decently struck shots into hazards. Take the monstrous, 604-yard, par-5 6th hole, for instance. The hole calls for a big tee shot, uphill over a lake, to a hogback fairway. The second and third shots are equally lengthy and demanding, with plenty of strategic interest, but lo and behold, if your approach misses slightly long and left—even if it hits the green—it is swept away, down a swale, through a hollow, and into waiting woods. Sure, it's easy to say,

"Then don't hit it there," but the hole is so long, with so many hazards, it's hard to be that precise.

Similarly thrilling but brutal are the uphill, 238-yard, par-3 8th, which asks for a forced carry over scrub-filled wetlands to a green with a steep falloff to the right, and the 441-yard, par-4 9th, which demands an uphill drive over a veritable desert followed by a healthy approach, to a green large enough to be home to three little greens. After all that work, three putting is more probable than possible.

Be that as it may, No. 8 is destined for greatness because it is memorable to a degree few courses will ever achieve. Accept that it's hard and that it's not No. 2, and enjoy it for what it is.

Insider Tips   Unlike No. 7, you don't want to play No. 8 when it's extra-firm unless you are an expert, low-single-digit handicapper. Get after it in the morning, or in summer when it requires a little extra water, to take some of the fearsome speed and firmness out of the greens.

Play this course first, before you play No. 2, to get you acclimated to the unique and difficult chipping experiences you will face at No. 2. If you're not going to play No. 2 on your visit, play another course before this one, just to be warmed up properly, because the shot-making demands are so severe.

Many of the greens on No. 8 slope hard to the sides and occasionally to the rear, rather than the more common back-to-front. As with course No. 2, they are seeded with G-2 grass, which keeps them firm and fast, even in summer. When in doubt, use one less club on your approaches, as the ball will run a ways once it hits the ground. Likewise, when you're chipping toward the hole, deliberately play it well short of the pin and let it run.

No. 8 can rightly brag about its superior clubhouse, practice facility, and amenities, but remember, it's a bit isolated and a little hard to find. Thus, you won't feel much of the historic aura, nor bask in the memorabilia, as you would at the main Pinehurst complex. In addition, its slightly more remote location makes it a little bit more of a chore to head elsewhere to take in another 18 holes. Then again, the other great Pinehurst courses are within 10 to 15 minutes, so the inconvenience is relative.

Bring extra balls to account for the hazards that populate the course. If you can afford a quality soft ball like the good players use, a balata-material ball or its synthetic equivalent, it will help when you're searching for extra spin and control on your approach shots to these firm greens.

Pine Needles Lodge & Golf Club

1005 Midland Rd., Southern Pines, NC 28387; phone (800) 747-7272 or (910) 692-8611

Tees:

> Gold: 6,708 yards, par-71, USGA rating 72.2, slope 131
>
> Blue: 6,318 yards, par-71, USGA rating 70.2, slope 126
>
> White: 6,003 yards, par-71, USGA rating 68.6, slope 124
>
> Red: 5,039 yards, par-71, USGA rating 68.4, slope 118

Challenge: ★★★½

Variety: ★★★

Terrain: ★★★★

Beauty/Visual Appeal: ★★★½

Pace of Play: ★★★

Golf Facilities: ★★★★½

14-Club Test: ★★★½

Intangibles: ★★★★½

Value: ★★★

Just the Facts Year Opened: 1927; Course Designer: Donald Ross; Walking: Yes; Greens Fee: $75–135 ; 9-Hole/Twilight Rate: Yes; Pull Carts: No; Practice Range: Yes; Club Rental: Yes.

Description and Comments Certain championship courses earn their status through fear and awe. Pine Needles, on the other hand, charms the socks off you. Typically, resort guests walk off the 18th green grinning ear to ear, saying, "I love this course! Can we play it again this afternoon?"

For the field in the 1996 U.S Women's Open, Pine Needles was set up at its sternest. Greens were firm and fast, the rough was up—par was a good score. Nevertheless, when the best women golfers in the world finished up their travails, their reactions were unanimous: "We love this course! When can we come back?"

Actually, the women are coming back to contest their national championship at Pine Needles in 2001. What's important here, however, is that it proves that Pine Needles is one of those truly rare birds: a course that can challenge the best, yet be enormously fun for Joe or Jane Average.

Pine Needles is located in Southern Pines, three pleasant miles down the road from the Village of Pinehurst. The word *hurst* means a wooded plot of rising ground. Throw some "pines" on top, and you have captured the look of Pine Needles perfectly. Legendary architect Donald Ross carved out his 18 gems from gently rolling, pine tree–covered sandhill terrain. Adding further spice to the cool green longleaf pines is around-the-calendar color bursts provided by magnolias and hollies, dogwoods, and azaleas, plus other flora. Quail, deer, foxes, and squirrels are frequent visitors to the Pine Needles course and an especially welcome guest is the endangered red-cockaded woodpecker, which has found a safe haven in Pine Needles.

If this setting seems incredibly idyllic—it is—the golf holes themselves offer more than just good looks—most are full of challenge and bite. Nevertheless, you'll have to determine for yourself whether Pine Needles is for you and worth its $135 price tag. After all, as with many Donald Ross classics, this course features much more steak than sizzle. Only three water hazards and fewer than 50 bunkers dot the landscape. Instead, the challenge—and pleasure—comes from maneuvering your ball through the pines, keeping it out of the occasionally fierce rough, and wielding a highly competent arsenal of short shots.

As is the case at Pinehurst No. 2, the virtues that lead to Pine Needles' high national rankings aren't readily apparent at first glance, but become quite clear as you ease into the round. The course opens with a benign, "shake-off-the-cobwebs" par-5, but its well-bunkered green, crowned (crested in the center with sharp dropoffs to the sides) in classic Donald Ross fashion, can turn "easy" birdies into disappointing bogies in a hurry.

The meat of this course lies in its steady succession of strong par-4s, beginning with the second hole, a rugged 451-yarder that plays slightly downhill to a green that slopes beguilingly away from the player. At the 4th, you are confronted with an uphill tee shot over a lake at the 416-yard par-4. Five other par-4s measure in the 430 yards or better range, where most golfers will do well to make par on any of them.

To reward you for your inevitable battles with the collection of par-4s, Ross has provided one of the finest quartets of par-3s around. The 207-yard 5th, played to a wildly undulating green and the rock-solid 189-yard 13th are memorable, but the hole at Pine Needles that will linger longest is the petite 3rd. Measuring only 134 yards from the back tees, the third features a wide teeing ground, with a backdrop of pines and shrubs, sitting slightly elevated above a small lake, which fronts the green. An arresting backcloth behind the green boasts towering pines and bursts of colorful dogwoods and flowers. To conquer the 3rd, however, you'll have to master the green, which slopes severely from back to front and is well fortified by bunkers. As with nearly every hole at Pine Needles, the 3rd is lovely and enticing, yet deceptively difficult. Every hole out here is completely playable, yet utterly bogeyable.

Insider Tips   Spend some extra time before and after your round at Pine Needles. There's a warmth and aura of good feeling about the whole place. There are hundreds of courses with more challenge and drama, including a half dozen in the Pinehurst area alone, but hardly a one is so rich in atmosphere. The easiest basis of comparison is the main complex at Pinehurst, which is absolutely marvelous, but is so large and efficient that it takes on the air of a gussied-up factory, almost a Hollywood conception of what the "Pinehurst experience" should be. Pine Needles boasts a first-class, challenging, tournament-caliber course, but in every other regard, it exudes a rustic, relaxed charm.

Much of the warmth of Pine Needles is traceable to the resort's family-run ownership, spearheaded by one of golf's leading ladies, Peggy Kirk Bell. A founding member of the LPGA, Bell is not only one of the most genial people in the business but also one of its finest instructors, famed for her "Golfari" clinics.

Thus, it comes as no surprise that the practice and teaching facility at Pine Needles is one of the best in golf. Included are three putting greens, practice bunkers, a double-ended driving range, and—perhaps best of all for fanatics who want to hit balls rain or shine—covered hitting stalls.

Bring a lofted fairway wood or trouble wood with you. More often than not, the combination of healthy rough bordering the fairways and firm, crowned greens require more loft and a higher ball flight than long and certain mid-irons are capable of providing.

For the ultimate challenge, to play Pine Needles when it's firm and fast, the way Donald Ross designed it, hit it in early autumn, but definitely call ahead to make sure they're not aerating the greens that week. At the very least, play it in the afternoon. Mornings are beautiful too, but in spring and summer, the moisture makes the already difficult rough wet and slightly softens the greens, making them slightly easier to negotiate. In summer, they've got to water the fairways and greens a fair amount to keep the grass healthy in the extreme heat, so the course won't play quite as "fast" at that time.

Take advantage of the practice facilities to work on your short game before your round. The green complexes here are not as severe as at Pinehurst No. 2, but they're still fairly demanding. When you're just off the green on a surface shaved smooth, when in doubt, choose the putter—it's the safest play.

Pace of play tends to be very respectable at Pine Needles, assuming you're not trapped in the rough or unduly menaced by the greens. Usually, an errant shot finds friendly brown pine straw, making your ball easy to find so you probably won't lose too many balls or spend much time looking. An added bonus to the reasonably high greens fee is that it tends to eliminate the casual duffer from showing up and clogging up the play. Consequently, it's easy to fit Pine Needles in a 36-hole day, whether you choose a replay here, or perhaps a round across the street at its sister property, Mid Pines.

The Pit Golf Links

Highway 5, Pinehurst, NC 28374; phone (800) 574-4653 or (910) 944-1600

How To Get On   Tee times can be made 90 days in advance.

Tees:

>   Championship: 6,600 yards, par-71, USGA rating 72.3, slope 139
>
>   Blue: 6,138 yards, par-71, USGA rating 70.2, slope 128
>
>   White: 5,690 yards, par-71, USGA rating 68.4, slope 121
>
>   Red: 4,789 yards, par-71, USGA rating 68.9, slope 120

Challenge: ★★★★	Golf Facilities: ★★★
Variety: ★★★	14-Club Test: ★★★
Terrain: ★★★½	Intangibles: ★★★
Beauty/Visual Appeal: ★★★	Value: ★★★★
Pace of Play: ★★½	

Just the Facts   Year Opened: 1985; Course Designer: Dan Maples; Walking: Yes; Greens Fee: $25–85; 9-Hole/Twilight Rate: Yes; Pull Carts: No; Practice Range: Yes; Club Rental: Yes.

Description and Comments   "Prepare to be amazed" at this most unique of Pinehurst area courses. So unusual and stark are The Pit's visual appeal and shot challenges that the course has polarized first-time players since its inception in 1985. You either love it or hate it, but without question, you'll react to it. Frankly, many more people love it than hate it. In fact, a minority of folks (call them heretics, if you will), actually place this as one of the region's top three courses. Others wouldn't play it again if you paid them. We think it fits somewhere in between, but much closer to the top than to the bottom.

Since the 1920s, the 230-acre site had been mined and excavated as a commercial sand pit. Along came architect Dan Maples, a local boy who knows the Pinehurst area as well as any architect alive, as both his father and grandfather worked under the legendary master himself, Donald Ross. Maples cast a discerning eye at the abandoned (by the 1980s) sand pit and envisioned a golf course.

The Pit earns its name as a links because fully half its holes play over and through sandy expanses and tall shaggy sandhills, many of which jut into the fairways, lending a certain Irish/Scottish flavor to the proceedings. Then again, there are nearly as many of these sandhills that are shaded by pines and carpeted in brown pine needles, a look that says we're definitely in Pinehurst. Then, boom! You're confronted with holes 11 through 13, which is pure Florida, including the 167-yard, island green, par-3 12th. Scrub oak and rumpled underbrush complete the one-of-a-kind landscape that is the Pit.

Where people get to debating the merits of The Pit is in the quirkiness of the holes themselves. Some find them unfair and exasperating, others find them supremely interesting and never dull. Some of the controversy stems from the fact that if you miss a shot at any time on most of the holes, it's gone. Don't even look for it, it's in so deep. To be fair, some of the more severe holes have been eased a bit in the last few years, adding to the course's playability. Plus, since the time The Pit debuted, many other "all-or-nothing" courses have sprung up throughout the United States, so the shock value has worn off a bit. It's one of those courses that may depend on how you're playing that day. It's also one of those courses you've got to come back and play a second time to figure out just what you need to do.

The Pit isn't exactly the Brad Pitt of Pinehurst, as it's probably the least attractive of the major courses in the area. Then again, after playing some of the more traditional-looking tests in the region, you may be perfectly ready to embrace this scruffy, rough-around-the-edges gem, whether it's because you're drawn to the raw, unkempt look or because you simply want a change of pace.

Insider Tips This course looks very short on the scorecard, but don't be deceived. It's an awfully tough test from the tips. You had either be very good or extremely accurate to tee it up from the "screw" tees, which are what the back tees here are perfectly called. Better you should enjoy the course from the spike tees, which check in at a manageable 6,138 yards and have fun. Because the penalties are so great for hitting it off line on nearly every hole at The Pit, keeping it in play is a must, so choose your club accordingly. Whenever possible, err on the conservative side. You'll spend a lot less time combing the unplayable areas for missing balls, and you'll enjoy the course a lot more.

Holes to pay attention to include the long par-3 4th, a brute from the 232-yard back tee; the controversial 8th, a short par-5 of only 480 yards that confounds players as it zigzags through the imposing mounds and buttonhooks to the left at the green, which is itself guarded by a handsome but annoying large tree; and finally, the distinctive downhill par-3 16th. Just 145 yards from the tips and 100 from the middle, this bunkerless mighty-mite is sunk into one of several abandoned pits on site.

By all means, spend some time at the range before you play The Pit. The balance between the nines is quite peculiar. The front nine weighs in at a hefty 3,528 yards from the tips, but the back nine measures just 3,072 yards. Thus, you'd better have your "A" game ready to roll when you reach the first tee.

Women, don't let the course's difficult surrounds frighten you away. The front tees make the course extremely playable. In a 1998 survey by a major golf publication, The Pit was ranked number 24 in the country of the 50 best places for women to play in the United States.

A Pinehurst Sampler
Beacon Ridge Golf & Country Club
6000 Longleaf Dr., West End, NC 27376; phone (800) 416-5204 or (910) 673-2950

Tees: Championship: 6,414 yards, par-72, USGA rating 70.7, slope 125,
Greens Fee: $15–40

Challenge: ★★½	Golf Facilities: ★★½
Variety: ★★★	14-Club Test: ★★½
Terrain: ★★★½	Intangibles: ★★½
Beauty/Visual Appeal: ★★★	Value: ★★★
Pace of Play: ★★★	

Description and Comments   Pleasant if unspectacular golf, but one of the genuine values in the Sandhills. Golf villas on site make course access easy. The watery par-4 13th, and the strong par-5 18th, are two of the most memorable holes.

The Carolina
277 Avenue of the Carolina, Whispering Pines, NC 28327; phone (888) PALMER2 or (910) 949-2811

Tees: Championship: 6,928 yards, par-72, USGA rating 73.9, slope 138
Greens Fee: $49–84

Challenge: ★★★★	Golf Facilities: ★★★
Variety: ★★★	14-Club Test: ★★★
Terrain: ★★★★	Intangibles: ★★★
Beauty/Visual Appeal: ★★★½	Value: ★★★½
Pace of Play: ★★½	

Description and Comments   As you can see by the phone number, the course has an Arnold Palmer connection—he and his company designed the course. It's only two years old, but it's vying admirably to be one of the region's best. Huge greens; wide, grass-dotted waste areas; and numerous wild flowers are only part of The Carolina scene. Preserved natural wetlands and several grand changes in elevation spice the play at The Carolina, already one of the most challenging, beautiful courses in the neighborhood.

The Club at Longleaf
2001 Midland Rd., Southern Pines, NC 28327; phone (800) 889-5323 or (910) 692-6100

Tees: Championship: 6,600 yards, par-71, USGA rating 70.9, slope 121
Greens Fee: $26–61

Challenge: ★★½	Golf Facilities: ★★★★
Variety: ★★★	14-Club Test: ★★★
Terrain: ★★★½	Intangibles: ★★★
Beauty/Visual Appeal: ★★★½	Value: ★★★★
Pace of Play: ★★★	

Description and Comments Another of the better bargains in the Pinehurst area, Longleaf is a true charmer. It's located a couple of intersections away from the Village of Pinehurst and occupies the site of the former Starland Farms, for years the training ground of some of the country's top thoroughbreds. As a nostalgic reminder, architect Dan Maples incorporated some of the fence and training track into the course's design. A tad schizophrenic, Longleaf offers a mildly rolling, open front nine, with a topsy-turvy, well-wooded back nine. Somehow the mix works.

Deercroft Golf Club

30000 Deercroft Dr., Wagram, NC 28396; phone (910) 369-3107
Tees: Championship: 6,745 yards, par-72, USGA rating 72.6, slope 125
Greens Fee: $25–65

Challenge: ★★½	Golf Facilities: ★★½
Variety: ★★½	14-Club Test: ★★½
Terrain: ★★★	Intangibles: ★★½
Beauty/Visual Appeal: ★★★	Value: ★★★
Pace of Play: ★★★½	

Description and Comments Located near the Sandhills' 10,000-acre wildlife refuge, Deercroft provides some attractive scenery amid the slash pines, a hybrid of the longleaf and shortleaf varieties. If you are accurate, you should score well here as the course is not overly long or extraordinarily difficult. However, the course is nicely bunkered, with narrow fairways, so if you stray, you'll see your score start to balloon. This is one of the Pinehurst area's hidden gems, so it tends to be less crowded than some big-name courses.

Foxfire Resort and Country Club, East Course

9 Foxfire Blvd., Jackson Springs, NC 27281; phone (800) 736-9347 or (910) 295-5555
Tees: Championship: 6,851 yards, par-72, USGA rating 73.5, slope 130
Greens Fee: $25–62

Challenge: ★★★	Golf Facilities: ★★½
Variety: ★★½	14-Club Test: ★★★
Terrain: ★★★	Intangibles: ★★½
Beauty/Visual Appeal: ★★★	Value: ★★½
Pace of Play: ★★★	

Descriptions and Comments   One of two solid tests of golf at this modest, comfortable resort. The East is slightly longer and slightly tougher than the West, but both are worth your while. Number one on the East is one of the region's most challenging opening holes, a watery par-5 with a green guarded by four traps. Recent renovations in 1998, including new irrigation, bunker sand, and fairway contouring, have improved the East course markedly.

Hyland Hills Golf Club

4100 U.S. 1 North, Southern Pines, NC 28387; phone (910) 692-3752
Tees: Championship: 6,726 yards, par-72, USGA rating 70.4, slope 124
Greens Fee: $20–55

Challenge: ★★	Golf Facilities: ★★★½
Variety: ★★★	14-Club Test: ★★½
Terrain: ★★★	Intangibles: ★★½
Beauty/Visual Appeal: ★★★	Value: ★★★★
Pace of Play: ★★★	

Description and Comments   Features the highest elevation in the region, though we're hardly talking nosebleed territory. This 27-year-old Tom Jackson design is especially playable for women. The emphasis here is on strategy and scenery, not power and distance. An excellent value.

Legacy Golf Links

U.S. Highway 15-501 South, Aberdeen, NC 28315; phone (800) 344-8825 or (910) 944-8825
Tees: Championship: 7,018 yards, par-72, USGA rating 73.2, slope 132
Greens Fee: $25–72

Challenge: ★★★	Golf Facilities: ★★★½
Variety: ★★★½	14-Club Test: ★★★★
Terrain: ★★★½	Intangibles: ★★★½
Beauty/Visual Appeal: ★★★	Value: ★★★★
Pace of Play: ★★★½	

Descriptions and Comments   Even in high season, Legacy is a value at $72. It's attractive, magnificently groomed, and offers a strong test for the scratch player while still being fun for the once-a-month golfer. The front nine features vast expanses of exposed-sand rough, and the back nine has water in play on all but one hole. Designer Jack Nicklaus II did a fine job, especially with the memorable 18th hole, a gorgeous par-4 that doglegs right over a pond. The United States Golf Association recently recognized the merits of The Legacy, awarding the course the 2000 Women's National Amateur Public Links Championship.

Little River Golf Club

500 Little River Farm Rd., Carthage, NC 28374; phone (910) 949-4600

Tees: Championship: 6,909 yards, par-72, USGA rating 73.6, slope 132
Greens Fee: $40–70

Challenge: ★★★½	Golf Facilities: ★★★½
Variety: ★★★★	14-Club Test: ★★★★
Terrain: ★★★½	Intangibles: ★★★★
Beauty/Visual Appeal: ★★★★	Value: ★★★½
Pace of Play: ★★★	

Description and Comments   This Dan Maples–designed course is draped over land that once was a horse farm, and much of the countryside is still visible from many of the holes—the clubhouse is a renovated hay barn. Beyond the great scenery, the course has a lot to offer. Tight fairways, water on six holes, and fast, severe greens create a supreme challenge. Little River Farm features a beguiling blend of open and wooded holes on rolling terrain. Because the soil here is more clay-based than sand-based, as is the case with most Pinehurst courses, there is a greater variety of trees to be found. Seventeen is the signature hole (485-yard, par-5), requiring a tee shot to an hourglass-shaped fairway surrounded by wetlands. For the second shot you must decide if you're going for the green, which is reachable but is well bunkered and guarded by a pond on the left, or play a more conservative lay-up shot.

Mid Pines Golf Club

1010 Midland Rd., Southern Pines, NC 28387; phone (800) 323-2114 or (910) 692-9362

Tees: Championship: 6,515 yards, par-72, USGA rating 71.4, slope 127
Greens Fee: $49–120

Challenge: ★★★	Golf Facilities: ★★½
Variety: ★★★	14-Club Test: ★★★½
Terrain: ★★★	Intangibles: ★★★★
Beauty/Visual Appeal: ★★★½	Value: ★★★
Pace of Play: ★★★	

Description and Comments   A classic 1921 Donald Ross design, Mid Pines is a well-preserved treat, a joy to play. Slightly easier—shorter, though tighter—than its sister course at Pine Needles, Mid Pines sports a couple of reachable par-5s, lively springtime blossoms, and a handsome par-4 finishing hole with the backdrop of the historic Mid Pines Inn. There are several odd, quirky holes here and some abrupt elevation changes, but all in all this is a soothing course for the ego.

The Plantation

1 Midland Rd., Pinehurst, NC 28374; phone (800) 633-2085 or (910) 695-3193

Tees: Championship: 7,135 yards, par-72, USGA rating 74.5, slope 140
Greens Fee: $60–115

Challenge: ★★★★	Golf Facilities: ★★★
Variety: ★★★½	14-Club Test: ★★★★
Terrain: ★★★★	Intangibles: ★★★★
Beauty/Visual Appeal: ★★★½	Value: ★★★
Pace of Play: ★★★½	

Description and Comments This 1993 Arnold Palmer design boasts absolutely superior greens and a terrific quartet of risk/reward par-5s. An extremely challenging course, much of the trouble is in the form of long par-4s on the back nine and forced carries over bunkers and water, to fairways and greens set on diagonals. It's a tough track, but not impossible. The club is mostly private these days, but some off-season outside play is permitted. Call ahead for availability—as one of the top 100 "public" courses in the country, it's truly worth the effort.

Pinehurst No. 4

One Carolina Vista, P.O. Box 4000, Village of Pinehurst, NC 28374; phone (800) 795-4653 or (910) 295-8141; www.pinehurst.com

Tees: Yardage, par, USGA rating, and slope not available at press time
Greens Fee: $70–110

Ratings not available at press time.

Description and Comments This is the crazy quilt of Pinehurst courses. It was originally designed by Donald Ross, then abandoned after World War II. It was then resurrected by Peter Tufts. In 1973, Robert Trent Jones Sr. changed several holes, and ten years later, his son Rees effected further modifications. All of this is merely trivia in 1999, because the course is in the middle of a complete makeover by modern golf's most honored designer, Tom Fazio. Call ahead to find out the opening date. It's Pinehurst and Fazio—it's probably going to be special. Ratings are not available until after the redesign is completed.

Talamore at Pinehurst

1595 Midland Rd., Southern Pines, NC 28387; phone (910) 692-5884
Tees: Championship: 7,020 yards, par-72, USGA rating 72.9, slope 142

Greens Fee: $39–87

Challenge: ★★★★

Variety: ★★★½

Terrain: ★★★½

Beauty/Visual Appeal: ★★★½

Pace of Play: ★★★

Golf Facilities: ★★★½

14-Club Test: ★★★★

Intangibles: ★★★½

Value: ★★★½

Description and Comments This is the course famous for its caddies—yes, llamas. Apparently, these are social animals as well as pack animals. As such, they only go out in pairs. Is it worth the extra $100? If you're into novelty, absolutely. The llamas have limited availability (late fall through early spring), so call ahead. But this Rees Jones–designed course offers much more than just novelty: It features a tough but fair layout with rolling terrain, many mounds, and an astonishing 122 bunkers. This is not a course for weaker players. Besides the multitude of bunkers, five holes require forced tee-shot carries over wetlands. At 623 yards from the tips, Talamore's opening hole is one of the region's finest.

Tobacco Road Golf Club

442 Tobacco Rd., Sanford, NC 27330; phone (877) 284-3762 or (919) 775-1940

Tees: Championship: 6,554 yards, par-71, USGA rating 73.2, slope 150

Greens Fee: $68–88

Challenge: ★★★★★

Variety: ★★★½

Terrain: ★★★★

Beauty/Visual Appeal: ★★★★

Pace of Play: ★½

Golf Facilities: ★★

14-Club Test: ★★★

Intangibles: ★★★★

Value: ★★★

Description and Comments The latest creation from golf's hottest modern architect, Mike Strantz, who also designed True Blue and Caledonia in Myrtle Beach and Royal New Kent and Stonehouse near Williamsburg, Virginia. This course represents one of the most unique designs in the history of golf. Folks either love it or hate it, though at the very least, good players appreciate the distinctiveness and artistry of the architect's efforts. Tobacco Road features towering sandhills, remarkable variety in landscape shaping and bunker design, and plenty of alternative routes to get from tee to green. The club's rustic clubhouse burned down in May 1999, but another is on the way. Unconventional and not for everyone's tastes, but if you appreciate innovative design Tobacco Road will prove quite addicting.

Whispering Woods Golf Club

26 Sandpiper Dr., Whispering Pines, NC 28327; phone (800) 224-5061 or (910) 949-4653

Tees: Championship: 6,324 yards, par-70, USGA rating 70.5, slope 122
Greens Fee: $25–50

Challenge: ★★	Golf Facilities: ★★★
Variety: ★★	14-Club Test: ★★
Terrain: ★★½	Intangibles: ★★★
Beauty/Visual Appeal: ★★½	Value: ★★★
Pace of Play: ★★★	

Description and Comments   This course underwent a facelift in 1994 and more trees and sand bunkers were added, thereby increasing the difficulty. However, it remains an easy, pleasant course that is not extremely long. Its par-70 features an interesting friendly mix of holes, with only three par-5s and five par-3s, making it a painless task to play to your handicap or better. It does have quite a few hills, which will affect your stance and make it more difficult to reach their very good greens. This would not be on our top five for your visit here, but if you're looking for a value at a very good price this is the place to start.

Woodlake Country Club

150 Woodlake Blvd., Vass, NC 28394; phone (800) 334-1126 or (910) 245-4686

Tees:
  Maples Course
  Championship: 7,012 yards, par-72, USGA rating 73.4, slope 134
  Palmer Course
  Championship: 7,150 yards, par-72, USGA rating 74.1, slope 134

Greens Fee: $30–70

Challenge: ★★★½	Golf Facilities: ★★★
Variety: ★★★	14-Club Test: ★★★
Terrain: ★★★	Intangibles: ★★★
Beauty/Visual Appeal: ★★★	Value: ★★★
Pace of Play: ★★★	

Description and Comments   One of the better holes in Greater Pinehurst is the second hole at Woodlake Country Club's original course (the Maples Course), a dogleg right, reachable par-5 that plays to an island fairway. Many of the holes here skirt the property's large and lovely man-made lake (the state's largest man-made lake). Arnold Palmer designed the second course at Woodlake, which also borders the club's mammoth lake and has huge greens, a difference from the original course, with heavy undulations. A good track, but honestly not in the same league as his other efforts in the Pinehurst area.

Lodging

EXPENSIVE

Pinehurst Resort & Country Club

One Carolina Vista, P.O. Box 4000, Village of Pinehurst; phone (800) ITS-GOLF or (910) 295-6811; www.pinehurst.com; Rates: $157–216 (standard hotel room)

The Pinehurst hotel, originally built as The Carolina in 1901, is nestled impressively at the end of a long, tree-lined lane in the heart of Pinehurst. It sits a three-minute drive down the same lane from the Pinehurst Country Club. The hotel is one of a handful of large, classic Southern "grand dames," resorts that include such distinguished names as The Cloister, The Homestead, and The Greenbrier. Early in 1999, as a nod to tradition, the folks at Pinehurst decided to switch the main hotel back to its original name: The Carolina.

Potentially, the problem with most of these types is that for all their emphasis on Southern grace and charm, they tend to be kind of stuffy, where the feeling is akin more to a private club than a place of public accommodation. Fortunately, the Pinehurst hotel is lovely in an old world way, but is no longer stuck in the past. The lobby is bright and accommodating, with easy check-in/check-out access. Service is excellent.

So that there's no mistaking that this is a hotel for serious golfers, the Ryder Cup lounge is located just off the lobby, with its nice assortment of memorabilia from golf's most ballyhooed team event.

Also conveniently located just off the lobby is the Carolina Dining Room, a jacket-required testament to good living and healthy appetites. If it's a tad overpriced, at least the setting is traditional and comfortable. Noteworthy is their fabled breakfast buffet, which for years was a monument to king cholesterol. In recent years, numerous healthy alternatives have popped up on the long, linen-lined serving tables. Calorie lovers needn't fret. The best biscuit and sausage gravy to be found in these parts can still be had each and every morning.

Note: You must be a guest of one of the Pinehurst Resort properties to play at the Pinehurst Country Club. This doesn't mean you have to stay at the Pinehurst Hotel (again, now known as The Carolina), however. Guests of the Manor Inn, a less expensive, less formal property owned by the Pinehurst Resort, also have full access. The Manor Inn opened in 1923, features 46 suites and parlors, and is home to a fun place for food and drink, Mulligan's.

Other lodging options at the Pinehurst Resort include fairway villas and condominiums, which may be just the ticket if you've brought your family along or are with a group of guys or couples. Finally, Pinehurst recently bought and refurbished the venerable Holly Inn, which dates to 1895. More intimate than The Carolina (85 rooms versus 220), this quaint, historic charmer will reopen in April 1999.

Golf Packages   Pinehurst offers seven different packages, including The Putterboy Package, which is a good value if you're going to golf marquee courses No. 2, No. 7, and No. 8. The package includes accommodations, dinner (beginning on day of arrival), and breakfast (through day of departure), daily golf (second round included), cart and practice range, sleeve of Titleist golf balls, club storage, fitness programs, and use of hotel fitness center.

Mid Pines Inn and Golf Club

1010 Midland Rd.; Southern Pines; phone (800) 323-2114 or (910) 692-2114; www.golfnc.com; Rates $60–95 (standard room)

Mid Pines Inn was built in the 1920s and is a grand Georgian-style hotel that seamlessly blends old-world charm and Southern hospitality. The hotel lies on the Donald Ross–designed golf course, which opened in 1921—it is the only course in the area that remains unchanged from the legendary master architect's original design.

The aura of golf history is felt as soon as you enter the Mid Pines driveway and intensifies as you step into the rotunda that serves as the hotel's lobby. No two rooms in this 118-room charmer are alike, but each captures the inn's graceful past. There's a very nostalgic feel to this property, as reflected by both interiors and exteriors. Narrow hallways tend to be graced with scores of historic photos. Porches tend to have screen doors that creak. If your tastes run to "comfortable as an old shoe," rather than "squeaky-clean modern," you'll enjoy Mid Pines. All of the public rooms at Mid Pines have recently undergone renovation, but the old-world appeal remains. In addition to the main hotel, there are also five Golf Course Villa homes along the 10th fairway, which can be ideal for families and groups.

Along with your golf clubs, make sure to bring a hearty appetite, as you will find the dining room off the main lobby featuring a wide variety of edibles throughout the day. Start your day with a visit to the expansive breakfast buffet that includes fruits, cereals, baked goods, and scrumptious made-to-order waffles. Lunch is also buffet-style with something for everyone. Dinner options are tasty and pleasant, but they fall short of memorable. After dinner, you can work some of those calories off in the game room, where you will find Ping-Pong, billiards, cards, and darts. To wet your whistle, stop by the Cosgroves Lounge after your round or for a nightcap and enjoy the collection of great golf memorabilia.

Golf Packages Mid Pines offers three golf packages: The Donald Ross (for the serious golfer), The Knollwood (the 18-hole package), and the Golf Lovers (the winter value package). All of the golf packages include room accommodations, three meals (except for the Golf Lover, which has two), golf each day at either Mid Pines or Pine Needles, cart (if desired), range balls, bag handling, transportation, and club storage. The number of rounds offered varies by package: Ross—two rounds per day; Knoll-wood—one round per day; Golf Lover—unlimited.

If you are only planning on playing one round or so during your stay, you also may want to look into the Bed & Breakfast and the Full American Plan packages. Because Pine Needles is a public course, with greens fees ranging from $80 to $135 depending on the time of year you play, this may be a more efficient option for your trip (you can make tee times for the day of play only).

Pine Needles Lodge & Golf Club

1005 Midland Rd., Southern Pines; phone (800) 747-7272 or (910) 692-7111; www.golfnc.com; Rates: call hotel

Like its sister hotel Mid Pines, Pine Needles Lodge & Golf Club also opened for business in the 1920s and has since grown into one of Southern Pines's most revered inns. The hotel is located adjacent to another one of Donald Ross's creations, which served as host for the Women's 1996 U.S. Open, as it will in 2001. Guests have easy access to the course as well as all of the resort's other amenities, including a swimming pool and grass tennis courts. Pine Needles also boasts a sensational golf school hosted by legendary golfer Peggy Kirk Bell, who owns Pine Needles and Mid Pines with her family.

Nearly all of the guest rooms have undergone some degree of renovation over the past three years. The charm of the original design remains, but there are now modern conveniences, such as in-room coffee service.

Dining at Pine Needles may be as memorable as the golf; okay, a close second. Breakfast includes the favorite omelet/waffle/pancake station where chefs await with pecans, chocolate chips, blueberries, strawberry butter, and more to create a customized masterpiece. It doesn't stop there: no visit to Pine Needles is complete until you have sampled their famous fried chicken—the specialty of the house. On the lighter side you will find fresh seafood, pasta, and vegetables.

For a post-round celebration there is a wonderful lounge overlooking the 1st and 18th holes where you can sit back and enjoy a libation (or two).

Golf Packages As with Mid Pines, Pine Needles offers three golf packages: The Donald Ross (for the serious golfer; detailed below), The Knollwood (the 18-hole package), and the Golf Lovers (the winter value package). All of the golf packages include room accommodations, three meals (except for the Golf Lover, which has two), golf each day at either Mid Pines or Pine Needles, cart (if desired), range balls, bag handling, transportation, and club storage. The number of rounds offered varies by package: Ross—two rounds per day; Knollwood—one round per day; Golf Lover—unlimited.

If you are only planning on playing one round or so during your stay, you also may want to look into the Bed & Breakfast and the Full American Plan packages. Because Pine Needles is a public course, with green fees ranging from $80 to $135 depending on the time of year you play, this may be a more efficient option for your trip (you can make tee times for the day of play only).

MODERATE

Foxfire Resort & Country Club

9 Foxfire Blvd., Foxfire Village; phone (910) 295-5555; fax (910) 295-6928; www.golfsouth.com; Rates: $95–100

Foxfire Resort is located six miles northwest of the Village of Pinehurst in a residential community. The resort is comprised of a series of condo units, ranging in size from one to two bedrooms, that are nicely appointed and come with a full kitchen and living room. The resort boasts two golf courses, a full-size pool, and two tennis courts. New management and substantial capital investments have made a measurable impact on Foxfire.

Golf Packages   Golf packages available; contact resort for details.

Pine Crest Inn

Dogwood Road, P.O. Box 879, Pinehurst, NC 28374; phone (800) 371-2545 or (910) 295-6121; www.pinecrestinnpinehurst.com; Rates: $49–103

This lovely inn was owned by Donald Ross for 27 years, until his death in 1948. Located in the heart of the Village of Pinehurst, the Pine Crest Inn provides easy access to the village's antique and specialty shops as well as sumptuous restaurants. In fact, its main dining room is the toughest reservation in town on Saturday nights, as it is highly popular with locals. One of the most popular traditions in town takes place at the Pine Crest: lobby chipping, a nightly ritual where contestants hit off the lobby carpet to a carpet-covered platform near the fireplace.

The inn has a modified American Plan, which includes a country breakfast and an evening dinner. Tee times for Pinehurst courses may be requested by the Pine Crest Inn three days in advance of play (day of play for No. 2). Times for most area courses may be made 60 days in advance of the day of play. For something special, consider the Telephone Cottage (once a switching station for the inn), which is a separate cottage steps away from the inn. This cottage offers privacy with all the amenities of the hotel. There are also five Corner Rooms in the inn, which are a little more spacious and have extra windows. The Standard Rooms are also spacious with deluxe features.

INEXPENSIVE

Marriott Residence Inn

105 Spruce Rd., Southern Pines, NC 28387; phone (888) 702-GOLF or (910) 693-3400; Rates: $79–110; Built: 1996; Renovations: None

Hampton Inn

1675 Highway 1 South, Southern Pines, NC; phone (800) 333-9266 or (910) 692-9266; Rates: $59–79; Built: 1998; Renovations: None

Dining

There's a little something for everyone looking for a good meal in the Sandhills region, just not an abundance of anything. North Carolina isn't quite the Deep South, but it's Southern enough to find good grits, biscuits, and red-eye sausage gravy at breakfast at most restaurants. As befits a high-end resort destination, there is a disproportionate smattering of "special occasion" restaurants; though expensive, not one is outrageously priced. Mostly, the cuisine and the prices are strictly middle America.

Cabin on the Green 4933 Highway 211 West, West End; phone (910) 673-3497. American/Continental; Moderate; Reservations recommended. Cozy spot. Rustic log cabin building tucked in pines, dates to 1911.

The Coves Market Square 1181 Market Square, Pinehurst; phone (910) 295-3400. Continental; Moderate; Reservations recommended. Perfect place for a post-round white wine libation.

The Lob-Steer Inn U.S. Highway 1, Southern Pines; phone (910) 692-3503. American; Moderate–Expensive; Reservations recommended. A steakhouse with character—a must for surf 'n' turf fans.

Longleaf Country Club 2001 Midland Rd., Southern Pines; phone (910) 692-4411. Family/golf grill; Moderate; Reservations suggested. Nice view of horse training track.

The Jefferson Inn 150 W. New Hampshire Ave., Southern Pines; phone (910) 692-5300. Continental; Expensive; Reservations required for dinner. Excellent steaks and patio dining in season.

Pine Crest Inn Dogwood Road, Pinehurst; phone (910) 295-6121. Continental; Expensive; Reservations recommended, especially for Saturday nights. This is the place to eat and be seen on Saturday nights. This is a charming old inn once owned by master architect Donald Ross.

Pine Needles Lodge 1005 Midland Rd., Southern Pines; phone (910) 692-7111. American; Expensive; Reservations recommended. The late award-winning golf writer Dick Taylor pronounced the resort's Southern fried chicken as "the best on earth." It is wonderful.

Pinehurst Resort and Country Club Carolina Vista Drive, Pinehurst; phone (910) 295-6811. Continental; Expensive; Reservations required for dinner; Jackets required at Carolina Dining Room at dinner. Hall-of-fame–quality breakfast buffet each morning.

Pinehurst Sundry & Soda Fountain 40 Chinquapin Rd., Pinehurst; phone (910) 295-3193. American; Inexpensive; Reservations not necessary. Old-fashioned soda fountain atmosphere in heart of the Village of Pinehurst. Burgers, wonderful shakes.

Pinehurst Track Restaurant Highway 5 (Race Track), Pinehurst; phone (910) 295-2597. Family; Inexpensive–Moderate; Reservations not necessary. The casual spot in town for breakfast meetings.

Activities

The drawback at Pinehurst is that they roll up the sidewalks awfully early. There's little in the region in the way of sightseeing or general family fun, unless the entire family is golf crazy. Horseback riding, boating and fishing at nearby lakes, horse-drawn carriage rides, and superb tennis top the list of activities in the Pinehurst area.

Nevertheless, if mom or dad wants to do 36 holes a day and the rest of the family pines for a breather from golf, here are a few suggestions:

Pottery Country Near the Sandhills town of Seagrove, this area is renowned for its hand-thrown pottery and dishware. Many of these independent pottery centers are open to the public, where you can see potters at work and can purchase their wares; phone (910) 873-8430.

Auto Racing: North Carolina Motor Speedway The famous Rockingham race track hosts NASCAR Busch Grand National and Winston Cup races. Guided tours available; phone (910) 582-2861.

Carriage Rides Through the Village of Pinehurst. Pinehurst Livery Stable; phone (910) 295-8456.

Miniature Golf Mini Pines, Southern Pines. Includes 800-foot go-cart track, baseball/softball batting cages. Lit for nighttime activity; phone (910) 692-4332.

Horseback Riding Ft. Bragg Riding Stables, Fayetteville. Open riding, lessons, pony rides, trail rides, and hay rides; phone (910) 396-4510.

Par-3 Golf Pine Horse Golf Club, Southern Pines. Real Bermuda fairways and water hazards, with synthetic turf tees and greens. Takes 45 minutes and costs $7; phone (910) 692-1941.

The 19th Hole

Wall-to-wall excitement Pinehurst is not. After golf, your options are pretty limited, especially if you're holed up in the Village of Pinehurst. Remember though, if you're in Pinehurst to begin with, you're there because you want to overdose on golf, not on nightlife. Be that as it may, there's a number of cozy spots where you can talk golf, watch sports, smoke cigars, and quaff your favorite beverages. Southern Pines and Aberdeen have more activity; Pinehurst has more class.

Pine Crest Inn Dogwood Road, Pinehurst; phone (910) 295-6121. If you want to head to a place for a brew or a cocktail and want to soak up the Pinehurst lore and legends, the bar here is the place. It remains the ultimate hangout for locals and tourists alike.

Squire's Pub 1720 U.S. 1 South, Southern Pines; phone (910) 695-1161. It serves up tasty British fare, but for those simply looking to wet the whistle after a full day of golf, Squire's features 56 kinds of beer, ale, stout, and porter.

Part Two

Western North Carolina

Overview

Okay, let's admit one thing right up front: When one mentions "golf vacation" and "North Carolina" in the same sentence, "Pinehurst" is what usually springs to mind. However, although Pinehurst is the state's leader in terms of golf options and history, it is not the only golf destination in North Carolina. Far from it. The area of western North Carolina, approximately an hour and a half drive west of Charlotte, is home to the Blue Ridge Mountains and some of the most scenic golf in the South, especially at fall foliage time. Unless you're a fan of high heat, humidity, and bugs, the happening summertime spot is the majestic breeze-fueled mountain areas of North Carolina, not the sizzling sandhills of Pinehurst.

Although construction and development has been the norm for many areas, nature is the focus and preservation the theme in western Carolina. As a result, golfers will find courses cut out from forests of birch, poplar, beech, hickory, and oak, with an abundance of wildlife only a sand wedge away. Golf here tends to be truly of the "relax and get away from it all" variety. There is a nice combination of resort and public golf courses in western North Carolina, though guest policies vary by course. For several of the top courses you will need to be a guest at the lodge or hotel to gain access.

As a group, the golf courses of western North Carolina are not as highly regarded as those in Pinehurst, Hilton Head, or northwest Michigan, for that matter. The attraction, frankly, is the region's weather, scenery, and relative proximity to major cities in the South, East, and Midwest. Be that as it may, there is an excellent variety of golf experiences from which to choose, some fair, others good, and a handful that are exceptional.

Courses tend to be shorter and tighter than in other areas due to construction limitations presented by the surrounding rocky shelves and dense forests, resulting in lower course ratings. However, there's plenty here to chal-

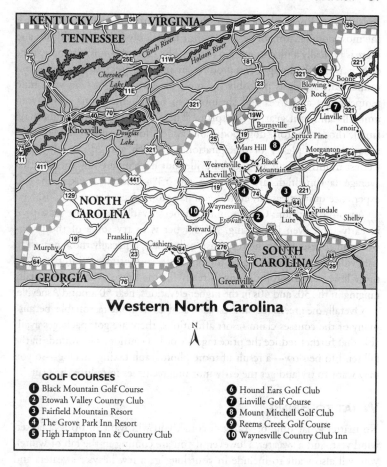

Western North Carolina

N
⋏

GOLF COURSES
1. Black Mountain Golf Course
2. Etowah Valley Country Club
3. Fairfield Mountain Resort
4. The Grove Park Inn Resort
5. High Hampton Inn & Country Club
6. Hound Ears Golf Club
7. Linville Golf Course
8. Mount Mitchell Golf Club
9. Reems Creek Golf Course
10. Waynesville Country Club Inn

lenge a good golfer. Water, especially mountain springs, comes into play throughout many of the courses, and the mountainous location will force golfers to overcome numerous uneven lies. Most courses in the region enjoy pleasant warm days and cool nights, making perfect conditions for good bentgrass greens that tend to be pretty quick and full of hard-to-read breaks. Because of the altitude, courses will play shorter than the scorecard indicates, so club accordingly. Also, your depth perception will be affected by the mountain vistas, so be sure to check your yardage before you swing away.

WHEN TO GO AND WHAT IT WILL COST

The majority of the courses in western North Carolina are open year-round, with the exception of the higher-altitude locations near Banner Elk and Blowing Rock, where snow is the norm during the winter. Summer is the most popular time of year—daytime highs only reach the mid-80s and there is typically a nice mountain breeze. The fall is the most dramatic time of year as the changing leaves produce an amazing visual backdrop to your round. Late-spring is probably the most pleasant time of year, with mild temperatures and trees and shrubbery in full bloom. Don't forget your umbrella and rain gear in the spring. There's a reason all that mountain laurel, rhododendron, dogwoods, and azaleas look so great in May—the mountains get plenty of precipitation in March and April. July is the wettest month in and around Asheville, but it's tempered by the fact that average daytime highs are 85 degrees with 73% humidity, making the golf experience quite pleasant, even if you have to dodge a few raindrops.

A word of caution: Courses in the higher elevations often are grass-poor in early- and even late-spring. A safer bet is to try some of the lower-elevation courses (or at the very least, call ahead), especially those nearest to Asheville if you're traveling to the region in springtime. Wintertime, for those lower-elevation locations, is really for the brave, with highs usually ranging in the 30s and 40s in the higher elevations, near 50 around Asheville.

Overall, the greens fees at these area courses are quite reasonable; because many of the courses claim resort affiliations, there are golf packages available that further reduce the price tag. A word of caution: The rounds in the fall tend to be slow—a result of more photograph taking, maybe—so you may want to try and get the early morning tee times to reduce the wait.

WHAT TO BRING

No matter what time of year you come, you will want to bring a jacket, wind vest, and a sweater. However, if you are coming in the fall or winter, you will also want to include in your luggage a few heavier sweaters and some gloves to ward off the possibly chilly temperatures. For spring and summer, you should also pack bug spray as well as some medicine if you tend to have allergies.

If you tend to hook or slice, you'll want to bring a few extra sleeves of balls, as the strays you hit may be hard to find in the surrounding forests.

As many of the courses tend to be short and narrow, your driver may stay in your bag more often than not. Perhaps tote an extra fairway wood in place of the driver. You may want to include an extra wedge (gap or lob) to take advantage of those short holes.

ONCE YOU'RE THERE

A multitude of golfing options abounds in western North Carolina. The number of rounds you decide to play will be dictated by the focus of your trip (that is, golf trip or family vacation), as well as the location of your accommodations. Many of the resorts in the area tend to be isolated, and playing a variety of courses may prove difficult and require a long commute. Thus, if you want to play more than just your own resort's course, you will have to plan your vacation carefully.

Basically, there are four general areas for golf in the mountains of western North Carolina. There is a cluster of courses in the greater Asheville region, plus additional clusters to the northeast, the south, and the west. It's not terribly difficult to combine the Asheville golf experience with one of the others, but it's somewhat impractical to combine any of the remaining three with each other. It's purely a matter of personal preference which individual destination you should choose. If you're seeking a true getaway filled with resorts that offer private club amenities and clientele, head to the northeast, where the Eseeola Lodge, with its Linville Golf Club and the Hound Ears Resort, offers the best one-two punch in the mountains.

A word to the wise: Driving in the region in broad daylight on a dry afternoon can be a thrill. At night, or in bad weather, navigating these twisting two-lane roads can be difficult at best, nightmarish at worst. Take it easy on the accelerator and you should be just fine.

One resort that offers top-notch accommodations and the opportunity to play other courses is the Grove Park Inn Resort. Located in Asheville, the heart of the area's cultural scene, Grove Park has a Donald Ross–designed course as well as a full menu of other courses within a 50-mile radius, including Etowah Valley Country Club, Mount Mitchell Golf Club, Reems Creek Golf Club, and Waynesville Country Club Inn.

Located deep in the Blue Ridge Mountains are two marvelous resorts: Eseeola Lodge, located in Linville (60 miles northeast of Asheville), offering play at Linville Golf Club; and Hound Ears near Valle Crucis (90 miles northeast of Asheville). In order to play these two courses, you must be a guest of the resort. Sixty-five miles south of Asheville, you will find the High Hampton Inn, a rustic, attractive golf resort.

GATHERING INFORMATION

For more information on western North Carolina in general:

> North Carolina Division of Tourism, Film and
>   Sports Development
> 301 N. Wilmington St., Raleigh, NC 27601
> Phone (800) 847-4862 or (919) 733-4171

For information on Asheville:

> Asheville Convention and Visitors Bureau
> 151 Haywood St. (P.O. Box 1010), Asheville, NC 28802
> Phone (800) 257-1300 or (828) 258-6101
> www.asheville-nc.com

Thomas Wolfe's *Look Homeward Angel.* Wolfe, a native of Asheville, writes about the town and its residents.

For information on Blowing Rock:

Blowing Rock Chamber of Commerce
Main Street (P.O. Box 406), Blowing Rock, NC 28605
Phone (800) 295-7851 or (828) 295-7851
www.blowingrock.com

For information on Boone:

Boone Area Convention and Visitors Bureau
208 Howard St., Boone, NC 28607
Phone (800) 852-9506 or (828) 264-2225

For information on Smoky Mountain Golf:

Great Smoky Mountain Golf Association
15 West Walnut St., Asheville, NC 28801
Phone (800) 799-5537 or (828) 258-0123
www.greatsmokiesgolf.com

The Major Courses

Etowah Valley Country Club

450 Brickyard Rd., Etowah, NC 28729 (18 miles southeast of Asheville); phone (800) 451-8174 or (828) 891-7141

How to Get On: Tee times can be made two days in advance.

North/West Course Tees:

Gold: 7,005 yards, par-73, USGA rating 73.1, slope 122

Blue: 6,700 yards, par-73, USGA rating 71.7, slope 124

White: 6,215 yards, par-73, USGA rating 69.6, slope 117

Red: 5,363 yards, par-73, USGA rating 70.2, slope 117

South/North Course Tees:

Gold: 6,911 yards, par-73, USGA rating 72.1, slope 121

Blue: 6,604 yards, par-73, USGA rating 71.0, slope 124

White: 6,156 yards, par-73, USGA rating 69.5, slope 118

Red: 5,391 yards, par-73, USGA rating 69.9, slope 115

West/South Course Tees:

Gold: 7,108 yards, par-72, USGA rating 73.3, slope 125

Blue: 6,880 yards, par-72, USGA rating 72.3, slope 123

White: 6,287 yards, par-72, USGA rating 70.3, slope 118

Red: 5,524 yards, par-72, USGA rating 70.3, slope 119

Challenge: ★★★	Golf Facilities: ★★★
Variety: ★★★½	14-Club Test: ★★★
Terrain: ★★★½	Intangibles: ★★★
Beauty/Visual Appeal: ★★★½	Value: ★★★★
Pace of Play: ★★½	

Just the Facts Year Opened: 1967; Course Designer: Edmund Ault; Walking: Allowed at times; Greens fee: $31; 9-Hole/Twilight Rate: Yes; Pull Carts: Yes; Practice Range: Yes; Club Rental: Yes.

Description and Comments Etowah has long been viewed as one of the best courses in the area, especially on the conditioning front, and this reputation has only grown with the 1988 addition of another nine holes. Each of the nines is distinctive and offers golfers varying terrain, from hilly to flat topography. No matter what combination you pick, you will be treated to a scenic test in excellent shape.

The original 18 holes, consisting of the West and South nines, are the longest and most demanding of the three course options, as reflected in the ratings and slopes for all tee boxes. The North course is an unusual par-37, with an extra par-5, and is maturing quite nicely. Thanks to its sensitive design, the North Nine is hardly an afterthought. On more rolling terrain it complements the two older nines wonderfully. You will find water coming into play on 12 of the 27 holes, as well as a variety of dogleg holes, so ball placement will be key. Greens tend to be well guarded by bunkers. Both greens and bunkers are larger on the West and North nines than on the South.

Insider Tips Etowah offers a "something-for-everyone" blend of holes: some open, just as many tree-lined, some flat, just as many hilly, so prepare yourself for an all-around test. This is really a "valley" course, laid out on more open, level terrain than many of its sister mountain courses. Combined with the fact that it's also one of the longer courses in the region, it practically begs for you to be able to smack your driver and play a power game. Many other courses nearby call for control rather than muscle. Still, a smattering of water hazards and dozens of bunkers will help keep the big bashers honest.

A final helpful hint: Try to block the mountains from your view as you select your club, as they have a curious habit of distorting your distance perception.

The Grove Park Inn Resort

290 Macon Ave., Asheville, NC 28804; phone (800) 438-5800 or (828) 252-2711

How to Get On: Resort guests can make tee times at any time; outside play is limited to three days' advance reservations.

Tees:

    Gold: 6,520 yards, par-71, USGA rating 71.7, slope 125

    Blue: 6,039 yards, par-71, USGA rating 69.4, slope 119

    Teal: 4,687 yards, par-71, USGA rating 68.6, slope 111

Challenge: ★★½	Golf Facilities: ★★
Variety: ★★★	14-Club Test: ★★
Terrain: ★★★	Intangibles: ★★★★
Beauty/Visual Appeal: ★★★★	Value: ★★½
Pace of Play: ★★	

Just the Facts Year Opened: 1899; Course Designer: Donald Ross; Walking: Allowed at times; Greens Fee: $66–80; 9-Hole/Twilight Rate: Yes; Pull Carts: No; Practice Range: No; Club Rental: Yes.

Description and Comments Known as the "Grand Old Lady of Sunset Mountain," Grove Park is North Carolina's oldest resort and was once the playground for the rich and famous. Names such as F. Scott Fitzgerald, Edison, Ford, Rockefeller, and no fewer than eight U.S. presidents have adorned the guest register. The golf course, the back nine of which is draped on a hillside in the shadow of the hotel, has played host to countless legends of the game, including Bobby Jones, Ben Hogan, Jack Nicklaus, and Arnold Palmer. The PGA Tour stopped here in the 1930s, 1940s, and 1950s. Clearly, the place is drenched in history. In short, the ambience for golf at the Grove Park Inn is remarkable. Alas, the golf course itself is not.

To be fair, recent renovations have strengthened this historic track, which owes most of its character to a Donald Ross redesign in 1924. Today, if it's not quite a "championship" course, it is truly a fun, interesting, scenic, and historic test.

Uneven lies are the common theme as the course is built on a series of rolling hills and the fairways tend to be narrow. You will encounter a winding stream on six of the holes as well as many bunkers on the majority of holes positioned in prime locations just waiting to envelop one of your shots. The front nine is flatter than the wildly hilly back side, allowing golfers to warm up a bit before encountering some of the more severe stances and lies the course will provide before round's end.

Memorable is the uphill, par-4 closing hole. You can practically snatch a cocktail off the resort's Sunset Terrace, so close is the 18th tee to the fabled drinking and dining establishment.

There is no range at Grove Park, but there is a very good pro shop as well as a teaching staff who conduct golf clinics, give swing analyses, as well as provide playing lessons. Make sure to bring a camera, as the views from this elevated course are spectacular.

Insider Tips If you can handle uphill, downhill, and sidehill lies, the course tends to be even easier than it looks on paper. Grove Park is a short course and plays even shorter because of the 3,000-foot elevation, with the obvious exceptions of the uphill holes. Also, because there is no driving range, it may take you a few holes to warm up. Given the fact that it is a short course, you might want to start off with a long iron or a three wood until you are ready to really swing away.

Because Grove Park is usually well conditioned and features a number of par-4s and par-5s that play shorter than advertised, you might find yourself having a lifetime's worth of birdie and eagle chances. If you get greedy, however, this little course can beat you up.

The Grove Park Inn does a roaring convention business, especially in the summer, so its one 18-hole course can get pretty clogged. Sadly, many of these conventioneers aren't really experienced golfers, so most likely, they'll slow things down. Thus, if you're looking to play at Grove Park, call ahead and find out when the convention groups are playing. Ask to tee off ahead of them or well after them.

Hound Ears Golf Club

P.O. Box 188, Blowing Rock, NC 28605; phone (828) 963-4321

How to Get On: You must stay in the Hound Ears lodge or rent one of the condos or villas on the property to get a tee time at the golf club. Club is open from April 1–November 15.

Tees:

> Back: 6,327 yards, par-72, USGA rating 69.4, slope 122
>
> Middle: 5,639 yards, par-72, USGA rating 67.3, slope 115
>
> Front: 4,959 yards, par-72, USGA rating 66.8, slope 110

Challenge: ★★	Golf Facilities: ★★★
Variety: ★★★½	14-Club Test: ★★
Terrain: ★★★½	Intangibles: ★★★½
Beauty/Visual Appeal: ★★★★	Value: ★★★
Pace of Play: ★★★	

Just the Facts Year Opened: 1963; Course Designer: George Cobb; Walking: Allowed at certain times; Greens Fee: $40–90; 9-Hole/Twilight Rate: Yes; Pull Carts: No; Practice Range: Yes; Club Rental: Yes.

Description and Comments Being a dog lover, I was naturally drawn to this resort. My disappointment on learning that the name of the club was not derived from man's best friend but rather a huge "ear-like" rock formation situated above the club was mitigated once I was able to experience the true essence of the Hound Ears Golf Club. The name isn't the only aspect to the course. Without sugar-coating anything, the golf course as Hound Ears is utterly charming—absolutely delightful. Is it for everyone? No. Longer, stronger players probably will gravitate to a more challenging layout. For most players, however, this bucolic retreat is pure fun.

At Hound Ears, trees line all fairways, tee boxes, and greens, yet the feeling is hardly claustrophobic. The fairways aren't that tight, unless you're a wild driver to begin with. You will find the Watauga River on most every hole as it winds its way through the course. The course provides a variety of different looks as it plays both in a valley as well as in the mountains.

Views are strong on this course so if the pace is slow, as it sometimes can be, at least you can enjoy your surroundings. The 15th hole, a 105-yard par-3, is especially beautiful with its waterfall, draping ferns, and downhill approach. Better players both praise and curse the par-5 12th hole, with its frightening triple-tiered green, which can reduce a poor putter to tears. Three putts here are the norm rather than the exception.

Insider Tips   If you are a wild driver, leave the big stick in the bag. You'll be fine with a three wood or long iron. As between brains and brawn, use the former and you'll probably post a better than average score. Unfortunately at Hound Ears, they'll only let you walk early in the morning or quite late in the afternoon. If you're physically up to handling a few mountain slopes, do yourself a favor and make the trek. It will truly invigorate you. Than again, Hound Ears tends to draw a well-heeled, older crowd, most of which favors golf in a cart.

Linville Golf Course

Linville Avenue, Linville, NC 28646; phone (828) 733-4363

How to Get On: You must be a guest of the Eseeola Lodge to have access to this private country club. Open from May 1–October 24.

Tees:

Long: 6,780 yards, par-72, USGA rating 72.0, slope 132

Middle: 6,279 yards, par-72, USGA rating 69.7, slope 126

Forward: 5,086 yards, par-72, USGA rating 69.3, slope 117

Challenge: ★★★★	Golf Facilities: ★★★
Variety: ★★★½	14-Club Test: ★★★
Terrain: ★★★★	Intangibles: ★★★★½
Beauty/Visual Appeal: ★★★★	Value: ★★★★
Pace of Play: ★★★½	

Just the Facts   Year Opened: 1924; Course Designer: Donald Ross; Walking: No; Greens Fee: $70–80 (no credit cards accepted); 9-Hole/Twilight Rate: Yes; Pull Carts: No; Practice Range: Yes; Club Rental: Yes.

Description and Comments   This course is pretty much unchanged from Donald Ross's original work, and golfers will encounter a fun yet demanding course, one that experts agree is one of the best mountain courses in the United States. The fairways roll, slope, and cling so closely to the natural contours of the property you'd think they've been there forever. Even stances may be the exception rather than the standard, and there are many changes in elevation. Greens are small and fast with slight undulations, so make sure to keep this in mind as you chip and putt.

Grandmother Creek, filled with trout, flows throughout the course and comes into play on 14 of the 18 holes. Linville's signature hole is number three, a 449-yard par-4 that requires a tee shot over the crest of a hill to a valley, followed by an uphill approach over a stream to a small, classic "inverted-saucer" green.

Insider Tips   The best time of the year to play Linville is September and October, when the leaves are turning and most of the tourists have departed. The course is pretty much as you see it—no tricks, just good (at times exceptional) golf. The greens are very tricky, so two putts are more than acceptable.

If you recall the 1999 U.S. Open at Pinehurst No. 2, Donald Ross was best known for designing "inverted-saucer" greens, which repel all but the most perfectly struck approach shots. There's a touch of that at Linville, but it's nowhere near as severe as his work elsewhere. Nevertheless, there is a premium on chipping or putting. Work on your short game at home before attempting to tackle Linville's greens.

Fairways are tree-lined, but feature friendly landing areas, so you can hit your driver on many of the holes. Rule of thumb: Don't hit your approach above the hole or you're facing a near-certain three putt.

Another observation: Anyone who can walk without crutches would love to walk this course, but they won't let you do it until late in the afternoon.

Mount Mitchell Golf Club

7590 Highway 80 South, Burnsville, NC 28714; phone (828) 675-5454

How to Get On: Tee times can be made two weeks in advance.

Tees:

Championship: 6,495 yards, par-72, USGA rating 70.0, slope 121

Middle: 6,125 yards, par-72, USGA rating 68.0, slope 116

Forward: 5,455 yards, par-72, USGA rating 69.5, slope 117

Challenge: ★★½   Golf Facilities: ★★
Variety: ★★½   14-Club Test: ★★★
Terrain: ★★★   Intangibles: ★★★
Beauty/Visual Appeal: ★★★★½   Value: ★★★
Pace of Play: ★★

Just the Facts   Year Opened: 1975; Course Designer: Fred Hawtree; Walking: Allowed at certain times; Greens fee: $35–60; 9-Hole/Twilight Rate: Yes; Pull Carts: No; Practice Range: No; Club Rental: Yes.

Description and Comments   Located in a valley below the 6,684-foot-high Mount Mitchell (the highest peak in the Eastern United States) and surrounded by the Pisgah National Forest, this course is a delightful play, especially in the fall. This bent grass course is basically flat, but don't let that lull you into a false sense of security. It's kind of bizarre actually. You're confronted with awe-inspiring vistas, probably the best in the region, but surprisingly most of the holes are dead flat. Mount Mitchell poses noteworthy challenges as golfers must maneuver around a crystal clear stream that comes into play on many holes. One of the best holes is number five, a 520-yard par-5, which features a stream that meanders down the right side of the fairway, then cuts in front of the kidney-shaped green. Another superb hole is the 14th, the hardest hole on the course. A 450-yard par-4, the 14th doglegs to the left and requires a solid tee shot that carries over the South Toe River.

Insider Tips   Simply because the course is so popular, a combination of stunning scenery (especially in autumn) and good value, the pace of play here tends to be slow. Thus, strive to get one of the first tee times of the day to ensure less than six hours to a round. You can leave your driver in the bag, except for a few holes, as the course tends to be short and tight. Tell yourself before you start the round to breathe deeply, ease off the accelerator, and play smart. Greens can get awfully quick and have pronounced undulations, so be careful with chipping and putting.

Reems Creek Golf Course

Pink Fox Cove Road, Weaverville, NC 28787; phone (828) 645-4393

How to Get On: Tee times can be made up to 30 days in advance.

Tees:

    Blue: 6,464 yards, par-72, USGA rating 70.5, slope 130

    White: 6,106 yards, par-72, USGA rating 69.0, slope 127

    Green: 5,357 yards, par-72, USGA rating 65.6, slope 119

    Forward: 5,455 yards, par-72, USGA rating 69.5, slope 117

Challenge: ★★★

Variety: ★★★★

Terrain: ★★★

Beauty/Visual Appeal: ★★★★

Pace of Play: ★★★

Golf Facilities: ★★★

14-Club Test: ★★★★

Intangibles: ★★★

Value: ★★★

Just the Facts   Year Opened: 1989; Course Designer: Martin Hawtree; Walking: No; Greens fee: $42–49; 9-Hole/Twilight Rate: Yes; Pull Carts: No; Practice Range: Yes; Club Rental: Yes.

Description and Comments   This is one of the newest and most talked about entries to the western North Carolina golf scene. Reems Creek offers golfers a solid test with many blind shots and fast but true greens. The course is very scenic, with eye-catching mountain views and a variety of lakes. These water hazards are scattered throughout the course, making ball placement key on many holes. Golfers will find further challenge battling the hilly terrain and the uneven lies, which often demand shots beyond the reach of most players. Reems Creek is sometimes frustrating—but always interesting. For better or worse, carts must stay on cart paths at all times.

Insider Tips   Spend a few extra bucks on a yardage book before you start your round. It might save you from an aggravating surprise later in the round. You will find this most helpful given the number of blind shots on the course. The key to Reems Creek is to stay in the fairway. The consequence of being in the bermuda rough will more than likely drive your score up into the "don't go there" range. Make sure to watch out for hole number four, a dogleg left perched on a bluff—if you don't know the bluff is there, it can be deadly on your scorecard.

This may sound like a recording, but Reems Creek is yet another mountain course where it's wisest to leave the driver at home. Another echo: The greens, especially in the fall, can get mighty quick, with tricky breaks and multiple tiers, so there's an emphasis here on putting.

A Western North Carolina Sampler

Black Mountain Golf Course

106 Montreat Rd., Black Mountain, NC 28711; phone (828) 669-2710

Tees: Championship: 6,181 yards, par-71, USGA rating 69.5, slope 128
Greens Fee: $30–35

Challenge: ★★½

Variety: ★★

Terrain: ★★★

Beauty/Visual Appeal: ★★★

Pace of Play: ★★½

Golf Facilities: ★½

14-Club Test: ★★

Intangibles: ★★

Value: ★★★

Description and Comments   This is your chance to play one of the longest par-6s in the country—the 17th hole at 747 yards. Outstanding scenery.

High Hampton Inn and Country Club

Highway 107 South, Box 338, Cashiers, NC 28717; phone (800) 334-2551 or (828) 743-2450

Tees: Championship: 6,327 yards, par-72, USGA rating 69.4, slope 122
Greens Fee: $28–48

Challenge: ★★½

Variety: ★★½

Terrain: ★★★

Beauty/Visual Appeal: ★★★★

Pace of Play: ★★★

Golf Facilities: ★★★

14-Club Test: ★★½

Intangibles: ★★★

Value: ★★★

Description and Comments   Rustic, scenic course that is fun but not extremely difficult to play, thanks in part to a total absence of sand bunkers. The 137-yard, par-3 8th hole, which plays to an island green, is one of the state's prettiest. Ladies be aware, there are no rankings for women's tees.

Apple Valley Golf Club, Fairfield Mountain Resort

201 Boulevard of the Mountains, Lake Lure, NC 28746; phone (828) 625-2888

Tees: Championship: 6,726 yards, par-72, USGA rating 72.6, slope 138
Greens Fee: $25–39

Challenge: ★★★½

Variety: ★★★

Terrain: ★★★

Beauty/Visual Appeal: ★★★½

Pace of Play: ★★★

Golf Facilities: ★★★½

14-Club Test: ★★★

Intangibles: ★★★

Value: ★★★★

Description and Comments   Narrow course with hilly terrain and amazing scenery. Resort was featured in the movie *Dirty Dancing*.

Bald Mountain Golf Club, Fairfield Mountain Resort

201 Boulevard of the Mountains, Lake Lure, NC 28746; phone (828) 625-2888

Tees: Championship: 6,575 yards, par-72, USGA rating 70.9, slope 125
Greens Fee: $25–39

Challenge: ★★★	Golf Facilities: ★★★½
Variety: ★★★	14-Club Test: ★★★
Terrain: ★★★	Intangibles: ★★★
Beauty/Visual Appeal: ★★★½	Value: ★★★½
Pace of Play: ★★★	

Description and Comments Challenging course that has a lot of water hazards and tight fairways.

Waynesville Country Club Inn

Ninevah Road, Waynesville, NC 28786; phone (828) 452-4617
Tees:
Carolina/Blue Ridge
Championship: 5,943 yards, par-70, USGA rating 66.9, slope 104
Carolina/Dogwood
Championship: 5,798 yards, par-70, USGA rating 66.4, slope 103
Dogwood/Blue Ridge
Championship: 5,803 yards, par-70, USGA rating 66.4, slope 105
Greens Fee: $44

Challenge: ★½	Golf Facilities: ★½
Variety: ★★★	14-Club Test: ★★½
Terrain: ★★★	Intangibles: ★★½
Beauty/Visual Appeal: ★★★½	Value: ★★½
Pace of Play: ★★★	

Description and Comments Three nines that play in three different combinations. The Carolina course is the flattest of the three courses and starts off with two par-4s that are very birdie-able. The Blue Ridge course provides the best views as it winds through the mountains. The first hole is a killer par-5 that will severely penalize you if you slice your tee shot. Dogwood is the newest of the nines and is also the shortest. Narrow fairways, three doglegs, and fast greens make it the most challenging.

Lodging

EXPENSIVE

Eseeola Lodge

175 Linville Ave., Linville, NC 28646; phone (800) 742-6717 or (828) 733-4311; www.eseeola.com; Rates: $270–300

Originally built in 1926 and then rebuilt in 1936 after a devastating fire, Eseeola is a rustic lakeside lodge open from mid-May to October. The lodge is situated 3,800 feet above sea level and thus provides a great escape from the summer heat. The best description of the rooms at Eseeola is upscale rustic accented with beautiful handmade quilts and furnished with authentic antiques. All rooms come with a private bathroom, hair dryer, and cable television; many of them have private porches that overlook the wonderfully manicured gardens. Other nice touches you will find at Eseeola are fresh flowers in your room, nightly turndown, bathrobes, and welcome gifts.

Breakfast and dinner are served in the lodge with a wonderful stone fireplace as a backdrop. Breakfast offers a wide range of appetizing delectables, from fresh mountain berries to made-to-order omelette and waffles. Dinner is an elegant four-course meal, jacket and tie required, where you will find a variety of French and new American entrees, everything from free-range chicken to rainbow trout.

The lodge is located smack dab in the middle of the Blue Ridge Mountains, so while you are staying at Eseeola you should make a point of exploring the lovely surroundings including hiking trails through Blue Ridge Mountains, Grandfather Mountain, Linville Falls and Linville Gorge, and the nearby artisan community of Penland, featuring antiques and mountain crafts.

Other activities offered nearby at the lodge are: a pool, eight tennis courts, croquet, boating, fishing, and children's programs.

Golf Package   Eseeola offers a good golf package, which is available Sunday–Thursday (May 31–June 30, excluding June 9th and 10th) and Sunday–Thursday after Labor Day until closing. It includes: lodging, one round of golf and one cart rental for each night's stay, daily breakfast and dinner in the Eseeola dining room, four-day advanced tee times, and all gratuities (taxes are additional).

Grove Park Inn Resort

290 Macon Ave., Asheville, NC 28804; phone (800) 438-5800 or (828) 252-2711; www.groveparkinn.com; Rates: Club Floor, $265–375; Main Inn, $90–240; Sammons and Vanderbilt Wings, $150–265

Grove Park Inn is perched high above Asheville (2,500 feet above sea level) and truly dominates the surrounding area. Construction on the Grove Park Inn began in 1909 and was completed in 1913. It was built by Edwin Grove, founder of Grove's Pharmacy, whose doctor suggested that he spend his summers in the midst of Asheville's fresh-mountain air due to a severe bronchitis problem. If you get a chance to stay at the Grove Park Inn, it may be the first time that you were grateful to someone for having bronchitis.

The hotel is dominated by the lobby area, which is, in short, stunning. It is a huge area featuring extremely high ceilings, stone walls, and sweeping views. It is where you will find Horizon's, the main dining area (see Dining section), and the Great Hall Bar. As you look at the boulders that comprise the walls of the lobby, it is almost incomprehensible when you realize that the building was constructed before cranes and other modern machinery existed. Rather, the inn was constructed using hundreds of mules, wagons, pulleys, and ropes to move the granite stones (some weighing 10,000 pounds). Make sure to take notice of the quotes/stanzas that are on some of the stones by notable authors, which further enhance the uniqueness and appeal of the great room.

The inn was recently renovated and features 510 tastefully appointed rooms, including 12 suites and 28 oversized Club Floor accommodations. All rooms feature a terrace so you can enjoy the wonderful views from the privacy of your room.

When you venture beyond your room, you will find a compelling menu of activities and beautiful grounds. Here's a little sampling of what you have to satisfy your appetite: There is the Donald Ross–built golf course, nine lit tennis courts (including three indoor), two pools (one indoor), a whirlpool, an indoor sports center, sauna, racquetball and squash courts, and a gym.

Golf Package   Includes two nights' accommodations, daily breakfast, unlimited golf and cart rental, daily cleaning and storage, bag tag and yardage book, 10% discount on golf shop merchandise (nonsale items), and 10% discount on all instruction.

High Hampton Inn

P.O. Box 338, Cashiers, NC 28717-0338; phone (800) 334-2551 or (828) 743-2411; www.highhamptoninn.com; Rates: $82–108

Nestled in the Blue Ridge Mountains, the High Hampton Inn is a 1,400-acre resort that once was a summer home of General Wade Hampton, who served as governor of South Carolina after the Reconstruction. It has since been turned into a handsome, rustic resort offering a wide variety of activities and amenities. Among those amenities however, you will not find telephones or televisions (what, no Golf Channel?). That's right—rooms do not come with either of these two modern concessions (they are available in the common areas).

Be aware, this resort is not for everyone. The rooms are not plush, but they are very comfortable. It's the scenery that can't be beat (and it is great for kids). Another rarity is that the inn advises its guests that tipping is not necessary, and no formal gratuity or service charge will be added to the bill. So if you feel like grabbing your sticks and heading for a unique and relaxing adventure, you can't go wrong with High Hampton Inn.

The inn serves as the central gathering point for the resort, with the lobby as the main stop. If you are there during the fall or winter, you will undoubtedly enjoy the stone chimney and its four fireplaces. The resort features 117 rooms, including 34 in the three-story inn (some suites are available), 15 cottages, and 37 homes. All rooms have private baths and are situated in close proximity to the dining room, lobby, and activity centers.

If you are traveling with a large group, you should consider the Colony Homes, which are located on wooded lots throughout the property. The homes range in size from two to four bedrooms, each with a private bath, and include a fireplace, fully equipped kitchen, outdoor grill, cathedral ceilings, VCR, phone, and daily maid service. These homes can be rented on a daily, weekly, or longer basis, with or without meals at the inn.

All accommodation packages include three meals daily, which are served buffet style and include a selection of wonderful dishes (coat and tie required for dinner). Mixed drinks are not allowed in the dining room; however, you can purchase beer and wine with your lunch and dinner if you desire. After dinner, you can adjoin to the lobby, where you will find entertainment each evening.

If you want to grab a drink, head to the Rock Mountain Tavern, where you can get a libation and enjoy soft music. Attire is casual before 6:30 p.m.; coat and tie afterward. Mixed drinks, beer, and wine can be purchased from 5 to 10 p.m.

Golf may be the main focal point of your vacation, but there are many other diversions: extensive hiking and jogging trails throughout the beautiful area; a 35-acre lake featuring fishing, boating, and sailing; six clay tennis courts; exercise room; archery; bicycle rentals; kids' programs; and lawn games.

Golf Packages   Package includes three nights/four days accommodations, daily greens fees, complimentary tennis, breakfast, lunch, and dinner (all buffet style).

Hound Ears Club

P.O. Box 188, Blowing Rock, NC 28605; phone (828) 963-4321; www.houndears.com; Rates: $110–145

Hound Ears is 700-acre resort nestled among the grand trees of the Blue Ridge Mountains and is perched 3,700 feet above sea level, providing outstanding views of Grandfather Mountain and the golf course below. The club is relatively small, with only 28 rooms located either in the main clubhouse or in the nearby lodge building. There is a variety of comfortable and nicely appointed rooms. Accommodations for longer stays are also available in both the clubhouse suites and privately owned chalet and condominiums near the golf course.

Penthouse Suite   This is the ultimate at Hound Ears. Located in the main clubhouse, the rooms are spacious and luxurious with a separate living room and a king-size bedroom. The suite comes with a private balcony overlooking the golf course and mountains.

Clubhouse Suites   Also located in the main clubhouse, suites include a large bedroom with two double beds and sitting area. Each suite comes with a private balcony overlooking the golf course and mountains.

Executive Suite   This suite is located in the lodge building and is comprised of two large bedrooms, each with two double beds, private bath, and dressing room. Sitting room with a private balcony overlooking the golf course and mountains is also included. Requires a minimum of four people.

Lodge Rooms   As the name indicates, these rooms are also located in the lodge building and include a large bedroom with two double beds opening onto a balcony overlooking the golf course and mountains.

Breakfast is casual, but dinner is formal and gentlemen are required to wear a jacket in both the dining room and lounge after 6:30 p.m. Both a jacket and tie are required for Saturday night only. Casual attire is accepted during the winter months beginning in November; blue jeans are not permitted at any time in the dining room or lounge. All meals are served in the main dining room.

Swimming is a unique experience in itself at Hound Ears, as the pool is located away from the main clubhouse in a huge rock grotto where wildflowers cascade over the rocks. A unique treat and, because the pool is heated constantly at 85 degrees, one that you can experience in all seasons. Other activities at the resort include tennis—six tennis courts, four clay surfaces, and two hard-court—children's activities, and fishing and horseback riding nearby.

Golf Packages   At Hound Ears, there are two golf packages, one for spring (April 2 to June 20) and one for fall (August 29 to November 7). They both included the following: 18 holes of golf per day including cart (additional holes may be played at the regular greens fee and unlimited golf for the month of April), complimentary use of the driving range and practice green, tennis (two court hours of tennis per day; complimentary use of the ball machine), breakfast and dinner with each night's stay, daily and evening maid service, and golf club storage.

Richmond Hill Inn

87 Richmond Hill Inn, Asheville NC 28806; phone (888) 742-4565 or (828) 252-7313; www.richmondhill.com; Rates: $145–400

This is a Victorian inn that once was the focal point of Asheville's social and political movements for many years. The inn is really three separate buildings, the Mansion, Croquet Cottages, and Garden Pavilion, which are interspersed among manicured gardens and wooded acres with walking trails. Guests at the inn enjoy a complimentary breakfast each morning as well as an afternoon tea. For dinner, try Gabrielle's (see Dining section), which has a strong menu and an equally impressive reputation. After dinner, guests can retire to the library, where there is a collection of books on western North Carolina.

Haywood Park Hotel

1 Battery Park Ave., Asheville, NC 28801; phone (800) 228-2522 or (828) 252-2522; www.haywoodpark.com; Rates: $130–300

Located in downtown Asheville, Haywood offers stylish rooms in this all-suite hotel. Rooms come with a wetbar, sitting area, spacious bathroom with garden tub, and Spanish tile (Jacuzzi suites are also available). A deluxe continental-style breakfast will be delivered each morning to your room, and there is a turndown service each evening that includes a special treat, chocolate truffles. The hotel also has a fitness facility and sauna that may come in handy after you get to experience the hotel's restaurant, 23 Page (see Dining section). This restaurant offers a memorable selection of seafood, pasta, and game, with lamb being a specialty of the house.

MODERATE

Chetola Mountain Resort

P.O. Box 17, North Main St., Blowing Rock, NC 28605; phone (800) 243-8652 or (828) 295-5500; www.chetola.com; Rates: rooms $330–390, condos $570–650

Chetola is a Cherokee word meaning "haven of rest" and that probably says it all. Located in the Blue Ridge Mountains, this 78-acre resort overlooks the Chetola Lake and is comprised of condos and rooms in the lodge; there are some suites available (when requesting a room, try for one that has a balcony and faces the lake). The resort has quite a few activities available to guests: indoor pool, hot tub, six tennis courts, gym, racquetball, boating, and hiking in nearby Moses H. Cone Park on the Blue Ridge Parkway.

Golf Package   Package includes two nights' accommodations (more nights can be added), gift of Chetola golf balls and tees, complimentary champagne on arrival, full use of Highland Sports and Recreation Center, and golf at the club of your choice: Jefferson Landing, Boone Golf Course, Hawksnet Golf, or Roan Valley Golf Estates.

Maple Lodge Bed & Breakfast

152 Sunset Dr., Blowing Rock, NC 28605; phone (828) 295-3331; www.maplelodge.net; Rates: $115–125

Maple Lodge was built in 1946 and is Blowing Rock's oldest bed-and-breakfast. There are ten rooms, which run to the small side, and one suite in Maple Lodge, all of which are attractively furnished with antiques and family heirlooms, goose-down comforters, four-poster or lace-canopy beds, private bathrooms, and fresh flowers.

The common rooms are really the high point of the lodge. The library has a stylish stone fireplace and offers guests a variety of games to choose from including backgammon and chess.

INEXPENSIVE

Best Western—Asheville Biltmore

22 Woodfin St., Asheville, NC 28801; phone (800) 528-1234 or (828) 253-1851; Rates: $59–75; Built: 1983; Renovated: 1999

Comfort Inn

800 Fairview Rd., Asheville, NC 28805; phone (800) 228-5150 or (828) 298-9141; Rates: $69–139; Built: 1985; Renovated: 1999

High Country Inn

1785 NC 105 South, Box 1339, Boone, NC 28607; phone (800) 334-5605 or (828) 264-1000; Rates: $34–74; Built: 1972; Renovated: 1997

Dining

Insider Tip The region has long catered to vacationers with a few extra pennies to spend, so there's plenty of sophisticated dining available at a variety of prices. When in doubt, the safest menu option is the specialty of the region, grilled mountain trout.

23 Page 1 Battery Park Ave., Asheville (in Haywood Park Hotel); phone (800) 228-2522 or (828) 252-2522. Continental; Expensive; Reservations suggested. Intimate dining—house specialty is grilled lamb chop with radicchio and artichoke mousse.

Café on the Square 1 Biltmore Ave., Asheville; phone (828) 251-5565. Continental; Inexpensive; Reservations accepted. The owners hail from California, and much of the selections on the menu reflect their heritage. Very fun menu and wonderful desserts.

Crippen's 239 Sunset Dr., Blowing Rock; phone (828) 295-3487. Continental; Moderate–Expensive; Reservations suggested. Located in Crippen's Country Inn, this restaurant has a wide variety of entrees, including the intriguing horseradish-encrusted salmon.

Daniel Boone Inn 130 Hardin St., Boone; phone (828) 264-8657. American; Inexpensive; No reservations needed. This restaurant features family-style meals and is known for its fried chicken.

Gabrielle's 87 Richmond Hill Inn, Asheville (in Richmond Hill Inn); phone (888) 742-4565 or (828) 252-7313. Continental; Expensive; Reservations suggested. Great fish and beef selections. Pianist Thursday–Monday accentuates atmosphere. Formal dining—jacket required.

Horizon's 290 Macon Ave., Asheville (in Grove Park Hotel); phone (800) 438-5800 or (828) 252-2711. Continental/American; Expensive; Reservations suggested. Formal dining (jacket required) with wonderful mountain and valley vistas below—very romantic. Unique menu including "lone star ostrich."

Mountain Smoke House 20 South Spruce St., Asheville; phone (828) 253-4871. American; Inexpensive–Moderate; Reservations accepted. One of the most unique restaurants in the area, combining barbecue specialties with bluegrass music. A local showcase for musicians, you won't forget your trip to this restaurant.

The Market Place on Wall Street 20 Wall St., Asheville; phone (828) 252-4162. Varied; Inexpensive–Moderate; Reservations accepted. There are two dining rooms at this restaurant. One serves a variety of selections, including seafood, lamb, and veal. The other one, named Pain and Vin (bread and wine), emphasizes the wine and serves a rotating menu that complements the day's selection. Outdoor seating available.

Windmill European Grill 85 Tunnel Rd., Asheville; phone (828) 253-5285. International/Continental; Moderate; Reservations accepted. This restaurant specializes in German, Italian, Middle Eastern, and Indian cuisine—Italian garners our vote as the best.

Activities

Chimney Rock Park An elevator takes you through a 26-story shaft of rock providing you with a an eye-popping view of Hickory Nut Gorge and its surroundings. You can also hike the trails that lead to Hickory Nut Falls, where *Last of the Mohicans* was filmed. US 64/74A, Chimney Rock; phone (800) 277-9611 or (828) 625-9611.

Canoeing and White Water Rafting Wahoo's Adventures, phone (800) 444-7238 or (828) 262-5774.

Folk Art Center Purchase authentic mountain crafts. MM 382 on Blue Ridge Parkway; phone (828) 298-7928.

Grandfather Mountain Just off the Blue Ridge Parkway, this mountain offers scenic hiking trails and is famous for its swinging bridge. There are also some animals for viewing, such as bears, otters, and a mountain lion.

Horseback Riding Pisgah View Ranch, Route 1, Cander; phone (828) 667-9100.

Linville Falls Only a half-mile walk from the Blue Ridge Parkway is one of North Carolina's most spectacular waterfalls. Route 1, Spruce Pine; phone (828) 765-1045.

Museum of the Cherokee Indian A great way to learn about the Cherokee tribe. US 441 at Drama Road, Cherokee; phone (828) 497-3481.

Biltmore Estate and Gardens Built in 1895 by George Vanderbilt, this amazing home is America's largest private residence. It is an architectural masterpiece and was, at the time of its construction, a site for unheard-of innovations, such as central heating, mechanical refrigeration, electric lights, and indoor bathrooms. Make sure to rent the headphones, which provide you with terrific insights into the home. The winery also is a charming spot to spend some time. During the spring and summer there is musical entertainment on the patio where you can purchase cheese and wine. One North Pack Square, Asheville; phone (800) 624-1575 or (828) 255-1700.

The 19th Hole

Gatsby's 13 W. Walnut St., Asheville, Features a range of musical entertainment from blues and jazz to alternative rock.

Great Hall Bar 290 Macon Ave., Asheville (in Grove Park Inn); phone (800) 438-5800 or (828) 252-2711. Wonderful views of valley below in a stunning setting.

The New French Bar 1 Battery Park Ave., Asheville (in Haywood Park Hotel); phone (800) 228-2522 or (828) 252-2522. An intimate bar.

Part Three

Charleston, South Carolina

Overview

The fanciful notion of the pre–Civil War South that Margaret Mitchell romanticized in *Gone with the Wind* endures in Charleston, South Carolina. This quaint, thriving coastal city is accessible by two major interstate highways (Interstates 26 and 95), and its magnificently restored historic district showcases more than 1,000 historically preserved Antebellum homes and buildings. Some of those buildings date back to the late 1600s.

An assortment of the most opulent homes is open to tours, and several restored buildings are now cozy restaurants and charming bed-and-breakfast inns. There are bars here where George Washington sipped suds, and the city is home to America's oldest synagogue, oldest museum, and oldest theater (the Dock Street Theater, still in operation with live performances). The elegant Mills House hotel was rebuilt after a fire early in the century, but it preserved the original balcony, which had adjoined the room that served as the headquarters of Robert E. Lee before the Civil War. When Lee was an officer in the U.S. Army, he would sit on that balcony at night, sip sherry, and smoke his cheroots.

In view of the famous Battery, out in the harbor, is Fort Sumter, which cadets from the nearby Citadel fired upon on April 12, 1861, to start the Civil War. And not far from downtown are some wonderfully preserved Antebellum plantation mansions, a tour of which reveals a good deal about what life was like for the landed gentry some 200 years ago.

Indeed, if Rhett Butler were ever to patch things up with Scarlet, he would definitely take her to Charleston for at least a long weekend. They would most certainly take their golf clubs along because Charleston has a strong line-up of extremely fine courses—particularly those that grace the nearby beautiful barrier islands.

Charleston has about everything that any vacationer would want—historical attractions, beaches and ocean, excellent deep-sea fishing, full-facility resorts, and an array of fine hotels and inns. It also has wonderful

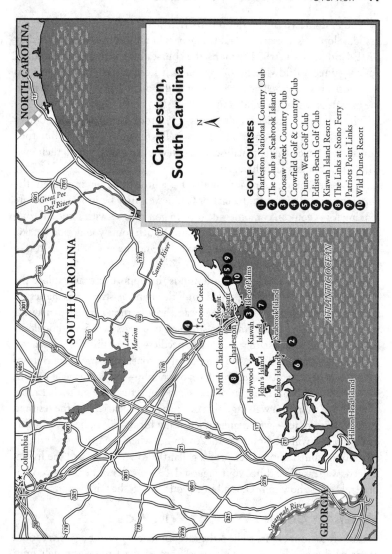

Charleston,
South Carolina

N

GOLF COURSES

1. Charleston National Country Club
2. The Club at Seabrook Island
3. Coosaw Creek Country Club
4. Crowfield Golf & Country Club
5. Dunes West Golf Club
6. Edisto Beach Golf Club
7. Kiawah Island Resort
8. The Links at Stono Ferry
9. Patriots Point Links
10. Wild Dunes Resort

live theater and concert facilities, an assortment of lively pubs and night-clubs, and some of the best restaurants on the entire eastern seaboard.

Within a 20-mile radius of the heart of Charleston are renowned resorts, numerous golf courses, and a variety of accommodations. If the focus of your stay is golf, golf, and more golf, or if you are looking for a vacation spot for you and your family, you will want to consider one of the world-renowned golf resorts outlined below.

The best known of Charleston's barrier island resorts is Kiawah Island, first developed as a resort by Arabian owners in the 1960s and purchased by AMF Companies in 1974. Among the courses here is the Ocean Course, which gained worldwide notoriety when it hosted the 1991 Ryder Cup Matches. This may well be the most difficult golf course in the world from the back tees when the wind is up.

The two other barrier island resorts—Seabrook Island and Wild Dunes on the Isle of Palms—may not be as well known as Kiawah, but they nonetheless have excellent facilities and golf courses that can hold their own with resort courses anywhere.

If you are looking for a vacation that has a little more "metropolitan" flavor along with some golf, the city of Charleston may be just what you are looking for—you can combine side trips to golf courses with some amazing sight seeing and fabulous dining. No matter which route you decide to take, make sure to devote at least one day to exploring the city of Charleston—it will be worth every minute.

The best part of being in Charleston is the opportunity to explore the city's nuances and environs. As you stroll through the streets of Charleston you will be overwhelmed by the beauty and architectural heritage that awaits you at every turn. Charleston has survived two wars, a 7.5 earthquake, a major fire, and a devastating hurricane; needless to say, this city is resilient.

Old-line Charlestonians who can trace their roots back several generations to the highborn are often thought of as a bit snobby—but it is generally a subtle snobbery that comes out in nuances and can actually be quite charming.

Carriage tours and walking tours of the historic district and the restored Antebellum homes—which are authentically furnished, right down to the dinnerware—will transport visitors to an era when the privileged aristocracy often valued honor over profit, gallantry was a given, and the living, indeed, was easy. We think your biggest decision will not be three wood or driver, but just how to pack it all in to your trip to the Charleston area.

WHEN TO GO AND WHAT IT WILL COST

Because the summers are so hot, the ideal time to come for a golf vacation, as far as the weather is concerned, is from early-October through mid-May. September (and sometimes October) is hurricane season, but the last time Charleston took a direct hit was in 1989 from Hurricane Hugo. The winters can be mild and pleasant, but January and February can be "iffy."

From the end of May until the end of June, the city celebrates music and the arts with the world-renowned, month-long Spoleto Festival, modeled after Gian-Carlo Menotti's festival in Spoleto, Italy. It may be worth suffering through hot weather on the golf course to take in this wonderful event. However, there are always lots of things to do and great things to see around Charleston, no matter what time of year you come.

The peak rate time at golf courses is generally from late-March through mid-April and from mid-September to mid-November. Resort and hotels with beach access tend to be priciest from mid-June to late-August, when family bookings are at their high point. Mid-April to the end of May is considered a shoulder season (between peak rates and low rates), as is late-August through October. The lowest rates are from November through March. For example, Seabrook Island Resort's golf package rates, per person, per day, based on double occupancy, run about $140 and $935 per week, from March 28 to May 1. From November 7 to February 12, these same packages run $96 per night and $655 for the week.

Weather in November and March is usually perfect for golf. These rate seasons may vary from resort to resort and from hotel to hotel. If you really want to play golf during a Charleston summer, pick one of the less tree-lined courses near the ocean to maximize the cooling breezes. Kiawah Island Resort's Ocean Course is the big-ticket course of choice in summer, whereas Patriot's Point is a good pick for those on a budget.

WHAT TO BRING

The wind can have an effect on the weather, as well as on the flight of your golf ball. Some winter and even early-spring and late-fall days can be downright bone chilling, especially around the ocean. You might wake to a warm, sunny day, but by the time you hit the back nine, you may wish you had a windbreaker or sweater, so make sure you always carry one in the cooler months. On the other hand, the summers are oppressively hot and humid. So if you're playing in the summer, tee up as early as you can, especially as most of the major moisture from July/August storms comes in the late afternoon. The humidity is usually high in the summer because of the ocean and the fact that two big rivers, the Ashley and the Cooper, come together in Charleston. So, in the winter months and the early- spring and late-fall, make sure you bring everything from short-sleeve shirts and shorts to windbreakers, lined jackets, and windshirts.

Bring a lot of golf balls, too, especially if you're going to be playing several of the oceanside courses and most especially if you plan to play the fabled Ocean Course at Kiawah Island. Also, because the ocean winds can play havoc with your golf ball, it would be a good idea to bring along your knockdown shot and your low-lofted driver.

ONCE YOU'RE THERE

The stretch of countryside from Charleston south to Hilton Head Island is commonly known as "the lowcountry." It is quite beautiful and unique. When you play golf here, one day you might be winding your way through avenues of old oaks dripping with Spanish moss. The next day, you could be taking a trip along the wetlands and coastal rivers that are edged with beautiful, golden marsh grasses. Another day, with the wind whipping, you might find yourself on some stunningly beautiful oceanside course. And on a couple of exceptional courses, you can get all those experiences in one day.

You have the choice of staying in downtown Charleston in the historic district, and having all of the nightlife and culture within walking distance, or out at one of the barrier island golf resorts. Where you should stay depends on what you want to do and see, which golf courses you want to play, and, of course, your budget. Kiawah Island Resort and Sea-brook Island Resort are both a 40- to 50-minute drive from downtown Charleston, depending on the traffic. The Isle of Palms, where Wild Dunes Resort is located, is about a 20- to 30-minute drive from downtown.

Some of the downtown hotels and bed-and-breakfasts can arrange golf at all three of those resorts for their guests, as well as at several other extremely good courses around Charleston.

If you have the time, stay a few days at one of the resorts and a few days downtown at one of the charming inns or fine hotels around the historic district. That plan gives you the best of both worlds.

For entertainment, there is no reason to leave the historic district. Most of the best restaurants and liveliest pubs are in and around the historic district.

Downtown provides an array of alternative lodging, from simple hotels to elegant ones like the Charleston Place, to historic inns furnished with reproduction antiques and providing wonderful touches like chamber music in the courtyards.

The golf courses here are extremely scenic, especially the coastal courses that are carved out along the Atlantic Ocean and the Intracoastal Waterway. These courses offer fabulous views of dunes, tidal marsh, and wildlife. These barrier islands are popular nesting spots for giant loggerhead turtles—and, if your timing is right, you might see schools of porpoises playing just a few yards off shore.

The one "must-play" in Charleston is the Ocean Course at Kiawah Island Resort, followed by the Links Course at Wild Dunes. For those on a budget, we'd pick one of those two to make your golf vacation truly mem-orable, then sample some of the best second-tier courses, such as Coosaw Creek or Dunes West. For superior low-country scenery with courses that won't beat you up on the scorecard or in the wallet, try the 36 holes at Seabrook Island.

GATHERING INFORMATION

Charleston Convention and Visitors Bureau
375 Meeting St., P.O. Box 975, Charleston, SC 29402
phone (800) 868-8118 or (843) 853-8000; charlestoncvb.com

Charleston Golf courses and hotel golf packages information.
phone (800) 247-5786; www.yourgolfpartners.com

South Carolina Department of Parks, Recreation, and Tourism
1205 Pendleton St., Columbia, SC 29201
phone (800) 868-2492 or (843) 734-0122

The Major Courses

Charleston National Country Club

1360 National Dr., Mt Pleasant, SC 29464; phone (843) 884-7799

How To Get On: Tee times can be made one year in advance.

Tees:

> Black: 6,975 yards, par-72, USGA rating 74.0, slope 140
>
> Green: 6,600 yards, par 72, USGA rating 72.4, slope 135
>
> White: 6,059 yards, par-72, USGA rating 69.4, slope 125
>
> Red: 5,045 yards, par-72, USGA rating 70.8, slope 126

Challenge: ★★★★	Golf Facilities: ★★★★
Variety: ★★★½	14- Club Test: ★★★★
Terrain: ★★★★	Intangibles: ★★★
Beauty/Visual Appeal: ★★★★	Value: ★★★½
Pace of Play: ★★★	

Just the Facts   Year Opened: 1990; Course Designer: Rees Jones; Walking: No; Greens Fee: $35–70; 9 Hole/Twilight Rate: Yes; Pull Carts: No; Practice Range: Yes; Club Rental: Yes.

Description and Comments   Originally built to be an exclusive private course, hard times brought on by Hurricane Hugo in 1989 delayed the opening of this course and forced the original owners out. The course is now semiprivate. This is a very scenic course, dotted with lagoons and a lot of nice visual touches, such as wooden bridges. The marshland comes into play, as do the water hazards. The greens are small and fast, and there are plenty of bunkers. Unless you are a single-digit handicapper, you should definitely avoid the back tees. But as with most of his courses, Rees Jones designed this one so it would be very tough from the back tees, but tamer, less demanding, and more fun for the average players from the forward sets of tees.

The course sits on three small islands that overlook Hamlin Sound and the Intracoastal Waterway. The wind can play a big part in how you score—it blows quite frequently and often briskly off the sound. There is an array of small pot bunkers and large mounds, and the wetlands come prominently into play on several holes, sometimes too prominently, as one complaint about Charleston National is the abundance of forced carries over marsh.

The wind has become more of a factor than Jones and the developers originally planned, because Hurricane Hugo came rolling into town and knocked down a lot of trees—and even many of the huge live oaks were stripped of most of their limbs and bent into strange positions.

The par-3s all play over wetlands and lagoons. Club selection is critical. Number five plays to a green that is tucked into a shallow island surrounded by marsh. The 9th is only 150 yards from the back tee and the green is big, but it's all carry over marsh with a big bunker guarding the back of the green. The 11th is a short hole (148 yards from the back) that requires a shot from one marsh island to another. The 16th is long and demanding (210 yards), with a two-club green protected by a pond on the right-hand side.

The 7th hole is not long, but it's a good position hole. Framed by old live oak trees, it offers a scenic look at the tidal creeks and saltwater marsh.

Number eight is the longest hole on the course and a genuine three-shot par-5 from the two back tees. But the 4th hole is the toughest on the course, a par-4 that plays 458 yards from the back tee. This hole brings the marsh into play and the wind can be a factor on this hole, especially if it's into the golfer's face.

Insider Tips   One key to scoring here is playing the par-3s well. All four of them require shots over water or marsh, and you can make big numbers if you pick the wrong clubs. That's easy to do, because these par-3s all sit down in little valleys. The wind is usually blowing harder than appears when you toss out some grass to test it. The thing to do here is watch the tops of the trees and see which way and how hard the wind is blowing them. You can easily encounter two-club winds on these holes, but you may not realize it until your ball disappears into a hazard.

This is an excellent layout. The only question may be the conditioning, which is occasionally not up to expectations. Ask around or check it out before you plunk down your greens fee.

Dunes West Golf Club

3535 Wando Plantation Way, Mt. Pleasant, SC 29464; phone (843) 856-9000

How To Get On: Tee times can be made one week in advance.

Tees:

Championship: 6,871 yards, par-72, USGA rating 73.4, slope 131

Men's: 6,392 yards, par-72, USGA rating 70.7, slope 125

Forward: 5,278 yards, par-72, USGA rating 69.2, slope 118

Challenge: ★★★½	Golf Facilities: ★★★★
Variety: ★★★	14-Club Test: ★★★½
Terrain: ★★★½	Intangibles: ★★★½
Beauty/Visual Appeal: ★★★★	Value: ★★★★
Pace of Play: ★★★½	

Just the Facts Year Opened: 1991; Course Designer: Arthur Hills; Walking: No; Greens Fee: $35–70; 9 Hole/Twilight Rate: Yes; Pull Carts: No; Practice Range: Yes; Club Rental: Yes.

Description and Comments This course occupies what was once part of historic Lexington Plantation, and the clubhouse was constructed on the site of the original plantation house. From the back tees it's quite formidable, but not so hard that it isn't fun to play. From the men's and forward tees, it's not hard to score if you keep the ball in play and if you can successfully negotiate the stretch run, from the 14th through the 18th.

Dunes West was named as one of the top 10 new resort courses by 2 of the major golf magazines when it opened in 1991. It is operated by Scratch Golf, a Florida-based company that has gained a very good reputation for running courses that are challenging, fun to play, and, above all, always well maintained. The course is set among bermuda-covered dunes and ancient live oaks. It is somewhat open and always extremely scenic, especially on the back nine, where the course meanders along tidal marshlands and the fairways are framed by moss-draped live oaks.

But even on the back nine, with all those natural hazards, the fairways are generous and allow you to score if you keep the ball in play and manage your game. The two par-5s on the front nine can be reached in two by moderately long hitters, but the par-5s on the back nine are long and demanding.

The stretch run, beginning with the 14th, is what usually stands in the way of a good score. The 14th is a long, tight par-4 that doglegs right and measures 474 yards from the back tee. The green is narrow and guarded by a bunker on the right and water behind it. The 15th is a long par-5 (560 yards) requiring a precise drive and a second shot to a double fairway separated by four long bunkers. The green is long, narrow, and surrounded by bunkers.

Number 16 is a dogleg-left par-4 that measures 404 yards from the back, but the drive must clear nearly 200 yards of marsh, with scrub brush on the right and trees on the left. The green is protected by bunkers in front, behind, and on the left. The 17th is a par-3 that plays 209 yards from the back tee, with water on the left about midway to the hole, and water on the entire right side of the green.

The 18th is a monster par-4, 454 yards from the tips. There is an alternate green that is used sometimes, but not often, which makes the hole some 80 yards shorter—but the green is well protected by bunkers. The primary green is wide but not very deep, and from about 85 yards out, is guarded on the left by marsh. It's a memorable finishing hole on an excellent and scenic golf course.

Insider Tips There are three things that you must do to score here: You must keep the ball in the fairways, which are fairly wide; you must avoid the trouble around the greens; and you must be able to read the subtle breaks on these greens. Without slowing down play, it would be a good idea to look at crucial putts from behind the hole, as well as looking at the hole from behind your ball. This is a favorite course of the pop rock group Hootie and the Blowfish, who live nearby, so don't be surprised if you see them—or hear them—at Dunes West.

Kiawah Island Resort, Ocean Course

1000 Ocean Course Dr., Kiawah Island, SC 29455; phone (800) 654-2924 or (843) 768-2121

How To Get On: Guests of the resort can make tee times 60 days in advance. Nonguests can book times five days in advance.

Tees:

> Orange: 7,395 yards, par-72, USGA rating 78.0, slope 152
>
> Blue: 6,861 yards, par-72, USGA rating 74.5, slope 142
>
> White: 6,252 yards, par-72, USGA rating 71.9, slope 134
>
> Red: 5,327 yards, par-72, USGA rating 72.9, slope 133

Challenge: ★★★★★	Golf Facilities: ★★★★½
Variety: ★★★½	14-Club Test: ★★★★
Terrain: ★★★★½	Intangibles: ★★★★★
Beauty/Visual Appeal: ★★★★★	Value: ★★★½
Pace of Play: ★★★½	

Just the Facts Year Opened: 1991; Course Designer: Pete Dye; Walking: At times; Greens Fee: $110–160; 9 Hole/Twilight Rate: Yes; Pull Carts: No; Practice Range: Yes; Club Rental: Yes.

Description and Comments This is arguably the toughest golf course in the world, and certainly the toughest resort course, especially when the wind blows, as it usually does. When they played the 1991 Ryder Cup Match, the famous "War on the Shore" ensued on this course. The United States bested the Europeans 14½–15½ in a thriller that went down to Bernhard Langer's final missed six-foot putt, but the course beat all of them. Interestingly enough, officials from both Ryder Cup sides wisely decided not to let their pros play this one from the back tees, which could have stretched the course to 7,884 yards tip to tip. They played the course at just over 7,000 yards, and it still made mincemeat out of them.

Even though this course was tamed down before the 1997 World Cup—fairways widened, some of the tall grass cut, and the waste areas grassed—it can still beat your brains in. One of the club pros, when asked about the Ocean Course, commented, only somewhat in jest, "They make me play it once a month."

This is not a course you would want to play every day of your vacation, let alone for the rest of your golfing life. In fact, if it were the only course you could play, you may want to trade your golf clubs for a bowling ball or a badminton racquet.

Yet this is a beautiful course, extremely well manicured on the wavy fairways and wildly rolling greens. Ten holes run right along the Atlantic Ocean, and the remaining eight provide great views of both the ocean and stunning tidal marshland, wild grasses, and exotic trees. It's nothing short of magnificent to behold. In the same way that a tank-town prizefighter might wonder what it would be like to get into the ring with the champ, most golfers long to know how they would fare up against the best the world has to offer. In either case, the challenger should expect to come away with some welts and bruises.

Great hole follows great hole here. Occasionally it's hard to remember one hole from the next, but individually each is rugged and beautiful. One of the most memorable is number 17, a par-3 that plays anywhere from 152 yards to 197 yards. This is certainly a hole that Mark Calcavecchia will never forget. Needing only a double bogey to win the his 1991 Ryder Cup match from Colin Montgomerie, who put his tee shot into the lagoon that runs from tee to green, Calcavecchia dunked it into the water about halfway to the green, made triple bogey, losing the hole and then the match. There are no real bail-out areas on this hole, although the green is extremely wide and there is some scrub and some dunes to catch a pulled shot. There is nothing to help a sliced shot here.

Another Ocean stunner is the par-4 13th, which normally plays 404 yards from the back tees, but which actually possesses a tiny "tiger" tee set way back in the trees, on the far side of the marsh. This stretches the hole to a mind-bending 478 yards. From whatever tees you pick, you'll face a forced carry tee shot over water. Woe to slicers, as wildlife-laced marsh lines the entire right-hand side. The long, narrow, lumpy green is guarded by mounds and bunkers left and by marsh on the right. At least it's open in front, allowing for the low, run-up approach.

There just aren't any "yawners," on this course. You have to stay alert and plot your shots from beginning to end. You may get pummeled, but you won't get bored.

Insider Tips Because club selection is so important here, shell out the money and buy the yardage book. It should really help, providing some inside tips on playing the toughest, trickiest holes.

The earlier you play, the better off you're likely to be, because you're more likely to escape the wind, at least on the front nine. And it's easier to putt the large greens when they are a little damp from late-night watering and early morning dew. Architect Pete Dye built a brute here, but it's mostly a fair brute. Due to strong coastal breezes, high approaches aren't as easy to play as low, running ones. Although Dye elevated most of the greens, at least he left most of them open in front. Thus, a Scottish-style bouncing approach into the green is often the smart and preferred tactic here.

On many holes at the Ocean Course, there is a requirement for certain shots to be equal parts power and precision. On the 525-yard, par-5, dogleg-left second hole for instance, there is a natural tendency on the tee shot to want to bite off more of the marsh than you can chew. But if you play too safe and bail out to the right, there is a good chance, at least from the "up" tees, that you can drive through the fairway into the marsh that guards the right side of the fairway. If you're not a long hitter, or if you haven't hit a particularly good drive, you're better off laying up short of the marsh (leaving an approach shot of from 125 to 160 yards) than trying to clear the marsh and have a short wedge into the elevated green. Many holes here offer these risk/reward decisions.

All of the greens and their surrounds feature funky slopes and swales, so it's wise to hone your chipping game before you tackle the Ocean Course. And for heaven's sake, choose the correct set of tees for your game. If you go back too far, you'll only anger the course ranger and the folks behind you with your slow play.

If you're coming to play the Ocean Course as an outsider, allow yourself at least 15 minutes to a half-hour extra driving time to get to the clubhouse. The Kiawah Island Resort is an enormous property, and all five courses feature separate clubhouses. The Ocean Course's facilities are by far the farthest away from the resort's main entrance. You've got to pass through two guard gates, then drive another 10 to 15 minutes through gorgeous, pristine low-country scenery, teeming with wildlife, until the road ends. You're there.

Kiawah Island Resort, Osprey Point Course

12 Kiawah Beach Dr., Kiawah Island, SC 29455; phone (800) 654-2924 or (843) 768-2121

How To Get On: Guests of the resort can make tee times 60 days in advance. Nonguests can book times five days in advance.

Tees:

    Gold: 6,678 yards, par-72, USGA rating 71.8, slope 124

    White: 6,015 yards, par-72, USGA rating 68.8, slope 118

    Forward: 5,122 yards, par-72, USGA rating 69.6, slope 120

Challenge: ★★★	Golf Facilities: ★★★★½
Variety: ★★★★	14-Club Test: ★★★★
Terrain: ★★★½	Intangibles: ★★★
Beauty/Visual Appeal: ★★★★	Value: ★★★★
Pace of Play: ★★★	

Just the Facts   Year Opened: 1988; Course Designer: Tom Fazio; Walking: Yes; Greens Fee: $59–139; 9 Hole/Twilight Rate: Yes; Pull Carts: No; Practice Range: Yes; Club Rental: Yes.

Description and Comments   Four big, natural lakes; inlets of saltwater marsh; and maritime forests of old live oaks, pines, palmettos, and magnolias gave Tom Fazio a great piece of land to work with. Osprey Point traverses a series of islands and you get from one golf hole to the next via a network of wooden bridges. This isn't a long course, but it has its share of tough holes. The ninth, for example, is a par-4 that plays 453 yards from the tips, and there are two par-3s that measure more than 200 yards each.

The beauty of this course, aside from the scenery, is the fact that there are so many short, strategic par-4s that tempt the long hitter into making greedy mistakes. This is a course where you have to keep your head about you, like playing an outdoor chess game. You have to study your moves carefully on nearly every hole.

For example, number seven measures only 328 yards from the back tee. Sounds simple enough. But it doglegs slightly to the right, around a big berm that is accented by sand bunkers. If you take the safe route and hit out to the left, you flirt with that berm and the sand bunkers. A big bunker guards the left-hand side of the green, making the landing area narrow if you come in from the left. If you are a big hitter, you can try to shorten the hole by cutting the dogleg with a drive at the hole. But if you gamble with your drive and don't succeed, you could end up out to the right in the deep woods.

Fazio put in a lot of moguls on this course, which are pleasing to the eye and make the course more challenging. There is water on 15 holes, and several long bunkers protect the greens. The fairways are generously wide, and the greens are big.

The 3rd hole plays over a protected marsh that requires a 175-yard carry from the back tee. The green is divided into two different sections by a ridge, and a long, deep bunker that is very hard to get up and down from runs the length of the green from the environmental area. Club selection on this long, narrow, diagonal green can vary as much as two or three clubs.

From the back tees, the par-4 9th plays 453 yards and requires a drive over water. You can cut off some yardage by cutting over the water, but no matter how much you cut off, you're still going to have a long shot into the green. To add to the difficulty, there is a big bunker in the middle of the fairway that swallows drives and makes it impossible to get to the green in regulation if you hit into it. Play to the left of the bunker and it's anywhere from 180 to 200 yards in; from the right side of the bunker, it's anywhere from 210 to 220 yards in.

Insider Tips The greens here are so big that you are going to have longer putts than you are accustomed to. You may hit more greens, but you may end up with more three putts than usual. So it's very important when you warm up to practice a lot of long lag putts to get the feel. Fazio used the water here more as an intimidation factor than a hazard, and you have to hit some pretty poor shots to get into them. So forget about the water and concentrate on making good lag putts.

All of the sprinkler heads are marked to the front, middle, and back of the greens. Depending on the hole location, club selection is very important, so check your yardages and pin placements carefully and take a yardage book with you. A marvelous clubhouse/dining/pro shop facility is worth your time at Osprey Point.

Kiawah Island Resort, Turtle Point Course

12 Kiawah Beach Dr., Kiawah Island, SC 29455; phone (800) 654-2924 or (843) 768-2121

How To Get On: Guests of the resort can make tee times 60 days in advance. Non-guests can book times five days in advance.

Tees:

> Gold: 6,925 yards, par-72, USGA rating 74.0, slope 142
>
> Blue: 6,497 yards, par-72, USGA rating 71.8, slope 134
>
> White: 5,986 yards, par-72, USGA rating 69.1, slope 125
>
> Red: 5,247 yards, par-72, USGA rating 71.1, slope 126

Challenge: ★★★★	Golf Facilities: ★★★
Variety: ★★★½	14-Club Test: ★★★½
Terrain: ★★★½	Intangibles: ★★★
Beauty/Visual Appeal: ★★★★	Value: ★★★½
Pace of Play: ★★★½	

Just the Facts Year Opened: 1981; Course Designer: Jack Nicklaus; Walking: Yes; Greens Fee: $79–139; 9 Hole/Twilight Rate: Yes; Pull Carts: No; Practice Range: Yes; Club Rental: Yes.

Description and Comments This was the toughest and most scenic of the Kiawah courses prior to the opening of the Ocean Course. Now nearly 20 years mature, what is perhaps most impressive about Nicklaus's work here is that he was able to blend the fairways and greens into the existing landscape without moving a lot of dirt and without resorting to a lot of artificial and radical undertakings, such as creating large mounds.

Though most of the talk about Kiawah these days is centered on the Ocean Course, Turtle Point is ranked among the best resort courses in the country and has been for several years. Although it is a formidable course, it is certainly much more fun to play, day in and day out, than the Ocean Course.

The course measures just over 6,900 yards from the back tees, but still requires accuracy and length off the tee and on approach shots. As with most Nicklaus courses, if you want to get on the back tees, you had better be able to play the game, or you could get your brains beat in all day. Move up to the next set of tees and you get a break. He leaves it all up to you.

Turtle Point zigzags through some lush vegetation and meanders along the marshes and out to the ocean. The fairways are surprisingly tight for a Nicklaus course, and the greens are small, requiring precise driving and accurate approach shots, which is vintage early Nicklaus.

What puts the frosting on the cake here are the three spectacular ocean holes: the 14th, 15th, and 16th. These holes are actually closer to the ocean than any of the holes on the Ocean Course. You can actually hit a sunbather if you yank a shot.

On the 14th, there is no easy pin placement. Because this hole usually plays into a headwind or with a prevailing wind—rarely a crosswind— wherever the pin, you're going to end up with a tough shot either way to get to the green or to hold the green.

On the 15th there is no room for error on your drive. You have to be precise, because the ocean is on the left side and homes line the right side. There is no room for error on the 16th either, as there is a bunker on the front right of this short par-3, and tall, thick grass to the left and in the back of a green that is severely undulating.

Insider Tips This course rewards a player who can hit a left to right ball, à la Nicklaus. But more important than working the ball is simply to hit it straight and keep it in the short grass. When you get to the three ocean holes—14, 15, and 16—keep in mind that the ball is going to break toward the water, even if it doesn't look like it will. Also, these three greens are considerably quicker than the others are, so keep that in mind when you line up your putts.

The greens at Turtle Point are shallow and often set at diagonals with hazards fronting them. You must hit it high to hold these greens. If you miss, you're better off erring to the open side in front of the green, away from the pin, to have yourself an easy chip shot. Unlike many Jack Nicklaus–designed courses, Turtle Point's greens are small and on the flat side. Accurate approach shots are critical here, whereas putting is pretty easy.

Turtle Point has its share of turtles, but more birds and an alarming number of alligators. Plenty of signs alert you to the gators' presence, but many people aren't fully cognizant of their abilities. They're not looking for conflicts—but give them a wide birth. They look slow, but they can run very fast for a distance of up to 60 yards.

Wild Dunes Resort, Links Course

5757 Palm Blvd., Isle of Palms, SC 29451; phone (800) 845-8880 or (843) 886-2164

How To Get On: Guests of the resort can make tee times 60 days in advance. Nonguests can book times 30 days in advance.

Tees:

    Blue: 6,722 yards, par-72, USGA rating 72.7, slope 131

    White: 6,131 yards, par-72, USGA rating 69.7, slope 121

    Gold: 5,280 yards, par-72, USGA rating 71.2, slope 125

    Red: 4,849 yards, par-72, USGA rating 69.1, slope 121

Challenge: ★★★½	Golf Facilities: ★★★★
Variety: ★★★★	14-Club Test: ★★★★
Terrain: ★★★★½	Intangibles: ★★★½
Beauty/Visual Appeal: ★★★★½	Value: ★★★★
Pace of Play: ★★★½	

Just the Facts Year Opened: 1981; Course Designer: Tom Fazio; Walking: Yes; Greens Fee: $50–150; 9 Hole/Twilight Rate: Yes; Pull Carts: No; Practice Range: Yes; Club Rental: Yes.

Description and Comments More than 200 years ago, Lord Cornwallis and his British troops stepped ashore on what is now the 18th hole on the Links Course at Wild Dunes Resort on the Isle of Palms. Because the Isle of Palms was one of the few barrier islands in the Deep South that wasn't cleared to grow sea island cotton in those colonial days, the mammoth sand dunes and thick stands of twisted oak live oak trees that greeted Cornwallis were still there when modern developers decided to build a golf resort on the island.

The abundance of live oaks and the massive sand dunes gave Tom Fazio a great piece of land on which to shape a seaside course. Fazio's end product is an incredibly beautiful, rolling layout ranked among the nation's best golf courses by all the major golf magazines and every credible course ranking system in America.

When Fazio first saw the land he was handed to build this course, he called it "an architect's dream." Although Hurricane Hugo rearranged some of this land in 1989—virtually destroying a few holes on the stretch run plus countless trees—it is still every bit as beautiful today. In fact, the Links Course underwent a major renovation not long after Hurricane Hugo came calling. The renovations actually improved the course, lengthening a few holes with the addition of some new tees and improving the angle of the approach shot into the beautiful 18th.

The Links Course is almost short by today's championship standards, measuring only 6,722 yards from the tips and 6,131 from the white tees. Nevertheless, it holds the big hitters at bay, thanks to ever-present coastal breezes, a multitude of well-placed trees, and a variety of additional hazards and landscape environments.

The par-3s here are exceptional and photogenic. Number four is not a long hole (170 yards), but water protects the entire right side. The eighth is the longest of the par-3s at 203 yards and doesn't have a lot of trouble, other than a small lagoon in front of the tees that eats topped shots, but the green is huge, extremely undulating, and contoured with tiers. The dramatically beautiful 12th plays a formidable 192 yards from the back tee and borders the ocean. The green is tucked right into the dunes, and the wind is always a factor. The 16th is built over the marsh with the ocean in the background and water all along the right side waiting to gobble up a slice.

Both nines finish in grand style. The par-4 9th is indeed a formidable foe from the back tee, at 451 yards. It is tamer from the forward tees, but water guards the green on either side like a fortress. The 18th is the most photographed and famous hole on the course, a great par-5 that isn't long (501 yards), but the wind and ocean always come into play. The hole doglegs severely to the right, requiring a tee shot perfectly placed on the left side of the fairway for any chance to reach the green in two. A hooked drive will definitely find the beach. If the wind is favorable, this hole will yield some eagles. But into a headwind or when the crosswinds start howling, it's an entirely different story. The massive green has some severe undulations and borders the dunes where Cornwallis and his men came ashore and, by the way, were defeated by the colonist troops at nearby Fort Moultrie in their first major victory of the American Revolution. Unfortunately, recent villa construction at the resort has eliminated the undisturbed naturalness the 18th once possessed, but it remains one of the most scenic closing holes on the East Coast.

The rolling mounds, sea oats, ocean, dunes, and the gnarled old live oaks add to the experience here and make the Links Course an unforgettable one that shouldn't be missed by any golfer on a trip to Charleston.

Insider Tips   The breeze is always a factor here, so practice your knockdown shots—you're going to need them, especially when you're playing into a headwind. If you don't play the wind here, it will play you.

The fairways are generous and they roll well though novices will have to cope with the vagaries of uneven lies, thanks to the topsy-turvy terrain. The real key to scoring here is how well you play your approach shots. The greens are extremely undulating, so work on your lag putting before you play, and take the time to read the greens to determine the subtle breaks that could be the difference between a two putt and a three putt.

A Charleston Sampler

The Club at Seabrook Island, Crooked Oaks Course

1002 Landfall Way, Seabrook Island, SC 29455; phone (843) 768-2529 or (843) 768-1000

Tees: Championship: 6,776 yards, par-72, USGA rating 71.9, slope 124

Greens Fee: $50–130

Challenge: ★★★	Golf Facilities: ★★★½
Variety: ★★★	14-Club Test: ★★★½
Terrain: ★★★½	Intangibles: ★★★
Beauty/Visual Appeal: ★★★★	Value: ★★★½
Pace of Play: ★★★½	

Description and Comments   This course would get a lot of votes to be a major course, rather than a sampler. One of two extremely good courses at Seabrook Island Resort (the other is Ocean Winds, discussed below), this Robert Trent Jones Sr. layout is the better of them, if for no other reason than it takes you on such a scenic journey through twisted old live oak trees, marshes, and the lush vegetation of the island's maritime forests of oaks, palmettos, magnolias, and pines. This is a true links-type courses, where the front nine goes out and the back nine comes back in the opposite direction. The greens at Crooked Oaks are classic Jones: large, elevated, and well-trapped. The par-3s aren't long, but in every case the greens are well guarded by marsh and lagoons.

This course just reopened after an extensive renovation. Specific hole descriptions were unavailable at the time of writing.

The Club at Seabrook Island, Ocean Winds Course

1002 Landfall Way, Seabrook Island, SC 29455; phone (843) 768-2529 or (843) 768-1000

Tees: Championship: 6,767 yards, par-72, USGA rating 72.0, slope 133
Greens Fee: $50–130

Challenge: ★★★½	Golf Facilities: ★★★½
Variety: ★★★	14-Club Test: ★★★
Terrain: ★★★½	Intangibles: ★★★½
Beauty/Visual Appeal: ★★★½	Value: ★★★½
Pace of Play: ★★★★	

Description and Comments The saltmarsh and dune ridges can play havoc on this Willard Byrd course where water hazards and marsh come prominently into play on 12 holes. Ocean Winds has a slightly higher slope rating than Seabrook's Crooked Oaks, as this course is more compact than Crooked Oaks, with more parallel fairways and more water hazards. The freshening breeze from the Atlantic, when it begins to howl, can wreak havoc with your game as you play out toward the ocean, turning peaceful tidal marshes into major hazards. For example, the 15th hole, 177 yards from the back tee, usually plays shorter because of a prevailing ocean wind. But the tee shot is all carry over tidal marsh, and a golfer is tested not only to carry the marsh but also to hit and hold the narrow green.

The finishing holes, the 16th, 17th, and 18th, are particularly good. Number 16 is a par-5 that isn't particularly long (492 yards from the back tee), but it is treacherous, with water hazards and marsh framing the entire fairway, from tee to green. The 17th is a tough par-4 that doglegs left and is protected by fairway bunkers and marsh on the left, and usually plays into a headwind. The final hole is a scenic par-4 that plays to the ocean, where the wind can play tricks on your approach shot.

Coosaw Creek Country Club

4210 Club Course Dr., Charleston, SC 29420; phone (843) 767-9000
Tees: Championship: 6,593 yards, par-71, USGA rating 71.3, slope 129
Greens Fee: $20–40

Challenge: ★★★	Golf Facilities: ★★★
Variety: ★★★	14-Club Test: ★★★½
Terrain: ★★★½	Intangibles: ★★★½
Beauty/Visual Appeal: ★★★½	Value: ★★★
Pace of Play: ★★★½	

Description and Comments This is a shotmaker's course, the type where a player that has a skillful short game might best a longer hitter. Arthur Hills designed this course so that golfers would have bail-out areas if they missed the greens; but these escape areas demand precise chip shots in order to make pars. The course is quite scenic with subtle mounds, rolling fairways, woods, wetlands, and gradual elevation changes. The back nine is much tougher than the front because there are more water hazards and wetlands on that side. There are also a few long, demanding holes, two of the toughest on the back side. The par-5 12th stretches to 596 yards and requires a drive over a lake and an approach shot that must avoid a stand of pine trees guarding the entrance to the green on the right. Into a headwind, this can be a four-shot hole.

The toughest hole on the course is the par-4 14th. From 100 yards out, the green is guarded in front and on the left by marsh that likes to suck up golf balls. The course is generally kept in very good condition.

Crowfield Golf and Country Club

300 Hamlet Circle, Goose Creek, SC 29445; phone (843) 764-4618
Tees: Championship: 7,003 yards, par-72, USGA rating 73.9, slope 139
Greens Fee: $37–75

Challenge: ★★★½	Golf Facilities: ★★★
Variety: ★★★	14-Club Test: ★★½
Terrain: ★★★	Intangibles: ★★★
Beauty/Visual Appeal: ★★★½	Value: ★★★★
Pace of Play: ★★★½	

Description and Comments　This isn't as much of a shotmaker's course as it is a slugger's course, but it is still a very good test of golf, a pretty one with a lot of moguls and mounding, large bunkers and multilevel greens. From the back tees, every par-4 on the back nine measures over 400 yards. But the greens are tricky, and what wins here is a good putting stroke and the ability to read the greens. The course, located about a half-hour from downtown Charleston, is situated on a former indigo plantation and was designed by Bob Spence, who now works with Davis Love III. The back nine is especially scenic because of an abundance of trees, lagoons, and lakes. The brick-work remains of the original Crowfield Plantation home, which dates back to the 1700s, is next to the 13th green.

The area around the course is quite scenic. There is an abundance of wildlife roaming the course, including white-tail deer, eagles, hawks, and alligators. The most memorable hole on the course is probably the 6th, a par-4 whose fairways are lined by sand bunkers on both sides and a multilevel green that is surrounded by water.

Edisto Beach Golf Club

24 Fairway Dr., Edisto Island, SC 29438; phone (843) 869-1111
Tees: Championship: 6,212 yards, par-71, USGA rating 69.5, slope 118
Greens Fee: $40–50

Challenge: ★★½	Golf Facilities: ★★
Variety: ★★★	14-Club Test: ★★½
Terrain: ★★★	Intangibles: ★★★
Beauty/Visual Appeal: ★★★★	Value: ★★★★
Pace of Play: ★★★★	

Description and Comments   This course is more than an hour from downtown Charleston, but well worth playing, just as the island is well worth seeing. Edisto Island is extremely scenic and peaceful and is a favorite stop for wildlife photographers who come from all over the world. It is also one of the favorite nesting places for the endangered giant loggerhead sea turtles, which weigh up to 600 pounds. The beach homes are understated, simple, wooden structures on stilts, not opulent multimillion-dollar extravaganzas. Many people find it a nice change of pace. The beach is unspoiled and pretty.

There is only one resort here, a very nice one called Fairfield Ocean Ridge, a cozy place that blends in with the trees and vegetation, as if it had sprouted right out of the woods. The golf course is not long, but it is nicely manicured, sporty, and fun to play. The scenery around the course is fantastic, and there are enough tough holes that you will not get bored playing it. Water on 14 of those holes and 59 bunkers scattered about the acreage add further interest.

The 6th hole is a 155-yard, par-3 island hole with a wide and shallow green. Most greens here are small, requiring precise iron shots.

Kiawah Island Resort, Cougar Point Course

12 Kiawah Beach Dr., Kiawah Island, SC 29455; phone (800) 654-2924 or (843) 768-2121
Tees: Championship: 6,861 yards, par-72, USGA rating 73.0, slope 134
Greens Fee: $100–125

Challenge: ★★★½	Golf Facilities: ★★★★
Variety: ★★★½	14-Club Test: ★★★½
Terrain: ★★★½	Intangibles: ★★
Beauty/Visual Appeal: ★★★★	Value: ★★★½
Pace of Play: ★★★	

Description and Comments   For years, the 1976 Gary Player Marsh Point course was the weak sister among Kiawah Island Resort's courses. It was relatively short and neither particularly imaginative nor very challenging. However, that's all changed now. Player came in and redesigned the course, lengthening it to 6,860 yards from the back tees, improving the landing areas, moving greens to put them into better and more scenic positions, and opening up fairways on the front nine to provide views of the Kiawah River. Fittingly, this new course carries a new name. Player—who one must assume knows as much about bunkers and bunkering as anyone alive because he plays them so well—added many bunkers to protect the outside of several of the doglegs. He also added some alternative routing into the par-5s.

A few years ago, we might have told golfers to save their time and money and play elsewhere, but Cougar Point is now a delight to play, quite a challenge, and a pretty walk through the woods and marsh, as well.

Kiawah Island Resort, Oak Point Course

4255 Bohicket Rd., Johns Island, SC 29455; phone (843) 768-7431

Tees: Championship: 6,759 yards, par-72, USGA rating 73.3, slope 137

Greens Fee: $50–79

Challenge: ★★★	Golf Facilities: ★★★½
Variety: ★★★	14-Club Test: ★★★½
Terrain: ★★★½	Intangibles: ★★
Beauty/Visual Appeal: ★★★½	Value: ★★★½
Pace of Play: ★★★	

Description and Comments This Clyde Johnston course was originally a real estate development course that lingered and was eventually bought by Kiawah Island Resort, which has considerably upgraded its condition. The somewhat cramped course is located a few miles outside the gates of the resort, adjoining the Kiawah River and tidal marshlands. The wind is a factor, especially on holes that open up to the marsh. Live oaks, magnolias, pines, and palmettos line several fairways. The greens and fairways are now in excellent condition, and the layout offers a lot of versatility, with a mix of long holes, short target holes, and scenic par-3s.

The 18th hole is the most memorable on the course. It runs out to the Kiawah and is extremely scenic, a par-4 that plays 406 yards from the back tees, with a tight fairway. The tee shot has to carry a sizable finger of the marsh, and the approach shot must carry a bulkhead into a green that is surrounded by big sand bunkers.

The Links at Stono Ferry

5365 Forest Oaks Dr., Hollywood, SC 29449; phone (843) 763-1817

Tees: Championship: 6,616 yards, par-72, USGA rating 70.9, slope 132

Greens Fee: $31–43

Challenge: ★★★
Variety: ★★★½
Terrain: ★★★½
Beauty/Visual Appeal: ★★★★
Pace of Play: ★★★

Golf Facilities: ★★★½
14-Club Test: ★★★
Intangibles: ★★★
Value: ★★★½

Description and Comments   Water, water everywhere. This is an extremely scenic and well-manicured Ron Garl–designed course that is located along the Intracoastal Waterway. Although it isn't a long course, it is still challenging. The front nine meanders through huge oaks and tall pines; the back nine offers panoramic views of the marsh and the Intracoastal Waterway. The surroundings are gorgeous, especially along the Intracoastal Waterway and the Stono River. This is one of the few courses where you might see a dolphin and an alligator swimming side by side, and there are a large number of giant live oak trees with hanging Spanish moss.

The fairways here are tight, and the rough is generally tough. There are also some treacherous par-3s that require shots over water to greens that are rolling and tricky to putt.

The long, par-4 6th hole is memorable, not only because it is demanding (440 yards from the back tee) but also because you will usually see wild horses roaming near the fairway. In the early mornings and late afternoons, you're likely to encounter herds of deer. The 14th is one of the toughest holes on the course from the back tees: a 168-yard par-3 that requires an all-carry shot over water into a green surrounded by large bunkers and rough-covered mounds.

Patriots Point Links

1 Patriots Point Rd., Mt. Pleasant, SC 29464; phone (800) 221-2424 or (843) 881-0042

Tees: Championship: 6,838 yards, par-72, USGA rating 72.1, slope 118
Greens Fee: $29–55

Challenge: ★★½
Variety: ★★★
Terrain: ★★½
Beauty/Visual Appeal: ★★★½
Pace of Play: ★★½

Golf Facilities: ★★½
14-Club Test: ★★★
Intangibles: ★★★
Value: ★★★

Description and Comments   Although there is nothing spectacular about the design of the course itself, its location along the banks of the beautiful Charleston Harbor, and the views of downtown Charleston, and the historic district make this Willard Byrd course worth playing. This isn't a particularly tough course, even from the back tees (118 slope), but it twists along tidal creeks and saltwater marshes and around lagoons. Those hazards, especially when the wind is up, keep it from being a pushover. Most of the hazards are lateral, however, and the greens are generously large, both of which are big pluses in the playability department. Wear a hard hat at Patriots Point—or at least keep an eye out, as wayward shots are frequent on these mostly parallel fairways.

The four finishing holes are the best and most memorable. They run along the Charleston Harbor. The 17th is a par-3 with an island green that sits right in the harbor and provides great views of downtown Charleston, Fort Sumter, and the neighboring sea islands. The 18th is a 500-yard par-5 that finishes along the harbor.

Wild Dunes Resort, Harbor Course

5881 Palmetto Dr., Isle of Palms, SC 29451; phone (800) 845-8880, (843) 886-2164, or (843) 886-2301

Tees: Championship: 6,446 yards, par-70, USGA rating 70.9, slope 124

Greens Fee: $40–90

Challenge: ★★★½	Golf Facilities: ★★★★
Variety: ★★★½	14-Club Test: ★★★★
Terrain: ★★★½	Intangibles: ★★★½
Beauty/Visual Appeal: ★★★★	Value: ★★★½
Pace of Play: ★★★½	

Description and Comments   This is a very underrated course because it is overshadowed by Wild Dunes's nationally ranked Links course, which gets most of the publicity. But the Harbor Course could easily pass inspection as one of Charleston's major courses. Like the Links Course, it was designed by Tom Fazio, but it plays along the Intracoastal Waterway, Morgan Creek, Waterway Island, and the marshlands, rather than along the ocean. Harbor requires accuracy over power, especially on the short front nine, more so than its sister, the Links Course. The yardage doesn't look like much on the card, but that is deceiving because par is only 70. Also, the bunkering is more extensive at the Links course. There is water and marsh on 17 holes; three holes parallel the Intracoastal Waterway, and the two marshfront finishing holes are as tough a test as you could ever ask for. The incoming nine launches at the resort's Yacht Harbor, which gives the course its name.

This course is extremely well cared for, with lush bermuda grass fairways and smooth, true greens. Because it gives you an entirely different type of test and an entirely different type of scenery, it is a perfect companion course to the Links Course, one that golfers will enjoy playing again and again.

Lodging

EXPENSIVE

The Governor's House Inn

117 Broad St., Charleston, SC 29401; phone (800) 720-9812 or (843) 720-2070; www.governorshouse.com; Rates: $165–330

Over 200 years ago this inn was once home to Governor Edward Rutledge, the youngest signer of the Declaration of Independence. Now a designated landmark, it is one of Charleston's more majestic B&Bs and a favorite among visitors. There are 12 rooms, all with private baths and hardwood floors.

Kiawah Island Golf and Tennis Resort

12 Kiawah Beach Dr., Kiawah Island, SC 29455; phone (800) 654-2924 or (843) 768-2121; www.kiawahresort.com; Rates: $135–225 (rooms), $175–500 (villas), $1,800–6,000 (homes)

If golf is your passion, Kiawah Resort will be nirvana. Kiawah is a barrier island located 21 miles from Charleston. There are more than 10,000 acres on the island, yet it remains a private community with access limited to property owners and guests of the resort or rental agencies. The resort is the only facility on this 10-mile stretch of beach (the only case of this in the world). On the island you will find a wide variety of flora and fauna spread out among the beaches, lagoons, and saltmarshes. By the way, don't be surprised if you see an alligator sunning on the banks of the lagoons as you tour around the island—and as the posted warnings indicate, they are dangerous, so don't try to pet one.

When deciding where to stay, you have a variety of options at Kiawah Resort. If you want a more conventional vacation, consider the Kiawah Island Inn, located adjacent to the beach, near many of the resort's restaurants, lounges, and shopping areas. In addition to room service, the inn offers its guests tennis courts and oceanside swimming pools. If you yearn for a little more room and privacy, you should check out the island's many villas; they are located all over the island, so you can choose not only the size of your villa but also the location. Finally, there are a number of resort homes around the island. The price tag on these homes is steep, but they are spectacular and include everything you could ever ask for in a dream home. Some even have a private dock so you may want to pack that 20-foot Boston whaler in your golf bag.

Besides golf, Kiawah offers an amazing array of outdoor activities designed to entertain and educate. The following is a smattering of what you will find on tap: Nature Excursions—Biking into History (learn about Native Americans that once inhabited the island), Wildlife in the Wetlands (seven-mile bike tour to study unique pond system), canoeing and kayaking, drawing and painting in the natural environment, night walks, saltwater fly-fishing, birds of Kiawah, cycling, full-service marina, and Kamp Kiawah.

A great way to get to experience Kiawah's golf courses and improve your game at the same time is through their respected golf school. The school runs from February through May and September through November.

For dining, Kiawah offers a wide variety of restaurants, outlined below.

Golf Packages   Packages include deluxe accommodations in the Inn or in a villa, daily golf at one of Kiawah's five premier golf courses, cart, range balls, breakfast buffet, taxes, and service charge.

Meeting Street Inn

173 Meeting St., Charleston, SC 29401; phone (800) 842-8022 or (843) 723-1882; www.aesir.com; Rates: $90–220

Located in the heart of the historic district, this inn will make you feel at home as soon as you step through the lobby. Each of the 56 rooms features antique reproductions and four-poster rice beds; you will no doubt enjoy the sunny garden courtyard, which includes a Jacuzzi.

The Mills House Hotel

115 Meeting St., Charleston, SC 29401; phone (800) 874-9600 or (843) 577-2400; www.millshouse.com; Rates: $195–225

If you are looking for a more conventional hotel, you can't miss with the Mills House. This grand Victorian hotel combines the charm of old-world Charleston with modern amenities. Each of the 214 rooms is individually decorated with period furniture including demi-canopied beds. You will also find a great sundeck and a pool for a little relaxation.

The Resort at Seabrook Island

1002 Landfall Way, Seabrook Island, SC 29455; phone (800) 845-2475 or (843) 768-1000; www.seabrookresort.com; Rates: $165–240

Seabrook Island may be only a short 30 minutes from Charleston, but the second you set foot on the property, you will feel a million miles away. Seabrook is a 2,200-acre private island nestled in the Low Country of South Carolina. Only resort guests and residents are granted access to the island, its facilities, and amenities. This resort is packed with activities, so if you are looking for a fun yet quiet site for your vacation, take a look at Seabrook.

Seabrook is ideal for groups and families, as all accommodations are villa style and range from one- to three-bedrooms with ocean, golf, and racquet/scenic area views. Each villa has a fully equipped kitchen, living room, and dining area. Along with two championship golf courses, Seabrook offers a wide variety of activities, including the Equestrian Center, 13 Har-Tru tennis courts, bike and jogging trails, fitness center, full-service marina, and a kids' club.

If you decide not to cook in your villa, you can choose from one of the restaurants on the island. The Island House Restaurant serves seafood and pasta in an elegant oceanside setting. Bohicket's Lounge/Seaview Restaurant also serves seafood and pasta, but in a more informal settings. Cap'n Sams offers up sandwiches and burgers.

Golf Packages   Seabrook offers the "Ultimate Golf Package" for those who want to play golf every day during their stay. It includes villa accommodations, daily greens fees, cart for 18 holes each day, arrival day golf at half price, club storage, full breakfast, and discounted replay rates.

Two Meeting Street Inn

2 Meeting St., Charleston, SC 29401; phone (843) 723-7322; Rates: $155–265

This mansion is arguably the most elegant inn in the city of Charleston. Located near the Battery, the inn was originally built in 1892 as a wedding gift from a bride's father and was converted to a B&B more than 60 years ago. There are nine bedrooms, each with a private bath and canopied four-poster beds. The common rooms are wonderfully decorated and may make it hard for you to head upstairs to your room.

Wild Dunes

5757 Palm Dr., Isle of Palms, SC 29951; phone (800) 845-8880 or (843) 886-6000; www.wilddunes.com; Rates: $125–375

Located on the northeast end of the Isle of Palms, Wild Dunes has it all: Two top-notch courses designed by Tom Fazio, two-and-a-half miles of beachfront, excellent accommodations, 17 tennis courts, 20 swimming pools, distinctive dining, and, if you can find time in your schedule, a fitness center.

On the accommodations side, Wild Dunes offers a variety of one- to four-bedroom villas, three- to six-bedroom homes. The views are spectacular no matter where the home is located, with choices of ocean, golf course, tennis court, lagoon, or marshland vistas. All villas are walking distance to the beach and restaurants.

If you love to be pampered you may want to try the newly built Board-walk Inn (93 rooms), where residents have access to room service, concierge, valet, and bell service. If you need more than one bed for your stay, you have a couple of options to consider: all king-size bedrooms also come with sleeper sofas; there are eight junior suites with separate sitting areas and additional balconies; and finally, there's the Presidential Suite for those who can afford the steep price tag.

As we mentioned in the opening paragraph, Wild Dunes is brimming with recreational options. The resort has 17 Har-Tru tennis courts (five lit for night play), miles of paved jogging/biking trails (bike and inline skate rentals available), fitness center, and the Wild Dunes Yacht Club. A variety of children's programs are available. If you feel like getting back to nature, check out the Naturalistic Wild Excursions, which take adventurers through the local waterways and to the neighboring barrier islands.

On the dining front, Wild Dunes features three restaurants from which to choose. The Grill at Boardwalk Inn specializes in seafood in a beautiful and relaxed setting; Edgar's Restaurant and Bar is located in the Links course clubhouse and serves breakfast, lunch, and dinner in a casual environment. Finally, the Grand Pavilion is a fine spot to grab a quick snack.

Golf Packages   Packages include lodging in a fully furnished villa, greens and cart fees for 18 holes per day, access to the fitness center, and a full breakfast. Golf packages can be customized, and the rate will be based on the number of players, rounds, and nights (a minimum stay is required and changes by season) as well as course selection and location of villa. Contact Wild Dunes and they will assist you with pricing your golf package.

MODERATE

Doubletree Hotels and Suites

181 Church St., Charleston, SC 29401; phone (800) 527-1133 or (843) 577-2644; www.doubletree.com; Rates: $109–229

Located in the heart of the market district, the Doubletree is an appealing option if you are traveling with your family—all accommodations in this hotel are two-room suites. There is a complimentary Southern breakfast and afternoon reception, fitness center, and valet parking. Golf packages are available.

Hampton Inn

345 Meeting St., Charleston, SC 29401; phone (800) 426-7866 or (843) 723-4000; www.hampton-inn.com; Rates: $89–159

This hotel was once an 18th-century burlap factory and features beautiful appointments, such as mahogany furnishings, pinewood floors, and an outdoor courtyard with a pool. The Hampton Inn is conveniently located in the Historic District (across from the Visitors Center) providing easy access to many of the city's great sights. Included in the room rate is a continental breakfast. Golf packages are available.

Hilton Charleston Harbor Resort

20 Patriots Point Rd., Charleston, SC 29401; phone (888) 856-0028 or (843) 856-9996; www.hilton.com; Rates: $145–195

The Hilton Charleston is the area's newest full-service resort located on the Charleston Harbor, a five-minute water taxi ride from the Historic District. The hotel has 131 rooms and six harborfront two-bedroom suites, which are each styled in an individual theme. Golf packages are available.

INEXPENSIVE

Best Western

1540 Savannah Hwy., Charleston, SC 29401; phone (800) 528-1234 or (843) 571-6100; Rates: $60–100; Built: 1950s; Renovated: 1999

Hampton Inn Riverview

11 Ashley Point Dr., Charleston; phone (800) 426-7866 or (843) 556-5200; www.hampton-inn.com; Rates: $75–100; Built: 1987; Renovated: 1998

Dining

82 Queen Street 82 Queen St.; phone (843) 723-7591. Low-Country fare; Moderate; Reservations suggested. A personal favorite—there are seven separate dining rooms as well as wonderful outside tables, which you should request if the weather is nice. As far as the food goes, no matter what you choose you can't go wrong, but the she-crab soup, duck, and bouillabaisse get our nod.

Andalucia 83 Cumberland St.; phone (843) 853-7445. Spanish; Moderate; Reservations suggested. Renovated house built in the 1700s located directly next to the Powder Magazine. Wonderful outdoor seating area—make sure to taste some of the sangria.

Anson 12 Anson St.; phone (843) 577-0557. Low-Country traditional; Expensive; Reservations suggested. Superior selection of appetizers.

Carolina's 10 Exchange St.; phone (843) 724-3800. Varied menu; Expensive; Reservations suggested. Not as quaint as some of the others in town, but convenient location near the Battery. Try the pecan brittle basket filled with vanilla bean ice cream and fresh seasonal berries.

Celia's Porta Via 49 Archdale St.; phone (843) 722-9003. Italian; Moderate; Reservations suggested. Italian arias provide authentic atmosphere.

Dining Room at Osprey Point Kiawah Island Resort; phone (843) 768-2777. Seafood; Moderate–Expensive; Reservations recommended. The island's most elegant dining experience—private club feel, yet it remains a relaxed environment. Serving breakfast and lunch daily, Sunday brunch, and dinner Wednesday through Sunday. Jacket required for dinner. Arrive early to have cocktails on the veranda, which features striking views of the Atlantic.

Hyman's Seafood Company 215 Meeting St.; phone (843) 723-6000. Family-style seafood; Inexpensive; Reservations not accepted. Expect waits up to one hour or more most of the day, but it's well worth the time investment. Outstanding service!

Indigo House Kiawah Island Resort; phone (843) 768-2768. Low-Country to Italian to Mediterranean; Expensive; Reservations suggested. Located in town center, serving family-style dinner amid tropical foliage.

Jasmine Porch Kiawah Island Resort; phone (843) 768-2768. Seafood; Expensive; Reservations suggested. Wonderful views of Atlantic Ocean—try the potato-crusted salmon.

Jestine's Kitchen 251 Meeting St.; phone (843) 722-7224. Seafood; Inexpensive; No reservations needed. Authentic native South Carolina dining—named for Jestine, who recently passed away at the age of 112!

The Library at the Vendue 23 Vendue Range; phone (843) 723-0485. Seafood; Moderate; Reservations suggested. A unique and fun culinary experience as the restaurant is comprised of several intimate dining rooms. Come early to have a drink at the rooftop bar, which features a wonderful view of the harbor.

The Ocean Course Restaurant Kiawah Island Resort; phone (843) 768-2768. Casual family dining; Inexpensive; Reservations not needed. Standard light lunch fare—if it's warm enough, request a table on the veranda so you can overlook the Atlantic while you eat.

The Peninsula Grill 112 N. Market; phone (843) 723-0700. Eclectic; Moderate; Reservations suggested. Considered by many as the best restaurant in town. Combines the best in cuisine from Los Angeles and New York—a memorable dining experience.

Slightly North of Broad 192 East Bay; phone (843) 723-3424. Low-Country; Moderate; Reservations suggested for parties of six or more. Terrific wine list and the "maverick grits" are amazing.

Sweetgrass Kiawah Island Resort; phone (843) 768-2768. American cafe; Moderate; Reservations suggested. Casual family restaurant located in the Straw Market. Check out the Italian herb– and Parmesan-encrusted shrimp.

Activities

Charleston has so many great sites and wonderful treasures that we recommend getting an overview of the city first. The best way to do this is either by one of the horse-drawn carriage rides or via a bus tour. Both might sound a tad touristy, but you will find that these are effective methods to see much of the city in a short time, orient yourself, get a history lesson, and acquire some useful local knowledge.

Within the City of Charleston:

- **Walk, walk, walk** Charleston is a city that is best seen on foot. Wonderful homes, churches, as well as the Historic District can all be easily covered via walking. This natural means of transportation allows you to enjoy the true ambience of the city. If you are not staying in a local hotel, it is recommended that you leave your car in the Visitors Center parking area as parking in this city is at a premium.

- **Waterfront Park** (the Battery)
- **The Historic Homes of Charleston:**
  Aiken-Rhett House 48 Elizabeth St.; phone (843) 723-1159
  Edmonsdston-Alston House 21 East Battery;
     phone (843) 722-7171
  The Nathaniel Russell House 51 Meeting St.;
     phone (843) 724-8481
- **The Citadel Dress Parade** Friday at 3:45 p.m. during the school year on the Citadel Campus. Phone (843) 953-6726.
- **The Powder Magazine** Built in 1709, this is the oldest remaining public building in either North or South Carolina. Phone (843) 805-6730.
- **The Market Area** Check out the sweetgrass baskets. East of Cooper River
- **Fort Moultrie/Fort Sumter National Monument** Located on Sullivan's Island (a 10-minute drive from Charleston), both these forts were built in the 1800s and served major roles in the Civil War. Fort Sumter is only accessible by a designated boat tour from Fort Moultrie. Phone (843) 883-3123.
- **Boone Hall Plantation** On the nearby island of Mount Pleasant, you will find Boone Hall Plantation, one of the area's more revered plantations. If you feel as though you recognize Boone Hall, you may have, as much of the miniseries *North and South* was filmed there and its avenue of oaks served as inspiration for Tara in the famed movie *Gone With the Wind.* Phone (843) 884-4371.
- **Patriots Point/The Yorktown** Home of the world's largest maritime museum and a World War II aircraft carrier, this is a great stop for both kids and adults alike. Plan on at least a couple hours to take it all in. Phone (843) 884-2727.

West of the Ashley River/North Charleston:
- **Magnolia Plantation and Garden** Magnolia is a 17th-century estate purchased and still owned by the Drayton family and has one of America's oldest gardens (developed around 1680). Only the grounds are accessible to the public, but Magnolia is definitely worth the trip to take in the beautiful blooms, especially in spring. Phone (800) 367-3517 or (843) 571-1266.
- **Middleton Place** A designated national landmark, this 18th-century plantation offers visitors the opportunity to view the beautiful grounds as well as the estate's home. Also, Middleton has a restaurant that serves lunch daily and dinner Tuesday through Saturday—a unique location for a meal to say the least. Phone (800) 782-3608 or (843) 556-6020.

- **Drayton Hall** This grand residence, built in 1742, is the only remaining house on the Ashley River that survived the American Revolution and the Civil War. Visitors have access to both the grounds as well as the Drayton house. Phone (843) 766-0188.

The 19th Hole

Bohicket's Lounge 1002 Landfall Way, Seabrook Island; phone (843) 768-3096. A nice, casual bar inside Seabrook Island Resort, overlooking the golf courses. Many TVs for viewing sports.

Charleston Chops 188 East Bay St., Charleston; phone (843) 937-9300. An upscale piano bar with a cigar room and good food.

Charleston Crab House 145 Wappo Creek Dr., Charleston; phone (843) 795-1963. Located on James Island, this is a fun bar on the water with excellent seafood.

Charleston Sports Bar 41 S. Market St., Charleston; phone (843) 853-2900. On the corner of State and South Market, there are pool tables and plenty of TVs to watch all the ball games and golf tournaments.

The Dining Room at Osprey Point 12 Kiawah Beach Dr., Kiawah Island; phone (843) 768-2121. Probably the best of several pubs at Kiawah Island Resort. Located in the clubhouse at the Osprey Point Course in a Tudor-style clubhouse. The bar is separate from the restaurant, in a beautiful living room setting with sofas, leather armchairs, and wingback chairs. A fireplace roars in the winter, there are TVs to watch sports, and soft, romantic lighting at night.

Edgar's Restaurant 5757 Palm Blvd., Isle of Palms; phone (843) 886-2260. A golfer's bar in the restaurant adjacent to the Links pro shop at Wild Dunes Resort.

Henry's on Market Street 50 N. Market St., Charleston; phone (843) 723-4363. Located in the historic district, this is a famous watering hole frequented by folks from age mid-20s to early-40s.

The Library 23 Vendue Range, Charleston; phone (843) 723-0485. A rooftop bar atop the Vendue Inn, overlooking the Cooper River and Charleston skyline.

The Mills House Hotel 115 Meeting St., Charleston; phone (843) 577-2400. The Best Friend Bar and the First Shot Lounge are located in this four-diamond hotel. The Best Friend Bar is named for the nation's first steam locomotive, based in Charleston, and contains an interesting collection of railroad artifacts. The First Shot Lounge is named for the first shot fired during the Civil War and overlooks a fountain courtyard.

Pusser's Landing 17 Lockwood Dr., Charleston; phone (843) 853-1000. Located at the City Marina near the hospital and Citadel campus. A fancy joint with a great view.

Shem Creek Located in Mt. Pleasant, this is an entire area of bars and restaurants along the Intracoastal Waterway.

South End Brewery 161 E. Bay St., Charleston; phone (843) 853-4677. A three-level microbrewery with pool tables, food, and live music.

Sullivan's Island Also located in Mt. Pleasant, this is another entire area of bars and restaurants.

Tommy Condon's 160 N. Church St., Charleston; phone (843) 577-3818. A genuine Irish pub with all the Irish beers to quench your thirst.

Wild Wing 36 N. Market St., Charleston; phone (843) 722-9464. Bands, wings, and inexpensive drinks. Usually a lively crowd. The disco upstairs is often packed.

The Windjammer 1000 Ocean Blvd., Isle of Dunes; phone (843) 886-8596. Just off the dunes near the water, about four miles from Wild Dunes Resort. A casual beach bar with a big volleyball court with tournaments. Live bands at night.

Part Four

Hilton Head, South Carolina

Overview

If you ever find yourself on *Jeopardy* and Alex Trebek asks you to name the second largest barrier island between New Jersey and Florida, make sure to answer, "What is Hilton Head?" Alex will surely be impressed with your geographic knowledge. Hilton Head is a 42-square-mile barrier island located an hour away from Savannah, Georgia, and is bordered by the Atlantic Ocean, Intracoastal Waterway, and the Calibogue (pronounced Cali-bogey) Sound. It is reachable from Interstate 95 via an expansive bridge on Highway 278. This bridge is the gateway to one of America's leading resort playgrounds, an area filled with white-sand beaches and some of the best Low-Country golf you will find anywhere.

Of course, green is the dominant hue on Hilton Head, thanks to acres of pines, moss-draped oaks, sturdy cabbage palmettos, and dense shrubbery—and the more than 400 golf holes scattered across the windswept island. It's also the color your friends' faces turn (with jealousy) when they hear you're headed there for a vacation.

Named for sea captain William Hilton, who claimed the island for England in 1663, Hilton Head originally thrived because its soil was ideal for such crops as sea island cotton and indigo and its waters brimmed with an abundance of seafood. This prosperity ended during the Civil War, when the island was the site of one of the largest naval engagements prior to World War II and a town of 40,000 residents, comprised of Union forces and freed slaves, served as one of the Union's Southern bases of operations. The island remained quiet and sleepy until the 1950s when Charles Fraser, a young South Carolina attorney, recognized that the same soil could yield something else of value: grass. Hilton Head's golf boom was born.

Given Hilton Head's present status as a true golf mecca, it may be hard to believe that the first course on Hilton Head was established not that long

Hilton Head, South Carolina

N

GOLF COURSES

1. Country Club of Hilton Head
2. Daufuskie Island Club & Resort
3. Eagle's Point
4. Golden Bear Golf Club at Indigo Run
5. Harbour Town Golf Links
6. Hilton Head National
7. Island West Golf Club
8. Ocean Creek Golf Course
9. Ocean Point Golf Links
10. Okatie Creek Golf Club
11. Old Carolina Golf Club
12. Old South Golf Links
13. Oyster Reef Golf Club
14. Palmetto Dunes Resort
15. Palmetto Hall Plantation
16. Port Royal Golf Club
17. Rose Hill Country Club
18. Sea Pines Plantation
19. Shipyard Golf Club

ago. Sea Pines opened its doors—or, more correctly, its greens and tee boxes—in 1960. In the relatively short time since then, golf has become as intrinsic to the island as wind is to Chicago. Today, there are more than 20 golf courses on Hilton Head and as many others within a 20-mile radius. Recently, a consortium of golf course owners banded together and have begun marketing Hilton Head as the "Golf Island."

In addition to golfers, this island attracts a wide variety of visitors: artists, athletes, and even presidents (President Clinton and family spend each New Year's here). No matter what their motive, these visitors all head to Hilton Head because it offers a wide range of recreational activities, pristine beaches, fine restaurants, superior accommodations, and quaint seaside villages. But all of this would be moot to us if it weren't for the awesome golf courses that are strewn throughout the island.

So many people have discovered Hilton Head's multiple charms that some contend the area has lost its "getaway" feel. That may be partially true, but its low-key nature still has strong appeal.

Accommodations of all kinds exist for families, couples, or for that male-bonding ritual of four to eight guys trying to squeeze in 36 holes a day. Whichever category you fit into, you'll find it on Hilton Head, although "active" nightlife can be a bit on the mild side for the "guys."

When to Go and What it Will Cost

Warmed by the Gulf Stream, Hilton Head Island is blessed with a sub-tropical climate, keeping it warm year-round. Spring, fall, and winter offer the most pleasant temperatures with mild days and crisp nights. Summer, however, can be a bear as both the heat and humidity will test your powers of positive thinking. Of course, the influx of tourists mirrors the weather, so you will find crowds flocking to the area when you can't necessarily cut the air with a knife. Another factor to keep in mind is hurricane season, which lasts from June to November, with the most treacherous period being August and September. Although it is extremely rare to have a full-blown hurricane roll through, the effects of nearby storms—high winds and lots of rain—are more common than you may think.

Weather-wise, the perfect time to come to Hilton Head for golf is the last two weeks in March and the first two in April. Daytime and nighttime temperatures are heavenly, and the azaleas and dogwoods are in full bloom. Unfortunately, that's when courses are most crowded—and most expensive. One more thing: The island hosts two major sporting events, the Family Circle Cup tennis tournament (late March/early April) and the MCI Classic PGA Tour golf event (mid-April). During these two events the island is buzzing with visitors and activity. They are quite exciting times, bit if you are looking to escape the hubbub, you may want to avoid traveling to Hilton Head during these events.

Early and mid-May is a terrific time to visit. It's still cool enough, the courses are still in excellent condition and it's right before school lets out, so crowds are down following the peak months of March and April and before the beach rush of summer. Mid- to late November is wonderful as well, with its cooling ocean breezes. By November, the tropical storm season is virtually over, and the low off-season rates start to kick in. Winter can actually be quite pleasant, but the lack of available daylight will prevent you from getting 36 holes in on most days. Frost is occasionally a problem in January and February, but it usually burns off by 10 a.m.

Be careful in June—courses get patchy as the transitional grasses emerge, with bermuda overtaking the winter rye. Also, call ahead if you're thinking about visiting from mid-September to mid-October. Although the weather tends to be gorgeous, that's when most courses start overseeding tees, fairways, and greens, so things can get a bit bumpy. Golfers should avoid July, which features high heat and humidity, late afternoon thunderstorms, and brutal armies of bugs. Finally, October in Hilton Head doesn't offer much fall foliage, but it ushers in the shrimp and oyster season. Try a Low-Country oyster roast, where you shuck your own for the true taste of the South.

Typical of major golf tourist destinations, Hilton Head is not inexpensive. In fact, it leans toward the pricey side. Bargain-basement greens fees are a rarity. Rather, you find yourself shelling out a minimum of $80 or more to play Hilton Head's marquee courses. Golf packages and off-season/shoulder-season rates are an alternative you may want to pursue to reduce the drain on your wallet. Also, if you are traveling with a group, the island boasts a number of condominiums and homes for rent, many of which can be incorporated into a golf package as well.

WHAT TO BRING

As is the case for most Southern cities, what you fill your suitcase with will be dictated by the time of year you visit. For all times of the year other than summer, you will want to make sure to have a sweater or a windshirt with you. For winter, you may even want to think about layers and pack a turtleneck and a sweater. During the summer, you certainly won't need that turtleneck, but you will want the lightest-weight clothes you can find. Shorts of Bermuda length are welcome at all Hilton Head courses throughout the year. As most of the island's facilities are upscale, shorter shorts are discouraged. No matter what time of year, you will want to stow a golf umbrella in your bag as well as a rain jacket.

You will also want to make sure to have a good bug repellent, because the no-see-ums and mosquitoes can eat you alive. Unfortunately, no-see-ums emerge at a certain pleasant temperature— around 60 degrees—at nice times of year, especially as the sun goes down and especially near marshes. When it's cooler than 60 degrees or if it's warmer than 75 degrees, they aren't as much of a problem. When the thermometer reads between 60 and 75, keep the repellent handy. The key is to keep moving, generally via golf cart—and hope for a breeze. If conditions are still, it's going to be rough where the bug factor is concerned.

A ball retriever is not a bad idea, as nearly every course in the area is loaded with lakes, lagoons, and wetlands. A lob wedge would be handy as well. There are so many water hazards and bunkers around the greens, you'll need that extra loft for your chip shots. A Tight Lies– or Orlimar-type fairway wood wouldn't be a bad idea either. The ball doesn't sit up as well on winter rye or seasonal bermuda fairways as well as it does in northern climes.

Something else you may consider is sticking a heavier putter in your bag. Virtually all of Hilton Head's public-access courses sport bermuda greens, which occasionally get grainy and slow. A heavier putter can often help provide the feel to counteract such conditions.

ONCE YOU'RE THERE

Packed into Hilton Head's 42 square miles are a plethora of golf resorts and courses that can keep even the most active golfer busy for weeks. At the top of the list is the Harbour Town Golf Links, located at the south end of the island in the Sea Pines Plantation. Sea Pines is the only real "city" that you will find once you cross that bridge from Highway 278. It is also home to the island's most identifiable landmark, a red and white lighthouse. Sea Pines is home to a number of fine restaurants as well as a collection of quaint shops—all only a stone's throw away from the Intracoastal Waterway.

Hilton Head was developed with the goal of establishing a vacation and residential community offering a variety of activities while preserving the natural environment. Construction was thus closely monitored; as a result, Hilton Head remains relatively "untouristy" in comparison to many similar destinations. That is not to say that tourists don't flock here—in fact at the height of tourist season, the population of Hilton Head swells from 25,000 regular residents to a few hundred thousand. However, most of the buildings tend to be low and unobtrusive, creating a relatively seamless blend between hotel developments and residential communities. Thus, it is common to find a major chain hotel snuggled next to a posh real estate development.

Located off the island, you will find two wonderful options for your adventures: Daufuskie Island Club and Resort and Fripp Island. The ferry ride and day of golf at Daufuskie is number two on our Hilton Head "must-dos," behind Harbour Town. Both destinations offer full-service resorts with accommodations as well as golf courses. However, both can be incorporated into day trips.

There are a couple of other wonderful day trips easily accessible from Hilton Head: Savannah, Georgia, and Charleston, South Carolina. Savannah's charms and eccentricities were fully revealed in the book (and subsequent movie) *Midnight in the Garden of Good and Evil.* Historic Savannah is comprised of 21 squares, all of which resemble mini-parks, each containing lovingly restored homes. Built on a bluff above the Savannah River in 1733, Savannah is most famous for River Street, which is always lively with its collection of bars and restaurants. However, it absolutely explodes on St. Patrick's Day, where it hosts one of America's three largest St. Paddy's Day celebrations.

Savannah is only a 45-minute drive from Hilton Head (perhaps an hour, tops), but go for the sight-seeing, not the golf. Quality public and resort golf facilities in Savannah are practically nonexistent, with only a couple of exceptions, notably the fine new Bob Cupp–designed course at the Westin Savannah Harbor Resort, which opened in January 2000.

Charleston, of course, is profiled elsewhere in another chapter. There are many wonderful courses to play in Charleston, some a moderate drive from Hilton Head, but Hilton Head's courses as a group are better, so you're better off touring Charleston's historic district then returning to Hilton Head for more golf.

Geographically, the easiest way to think of Hilton Head is that it's shaped like a foot. Its major resort developments are comprised of "plantations." Sea Pines Plantation, for instance, home to the famous Harbour Town Golf Links, is located at the "toe" of the island, and Palmetto Dunes is at the "heel."

Two words to the wise: First, if you're looking to get from the north end of the island to the south, or vice versa, take the new (January 1998) Cross-Island Expressway instead of the William Hilton Parkway (Highway 278 Business). It will easily save you 20 minutes of traffic and stop light time in peak seasons. Second, if you're staying in any of the resort developments in any island plantation, don't expect to find it easily for the first time at night. There are few if any street lights in these plantations or at most spots on the island, so do your exploring during the day. On the bright side, nighttime stargazing on Hilton Head is sensational.

Where you stay on Hilton Head depends on what you like and who you're traveling with. For a family golf vacation or if you're part of a group, you may prefer the comfort, convenience, and roominess of a villa. Palmetto Dunes offers superior beach access and great golf, but limited nightlife. At Sea Pines, the golf is also wonderful. Beach access isn't quite as good, but in season, the Harbour Town marina area buzzes with activity.

If you prefer room-service pampering, on-site dining, and poolside bars, one of the major hotels is the way to go. The Westin Port Royal is the ritziest, followed closely by the Hyatt Regency and Hilton, both in Palmetto Dunes, and by the Crystal Sands Resort in Shipyard Plantation.

At first glance, you wouldn't even know that Hilton Head has beaches, because they're obscured by the trees. Just ask a local for directions or else pick up a map and take a side street off the William Hilton Parkway (Highway 278). Wherever you're staying on Hilton Head, you're no more than a 10-minute drive from the beach. The major resorts have them in their backyards. If there's one "must-do" in Hilton Head, it is 18 holes at Harbour Town, on a warm, late spring day, followed by a libation at the Quarterdeck Restaurant, underneath the famed lighthouse. Accomplish this task and your memories of Hilton Head are that much sweeter.

GATHERING INFORMATION

Greater Beaufort Chamber of Commerce
1006 Bay St., P.O. Box 910, Beaufort, SC 29901; phone (843) 524-3163

Hilton Head Chamber of Commerce
1 Chamber Dr., P.O. Box 5647, Hilton Head, SC 29938; phone (843) 785-3673

Island Visitors Information Center
U.S. Hwy. 278 at S.C. 46; phone (888) 741-7666 or (843) 785-4472

Web sites:
hiltonheadisland.com; aesire.com/hiltonhead;
www.golfisland.com (phone (888) GOLF ISLAND)

The Major Courses

Daufuskie Island Club and Resort, Melrose Course

Daufuskie Island, Hilton Head Island, SC 29925; phone (843) 842-2000

How To Get On: Guests of the resort can book tee times when they make reservations. Nonguests can make tee times one week in advance.

Tees:

Gold: 7,081 yards, par-72, USGA rating 74.2, slope 138

Blue: 6,688 yards, par-72, USGA rating 72.4, slope 130

White: 6,245 yards, par-72, USGA rating 70.3, slope 121

Red: 5,575 yards, par-72, USGA rating 72.3, slope 126

Challenge: ★★★★	Golf Facilities: ★★★½
Variety: ★★★★	Whole Bag Test: ★★★★
Terrain: ★★★½	Intangibles: ★★★★½
Beauty/Visual Appeal: ★★★★½	Value: ★★★½
Pace of Play: ★★★★	

Just the Facts   Year Opened: 1987; Course Designer: Jack Nicklaus; Walking: Yes; Greens Fee: $80–155; 9 Hole/Twilight Rate: No; Pull Carts: No; Practice Range: Yes; Club Rental: No

Description and Comments   Daufuskie Island is separated from Hilton Head Island by one nautical mile. But that mile helps make Daufuskie special. Daufuskie is accessible only by boat—an enchanting 30 to 40 minute ride by private or public ferry, or a 10-minute water taxi excursion from Harbour Town. There's not a single paved road or street light on Daufuskie and only a handful of cars on the entire island. It wasn't until

1953 that it had electricity, 1973 for telephone service. In other words, this place is flat-out peaceful and rustic. If you want an idea of what Hilton Head was like 40 years ago, spend some time on Daufuskie.

The island is home to a charming, full-service resort, which includes a main lodge and 37 cottages, plus such amenities as restaurants and a swimming pool. For golfers, the chief amenities are its two 18-hole golf courses, Bloody Point (described in the Sampler section) and Melrose. If Bloody Point is Daufuskie's subtle siren, the Melrose Club is bells and buzzers and whistles, especially the final three holes. This impressive trio gives Harbour Town a run for its money as the most spectacular finish in the Low Country.

The 16th is a 187-yard par-3, and the 17th a 400-yard par-4 that regularly play into daunting crosswinds in full view of the beach, whereas the 18th is an incredible 560-yard par-5 that has the Atlantic Ocean lapping at its right side from tee to green. The hole features a wide fairway split in two by a tree and bunker complex. If you dare challenge the sliver of fairway that runs along the water's edge, you can get home in two.

Unfortunately, the other 15 holes are a mixed bag of handsome scenery and quirky design, which keeps Melrose off the list of truly great courses. Designed by Jack Nicklaus in 1987, Melrose originated as an extremely exclusive club favored by better players. As such, many of the holes feature interesting but excessive design features. There's not a dull hole out here, but there are one too many frustrating ones.

For starters, most of the greens are shallow and placed on a diagonal, then surrounded by sand, water hazards, and gnarly, bermuda rough-covered mounds. If your approach shots can soar high, then land softly, as Nicklaus used to do, you're fine. For most of us, however, that's impossible, resulting in many a nearly good shot finding hazards or else facing a brutal recovery shot. At times on the densely wooded front nine, it's almost unfair for the average golfer, such as at the question mark–shaped third hole. At the third, the good player has a chance to carry a pond and go for the green in two, but the "safe" play calls for such a demanding shot so far away from the green that the majority of golfers will be blocked by tall trees on their approach to the green even after hitting two good shots.

The 398-yard, par-4 seventh is similarly exciting but frustrating to play, as a tree and bunker complex sits right in the middle of the fairway on this dogleg left, exactly where the majority of golfers' optimum drive would wind up.

The monstrous 584-yard, par-5 ninth—where marsh lined with swaying grasses must be crossed twice—is the same way. Its shot values are simply too demanding for most golfers. It's safe to say that the ninth yields more double and triple bogies than any hole in the Low Country.

In spite of Melrose's frustrating design aspects, it remains a memorable experience overall, thanks to the ferry ride, the seclusion, the challenge, and the fantastic finish along the Atlantic Ocean. It ranks number two, after Harbour Town, on the public-access "must-play" list in the Hilton Head area.

Insider Tips   Just getting to Daufuskie Island to play the Melrose Course is half the fun. You have to check in for your ferry ride a half-hour early, and remember, check-in is at a facility on the north end of Hilton Head Island. Do not be late. The boats leave on-time—period.

Another tip: You and your clubs will likely be separated until you arrive at the course. Do yourself a favor and make sure your golf bag is properly marked and loaded, both going and coming back. Clubs are never lost, but due to the nature of the process, delivery can be delayed. Keep an eye out.

The narrow front nine is edged with ball-grabbing, club-twisting bermuda rough and plays through thick forest and along a tidal marsh. It's a veritable wildlife preserve, with deer, ospreys, alligators, sea turtles, and the occasional bald eagle making appearances, but it's no place for you to be the least bit wild—keep the driver in the bag.

Beware of deceptive design tricks. There's an apparent shortcut to the left of the tree and bunker complex in the middle of the seventh fairway. Don't take it. It's way too narrow and risky as it's partially hidden by marsh grass and there's a sea of inescapable marsh that edges the fairway. Take one more club at the 184-yard, par-3 13th. From the tee, the bulkheaded water hazard looks like it cuts straight across, but in reality the middle of it juts into the wing nut–shaped green, right at your aiming point.

There's a chance to get home in two if you play down the skinny right-side fairway that sits next to the beach at the par-5 18th, but it's a strange risk/reward situation. Nicklaus blocked the entrance to the green from this side with sand, so there's no real percentage in going this route.

If you have small children or are simply out looking to enjoy a bit more golf and the stunning scenery, there's a marvelous nine-hole pitch-and-putt course that plays through the trees, in full view of the beach, ocean, and resort. From an aesthetic standpoint, the entire Melrose experience is unforgettable.

Harbour Town Golf Links

11 Lighthouse Lane, Hilton Head Island, SC 29928; phone (800) 955-8337 or (843) 363-4485

How To Get On: Tee times can be made two weeks in advance.

Tees:

> Heritage: 6,916 yards, par-71, USGA rating 74.0, slope 136
>
> White: 6,119 yards, par-71, USGA rating 70.0, slope 126
>
> Red: 5,019 yards, par-71, USGA rating 69.0, slope 117

Challenge: ★★★★
Variety: ★★★★★
Terrain: ★★★★
Beauty/Visual Appeal: ★★★★★
Pace of Play: ★★★½

Golf Facilities: ★★★★½
Whole Bag Test: ★★★½
Intangibles: ★★★★★
Value: ★★★★

Just the Facts   Year Opened: 1969; Course Designer: Pete Dye; Walking: At times; Greens Fee: $110–200; 9 Hole/Twilight Rate: Yes; Pull Carts: No; Practice Range: Yes; Club Rental: Yes

Description and Comments   Any mention of golf in Hilton Head must start at the Sea Pines Plantation, which is where the game began on the island. Sea Pines can claim Hilton Head's oldest course, the Ocean, which opened in 1960, and the area's second oldest, Sea Marsh, which made its debut in 1966. It was Sea Pines's third course, however, that stamped Hilton Head Island as a "must-do" golf destination. From the day Harbour Town Golf Links opened in 1969, critics hailed the Pete Dye/Jack Nicklaus creation as one of the nation's top 10 courses. It didn't hurt that Arnold Palmer broke out of a long slump that fall with a win here at the inaugural Heritage Classic. The PGA Tour soon switched the event to springtime; the warm breezes, blooming azaleas, and view of the sound, harbor, and lighthouse have enchanted players and television viewers ever since.

When Harbour Town opened, it bucked a 25-year trend of longer, bigger, boring courses. Architects Dye and Nicklaus hatched a short, tight, Low-Country gem that ribbons through forests of live oaks, pines, palmettos, and magnolias. Holes culminate in greens that were tiny for their era and even now remain among the smallest on the PGA Tour.

Such are the shotmaking demands that only the best players seem capable of conquering the 6,916-yard, par-71 track. Among the names who have graced the champions roll at Harbour Town besides Palmer are Jack Nicklaus, Tom Watson, Nick Faldo, Greg Norman, Fuzzy Zoeller, Johnny Miller, Hale Irwin, the late Payne Stewart, and of course Davis Love III, who's won here four times. Not many courses of this stature are open for public play—Pebble Beach, Pinehurst No. 2, and the TPC at Sawgrass spring to mind—but it's not often you can walk (or ride) in such famous footsteps.

What makes Harbour Town so great is its endless variety, both in scenic value and in playing value. You'll remember almost every hole easily long after you've departed the grounds. As a group, the quartet of par-3s is as good as any in the country, even if they play a bit similarly. As a group, the collection of par-4s is one of the best in golf, hampered only by the geographic limitation—or rather topographical limitation—of flat fairways.

Some of the holes appear quiet and still, tucked into the pines and live oaks, which are dripping with Spanish moss. The moss radiates an eerie beauty as it clings like tinsel on a Christmas tree. Other holes are open, with expansive views of Calibogue Sound, with expansive breezes to match.

In terms of playing value, the shot-making skills required to tame this test are almost unparalleled. The par-36 front nine is full of gently turning holes hemmed in by trees, which makes placement off the tee a premium. Most memorable are the par-3 seventh, the par-4 eighth, and the par-4 ninth. Seven measures 180 yards and features a green ringed with sand. Posing even stronger peril are the trees, whose limbs overhang the putting surface and steal away shots like Shaquille O'Neal. Eight is the number-one handicap, a stout 466-yarder that swings left around a lagoon. Two intrusive pines in the fairway force a precise drive. The ninth is a mixed bag. It suffers from having the practice range adjacent to the left. However, the exacting approach to this mighty-mite par-4 of 337 yards is one you won't soon forget. They tiny green is U-shaped and is a tough putting surface to hold, no matter what club you're approaching with. Fronting the green is a yawning, cavernous bunker, and tucked in the gap of the U behind the green is one of the smallest, meanest pot bunkers this side of Scotland. Further behind the green is the handsome pro shop/clubhouse.

The par-35 back nine opens with four superb par-4s, followed by the lovely but lethal 165-yard, par-3 14th, where Ben Crenshaw once dunked four balls on his way to a 12. All throughout the round, precision is favored over power; gentle fades and controlled draws are the order of the day. Like an old-fashioned course, Harbour Town forces a golfer to work the ball, shaping and carving shots rather than simply pounding them.

Lee Trevino loves the 575-yard, par-5 15th with its overhanging palms and pines. It's so long, he says, that "even King Kong couldn't get on the green in two."

Sixteen measures just 376 yards, but its fairway zigzags through tall pines before bending left around an enormous waste bunker. The 17th is one of golf's great par-3s—192 yards over a lagoon and a 90-yard bunker to a banana-shaped green. Beyond the green is a marshy slope, which leads to the waters of the Calibogue Sound.

Finally, we arrive at one of the world's most spectacular holes, a 478-yard par-4. To the left of the entire hole lies one of golf's most attractive hazards, the aforementioned Calibogue Sound. To the right lies trees, condos, and out-of-bounds. In the distance looms Harbour Town's most enduring symbol, a candy cane–striped lighthouse, along with a marina filled with boats owned by the kind of people who can afford to play Harbour Town every day.

A generous landing area awaits the tee shot, but the wind can shrink the safe zone dramatically. A tailwind can allow the hole to be played with as little as a three wood, eight iron, but more typically, crosswinds blow left to right, off the sound.

According to Davis Love III, the second shot is actually the key to the hole. The approach must carry a vast sand bunker that skirts the golden marsh grasses of the sound. But you don't want to overcook it, either, as a nasty trap lurks immediately behind the green. Miss the mostly round, flat green to the left and you're wet.

The heroic 18th concludes your round at the number one "must-play" course on the southeast coast. Don't just take our words for it; take Tom Watson's. Come April 2000, they're going to shut down Harbour Town for 9 to 12 months. After 30 years, it's time for some renovations. As to these developments, Watson said recently, "I just hope when they renovate the golf course, they don't screw it up. That's imperative, because they have a wonderful golf course here. This is one of my favorite golf courses in the world." Countless golfers could not agree more.

Insider Tips   Harbour Town is the pint-sized superstar of the PGA Tour. Tom Watson, Lee Trevino, Curtis Strange, Davis Love III, and many other tour greats finger Harbour Town as one of their favorite courses anywhere. Of course, you don't have to have a major championship on your resume to identify this course as one of the world's most scenic, challenging, and historic public-access courses. Consequently, everybody wants to play Harbour Town at least once. Thus, demand is quite high, even at a price tag that's awfully hefty—$150 to $200 for 18 holes. Here are some suggestions for getting the most out of your Harbour Town experience.

If there have been complaints over the years about Hilton Head's one "must-play" course—and they're legitimate—they concern slow play and course maintenance. Obviously, chronically slow play detracts from the overall playing experience. It's impossible to maintain any kind of rhythm and tempo when you have to stop and wait five to ten minutes on every shot.

In recent years, pace of play has improved somewhat. Understand that at courses like Harbour Town, play is always going to be slow. It's a difficult test of golf; it's open to public and resort play; and because it hosts a PGA Tour event, it's always in demand. On the one hand, it's not a bad place to be taking frequent pauses, as it enables you to soak up the atmosphere and drink in the scenery. On the other hand, there are several ways to get around the slow play problem. First, try your luck in winter, when demand is lower. Not as many folks want to brave the elements (50 to 65 degrees) for such a heady tariff, so you might have more room to move.

Another possibility is to play the course in mid-May (our personal preference) or mid-September. In mid-May, it's just after the peak golf weather, but mid- to high 80s with coastal breezes isn't all bad. You also have much more daylight than you did a month or two before, so many times you can start a round at 3:30 p.m., buzz around, and still finish in twilight.

One of the drawbacks to a late-afternoon finish at Harbour Town is that two of the best holes—the approach to the par-4 16th and the par-3 17th—play directly into a nearly blinding setting sun, so not only do you get cheated with respect to the lovely aesthetics but it's hard to see where your target is and where your ball lands.

As to course conditioning, we'll freely admit that day in and day out, the course is not as well-groomed as most "Top 100" courses. We're talking tee boxes, fairways, and greens. However, things have improved dramatically in the past few years. Three to five years ago, conditioning was deplorable. It was like playing a municipal course—for $150 bucks. Today, it's much better. If you truly want optimum playing conditions, tackle it a couple of weeks before or within a couple of weeks after the PGA Tour has come to town, which takes place in mid-April.

As far as playing tips go, remember that placement is much more important than power here. Fairways are narrow, so most good players hit three woods or long irons off many tees and leave the driver in the bag. These narrow fairways also dogleg, dodging hazards and overhanging live oak limbs in the process, so it's important to find not only the fairways but also proper side of the fairway, or else risk being blocked out on your approach.

Another aspect of your game to focus on is your pitching and chipping. Harbour Town's greens are about 20 percent smaller than at most tournament courses, so it figures that you're going to miss more greens than normal. Thus, you'll have more short game work to do.

An oddity in this day and age is that Harbour Town offers only three sets of tees. The problem is that it's too short from the White tees for many decent golfers, but too long and tough from the tips. A practical solution is for them to establish a course that plays in between, at say 6,400 or 6,500 yards, but until they do, you may—just for fun and maximum enjoyment—mix and match some tees. That is, play certain holes from the Whites and others, where it makes sense, from all the way back.

Finally, it's not a bad idea to pick up a souvenir in the excellent pro shop. Logo items are reasonably priced compared to many PGA Tour stops, and the lighthouse logo is quite distinctive . . . a wonderful conversation starter when you're out and about.

Palmetto Dunes Resort, Arthur Hills Course

7 Trent Jones Lane, Hilton Head Island, SC 29928; phone (800) 827-3006 or (843) 785-1140

How To Get On: Resort guests can make tee times 90 days in advance. Nonguests can book tee times 60 days in advance.

Tees:

> Blue: 6,651 yards, par-72, USGA rating 71.4, slope 127
>
> White: 6,122 yards, par-72, USGA rating 69.3, slope 120
>
> Red: 4,999 yards, par-72, USGA rating 68.5, slope 113

Challenge: ★★★	Golf Facilities: ★★★★
Variety: ★★★★	14-Club Test ★★★½
Terrain: ★★★★	Intangibles: ★★★★
Beauty/Visual Appeal: ★★★★	Value: ★★★★
Pace of Play: ★★★½	

Just the Facts   Year Opened: 1986; Course Designer: Arthur Hills; Walking: Yes; Greens Fee: $75–115; 9 Hole/Twilight Rate: Yes; Pull Carts: No; Practice Range: Yes; Club Rental: Yes

Description and Comments   The Arthur Hills Course at Palmetto Dunes is one of Hilton Head's most popular courses. After just one trip around, it's easy to see why. How good is the Hills? Put it this way: The Palmetto Dunes resort's first course (described below) is one of the island's oldest and was designed by the dean of modern architecture, Robert Trent Jones in 1969. The resort's second course (also described below) was designed by George Fazio in 1974 and logged several years as a member of the most prestigious Top 100 courses list in the country. Yet neither of these are the signature course at Palmetto Dunes. That honor falls to the Arthur Hills Course.

Short by contemporary standards—6,651 yards, par-72 from the tips— the emphasis at Hills is on strategy. Well, that's not entirely true—there's equal emphasis on beauty. Heavily wooded with pines, oaks, and, as you might expect, palmettos, the Hills course also weaves through natural sand dunes and lagoons, all in splendid isolation. Elevation changes, ocean breezes, and a paucity of rough and fairway bunkers invigorate this course.

There are many reasons why Hills is so wildly popular. First, it's generally in excellent condition. Its sandy subsoil is perfect for effective drainage, so you can generally enjoy good playing conditions even after a heavy rain. In addition, the course converted its greens in 1995 from 328 bermuda to Tifdwarf bermuda, a finer, more weather-resistant strain that provides smoother putting surfaces.

A second reason for Hills's popularity is its setting—pure Low Country— which provides for a unique experience for vacationers. Its unique character encompasses huge, rolling dunes often covered with dense clumps of love grass, lovely salt marshes, and lagoons in play on ten holes.

Finally, the course serves up tremendous variety for most golfers. Few courses call for such a blend of power and precision, which keeps all sorts of players interested at all times.

If there's been a criticism leveled at the Hills course, it's that it gets tricky in spots. Sometimes it's difficult to discern how the greens are configured from the middle of the fairway. What you think may be a good shot instead winds up away from the pin or even off the green. Moreover, some of the holes, such as 2, 12, and 13, curve awkwardly and deceptively around water hazards, making it tough to figure out where you're supposed to land the ball.

Nevertheless, most of the holes offer supreme shot-making opportunities. The aforementioned 399-yard, par-4 12th is one of the more memorable holes, as it calls for an exquisitely precise drive over a lake into a narrow fairway, followed by a difficult approach. If the second shot is pushed by a whisker, it's in the lake.

Other fine holes are the risk/reward par-5s that conclude each nine, and the 5th and 15th, which play to greens that nestle into the shadows of the Leamington lighthouse, a historic landmark listed on the National Register.

Without hesitation, however, the best hole on the Arthur Hills Course at Palmetto Dunes is the 17th, a 380-yard par-4. This is a pressure-packed tiny terror. You'll react to it like a kid on a roller coaster: screaming that you can't wait 'til it's over, then screaming that you can't wait to do it again.

A 160-yard carry over water awaits from the back tees (a less terrifying 110 yards from the white markers) to a bowl-shaped fairway. A hooked drive will surely find the lagoon, which snakes its way up the left side of the hole and crosses directly in front of the small, shallow green. The all-carry approach to this bunkerless green tucked in the trees is usually into the breeze. Don't be short!

Insider Tips   Before or after your round, spend some time at the pro shop, which is annually selected as one of America's 100 best. During your round, make note of several things. For starters, on a pleasant day, you may want to walk the course, as Palmetto Dunes is one of the few great resorts in the South that will let you do so. At times, there are some long hikes over bridges and on cart paths to carry you over and through the lagoons and wetlands, but all told, you needn't be a health fanatic to enjoy this walk through the woods.

If you are walking—or riding, for that matter—keep your eye out for alligators. Especially as you walk off the 12th tee or as you make your way up the 13th, take care to watch for the gators, which can move surprisingly fast if provoked.

This may be a course where it's wisest to leave the driver in the bag on at least half of the par-4s and 5s. At only 6,651 yards from the tips, you can tell right away that the premium here is not on distance, but rather on strategy and course management.

Finally, the Hills Course at Palmetto Dunes is home every year to one of college golf's most prestigious tournaments. Tiger Woods played here in

1995 and 1996 and never did conquer the course. Most amazing might have been the feat a couple of years before of Arizona State's left-hander Phil Mickelson, who actually drove the green on the dogleg left, 380-yard, water-logged, par-4 17th. "Impossible" doesn't seem to be in Lefty's vocabulary.

Palmetto Dunes Resort, George Fazio Course

7 Trent Jones Lane, Hilton Head Island, SC 29928; phone (800) 827-3006 or (843) 785-1130

How To Get On: Resort guests can make tee times 90 days in advance. Nonguests can book tee times 60 days in advance.

Tees:

> Gold: 6,873 yards, par-70, USGA rating 74.2, slope 132
>
> Blue: 6,534 yards, par-70, USGA rating 72.6, slope 126
>
> White: 6,239 yards, par-70, USGA rating 71.2, slope 123
>
> Red: 5,273 yards, par-70, USGA rating 70.8, slope 127

Challenge: ★★★★	Golf Facilities: ★★
Variety: ★★★	14-Club Test ★★★
Terrain: ★★★	Intangibles: ★★★½
Beauty/Visual Appeal: ★★★	Value: ★★★½
Pace of Play: ★★★	

Just the Facts Year Opened: 1974; Course Designer: George Fazio; Walking: At times; Greens Fee: $50–90; 9 Hole/Twilight Rate: Yes; Pull Carts: No; Practice Range: No; Club Rental: Yes

Description and Comments Of the three courses at Palmetto Dunes, if the Robert Trent Jones course (described below) is memorable for the ocean-view 10th and the "fun" factor, and the Arthur Hills course (described above) is memorable for its strategic options and Low-Country scenery, then the George Fazio course is memorable for its fearsome and massive bunkers.

Strong golfers relish play at the Fazio course. That's not to say mid- and high-handicappers wouldn't appreciate this testing track, merely that your "A" game better be an "A+" to score well here. The Fazio course features a seemingly endless profusion of large, cookie cutter–style bunkers, a Fazio trademark, along with a numbing succession of long, tree-lined par-4s that will earn you a ticket on a speeding train to Bogeyville. Par is a stern U.S. Open–style 70 on this 6,873-yard course. Sharpen your long irons, fairway woods, and sand play before taking on the Fazio. No fewer then eight par-4s measure at least 400 yards from the Gold tees. Tougher still is that if you move up to the Blues, six of them still check in at 400 yards plus.

This is not to say that the Fazio is simply a dull slog of hard, boring par-4s. In fact, there's plenty of character in the layout, as the terrain dips and rolls through heavily forested areas, emerging from the trees now and again. Understandably, the open holes are more wind-influenced, whipped by the breezes from the nearby Atlantic.

Classic Fazio touches include liberal, intrusive trapping and greens that crest in the middle, falling away on either side, such as the humpbacked specials at the 562-yard, par-5 second and the 445-yard, par-4 15th. Another Fazio trademark is his imaginative shaping of teeing areas, which helps provide memorability, variety, and flexibility.

Opened for play in 1974, Fazio became the youngest layout ever to be named to golf's most prestigious Top 100 Courses ranking list, a distinction earned primarily due to its relentless challenge. Virtually every hole runs parallel to another on its right and there's out-of-bounds to the left of every hole except the 3rd and the 16th. Perhaps the Fazio course has slipped a bit in the rankings over the years because there's not a lot of variety (sand everywhere, many similar long par-4s, only two par-5s) and the greens themselves aren't particularly interesting with the exception of the three-tiered putting surface at the 205-yard, par-3 fourth. Still, it's undeniable that the George Fazio course at Palmetto Dunes is an attractive, straightforward test. And the finishing holes are as tough a stretch to par as you'll find in the Low Country.

The 445-yard 15th demands an approach to an elevated green squeezed by enormous traps left and right—and it's the easiest of the final four. At the 425-yard 16th, another meaty par-4, you stare from the tee into a sea of sand. At first glance, you're not even sure there's a fairway out there because the square footage of sand seems to outnumber the square footage of grass. Your second shot should head in the direction of a deceptively long green (it runs into the putting surface of the 11th hole, creating an odd double green). Guarding the green are three more traps and a lagoon to the right. Oh, by the way, pull your drive and you'll find a wide, watery canal.

Fazio's 17th is infamous as one of Hilton Head's hardest par-3s. If you're thinking of a run-up to this 230-yard monster, forget it. The hole demands a thrilling "Honey, I made it!" kind of carry over a wide, diagonal neck of water to a huge green further protected to the left by woods and, yes, another bunker. The 18th is just a basic brute, a 462-yard par-4 that calls for a drive over a sandy waste area. From there, the hole turns to the right as a slight dogleg and culminates in a sand-filled adventure, out of which bubbles up a narrow, deep green.

Insider Tips Needless to say, warm up your sand wedge and the rest of your clubs for some serious sand play. No course in the Low Country is as sternly bunkered. Likewise, skip the practice with your short and mid-irons. There are so many long par-4s (plus two par-3s of 200-plus yards) that your driver, fairway woods, and long irons are going to be your key weapons in this battle.

To that end, don't kid yourself. Pick the correct and appropriate set of tee boxes. Why bother playing from the tips if you can't reach half the par-4s in regulation even after driving it your Sunday best? From the right set of tees, this course is actually pretty fun.

If you like to walk, they'll let you do it here, and it's a fun experience. Also, Fazio enjoys fine sandy subsoil, so tees, fairways, and greens drain quite well, making this a good choice for prime playing conditions, even after a heavy rain.

Among the drawbacks to Fazio are no practice range, no locker room, and a cramped pro shop. So do your practicing, changing, and shopping somewhere else. But if you want a supreme test of your long game and sand shots, Fazio's the place.

Palmetto Dunes Resort, Robert Trent Jones Course

7 Trent Jones Lane, Hilton Head Island, SC 29928; phone (800) 827-3006 or (943) 785-1136

How To Get On: Resort guests can make tee times 90 days in advance. Nonguests can book tee times 60 days in advance.

Tees:

> Blue: 6,710 yards, par-72, USGA rating 72.2, slope 123

> White: 6,148 yards, par-72, USGA rating 69.3, slope 119

> Red: 5,425 yards, par-72, USGA rating 70.7, slope 117

Challenge: ★★½	Golf Facilities: ★★★½
Variety: ★★★	14-Club Test ★★★
Terrain: ★★½	Intangibles: ★★★
Beauty/Visual Appeal: ★★★½	Value: ★★★
Pace of Play: ★★★	

Just the Facts   Year Opened: 1969; Course Designer: Robert Trent Jones Sr.; Walking: Yes; Greens Fee: $50–90; 9 Hole/Twilight Rate: Yes; Pull Carts: No; Practice Range: Yes; Club Rental: Yes

Description and Comments   Perhaps the most benign course at Palmetto Dunes is the Robert Trent Jones course—incredible, considering the architect's fearsome reputation. In reality, Jones crafted not a championship course but a wonderful resort course—scenic, with lots of trees, lakes, and bunkers—but without being so taxing that you'd need an extra box of balls to finish 18 holes. In many respects, the Jones course is the quintessential Hilton Head layout—punctuated with mature stands of pines, live oaks, and palmettos and criss-crossed with a network of lagoons that comes into play on 11 holes.

Even if this course represents a kinder, gentler Jones, his classic signature touches appear throughout the layout. Among these are liberal use of strategically deployed water hazards,; "airport runway" tee boxes, such as the ones at the 201-yard par-3 fifth; and artfully sculpted, huge bunkers, such as the fairway traps on the 361-yard, par-4 3rd and the deep green-side bunker to the right of the 378-yard, par-4 16th.

Frankly, the front nine at the Jones is disappointingly dull. Fairways are mostly tabletop flat, providing little variety in lies and stances. Holes four, five, six, seven, and eight head in exactly the same direction, providing little variety with respect to the wind. Even worse, they all play adjacent to busy Highway 278, the William Hilton Parkway, Hilton Head's main drag. At least the eighth is a fun hole, a 198-yard par-3 over water to an elevated green that is surrounded by four deep traps.

Thankfully, this 30-year-old course gets completely enjoyable on the back nine, beginning with the all-star 10th hole, a 540-yard par-5 that starts slowly but culminates in one of the most photographed greens in the Low Country. Six bunkers menace play throughout the hole, but what you'll remember here is the breezy approach into the green, which is perched merely a pitch shot away from the rolling surf of the Atlantic Ocean. The 10th is one of only two holes on Hilton Head Island that takes you beachside to the Atlantic, the other being the par-3 15th at the Sea Pines Ocean Course.

The remainder of the back nine journeys through the woods and over and alongside the winding lagoons and is a joy to play. It's totally fun, scenic, and not terribly difficult, with its mostly short par-4s. The Robert Trent Jones course at Palmetto Dunes is hardly Hilton Head's most memorable or challenging track, but for golfers whose handicaps range from 0 to 36, it might be the most enjoyable.

Insider Tips If you're prone to serious hooks, you may want to avoid the front nine entirely, as holes four through eight feature Hilton Head's busiest, noisiest thoroughfare to the left side. If slicing is your problem, take some extra balls for the back nine, as there's water trouble to the right of holes 11, 12, 13, 14, and 15.

For those of you who don't like surprises, you can get a glimpse of half the holes on the front nine just driving by them on Highway 278.

For those who absolutely love to whack their drivers, you've come to the right place. Amid all the trees and bunkers and lagoons are a set of the widest, flattest, friendliest fairways on the island, so smash away.

The Jones course winds in and around a handsome low-key residential and resort development, so early in the morning and in late afternoon keep your eyes peeled for cyclists, dog walkers, and joggers.

Finally, enjoy your putting experience at the oceanside 10th green. The hole isn't as spectacular as it looks in the brochures because the fairway is flat and the green slightly elevated. This means you can't see the beach until you're practically on the green; the brochure guys took their photos from a crane or plane.

Palmetto Hall Plantation, Arthur Hills Course

108 Fort Howell Dr., Hilton Head Island, SC 29926; phone (800) 827-3006) or (843) 689-4100

How To Get On: Tee times can be made 60 days in advance.

Tees:

    Gold: 6,918 yards, par-72, USGA rating 72.2, slope 132

    Blue: 6,582 yards, par-72, USGA rating 70.5, slope 123

    White: 6,257 yards, par-72, USGA rating 68.9, slope 117

    Red: 4,956 yards, par-72, USGA rating 68.6, slope 126

Challenge: ★★★½	Golf Facilities: ★★★★
Variety: ★★★★	14-Club Test ★★★★
Terrain: ★★★½	Intangibles: ★★★
Beauty/Visual Appeal: ★★★½	Value: ★★★★
Pace of Play: ★★★½	

Just the Facts   Year Opened: 1991; Course Designer: Arthur Hills; Walking: No; Greens Fee: $65–100; 9 Hole/Twilight Rate: Yes; Pull Carts: No; Practice Range: Yes; Club Rental: Yes

Description and Comments   This semi-private course is one of the more sought-after courses among locals and visitors alike. This is a very difficult course because there are so many elevated, multitiered greens and you have to carry the ball up onto them, rather than hitting bump-and-run shots. But it is also a very fair course provided you can drive the ball in the fairways and hit the landing areas. Even though it is in a residential community, the homes are set far enough back that they aren't visually bothersome, allowing you to yank one or push one here and there and not have to worry about out-of-bounds stakes that edge up to the second cuts of rough.

Because of its tree-lined fairways and an abundance of water hazards, this is also a very interesting course, though really a brute from the back tees, because so many lagoons come into play off the tees. It's one where you will usually use all 14 clubs in the bag. There is a well-balanced mix of good par-3s, par-4s, and par-5s. But you had better come ready to play, because right out of the chute is one of the toughest par-4s in South Carolina, a perhaps too-demanding 420-yard par-4.

The 14th is an even tougher par-4, maybe the hardest hole on the course, even though the handicapping on the scorecard doesn't indicate it. From the back tee, this hole plays 442 yards and can be a monster when you're playing it upwind. The fairway doglegs left and is heavily bordered by trees on either side. On the left side, between the tree line and the fairway, a waste bunker runs down the entirety of the hole. A strong, accurate tee shot on this hole is a must if you're going to have a decent chance at making par.

The best of the par-3s is the moderately long third hole, which features a tiered green that is very narrow on the forward pin positions and very wide on the second tier. There is also a bunker that runs all the way from the wetlands down the right-hand side of the hole, through the right side of the green. When you're standing on the tee getting ready to hit, the bunker looks like a full acre of sand.

Perhaps the most scenic hole is the par-5 15th, which features a gradual sloping dogleg that turns right about 200 yards off the tee. A lagoon parallels the fairway all the way through the green on the right and the hole is heavily treed on the left. Because there are no houses around this hole, you are afforded a peaceful look across the lagoon at unspoiled wilderness. You can also birdie this hole, or even eagle it, as it plays only 490 yards from the tips.

The frosting on Arthur Hills's cake is the 18th, definitely his signature hole—a par-4 that stretches 434 yards from the back tee. A lagoon lurks all the way down the left-hand side, and the elevated green slopes heavily toward the water.

If you keep the ball in play here, you have a chance to score well. But if you get off the beaten path, you pay the price, because beyond the rough is a jungle of heavy woods, lagoons, and wetlands.

Insider Tips   This is position golf. One of Arthur Hills's trademarks is to place trees strategically so that they come into play and penalize you if you're not in the proper position. If you can work the ball or pinpoint your tee shots, that sets the table at this course. So if you don't have a lot of confidence in your driver, pull out a three , four, or five wood or a long iron. Otherwise, you may spend your day going over and around trees or fishing your ball out of lagoons. When you come to the fourth hole, there is a lagoon that comes into play about 230 yards from the back tee. If you use a driver on this hole and you don't hit it in the right spot, you're in trouble. So calculate the distance accordingly.

There are many knowledgeable golfers who rank the Hills course at Palmetto Hall as the best of the five Palmetto Dunes/Palmetto Hall courses and as perhaps the number two public-access course in the Hilton Head area (behind Harbour Town), thus according it "must-play" status. Others, however, deem it a bit too difficult for the average golfer with its profusion of water holes and wetlands. In fact, the course is routed around so many wetlands that it's the only Palmetto Dunes/Palmetto Hall course where carts are mandatory. Our opinion? If you can carry the ball 150 to 200 yards in the air, you'll love Palmetto Hall's Hills Course.

Palmetto Hall Plantation, Robert Cupp Course

108 Fort Howell Dr., Hilton Head Island, SC 29926; phone (800) 827-3006 or (843) 689-4100

How To Get On: Tee times can be made 60 days in advance.

Tees:

> Gold: 7,079 yards, par-72, USGA rating 74.8, slope 141
>
> Blue: 6,524 yards, par-72, USGA rating 70.1, slope 126
>
> White: 6,042 yards, par-72, USGA rating 68.4, slope 120
>
> Red: 5,220 yards, par-72, USGA rating 71.1, slope 126

Challenge: ★★★★	Golf Facilities: ★★★★
Variety: ★★★½	14-Club Test ★★★★
Terrain: ★★	Intangibles: ★★★★
Beauty/Visual Appeal: ★★½	Value: ★★★
Pace of Play: ★★★	

Just the Facts   Year Opened: 1993; Course Designer: Robert Cupp; Walking: Yes; Greens Fee: $55–100; 9 Hole/Twilight Rate: Yes; Pull Carts: No; Practice Range: Yes; Club Rental: Yes

Description and Comments   As one wag put it, "If you aced high school geometry, you'll like the Cupp course." That may or may not be true, but there's a kernel of wisdom in the humor. Few golf courses in the world were as controversial on the day they opened as the Robert Cupp course at Palmetto Hall.

Palmetto Hall Plantation is a residential community owned by Greenwood Development Corp., which also owns Palmetto Dunes. Golfers at Palmetto Hall can choose from two distinctive courses—the traditionally designed, soft-contoured Arthur Hills course, which dates to 1991; and the completely unique Cupp course, which debuted a year later.

The Cupp course is unlike anything you've ever seen. A tough track of nearly 7,100 yards, the Cupp was designed on computer, with the results replicated in the field. Thus was born the first geometric golf course with square and rectangular tees and greens, trapezoidal bunkers, and grass pyramids on the sides of many fairways. It may be the only course in golf where you need a protractor and compass to break par.

Several things must be noted about Cupp's radical design. First, realize that this is a traditional Low-Country golf experience in many respects. Overall there's a graceful flow to the routing, if not to the features of the individual holes themselves. Holes wind over terrain that's pure Hilton Head—flat, with any number of ponds, wetlands, and marsh areas and through avenues of palmettos, oaks, and pines. Because the existing terrain was so flat to begin with, the artificial conical mounds look even more unnatural than they might otherwise.

Be that as it may, the jagged lines, harsh edges, and right angles of the bunkers, mounds, tee boxes, and water hazards are nowhere near as pronounced from eye level on the fairway as they are when photographed from above for brochures.

In time, the Cupp has come to be recognized as another excellent Hilton Head course, albeit one with a few quirks. Realize that it's not for everybody.

One of the truly appealing aspects to the course is that it's a monster from the tips, an irresistible challenge for those talented enough to play from all the way back, but move it up to any of the other sets of tees and it's generally playable. For instance, the number one handicap hole, the 435-yard third, calls for a 240-yard carry from the Gold tee; move it up to the Blues and you shave 50 yards off the still formidable but manageable carry. It's even more extreme at the brutal 472-yard ninth, which asks for a 250-yard carry. From the Blue tee, however, the hole shrinks by nearly 100 yards.

Perhaps the best hole on the Cupp is the 440-yard, par-4 13th, which is a classic "Cape" hole, with water to carry off the tee that extends up the left side on this dogleg left. The classic risk/reward decision is of the "bite-off-as-much-as-you-can-chew" variety: Play it safe, further right of the water, and you'll have a really long second shot to the green.

Insider Tips   It's worth repeating, so listen up: Leave your ego at the door when playing the Gold tees. From there, it's the toughest public-access course in the Hilton Head area.

Walking is permitted at the Cupp Course, and it's not a bad one for doing so, except when you have to climb one of the pyramids. If you're hoofing it, pay heed to the numerous alligators, which can be found sunning themselves adjacent to the course's many water hazards. Most folks prefer to ride, but a friendly warning: Don't take the carts where they don't belong. Sometimes it's hard to execute the three-point turns required by the cart path routing, but try to avoid the temptation to take shortcuts. We've actually witnessed carts getting stuck, perched precariously, all four wheels off the ground, on top of a fairway pyramid.

A final suggestion: Get a yardage book and select your clubs carefully. Due to the bizarre landscape features, depth perception is difficult here. Note that Palmetto Hall also has a private membership. The Cupp Course alternates with the Hills Course, with one private, one public, depending on the day. Call ahead. Do yourself one final favor: Spend some time in the magnificent clubhouse.

A Hilton Head Sampler

Country Club of Hilton Head

70 Skull Creek Dr., Hilton Head Island, SC 29926; phone (843) 681-4653

Tees: Championship: 6,919 yards, par-72, USGA rating 73.6, slope 132

Greens Fee: $50–85

Challenge: ★★★½

Variety: ★★★½

Terrain: ★★★½

Beauty/Visual Appeal: ★★★★

Pace of Play: ★★★★

Golf Facilities: ★★★½

14-Club Test ★★★½

Intangibles: ★★★½

Value: ★★★★

Description and Comments Despite its forbidding name, the Country Club of Hilton Head actually welcomes public play, though clubhouse access is limited and talk remains that the course may one day be completely private. Be that as it may, it's worth your while to hustle over and see this one, because it's one of Hilton Head's best.

Rees Jones designed this course in 1986 in his "heavy mounding" period, but here the grassy mounds manage to blend nicely with what nature has provided, including marshland, magnolias, live oaks, pines, and palmettos. The result is a fun, pretty course that's a strong challenge from any set of tees. Most of the greens here are slightly elevated and well bunkered, placing a premium on approach shots. Take care to play smart. If you feel you might miss a green, miss it on the correct side, as the mounds and bunkers in play make for some dicey chipping opportunities.

What makes the Country Club of Hilton Head so good is its variety. Almost every hole doglegs, but as many to the left as to the right. Some are gentle, but others turn abruptly. Holes alternate between open and tree-lined; it's the open nature of the course that makes it popular in summer because it allows for the coastal breezes to make your round just a little bit more tolerable.

The back nine is the more scenic and interesting of the two. Easily the best hole is the gargantuan, par-5 12th, which at least plays ever so slightly downhill for its 575-yard journey. From the fairway landing area on this dogleg left, you can drink in a view from atop the highest point in Hilton Head—28 feet above sea level! What you'll see is a plethora of bunkers guarding both fairway and green, a marshy hazard blocking the left front of the green, and stirring glimpses of the Intracoastal Waterway and Skull Creek behind the green.

Another intriguing hole is the 17th. From the gold and blue tees, this par-4 measures roughly 400 yards and calls for a precise drive over marsh and through a chute of trees. Form the White tee, however, it's just a cute little thing at 286 yards, which changes the complexion of the hole entirely. Throw in a fine quartet of all-carry par-3s and you've got one excellent course. Tucked way back into Hilton Head Plantation, it's not the easiest course to find. Better to have someone direct you to the plantation's back-gate entrance. From there, it's easy.

Daufuskie Island Club and Resort, Bloody Point Course

Daufuskie Island, Hilton Head Island, SC 29925; phone (843) 842-2000

Tees: Championship: 6,900 yards, par-72, USGA rating 73.2, slope 135

Greens Fee: $80–155

Challenge: ★★★½

Variety: ★★★½

Terrain: ★★★½

Beauty/Visual Appeal: ★★★★

Pace of Play: ★★★★½

Golf Facilities: ★★★

14-Club Test ★★★½

Intangibles: ★★★★

Value: ★★★

Description and Comments   With a name like "Bloody Point," this has to be an interesting golf experience. In truth, the experience is better than the course itself.

By any objective standard, Bloody Point is a fine course and a good test for any level of player. It's renowned for its subtle challenges and quiet, unspoiled beauty. Most of the holes ease gracefully past tidal marshes and ancient live oaks. Although water comes into play on nearly half the holes, there is usually an alternate, safe way to approach the green.

The 420-yard, par-4 13th is an exception. Framed by tidal marshes and offering river and ocean views, this gorgeous hole will prove to be very unlucky for those who fail to clear the water with their second shots. Other memorable holes include a pair of watery front-nine par-3s, the 165-yard 4th and the all-carry, 160-yard 7th; the 14th and the 16th, a pair of brutally long par-4s (475 and 460 yards, respectively) that often play into the wind; and the two par-5s that finish each nine.

Nevertheless, the best hole is the 190-yard, par-3 17th, which heads straight out to the Mungen River, which flows into the nearby Atlantic. Two big bunkers guard the green, one poised short-right and one flush left of the putting surface. Ocean breezes almost always affect club and shot selection.

Bloody Point enjoys so many wonderful trappings: It is accessible only via a 40-minute ferry ride from Hilton Head Island; it's handsome and fun to play for all classes of golfers; it's plenty challenging; it enjoys a strong architectural pedigree in Tom Weiskopf and Jay Morrish; and it's seldom crowded, so you can usually buzz around pretty quickly.

Be that as it may, Bloody Point disappoints slightly because it simply lacks the drama or jaw-dropping views that would befit this island setting. Unlike its sister course, Melrose (described above in the Major Courses section), there are no ocean holes, and few of them even offer the views one might expect. If you could only play one course on your trip to Daufuskie, make it Melrose. Better yet, though, make time to play them both, even on the same day. It's a superb golf experience.

Eagle's Pointe

1 Eagle's Pointe Dr., Bluffton, SC 29910; phone (888) 325-1833 or (843) 686-4457

Tees: Championship: 6,738 yards, par-71, USGA rating 72.5, slope 130

Greens Fee: $59–79

Challenge: ★★★	Golf Facilities: ★★★
Variety: ★★★	14-Club Test ★★★½
Terrain: ★★★	Intangibles: ★★½
Beauty/Visual Appeal: ★★★	Value: ★★★½
Pace of Play: ★★★½	

Description and Comments   This relatively new course was designed by Davis Love III and is located off-island about midway between Hilton Head Island and I-95 on Highway 278. Eagle's Pointe is a good course for the average golfer because it's not overly difficult from the forward tees, yet it challenges single-digit handicappers from the tips. Nearly all of the fairways here are bordered by hardwood trees, especially oaks, mixed with pines. Although there is nothing spectacular about the topography—no ocean, marshes, rivers, or canals—there is a very good mix of holes. A long, straight hole might be followed by a short, tight hole or a testy dog-leg. For example, the 16th, which measures a hefty 440 yards, is perhaps the toughest hole on the course because of its length and because there is water nearly all the way up the left side. But in his wisdom, Love made the 17th relatively short at 377 yards, and this is one hole where everyone can birdie, provided they can hit a narrow fairway bordered by woods on the right and a lagoon on the left.

The par-4 ninth, 442 yards from the back tees, is one of the more interesting holes on the course because of a huge live oak tree in the middle of a fairway guarded by woods on the left and water on the right. But the short, par-4 sixth (only 329 yards from the back tee) may well be the pivotal hole on the course. There are woods on the left and water on the right; the farther you hit your tee shot, the tighter the fairway gets. A birdie isn't all that hard to come by, but neither is a triple bogey.

The facilities here are very nice, the staff is country-club courteous, and the course has 18 very distinctive holes. You never get the feeling late in the round, as you do on some courses, that when you come to a particular hole, you have already played it. If the course can be distinguished from others in the neighborhood, it is due to its mostly huge greens, many of which are well guarded by surprisingly large, deep bunkers. Normally at a modest semi-private course, the trapping is much more benign. By the way, they'll let you walk here, but don't bother. It's a tough slog—not because of the terrain, which is mostly flat, but because of vast distances between previous green and next tee.

Golden Bear Golf Club at Indigo Run

72 Golden Bear Way, Hilton Head Island, SC 29928; phone (843) 689-2200

Tees: Championship: 7,014 yards, par-72, USGA rating 73.7, slope 132

Greens Fee: $35–70

Challenge: ★★★½	Golf Facilities: ★★★★
Variety: ★★★½	14-Club Test ★★★½
Terrain: ★★★	Intangibles: ★★★
Beauty/Visual Appeal: ★★★½	Value: ★★★★
Pace of Play: ★★★	

Description and Comments   As its name would indicate, this course is the architectural handiwork of the Jack Nicklaus organization. In reality, design credit goes to Nicklaus associate Bruce Borland, who died tragically in the same plane crash that took the life of PGA Tour star Payne Stewart. If Golden Bear is any indication, Borland would have had a fine design career ahead of him.

Borland and the Nicklaus team were saddled with a very tight routing done by William Byrd, another prolific designer who is better respected for his land planning and landscape architecture than for his golf course architecture.

Golden Bear more closely resembles an old-fashioned classic parkland course than any built in the Hilton Head area in the past 10 years. Opened in 1992, Golden Bear demands proper tee shot placement, more because of trees than multiple wetlands. Thus, the occasional ground ball or topped shot doesn't get punished as severely as a big slice or hook, making the course quite fun and playable for mid- and high handicappers. Yet it's plenty tough from the tips, thanks to the presence of countless pines and live oaks, numerous lagoons and a number of well-placed bunkers.

Part of the reason Golden Bear is such a pleasure to play is that many of the lagoons and other water hazards are positioned more for aesthetic value, rather than being directly in the line of play. Also, the gently rolling fairways and gently contoured greens are kept in excellent condition.

A pair of watery front-nine par-3s will grab your attention—the 199-yard 4th and the 183-yard 8th—but the two holes that will linger a while are the par-5 9th and par-5 18th. Both are reachable by big hitters, but you must risk putting it in the water on both holes.

Golden Bear offers good value in a pleasant setting. Carts are outfitted with the Pro Shot Electronic Yardage and Course Information Monitor, which helps with club selection and course management. They've got an excellent large practice range and putting green. It's all pretty darn good.

Hilton Head National

U.S. Hwy. 278, Bluffton, SC 29910; phone (888) 955-1234 or (843) 842-5900

National Course

Tees: Championship: 3,261 yards, par-35, USGA rating 35.9, slope 121

Greens Fee: $30–85

The Player Course

Tees: Championship: 3,298 yards, par-36, USGA rating 36.1, slope 134

Greens Fee: $30–85

The Weed Course

Tees: Championship: 3,357 yards, par-36, USGA rating 35.6, slope 129

Greens Fee: $30–85

Challenge: ★★★
Variety: ★★★★
Terrain: ★★★★
Beauty/Visual Appeal: ★★★★
Pace of Play: ★★★½

Golf Facilities: ★★★★
14-Club Test ★★★½
Intangibles: ★★★
Value: ★★★★

Description and Comments   Here we go again with another pretentious-sounding name for a public golf course. At least in this case, however, we're dealing with a very good 27-hole complex with amenities to match.

Golf legend Gary Player crafted the club's original 18 holes in 1989. From its inception, Hilton Head National has been renowned for its excellent service, superior course conditioning, and pristine playing environment, thanks to an abundance of trees and marshland and an absence of intrusive housing developments. To enhance playability, Player positioned most of the hazards to the sides of play, with, of course, some interesting exceptions. Tee boxes and fairways are edged by mounds and tall, wavy marsh grasses, providing an attractive look. On the open holes, the mounds and grasses lend a linksy feel to the proceedings, especially if the wind is blowing.

Neither the bunkering nor green design is especially exciting, but at least it's inoffensive, unlike so many of the weird and wild greens and bunker complexes built in the late 1980s. Among the favorites on the original 18 are the 440-yard, par-4 9th, with its 175-yard marsh carry from the back tee, and the 521-yard, par-5 18th, with wetlands in play on the left side. Both holes culminate in a shared double green.

In 1999, Hilton Head National opened a third nine, designed by Bobby Weed. It's appropriately called the Weed nine. The old front nine is now known as the National, and the old back nine is called the Player. The new Weed nine blends beautifully in appearance with its older siblings, but plays vastly different and faster—more bouncy, with loads of shot-making options—giving Hilton Head National tremendous variety.

Greens on the Weed nine are firmer, as they're turfed with Tifeagle bermuda, and the Player and National nines are carpeted with Tifdwarf. Taken together, they're the best-maintained resort greens in the region.

Which nines should you play? The Weed nine is a bit different, but tee through green, it's the most intriguing. You'll also want to play the Player nine, with its awesome 175-yard, pond-guarded, par-3 eighth hole—which you can see from Highway 278—and its welcoming fountain. What the heck—all three nines are worth your while and worthy of your dollars.

Island West Golf Club

U.S. Hwy. 278, Bluffton, SC 29910; phone (843) 689-6660

Tees: Championship: 6,803 yards, par-72, USGA rating 72.1, slope 129;

Greens Fee: $40–70

Challenge: ★★★	Golf Facilities: ★★½
Variety: ★★½	14-Club Test ★★★
Terrain: ★★★	Intangibles: ★★½
Beauty/Visual Appeal: ★★★	Value: ★★★
Pace of Play: ★★½	

Description and Comments   One of the better bargains in the Hilton Head area, Island West is a 1991 collaboration between designer Clyde Johnston and his consultant, PGA Tour star Fuzzy Zoeller. Located 10 miles from the bridge that connects the island to the mainland, the course doesn't exactly blow you away with memorable golf holes, but without question, it's a fun, fair test of golf.

Routing the course wasn't an easy task, as the site had 70 acres of protected wetlands and 25 acres of ponds. All this wet stuff serves more as an attractive nuisance; only twice in the round do you face a forced carry.

The back nine is the stronger of the two, more scenic and more challenging. Noteworthy are the 8th and 17th holes, a pair of side-by-side par-3s that play over water to a 125-yard-wide double green.

Island West long had a dubious reputation as having the rudest personnel in the area, from pro shop clerks to starters. Reports indicate that a recent management change has resulted in friendlier folks.

Ocean Creek Golf Course

908 Ocean Creek Blvd., Fripp Island, SC 29920; phone (800) 933-0050 or (843) 838-1576

Tees: Championship: 6,510 yards, par-71, USGA rating 71.4, slope 131

Greens Fee: $50–75

Challenge: ★★★

Variety: ★★★

Terrain: ★★★★

Beauty/Visual Appeal: ★★★★½

Pace of Play: ★★

Golf Facilities: ★★★

14-Club Test ★★★

Intangibles: ★★★★

Value: ★★★½

Description and Comments　Let's start with the notion that if you're looking for truly spectacular Low-Country scenery, this is the place for it. Pure visual splendor alone is reason enough to make the hour-and-fifteen-minute drive from Hilton Head, via the scenic, historic town of Beaufort.

So striking is the exotic landscape at Ocean Creek that prior to the course being constructed, it was used for the Vietnam scenes in the movie *Forrest Gump,* and it showed up on numerous occasions in the Disney live-action film *The Jungle Book.*

Ocean Creek, the newer of the two courses at Fripp Island Resort, opened in 1995. It was the first signature design by PGA Tour star Davis Love III, no stranger himself to the Low Country. Love won the Heritage event at Hilton Head's Harbour Town three times before designing this course, and he lived at the southern tip of the region, at Sea Island, Georgia. Thus, Love and his crew had a special affinity for the site even before construction began.

Nature, obviously, is the dominant feature of the Ocean Creek course. The land is framed by what aquatic explorer Jacques Cousteau called some of the most fertile and pristine salt marshes in the world. Four distinct rolling dune lines, some as high as 15 feet, bisect the otherwise flattish terrain, lending additional drama to the setting.

Love routed many holes on the front nine around and over these lagoons and marshlands, creating a series of short but spectacular holes. At the 423-yard, par-4 fifth, you can see the Forrest Gump backdrop from the island tee box. Six and seven are even more spectacular, a 185-yard par-3 and a 409-yard par-4, respectively. On the back nine, the appealing Jungle Book lake where Mowgli and Kitty walk is a critical element of the 11th hole.

Unfortunately, negotiating all of these impressive hazards can be a nightmarish proposition for most golfers, especially when the breeze is up. The holes themselves, connected via a network of bridges and wooden walkways, are really memorable, but not necessarily roomy enough to accommodate golf shots. Bring lots of film—and plenty of extra balls.

Ocean Point Golf Links

250 Ocean Point Dr., Fripp Island, SC 29920; phone (800) 845-4100 or (843) 838-2309

Tees: Championship: 6,590 yards, par-72, USGA rating 72.2, slope 129

Greens Fee: $45–65

Challenge: ★★★	Golf Facilities: ★★★
Variety: ★★★	14-Club Test ★★★
Terrain: ★★★	Intangibles: ★★★½
Beauty/Visual Appeal: ★★★★	Value: ★★★½
Pace of Play: ★★½	

Description and Comments   Possessing little of the unique Low-Country dense foliage of its sister course, Ocean Creek, Ocean Point course at Fripp Island nonetheless boasts some outstanding scenery of its own. Ocean Point lives up to its name—one of the rare courses in this part of the world that not only offers frequent glimpses of the Atlantic but also features two holes that play alongside: the dogleg left, 365-yard, par-4 9th and the 486-yard, par-5 18th.

So why isn't Ocean Point better known? Partly because of its remote location— 19 miles from Beaufort and nearly an hour and a half from Hilton Head. Also, intrusive condo developments compete for your visual attention, blocking or at least partially obstructing what otherwise would be staggering beach and ocean views.

Moreover, the course design itself is fairly ordinary. Terrain on the 1964 George Cobb design is flat, and targets aren't particularly well defined. Bunkers are mostly old-fashioned ovals, and the bermuda greens are mostly benign, characterless, and of medium speed. Still, Ocean Point enjoys a good, rugged set of par-3s, three beefy par-4s, and it's challenging for all when the wind is up, which is often. Frequent wildlife sightings include deer, birds, and alligators. It may seem odd to have to drive an hour and a half from Hilton Head just to play golf on the ocean, but this trip is worth the time. Perhaps make it an overnight side trip, staying at the family-oriented Fripp Island Resort, or else explore the myriad options in nearby Beaufort.

Okatie Creek Golf Club

60 Sun City Club Lane, Bluffton, SC 29910; phone (843) 705-4653
Tees: Championship: 6,724 yards, par-72, USGA rating 71.9, slope 130
Greens Fee: $34–54

Challenge: ★★½	Golf Facilities: ★★★½
Variety: ★★½	14-Club Test ★★½
Terrain: ★★	Intangibles: ★★
Beauty/Visual Appeal: ★★½	Value: ★★½
Pace of Play: ★★★	

Description and Comments   It used to be that if you told folks you were moving to a Sun City development, it meant you realized you had made it to the finish line and were ready to climb off life's roller coaster. Not so anymore. The Del Webb Corporation is redefining retirement with a mushrooming family of communities, including the new Sun City Hilton Head, that emphasize the active life. And at Sun City that means a lot more than shuffleboard.

Located approximately 13 miles west of Hilton Head Island in the town of Bluffton, Sun City Hilton Head unfolds over a spacious 5,600 acres. Plans call for 63 holes of golf—two 18-hole courses and one with 27.

Eighteen holes are open for play now—Okatie Creek Golf Club—with public access to players of all ages. The course was designed by PGA Tour player Mark McCumber, who will also forge the development's second 18 holes. McCumber knows a good course when he sees it; after all he's won tournaments at classic courses, such as the TPC at Sawgrass, the Olympic Club, and the Blue Monster at Doral.

McCumber draped the course over typically flat Low-Country terrain and carved it from pine forests. The 115 turfed acres have been adorned with 4,500 azaleas, plus numerous crepe and wax myrtles. A smattering of bunkers and water hazards add further spice.

Perhaps Okatie Creek's most rigorous hole is the sixth, a rugged par-5 of 549 yards that features a double dogleg, first to the left, then to the right. The course also boasts an outstanding quartet of par-3s, including the particularly stimulating 205-yard 12th, which calls for a long iron or fairway wood to a well-bunkered green further protected by a serpentine lagoon along the right side of the hole.

Another much-talked-about hole is the meaty 439-yard, par-4 14th, which forces a tough strategic decision on how best to negotiate a lone pine tree in the center of the fairway.

There are two ways of looking at Okatie Creek: To some, this flat course, with its flat bunkers that ribbon through cookie-cutter homes is an unattractive snooze, a "why waste your time when there are so many other courses to pick from" situation. To others, it's a stress-free romp where you can finish with the same ball you started with. We think it fits somewhere in between.

Old Carolina Golf Club

90 Buck Island Rd., Bluffton, SC 29910; phone (888) 785-7274 or (843) 785-6363

Tees: Championship: 6,805 yards, par-72, USGA rating 73.1, slope 142

Greens Fee: $50–85

Challenge: ★★★★	Golf Facilities: ★★★
Variety: ★★★	14-Club Test ★★★½
Terrain: ★★★½	Intangibles: ★★★
Beauty/Visual Appeal: ★★★½	Value: ★★★½
Pace of Play: ★★	

Description and Comments   Unusual for a Low-Country course, Old Carolina is a rolling, mounded layout with undulating greens. Located six miles west from the bridge to Hilton Head Island, Old Carolina was designed by Clyde Johnston in "modern links style," which is brochure-speak for a layout that is long on mounds and short on trees.

In truth, Old Carolina embodies almost none of the virtues of links golf, which traditionally features few forced carried and favors low-running approach shots. At Old Carolina, there are many forced carries, some of them nearly unfair for most levels of players, either because they're too daunting or because they involve hazard placement that's difficult to discern. The 8th, a 550-yard par-5, and the 9th and 18th holes, a pair of medium-long par-4s, are the most notorious offenders. As attractive as each of those holes are, they're ridiculously difficult, with huge, poorly placed water and sand hazards and shallow greens not particularly well designed for the shot they're supposed to accommodate. Two other par-5s, the 565-yard 12th and the 510-yard 15th, also feature forced carries and ill-defined landing areas.

Make no mistake. This is a hard course. It's only 6,805 yards from the tips, yet it's sloped at a fearsome 142 rating. Simply stated, Old Carolina never lets up, with one shot after the next over lakes, wetlands, mounds, and bunkers.

Nevertheless, many vacationing golfers love Old Carolina. Unlike some of Hilton Head's older courses, it's interesting and visually stimulating at every turn. The greens sport wonderful contouring and gentle containment mounds help keep wayward balls in play. Without question, you'll encounter many memorable holes, such as the 370-yard, par-4 13th, a dogleg left that features a green protected by water and no fewer than 11 bunkers!

If you're prepared to part with a few balls and put up with a beautiful but frustrating holes, you'll find that Old Carolina will keep you on your toes and entertained for the entire four-and-a-half-hour journey.

Old South Golf Links

50 Buckingham Plantation Dr., Bluffton, SC 29910; phone (800) 257-8997 or (843) 785-5353

Tees: Championship: 6,772 yards, par-72, USGA rating 72.4, slope 129

Greens Fee: $53–82

Challenge: ★★★	Golf Facilities: ★★★½
Variety: ★★★★	14-Club Test ★★★½
Terrain: ★★★½	Intangibles: ★★★½
Beauty/Visual Appeal: ★★★★	Value: ★★★★
Pace of Play: ★★★	

Description and Comments   Since its 1991 opening, this Clyde Johnston design has proved to be one of the Hilton Head area's most popular courses. There are very good reasons for this: It's scenic, challenging, and fun. Old South is definitely one of the best values in all the Low Country. Nearly half the holes are draped over terrain that skirts the broad waters of the May River. Many holes feature dramatic vistas of Hilton Head proper, across the Calibogue Sound. The opening holes on both nines play through live oak forests and along lagoons, then holes move out onto narrow strips of turf that edge saltwater marshes. Still other holes ease through sparsely treed open pasture. The variety is outstanding.

For the scratch or very good player, Old South isn't the formidable challenge its sister course (Old Carolina) is, unless there is a strong breeze. When conditions are moderately calm, Old South is plenty challenging, yet still fun for all classes of golfers. When the wind is up, it becomes a stern test, especially on the back nine, which is more open than the heavily wooded front nine. It's this breezy, open nature, however, that makes Old South a highly recommended course in summer's sweltering heat.

Understand that as attractive and playable as Old South is, it is still target golf, with numerous mandatory forced carries, so the course is not recommended for beginners. Even intermediates (10–15 handicap) should expect to lose a few balls in the many hazards that dot the landscape.

Whether you lose one ball or a dozen, you're certain to enjoy Old South. Front nine favorites include the lagoon-laced, 530-yard, par-5 third and 167-yard, par-3 fourth, plus the dogleg-right, 370-yard, par-4 seventh, which plays to an island fairway in the tidal marsh then over more wetlands to a peninsula green backed by stands of palmettos.

Still, it's the back nine that folks rave about (or curse), thanks to holes like 16 and 17. The par-4 16th measures 417 yards and hopscotches the marsh to a two-tier island green, backed, appropriately enough, by an enormous beach bunker. Seventeen is a 180-yard par-3 composed of a tee box and green sited on bluffs and separated by marsh.

Thanks to its design, scenery, and facilities, Old South is clearly one of the best courses in the "New" South.

Oyster Reef Golf Club

155 High Bluff Dr., Hilton Head Island, SC 29925; phone (843) 681-7717

Tees: Championship: 7,027 yards, par-72, USGA rating 73.7, slope 131

Greens Fee: $50–85

Challenge: ★★★½

Variety: ★★★½

Terrain: ★★★½

Beauty/Visual Appeal: ★★★★

Pace of Play: ★★★★

Golf Facilities: ★★★½

14-Club Test ★★★½

Intangibles: ★★★

Value: ★★★★

Description and Comments　Without question, one of Hilton Head's unsung gems is Oyster Reef. Don't let its lack of high visibility fool you, however. This is a wonderful track, one of the region's best.

"The Reef," as locals call it, enjoys a gorgeous, secluded location deep in the heart of Hilton Head Plantation on the island's north end. This plantation tends to be quieter and less tourist-oriented than the others because of the paucity of commercial development. There are no hotels or resort villas and only a single acclaimed restaurant, the marvelous Old Fort Pub.

Many factors distinguish Oyster Reef from others in the area. First and foremost, it is the only public-access course in the region that sports bentgrass greens. Late in 1997, Crenshaw bent was planted, a hardier strain than older models, which would typically wilt in summer's heat and humidity and high nighttime temperatures. Good bent is preferred over bermuda, because with its thinner blade, it is less grainy and when shaved smooth, putts faster and truer. At Oyster Reef, so far so good—an unexpected treat in this part of the country.

Oyster Reef is a typical early 1980s Rees Jones design. It's long—one of the longest in Hilton Head—but extremely fair. Strategically placed mounds, a Rees Jones trademark, line most of the holes, as do moderately thick stands of live oaks and Carolina pines. Most of the holes dogleg one way or the other, placing a premium on precise driving. Water on half the holes, plus 68 bunkers reinforce the "accuracy" theme, but you'll need to use your driver a lot, as Oyster Reef stretches more than 7,000 yards from the tips. Many tees are slightly elevated, giving good views of what's to come.

Most memorable—and one of Hilton Head's best holes—is the 192-yard, par-3 sixth. Overhanging oak limbs, a huge splash of sand fronting the green, and an outstanding view of the Port Royal Sound in the background combine to make this a great hole. Oyster Reef's macho finish includes the 453-yard 17th and the 461-yard 18th, a pair of burly par-4s. The dogleg-left, 541-yard 15th and the 209-yard, par-3 16th are both watery gems. This "Final Four" may not be as exciting as the NCAA hoops, but in golf circles, it's a fantastic finish. Oyster Reef hosted a national junior event from 1987 to 1991. During that time, only one golfer broke 70—a youngster named David Duval.

Port Royal Golf Club, Barony Course

10A Grasslawn Ave., Hilton Head Island, SC 29928; phone (800) 234-6318 or (843) 681-1760

Tees: Championship: 6,530 yards, par-72, USGA rating 71.6, slope 129

Greens Fee: $50–89

Challenge: ★★★

Golf Facilities: ★★★★

Variety: ★★½

14-Club Test ★★½

Terrain: ★★½

Intangibles: ★★½

Beauty/Visual Appeal: ★★★

Value: ★★½

Pace of Play: ★★★

Description and Comments Port Royal Plantation is home to Hilton Head Island's best resort hotel, the Westin. Its golf clubhouse is one of the finest public-access facilities in the region. It's worth noting—just in case—that they serve up a great Bloody Mary. Unfortunately, none of Port Royal's three 18-hole courses measure up to the setting and surrounding facilities.

Be that as it may, Port Royal boasts three good golf courses—Barony, Planter's Row (described below), and Robber's Row (also described below), though not one is great. Barony is the oldest, a 1968 George Cobb design. If only "average" by Hilton Head standards, in the grand scheme, it's still a fine course. It's likely the most forgiving of Port Royal's trio, as it's the most open, with medium-size, friendly greens. Nevertheless, it's hardly a pushover. Large oaks, deep bunkers, and shaggy bermuda rough keep big hitters honest.

In many respects, Barony is the classic Hilton Head resort course: It's fun to play without being particularly memorable, and it's scenic with magnolias, lagoons, and moss-draped oaks without being spectacular. It's a terrific course with which to start your vacation, as it will give you a true taste of Hilton Head without beating you up.

The terrain itself is table-top flat, but there's some memorability and variety, thanks to the numerous doglegs, the intrusive flower beds, and the solid greenside bunkering. Flower beds and gardens add splashes of color to the experience and additional character comes in the form of Civil War memorabilia. Port Royal was the site of several battles; the club pays homage via plaques and commemorative tee markers.

Perhaps the strongest hole on Barony is the 428-yard, par-4 12th. Water runs up the entire right side of the hole, and a lake menaces a hooked approach to the flat green, which itself is pinched by three bunkers. The 12th plays toward the ocean, so it's usually into the wind.

Port Royal has a small but vibrant membership, in addition to being open for public and resort play, the result being that at any given time, one of the three courses is closed to outside play. If that's a concern, call well ahead of time, so there won't be any surprises when you arrive for your golf vacation.

Port Royal Golf Club, Planter's Row Course

10A Grasslawn Ave., Hilton Head Island, SC 29928; phone (800) 234-6318 or (843) 686-8801

Tees: Championship: 6,625 yards, par-72, USGA rating 71.7, slope 133

Greens Fee: $50–89

Challenge: ★★★	Golf Facilities: ★★★★
Variety: ★★½	14-Club Test ★★½
Terrain: ★★★	Intangibles: ★★½
Beauty/Visual Appeal: ★★★½	Value: ★★½
Pace of Play: ★★★	

Description and Comments   Planter's Row is the newest of Port Royal's three courses, a 1983 creation of Willard Byrd. In 1985, the course hosted the Senior PGA Tour's Hilton Head Seniors International. Most of the players undoubtedly kept their drivers in their bags, because Planter's Row is strictly bow-and-arrow golf through the trees.

As tight and flat as a gymnast's stomach, Planter's Row is a straight hitter's dream—and a wild hitter's nightmare. If you tend to spray the ball, either go play elsewhere or be prepared to listen for your errant shots as they bounce off tree trunks and the numerous live oak limbs that overhang in (and practically overwhelm) the fairways.

Mind you, despite having fairways the width of a bowling alley, Planter's Row is hardly a one-dimensional course. A handsome lagoon influences a couple of holes on the front side and a half-dozen on the back. Bunkering throughout the course shows excellent variety and greens are large, with pronounced undulations. Shot-making opportunities abound, along with an emphasis on chipping, putting, and recovery shots.

Planter's Row enjoys a pristine environment, as it's free of housing developments. Pines, palmettos, flowers, and shrubs grace every hole, along with those ubiquitous moss-drenched live oaks. Once in a while, however, the outside world intrudes, as the noise from nearby Highway 278 can be a distraction, as can the roar of small jets taking off and landing at nearby Hilton Head Airport.

Two holes stand out at Planter's Row. The 12th is a nasty, narrow, 424-yard par-4 that features a pair of traps on the left side of the fairway landing area and an approach over two separate ponds. Perhaps the most intriguing hole is the par-5 18th. Most folks play this one at 480 yards, but highly skilled golfers (or nut jobs) can hike back in the trees and play it at 552 yards. Water on the right and a bunker on the left conspire to squeeze the landing area for the second shot to the size of Kate Moss's waist.

Great is not an adjective you'd use to describe Planter's Row. If you can keep it straight, however, you'll enjoy your journey to Port Royal's wonderful Antebellum-style clubhouse.

Port Royal Golf Club, Robber's Row Course

10A Grasslawn Ave., Hilton Head Island, SC 29928; phone (800) 234-6318 or (843) 681-1760

Tees: Championship: 6,642 yards, par-72, USGA rating 72.6, slope 134

Greens Fee: $50–89

Challenge: ★★★½	Golf Facilities: ★★★★
Variety: ★★★½	14-Club Test ★★★
Terrain: ★★★	Intangibles: ★★★★
Beauty/Visual Appeal: ★★★½	Value: ★★★½
Pace of Play: ★★★	

Description and Comments For the better player, Robber's Row is definitely the supreme challenge at Port Royal. It's also the best of the three courses, period. Originally a mid-1960s design from George Cobb and Willard Byrd, Robber's was reworked in 1993–94 by Pete Dye and his wife, Alice, an accomplished golfer and architect herself. The result is a relatively new, challenging, yet fun-to-play layout that is draped over truly historical terrain.

Robber's Row is laid out on the marsh side of the Port Royal Plantation community, atop land that holds remains of Civil War fortresses and encampments. In 1861, this area was part of the town of Port Royal, and tent cities were erected here after the Union soldiers took over Hilton Head Island in the 1861 Battle of Port Royal. Not every hole in your round here will call for hand-to-hand combat, but each tee box features a marker detailing the significance of the site.

More open than Planter's Row, Robber's is still a tight track, demanding precise iron play, and is full of Low-Country character. Countless live oaks, magnolias, and bunkers line the fairways and surround the greens. The Dyes added several water hazards in their redesign, lengthened the second hole to a par-5, and reduced the pushover par-5 10th to a now rugged par-4. Perhaps the Dyes' strongest influence was on the greens, which they reworked to provide far more interest than their predecessors. One thing they couldn't do was eliminate some trees and villas to provide ocean views. Instead, we get ocean breezes, but not a single glimpse of the Atlantic.

Robber's Row today is renowned for its clubhouse, facilities, difficult set of greens, and outstanding quartet of par-3s. Two of the best are the 197-yard fourth, with water down the left side, and the 15th, which plays nearly as long, but to a green encircled by sand.

Again, membership at Port Royal has exclusive access to Robber's Row from time to time. Call ahead if you definitely want to include this course on your Hilton Head vacation itinerary.

Rose Hill Country Club

One Clubhouse Drive, Bluffton, SC 29910; phone (843) 757-2160 or (843) 842-3740

Tees: Championship: 6,808 yards, par-72, USGA rating 72.9, slope 126

Greens Fee: $32–50

Challenge: ★★★	Golf Facilities: ★★½
Variety: ★★½	14-Club Test ★★½
Terrain: ★★½	Intangibles: ★★
Beauty/Visual Appeal: ★★★	Value: ★★★★
Pace of Play: ★★★	

Description and Comments   Six miles west of the bridge that connects Bluffton to Hilton Head Island is the 27-hole Rose Hill Country Club. The three nines sit on the opposite side of Highway 278 from the entrance to Rose Hill Plantation. Both real estate community and golf course are kind of "second-tier" in the Hilton Head market, but they're still quite handsome.

Rose Hill isn't even that well known to Hilton Head regulars, but word is getting out. Several years ago, we encountered a gentleman at an old club in western Wales who happened to be wearing a Rose Hill logo shirt. Sure enough, he had played in Hilton Head and at Rose Hill and enjoyed it very much. Understand that Rose Hill isn't a top-tier course and you'll probably enjoy it, too.

Gene Hamm, one of the most prolific architects in the Carolinas, crafted Rose Hill with an emphasis on playability. Although there's water on 25 of the 27 holes, seldom is a forced carry necessary.

This traditional design is mostly wall-to-wall grass. Hamm moved enough dirt to create a gently rolling landscape. Much of the dirt he excavated to create the lakes he piled up in the form of grassy mounds that frame the fairways and edge the greens. Also framing fairways and greens are towering pines, live oaks, and sturdy magnolias.

The West nine is the newest of the three and is more challenging than its elder siblings, the South and the East. Lakes, mounds, smallish pot bunkers, and smallish, well-bunkered greens spice the play on all 27 holes, but what you'll remember from Rose Hill are the testy par-3s and the monstrous 600-yard par-5 second hole on the West.

One of the best bargains in Hilton Head, Rose Hill serves up afternoon specials and price breaks to locals nearly year-round. For cost and playability reasons, it's a good fit for mid- and high handicappers.

Sea Pines Plantation, Ocean Course

100 N. Sea Pines Dr., Hilton Head Island, SC 29928; phone (800) 955-8337 or (843) 842-1894

Tees: Championship: 6,906 yards, par-72, USGA rating 72.8, slope 133
Greens Fee: $80–95

Challenge: ★★★	Golf Facilities: ★★★½
Variety: ★★★	14-Club Test ★★★
Terrain: ★★½	Intangibles: ★★★½
Beauty/Visual Appeal: ★★★★	Value: ★★★
Pace of Play: ★★½	

Description and Comments If you must see the Atlantic Ocean while playing golf on Hilton Head, you have only two slender options. There's the par-5 10th at Palmetto Dunes's Jones course, and one other: the par-3 15th at Sea Pines's Ocean course.

Ocean was designed by George Cobb in 1960 and claims the distinction of being Hilton Head's first golf course. It's located in the heart of Sea Pines Plantation, at the geographical "toe" at the southwesternmost end of the foot-shaped Hilton Head Island. In 1995, PGA Tour player–turned-architect Mark McCumber redesigned Ocean, stretching the course some 300 yards to 6,906 from the "McCumber" tees.

What McCumber also did was retool the course's signature 15th hole, enhancing not only its playing value but also its scenery . The 15th measures 210 yards from the back tee. McCumber raised the tee and lowered the green from the original design, so now when you're standing on the tee you have a wide beach and the lapping waves of the Atlantic in the background. The wide, large green at 15 is protected by two flattish bunkers on the right side. Behind the green are a couple of stubby palmettos, separated as if they were football goal posts, plus a low line of shrubbery. Thus, along with ocean views, you get ocean breezes. No matter how many great holes you've seen or played, this stirring one-shotter will linger long in your memory.

Naturally, the rest of the course can't come close to measuring up to the 15th hole. Conditioning isn't as consistently good as it should be for a course with this price tag; many holes are only ordinary in design, and pace of play can be on the slow side. Still, the finish is excellent. The 17th is a brutal par-4, 455 yards from the tips with water left and right and 18 is a big 560-yard par-5, with water all the way up the right-hand side and bunkers throughout.

The Ocean Course at Sea Pines is certainly a pleasant track, with palms, pines, live oaks, and lagoons, but hardly spectacular—with one glorious exception.

Sea Pines Plantation, Sea Marsh Course

100 N. Sea Pines Dr., Hilton Head Island, SC 29928; phone (800) 955-8337 or (843) 842-1894

Tees: Championship: 6,515 yards, par-72, USGA rating 70.0, slope 120

Greens Fee: $70–95

Challenge: ★★½	Golf Facilities: ★★★½
Variety: ★★½	14-Club Test ★★½
Terrain: ★★½	Intangibles: ★★★
Beauty/Visual Appeal: ★★★½	Value: ★★½
Pace of Play: ★★★	

Description and Comments   Sea Marsh is Hilton Head's second oldest course, dating to 1966. Although many "new kids" in the region are more dramatic, this elder statesman more than holds its own in the enjoyment department.

Of the three public-access courses in Sea Pines (Harbour Town and Ocean are the others), Sea Marsh is by far the easiest, from any set of tees. Ample fairways and flattish, medium-size greens are nestled spaciously into dense stands of pines, live oaks, and palmettos. Marsh and lagoons affect play on half the holes, but because most of the holes are so modest in terms of yardage, they don't really bother anybody, except beginners and intermediates who have trouble getting the ball airborne.

Designed by George Cobb, Sea Marsh was redesigned by Clyde Johnston in 1990, who made the hazards more visible and improved bunkers, greens, and irrigation, making everything drain better after a soaking. He also tweaked a number of holes in the renovation, making them more interesting and playable.

Sea Marsh begins in unusual fashion. On paper, the 366-yard, par-4 first hole doesn't seem that difficult, but the opening tee shot must carry a vast expanse of lagoon, an intimidating prospect for many on the first shot of the day. Another intriguing hole is the ninth, a short, 505-yard par-5, which doglegs 90 degrees to the left following a perfectly placed tee shot. Any topped or sliced second shot will find water.

Sea Marsh is characterized by well-crafted, well-placed bunkers throughout, nowhere more so than at its signature hole, the 163-yard, par-3 13th. The well-bunkered green is guarded by live oaks to the side and by water short and left.

No one will ever confuse Sea Marsh with a Top 100 course. However, it's attractive and fun to play, especially for vacationers who may otherwise be a bit rusty. The late Dave Marr, former broadcaster and PGA champion, holds the course record with a 62.

Shipyard Golf Club

45 Shipyard Dr., Hilton Head, SC 29938; phone (843) 686-8802
Shipyard Golf Club features three nine-hole courses.

Brigantine/Clipper Combination

Tees: Championship: 6,818 yards, par-72, USGA rating 73.0, slope 128

Greens Fee: $60–95

Clipper/Galleon Combination

Tees: Championship: 6,830 yards, par-72, USGA rating 73.0, slope 129

Greens Fee: $60–95

Galleon/Brigantine Combination

Tees: Championship: 6,716 yards, par-72, USGA rating 72.6, slope 128

Greens Fee: $60–95

Challenge: ★★★½	Golf Facilities: ★★★★
Variety: ★★½	14-Club Test: ★★★
Terrain: ★★½	Intangibles: ★★★
Beauty/Visual Appeal: ★★★½	Value: ★★★
Pace of Play: ★★½	

Description and Comments   Close to where the "heel" and the "instep" merge on foot-shaped Hilton Head is a longtime favorite, Shipyard Golf Club. Managed by American Golf Corporation, the club's three nine-hole courses—Galleon, Brigantine, and Clipper—weave through a multitude of magnolias, pines, and oaks, with liberal splashes of sand and water thrown in for good measure.

Shipyard fits the bill for a typical American Golf property in that every aspect of the golf experience will be satisfactory—from snack bar food to course maintenance—but seldom is any one aspect outstanding. Always, however, Shipyard is pleasing to the eye.

There's a very lush, mature feel to Shipyard, principally because two of the nines, Galleon and Clipper, date back to the late 1960s. Stately pines; gnarled, mossy live oaks; quiet lagoons; and pockets of wildflowers are everywhere. Homes and villas are everywhere as well, but they're not as obtrusive as many other developments in the Low Country. Occasionally the course touches busy Highway 278, but mostly you're in for a secluded nature walk. By the way, watch where you walk—seriously—as Shipyard is home to an abundance of alligators.

Shipyard suffers from a certain sameness in look because nearly all of the 27 holes are sidewalk-flat, laced with lagoons, and carved from the same tall timber. Thus, most of the holes are pleasant and scenic, if not memorable. What is memorable are the club's excellent pro shop, practice facility, and learning center.

Try to avoid Shipyard after a good rain, as its flat fairways are 30 years old and were not built on sandy subsoil, so drainage is often poor. Also try to avoid the Brigantine nine, which was added in 1985 by Willard Byrd. It's too tight, with too many water hazards for the average golfer. You could easily lose nine balls in nine holes.

The Senior PGA Tour pros played here from 1982 through 1984 over the Galleon/Clipper combo. Among their favorite holes were Galleon's second, a short, classic risk/reward par-5 that doglegs left, with water and sand everywhere, and Clipper's fourth, a 178-yard par-3 that calls for a mid-iron over a lagoon to a green protected by four bunkers.

Lodging

To say that Hilton Head offers a diversity of accommodations is an understatement. Visitors to the island can choose from hotels at all price levels, motels, vacation-ownership resorts, private homes, villas, and condos. A collection of the "best of the best" follows, but first a word of caution: Availability and prices will be at a premium during the Family Circle Cup tennis tournament (late March/early April) and the MCI Classic PGA Tour golf event (mid-April). The island is certainly filled with a lot of energy during these events, but you will need to book early during these periods, or you may want to avoid them altogether if you prefer avoiding the crowds.

EXPENSIVE

Hilton Oceanfront Resort

23 Ocean Lane, P.O. Box 6154, Hilton Head Island, SC 29938; phone (843) 842-8000 or (800) 845-8001; www.hiltonheadhilton.com; Rates: $135–240

The Hilton Oceanfront is located within the Palmetto Dunes development and is accessible only via a security gate. This separation results in less traffic (both car and sight-seer) than many of the other major hotels on the island. The added tranquility provides guests with an increased sense of relaxation and a feeling that they are almost on an island within an island.

There are 324 rooms at the resort, including 32 suites, all of which are attractively furnished (part of a recently completed $5.5 million renovation) and offer close proximity to beaches and golf. Each room includes a kitchenette, dining and living areas, as well as a private balcony. All guests will have access to health club, kid's camp and childcare, concierge services, and complimentary shuttle within Palmetto Dunes to and from Shelter Cove Harbour, a waterside plaza with an assortment of shops and restaurants. The grounds at the Hilton are magnificently landscaped, and guests will find almost every sports activity imaginable just a gimmie putt away, including tennis, lawn games, a gym, a sauna, boating, and fishing.

Golf Packages There are two golf packages offered through the Hilton: the Value Golf Package and the Deluxe Golf Package, with play allowed on the following island courses: Island West, Old Carolina, Old South, Rose

Hill, Okatie Creek, Oyster Reef, Eagle's Point, Arthur Hills at Palmetto Dunes (surcharges required), George Fazio, Robert Trent Jones, Robert Cupp, Arthur Hills at Palmetto Hall, Shipyard Golf Club, Planter's Row, Barony, Robber's Row, Golden Bear at Indigo Run, and Country Club of Hilton Head.

Hyatt Regency Hilton Head

1 Hyatt Circle, Hilton Head, SC 29928; phone (800) 554-9288 or (843) 785-1234; www.hyatthiltonhead.com; Rates: $200–285

The Hyatt Regency was the first landmark hotel built on Hilton Head and thus became the benchmark for all other developments that followed. As soon as you enter the hotel, you will surely agree that the competition had a lot to live up to. Once again, Hyatt built a lobby that takes your breath away as soon as you enter, reminding you (if you hadn't realized yet) that you are on vacation and have arrived in a special place.

The Hyatt is also located in Palmetto Dunes, although you do not have to go through a security gate to get there. There are over 450 rooms at the Hyatt, each with a private balcony and top-drawer amenities. When making reservations, request a top-floor room so you can get the superior view.

As nice as the rooms are, what waits outside is also spectacular. There are five championship golf courses at Palmetto Dunes; three miles of pristine beach (many say the best beach on the island); 25 world-class tennis courts (six lit for night play); Camp Hyatt for the young ones; a magnificent health spa with whirlpool, sauna, and massage therapist; and indoor and outdoor pools. As if that were not enough, the Hyatt is located near Shelter Cove Marina, so there is also easy access to sport fishing, boat trips, and yachting.

Golf Packages The Hyatt golf package includes accommodations with a private balcony, $10 food and beverage coupon per day, guaranteed tee times each day at one of Palmetto's five courses, shared golf cart for each round, turndown service on request, and access to Hyatt Spa health club. Note: There is an additional surcharge for Arthur Hills courses at both Palmetto Dunes and Palmetto Hall.

Sea Pines

32 Greenwood Dr., Hilton Head Island, SC 29928; phone (800) 732-7463 or (843) 785-3333; www.seapines.com; Rates: $145–300

When you mention Hilton Head to most people, the first image that pops into their minds is the Harbour Town Lighthouse. This lighthouse is the focal point of the Sea Pines Plantation, a 5,000-acre development located at the southern tip of Hilton Head. Sea Pines was America's first master planned community, and the developers got it right from the start.

Sea Pines is the location of the signature golf course on the Island, the Harbour Town Golf Links, site of the MCI Classic—The Heritage of Golf.

In addition, there are two other courses at Sea Pines, Sea Marsh and Ocean. But golf is just one of the activities available to you here. You will also find more than 80 tennis courts (Sea Pines is the site of the Family Circle Cup professional women's tennis tournament), two major harbors, and a 600-acre forest preserve.

Sea Pines offers a wide variety of accommodation options. You can choose from a home or a villa, each with one to six bedrooms and ocean, fairway, Harbour Town Lighthouse, or lagoon views. All vacation homes require a one-week stay in all seasons, with the exception of some homes in the Harbour Town area. Generally, most homes rent Saturday to Saturday; between November and March, many homes are available on a monthly basis.

By booking through Sea Pines, guests will receive complimentary tennis, preferred tee times, reduced greens fees, pool and charging privileges, and discounted rates for bike rentals. In addition, resort guests also have access to the Sea Pines Beach Club.

Golf Packages　Sea Pines' "Best of Southern Golf" package includes private villa accommodations, one round at Harbour Town Golf Links, one round at Sea Marsh or Ocean Course (or both), and one round per day at one of the following: Hilton Head National, Country Club of Hilton Head, Old South, Golden Bear at Indigo Run, Robber's Row, Planter's Row, Barony, Oyster Reef, Island West, Eagle's Pointe, Old Carolina, and Shipyard.

Palmetto Dunes Resort

4 Queens Folly Rd., Hilton Head Island, SC 29928; phone (800) 845-6130 or (843) 785-1161; www.palmettodunesresort.com; Rates: $125–440

Palmetto Dunes is a 2,000-acre oceanfront development located on the east side of the island. The resort is one of the more tasteful on Hilton Head, as there is a strict architectural review board that oversees the design and building of the villas and homes within the development. In addition to 450 "architecturally endorsed" villas and homes, there is also three miles of beach, three golf courses, a 25-court tennis facility, and 30 swimming pools. The villas and homes vary in size from one to six bedrooms, and all are nicely equipped with a full kitchen, living room, dining area, balcony, and patios. The resort has a distinct "beachy" feel, but don't be fooled—despite the proximity to the beach, very few of the homes are located right on the water. Rather, the majority are tucked within dense forest, which provides a canopy feel. Don't get us wrong—this resort is one of Hilton Head's best, but if you are expecting to be lulled to sleep by the waves of the ocean, you will have to bring along a CD to play in the stereo system.

Golf Package   Golf packages are available at more than 20 area courses. These packages are very flexible and will be customized based on the number of golfers, accommodations selected, courses selected, and number of rounds planned. Your best bet is to contact the resort directly; they can develop more accurate costs for you.

The Westin Resort

2 Grasslawn Ave., Hilton Head Island, SC 29928; phone (800) 228-3000 or (843) 681-4000; www.westin.com; Rates: $250–350

The Westin is the island's most luxurious hotel. This newly renovated, 24-acre oceanfront resort is located within Port Royal Plantation and combines the feel of old-fashioned Southern hospitality with modern amenities. The hotel itself is five stories tall and was built in a U-shape, which provides for striking ocean views from its rooms.

The hotel features standard rooms and suites as well as two- and three-bedroom villas. All of the hotel rooms have private balconies; there are six different floor plans to choose from for the suites. What's on the inside is only half of the story, as the Westin also has an amazing array of fun and games. There are three award-winning golf courses; a top tennis facility with three different grand-slam surfaces; a fitness center with massage, personal trainer, and spa treatments; bike paths; volleyball; kayaking; and sailing. To sum up, the hotel has it all. If you can afford the higher price tag, you can't miss with the Westin.

Golf Packages   The Westin golf package includes: guest room with private balcony; 18 holes of golf daily at many of Hilton Head's golf courses with a shared golf cart, range balls daily, golf bag, and club storage at the hotel; golf gift on arrival; daily buffet breakfast at the Carolina Café; access to the fitness center, including the sauna, steam room, whirlpool, and indoor pool; and free Hilton Head airport and resort shuttle.

There are many great resorts in close proximity to Hilton Head that would be a great addition/supplement to your vacation. Here are two that we recommend you consider.

Daufuskie Island Club and Resort

1 Seabrook Dr., Hilton Head Island, SC 29926; phone (800) 648-6778 or (843) 842-2000; ww.daufuskieresort.com; Rates: $150–260 (room), $270–500 (two-bedroom cottage)

Daufuskie Island is a barrier island that lies one mile off the coast of Hilton Head. Accessible only via a short boat ride from Hilton Head, Daufuskie Resort offers a wonderful opportunity to escape into an isolated world of golf and relaxation.

Visitors to the resort can choose from one of the well-appointed rooms (most with ocean views) in the Melrose Inn or from one of the cottages on the property. The cottages range from two to four bedrooms and include a living room, dining room, full kitchen, washer/dryer, and a porch with ocean or marsh views.

The island boasts many activities that can keep you quite busy. There are two championship golf courses, horseback riding, tennis at the Stan Smith Tennis Center, oceanside swimming pools, lawn games including croquet, a pitch-and-putt course, fishing, and a fitness center.

Golf Packages Packages include premium accommodations, unlimited ferry passage, one round of golf per night including cart, and bellman, housekeeping, and golf gratuities.

Fripp Island Resort

One Tarpon Blvd., Fripp Island, SC 29920; phone (800) 845-4100; www.frippislandresort.com; Rates $130–900

Fripp Island is an oceanfront resort located 55 miles north of Hilton Head. The island boasts a variety of activities, including three golf courses, a 10-court tennis complex, an extensive teen and children's program, volleyball, fitness center, and boat rentals.

On the accommodation side, Fripp has a variety of villa and patio homes strewn throughout the island in a variety of settings. Each villa comes with a fully stocked kitchen.

Golf Packages Package is valid during sports season only and includes the following: lodging in a three-bedroom villa, guaranteed tee times booked in advance, 18 holes of golf per day with cart, daily choice of breakfast or lunch, free bag of range balls daily, and daily maid service. Call Fripp directly to determine rates.

MODERATE

Holiday Inn Oceanfront Resort

1 South Forest Beach Dr., Hilton Head Island, SC 29928; phone (800) 423-9897 or (843) 785-5126; Rates: $160–230

Located on the beach, Holiday Inn Oceanfront is an affordable yet notable hotel. It is located directly on the beach and offers spacious, contemporary designed rooms. A great place for kids with the "kids stay and eat free" program—there is a Pizza Hut, ice cream parlor, and gift shop on property.

Golf Packages Holiday Inn's golf package includes guaranteed tee times, greens fees, cart, and taxes at more than 23 golf courses; welcome golf survival kit; "Sunrise 7" daily breakfast in Grouper's Restaurant; and complimentary drink coupon on arrival.

Residence Inn by Marriott

12 Park Lane, Hilton Head Island, SC 29928; phone (800) 331-3131 or (843) 686-5700; www.marriott.com; Rates: $140–170

The Residence Inn is ideal for families, as all of the 156 rooms are suites with fully equipped kitchens, balconies, and some even have fireplaces. There is also a heated pool and hot tub, lighted tennis courts, and a complimentary beach shuttle.

Golf Packages The golf package includes 18 holes of golf and cart daily, access to 20 golf courses on Hilton Head, guaranteed tee times, deluxe continental breakfast daily, and a welcome gift on arrival.

Condos, Homes, and Villas

There are more than 40 companies that handle home and villa rentals on Hilton Head Island. The accommodations range in size and location, and many offer golf packages. Your best bet is to contact the agency, lay down your parameters, and let them do the work.

Adventure Inn Villa Rentals (800) 662-7061
Beach Properties of Hilton Head (800) 671-5155
Fiddler's Cove (800) 321-1611
Hilton Head Condo Hotline (800) 258-5852
Hilton Head Discount Rentals (800) 445-8664
Hilton Head Vacation Rentals (800) 732-7671
Prestige Vacation Rentals (800) 633-4461
Shoreline Rentals (800) 334-5012
Vacations on Hilton Head (800) 232-2463
Vacation Villa Rentals (877) 445-8664

INEXPENSIVE

Comfort Inn

2 Tanglewood Dr., Hilton Head Island, SC 29928; phone (800) 228-5150 or (843) 842-6662; www.comfortinn.com; Built: 1987; Renovated: 1999; Rates: $60–150

Fairfield Inn

9 Marina Side Dr., Hilton Head Island, SC 29928; phone (800) 833-6334 or (843) 842-4800; Built: 1989; Rates: $70–90

Hampton Inn

1 Dillon Rd.; Hilton Head Island, SC 29928; phone (800) HAMPTON or (843) 681-7900; www.hampton-inn.com; Built: 1990; Renovated: 1999; Rates: $80–100

Dining

Alexanders 76 Queens Folly Rd.; phone (843) 785-4999. Continental; Expensive; Reservations suggested. Located in Palmetto Dunes, this restaurant has a strong menu and beautiful views of the adjacent lagoon.

Brians 1301 Main Street Village; phone (843) 681-6001. French/American; Expensive; Reservations suggested. Varied menu—check out the wild mushroom–crusted rack of lamb.

Brick Oven Café Park Plaza, Unit 224; phone (843) 686-2233. American; Inexpensive; Reservations suggested. Great food and fun setting—decorations are very 1940s and the Velvet Room features live music Monday though Sunday.

CQ's 140 Lighthouse Rd., Harbour Town; phone (843) 671-2779. American; Moderate–Expensive; Reservations suggested. Delightful restaurant offering a splendid menu and setting.

Café Europa next to the Harbour Town Lighthouse; phone (843) 671-3399. Seafood; Expensive; Reservations recommended. Setting and view can't be beat—good wine list.

Café at Wexford Village at Wexford; phone (843) 686-5969. French; Expensive; Reservations suggested. Romantic atmosphere—favorite among islanders.

Crabby Nick's Highway 278, Mid-Island; phone (843) 842-2325 Seafood; Moderate; Reservations suggested. Casual, family-style restaurant serving large portions.

Di Vino 5 Northridge Plaza; phone (843) 681-7700. North Central Italian; Expensive; Reservations recommended. Intimate—only 14 tables—this restaurant has a well-deserved reputation along with a nice selection of Italian wines.

Fitzgeralds 41 S. Forest Beach Dr.; phone (843) 785-5151. Continental; Expensive; Reservations suggested for parties of five or more. Family-owned and operated—classic seafood menu.

Harbourmasters 1 Shelter Cove Lane; phone (843) 785-3030. Continental; Moderate; Reservations suggested. Make sure to arrive early so you can take in the beautiful views. Try the blackened tuna.

Hemingway's located in the Hyatt Regency; phone (843) 785-1234. American; Expensive; Reservations suggested. Great variety of seafood. Overlooks Hyatt's wonderful gardens and the Atlantic Ocean.

Hilton Head Brewing Company Hilton Head Plaza; phone (843) 785-2739. American; Moderate; Reservations not necessary. Tasty appetizers, sandwiches, and seafood dishes. Microbrewery on premises.

Hilton Head Diner Hwy. 278 at Yacht Cove Drive; phone (843) 686-2400. American; Inexpensive–Moderate; Reservations not necessary. Open 24 hours a day, this super-popular diner offers a wide variety of menu items in a fun and casual atmosphere. Expect a wait during mid-mornings on weekends. Take-out available.

The Kingfisher 18 Harbourside Lane; phone (843) 785-4442. Seafood; Moderate; Reservations suggested. Memorable views of Shelter Cove Harbor; specialties include fish and Black Angus steak.

Kurama 9 Palmetto Bay Rd.; phone (843) 785-4955. Japanese/Sushi; Moderate–Expensive; Reservations accepted. This ranks up there as one of the best sushi restaurants we have ever encountered anywhere. Each dish was delightful. If you like sushi, don't miss this restaurant.

Little Venice Shelter Cove; phone (843) 785-3300. Italian; Expensive; Reservations suggested. A wide selection of Italian favorites served overlooking the Shelter Cove Harbour. Outside seating available.

Primo Orleans Plaza; phone (843) 785-2343. Seafood; Moderate–Expensive; Reservations suggested. Zesty pasta and seafood; casual yet refined atmosphere.

Spartina Grill 70 Marshland Rd.; phone (843) 689-2433. American; Inexpensive–Moderate; No reservations necessary. Restaurant offers "little plates" to encourage you to try a bunch of menu items.

Two Eleven Park 211 Park; phone (843) 686-5212. American; Moderate–Expensive; Reservations accepted. Menu combines American, Southern, and Italian items. More than 75 wines available by the glass and in excess of 200 by the bottle. Salud!

W. G. Shucker's Palmetto Bay Marina; phone (843) 785-8050. Seafood; Moderate; Reservations suggested. Eye-catching views of Palmetto Bay Marina. Raw oysters the specialty; crab races on Wednesday.

Activities On the Island

Bike Rentals Hilton Head Bicycle Company, phone (843) 686-6888; Harbour Town Bikes, phone (843) 785-3546; South Beach Cycles, phone (843) 671-2453.

Boat Rentals Island Water Sports, phone (843) 671-7007 or (843) 842-8181. Powerboat, parasailing, waverunners, water-skiing, and sailing.

Boat Cruises Adventure Cruises, phone (843) 785-4558. Sight-seeing, Daufuskie Island Ferry, dinner cruises (in season), deep-sea fishing, sunset cruises, dolphin-watch tours.

Fishing Palmetto Bay Marina, phone (843) 842-7433. Half-day charters.

Horseback Riding Happy Trails Stable, phone (843) 842-7433; Lawton Stables, phone (843) 671-2586. Rides through pristine landscape, including horseback-only areas.

In-Line Skate Rentals Outside Hilton Head, phone (843) 671-2643 or (843) 686-6996.

Driving Range; Miniature Golf Island Putt & Drive, phone (843) 686-3355. Hilton Head's only lit driving range, video games, miniature golf, and batting cages. Pirate's Island Adventure Golf, phone (843) 686-4001.

Kayak Rentals/Nature Tours Adventure Kayak Tours, phone (843) 816-5686. Closely observe dolphins, otter, ospreys, and other wildlife with an interpretive naturalist.

Windsurfing Outside Hilton Head, phone (843) 671-2643 or (843) 686-6996.

Activities Off the Island

Beaufort

Located 40 miles north of Hilton Head, Beaufort (pronounced BYEW-fort) is South Carolina's second oldest town, founded in 1710. Visitors will find wonderful Antebellum architecture as many of the town's 18th- and 19th-century homes remain. If you are a history buff (and even if you are not), this town is worth a stop on your tour as it's great example of the Old South. While there, check out:

Beaufort Museum 703 Craven St., Beaufort; phone (843) 525-7077. Displays of Native American pottery, antiques, and Civil War exhibits.

John Mark Verdier House Museum 801 Bay St., Beaufort; phone (843) 524-6334. This house was the headquarters for Union forces during the Civil War and is now restored and furnished as if you were arriving in 1790. Open Tuesday–Sunday.

The 19th Hole

Callahan's Sports Bar & Deluxe Grill 49 New Orleans Rd.; phone (843) 686-7665. This is the one of two places on the island to watch sports. Multiple pool tables and traditional pub games, such as darts.

Caseys 37 New Orleans Rd.; phone (843) 785-2255. This is the other place on the island to watch sports—check out the great sports memorabilia.

Harbour Town Grill 11 Lighthouse Lane; phone (843) 842-8484. The place to grab you're first cold one and toast your round at Harbour Town, which sits adjacent.

Monkey Business Park Plaza; phone (843) 686-3545. Dance nightclub for the younger set.

Quarterdeck Restaurant Sea Pines; phone (843) 671-2222. Sensational setting underneath the famed Harbour Town Lighthouse.

Regatta 23 Ocean Lane; phone (843) 842-8000. Located in the Hilton; live music nightly.

Reilley's Hilton Head Plaza at Sea Pines Circle; phone (843) 842-4414; Port Royal Plaza; phone (843) 681-4153. Solid menu and warm atmosphere. Perfect lunchtime spot, too.

Signals 130 Shipyard Dr.; phone (843) 842-2400. Nightly entertainment at the Westin Hotel.

Part Five

Myrtle Beach,
South Carolina

Overview

If it hadn't snowed one year in Pinehurst, it's hard to say where Myrtle Beach and the famous Grand Strand might be today.

Back in the early 1960s, when a freak snowstorm hit Pinehurst, North Carolina, a group of vacationing golfers panicked and started calling towns south of Pinehurst to determine where the snow belt ended and who might have a golf course open and would let them play it.

The snowstorm had missed Myrtle Beach, South Carolina, which is located just below the North Carolina border. Someone from the mayor's office or the chamber of commerce—the story gets fuzzy after years of telling—said to come on, that the hotels were empty and there would be no problem getting the group on the handful of courses in the city.

Myrtle Beach was then a summer resort. Families came for the beaches, and teenagers came to cruise the streets, dance the shag, and tip soda pop machines over into swimming pools. From Memorial Day to Labor Day, it would be so packed that you'd have to bribe someone to get a room. But, after Labor Day, when school started and the summer beach crowd took off, you could fire a cannon down the main street on a Saturday night and probably not hit anyone.

To make a long story slightly shorter, the Pinehurst group came down in a chartered bus, stayed several days, and played the three or four courses around Myrtle Beach. They had a great time and the price was right, so they came back again the next year and brought more people with them. And they returned the year after that and brought even more people.

Right about in the middle of all that, a few city fathers saw the gold glittering in the rough and realized that catering to golfers would be a way to stretch the season. They built a few more courses and began to advertise nationally. More people came, more people followed, and it wasn't long before the summer season had been stretched to include a pretty lively

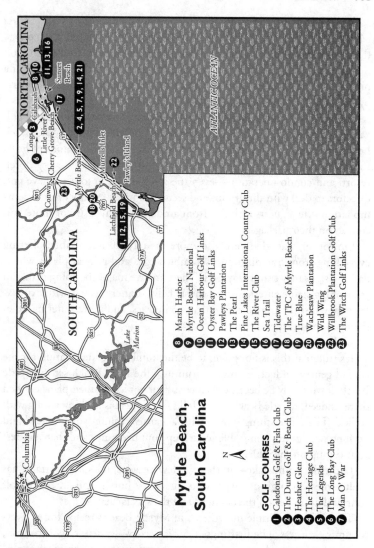

spring and fall business as well. And it wasn't long after that when the snow-birds started coming for extended stays in the winter.

Today, there are well over 100 courses in the vicinity of the 60-mile stretch of coastline that the chamber of commerce marketeers named "the Grand Strand." Officially, the Grand Strand, still referred to by the generic term of "Myrtle Beach," begins in Georgetown, South Carolina, and ends in Southport, North Carolina.

The Grand Strand has its share of detractors, and deservedly so. As Myrtle Beach and the towns around it blossomed from the influx of golfers, there weren't adequate zoning laws to govern the growth. As a result, you might find a T-shirt shop or a tattoo parlor next door to a snazzy hotel or a nice resort. In fact, some people like to refer to the Grand Strand as "Kmart-by-the-Sea."

But make no mistake about it: Myrtle Beach is *the* most successful golf vacation destination in the world. In the past decade alone, Myrtle Beach has grown nearly 25 miles north *and* south. There are thousands of hotel rooms, resort villas, and rental condominiums, and nearly every hotel, resort, and condo operation—even the mom-and-pop joints—have golf directors to deal with the groups and secure tee times. Nearly every accommodation offers guests a choice from among as many as 60 or more golf courses on their packages.

On top of that, there are also more than 1,500 restaurants, offering everything from fine dining to scrambled eggs and grits at places whose flashing signs may simply say EAT. There are five major shopping malls, an array of big-name entertainment music halls, dinner theaters with extravagant shows, sprawling entertainment complexes, and more watering holes than you might care to remember.

All because it snowed one winter in Pinehurst.

It's true that this is not going to be the number-one destination for the landed gentry. In fact, if you ever run into the Palm Beach set in Myrtle Beach, it will likely be because their chauffeur got lost or their plane crashed there. Indeed, Myrtle Beach is for "folks," and there is nothing wrong with "folks." There is nothing wrong with a waitress calling you "Sugah" and nothing wrong with being able to kick up your heels now and then and rest your feet up on the table.

But make no mistake—in the past few decades, the Grand Strand has built some very high-quality resorts, first-class hotels, and a bevy of golf courses that border on the fabulous and the spectacular.

There are two simple ingredients in Myrtle Beach's recipe for its overwhelming success. The first ingredient is *variety*—variety of golf courses, variety of accommodations, variety of restaurants, and variety of entertainment choices. The second ingredient is the contrast between the high season for the hotels and the high season for the golf courses. In the summers, when the hotel rates are at their highest, the golf courses are practically begging people to play. In the spring and fall, when golf is in great demand and is a high-ticket item, the hotels are offering bargain rates. And in the winter, both the golf courses and the hotels are crying to be occupied.

The result of those seasonal contrasts is that nearly every hotel, resort, and villa in Myrtle Beach can offer bargain golf packages.

And though it's a fact that some people look upon all of the flashing neon, those amusement parks, the "goony golf" putt-putt courses, and the T-shirt emporiums as tacky, one thing remains as gospel. If you come to Myrtle Beach armed with a little local knowledge, you can easily find quality lodging, excellent restaurants, fun places to take the kids, a myriad of things to do at night, extremely nice beaches, and—at the very minimum— a handful of golf courses that will probably thrill you to death.

WHEN TO GO AND WHAT IT WILL COST

Yes, it's the sunny South, but it is not so far south that the weather isn't "iffy" from December through February. But with the hotels and golf courses in their lowest-rate season, you can buy a bargain vacation here in the winter. An added bonus: The traffic will be light and the best restaurants will not have waiting lists.

A winter vacation here is recommended over a summer trip. It's insufferably hot and humid in the summer. It's not bad weather if you're splashing in the ocean, but if you're on a golf course in the middle of the day with no breeze, it's miserable. On top of that, the traffic is murder with all the beach vacationers roosting here, and there will be waits at most good restaurants during prime dinner hours. If you do come in the summer, get the earliest tee times you can, then head for a pool or the beach in the afternoons.

Weather-wise, the best time for golf in Myrtle Beach is definitely spring and fall. Actually, the golf package rates are highest from about mid-March until the end of April. For example, Condotels in Surfside Beach, just south of downtown Myrtle Beach, prices its golf packages at $83 per person for four golfers in a four-bedroom condo from March 17 through April 30, as opposed to just $33 per person from November 29 to January 27. If you come in May, the weather should still be pleasant and the rates will be slightly lower than during the peak golfing season. If you visit here between Thanksgiving and Christmas, the weather is usually more predictably nice, and the rates are in low season.

Spring is usually the time when groups of male-bonding buddies—many from the Northeast and Midwest, itching to play after winter's hibernation—come here and play 36 holes a day. Fall is traditionally when couples take golf vacations here, once they've got the kids back in school.

WHAT TO BRING

If you come in the winter, take a good mix of clothing—some short-sleeve shirts, sweaters, windshirts, windbreakers, a rain suit, and a warm jacket for evening. The weather is unpredictable and can turn on you like a bad day on Wall Street.

Fall and spring days are usually pleasantly mild, but the wind can blow, especially in the spring, so it's a good idea to bring a sweater and windbreaker along. If you tee off at midday in the early spring or late fall, it may be warm when you start but chilly when you're on the finishing stretch of holes.

If your home area has a lot of flat approach areas, be forewarned that these greens are elevated and often guarded by water and deep bunkers; leave that "chipper" at home. A 60-degree wedge can turn out to be the best friend you have in your bag.

ONCE YOU'RE THERE

With more than 60 miles of hotels and resorts, the hard part is deciding where to stay. The northernmost and southernmost reaches are quieter and less crowded than Myrtle Beach proper. But because of the sheer volume, no matter where you stay, you can find hotels and courses priced up and down the scale and usually not far away. What you want to do and see and where you want to play golf should determine the area where you choose to stay.

Downtown Myrtle Beach traffic can get quite congested during the peak seasons, but downtown also offers a great variety of restaurants and night spots and puts you in a position where you can play courses far to the north and far to the south. Before you choose what golf courses you're going to play on your package, know their location. If you decide you want to play 36 holes one day (or every day), you may be hard pressed to make your tee time if you choose one course on the south end of the Strand and another on the north end. If you want to play 36 a day, schedule courses that are reasonably close to one another.

Speaking of traffic, it would be a good idea to become acquainted with the roadway called "The Bypass" (Highway 501 Bypass), which can get you to a lot of courses, restaurants, and so on, and take you around the downtown traffic and rush-hour jams.

Picking which golf courses to play can be almost as challenging as playing them. Be forewarned that most of the older courses are yawners—often flat and lacking character and imagination. There are a few exceptions, however, including the venerable Dunes Club. This Robert Trent Jones gem, which opened in 1949, is ranked among the best in the nation and is a challenge and a joy to play. Pine Lakes International, a.k.a. "The Granddaddy," is not quite the course that the Dunes Club is, but it provides an overall golfing encounter unlike most others you'll come across.

As far as lodging goes, the knock on Myrtle Beach used to be that the hotels were mostly mom-and-pop places, but that has changed dramatically, especially in the past decade. Litchfield Beach and Golf Resort, for example, offers a top-notch seaside resort in the south end of the Strand, near Pawleys Island. The accommodations in hotel rooms and villas are first-class, and the resort has three extremely good golf courses. Nearby Pawleys Plantation offers luxury accommodations in a gated community, a beach club, peace and quiet, and a highly rated Jack Nicklaus golf course.

Closer to downtown, Condotels in Surfside Beach and adjacent to Deer Track Golf Club offers dozens of golf courses on its packages, as well as condominium accommodations with hotel services (restaurant, daily maid service, etc.). The Legends, a self-contained resort located just off the Bypass, includes three Scottish links–type courses that are extremely well manicured and exciting to play. The Legends also has some very charming and upscale condos.

Kingston Plantation, on the beach in Myrtle Beach, is a very upscale resort that has deluxe villas, high-rise condominium suites, and an Embassy Suites hotel. Farther to the north, Sea Trail Plantation and Golf Resort, in Sunset Beach, North Carolina, has very nice, fully equipped villas and one of the better courses on the Grand Strand.

There are hotels, condos, villas, full-service resorts, and golf course after golf course virtually everywhere along this 60-mile golf haven. There are plenty of no-frills, "mom-and-poppers" if you're on a tight budget and a broad range of very good hotels priced in the mid-range category. The Breakers and the Swampfox, both on the beach near downtown, are moderately priced hotels that have tower suites with full kitchens and living rooms.

There is the full range of chain hotels and motels, including three Hampton Inns. Like nearly all hotels here, the Hampton Inns (one near downtown and two farther north) have golf directors to help book tee times and make sure everything runs smoothly for golf groups. What make them especially appealing (one of the strengths of this chain) is that they are consistently good, moderately priced, and include complimentary daily breakfast. The Caravelle Golf and Family Resort is a nice, moderately priced hotel that offers nothing out of the ordinary in the way of accommodations, but it is a recommended choice because it is one of only six hotels (also including The Breakers) that offer the Dunes Club on its golf packages.

All hotels here and even the self-contained resorts offer a broad choice of golf courses on their packages. Some of the best of them, however, come with a surcharge on the package. During peak golf course rate periods (primarily in the spring) those surcharges can be quite high.

There is almost every imaginable type of restaurant along the Grand Strand, all the way from Georgetown, South Carolina, to Sunset Beach, North Carolina. Murrells Inlet, near Georgetown, is well known for its seafood restaurants, and there is one area in North Myrtle Beach known as Restaurant Row. But if there is one restaurant, one dining experience, that really captures the spirit of golf and pays homage to the game, it is The Old Pro's Table in North Myrtle Beach. The steak and seafood is terrific, but the atmosphere makes it a standout. Owner Joe Hackler has a magnificent collection of antique golf clubs and golf memorabilia, some of which is on display in the restaurant, including antique clubs and balls, a large library of golf books, and framed golf magazine covers and golfing scenes covering the walls. In the same vicinity is a Sam Snead's restaurant, which is worth a stop if for no other reason than to see all of the Sam Snead memorabilia and old photos on the walls.

One intangible about Myrtle Beach that proves enticing to a golfer, besides all the variety of golf courses, is that the golfer is king here and is treated like one. In Myrtle Beach, they know exactly who brings the butter to their bread.

GATHERING INFORMATION

The best source of information for the Grand Strand is a group called Myrtle Beach Golf Holiday, which is the marketing arm of nearly 100 courses, hotels, and resorts. The group publishes a pretty comprehensive guide that you can order for free, but be forewarned that because the courses and hotels pay the organization, their guide does not comment on quality or lack thereof. However, we do that for you in the following section.

The Myrtle Beach Convention and Visitors Bureau should be able to provide you with any specific information that Myrtle Beach Golf Holiday may not have.

Myrtle Beach Golf Holiday
Phone (800) 845-4653

Myrtle Beach Convention and Visitors Bureau
1200 N. Oak St., P.O. Box 2115, Myrtle Beach, SC 29578
Phone (800) 356-3016 or (843) 236-6152
www.myrtlebeachlive.com

The Major Courses

If there is one course to avoid, it's a course called Wicked Stick in Myrtle Beach. Clyde Johnston has designed a lot of good courses, but this is not one of them. John Daly consulted with him, and perhaps it was Daly's British Open win that made them try to force so much Scotland into South Carolina. The layout is erratic and amateurish, and it isn't much fun to play. Insider tip: Don't play it.

Caledonia Golf and Fish Club

369 Caledonia Dr., Pawleys Island, SC 29585; phone (843) 237-3675
How to Get On: Tee times can be made through various hotel packages or on a daily fee basis, one year in advance.
Tees:

   Pintail: 6,526 yards, par-70, USGA rating 70.9, slope 132
   Mallard: 6,121 yards, par-70, USGA rating 68.8, slope 122

Wood Duck: 5,710 yards, par-70, USGA rating 66.7, slope 114

Redhead: 4,957 yards, par-70, USGA rating 68.2, slope 113

Challenge: ★★★½	Golf Facilities: ★★★★
Variety: ★★★★	Whole Bag Test: ★★★
Terrain: ★★★★	Intangibles: ★★★★
Beauty/Visual Appeal: ★★★★	Value: ★★★★
Pace of Play: ★★★½	

Just the Facts   Year Opened: 1994; Course Designers: Mike Strantz and Forest Fezler; Walking: No; Greens Fee: $70–130; 9 Hole/Twilight Rate: No; Pull Carts: No; Practice Range: Yes; Club Rental: Yes.

Description and Comments   All major golf publications have golf course ranking systems and special awards that recognize courses in the private, public, and resort categories. Caldedonia Golf and Fish Club has drawn praise and high rankings from nearly all of them as well as from the golfers who have had the pleasure to play it ever since it opened in 1994. And the awards keep coming in.

Designed by Tom Fazio protégé Mike Strantz, who was assisted by 1970s PGA Tour notable Forest Fezler, this course, laid out along the Waccamaw River, is gorgeous. Strantz did a great job, especially when you consider that he only had 125 acres to work with. This Pawleys Island beauty, located south of Myrtle Beach, was built on the site of a former rice plantation of the same name (Caledonia was the Roman name for Scotland).

The course itself meanders along lakes, streams, and stands of hardwood trees and imposing old live oaks. The big trees come into play on several holes, and there is a lot of water; yet this isn't one of those killers that is likely to chop you up and have you for lunch. But because there is so much water and so many waste bunkers, it does require careful club selection and straight hitting if you're going to score well. Water comes into play on nine holes, and the waste bunkers can be quite intimidating.

The interior holes—from the 7th through the 14th—are especially beautiful, and all the way around you are likely to see a lot of pretty flowers and plants and all sorts of wildlife, from whitetail deer to ducks, doves, and quail. Accordingly, the four sets of tees are named after indigenous birds—Pintail, Mallard, Wood Duck, and Redhead.

Though the course isn't long (6,500 yards from the back tees, down to 4,950 from the women's tees) the length, or lack of it, is deceptive, since par is only 70. Two of the holes were selected by a local newspaper to the Grand Strand's "Dream 18." One of those holes is number 11, a sneaky par-3 that is only 156 yards from the back tee, but the long, narrow green is protected by a big lagoon that guards both its entire left side and front edge.

The back nine is longer and tougher than the front and includes a long, memorable dogleg par-5 in which a waste bunker runs down the right side from nearly 200 yards, all the way up to the green. The approach shot is particularly difficult because the waste bunker on the right tends to make a player want to steer the shot left to avoid it, but, anticipating that, Strantz placed two bunkers to protect the left side of the green.

This is a surcharge course and extremely popular. Nearly everybody has heard about it and wants to play it, and they include it in their golf package. Because the course is offered by dozens of hotels, it's best to put this one in the starting line-up as soon as you book your trip. By unanimous acclaim, it's a Myrtle Beach "must play."

Insider Tips   The monstrous dogleg-left 15th hole, at 462 yards from the tips, is tough enough even when you know how to play it. The large bunker on the left-hand side is intimidating and you may tend to steer away from it. But to have a chance for par on this hole, or even birdie, you need to drive the ball as far toward that left bunker as you can, without going at it, so you can have a decent shot at the hole and a chance to get home in two.

The par-3s here have very deep greens, so you should pay very careful attention to the pin placements so that you don't select the wrong club and guarantee yourself a three putt.

The Dunes Golf and Beach Club

9000 North Ocean Blvd., Myrtle Beach, SC 29572; phone (843) 449-5914
How to Get On: This great old club, otherwise private, is open to guests of six member hotels: The Breakers, The Caravelle, The Caribbean, The Driftwood-on-the-Ocean, South Wind Villas, and Dunes Village.
Tees:

Gold: 7,015 yards, par-72, USGA rating 75.4, slope 141

Blue: 6,417 yards, par-72, USGA rating 72.1, slope 132

White: 6,010 yards, par-72, USGA rating 69.7, slope 121

Forward: 5,243 yards, par-72, USGA rating 72.3, slope 132

Challenge: ★★★★½	Golf Facilities: ★★★½
Variety: ★★★★	14-Club Test: ★★★★½
Terrain: ★★★½	Intangibles: ★★★★
Beauty/Visual Appeal: ★★★★	Value: ★★★½
Pace of Play: ★★★★	

Just the Facts   Year Opened: 1949; Course Designer: Robert Trent Jones Sr.; Walking: No; Greens Fee: $80–135 (surcharge course on packages with the six hotels mentioned above); 9 Hole/Twilight Rate: No; Pull Carts: No; Practice Range: Yes; Club Rental: Yes.

Description and Comments   As the slope and course rating indicate, this is a real test, right from the get-go, the long, narrow, par-4 first hole, which requires a tee shot over water and demands an approach to a severely contoured green protected by deep bunkers.

What makes the Dunes Club especially delightful to play is that it is truly a fair test for all skill levels. This was no accident—Jones planned it and designed it that way. This is a course that rewards the successful gambler, but always offers a way out for those who want to play conservatively. For example, short hitters do not have to get their brains beat in, but they do have to use their heads, play strategically, and figure out the alternate routes that Jones carved out.

The design provides a great mix of holes, from straight-away, "pound it" holes and short holes requiring strategically placed drives, to savage monsters like the par-5 13th, called "Waterloo," which plays 590 yards from the back tee, doglegs severely (110 degrees) from left to right, and has a lake that breathes down your neck down the entire right side.

Numbers 10 through 13 are known as "Alligator Alley." This stretch can make or break a golfer's round. From all the way back, they are, in order, a tricky and treacherous 380-yard par-4 that requires a gutsy approach shot over a lagoon, with water also on the left; a dogleg right, 430-yard par-4 where water threatens the approach shot and looms behind the green; a 245-yard par-3 with a sloping green and water all along the right side; and that dogleg, 590-yard par-5 with the lake that looms from tee to green down the right side. The three other sets of tees are a little tamer, but these holes are no less intimidating. However—and here again is the genius of Jones's masterful design—he leaves a lot of bail-out areas and lay-up options for golfers whose games might not be so stout as to let it all out on these holes.

The difficulty of the holes themselves isn't all that makes this course such a formidable opponent and so interesting to play. The greens, most of them elevated, provide a tremendous variety of forward slopes, backward slopes, elevations, and undulations. Ultimately, this is a fair course where you are rewarded for a good shot.

Insider Tips   Play within yourself and don't take chances unless you know you can make the shots. Laying up, finding bail-out areas, or hitting a fairway wood or an iron off the tee on the narrowest holes allows you to avoid big numbers and, as they say, live to fight another day. On some of the tough holes, it may be wiser to play with the conservatism of Hogan than the unbridled fury of Palmer.

Another tip is to avoid an early morning tee time, when the dew and the water from the sprinkling system the night before are still on the fairways. The rolling fairways don't allow the ball to roll a long way even when they are dry—and almost not at all when they are wet. Nearly all of the greens are elevated, so you'll need an extra club into most holes, even on the driest day. The Dunes Club has hosted many important tournaments, including the U.S. Women's Open and the past seven Senior PGA

Tour Championships, and boasts a tremendous classic design. It's worth staying in one of the six member hotels at least once just to be able to play this storied course.

Heather Glen

Highway 17, Little River, SC 29568; phone (843) 249-9000

How to Get On: Tee times can be made via packages with various hotels or on a daily fee basis, up to a year in advance.

Tees:

> Blue: 6,769 yards, par-72, USGA rating 72.0, slope 130
>
> White: 6,310 yards, par-72, USGA rating 70.3, slope 123
>
> Red: 5,052 yards, par-72, USGA rating 69.0, slope 118

Third Nine Tees:

> Blue: 3,405 yards, par-36
>
> White: 3,183 yards, par-36
>
> Red: 2,517 yards, par-36

Challenge: ★★★½	Golf Facilities: ★★★★
Variety: ★★★★	14-Club Test: ★★★½
Terrain: ★★★½	Intangibles: ★★★½
Beauty/Visual Appeal: ★★★★	Value: ★★★½
Pace of Play: ★★★½	

Just the Facts Year Opened: 1987; Course Designers: Willard Byrd and Clyde Johnston; Walking: No; Greens Fee: $30–85; 9 Hole/Twilight Rate: No; Pull Carts: No; Practice Range: Yes; Club Rental: Yes.

Description and Comments When Heather Glen opened in 1987, it was a major golf publication's choice as the best new public course in America. This is certainly the number one course in the northern reaches of the Grand Strand. Located in the Little River area, this course borrowed something from Pine Lakes International—men in Scottish kilts greet you in the parking lot. The replica 1800s clubhouse also has a Scottish flair in its design. Naming nearly all the holes with some sort of Scottish phrase may have been a bit much, however; in spite of the fact that somebody got a little carried away on that one, this does nothing to detract from the greatness of the course.

There are three nines here, so you have a lot of variety. If you want to play 27 holes, you don't have to leave the property or play another nine over again. The courses features a lot of hardwood trees, love grass, Scotch broom, some severe mounds, long waste bunkers, and several pot bunkers that look like moon craters.

The second nine is the most dramatic and most beautiful and is heavily accented by water and deep pot bunkers. It plays 3,400 yards from the back tees, and water comes into play on every hole on this nine with the exception of the 12th (3rd hole on the nine). If you want to play 36 here, it would be a good idea to play all three nines and then go back and play the second nine again.

Number 8 is one of the greatest and most difficult par-3s on the Grand Strand. It measures 224 yards from the back (blue) tee and 191 from the white tee. The women get a break here at 110 yards. Water comes into play from about midway to the hole, the entirety of the fairway, all the way to a green that is surrounded by bunkers.

Number 9 is a monster—447 yards from the blue tee, 407 from the white, and 309 from the red—but water only comes into play if you yank your approach shot to the right.

Number 6 provides the best opportunity for an eagle on the first two nines. From the blue tee it measures 484 yards, and 461 from the white tee. There is a modicum of trouble on the right-hand side, but if you can place your drive in the fairway and if you don't get intimidated by the long waste bunker that runs down the better part of the right side, you can knock it on in two.

The finishing hole on the second nine is perhaps the best hole on the course. A par-5 of 587 yards from the blue tee, 558 from the white, and 462 from the red, the fairway provides alternative routing. If you can pound the ball somewhere out into Tiger Woods territory and if you can hit a fade down the right-hand side and not be afraid to flirt with the water, you gamble with a second shot that must carry over water the entire way to the green. Not many people can do that. The smart play is to take it down the left side with two strong shots, then play a shot into a green that sits at a right angle from the end of the fairway and is all carry over water.

Willard Byrd and Clyde Johnston put a lot of careful thought into the details of this course, such as where every bunker and green should be placed to provide the ultimate golfing experience. If you're really ambitious and energetic, you can play 27 holes here, then go across the road and play Glen Dornoch, Clyde Johnston's relatively new 6,850-yard track that has been getting some good reviews from golf writers and players alike.

Insider Tips If you're going to play two of the three nines at Heather Glen, make sure one of them is the second nine. It is clearly the best of the three. Also, there are numerous pot bunkers. With typical Scottish pot bunkers, sometimes your only way out is to hit it sideways or backward. Here, the pot bunkers are not quite as severe, but it is always prudent to think long and hard when contemplating what sort of shot will extricate yourself from these tiny terrors.

The Heritage Club

Hwy. 17 S., River Road, Myrtle Beach, SC 29585; phone (843) 237-3424

How to Get On: Tee times can be made via packages with various hotels, or on a daily fee basis, up to nine months in advance.

Tees:

    Gold: 7,100 yards, par-71, USGA rating 74.1, slope 142

    Blue: 6,575 yards, par-71, USGA rating 72.0, slope 132

    White: 6,100 yards, par-71, USGA rating 69.6, slope 129

    Red: 5,315 yards, par-71, USGA rating 71.0, slope 125

Challenge: ★★★★½	Golf Facilities: ★★★★
Variety: ★★★	14-Club Test:★★★½
Terrain: ★★★★	Intangibles: ★★★½
Beauty/Visual Appeal: ★★★★	Value: ★★★½
Pace of Play: ★★★	

Just the Facts Year Opened: 1986; Course Designer: Dan Maples; Walking: No; Greens Fee: $30–75; 9 Hole/Twilight Rate: Yes; Pull Carts: No; Practice Range: Yes; Club Rental: Yes.

Description and Comments Immaculately conditioned and beautifully landscaped, the Heritage Club course is among a handful of the best courses on the Grand Strand. Built on what was once two working rice plantations, owner Larry Young (who also owns The Legends Resort) did a good job of re-creating the look of the antebellum South with his colonial clubhouse, which features a wooden porch, green gables, and a spiral staircase inside. Like an old plantation, an avenue of live oak trees leads along the approach road to the clubhouse, and live oaks, magnolia trees, dogwood trees, and azaleas grace the grounds and the golf course.

This is an extremely difficult course, evidenced by the fact that in 14 years of play, the course record from the back tees over this par-71 layout is just two under par—a 69 shot by Senior PGA Tour star Leonard Thompson.

This is certainly one of designer Dan Maples's best courses—and he has built a bevy of good ones. The greens are big and undulating, the three par-5s are long and demanding, and the par-4s are monsters. From the back tees (gold) nine of the par-4s are 400 yards or longer (four of them measure 440 yards each, and one stretches to 460 yards). One of the par-5s plays 610 yards. The next two forward sets of tees are more forgiving, but there are still six par-4s measuring over 400 yards from the blue tees, as well as a par-3 that plays 200 yards.

Even the shorter par-4s aren't all that easy. The ninth, for instance, plays just 370 yards from the gold tee, 350 from the blue tee, and 330 from the white tee. But the green here is the true guardian of par. It is so severely undulating that if you aren't paying close attention to the breaks and read them correctly, or if you haven't brought your "A" putting stroke with you, you could take three or four putts to hole out.

The 13th is one of the most beautiful and interesting holes on the course. It is a par-3 that plays a whopping 235 yards from the gold tee, onto an island green that is guarded like dragons by pot bunkers and a huge sand trap.

A total of nine holes run along the saltwater marshes and overlook Caledonia Creek and the expansive Waccamaw River.

The 18th is a great finishing hole, especially when the bets are down and the press is on. It's a dramatic par-5 reachable by long knockers who want to take the gamble, but the second shot—the approach shot for those who lay up—must carry over water and saltwater marsh to an hourglass-shaped green.

Insider Tips   At 7,100 yards and par-71, this is a monster from the back tees. With all of the saltwater marsh, be sure to take plenty of golf balls. But don't try this course from the back tees if you are 1) a high handicapper, or 2) even a mid-range handicapper who isn't a long hitter. Note that virtually every green at The Heritage Club is enormous, with up to three and four tiers apiece. As interesting as the concept is, it almost gets repetitive after a while. If greens such as these are not your cup of tea, you might be in for a long day here.

The Legends, Heathland Course

U.S. 501, P.O. Box 2038, Myrtle Beach, SC 29578; phone (800) 377-2315 or (843) 236-9318

How to Get On: Tee times can be made via packages with The Legends Resort, with various hotels in the area, or directly with the course nine months in advance.

Tees:

Tour Gold: 6,785 yards, par-71, USGA rating 72.3, slope 127

Green: 6,190 yards, par-71, USGA rating 69.0, slope 117

Red: 5,060 yards, par-71, USGA rating 71.0, slope 112

Challenge: ★★★½	Golf Facilities: ★★★★
Variety: ★★★★	14-Club Test:★★★½
Terrain: ★★★½	Intangibles: ★★★★
Beauty/Visual Appeal: ★★★★	Value: ★★★★
Pace of Play: ★★★★	

Just the Facts   Year Opened: 1990; Course Designer: Tom Doak; Walking: No; Greens Fee: $50–105; 9 Hole/Twilight Rate: Yes; Pull Carts: No; Practice Range: Yes; Club Rental: Yes.

Description and Comments   All three 18s at The Legends Resort are extremely good, but Heathland is truly outstanding and was rated among the top 10 new resort courses in the world when it opened in 1990.

Heathland, as its name suggests, and in keeping with the theme of the entire resort, is a bit of Scotland imported to South Carolina. The courses, the gigantic clubhouse, and the charming resort village here have an unmistakable Scottish flair. The trees have been yanked to allow the wind to blow with Scottish fury in the afternoon, and you will encounter deep pot bunkers, heather, gorse, and berms along these 45 fairways. You will hear the sound of pipers playing intermittently from the clubhouse. This may be as close to Scotland as you're going to get without actually going across the pond.

Heathland's architect, Tom Doak, patterned several of the holes after famous holes on traditional British and Irish courses like St. Andrews and Lahinch. If you're going to score well here, you had better be a good lag putter, for the greens are enormous. Being faced with 90- or 100-foot putts is not uncommon. But, like traditional Scottish courses, there are long aprons and no bunkers obstructing pitch and chip shots, so that you can hit bump-and-runs and recover from botched approach shots.

Many of the fairways are wide, but you have to know which side of the fairways will give your ball roll and which side will curtail the roll. If there is a signature hole on this course, it is the 6th, which is the most rugged hole on the course and the only one where trees come into play. Your tee shot comes out of a narrow chute and must carry nearly 200 yards to clear the trees, if you are going to take that route. You can take a longer route if you don't want to fool with the trees, but this hole plays a whopping 460 yards from the back tees. The 6,765 yards from the tips and the 6,190 from the men's forward tees are deceptively long, since there are only three par-5s—two of which are extremely long.

The par-5 13th, however, can be reached in two by moderately long hitters, even though it plays considerably long (535 from the back tee, 510 from the men's forward tee), because the fairway runs severely downhill.

Your best chance for an eagle will be on number seven, a par-5 that plays just 460 yards from the back tee and a very tame 425 from the next forward tee. The landing area is tight and guarded by bunkers on the right side, but there is otherwise little trouble other than a deep, riveted bunker in front of the green. If you can hit it straight, you can probably hit it in two. This hole was patterned after the famous Road Hole number 17 at St. Andrews, Scotland.

Insider Tips   Heathland is an authentic links-style golf course, but, unlike links courses in the British Isles, the greens here are big and soft enough that you can fly the ball to the hole, rather than having to bounce it in.

Don't be afraid to hit it to the stick, keeping in mind that the huge greens could produce a two-, three-, or four-club difference from the front of the green to the back.

Also keep in mind that the best time of the day to play, if you want to score well, is morning or evening, because with the lack of trees the wind can dramatically change the character of this course. Heathland can be a puppy in the morning and a very mean dog by the afternoon.

Larry Young, the golf entrepreneur who owns The Legends, also owns three other extremely good courses in Myrtle Beach—Marsh Harbor, Oyster Bay, and The Heritage courses. The resort can put together a package that includes all of these courses and can also book tee times at myriad other Grand Strand layouts. The practice facilities here, by the way, are outstanding, and the greens are equipped with satellite systems to give you exact yardage everywhere, all the time.

Oyster Bay Golf Links

614 Shore Dr., Sunset Beach, NC 28469; phone (843) 236-9318

How to Get On: Tee times can be made via various hotel packages, on a daily fee bases (180 days in advance), or as a guest of The Legends Resort.

Tees:

> Blue: 6,685 yards, par-70, USGA rating 71.6, slope 134
>
> White: 6,355 yards, par-70, USGA rating 69.7, slope 125
>
> Red: 4,665 yards, par-70, USGA rating 68.0, slope 118

Challenge: ★★★	Golf Facilities: ★★★★
Variety: ★★★★½	14-Club Test:★★★½
Terrain: ★★★½	Intangibles: ★★★★
Beauty/Visual Appeal: ★★★★	Value: ★★★★
Pace of Play: ★★★	

Just the Facts Year Opened: 1983; Course Designer: Dan Maples; Walking: No; Greens Fee: $70–80; 9 Hole/Twilight Rate: Yes; Pull Carts: No; Practice Range: Yes; Club Rental: Yes.

Description and Comments For more than 15 years, Oyster Bay has been one of the most sought-after courses by visitors and one of the most consistently highly ranked by the golf publications. One of the leading golf publications has ranked this one as the best resort course in America.

As its name suggests, there are oyster shells everywhere, including the approach road to the clubhouse and the clubhouse driveway. In some cases, oysters even shore up the greens and wall the tees.

But it's not the oyster shells that make this course so outstanding—it is the design and the land itself. The way the course is laid out, you never get tired of playing it. There is nothing boring about this one. There is a good mix of length on the various holes, as well as several good water hazards, strategically placed bunkers, and tricky, rolling greens.

At first glance at the scorecard, Oyster Bay doesn't appear all that imposing. It is only 6,695 yards from the back tees. But par here is 70, so that length is deceptive. Even the shorter par-3s are very challenging. Number 6, for example, plays only 165 yards from the back tee, but it features a huge bunker that runs the entire left side, from tee to green, and a big bunker on the right near the green that often catches shots steered away from the bunker on the left. And the 8th, which plays only 160 yards, has a green that is protected on the left by the marsh. The 17th, 165 yards from the back tee, is an island green, and it's all carry over the water.

The par-4s here are terrific. Numbers 2 and 3 are especially difficult— back-to-back monsters that play 450 and 470 yards, respectively, from the back tees, and 420 from the next forward tee. The approach shot to the 3rd is a toughie, because the green is surrounded in front and on each side by a lake. The 18th, though not as long as the 2nd and 3rd holes (400 yards from the back tee), is nonetheless a great finishing hole, with marsh protecting the green across the entirety of the fairway.

The 15th is another memorable hole, a par-3 that plays 210 yards from the back tee into another island green that leaves only a small bit of dry land on the left as a bail out area.

Insider Tips   The best tip here is to plot your shots from the tees. The name of the game is strategy, especially on holes where the marshland comes into play (numbers 3, 4, 5, 7, 8, 9, and 10) and where the large lakes come into play (1, 2, 14, 15, and 16). Look at the fairway and the layout on the tee markers or the scorecard, and try to place your drives where you won't be hitting at trouble on your approach shots.

Oyster Bay provides some beautiful vistas and is fun as well as challenging. If you come down during peak periods and you want to play this one, it would be a good idea to book your tee time well in advance.

This is a sister course to the courses at The Legends Resort as well as The Heritage Club and Marsh Harbor.

Two cautionary observations: First, hit the range before you start a round here, because the first four holes are brutal, especially numbers 2 and 3. Second, play may slow down a bit for pictures at the course's signature hole, the short, par-4 13th, which doglegs right out toward the bay and features a slightly elevated green shored with a wall of oyster shells.

Pawleys Plantation

70 Tanglewood Dr. (Highway 17), Pawleys Island, SC 29585; phone (800) 367-9959 or (843) 237-1736

How to Get On: Tee times can be made via packages with various hotels or on a daily basis, one year in advance.

Tees:

> Gold: 7,026 yards, par-72, USGA rating 74.8, slope 140
>
> Blue: 6,522 yards, par-72, USGA rating 71.9, slope 133
>
> White: 6,127 yards, par-72, USGA rating 70.5, slope 125
>
> Red: 5,572 yards, par-72, USGA rating 73.0, slope 130

Challenge: ★★★★	Golf Facilities: ★★★★
Variety: ★★★½	14-Club Test: ★★★½
Terrain: ★★★★	Intangibles: ★★★★
Beauty/Visual Appeal: ★★★½	Value: ★★★½
Pace of Play: ★★★★	

Just the Facts Year Opened: 1988; Course Designer: Jack Nicklaus; Walking: No; Greens Fee: Surcharge course based on packages with the six hotels mentioned above; 9 Hole/Twilight Rate: Yes; Pull Carts: No; Practice Range: Yes; Club Rental: Yes.

Description and Comments This is a beautiful course located inside a gated resort community on the quieter south end of Myrtle Beach. This is a very tough test of golf, especially from the back tees. As with most Nicklaus courses, the back tees will challenge the best players, including Jack himself. Besides the length, there is a lot of marshland that comes into play on the back nine.

Jack also is fond of constructing double greens, as he did here on the par-3 13th and the long, par-4 16th, which share a monstrous green. The 16th is one of the toughest holes on the course, a par-4 that stretches to 444 yards from the back tee, 423 from the blue tee, and more than 400 yards from the white tee.

The par-5s are unusually long from the back tees. If you're going to hit the greens in two from the back tee, you're going to have to really rock a couple of drives and second shots. Number 1 plays 511 yards, number 4 plays 543, the 11th measures a whopping 563, and the 14th is 525. From the blue and white tees, these par-5s are reachable in two by moderately long hitters, with the exception of the 11th, which plays 542 yards even from the white tee.

The final hole is an extremely good finishing hole, a par-4 that plays 443 yards from the back tees, doglegging left with marsh guarding the left side of the fairway and a lake guarding the approach shot to the green.

The 13th hole is out in the middle of the marshland, with a cart path built across a dike that was part of the historic rice plantation on which the golf course sits. The green is surrounded by marsh and shored up by railroad ties. Although the hole measures only 145 yards from the gold tee, 115 from the blue tee, and only 69 from the white tee, there is no room for error; this hole will make you swallow hard before you hit your tee shot, especially if the wind is up.

Besides being a challenging and well-kept course, Pawleys Plantation deserves a lot of praise for its visual appeal. The marshlands here are hauntingly lovely, the ocean comes into view on several holes, and there is an abundance of wildlife around the course.

Insider Tips This is a course that demands accuracy. The penalties for spraying the ball all over the park are severe. A tip on the island hole, the 13th: Hit for the center of the green, no matter where the flagstick is. Unlike most courses that Nicklaus builds, which are set up for his fade, this is a course where you need to bring your draw, because most of the holes go from right to left.

Pine Lakes International Country Club

5603 Woodside Dr., Myrtle Beach, SC 29577; phone (800) 446-6817 or (843) 449-6459

How to Get On: Tee times can be made through various hotel packages or on a daily fee basis, up to one year in advance.

Tees:

> Blue: 6,609 yards, par-71, USGA rating 71.3, slope 121
>
> White: 6,176 yards, par-71, USGA rating 69.4, slope 115
>
> Red: 5,376 yards, par-71, USGA rating 71.2, slope 118

Challenge: ★★½	Golf Facilities: ★★★★
Variety: ★★★	14-Club Test:★★★
Terrain: ★★★	Intangibles: ★★★★½
Beauty/Visual Appeal: ★★★★	Value: ★★★★½
Pace of Play: ★★★★	

Just the Facts Year Opened: 1927; Course Designer: Robert White; Walking: No; Greens Fee: $52–106; 9 Hole/Twilight Rate: No; Pull Carts: No; Practice Range: Yes; Club Rental: Yes.

Description and Comments They call this one "The Granddaddy" because it is the oldest course in Myrtle Beach, and—as you are likely to agree when you finish playing—it is also the most memorable. The Granddaddy provides not only 18 holes of golf but also a golfing experience that you're not likely to forget.

Opened in 1927 as the Ocean Forest Club, this club has entertained the deep pockets of several generations. They say that the Vanderbilt family took supper with the Roosevelts here and that Rockefeller golfed with Sarazen. Legend also has it that the idea for *Sports Illustrated* was hatched in the clubhouse bar here in the 1950s.

All that lore is great stuff for cocktail patter, but what makes the experience truly memorable are touches like these: When you open your door in the parking lot, men in knickers and red jackets greet you. The employees working in the grill room and in the pro shop are smartly dressed in tams and Scottish kilts. On chilly days, you're served complimentary hot chocolate on the 1st tee, and, as part of the tradition, on the 10th tee you will be served a cup of complimentary homemade chowder, straight from the kitchen fire. Even the rangers here wear kilts, tams, and bright red jackets. These costumes pay homage not just to golf's roots but to the Scottish heritage of the course, which was designed by Scotsman Robert White, with his legendary countryman Donald Ross consulting.

Before you get lost in all of the pomp, be assured that Pine Lakes International is also a very good test of golf. The course record from the back tees is 65, which is impressive considering that in its 70-plus years it has survived assaults from some of the finest players in the world, including Gene Sarazen and Bobby Jones. One reason that this course isn't likely to yield a lot of low numbers is that you cannot recover from a missed approach shot with a run-up shot. Bunkers or cuts of rough protect nearly all the greens. Although the course is only moderately long (6,609 yards from the tips), the par-5s are extremely difficult to hit in two—meaning that birdies must be earned with accurate approach shots—and two of the par-3s stretch to more than 200 yards. Four of the par-4s are over 400 yards, and the 18th, though only 370 yards from the back, is an extremely tough hole to par due to an assortment of hazards.

The stretch run here can clobber you if you're not on your toes and on your game. Number 15 measures 200 yards from the back tees. Number 16, though only 379 from the back tee, requires an intimidating drive over a large body of water, which also comes into play on the left. The 17th is 442 yards from the back tee and it doglegs left with a lake protecting the left side of the fairway, ready to swallow a pulled shot. The 18th requires careful placement to avoid the water on both sides of the fairway and a series of bunkers.

There might be newer courses around here that are snazzier, but this fine test of golf, which provides a wonderful slice of tradition, should not be missed.

Insider Tips   All of the greens on this circa-1920s layout are traditionally small, so a good tip is to play to the center of the greens, rather than trying to nibble on the corners, to use baseball terminology. You don't have a lot of margin for error if your shots hit the left or right side of these greens, so you could end up hitting a decent shot and still missing the green and making bogey.

The TPC of Myrtle Beach

P.O. Box 159, Murrells Inlet, SC 29576; phone (888) 742-8721

How to Get On: Tee times can be made via various hotel packages or on a daily fee basis, up to a year in advance.

Tees:

Black: 6,950 yards, par-72, USGA rating 74.0, slope 145

Gold: 6,600 yards, par-72, USGA rating 72.2, slope 136

Blue: 6,193 yards, par-72, USGA rating 70.4, slope 125

White: 5,783 yards, par-72, USGA rating 68.4, slope 121

Red: 5,118 yards, par-72, USGA rating 70.3, slope 125

Challenge: ★★★★

Variety: ★★★★

Terrain: ★★★★

Beauty/Visual Appeal: ★★★½

Pace of Play: ★★★½

Golf Facilities: ★★★★★

14-Club Test: ★★★½

Intangibles: ★★★★

Value: ★★½

Just the Facts Year Opened: 1998; Course Designer: Tom Fazio; Walking: No; Greens Fee: $100–160; 9 Hole/Twilight Rate: Yes; Pull Carts: No; Practice Range: Yes; Club Rental: Yes.

Description and Comments This course was a joint project between the PGA Tour and Myrtle Beach Golf Holiday, the latter of which is the marketing arm of more than 90 courses and dozens of hotels and resorts in the Myrtle Beach area. That fact irked many golf course owners, who felt (rightly so) that Myrtle Beach Golf Holiday went into direct competition with them and had a conflict of interest.

All those local politics aside, Tom Fazio, in cahoots with PGA Tour star Lanny Wadkins, built an extremely fine course on an extremely nice piece of land near the southern end of the Grand Strand. In general, TPC courses are noted for having fine facilities, but also for charging high prices for everything. Anyone who has ever bought a candy bar and some crackers on the TPC Stadium Course in Ponte Vedra, Florida, can testify to that. Make no mistake about it, the PGA Tour is a business, not a service, and they are in it to make a profit, even if it ends up gouging the average golfer. The greens fees here during the peak rate periods of mid-September to November and mid-February through May are a whopping $140. One good thing about all of the competition here is that price gouging doesn't work. People can, and do, literally go across the street to do business with the competition. If money is no object, this recently opened course is a dandy, although there are many courses in the area that are every bit as good.

What's most exciting about this course is the terrain and the landscaping. There are rolling fairways and an emphasis on accurate driving. Unlike Pete Dye's TPC Stadium Course, you won't come away with the feeling that you've just played something that's tricked up. Water comes prominently into play here, as do a variety of environmental grasses and hardwood trees. There is nothing tricky about this course. There is a good mix of long holes and shorter holes, and five sets of tees. The number-one handicap hole is the 9th, a whopper of a par-4 that plays 472 yards from the back (black tee) and 457 from the next forward set of tees (gold). The second hole is an interesting par-5 where water comes into play not once but twice—on the drive and the approach shot. The 5th is a testy little par-3 that is only 158 yards from the back tee, but it's all carry over water.

The finishing hole is a beauty, a par-5 that plays 538 yards from the back tees and 515 yards from the next forward set of tees. Water runs all the way down the left side and cuts in front of the green and around its left side.

This is obviously a course well worth playing. But a TPC label is somewhat akin to a Polo label on a shirt. Take the little polo player off the shirt and it probably sells for $25 less.

Insider Tips　Don't play the back tees unless you are a long, straight hitter. Accuracy off the tees is extremely important. The greens hold very well, so don't be timid about going for the flags. However, these are extremely big greens, so check your pin placements and your yardage carefully. You don't want to end up with putts of 20 or 30 feet or more because these greens aren't always easy to putt.

Tidewater

4901 Little River Neck Rd., Cherry Grove Beach, SC 29582; phone (800) 446-5363 or (843) 249-3829

How to Get On:　Tee times can be made via packages with various hotels, as a resort guest at Tidewater, or on a daily fee basis, one year in advance.

Tees:

Black: 7,020 yards, par-72, USGA rating 74.3, 73.7, slope 134

Blue: 6,505 yards, par-72, USGA rating 74.3, 71.2, slope 126

White: 6,030 yards, par-72, USGA rating 74.3, 68.7, slope 118

Gold: 5,100 yards, par-72, USGA rating 74.3, 70.2, slope 132

Forward: 4,765 yards, par-72, USGA rating 74.3, 67.5, slope 127

Challenge: ★★★½

Variety: ★★★★

Terrain: ★★★★

Beauty/Visual Appeal: ★★★★

Pace of Play: ★★★½

Golf Facilities: ★★★★

14-club Test: ★★★★

Intangibles: ★★★

Value: ★★★★

Just the Facts　Year Opened: 1990; Course Designer: Ken Tomlinson; Walking: At times; Greens Fee: $80–145; 9 Hole/Twilight Rate: No; Pull Carts: No; Practice Range: Yes; Club Rental: Yes.

Description and Comments　If someone told you that the course you were about to play was designed by a former accountant, you might consider turning around and going home. But in the case of Tidewater, that would be a mistake. In fact, there are a lot of golfers, including some tour players, who will tell you that this is the best course on the whole Grand Strand.

Ken Tomlinson, who owns a CPA firm, is the owner and designer of the golf course—although Hale Irwin did some consulting, and Tomlinson does have a golf background, having played college golf. When the course first opened in 1990, it was named as the best new public golf course in America by both major golf publications.

What Tomlinson had going for him here was the combination of a vision and a magnificent piece of land—over 500 acres of rolling land that meanders along the Intracoastal Waterway, the saltwater marshes, and the Atlantic Ocean. The vision was that nature should determine what kind of course this would be. Although he enhanced the landscape, he didn't really alter it. There are a number of elevation changes that are uncommon in this part of the country. In building the fairways, Tomlinson designed multiple landing areas. Thick groves of trees border many of the fairways.

If there is anything resembling a signature hole, it would have to be the 4th, a par-4 that plays 420 yards from the back tee and is the one that most photographers are drawn to. The fairway is elevated and borders a cliff, with a long, crescent-shaped bunker that can stop a ball from going over the cliff.

The 4th is one of four ocean-view holes, all of them gorgeous. Others include the 3rd, a 150-yard par-3 that looks out from the tee over the marsh on the golfers' left. The 12th, a 180-yard par-3, and the 13th, a long par-5 (580 from the back, a milder 480 from the next forward men's tee), bring you back to a view of the Atlantic Ocean. Five more holes look out to the Intracoastal Waterway—numbers 8, 9, 16, 17, and 18. The 8th is a reachable par-5 for long knockers, but the saltwater marsh guards the entire left side of the hole. The stretch run—16, 17, and 18—is a tough and beautiful test of golf. Sixteen is a long par-5 (570 yards) that runs dramatically downhill to a green that is backed up by the Intracoastal Waterway. Number 17 is a par-3 that plays 210 yards all the way back, and number 18 gives golfers a rugged and beautiful finishing hole. The 18th measures 440 yards from the back tee. It is rated as the number-6 handicap hole on the course, but it is probably the second or third toughest hole. The saltwater marsh runs all the way down the right side and crosses in front of the green, making for a very difficult shot for those who are able to hit a long enough drive to reach it in two.

In nearly 10 years, the best score at Tidewater has been 67. This is a tough course, but a fair one and a beautiful one as well. Even if you didn't play it, you would probably love just walking it.

Insider Tips   There is a usually a lot of wind out here, especially along the bluffs that overlook Cherry Grove Inlet. It would be a good idea to practice hitting low, knockdown shots before you play here. The second shots here are very demanding and require that you carry a lot of trouble in front of the greens. If anything, if you are in doubt, err long and take more club than you might think you need. Better to be on the back of the green than in a deep front bunker or in some saltwater marsh.

A Myrtle Beach Sampler

The Long Bay Club

Highway 9, P.O. Box 330, Longs, SC 29568; phone (800) 344-5590 or (843) 399-2222

Tees: Championship: 7,021 yards, par-72, USGA rating 73.0, slope 129

Greens Fee: $40–90

Challenge: ★★★	Golf Facilities: ★★★½
Variety: ★★★½	14-Club Test:★★★★
Terrain: ★★★	Intangibles: ★★★
Beauty/Visual Appeal: ★★★★	Value: ★★★½
Pace of Play: ★★★	

Description and Comments   One of the most challenging courses around. None but the brave and the foolish take on this Jack Nicklaus monster from the back tees. Three other sets of tees make it a more civilized and enjoyable experience. The greens are typical Nicklaus, in that you can't roll the ball up, you have to fly it there. In additionally, they are often shallow and set on a diagonal, so you not only have to fly it there but fly it high and make it stop on a dime or you will run into what is usually severe trouble behind the green. The course is replete with hazards—big lakes, long waste bunkers, many sand traps, and tree-lined fairways.

Perhaps the most unusual and memorable hole is the 10th, a short par-4 that may give you the sensation that you are playing on the moon. The entire left side is lined with crater-like mounds, all the way to the green, and a waste bunker frames the tight fairway in a horseshoe that runs nearly the entire way to the green and turns the fairway into a peninsula surrounded by sand. In a humorous, bizarre touch, you actually get to drive your cart through the sand to get to the green.

The finishing holes on each nine are extremely good, because they require challenging approach shots over large lakes.

Man O' War

5601 Leeshire Blvd., Myrtle Beach, SC 29579; phone (843) 236-8000

Tees: Championship: 6,967 yards, par-72, USGA rating 72.4, slope 130

Greens Fee: $40–90

Challenge: ★★★½	Golf Facilities: ★★★½
Variety: ★★½	14-Club Test:★★★½
Terrain: ★★★	Intangibles: ★★★½
Beauty/Visual Appeal: ★★★★	Value: ★★★½
Pace of Play: ★★★½	

Description and Comments This Dan Maples beauty is worth playing if for no other reason than to putt these gigantic, incredibly smooth greens. On some of the biggest of them, you may feel like the Incredible Shrinking Man or a Lilliputian encountering Gulliver. This course may also look like the land of a thousand lakes. The entire course was created in the middle of a 100-acre lake. You will probably use every club in the bag, no matter which of the four tees you play, and there are back-to-back island greens that will dazzle you and perhaps give you fits, and a par-4 9th hole that is indeed an island, all the way from the tee to the green.

Maples has provided some very generous landing areas, but all of that water can be a solid psychological intimidation. The best bet here is to just let it go with your normal swing rather than to start aiming the ball. Although you may not consider Man O' War to be a great course, it is certainly a unique course and one that you should play at least once.

Marsh Harbor

Highway 179, Calabash, NC (P.O. Box 65, North Myrtle Beach, SC 29597); phone (843) 249-3449

Tees: Championship: 6,690 yards, par-71, USGA rating 72.4, slope 134

Greens Fee: $30–75

Challenge: ★★★½	Golf Facilities: ★★★★
Variety: ★★★½	14-club Test: ★★★½
Terrain: ★★★★½	Intangibles: ★★★
Beauty/Visual Appeal: ★★★★	Value: ★★★½
Pace of Play: ★★★½	

Description and Comments Located on the northern end of the Grand Strand, this course is under the umbrella of The Legends Resort and can be played on a resort package at The Legends, along with packages from various other hotels in the area and for a daily fee. When it first opened in the late 1980s, Marsh Harbor achieved the distinction of being rated among the top 25 public courses in America by one of the leading golf publications. The scenery, with lakes and streams, the Intracoastal Waterway, the yacht basin, and marshlands, is hard to beat. The total yardage is deceptively long because par is only 71. The stretch run on the front nine and several holes on the back nine are carved right out of the marsh. Perhaps the toughest and most memorable hole on the course is the par-5 17th. This hole requires some decision making because the marsh on one side, trees on the other, and huge bunkers all figure into the equation. The tee shot, the second shot, and the approach shot must each carry marsh. The hole plays 570 yards from the back tee, and the wind is normally into the golfer's face. This course is definitely a keeper.

Myrtle Beach National, Kings North

4900 National Dr., Myrtle Beach, SC 29579; phone (800) 344-5590 or (843) 448-2308

Tees: Championship: 7,017 yards, par-72, USGA rating 72.6, slope 136

Greens Fee: $100–115

Challenge: ★★★	Golf Facilities: ★★★★
Variety: ★★★★½	14-club Test: ★★★★
Terrain: ★★★½	Intangibles: ★★★
Beauty/Visual Appeal: ★★★★	Value: ★★★½
Pace of Play: ★★★	

Description and Comments Arnold Palmer designed all three courses at Myrtle Beach National between 1973 and 1975, before he started working exclusively with Ed Seay, his longtime design partner. The best of these courses is King's North, the original course. The three courses underwent a renovation to the tune of nearly $5 million just a few years ago and are superbly conditioned. Arnie redesigned and rerouted his King's North course. This is one of the most challenging courses on the Grand Strand, as well as one of the most popular. The 18th hole is magnificent, with 42 sand bunkers guarding both the fairway and the green and a long waste bunker and a lake protecting the right side almost from tee to green. Number six is Arnie's kind of hole, a par-5 of considerable length (568 from the back tees, but much tamer from the forward tees) that requires a long accurate drive and then a second shot down a fairway that doglegs left to a green that is surrounded by water on three sides and large bunkers on the other side. An alternate, island fairway exists to the left of the traditional fairway, which shortens the hole but brings more trouble into play. It is a hole where Arnie would certainly take a gamble and go for it in two.

Ocean Harbour Golf Links

Highway 179, Calabash, NC 28459; phone (843) 448-8398

Tees: Championship: 7,004 yards, par-72, USGA rating 74.2, slope 138

Greens Fee: $50–70

Challenge: ★★★★	Golf Facilities: ★★★½
Variety: ★★	14-Club Test: ★★½
Terrain: ★★★½	Intangibles: ★★★
Beauty/Visual Appeal: ★★★★	Value: ★★★
Pace of Play: ★★	

Description and Comments   Ranked among the best resort and public courses when it opened in 1989, Ocean Harbour is breathtakingly beautiful. It is also breathtakingly frustrating, thanks to its endless profusion of semiblind hazards. The course borders the Intracoastal Waterway and is flanked by the Calabash River, the Little River Inlet, and an abundance of tidal marshland. This is a course that requires pinpoint accuracy on most of the holes because water hazards and marsh are everywhere. This course is right on the border of the two Carolinas, and there are holes in each state. Nearly everybody who plays this course will talk about number 4, a long par-4 in which the Intracoastal Waterway comes into play. Part of the hole is in North Carolina, and part is in South Carolina. But that's not what makes it memorable. The visual aspects are spectacular, with a view from the tee of huge old live oak trees, the Intracoastal Waterway, and tidal marshland. And, just to the right of the green, you can see the Atlantic Ocean. The finishing holes are quite a test, from 14 all the way home, because they are played through the marshlands and are relatively long, except for the par-3 15th, which is only 165 yards from the back tee but is all carry over marsh.

The Pearl, East Course

1300 Pearl Blvd., Sunset Beach, NC 28468; phone (843) 272-2580
Tees: Championship: 6,750 yards, par-72, USGA rating 73.1, slope 135
Greens Fee: $35–70

Challenge: ★★★★	Golf Facilities: ★★★½
Variety: ★★★★	14-Club Test: ★★★★½
Terrain: ★★★★	Intangibles: ★★★
Beauty/Visual Appeal: ★★★★½	Value: ★★★★
Pace of Play: ★★★★½	

Description and Comments   About a driver and a wedge across the North Carolina border, The Pearl's East Course is challenging, exciting, and beautiful. Dan Maples did a masterful job building two courses here that were both of such high quality that they received nominations for America's best new courses when they opened 12 years ago. The East Course takes advantage of a lot of water and marshland. Water comes into play on 11 holes, and the marshland is a factor on the three finishing holes.

The result of Maples's prudent design is a course that gives you a lot of variety, challenge, and visual appeal. Numbers 17 and 18 are great finishing holes. The 17th is a long par-4 (418 from the back tee) whose left side flirts with marsh all the way from tee to green, and a waste bunker also guards the left side of the fairway, nearly the entirety of the hole. If you bail out to the right, mounds can stymie you. The 18th is an extremely long par-5 (572 from the back) that doglegs left. A waste bunker can catch a pulled tee shot, water guards the approach on the left, and marshland runs all the way from tee to green.

The Pearl, West Course

1300 Pearl Blvd., Sunset Beach, NC 28468; phone (843) 272-2580
Tees: Championship: 7,005 yards, par-72, USGA rating 73.2, slope 132
Greens Fee: $30–70

Challenge: ★★★★	Golf Facilities: ★★★★
Variety: ★★★★	14-Club Test:★★★★
Terrain: ★★★★	Intangibles: ★★★
Beauty/Visual Appeal: ★★★★	Value: ★★★
Pace of Play: ★★★½	

Description and Comments   This is an ever-so-slightly longer course than the East Course, but not necessarily a more difficult one. The slope rating is slightly lower on the West, but the course ratings are about the same. This course is memorable not only for its beauty but for two monstrous par-5s on the back nine—numbers 14 and 16. If you're fatigued coming into the stretch, these two holes can be killers. Even from the next two forward sets of tees, the 14th plays 605 and 571 yards, respectively. And sandwiched between these two formidable par-5s is a long par-4 (443, 436, 407, 370 yards), which is probably tougher than the two par-5s that flank it. If you pull or hook your shots or push or slice them, you can be in big trouble because there is danger lurking on both sides. The green is double-tiered and has some severe slopes.

Like the East Course, this is a pleasure to play because it is so lovely, with all the water and marshland and the wonderful landscaping that is highlighted by beautiful pampas grass.

The River Club

Pine Drive, P.O. Box 379, Pawleys Island, SC 29585; phone (843) 237-8755
Tees: Championship: 6,669 yards, par-72, USGA rating 72.4, slope 128
Greens Fee: $90–100

Challenge: ★★★   Golf Facilities: ★★★½

Variety: ★★★★   14-Club Test: ★★★

Terrain: ★★★   Intangibles: ★★★½

Beauty/Visual Appeal: ★★★   Value: ★★★

Pace of Play: ★★★½

Description and Comments   This is a sister course to Litchfield Golf and Beach Resort's Willbrook Plantation and Litchfield Plantation courses. The yardage and the slope rating are deceiving, because there is so much water that can drive your score up. Tom Jackson did a masterful job of designing this scenic layout in which water comes into play on 15 holes.

There are varying opinions as to which hole is the hardest or the best on the course. Number 11, a par-5, is usually prominently in the discussions because it is moderately long (546 from the back tee) and requires a delicate approach shot into a green that is surrounded by water, except for a small opening in front. The 15th is a demon of a par-4, 412 from the back. But it isn't the length that makes it so tough—it's the water that runs along the left side, from tee to green, surrounding the green in front, in back, and on the left.

The par-3s here are also extremely challenging, especially the 14th, which is almost all carry over water to a green that is nearly encircled by it and is protected by eight bunkers.

Sea Trail, Rees Jones Course

211 Clubhouse Rd., Sunset Beach, NC 28468; phone (800) 546-5748 or (910) 287-1122

Tees: Championship: 6,761 yards, par-71, USGA rating 72.4 slope 132

Greens Fee: $30–70

Challenge: ★★★★   Golf Facilities: ★★★★

Variety: ★★★   14-Club Test: ★★★½

Terrain: ★★★½   Intangibles: ★★★½

Beauty/Visual Appeal: ★★★½   Value: ★★★½

Pace of Play: ★★★½

Description and Comments   This popular resort on the northern end of the Grand Strand also has courses designed by Dan Maples and Willard Byrd. But the Jones is probably the best of the three, because it is a little tougher. The greens are elevated, and many of them are guarded by water hazards. There is water on 11 holes, and the par-3s are some of the most memorable on the entire Grand Strand. Even the shorter par-4s are challenging, such as the 10th, which plays only 345 yards from the back tee. Number 10 has a severe dogleg-right fairway bordered by a large lake down the entire right side. The layout of the hole entices the golfer to try to cut the dogleg, but the smart shot is placed on the left side and offers a good look at and a good shot into a hole that is surrounded on both sides and in back by water. This is a course that will truly make you think, all the way around—like a chess game with golf clubs.

True Blue

900 Blue Stem Dr., Pawleys Island, SC 29585; phone (888) 483-6800 or (843) 483-6801

Tees: Championship: 7,060 yards, par-72, USGA rating 74.3, slope 145

Greens Fee: $45–90

Challenge: ★★★★½	Golf Facilities: ★★★★
Variety: ★★★½	14-Club Test:★★★½
Terrain: ★★★½	Intangibles: ★★★★
Beauty/Visual Appeal: ★★★★	Value: ★★★½
Pace of Play: ★★★	

Description and Comments   This is one of the real beauties, designed by up-and-coming young architect Mike Strantz. An open course with a lot of scrub and natural sandy areas, what makes it tough is also what makes it so visually appealing—the extremely large lakes and the marshland. It's hard to pick out a signature hole, because there are so many good and memorable holes here. The opening hole is the number-one handicap hole on the course, a par-5 that is extremely long (624 from the back tee). Right out of the chute, you have to tee off over the marsh, which comes into play farther down the left side of the fairway. But the 15th may be the most exciting hole on the course because of all of the sand in the waste bunkers bordering both sides of the fairway, which also comes into play prominently on the approach shot to this long par-5 (602 yards from the back tee). The stretch run (16, 17, and 18) is very difficult because of all of the water that comes into play. This is an extremely tough course from the first two sets of tees; higher handicappers should move up. Even from the third set of tees (white), at 6,488 yards, this is no pussycat. All in all, this is a great course to play, though it has polarized the masses in its short life. Some find it absurd, too tough, with blind shots, whereas others embrace it for its supreme challenge and unique design features. It's controversial—but unforgettable.

Wachesaw Plantation, East Course

911 Riverwood Dr., P.O. Box 1578, Murrells Inlet, SC 29576; phone (888) 922-0027 or (843) 357-2090

Tees: Championship: 6,933 yards, par-72, USGA rating 73.6, slope 135

Greens Fee: $55–99

Challenge: ★★★½

Variety: ★★★★½

Terrain: ★★★½

Beauty/Visual Appeal: ★★★½

Pace of Play: ★★★

Golf Facilities: ★★★

14-Club Test:★★★½

Intangibles: ★★★

Value: ★★★★

Description and Comments   Located on an otherwise private development with a members-only Tom Fazio course, Wachesaw Plantation's East Course was built to accommodate daily-fee play. Clyde Johnston, who designed the East Course, need not take a back seat to Fazio here. This is a fine course, one of the best on the Grand Strand. The LPGA plays a tournament here every year. This is a course that has a Scottish flair, but what makes it great is that it has a combination of several hazards—ponds, wetlands, bunkers, mounds, and waste bunkers. This course provides a lot of variety. Its tree-lined fairways are well defined by water hazards and marshland, and the bentgrass greens are big and well kept. There are many extremely good holes here, one of the most interesting being the long, challenging, double-dogleg, par-5 seventh, which measures 580 yards from the back tees. The finishing hole is also a beauty, a par-4 that stretches to 430 yards from the back tee. The tee shot on 18 has to clear water, the fairway doglegs severely left, and the green is protected by water.

Wild Wing, Avocet Course

Highway 501, Myrtle Beach, SC 29578; phone (800) 736-9464 or (843) 347-9464

Tees: Championship: 7,127 yards, par-72, USGA rating 74.2, slope 128

Greens Fee: $100–110

Challenge: ★★★½

Variety: ★★★★½

Terrain: ★★★½

Beauty/Visual Appeal: ★★★★

Pace of Play: ★★★½

Golf Facilities: ★★★★

14-Club Test:★★★★

Intangibles: ★★★

Value: ★★★½

Description and Comments   Larry Nelson's creative and scenic course that is chockfull of elevated tees and greens, grass bunkers, double fairways, and double greens. Ranked among the nation's best new courses when it opened in 1994, it is one of the state's best. One of four 18-hole courses at this resort complex, Avocet is a traditional design featuring several water holes and fairways that require accuracy and strategic placement. The finishing hole provides a thrilling experience, a par-4 that plays 450 yards from the back tee and invites you to bite off as much as you can chew on the drive. The fairway is bordered on one side by marshland and on the other side by water, with a huge bunker in front of the green, looming like a dragon guarding a cave of hidden treasure. This is definitely the best of the four Wild Wing courses.

Wild Wing, Falcon Course

Highway 501, Myrtle Beach, SC 29578; phone (800) 736-9464 or (843) 347-9464

Tees: Championship: 7,082 yards, par-72, USGA rating 74.4, slope 134
Greens Fee: $100–110

Challenge: ★★★½
Variety: ★★★
Terrain: ★★★
Beauty/Visual Appeal: ★★★½
Pace of Play: ★★★½

Golf Facilities: ★★★★
14-Club Test: ★★★
Intangibles: ★★★
Value: ★★★½

Description and Comments   This is the toughest of the four Wild Wing courses, but by no means is it better than the other courses here. The greens that designer Rees Jones built here are excellent and consistent. This course includes a 320-yard-long sand bunker that separates the 12th and 13th holes, a par-5 and a par-4, respectively. But the best hole is probably the 18th, a monster of a par-4 that is one of the best finishing holes on the entire Grand Strand. The green is surrounded by no fewer than 13 bunkers, it plays 471 yards from the back tee and usually plays into a headwind. If you earn a par on this one, it will be hard earned and you'll deserve a pat on the back.

Wild Wing, Wood Stork Course

Highway 501, Myrtle Beach, SC 29578; phone (800) 736-9464 or (843) 347-9464

Tees: Championship: 7,044 yards, par-72, USGA rating 74.1, slope 130
Greens Fee: $100–110

Challenge: ★★★½
Variety: ★★★★
Terrain: ★★★★
Beauty/Visual Appeal: ★★★★
Pace of Play: ★★★½

Golf Facilities: ★★★★
14-Club Test: ★★★½
Intangibles: ★★★½
Value: ★★★★

Description and Comments   Willard Byrd's course was the first of the four Wild Wing courses. The fairways are wide open, but strategically placed lagoons and lakes negate any advantage that the generous fairways provide to the wild swinger. You will be tempted to hit with Palmer-like fury, but your best bet is to play smart shots. Water comes into play on nearly every hole. The 13th features water on the entire right side from tee to green and a long waste bunker that runs the entire length of the left side. Although this is a very long course from the back tees, the forward tees give the higher handicappers a break. Wood Stork is definitely one of the most beautiful, peaceful courses in all of Myrtle Beach.

Willbrook Plantation Golf Club

Highway 17, Litchfield Beach, SC 28585; phone (843) 237-4900

Tees: Championship: 6,674 yards, par-72, USGA rating 72.5, slope 131

Greens Fee: $90–100

Challenge: ★★★½	Golf Facilities: ★★★★
Variety: ★★★★	14-Club Test:★★★½
Terrain: ★★★	Intangibles: ★★★
Beauty/Visual Appeal: ★★★★	Value: ★★★★
Pace of Play: ★★★	

Description and Comments   On the peaceful and scenic southern end of the Grand Strand, Willbrook Plantation is one of the better designs by a relatively unsung architect, Dan Maples. One of three fine courses at Litchfield Golf and Beach Resort, which was once a rice plantation, Willbrook Plantation is fraught with saltwater marsh hazards that come prominently into play on eight holes. This is an enjoyable and extremely scenic course that can be tamed by low handicappers from the back tees and midrange handicappers from the two forward tees (white and red). You will encounter one of the tougher par-4s right out of the box: Number one plays 428 from the back tee and the drive must clear the marsh. It's a very intimidating opener.

The finishing hole is a beauty—a moderately long par-5 that doglegs right and is protected by marshlands all the way down the right side and has a lagoon that comes into play on the right side as a hazard to second shots.

The Witch Golf Links

1900 Highway 44, Conway, SC 29526; phone (843) 448-1300

Tees: Championship: 6,702 yards, par-71, USGA rating 71.2, slope 133

Greens Fee: $45–95

Challenge: ★★★	Golf Facilities: ★★★
Variety: ★★★½	14-Club Test:★★★½
Terrain: ★★★½	Intangibles: ★★★½
Beauty/Visual Appeal: ★★★★	Value: ★★★½
Pace of Play: ★★★	

Description and Comments   On the southwestern gateway to the city of Myrtle Beach, The Witch is another Dan Maples beauty. There are no homes intruding on this course, only acres and acres of wilderness, wetlands, and marshland. They didn't have to move a lot of dirt here. The course follows the natural route of an extremely good piece of land. The front nine, though flat, is a good and enjoyable test. The back nine has several elevation changes, uncommon to this part of the country.

The toughest hole on the course—at least, the one with the number one rating on the card—is the opening hole, which is totally surrounded by wetlands hazards. From the back tee, it plays 420 yards. It isn't long from the member tee (384), but the hole is fraught with trouble due to the marsh and wetlands, which will swallow any shot that's sliced or badly hooked.

One word of advice: As pretty as this course is, because it has been laid out directly along the wetlands, you're likely to encounter a lot of bugs, especially in the mornings before the breezes come up. Either avoid playing it early or be aware that the best weapon you have, other than the 14 in your golf bag, is a bottle of bug spray. Save some pennies for a shirt or cap here. The club's "witch on a broomstick" logo is one of the most memorable anywhere.

Lodging

As with Hilton Head, visitors have a wide range of lodging options in Myrtle Beach with over 60,000 rooms to choose from in the area. One thing Myrtle Beach has always lacked is the five-star type of luxury accommodations, but that too may be changing soon. There are hotels priced for everyone's pocketbook—motels, villas, and cottages. Most of the beachfront hotels are high-rise buildings yielding amazing views of the beaches and Atlantic Ocean below. In addition, there are two full-service golf resorts located on nearby Pawleys Island that you may want to consider for your vacation.

EXPENSIVE

Beach Cove Resort

4800 S. Ocean Blvd., North Myrtle Beach, SC 29582; phone (800) 331-6533 or (843) 918-9000; www.beachcove.com; Rates: $148–295

Water is the theme of this hotel. First, there is its location—right on the ocean. Then there are the pools (four outdoor and one indoor), followed by a 350-foot lazy river ride, which you can float on as it tours through the grounds of the hotel. Finally there are numerous whirlpools, both indoors and outdoors.

Located in the northern section of the Grand Strand, the Beach Cove Resort has twin 15-story buildings that house 260 suites, each with a fully equipped kitchenette, living area with sofa bed, and a dining area. There is also a new third tower with 70 two- and three-bedroom condos with spacious rooms and baths, living rooms, and full kitchens. Besides the wonderful pool complex, Beach Cove also has racquetball, men's and women's saunas, beach volleyball court, and covered parking.

Golf Packages   Beach Cove's Pro Golf Package includes luxury oceanfront accommodations, one round of golf per day at a premium rated course, buffet breakfast, golf cart, pro package gift, and *USA Today* newspaper; Tradewinds Café dinner option available on request.

Embassy Suites Kingston Plantation

9800 Lake Dr., Myrtle Beach, SC 29572; phone (800) 876-0010 or (843) 449-0006; www.kingstonplantation.com; Rates: $209–289

This is Myrtle Beach's most luxurious hotel, nestled within 145 acres of manicured gardens, lakes, and woods. The hotel is comprised of 255 suites and 1- to 3-bedroom condos. All of the rooms have a living room, dining area, and balcony and feature sweeping views of the Atlantic. There is also an indoor lap pool, squash, racquetball court, aerobics studio, weight training and cardio equipment, sauna, and whirlpool.

Golf Packages   Packages can be customized and include accommodations, breakfast, taxes, and greens fees. Carts and surcharges are extra and will be incorporated into the package when you contact Kingston.

Wyndham Myrtle Beach Resort

1000 Beach Club Dr., Myrtle Beach, SC 29572; phone (800) 248-9228 or (843) 449-5000; www.wyndham.com; Rates: $99–289

The Wyndham is located directly on the beach and features 385 oceanview rooms. All the rooms have a private balcony, refrigerator, coffee maker, in-room safe, hair dryer, and iron/ironing board. The advantage of this hotel is that the Arcadian Shores Golf Club is on the premises, so golf is closer than ever. In addition, there are pools, a Jacuzzi, a gym, and a kids' club.

Golf Packages   Wyndham's golf package includes ocean-view accommodations, daily breakfast (including gratuities), greens fees, and taxes (cart fee not included, and some courses have surcharges).

MODERATE

Breakers Resort Hotel

2006 N. Ocean Blvd., P.O. Box 485, Myrtle Beach, SC 29578; (800) 953-1135 or (843) 626-5000; www.breakers.com; Rates: $103–202

The Breakers is one of the "Grand Old Dames" of Myrtle Beach. It was built 65 years ago, but has since been updated and remains one of the area's best hotels. It was the first hotel in Myrtle Beach that incorporated a golf package offering access to all the area courses, including the exclusive Dunes Golf and Beach Club.

Four separate high-rise buildings, ranging from 11 to 15 stories, feature spacious one-, two-. or three-bedroom suites decorated in a contemporary theme with many having balconies and kitchenettes. The resort has indoor and outdoor pools, a whirlpool, an exercise room, and a sauna.

Golf Packages   The Breakers resort offers the VIP Package, which consists of lodging for six nights in a two-room suite with kitchenette; choice of all courses (surcharge for Caledonia, Tidewater, TPC, and True Blue); electric cart; six buffet breakfasts; six full dinners; golf shirt and cap with logo; sleeve of golf balls and towel; unlimited use of fitness center, saunas, and whirlpool; advanced reserved tee times; and free tennis—up to two hours daily.

Four Points Hotel by Sheraton

2701 S. Ocean Blvd., Myrtle Beach, SC 29577; phone (800) 992-1055 or (843) 448-2518; www.sheratonresort.com; Rates: $148–170

Four Points offers a wide variety of amenities at an affordable price. There are 219 rooms in this 16-story high rise, some of which are efficiencies and some of which are suites, and it is located directly on the beach. Each room has a refrigerator, microwave, coffee maker, cable television, electronic safe, and iron/ironing board. The resort has two pools (one indoor and one outdoor), a whirlpool, a health club, a sauna, a supervised kids' program in season, free covered parking, and tennis club privileges.

Golf Packages   The Four Points "Masters Package" includes four nights' accommodations, four rounds of golf at a choice of many area courses, four breakfasts, access to in-house golf specialist, and a free welcome gift.

Patricia Grand Hotel

2710 N. Ocean Blvd., P.O. Box 1855, Myrtle Beach, SC 29578-1855; phone (800) 255-4763 or (843) 448-8453; www.patricia.com; Rates: $35–160 (ocean front room)

Patricia Grand North

6804 N. Ocean Blvd., P.O. Box 1829, Myrtle Beach, SC 29578-1829; phone (800) 255-4763 or (843) 449-4833; www.patricia.com; Rates: $40–190 (ocean front king end suite)

These sister hotels offer another great option for your stay in Myrtle Beach. Both are situated right on the beach and have solid reputations. On the amenity side, they have indoor and outdoor pools, a "lazy river" that winds through the hotel area, and indoor and outdoor whirlpools. The rooms vary in size, but all are nicely appointed.

Golf Packages   Eighteen holes of golf per day at selected golf courses (some courses require surcharges).

Serendipity Inn

407 71st Ave., Myrtle Beach, SC 29572; phone (800) 762-3229 or (843) 449-5268; www.serendipityinn.com; Rates: $80–130

This inn is a family owned and operated bed-and-breakfast that offers a unique alternative to the large hotels that dominate the area. Serendipity is located in a quiet neighborhood and is more peaceful than many Myrtle Beach accommodations, and it is only 300 yards from the beach. The rooms range in size from queen beds to full-size apartments. All rooms are individually decorated in a different theme that reflects varying historical periods.

Golf Packages   Golf packages are available, but the inn suggests that you contact them directly so that they can develop the best one for you.

INEXPENSIVE

Fairfield Inn

1350 Paradise Circle, Myrtle Beach, SC 29577; phone (800) 217-1511 or (843) 444-8097; www.thefairfieldinn.com; Rates: $85–105; Built: 1997

Landmark Resort Hotel

1501 S. Ocean Blvd., Myrtle Beach, SC 29577; phone (800) 845-0658 or (843) 448-9441; www.landmarkresort.com; Rates: $30–189; Built: 1973; Renovated: 1997

Palm Crest Motel

701 S. Ocean Blvd., Myrtle Beach, SC 29577; phone (800) 487-9233 or (843) 448-7141; Rates: $57–78; Built: 1961; Renovated: 1999

MYRTLE BEACH VILLAS & CONDOS

There are many companies that specialize in villa and condo rentals if you are considering this type of accommodation for your stay. We recommend that you contact these agencies so that they can develop a golf package for you.

Beach Vacations Inc., phone (800) 449-4005
Chicora Beach Holiday, phone (800) 845-0833
Condos of Myrtle Beach, phone (800) 756-4579
Dunes Beach Home Rentals, phone (800) 779-3947
Grand Strand Vacations, phone (800) 722-6278
Ocean Resorts Rental Management, phone (800) 334-5015
Re/Max Ocean Forest, phone (843) 497-7369
Vacation Rentals and Travel, phone (800) 318-4397

PAWLEYS ISLAND

Litchfield Beach and Golf Resort

P.O. Box 320, Highway 17 South, Pawleys Island, SC 29585; phone (888) 714-5992 or (843) 237-3000; www.litchfieldbeach.com; Rates: $59–190

Located on Pawleys Island, a short distance from the heart of Myrtle Beach, lies the Litchfield Beach Golf Resort. This resort exudes "Low-Country charm" and is a great alternative if you want to avoid the hubbub of Myrtle Beach and have a more laid-back, golf-oriented vacation.

Litchfield has a plethora of amenities, including three on-site courses, The Litchfield Country Club, River Club, and Willbrook, as well as the Bryan Van Der Riet Golf Academy. In addition, you will find the Litchfield Racquet Club and Tennis School, indoor and outdoor pools, Summer Adventure Camp for Kids, and a full-service health and beauty spa.

The accommodations at Litchfield are top-notch, with a choice of cottages, condos, villas, suites, and houses. All are beautifully furnished and offer a variety of views including fairway, ocean, and scenic.

Golf Packages There are many factors that will affect the pricing, including your choice of accommodation type (condo versus cottage, etc.), view, time of year, and number of rounds selected. There are also a number of packages offered, but the one that is most popular is the "Resort Package," which includes accommodations, buffet breakfast each day, and greens fees at the resort's three courses. Carts, taxes, and surcharges for other Myrtle Beach courses added to the package are extra.

Pawleys Plantation Golf and Country Club

70 Tanglewood Dr., Pawleys Island, SC 29585; (800) 367-9959 or (843) 237-6009; www.pawleysplantation.com; Rates: $105–150 (one-bedroom villa)

Pawleys is a 582-acre resort that lies in the middle of Pawleys' marshlands and lakes. The resort is said to be the oldest in the United States and was once an 18th-century plantation where the elite came from the North.

Accommodations on the island range from one- to three-bedroom luxury villas nestled on the fairways of the golf course. All villas have private entrances, large living rooms, fully equipped kitchens (including microwave and coffee maker), dining areas, and screened-in verandas. There is also a select group of deluxe villas that have fireplaces, wet bars, formal dining rooms, private master suites, and open-air patios.

Besides golf, Pawleys also offers lit HydroCourt tennis courts, wooded paths for jogging and walking, fishing, and special guest rates at the Health-Point spa.

Golf Packages The "Plantation Platinum" package includes four nights' accommodations, four rounds of golf, and four breakfasts.

Dining

Collector's Café 7726 N. Kings Highway; phone (843) 449-9370. Seafood; Moderate; Reservations suggested. A restaurant with an art gallery—try the crab cakes.

Damon's 4810 Highway 17 S.; phone (843) 238-2421. American, Moderate; Reservations accepted. Great place for ribs.

Fuscos 5308 N. Ocean Blvd.; phone (843) 449-4010. American; Moderate; Reservations suggested. Wonderful views of the ocean.

Joe's Bar & Grill 810 Conway Ave.; phone (843) 272-4666. American; Moderate–Expensive; Reservations suggested. Try the lobster tail and outdoor dining.

Latif's 503 61st Ave.; phone (843) 449-1716. American; Moderate; Reservations accepted. French bistro atmosphere; good chicken salad.

Oak Harbor Inn 1407 13th Ave. N; phone (843) 249-4737. American; Moderate; Reservations suggested. Open and airy restaurant that overlooks the marina.

Rosa Linda's Café 4715 U.S. 17 N.; phone (843) 272-6823. Mexican /Italian; Inexpensive; No reservations needed. Fun combination of food types—good pasta and fajitas.

Sea Captain's House 3000 N. Ocean; phone (843) 448-8082. Seafood; Moderate; Reservations accepted. Restaurant overlooks ocean; fireplace adds atmosphere. Good crab casserole.

Tony's 1407 U.S. 17 N.; phone (843) 249-1314. Italian; Moderate–Expensive, Reservations suggested. Good pasta and veal in a nice Mediterranean decor.

Activities

Alligator Adventure 4604 Hwy. 17 S, N. Myrtle Beach; phone (843) 361-0789. Reptile show and alligator-feeding demonstration.

Balloon Rides Awesome Balloon Flights, 401 Ashwood Lane, Myrtle Beach; phone (843) 215-7990. See the area from a unique perspective.

Bicycle Rental The Bike Doctor, 315 Sea Mountain Hwy. N, Myrtle Beach; phone (843) 243-8152. A terrific means to explore Myrtle Beach.

Canoe/Kayak Rentals & Tours Black River Outdoors Center Expeditions, 21 Garden Ave., Hwy. 701 N, Georgetown; phone (843) 546-4840.

Wind N Sea Outfitters, 6104 Frontage Rd., Myrtle Beach; phone (843) 692-0089. Explore the watery environs of Myrtle Beach.

Dinner Theaters Carolina Opry, 8901 A Hwy. 17 N., Myrtle Beach; phone (800) 843-6779. Dixie Stampede, 8901-B Hwy. 17 Business, Myrtle Beach; phone (800) 433-4401. Myrtle Beach is known for its dinner theaters.

Myrtle Beach Pavillion Amusement Park 9th Ave. N. and Ocean Blvd.; phone (843) 488-6456. Thrill and kiddie rides, video games, teen nightclub.

Myrtle Beach Grand Prix 3201 Hwy. 17, phone (843) 238-2421. Go-carts and speedboats.

Parasailing, Boat Charters, Wave Runners Captain Dick's Marina, 4123 Hwy. 17 Business, Murrells Inlet; phone (843) 344-3474.

Ripleys Aquarium 9th Ave. N. and U.S. 17 N. Bypass; phone (843) 916-0888. See sea creatures up close.

Sailboat Charters Downwind Sails, 29th Ave. S., Myrtle Beach; phone (843) 448-7245.

Wild Water A fine place to escape the heat and have some fun. 910 U.S. 17 S., Surfside Beach; phone (843) 238-9453.

Country and Western Shows Carolina Opry, 82nd Ave.; phone (843) 238-8888.

Dolly Parton's Dixie Stampede 8901-B U.S. 17 Business; phone (843) 497-9700.

House of Blues 4640 U.S. 17 S.; phone (843) 272-3000. Great music entertainment.

The 19th Hole

Starting on the south end of the Grand Strand and working north, check out:

Webster's Phone (843) 237-3000 near Pawleys Island, a nice golfer's pub and restaurant inside Litchfield Plantation and open to the public.

Mingo Moe's Phone (843) 235-0422 at Litchfield Plaza, provides a tropical decor and caters to the 40+ crowd with swing music, shag dancing, and big band sounds.

Fordy's Irish House Phone (843) 651-2265 on Highway 17 in Murrells Inlet is a casual, fun sports bar that has more than 40 TVs to watch all the games and all the Irish and domestic beers to help you kill time while you're doing it.

The Legends Resort On the Bypass south of downtown Myrtle Beach; phone (843) 236-9318. **The Pub** at the golf clubhouse has a variety of domestic and imported beers and a cigar humidor. **The Ailsa Pub** is in the resort village and is for resort guests and members only. It is named after the famous Ailsa Rock in Scotland and features a fireplace, a romantic setting, a cigar humidor, and several Scottish beers.

Broadway at the Beach Just south of downtown Myrtle Beach located on North Oak Street; phone (843) 448-5123. A huge entertainment complex with a special nightclub district called Celebrity Square.

Studebaker's On 21st Avenue N. and Business 17; phone (843) 448-9747. A good singles-mingling dance club where DJs play swing, shag, rock, and golden-oldies music.

Barefoot Landing Entertainment and shopping complex on Highway 17 in North Myrtle Beach, houses several bars and restaurants, among them **Dick's Last Resort;** phone (843) 272-7794, a funky, fun pub that is popular with both locals and visitors and that gets lively crowds for happy hour and after the sun goes down.

Restaurant Row Highway 17 in North Myrtle Beach is home to the bar at **The Old Pro's Table Restaurant;** phone (843) 272-6060. Though it exists more to serve the restaurant than as a meeting and mingling spot, it's worth a visit just to look at the fantastic collection of golf memorabilia. Nearby is **Sam Snead's Tavern;** phone (843) 497-0580, whose walls are smothered with a good deal of interesting memorabilia of the great Slammer.

Provisions On Bay Street in Sunset Beach, North Carolina; phone (910) 457-0654, is a restaurant with a nice, casual bar whose special feature is that it overlooks the ocean and is a great place to watch a sunset.

Part Six

Alabama

Overview

Since the beginning of the interstate highway system, Alabama has been the state that golf travelers just passed through on their way to their final golf destination. Sure, there were a few courses in the state, but overall it was virtually barren of worthy choices. Then along comes Dr. David G. Bronner, CEO of Retirement Systems of Alabama.

Dr. Bronner was looking to invest the state's rather large pension fund and wanted to make sure that his investment would benefit Alabama's image, economy, and citizens. He turned to golf and to Bobby Vaughan of SunBelt Golf Corporation to meet his goals. What Bronner had in mind had not been attempted, from scratch, in any other state. He wanted to build a series of courses throughout the state that were easily reachable, were challenging, and would provide visitors with a "country club for the day" feeling, thereby increasing the state's tourism, bringing in new industry, attracting retirees, and improving the quality of life for its citizens.

To accomplish all these goals, Vaughan turned to Robert Trent Jones Sr., the dean of American golf architects. Jones got to work; by all accounts he not only met but far exceeded Bronner's objectives. The project is known as the Robert Trent Jones Golf Trail, or just the Trail. Presently there are seven sites (with another on the way), each of which is located no more than 30 minutes from the interstate and within a two-hour drive from another Trail course. Four of the sites make up a 54-hole complex (Grand National, Hampton Cove, Magnolia Grove, and Oxmoor Valley) comprised of two 18-hole courses and an 18-hole short course. The other three sites (Cambrian Ridge, Highland Oaks, and Silver Lakes) are made up of three 9-hole full-scale courses, which are played in three different 18-hole combinations, and a 9-hole short course made up of par-3s ranging from 90 to 250 yards. Needless to say, golfers are no longer just passing through. They now stop, play, and enjoy all that Alabama has to offer.

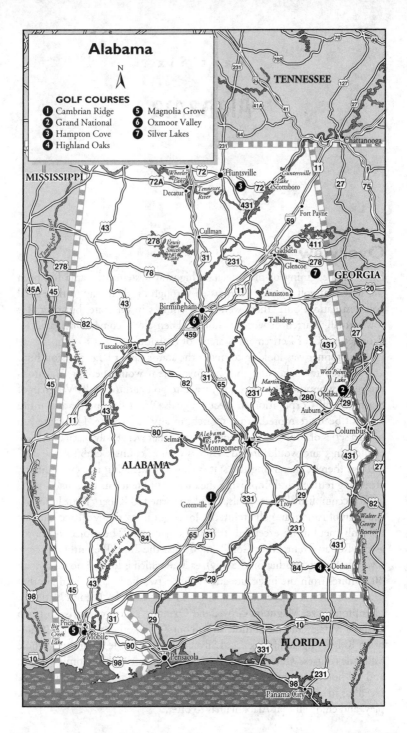

A couple of tidbits worth knowing: Everyone involved, from the developers to the architects, had to get the entire Trail project started and going in a hurry. Admittedly, there was a lot of pension fund money to be spent— a few hundred million—but there was an open-window time period in which it had to be spent. With a new administration, the window could have closed, and funding for the project could have been halted during construction, leaving some half-built courses and clubhouses. Fortunately, the money was spent; Robert Trent Jones, Roger Rulewich (Jones's lead architect), and their crew got the courses completed fairly quickly. As a result of their haste, however, there are some rough edges, some unpolished spots, and at least one goofy hole on nearly every Trail course.

Generally speaking, there's a certain similarity in the Trail sites in that the clubhouses are identical and nearly all of the courses are built in floodplains, fairways can be damp, and many tees and greens are elevated. This makes for attractive tee shots and difficult approaches. The Trent Jones–style, tattered-edge bunkers are common in these courses.

The final common element is that as a group, these courses are simply very difficult. They're not impossible, especially as each course has four sets of tees, but they're all pretty tough—long, with lots of large, deep bunkers and huge, multitiered greens. Frankly, if you're a lousy golfer or one whose ego needs stroking on the scorecard, you may want to go somewhere else for your golf vacation. In truth, these courses are perfect for a good or decent player who wants championship-caliber golf at bargain-basement prices.

By the same token, the variety of site selections for the different facilities is outstanding. No two sites look alike in landscape and terrain, so the only sense of déjà-vu you will get is from the cookie-cutter clubhouses.

No matter how analytical or nitpicky about the Trail courses you get, the one thing—the only thing—that matters is that the courses on the Robert Trent Jones Trail offer some of the best values of any public-access golf experiences in the United States. In a nutshell, the Trail offers world-class golf at municipal course–type prices. The quality of design, course maintenance, service, and amenities is remarkably consistent from one facility to the next, so you can't really go wrong whichever Trail course you choose.

Let's not forget that there's more top-notch, public-access golf in Alabama besides the Trail courses. One worthwhile detour: While driving south on Interstate 65 from Montgomery to Mobile, take a few days to sample the historic courses and lodging at the Marriott Grand Hotel in Point Clear and especially at Gulf Shores, which has several fine tracks, most notably the truly superb Kiva Dunes layout designed by Jerry Pate. Nevertheless, the prime golf vacation attraction in Bear Bryant Country is the Trail itself.

On the accommodations side, we have included information for four cities: Birmingham, Mobile, Montgomery, and Huntsville. These cities have been selected because they provide easy access to the Trail's courses and also offer a variety of accommodation, dining, and activity options.

When to Go and What it Will Cost

The courses on the Trail offer a private club feel at a municipal course rate. The land for each of the Trail courses has been either donated or leased for a dollar to the community in which it was built, so courses are able to keep prices down: greens fees range from $20 to $50 (not including a cart). Thus, it is a great place to head to experience a variety of notable courses without laying out a ton of cash. To reduce costs even more, the Golf Trail can create a custom package for you that includes greens fees and accommodations. Whatever route you decide to take, you will find that the Trail is a grand bargain in comparison to surrounding golf destinations.

As is typical of the South, spring and fall are the most popular times of the year to vacation in Alabama. Autumn gets our nod for the best time to head to Alabama as it is lovely, temperature-wise (highs reach into the mid-70s and lows in the 50–60s range), as well as in the scenery department, with a bit of changing fall foliage. Spring arrives early in Alabama—temperatures hit the 60s by March. Winter can be chilly, but still playable in a sweater. If you head here during the summer, you certainly won't need that sweater. On the contrary, highs are typically in the upper 80s to low 90s, and high humidity is quite common. Oddly enough, if you want to hit the Trail during summer, you're better off heading further south to, say, Mobile's Magnolia Grove or Dothan's Highland Oaks, where at least you have a prayer of breezes off the nearby Gulf to help cool things a bit. Up north, you'll need more luck than prayer to get any summertime relief.

What to Bring

What goes into the suitcase will be dictated by when you are heading for 'Bama. If you are coming during the fall or spring, you will want to include a light sweater and a wind jacket. For the winter months, pack a heavier sweater as well as the wind jacket, and you will want to have an umbrella, just in case. For the summer, lightweight clothes are the ticket. No matter what time of the year you come, make sure you have sunscreen and bug spray—these two items are essential.

The courses tend to be difficult, with many having water in one form or another as well as other natural hazards, so you will want to have a few extra sleeves of balls with you. During the summer, make sure to pack a couple of extra gloves, as the humidity will cause your hands to sweat. Many of the courses allow walking but do not have pull carts, so if you enjoy walking, make sure to bring a light bag to make your trek easier. Also, comfortable shoes are important as well as a couple of extra pairs of socks, especially if you are playing in the morning when it is damp or after it has rained.

ONCE YOU'RE THERE

As you travel from one course to the other (as you probably already inferred, a rental car is a must for your Trail odyssey), you may feel as though you are experiencing déjà-vu. No, it is not your imagination, all the clubhouses were built with the same floor plan to save money. Luckily, however, this cookie-cutter approach was not extended to the courses. A major concern when the sites were being developed was that because they were all being designed by the same person at the same time, they would all look and play alike. We are happy to report this is not the case. Each of the sites—and in fact each of the courses—has its own personality, ensuring that golfers won't quickly adopt a "been here, played it" attitude. Also, each of the courses has multiple tee boxes, making the courses ideal no matter what your handicap. Make sure to check the sign at the first tee, which provides information on which tees will be appropriate for your skill level.

Birmingham has the biggest airport, although commuter flights can take you around the state. Where you start on the Trail is up to you, but try to incorporate Grand National in Opelika (near Auburn) and Cambrian Ridge in Greenville, as these are two of the best sites on the Trail. If you only had time to visit two Trail sites, we'd recommend these two, given their high quality and proximity to each other. On a side note, many of the courses are only a short drive away from other states' golf destinations, such as Mississippi's Gulf Coast and Florida's Panhandle, so if you have the time, you might want to plan a trip that crosses state lines.

As we have mentioned, Alabama has not historically been much of a tourist destination. This is both good and bad for you. On the plus side, you'll find that prices for accommodations and dining are reasonable in comparison with other golf meccas. The down side is the fact that the lodging has not caught up with the golf, and thus it is hard to find premiere hotels or world-class resorts in most of the cities where the courses are located. That is not to say that these accommodations there are not acceptable, but don't expect the Hilton Head–like options.

GATHERING INFORMATION

Golf Trail Information: If you are considering a trip on the Robert Trent Jones Golf Trail, your first call should be to the Trail's main offices, which can assist you in developing an itinerary as well as comprehensive golf packages that meet your needs. They can be reached at (800) 949-4444 or via their Web site at www.rtjgolf.com.

For information about Alabama contact:
Alabama Bureau of Tourism and Travel
401 Adams Ave., Montgomery, AL 36103
Phone (800) 252-2262 or (334) 242-4169.

The Major Courses

Cambrian Ridge Golf Course

101 SunBelt Parkway, Greenville, AL 36037; phone (800) 949-4444 or (334) 382-9787

Located 40 miles south of Montgomery, the three nines at Cambrian Ridge (which play in three different 18-hole combinations) are very diverse in their terrain—from rolling fairways to hilly and flat ones. Nowhere else on the Robert Trent Jones Golf Trail will you find the dramatic differences you will at Cambrian Ridge. As is the case with many of the Trail courses, water comes into play on many of the holes, and the patented Robert Trent Jones bunkers (large and gaping, with lacy edges) are everywhere. The course also features a nine-hole short course, composed entirely of challenging par-3s.

Greenville's Cambrian Ridge is truly the hidden gem of the Trail. Then again, hidden may be the operative word here. There's just not much happenin' in sleepy ol' Greenville. As one former Alabaman put it, "If you're into doing anything else but playing golf, you've come to the wrong place." The only nearby attraction is the Hank Williams Sr. museum, but even that is pretty much skippable unless you are truly a Williams fanatic who wants to pay your respects. Cambrian Ridge is one of the Trail's "must-plays," but your best bet is to sample it while commuting from Montgomery.

How To Get On: Tee times can be made seven days in advance—longer if the Trail's central booking department creates your itinerary.

Canyon Course Tees:

    Purple: 3,746 yards, par-36, USGA rating 38.0, slope 74

    Orange: 3,490 yards, par-36, USGA rating 36.9, slope 72

    White: 3,058 yards, par-36, USGA rating 35.8, slope 70

    Teal: 2,422 yards, par-36, USGA rating 34.4, slope 68

    Women's Teal: 2,422 yards, par-36, USGA rating 33.9, slope 59

Loblolly Course Tees:

    Purple: 3,551 yards, par-36, USGA rating 36.6, slope 66

    Orange: 3,295 yards, par-36, USGA rating 35.6, slope 63

    White: 3,078 yards, par-36, USGA rating 34.7, slope 61

Teal: 2,350 yards, par-36, USGA rating 33.4, slope 58

Women's Teal: 2,350 yards, par-36, USGA rating 33.5, slope 54

Sherling Course Tees:

Purple: 3,681 yards, par-36, USGA rating 37.4, slope 67

Orange: 3,423 yards, par-36, USGA rating 36.3, slope 65

White: 3,028 yards, par-36, USGA rating 34.9, slope 62

Teal: 2,435 yards, par-36, USGA rating 33.7, slope 60

Women's Teal: 2,435 yards, par-36, USGA rating 34.3, slope 57

Challenge: ★★★★½	Golf Facilities: ★★★★
Variety: ★★★★	14-Club Test: ★★★★
Terrain: ★★★★½	Intangibles: ★★★★
Beauty/Visual Appeal: ★★★½	Value: ★★★★
Pace of Play: ★★★	

Just the Facts   Year Opened: 1993; Course Designer: Robert Trent Jones Sr.; Walking: Yes; Greens Fee: $44; 9 Hole/Twilight Rate: Yes; Pull Carts: No; Practice Range: Yes; Club Rental: Yes.

Description and Comments   Cambrian Ridge probably is the most dramatic of all of the Trail sites, with the most attractive vistas, steepest terrain, boldest bunkers, and tallest trees. The most common pairing at Cambrian Ridge is between the Sherling and Canyon nines. The Sherling course starts off innocently enough with a strong yet manageable par-5 followed by a mellow par-3. Then comes the drama. The 3rd hole is a striking par-4 (428 yards) that features stunning views as it plays downhill to Sherling Lake. Keep your camera out for the next three holes as they wind around the lake. The hardest hole on this course is the 8th, a brutal par-5 that plays 636 yards from the tips and features a fistful of yawning fairway bunkers. The enormous green is multitiered and often results in three putts. Now comes the hard stuff.

The Canyon Course is the most demanding nine at Cambrian and requires golfers to play "target" golf. It starts out with a downhill dogleg right that plays 501 yards from the tips—not too bad for a par-5, but this hole is a par-4! Even if you hammer your drive, you still have a lot of ground to cover (uphill to boot) to reach the shallow green. Needless to say, bogey is an acceptable score here. We're sorry to say that the second hole offers no respite. From the tips, it measures an almost incomprehensible 275 yards. One of the criticisms of the Robert Trent Jones organization over the years has been its inability to build interesting short or medium-length par-3s. Critics will work themselves into a frenzy at Cambrian Ridge's Canyon nine. As if the par-3 2nd isn't bloated, the second par-3, the 8th, is in the behemoth range as well, at 258 yards. As crazy as that appears to be, the redeeming features of the holes are that they can be played at 163 and 152 yards, respectively, from the white tees.

The Loblolly nine is much easier than the other two courses as it is relatively flat and shorter from most of the tees. It is, however, still worthy of your time. Loblolly features gently rolling terrain, majestic trees, and greens guarded by water. Although much less intimidating than the other two nines, it still requires skillful play. Our recommendation: Play all 27 holes—they all are unique and provide a strong challenge.

Insider Tips   OK, first the good news. The course is pretty wide open off the tees, so you can use your driver. Now the bad news: You'll need to smash your driver throughout the round, including on both of Canyon's par-3s. Some other tips that can make your round a little less painful: On Sherling's 5th hole, make sure to keep all your shots to the right side to avoid the gaping lake on the left. For the 9th hole, the left-hand side is the place to be. Also, add a club or two more to your approach shot to the tri-tiered green. A hint for first-time visitors: For Canyon's 4th through 6th holes, a trio of shortish par-4s, a rule of thumb is to play conservatively, using the striped 150-yard post perched in the fairway center as a guide. Any drive played to the vicinity of the marker will result in a favorable approach to the greens without endangering your tee shot and leave you with a level lie.

Grand National Golf Course, Lake and Links Courses

3000 SunBelt Parkway, Opelika, AL 36801; phone (800) 949-4444 or (205) 749-9042

Grand National is the flagship of the Trail and is reportedly the single most impressive site that Robert Trent Jones Sr. had ever seen. In fact, the Grand Old Man of modern architecture went on record calling Grand National "The most spectacular golf site in the world." Pretty high praise indeed, given the other jewels he has worked on, such as California's Spyglass Hill, The New Course at Ireland's Ballybunion, and Spain's Ryder Cup site, Valderrama, just to name a few. The site, located near Auburn, is comprised of two 18-hole regular courses and one 18-hole short course, all built on surprisingly gentle terrain. The challenge at Grand National comes in the form of 600-acre Lake Saughahatche. Thirty-two of the 54 holes play alongside this lake, creating quite a few tricky water hazards. In 1997, Grand National hosted the Nike Tour Championship; in 2000 it will host the NCAA Men's Division 1 Championship. Grand National offers challenging golf and scenic vistas—it is one stop on the Trail you don't want to miss.

How To Get On: Tee times can be made seven days in advance—longer if the Trail's central booking department creates your itinerary.

Lake Course Tees:

> Purple: 7,149 yards, par-72, USGA rating 74.9, slope 138
>
> Orange: 6,488 yards, par-72, USGA rating 72.3, slope 134
>
> White: 5,948 yards, par-72, USGA rating 69.9, slope 129
>
> Teal: 4,910 yards, par-72, USGA rating 68.7, slope 117
>
> Women's Teal: 4,910 yards, par-72, USGA rating 68.0, slope 119

Challenge: ★★★★	Golf Facilities: ★★★★
Variety: ★★★½	14-Club Test: ★★★★
Terrain: ★★★★★	Intangibles: ★★★★
Beauty/Visual Appeal: ★★★★½	Value: ★★★★½
Pace of Play: ★★★½	

Just the Facts   Year Opened: 1992; Course Designer: Robert Trent Jones Sr.; Walking: Yes; Greens Fee: $39–49; 9 Hole/Twilight Rate: Yes; Pull Carts: No; Practice Range: Yes; Club Rental: Yes.

Description and Comments   The Lake Course . . . do you think there might be water? Good guess. Water is the predominant theme on this tract, with eight lakeside holes, four on each side, creating lovely scenery as well as the potential for many lost balls.

You won't get much of a chance to warm up before you encounter your first water test. Lake Sugahatchee plays along the entire left side of the second hole, a 428-yard par-4. The right-hand side is no bargain either, with bunkers crowding the landing area. Lakeside breezes will complicate the approach to a peninsula green, making the hole play more difficult than it appears on paper. Par is an excellent score on this hole. It doesn't get any easier from here.

There are numerous other challenging and scenic holes that we could outline here, but the two that are the most dramatic and most memorable are the par-5 12th and the par-3 15th. As you stand on the 12th tee, you may feel as though you are 3,000 miles away on Pebble Beach's famed 18th. The hole is a boomerang shape and hugs the shoreline along the entire left side and plays 522 yards from the tips. It is a great risk/reward test, as cutting off yardage over the water on both sides of the boomerang can bring you to birdie range. The 15th is a par-3, 230-yard hole where the tee shot is all carry over the lake to a long and narrow island green.

Insider Tips   On this course, as well as at the Links Course (see below), our best recommendation is that you select the appropriate tees for your game. If you play from the correct tees, you at least have a fighting chance. Here's a tip that will let you have more fun not only at this course, but at others on the Trail: Mix and match which tees you play. You obviously can't do this in a tournament or when posting a score, but when you're just out having fun, you may enjoy playing certain holes from the purple, others from the orange, and perhaps others from the white. Beyond that, course management will be the key. With water coming into play on so many holes, you will need to think two shots ahead. Before you tee off, consider not only where the water is for this first stroke but also where it comes into play on the rest of the hole. Pick a line that is most advantageous for the entire hole.

Another piece of advice for the Lake Course: If you're playing this one shortly before or soon after it hosts a tournament, prepare to score at least 10 shots higher than your usual tally. The greens are harder, the rough is higher, the sand softer. This is true for any of the Trail courses that hosts big events. Call ahead to find out when these events are taking place. If you relish that sort of challenge, you'll love these setups. If you don't, you may want to try one of the other courses.

Links Course Tees:

Purple: 7,311 yards, par-72, USGA rating 74.9, slope 141

Orange: 6,574 yards, par-72, USGA rating 72.7, slope 136

White: 6,052 yards, par-72, USGA rating 70.2, slope 131

Teal: 4,843 yards, par-72, USGA rating 69.6, slope 113

Women's Teal: 4,843 yards, par-72, USGA rating 70.4, slope 120

Challenge: ★★★★½	Golf Facilities: ★★★★
Variety: ★★★★	14-Club Test: ★★★★½
Terrain: ★★★★	Intangibles: ★★★★
Beauty/Visual Appeal: ★★★★	Value: ★★★★½
Pace of Play: ★★★½	

Just the Facts   Year Opened: 1992; Course Designer: Robert Trent Jones Sr.; Walking: Yes; Greens Fee: $39–49; 9 Hole/Twilight Rate: Yes; Pull Carts: No; Practice Range: Yes; Club Rental: Yes.

Description and Comments   The Links Course is the cornerstone of Grand National and is Trail developer Bobby Vaughan's favorite course. The Links has a little bit of everything—trees, wetlands, topsy-turvy terrain, elevation changes, more of Lake Sugahatchee, big brassy bunkers, and wildly rolling greens—all combining to make this an incredibly tough and stimulating test of golf. Some experts claim that Links is the hardest but most fair to play of all the Trail courses.

As with the Lakes, golfers will encounter hardy holes early on. The 2nd hole is a par-5, 556-yard dogleg gem with a mogul-filled fairway. If you smack a good drive, the green is reachable in two—but it is a risk/reward decision. The green is well bunkered and protected by water on the right. So, if you hit it well, you can be a hero with a birdie. Hit it off line, and, well, let's just say you could be flirting with disaster.

The 18th hole (par-4, 471 yards) is an amazing finishing hole—easily the best on the trail. Golfers must confront Lake Sugahatchee not once but twice to reach the hole's football field–sized green. Off the tee, you will want to aim just left of the bunker on the right. You then face a killer approach over water and rocks. Pull it off and you'll achieve "legend" status, but for the prudent player, lay-up could be the better way to go.

Insider Tips   Like all of the courses on the Trail, there are four tees at the Links. In a departure from many of the courses on the Trail, there's a wide disparity in yardage and difficulty between the purple (back) tees and the orange (second from the back). The purple tees stretch nearly 750 yards longer than the orange ones, so unless you are "Tigerish" off the tee and can really crank your drives, you will want to select the orange teeing ground. What we're really asking is do you really want to play the par-3 11th over marsh and bunker from the back tee of 260 yards? Have some fun and move up.

The best scoring opportunities occur from holes six through thirteen, which tend to yield more birdies than elsewhere on the course. This is relative, however, and applies only to great players. The Links Course can be terribly punishing to average golfers, especially those who haven't brought their "A" games with them. Conversely, the final five holes are the most challenging. Once again, course management is the key to your success here. Also, atypical of a links-style course, this layout has quite a few elevation changes, so you will need to make adjustments with your yardages.

Hampton Cove Golf Course

450 Old Highway 431 S., Owens Cross Road, Huntsville, AL 35763; phone (800) 949-4444 or (256) 551-1818

Hampton Cove is the northernmost site on the Trail, located near Huntsville, and consists of two 18-hole courses, The Highlands and River Courses, as well as a Short Course all located among surrounding mountains. Although southern in its roots, its terrain is reminiscent of a Colorado course. It probably is one of the most well-developed layouts, as indicated by the huge homes that line the first few holes of the Highlands Course.

This site suffers a bit when it takes some rain because the course sits so low in a mountain valley. It was built in a low-lying flood plain, necessitating the creation of elevated tee boxes and greens on every hole. This leads to some monotony in appearance and playing value, but at least the tees and greens stay drier as the rainwater drains off. Fairways, unfortunately, can get awfully mushy.

Hampton Cove should probably be last on your list of Trail courses to sample in mid-summer, though the Birmingham-area courses aren't much better. We're not saying that you shouldn't attempt it, just remember, we're talking miserably hot, "can't catch your breath" kind of heat and humidity.

How To Get On: Tee times can be made seven days in advance—longer if the Trail's central booking department creates your itinerary.

Highlands Course Tees:

  Purple: 7,262 yards, par-72, USGA rating 75.0, slope 133

  Orange: 6,620 yards, par-72, USGA rating 72.1, slope 124

  White: 6,004 yards, par-72, USGA rating 69.4, slope 117

  Teal: 4,765 yards, par-72, USGA rating 66.0, slope 118

  Women's Teal: 4,765 yards, par-72, USGA rating 68.3, slope 113

Challenge: ★★★½	Golf Facilities: ★★★★
Variety: ★★★	14-Club Test: ★★★½
Terrain: ★★★½	Intangibles: ★★★
Beauty/Visual Appeal: ★★★★	Value: ★★★★½
Pace of Play: ★★★½	

Just the Facts   Year Opened: 1992; Course Designer: Robert Trent Jones Sr.; Walking: At certain times; Greens Fee: $20–27; 9 Hole/Twilight Rate: Yes; Pull Carts: No; Practice Range: Yes; Club Rental: Yes.

Description and Comments   Highlands is a links-style course that, with the exception of a few holes, plays through a river valley. Its first few holes play through a meadow lined with fescues and sand bunkers. The terrain quickly changes with the 4th, a par-3 that plays along a hillside through trees. The 5th hole is especially eye-catching: The green is framed by an old barn on the right-hand side, and a stream runs through the hole. This course provides the most variety in terms of landscape—the only drawback is the fact that the first three holes play through a housing development, detracting from the course's beauty.

Insider Tips   Although there are many hazards throughout the course, landing areas remain generous. However, because the course features rolling terrain and grassy mounds, you will have an uneven lie for the majority of your shots, so be careful on your second shot. The most difficult hole is the 3rd hole, so make sure you are warmed up—as much mentally as physically—by the time you get there. It boasts many strategic options and calls for well-thought-out choices. It is a 518-yard par-5 that features a stream flowing right down the center and in front of the green. The 9th hole is also very difficult—another par-5 (511 yards) that plays uphill all the way from tee to a well-protected green.

River Course Tees:

  Purple: 7,667 yards, par-72, USGA rating 76.0, slope 130

  Orange: 6,764 yards, par-72, USGA rating 71.3, slope 123

  White: 6,111 yards, par-72, USGA rating 68.7, slope 116

Teal: 5,278 yards, par-72, USGA rating 67.0, slope 118

Women's Teal: 5,278 yards, par-72, USGA rating 70.4, slope 119

Challenge: ★★★★	Golf Facilities: ★★★★
Variety: ★★½	14-Club Test: ★★★
Terrain: ★★½	Intangibles: ★★★
Beauty/Visual Appeal: ★★★	Value: ★★★★
Pace of Play: ★★★½	

Just the Facts Year Opened: 1993; Course Designer: Robert Trent Jones Sr.; Walking: Yes; Greens Fee: $20–27; 9 Hole/Twilight Rate: Yes; Pull Carts: No; Practice Range: Yes; Club Rental: Yes.

Description and Comments At first glimpse of the River Course you might think that this is a boring layout. The course was built on a former soybean field and tends to be flat, except for some mounds in the fairway. It also is the only course on the Trail (and one of few championship courses anywhere) without any bunkers. This is due to the fact that the course was laid out on such low-lying ground that they couldn't dig in to create bunkers or they would have hit the water table. So why should you play here? The challenge comes from the thick forests that line the fairways and a river that winds its way through 16 of the holes, creating 26 water hazards. Greens are triple-tiered, are extremely undulating, and sit atop knolls to create quite a putting threat. When you reach the 18th green, make sure to take note of the 250-year-old oak tree behind the putting surface.

Insider Tips Control and a solid short game are the keys to scoring well on this course. If you keep out of the rivers and trees (no easy task given the prolific amount on the course of each hazard) you've won half the battle. That just leaves chipping and putting. The fact that the greens are perched on pedestals make it critical for you to get the ball there—short shots will be punished severely and may end up exactly where they started. Be certain of your yardage before you make your approach, and check pin placements. One of the hardest holes on the course is number seven, a 433-yard par-4 that has water protecting the green and is made more difficult when the wind comes up. It is often wise to lay up on this hole and hope for a great up and down.

Try to avoid this low-lying course after a good rain. If you are forced to play it in these soft conditions, think about picking the ball cleaner than usual off the fairway with your irons. Take a shallower divot with less grass displaced.

Highland Oaks Golf Course

904 Royal Parkway, Dothan, AL 36301; phone (800) 949-4444 or (334) 712-2820

Highland Oaks, located in the southeast corner of Alabama, is just this side of Florida and is quickly gaining recognition normally reserved for courses located in its more golf-friendly neighbor. For instance, the Nike Tour Championship was contested at Highland Oaks in 1999. Although we recognize that this isn't the U.S. Open, it is further evidence that Alabama is on the golfing map. Highland Oaks has three 9-hole courses that play in 3 18-hole combinations, as well as a 9-hole short course.

How To Get On: Tee times can be made seven days in advance—longer if the Trail's central booking department creates your itinerary.

Highlands Course Tees:

> Purple: 3,892 yards, par-36, USGA rating 38.6, slope 70
>
> Orange: 3,580 yards, par-36, USGA rating 37.1, slope 68
>
> White: 3,296 yards, par-36, USGA rating 35.8, slope 66
>
> Teal: 2,554 yards, par-36, USGA rating 34.3, slope 63
>
> Women's Teal: 2,554 yards, par-36, USGA rating 35.0, slope 64

Marshwood Course Tees:

> Purple: 3,812 yards, par-36, USGA rating 38.3, slope 68
>
> Orange: 3,492 yards, par-36, USGA rating 36.8, slope 65
>
> White: 3,158 yards, par-36, USGA rating 35.3, slope 63
>
> Teal: 2,531 yards, par-36, USGA rating 34.0, slope 60
>
> Women's Teal: 2,531 yards, par-36, USGA rating 34.5, slope 62

Magnolia Course Tees:

> Purple: 3,699 yards, par-36, USGA rating 37.4, slope 65
>
> Orange: 3,404 yards, par-36, USGA rating 36.1, slope 62
>
> White: 3,090 yards, par-36, USGA rating 34.7, slope 59
>
> Teal: 2,471 yards, par-36, USGA rating 33.3, slope 56
>
> Women's Teal: 2,471 yards, par-36, USGA rating 34.0, slope 59

Challenge: ★★★★½	Golf Facilities: ★★★★
Variety: ★★★★	14-Club Test: ★★★★
Terrain: ★★★½	Intangibles: ★★★½
Beauty/Visual Appeal: ★★★★	Value: ★★★★½
Pace of Play: ★★★½	

Just the Facts Year Opened: 1993; Course Designer: Robert Trent Jones Sr.; Walking: Yes; Greens Fee: $20–27; 9 Hole/Twilight Rate: Yes; Pull Carts: Yes; Practice Range: Yes; Club Rental: Yes.

Description and Comments Overall, these courses tend to be the most classically designed on the Trail, featuring many sand bunkers, large greens with undulations, and tree-lined fairways. The three nines are also the longest courses you will find on your Trail adventure. The Highlands nine is really the core course at this site (the Highlands and Magnolia courses tend to be the favored combination at Highland Oaks, played in that order) and features fairly open fairways with water hazards (in the form of lakes) coming into play on several holes.

Getting to the Magnolia nine is almost as fun as playing as you must traverse a 1,000-foot-long wooden bridge that spans a marsh. The Magnolia nine is aptly named: It sports many of these stately trees throughout the course. The Marshwood Course has gained notoriety for its 6th hole, an incredibly long par-5 playing an unfathomable 701 yards from the tips. However, the best hole on the course is its finishing hole, a 422-yard dogleg-right par-4 that plays to a slanted, elevated green that rises above the wetlands.

Insider Tips   Given the open fairways and long yardages, make sure you have your driver working before you get to the first tee. An effectively hit tee shot will make a big difference in your score. On the Highlands course, the 3rd hole is the hardest and requires a tee shot over water to a landing area. Your approach shot must also clear a second body of water to reach the large, concave green. It is important that you pick the right club off the tee—check the yardages from your tee—you don't want to be too long, but then again, you want to have a nice short approach shot that you can nestle near the flag. On Marshland's 701-yard hole, the best advice is to carry the fairway bunkers. Then you will get the downhill roll, accruing you some much-needed yardage.

Magnolia Grove Golf Course

7000 Lamplighter Dr., Mobile, AL 36575; phone (800) 949-4444 or (334) 645-0075

Located in the southwest corner of the state just outside of Mobile lies Magnolia Grove, another Trail course that is earning widespread recognition. Magnolia Grove resembles Florida's terrain more than Alabama's, with sandy soil and rolling fairways lined by pine trees. In 1998 it hosted the Nike Tour Championship (played at Highland Oaks in 1999) and in 1999 the AFLAC LPGA Tournament of Champions. Magnolia Grove consists of two 18-hole regular-length courses, Crossings and Falls, and one 18-hole short course. All three courses cover a variety of terrain, including creeks, lakes, marshland, and forests. The greens at Magnolia Grove tend to be the most forgiving and puttable of all the Trail courses.

How To Get On: Tee times can be made seven days in advance—longer if the Trail's central booking department creates your itinerary.

Crossings Course Tees:

Purple: 7,151 yards, par-72, USGA rating 74.6, slope 134

Orange: 6,560 yards, par-72, USGA rating 71.6, slope 132

White: 6,063 yards, par-72, USGA rating 69.0, slope 128

Teal: 5,184 yards, par-72, USGA rating 67.9, slope 123

Women's Teal: 5,184 yards, par-72, USGA rating 70.4, slope 131

Challenge: ★★★½   Golf Facilities: ★★★★

Variety: ★★★   14-Club Test: ★★★½

Terrain: ★★★½   Intangibles: ★★★★

Beauty/Visual Appeal: ★★★½   Value: ★★★★

Pace of Play: ★★★½

Just the Facts   Year Opened: 1992; Course Designer: Robert Trent Jones Sr.; Walking: Yes; Greens Fee: $34–44; 9 Hole/Twilight Rate: Yes; Pull Carts: No; Practice Range: Yes; Club Rental: Yes.

Description and Comments   Crossings derives its name from the fact that you must cross a set of railroad tracks to reach the 13th through 15th holes. Along the way, you must also cross quite a few hazards in the form of water, marshland, and sand as you negotiate your way around this 18-holer. The course starts out pretty gently and allows you to get warmed up before the real test starts. The 4th hole, a 525-yard par-5, plays up and over a crest of a hill to a tight, well-guarded green with a pond in front and railroad tracks in back.

The course plays relatively flat, with the only uphill tee shots coming on the 10th and 11th holes. The back nine is where you will find most of the water hazards that you must negotiate. The 14th, a par-3, requires a tee shot over marshland to a heavily bunkered green, whereas the 15th, a short dogleg hole (430 yards), has marshland in front of the green. The final hole is a **V** shape with a tee shot down a hill and a second back up another hill to the green.

Insider Tips   You will want to be very selective in using your driver. On many of the holes, you can reach the trouble area off the tee with a solidly hit ball, so make sure to refer to the yardage book before you swing away. If you end up in the trees, you will want to take your medicine and hit a safe shot out and play for bogey. Attempted heroics can lead to sudden disaster.

Falls Course Tees:

Purple: 7,239 yards, par-72, USGA rating 75.1, slope 137

Orange: 6,558 yards, par-72, USGA rating 71.9, slope 131

White: 6,070 yards, par-72, USGA rating 69.7, slope 126

Teal: 5,253 yards, par-72, USGA rating 68.1, slope 124

Women's Teal: 5,253 yards, par-72, USGA rating 71.0, slope 126

Challenge: ★★★★   Golf Facilities: ★★★★

Variety: ★★★   14-Club Test: ★★★½

Terrain: ★★★½   Intangibles: ★★★★

Beauty/Visual Appeal: ★★★½   Value: ★★★★

Pace of Play: ★★★½

Just the Facts   Year Opened: 1992; Course Designer: Robert Trent Jones Sr.; Walking: Yes; Greens Fee: $34–44; 9 Hole/Twilight Rate: Yes; Pull Carts: No; Practice Range: Yes; Club Rental: Yes.

Description and Comments   The Falls is the harder and, in our opinion, better of the two courses at Magnolia Grove. Falls plays out to a lake and then makes a turn at the 10th and plays back in. The holes are characterized by their many contoured bunkers and the relatively forgiving, elevated greens. The signature hole is the 10th, a 570-yard par-5, at which golfers play to a peninsula green accented by a cascading waterfall. But it is the stretch of par-4s from holes 14 to 17 that really gets our attention. These four are an extremely hard string of holes, especially the marsh-laden, 437-yard, dog-leg 16th.

Insider Tips   As is the case with the Crossings course, you will want to use your driver with discretion. If you do end up in the trees or in another of the many hazards, you will face severe penalties. The terrain on the Falls is gently rolling, and thus you will encounter many sidehill lies.

Oxmoor Valley Golf Course

100 SunBelt Parkway, Birmingham, AL 35211; phone (800) 949-4444 or (205) 942-1177

Oxmoor Valley is built on land donated by U.S. Steel in Birmingham and is comprised of two regular 18-hole courses, Ridge and Valley, and one 18-hole short course. The courses are built in the peaks and valleys of the Appalachian Mountains, providing numerous elevation changes and scenic forests.

How To Get On: Tee times can be made seven days in advance—longer if the Trail's central booking department creates your itinerary.

Ridge Course Tees:

Purple: 7,055 yards, par-72, USGA rating 73.5, slope 140

Orange: 6,527 yards, par-72, USGA rating 71.6, slope 136

White: 6,148 yards, par-72, USGA rating 70.1, slope 133

Teal: 4,974 yards, par-72, USGA rating 69.1, slope 122

Women's Teal: 4,974 yards, par-72, USGA rating 70.2, slope 130

Challenge: ★★★★	Golf Facilities: ★★★★
Variety: ★★★½	14-Club Test: ★★★★
Terrain: ★★★½	Intangibles: ★★★½
Beauty/Visual Appeal: ★★★★	Value: ★★★★
Pace of Play: ★★★	

Just the Facts   Year Opened: 1992; Course Designer: Robert Trent Jones Sr.; Walking: Yes; Greens Fee: $39–49; 9 Hole/Twilight Rate: Yes; Pull Carts: No; Practice Range: Yes; Club Rental: Yes.

Description and Comments   Appropriately named, the Ridge Course plays along a succession of mountain ridges, at times atop the remains of old coal mines. Needless to say, it is a scenic layout with wonderful views of the land beyond and below. The fairways tend to be extremely rolling, almost like a roller coaster, but are surprisingly generous. This is comforting given the fact that you must hit a lot of your blind shots up and over mounds. The fairways are lined by forests, so be certain of your aim before you swing.

One of the most difficult holes on this course is the par-5 9th, a 592-yarder that features a well-guarded green positioned on a plateau. The most scenic hole is the 17th, a 176-yard par-3 where the green lies 90 feet below the tee—make sure to have your camera for this one. Unique is the green at the par-5 12th and the tee box at the par-4 13th, both of which are located on top of a gray shale mesa left over from long-ago mining operations.

Insider Tips   The fairways are peaked in the center, so your drives will need to be very accurate or your tee shot will run down either side of the peak into the forest or other hazards. The greens are large and undulating and have many subtle breaks—three putts are the norm rather than the exception. Also, this course is only walkable if you are training for or have recently run a marathon. If not, don't even think about it, as you will not enjoy the round.

Valley Course Tees:

    Purple: 7,292 yards, par-72, USGA rating 73.9, slope 135

    Orange: 6,631 yards, par-72, USGA rating 70.8, slope 129

    White: 6,059 yards, par-72, USGA rating 68.1, slope 123

    Teal: 4,899 yards, par-72, USGA rating 69.4, slope 122

    Women's Teal: 4,899 yards, par-72, USGA rating 70.6, slope 131

Challenge: ★★★★	Golf Facilities: ★★★★
Variety: ★★★½	14-Club Test: ★★★½
Terrain: ★★★½	Intangibles: ★★★½
Beauty/Visual Appeal: ★★★½	Value: ★★★★
Pace of Play: ★★★½	

Just the Facts   Year Opened: 1992; Course Designer: Robert Trent Jones Sr.; Walking: Yes; Greens Fee: $39–49; 9 Hole/Twilight Rate: Yes; Pull Carts: No; Practice Range: Yes; Club Rental: Yes.

Description and Comments   As you approach the 1st tee you will think that the Valley Course is similar to the Ridge. But besides this first hole, where you drop 250 feet from the first tee to the first green, the rest of the course is mostly flat as it winds its way along the valley floor between two mountain peaks. The Valley Course is a links-style layout that features rolling terrain and lakes that come into play on many holes. The biggest challenge will come from your flat stick as the greens are, in short, scary. They are wide, deep, undulating, and very swift.

The 18th hole is one of the most memorable on the course. A 414-yard par-4 nicknamed "the assassin" that plays dramatically up to the clubhouse located just beyond the green.

Insider Tips The dramatic difference between the two courses makes this stop on the Trail quite memorable. The Valley Course is the easier of the two layouts, as illustrated by the slopes and ratings, but it is actually longer from the tips. Regardless of what the statistics show, it is the more playable of the two, but it is still quite a challenge. Walking here is also very tough, although easier than the Ridge Course, but we still recommend taking a cart.

Silver Lakes Golf Course

1 SunBelt Parkway, Glencoe, AL 35905; phone (800) 949-4444 or (256) 892-3268

Silver Lakes is located near Birmingham and is comprised of three 9-hole courses played in three 18-hole combinations. In addition, there is a short course.

How To Get On: Tee times can be made seven days in advance—longer if the Trail's central booking department creates your itinerary.

Backbreaker Course Tees:

Purple: 3,846 yards, par-36, USGA rating 38.2, slope 63

Orange: 3,385 yards, par-36, USGA rating 35.4, slope 58

White: 2,927 yards, par-36, USGA rating 33.8, slope 56

Teal: 2,364 yards, par-36, USGA rating 33.1, slope 54

Women's Teal: 2,364 yards, par-36, USGA rating 33.7, slope 60

Heartbreaker Course Tees:

Purple: 3,828 yards, par-36, USGA rating 38.5, slope 68

Orange: 3,301 yards, par-36, USGA rating 35.5, slope 60

White: 2,967 yards, par-36, USGA rating 34.1, slope 59

Teal: 2,543 yards, par-36, USGA rating 34.3, slope 57

Women's Teal: 2,543 yards, par-36, USGA rating 34.3, slope 62

Mindbreaker Course Tees:

Purple: 3,579 yards, par-36, USGA rating 37.0, slope 64

Orange: 3,215 yards, par-36, USGA rating 35.4, slope 60

White: 2,987 yards, par-36, USGA rating 34.2, slope 58

Teal: 2,322 yards, par-36, USGA rating 33.8, slope 56

Women's Teal: 2,322 yards, par-36, USGA rating 34.0, slope 62

Challenge: ★★★★½

Variety: ★★★★

Terrain: ★★★★

Beauty/Visual Appeal: ★★★★

Pace of Play: ★★★

Golf Facilities: ★★★★

14-Club Test: ★★★★

Intangibles: ★★★½

Value: ★★★★

Just the Facts Year Opened: 1993; Course Designer: Robert Trent Jones Sr.; Walking: Yes; Greens Fee: $29–39; 9 Hole/Twilight Rate: Yes; Pull Carts: No; Practice Range: Yes; Club Rental: Yes.

Description and Comments As the names of the three nines indicate, Silver Lakes tends to be the hardest course on the Trail, but the beauty of the surrounding areas may quickly ease your stress. Even the lead architect of the Trail's courses feels that this one poses the toughest challenge on the entire Trail. The course is located in the foothills of the Appalachians and at the edge of Talladega National Forest, which is particularly striking during the fall.

The Backbreaker nine is the most scenic, featuring magnificent views of the Appalachians from the course's elevated tees. A 75-acre lake comes into play on quite a few holes, as it does on the other two nines.

Heartbreaker is aptly named—many consider it the hardest test on the Trail. Evidence of this moniker is the par-4 9th hole that plays 450 yards from the tips. Although the length is tough on its own, it is the water that winds its way down the entire left-hand side of the hole that really wreaks havoc.

The final nine, Mindbreaker, sounds more like a title for a Stanley Kubrick movie rather than a golf course, but let us assure you it is the latter. Considered the easiest of the three nines, it still demands your attention as well as your shotmaking ability.

Insider Tips All of the nines are fairly wide open, and many of the holes play uphill, so if you can swing a driver safely off the tee, let 'er rip. Greens tend to be undulating with many tiers, so make sure to check pin placements and refer to the yardage book provided at the start of your round to make yardage adjustments. Although walking is allowed, there are quite a few elevation changes; you may want to rethink walking unless you love a good workout while you play. Oh, one more warning—watch out for poisonous snakes near the lakes.

Lodging in Birmingham

When you look at the city of Birmingham today, it's hard to believe that it wasn't always a prosperous city. One indication of how inconsequential the city was: a comment made by a Union general during the Civil War who decided that Birmingham "deserved no attack as it is a poor, insignificant southern village." This attitude explains why Birmingham suffered very little damage during the Civil War.

The city of Birmingham really came into its own during the 1900s when it became the South's foremost industrial city with strong iron and steel production. The success of the city continued until the Great Depression, when the industries that sustained the economy of the city were drastically affected. The city has since developed into a medical and educational center with the University of Alabama at Birmingham becoming the city's largest employer and fastest-growing medical center.

Birmingham, however, is probably best known for the race relations problems that burst into the national conscientiousness in the 1960s and for the horrible images of fire hoses and protests. Birmingham was the focal point for much of the civil rights activity. This is where Dr. Martin Luther King Jr. was jailed for his fight for racial equality.

Happily, Birmingham's troubles are in the past and today it is recognized as a warm and inviting city. No doubt its close proximity to Oxmoor Valley is ideal for your Robert Trent Jones Golf Trail experience, but there is a lot in the city that you will want to incorporate into your trip. Civil rights memorials, historic landmarks, and other sites around the town will no doubt convince you that Birmingham has certainly shed that image of "an insignificant southern village."

EXPENSIVE

Pickwick Hotel

1023 20th St. S., Birmingham, AL 35205; phone (800) 255-7304 or (205) 933-9555; Rates: $90–130

This was originally an office building, but was transformed into a hotel in 1986. The 35 rooms (28 suites) at Pickwick are decorated in an art deco style. A fun place to stay.

Wynfrey Hotel

100 Riverchase Galleria, Birmingham, AL 35244; phone (800) 323-7500 or (205) 987-1600; www.wynfrey.com; Rates: $90–130

An elegant lobby sets the tone for this centrally located hotel, which is within walking distance of the city's main shopping area. Elegant furnishings lean toward traditional and French styles for the 310 rooms and 19 suites. Located at the hotel are a pool, fitness center, and hot tub.

MODERATE

Radisson Hotel

808 South 20th St. S., Birmingham, AL 35205; phone (205) 933-9000; www.radisson.com; Rates: $80–110

This is a traditionally designed 14-story hotel that features 287 rooms including 11 suites. An inviting lobby greets visitors and provides a pleasant central meeting spot as well as a good site for a nightcap in the piano lounge. Rooms are more than acceptable and are decorated in a contemporary theme. The hotel also features a pool, sauna, and steam room.

Sheraton Perimeter South Park

8 Perimeter Dr., Birmingham, AL 35243; phone (205) 967-2700; www.sheraton.com; Rates: $60–130

This hotel recently went through a major reconstruction with all rooms being updated. Decorated in a typical hotel motif, this Sheraton is very acceptable and offers other amenities, such as an indoor pool, sauna, and health club.

INEXPENSIVE

Comfort Inn Oxmoor

195 Oxmoor Rd., Birmingham, AL 35209; phone (800) 228-5150 or (205) 941-0990; Rates: $69–99; Built: 1994; Renovations: None.

Hampton Inn Mountain Brook

1466 Montgomery Highway, Birmingham, AL 35216; phone (800) 426-7866 or (205) 822-2224; Rates: $68–78; Built: 1983; Renovations: 1998.

Dining in Birmingham

Arman's at Parklane   2117 Cahaba Rd.; phone (205) 871-5551. Continental; Moderate–Expensive; Reservations required. Located in Birmingham's former English district, the restaurant still has a European flair in both atmosphere and taste.

Fish Market Restaurant   611 21st St. S.; phone (205) 322-3330. Seafood; Inexpensive–Moderate; Reservations not accepted. A restaurant as well as a fish market, this site has some of the best seafood in town. You can't go wrong with anything on the menu.

Highlands   2011 11th Ave. S.; phone (205) 939-1400. Southern/French; Expensive; Reservations required. This is the city's best restaurant, offering a variety of French flavored dishes with a southern flair. Great wine list.

Meadowlark Farms   U.S. 31, Alabaster; phone (205) 633-3141. Continental; Expensive; Reservations required. Located in a former farmhouse that has been transformed into a European-style inn. An intimate dining experience with traditional selections including duck and lamb.

Activities in Birmingham

16th Street Baptist Church   1530 6th Ave. N.; phone (205) 251-9402 for an appointment. Site of the tragic bombing in 1963 where four young girls were killed.

Alabama Jazz Hall of Fame   1631 4th Ave. N.; phone (205) 254-2731. A celebration of Alabama's great Jazz musicians, including Lionel Hampton and Nat "King" Cole.

Alabama Sports Hall of Fame   22nd Street N. and Civic Center Boulevard; phone (205) 323-6665. Great display of sports memorabilia of Alabama's athletic superstars, including Paul "Bear" Bryant, Jesse Owens, and Willie Mays.

Arlington Antebellum Home & Garden   331 Cotton Ave. SW; phone (205) 780-5656. The city's only antebellum mansion is now a decorative arts museum displaying wonderful examples of nineteenth-century furniture.

Birmingham Botanical Gardens   2612 Lane Park Rd.; phone (205) 879-1227. Spend time among wonderful foliage at this extensive 67-acre botanical gardens (located near the Birmingham Zoo).

Birmingham Civil Rights Institute   520 16th St. N.; phone (205) 328-9696. Journey through the civil rights movement from the 1920s to the present.

Birmingham Civil Rights District   A six-block-long celebration of human rights near the Civil Rights Institute.

Birmingham Zoo   2630 Cahaba Rd.; phone (205) 879-0409. Don't miss the white rhinoceroses.

Ruffner Mountain   1214 81st St. S.; phone (205) 833-8112. 538 acres of great hiking and walking trails.

Sloss Furnaces   20 32nd St. N.; phone (205) 324-1911. Once a huge ironworks plant, now a museum celebrating the history of Birmingham's industry.

Lodging in Huntsville

Today, Huntsville is northern Alabama's biggest and one of the South's fastest-growing cities. It is also one of the stops on the Robert Trent Jones Golf Trail, where you will find the Hampton Cove Golf Course. No doubt these developments would shock John Hunt, who in 1805 built a log cabin on a local river and became the first resident. As you may have guessed, the town was named after him.

For many years the only industry in Huntsville was cotton, but that changed when Senator John Sparkman, a resident of Huntsville, brought a German delegation of rocket scientists to the city. They decided that Huntsville was an ideal location for their facilities, and thus it is in this city that Wernher Von Braun and his comrades put America's space program on the front page. Today, the U.S. Space and Rocket Center is the site of one of NASA's key research and development departments.

Expensive

The Huntsville Hilton

401 Williams Ave., Huntsville, AL 35801; phone (256) 533-1400; www.hilton.com; Rates: $60–130

Conveniently located near Huntsville's historic district and the Big Springs Entertainment Park, this Hilton offers large rooms that are nicely furnished as well as a pool, hot tub, and gym. There are 268 rooms and nine suites in this hotel, which also features a nice lobby with a piano and entertainment most evenings.

Moderate

The Executive Lodge Suite Hotel

1535 Sparkman Dr., Huntsville, AL 35816; phone (800) 248-4722 or (256) 830-8600; www.executivelodge.com; Rates: $69

Huntsville's largest hotel featuring 313 "all-suite" rooms, which are nicely appointed and include a sitting area as well a patio or balcony. The hotel also has a pool.

Inexpensive

Comfort Inn

3788 University Dr., Huntsville AL 35816; phone (800) 654-6200 or (256) 533-3291; Rates: $50–65; Built: 1987; Renovations: 1998.

Hampton Inn

4815 University Dr., Huntsville AL 35816; (800) 426-7866 or (256) 830-9400; Rates: $60–65; Built: 1986; Renovations: 1997.

Dining in Huntsville

Café Berlin　505 Airport Rd.; phone (256) 880-9920. German; Moderate; Reservations accepted. If you like German food, this is the place for you—excellent food and a fun, German-themed atmosphere. Save room for the restaurant's mouth-watering Black Forest cake for dessert.

Greenbrier Restaurant　27028 Old Highway 20, Madison; phone (256) 351-1800. Southern; Inexpensive; Reservations accepted. A tad out of the way, but as soon as you sink your teeth into the ribs you will know that the drive was worth it.

Activities in Huntsville

Alabama Constitutional Village　109 Gates Ave.; phone (256) 535-6565. Visitors can participate in demonstrations of the cotton gin, wheel lathe, butter churn, and candle dipping at the site of Alabama's Continental Congress.

Early Works Museum   404 Madison St.; phone (800) 678-1819 or (256) 564-8100.An interactive museum that allows visitors to experience pioneering life.

Huntsville Botanical Gardens   110-acre garden located near the Space and Rocket Center—great place to walk and spend some time smelling the roses.

Huntsville Depot Museum   320 Church St.; phone (800) 678-1819. This is the country's oldest remaining railroad depot and is great for kids since they can climb on locomotives. Adults will no doubt enjoy the side trip on the Huntsville Trolley, which takes visitors on a tour of the city's historic district.

U.S. Space and Rocket Center   1 Tranquility Base; phone (800) 637-7223 or (256) 837-3400. A marvelous place for kids and adults alike to experience many aspects of space exploration. Don't miss the Omnicon Theatre and the side trip via bus to the Marshall Space Flight Center, where visitors can see the International Space Center currently under construction.

Lodging in Mobile

When planning your Robert Trent Jones Golf Trail adventure, you may want to consider the spring for your trip so you can enjoy Mobile's Azalea Trail Festival. That's right, we are recommending you plan your vacation around some flowers—and we guarantee it will be worth your time. In fact, Mobile is known as the "Azalea City," and the Spring Spectacular, held annually during March and April at the Bellingrath Gardens and Home, is a veritable floral extravaganza.

Mobile is a Southern melting pot with a mixture of Spanish, French, African, and Creole heritage. This combination of influences is reflected in many aspects of the city: the architecture, cuisine, and dialect to name a few. Originally, Mobile prospered because of its strategic location on the coast and became one of the South's key shipping points. Today, Mobile is truly a majestic city and a memorable stop on your golf adventure.

EXPENSIVE

Adam's Mark Mobile

64 S. Water St., Mobile, AL 36602; phone (334) 438-4000; Rates: $60–160

Spectacularly located right on the water, the 375 rooms at Adam's Mark are well appointed, offering beautiful views of Mobile Bay and downtown from their immense windows. The hotel has a pool, hot tub, sauna, and gym, as well as evening entertainment.

MODERATE
Radisson Admiral Semmes Hotel

251 Government St., Mobile, AL 36602; phone (334) 432-8000; Rates: $60–120

Located in the heart of Mobile's historic and government districts, this Radisson attracts many local politicians both at lunch and after work (but don't let that scare you away). Accommodations are spacious, and furnishings are adequate but not too inspiring.

INEXPENSIVE
Clarion Hotel at Bel Air Mall

3101 Airport Blvd., Mobile, AL 36606; phone (800) 252-7466 or (334) 476-6400; Rates: $50–86; Built: 1979; Renovations: 1998

Hampton Inn—Tillmans Corner

5478 Inn Rd., Mobile, AL 36619; phone (800) 426-7866 or (334) 660-9202; Rates: $55–60. Built: 1994; Renovations: none.

Dining in Mobile

La Louisiana 2400 Airport Blvd.; phone (334) 476-8130. Italian; Moderate; Reservations accepted. A family-owned restaurant where a lot of care goes into all the dishes. Located on the edge of town—gumbo is the specialty.

Pillars 1757 Government St.; phone (334) 478-6341. Continental; Moderate; Reservations accepted. Delightful atmosphere in this old mansion with large porches and antiques. Broiled snapper and rack of lamb two of the best items on the menu.

Roussos Restaurant 166 S. Royal St.; phone (334) 433-3322. Seafood and steaks; Moderate–Expensive; Reservations accepted. Known for its crab claws, Roussos is a local favorite.

Activities in Mobile

Condé-Charlotte Museum House 104 Theatre St.; phone (334) 432-4722. Located next to Fort Condé, this museum showcases the furniture and furnishings of different eras of Mobile's growth.

Dauphin Island Located on the south end of State Highway 193, Dauphin is a 15-mile-long island that has a variety of attractions, including Fort Gaines, prehistoric Indian Shell Mound, and the highly regarded sea lab (see below).

Estuarium at the Dauphin Island Sea Lab   101 Bienville Blvd.; phone (334) 861-7500. Newly built, the Estuarium is a great stop for both kids and adults with exhibits on Mobile, the barrier islands, and the Gulf of Mexico's ecosystems; the history of the salt marsh; and two giant aquariums.

Fort Condé   150 S. Royal St.; phone (334) 434-7304. Originally an eighteenth-century fort that was discovered 150 years after it was destroyed during construction of Interstate 10. The fort was reconstructed to reflect its original design (on a smaller scale) and is now the home to Mobile's Visitor Center as well as a museum.

Fort Gaines   Fort Gaines, built in 1821, is located on the east end of Dauphin Island and was at one time a prime coastal defense point against foreign aggression. It was also a key site during the Civil War's Battle of Mobile Bay. Phone (334) 861-6992.

Oakleigh Period House Museum   350 Oakleigh Pl.; phone (334) 432-1281. A beautiful antebellum home, Oakleigh showcases beautiful period furniture and furnishings. The Greek revival–style home was built in 1833, survived the ravages of the Union soldiers, and then became a focal point for Mobile's social life following the Civil War. The Cox-Deasy House located next door is also worth a look.

Richards–DAR House Museum   256 N. Joachim St.; phone (334) 434-7320. This home was originally built in 1860 and is a beautiful example of the Italianate style. Take notice of the cast-iron gates, which depict the four seasons.

USS Alabama **Battleship Memorial Park**   This battleship was the winner of nine battle stars in World War II and today provides visitors with a glimpse into life at sea. Also at the park are the *USS Drum,* a submarine; *Calamity Jane,* a B-52 bomber; and a P-51 fighter plane.

Lodging in Montgomery

Montgomery is home to both the Civil War and civil rights. As you may remember from high school civics class, the city was the site where Jefferson Davis took his oath of office to become the president of the Confederate States of America. It also was where Dr. Martin Luther King Jr. and Rosa Parks defined what a hero is through their actions and words.

None of the courses on the Robert Trent Jones Golf Trail are located in Montgomery; however, it is within an hour to an hour and a half from three of the courses, Grand National, Cambrian Ridge, and Highland Oaks, and thus can be a great base of operations for your Trail adventure.

EXPENSIVE
Embassy Suites

300 Tallapoosa St., Montgomery, AL 36104; phone (334) 269-5055; www.embassysuites.com; Rates: $89–129

A downtown location and a spectacular lobby make this a perfect hotel for your stay in Montgomery. All of the 237 rooms are well-appointed suites, and the hotel also has indoor pool, hot tub, sauna, steam room, and gym. A good place for kids as breakfast is free (and quite an impressive spread, too). There also is a manager's cocktail reception each evening.

MODERATE
Marriott Courtyard

5555 Carmichael Rd., Montgomery, AL 36117; phone (334) 272-5533; Rates: $75–100

The 146 rooms at this Courtyard are more than acceptable, but don't expect the Ritz—of course, the prices are a lot easier to swallow. Also located at the hotel are a pool, hot tub, gym, and restaurant.

INEXPENSIVE
Comfort Inn

1035 W. South Blvd., Montgomery, AL 36117; phone (800) 228-5150 or (334) 281-5090; Rates: $50–65; Built: 1984; Renovations: 1995

La Quinta Inn

120 Madison Ave., Montgomery, AL 36104; phone (334) 264-2231; Rates: $60–90; Built: 1986; Renovations: 1997

Dining in Montgomery

Corsino's   911 S. Court St.; phone (334) 263-9752. Italian; Inexpensive–Moderate; Reservations not accepted. A relaxed and casual family-owned restaurant that serves delectable Italian favorites. A local hot spot—you should expect a wait for a table.

Martin's Restaurant   1796 Carter Hill Rd.; phone (334) 265-1767. Southern; Inexpensive; Reservations not needed. Stop by Martin's to have some down-home cooking. Favorites include catfish and fried chicken. No credit cards accepted.

Sahara Restaurant   511 E. Edgemont Ave., Cloverdale; phone (334) 262-1215. Southern; Moderate–Expensive; Reservations accepted. Montgomery's best restaurant serving traditional Southern favorites in a sophisticated atmosphere. Snapper and grouper are two of the best items on the menu.

Activities in Montgomery

Alabama Shakespeare Festival 1 Festival Dr.; phone (800) 841-4273 or (334) 271-5353. This is America's fifth largest Shakespeare festival with almost year-round shows.

Alabama State Capitol Bainbridge Street and Dexter Avenue; phone (334) 242-3935. The Designated National Landmark where Jefferson Davis took his oath of office to become the Confederacy's president.

Civil Rights Memorial 400 Washington Blvd. Designed by Maya Lin, the architect of the Vietnam War Memorial in Washington D.C., this memorial honors the 40 individuals who lost their lives in the battle for equal rights.

Dexter Avenue King Memorial Baptist Church 454 Dexter Ave.; phone (334) 263-3970. This was Dr. King's first pulpit and was where he led the Montgomery bus boycott—a protest touched off when Rosa Parks refused to move to the back of the bus.

First White House of the Confederacy 644 Washington Ave.; phone (334) 242-1861. The home that Jefferson Davis lived in during the organization of the Confederacy (located across the street from the state Capitol).

Jasmine Hill Gardens and Outdoor Museum 3001 Jasmine Hill Rd.; phone (334) 567-6463. Bring your walking shoes so you can enjoy the 20 acres of beautiful gardens, which feature year-round floral displays. Also, take note of the replicas of Greek sculptures and the ruins of the Temple of Hera.

Martin Luther King's Former Home 309 S. Jackson St. Built in the 1920s, this was where Dr. King lived from 1954 to 1960.

Montgomery Zoo 2301 Coliseum Parkway; phone (334) 240-4900. A 40-acre zoo that is home to more than 800 different animals.

Murphy House 22 Bibb St. This antebellum mansion housed Union troops during the Reconstruction.

F. Scott and Zelda Fitzgerald's Museum 919 Felder Ave.; phone (334) 264-4222. Zelda grew up in Montgomery and become half of arguably the most interesting couple in America's literary history. The museum showcases their belongings and includes a video of their life in Montgomery. A fun stop for all you *Great Gatsby* fans.

The 19th Hole

Each stop on the trail features a fine 19th hole to retire and sip a little after-round libation.

Part Seven

Georgia

Overview

If you ask any serious golfer what first pops into their minds when they think of Georgia, you will probably get a one-word answer: Augusta. Its legendary golf course, Augusta National Golf Club, is home to The Masters Tournament, which focuses the eyes of the golfing world on Georgia for one magical week every April. Unfortunately, the television set will probably be as close as most golfers will ever get to this fabled course—tickets to the tournament are extremely hard to obtain and actually playing the course next to impossible.

The club was conceived in the late 1920s by the great Bobby Jones, an Atlanta native, who chose Augusta for his "dream" course in part because of the city's resort-like ambience and climate. Oddly, despite boasting the presence of one of the most hallowed golf courses on the planet, Augusta never developed as a prime destination for vacationing golfers. Luckily however, Augusta is not the only game in town. There are many superb resorts and courses located throughout the state offering golfers a remarkable variety of challenges and topography.

Georgia is a state that offers visitors diversity. There are the metropolitan cities of Atlanta and Athens, and then there is the rural, off-the-beaten-path towns and cities spread throughout the state. Visitors can hike to the peaks of Appalachian Mountains or dip into the Atlantic Ocean on the eastern side of the state. Georgia is unique in how it embraces both big-city sophistication and old Southern charm.

Many of Georgia's most acclaimed courses are draped over rolling terrain composed of red-clay soil and are lined with pines and hardwoods. On the east coast, soil is sandier so the courses drain better and are framed with vegetation that more closely resembles the Low Country of South Carolina. We have divided the "Peach state" into four sections: north of Atlanta, west of Atlanta, east of Atlanta, and the Golden Isles near Brunswick. We have

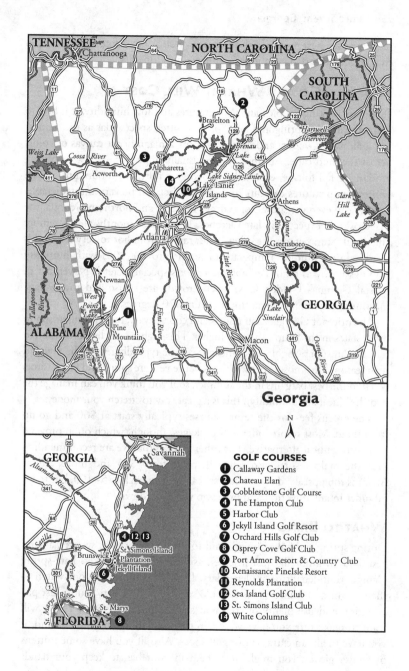

Georgia

N

GOLF COURSES

1. Callaway Gardens
2. Chateau Elan
3. Cobblestone Golf Course
4. The Hampton Club
5. Harbor Club
6. Jekyll Island Golf Resort
7. Orchard Hills Golf Club
8. Osprey Cove Golf Club
9. Port Armor Resort & Country Club
10. Renaissance PineIsle Resort
11. Reynolds Plantation
12. Sea Island Golf Club
13. St. Simons Island Club
14. White Columns

identified the best resorts in those areas as well as other fine nearby courses that would be prized additions to your golfing itinerary.

WHEN TO GO AND WHAT IT WILL COST

If you are looking for pleasant temperatures and low humidity, it is best to come during the spring and fall. Spring is often spectacular as the blooming azaleas, dogwoods, and camellias paint a magnificent canvas of colors across the landscape. Autumn is also visually appealing with a surprising amount of fall foliage, especially in Georgia's northern mountains. In the winter, temperatures can dip, and the weather can be very unpredictable. Atlanta can even get snow. For central, western, and northern Georgia, the first frosts are expected in late October. The wettest months are December and April. Summer, on the other hand, ranges from hot to very hot and is nearly always humid. Temperatures reach into the 100s with humidity readings nearly as high. Perhaps the region's special secret is November in coastal Georgia's Golden Isles, when crowds are sparse and the average maximum daytime temperature is a balmy 70 degrees.

The prices at Georgia's golf resorts and courses vary, but in comparison to other states in the South, they are higher. This higher cost, however, is often reflected in superior golf. The prices at resorts typically reflect the low and high season—the most expensive times of the year are spring and fall. Visitors will find the best bargains in the summer, so if you think you can manage the two "h's" (heat and humidity), this is a great way to stretch your money.

The greens fees for the resort courses typically start at $60 and go up from there. Most resorts offer golf packages, though, which often proves a more economical alternative. The other courses that we are recommending near the main resorts also range in price from $25 and more. Metro Atlanta's top upscale, daily-fee courses can set you back $75–100, but travel 60 miles in any direction and prices go way, way down.

WHAT TO BRING

During spring and fall, you will want to pack a lightweight sweater, a wind vest, and an umbrella (just in case), as well as a wind jacket. Late-spring Georgia thunderstorms are legendary. In April you can set your watch to them, right at 4 p.m. May is tornado season in the Deep South. Just pay attention and use plenty of common sense. During the winter, you will want to make sure you have your rain gear, including an umbrella and, if you have them, an extra pair of golf shoes. Also, if you have some mittens or winter gloves, you might toss them in your bag to keep your hands warm. For the summer, short and lightweight garments are the ticket. Make sure to bring a backup glove in your bag, as your hands will perspire in the heat.

The courses in the area are diverse, but many have quite a few water hazards on them, plus thickets of dense woods, so a few extra sleeves of balls are in order. For club selection, the rough on some of the courses can be difficult and thus a seven-wood may be your salvation. Georgia's best courses are notorious for the bermuda rough that lines the fairways and edges the greens. It's not fierce looking at first glance, but the grass is tough and wiry and the ball inevitably settles down deep into it. Bring a trusty sand wedge as well as your seven-wood.

We have to emphasize one thing (and this could be the most important): Put a can of bug spray in your bag if you are heading for Georgia in either the spring or summer. This may be the most valuable weapon you bring.

ONCE YOU'RE THERE

Georgia has a variety of high-profile resorts offering marvelous golfing experiences. Wherever you decide to go, whether to a resort in relatively close proximity to Atlanta or somewhere a little more remote, you will find both resort and public courses in the area that will challenge you. Even if you want an urban vacation, where you sightsee in Atlanta, a number of excellent courses await in the vicinity, almost all of them having sprung up in the past 10 years. Unless you have a few weeks to spend in Georgia, you're not going to be able to sample all of the state's top courses, so our advice is to spend a couple of days in Atlanta, then head either to the Lake Oconee region or to the Golden Isles. The northern mountains offer some of the state's best bargains, such as at the Brasstown Valley resort in Young Harris. If there's been heavy rain, the sandier soil of the Golden Isles is your best bet because most of Georgia's red clay soil–based courses don't drain particularly well.

The variety of climates and topography in Georgia means that you'll get both bentgrass and bermuda grass experiences, depending on where you are in the state. Generally, all the bentgrass greens in the state are north of Macon, where nights are cooler and "traditional" four seasons are the norm, as opposed to the southern part of the state and the eastern coastline, which remain temperate year-round.

For the bermuda grass courses, Georgia is like most southern states. When the grass goes dormant in late fall, it turns brown, or rather straw-colored, a generally unappealing hue for golfers who like deep, bright greens. Three words of advice: Get over it.

Though not visually appealing, this dormant bermuda provides an excellent playing surface—the ball sits up perfectly every time. Some courses overseed in the fall with a more eye-catching rye grass, which greens up southern courses in winter. Some clubs overseed only tees and greens, leaving fairways and rough with that "burned-out" look. Others overseed wall-to-wall.

Others do fairways, but leave the roughs alone. If color is a concern for you, call ahead.

As far as what time of day is best, the general rule of thumb is the earlier in the day you can get out, the better off you are, no matter what time of year you go. It's easy to take that sweater off after the front nine, and you miss those late afternoon thunderstorms. From the middle of the state northward, if you get a good rain, your golf is done for the day. From Vidalia to the south, the soil is sandier and thus drains better after a rainstorm.

GATHERING INFORMATION

For more information about travel and golf in Georgia, you can contact:

> Atlanta Convention and Visitors Bureau
> 233 Peachtree St., Suite 2000, Atlanta, GA 30303
> Phone (800) 285-2682 or (404) 222-6688

> Brunswick/Golden Isles Visitors Bureau
> 4 Glynn Ave., Brunswick, GA 31528
> Phone (800) 933-COAST; www.bgislesvisitorsb.com

> Georgia Department of Industry, Trade, and Tourism
> Box 1776, Atlanta, GA 30301
> Phone (800) 847-4842 or (404) 656-3590
> www.gomm.com; visitga@itt.state.ga.us

To get a feel for the way Georgia used to be, and in some regards, remains, watch or read *Gone with the Wind.*

The Major Courses

THE GOLDEN ISLES

Though you probably hear more about the beaches of Florida and South Carolina, Georgia actually has a fine coast as well. About midway between Savannah and Jacksonville, near the historic gateway town of Brunswick—the shrimp capital of the world and the birthplace of Brunswick Stew—are Georgia's Golden Isles. They're incredibly cozy islands with superb golf resorts, snug little cafes and pubs, splendid restaurants, and a preserved history that dates back to the colonization during the early 1700s. Countless marsh inlets and lagoons are interspersed with lovely, oak-lined golf holes, and the islands are kept mercifully free of billboards, neon, and high-rises.

Jekyll Island Golf Resort, Indian Mound Course

322 Captain Willy Rd., Jekyll Island, GA 31527; phone (912) 635-2368

Golf at Jekyll Island dates back to 1898. Today, remnants of those ancient links appear in Jekyll's 9-hole course, formerly known as Oceanside, now known as the Great Dunes course. Jekyll's three championship courses and its 9-holer offer the best bang for your buck in Georgia. It's good, inexpensive, state-run golf.

How to Get On: Reservations can be made up to six months in advance.
Tees:

> Blue: 6,596 yards, par-72, USGA rating 71.3, slope 127
> White: 6,282 yards, par-72, USGA rating 69.0, slope 124
> Red: 5,345 yards, par-72, USGA rating 70.0, slope 122

Challenge: ★★★	Golf Facilities: ★★★
Variety: ★★★	14-Club Test: ★★★
Terrain: ★★★	Intangibles: ★★★
Beauty/Visual Appeal: ★★★	Value: ★★★★
Pace of Play: ★★★	

Just the Facts Year Opened: 1975; Course Designer: Joe Lee; Walking: Yes; Greens Fee: $29; 9-Hole/Twilight Rate: Yes; Pull Carts: Yes; Practice Range: Yes; Club Rental: Yes.

Description and Comments As you look at the stats or at the scorecard when you arrive you will see that this is the shortest and probably the most forgiving of the three courses at Jekyll Island. But don't let these facts fool you—there still is a lot of challenge that awaits you, whether you are a low or high handicapper. The course has wide, mostly flat fairways, but they are carved through pine trees and marshlands—accuracy still plays a role. There are many bunkers on the course as well as five lakes that come into play on eight holes—placing further demands on your shotmaking ability. The signature hole, which is atypically also the easiest hole on the course, is the 176-yard, par-3 12th, though equally memorable is the very scenic 14th, a 322-yard par-4 that commences from an elevated tee, then doglegs left around a large lake.

Insider Tips The wind and the time of year you are playing this course (as for all the courses in the area) will affect your club selection. Make sure to pay special heed to the tricky breezes and club accordingly. Indian Mound's large, sloping greens place a premium on accurate approaches and good lag putting.

A note about course conditioning: Because Indian Mound, like the other Jekyll Island courses, is state-owned, and thus state-maintained, it won't be as plush as those up the road at Sea Island. On the other hand, the greens fees at the Jekyll Island courses are only a fraction of what they are at Sea Island. They're both good values, in their own way.

Jekyll Island Golf Resort, Oleander Course

322 Captain Willy Rd., Jekyll Island, GA 31527; phone (912) 635-2368
How to Get On: Reservations can be made up to six months in advance.

Tees:

Blue: 6,679 yards, par-72, USGA rating 71.8, slope 128

White: 6,241 yards, par-72, USGA rating 69.4, slope 120

Red: 5,654 yards, par-72, USGA rating 72.6, slope 124

Challenge: ★★★	Golf Facilities: ★★★
Variety: ★★★	14-Club Test: ★★★
Terrain: ★★	Intangibles: ★★★½
Beauty/Visual Appeal: ★★★★	Value: ★★★★½
Pace of Play: ★★★	

Just the Facts   Year Opened: 1964; Course Designer: Dick Wilson; Walking: Yes; Greens Fee: $29; 9-Hole/Twilight Rate: Yes; Pull Carts: Yes; Practice Range: Yes; Club Rental: Yes.

Description and Comments   The original 18-hole championship course at Jekyll Island, Oleander is a solid, straightforward test that can stiffen in a hurry when the wind is up. Accuracy and touch are the secrets to success here. The course traverses woodlands and marshlands, and visitors may feel as though they are at the local zoo as sightings of deer, wild turkeys, and alligators are common.

Fairways are very playable, if you stay in them, but you can definitely feel free to bang the driver on most holes. However, the course has many hazards, in the form of sand, trees, and water, awaiting balls that venture off the recommended path. Throw in a few doglegs and you will know why this is the hardest of the Jekyll courses to score on. The 12th hole, a 443-yard par-4, is recognized as one of Georgia's strongest holes open to the public—the second shot features a healthy carry over a lake to a shoebox-sized green.

Insider Tips   Oleander is quite playable, but it calls for astute course management in order to score well. On most of the holes, you can let your driver fly within reason, as the fairways are amply wide. However, there are some holes on which it is advisable to play conservatively—your mantra at this course should be accuracy and finesse. One other point in your favor, the greens are not as demanding as some in the area, and thus you can pick up some strokes with your flat stick. From the "airport runway" tee boxes to the fairly flat greens, this isn't a terribly memorable course, but given its setting, challenge, and price, it turns into one of the best values around.

Jekyll Island Golf Resort, Pine Lakes Course

322 Captain Willy Rd., Jekyll Island, GA 31527; phone (912) 635-2368

How to Get On: Reservations can be made up to six months in advance.

Tees:

Blue: 6,802 yards, par-72, USGA rating 72.2, slope 130

White: 6,379 yards, par-72, USGA rating 70.4, slope 124

Red: 5,742 yards, par-72, USGA rating 71.9, slope 124

Challenge: ★★★
Variety: ★★★
Terrain: ★★½
Beauty/Visual Appeal: ★★★
Pace of Play: ★★★½

Golf Facilities: ★★★
14-Club Test: ★★★½
Intangibles: ★★★½
Value: ★★★★

Just the Facts   Year Opened: 1968; Course Designer: Joe Lee; Walking: Yes; Greens Fee: $29; 9-Hole/Twilight Rate: Yes; Pull Carts: Yes; Practice Range: Yes; Club Rental: Yes.

Description and Comments   As the name implies, tall pines are the prominent feature on this layout, resulting in the tightest (and longest) of the three courses at Jekyll Island. The trees are not the only concern here, though—bunkers protectively guard almost every green on the course and there is a large lake bordering the 18th hole. Fairways are moderately mounded and feature many doglegs.

Insider Tips   You have heard it a million times, but if you keep it in play at Pine Lakes, you will score well. If you don't, you may find a big number or two littering your scorecard. If you do venture into the woods, our recommendation is to take your medicine, pitch out, and play it from there, as the forest is pretty thick. Trying to make a miracle shot will probably put you even deeper into the dark woods. This is not the most memorable course you'll ever play, but the price is so good, you'll want to play it over and over.

Sea Island Golf Club, Plantation Course

100 Retreat Ave., St. Simons Island, GA 31522; phone (800) 732-4752 or (912) 638-5118

Note: Sea Island Golf Club is currently undergoing a redesign of their Seaside and Marshside nines. These 2 courses will be combined into one 18-hole course (named Seaside) by Tom Fazio. It is due to open in late fall 1999. At the time of this writing, no details were available. Contact Sea Island Golf Club for details.

How to Get On: You must be a guest of The Cloister resort to play this private country club.

Tees:

    Back: 6,549 yards, par-72, USGA rating 73.9, slope 135
    Middle: 6,068 yards, par-72, USGA rating 71.4, slope 130
    Forward: 5,194 yards, par-72, USGA rating 69.8, slope 124

Challenge: ★★★½
Variety: ★★★½
Terrain: ★★★½
Beauty/Visual Appeal: ★★★★
Pace of Play: ★★★★

Golf Facilities: ★★★★
14-Club Test: ★★★½
Intangibles: ★★★★½
Value: ★★★½

Just the Facts   Year Opened: 1997; Course Designer: Rees Jones; Walking: At times; Greens Fee: $90–125; 9-Hole/Twilight Rate: Yes; Pull Carts: No; Practice Range: Yes; Club Rental: Yes.

Description and Comments   Sea Island boasts an outstanding legacy. It was one of Bobby Jones's favorite courses and is the playground for many of America's industrial leaders. The Cloister was the site of President George Bush's honeymoon and 50th wedding anniversary celebration. Davis Love III calls Sea Island home. Quite a lot to live up to, which is not a concern for this venerable site.

Sea Island Golf Club is one of the South's most esteemed private clubs. It is, however, accessible to guests of the posh, equally esteemed Cloister resort, located a 10-minute drive away on St. Simons Island. The club is tucked away all by its lonesome at the end of a quiet avenue shaded by a canopy of handsome, ancient, live oak trees dripping with Spanish moss. The club once was made up of four distinct nine-hole courses, two of which dated to the 1920s. In 1997, the club decided to pair two of the nines together (The Plantation and The Retreat) and create The Plantation Course. This "new" course was reshaped under the watchful guidance of Rees Jones, the "U.S. Open doctor," who was able to retain Sea Island's golf history and blend it seamlessly with a modern-day design.

Today, the revised Plantation Course unfolds on a lovely parkland setting with holes framed by lush vegetation, including oleanders, crepe myrtles, palms, century-old oak trees, and gorgeous panoramic views of St. Simons Sound. Fairways are relatively wide to accommodate the ever-present breezes, and they are also fairly flat. Greens tend to be elevated, but run-ups are possible on most holes, reflecting the Old World flavor of the course.

Jones saved the best for last—the 520-yard, par-5 18th will no doubt be one hole you will remember. It typically plays into the wind and is a great example of a risk/reward hole. Far off in the distance is one of the many lakes. From the tee box you will see a lake that lines the fairway along the entire left-hand side and far in the distance is the green, jutting out into this same lake. If you are a long hitter and rip a good tee shot, you can try to go for it in two. If you are in doubt, there is a perfectly positioned lay-up area for more conservative play. Either way, it will be hard to wipe that smile off your face when you sink the final putt.

Sea Island Golf Club is also home to a superb teaching facility featuring an expansive driving range, short-game area, and a learning center headed up by LPGA Hall of Famer Louise Suggs.

Insider Tips   Jones's mission is to design courses that require quality shotmaking while also maintaining playability. Plantation achieves both objectives. You can score well on this course if you mind your course management. The biggest factor probably will be the wind, so make sure to adjust as needed to compensate for the often-blowing gusts off the St. Simons Sound. Lower handicappers who want more of a challenge will want to play from the tips, a formidable test. Pay special attention to the bunkering, which is done up in neoclassic style typical of Rees Jones, whereby he gives you a hint of bunker by flashing a little bit of sand back at you, but be aware that there's more bunker than meets the eye.

Sea Island has an old-money, upscale feel that appeals especially to Society Register folks and those who aspire to be. This is not the kind of place where Joe Sixpack is going to feel all that comfortable. To enhance the "private-club" feel, Sea Island makes caddies available during certain months. If you get the chance, try the caddie route. It's the ultimate way to play, a rare pleasure at a resort. The course is easy to walk, and you'll get some excellent advice on club selection and green reading.

Spring and fall are the best times to sample Sea Island. Big banks of blooming azaleas make spring particularly delightful. Sea breezes can make midsummer golf somewhat bearable, but likewise can make winter golf a brute.

St. Simons Island Club

100 Kings Way, St. Simons Island, GA 31522; phone (912) 638-5130
How to Get On: Guests of the Cloister can make tee times with their reservations. Nonguests can book tee times one day in advance.
Tees:

    Blue: 6,490 yards, par-72, USGA rating 71.0, slope 133

    White: 6,114 yards, par-72, USGA rating 70.1, slope 129

    Red: 5,361 yards, par-72, USGA rating 70.0, slope 120

Challenge: ★★★	Golf Facilities: ★★★½
Variety: ★★★½	14-Club Test: ★★★½
Terrain: ★★★½	Intangibles: ★★★
Beauty/Visual Appeal: ★★★★	Value: ★★★
Pace of Play: ★★★½	

Just the Facts   Year Opened: 1974; Course Designer: Joe Lee; Walking: Allowed at certain times; Greens Fee: $80–100; 9-Hole/Twilight Rate: Yes; Pull Carts: No; Practice Range: Yes; Club Rental: Yes.

Description and Comments   Although Sea Island Golf Club receives most of the attention and notoriety, St. Simons certainly is no slouch when it comes to golfing in the Golden Isles. As you glance at the scorecard of the Island Club, as the locals call it, you will see that the course is relatively short. You will also notice the slopes. So where does the challenge come from?

The answer is in the tight fairways and abundant grass and sand bunkers on both the fairways as well as adjacent to the greens. Throw in a few water holes, a handful of elevation changes, and some moderately hilly terrain and you've got a sizable challenge, albeit in a compact, comfortable package. Particularly memorable is the 382-yard, par-4 6th, which flirts with lake, marsh, and bunkers in its dogleg journey to the left. Another dandy is the tough 373-yard, par-4 18th, which is narrowed by water on the left and trees on the right.

Insider Tips You really don't need to be long off the tee to score well here. You do, however, need to be accurate, so you may want to avoid that driver and bring out the long iron or the three-wood. Also, there are typically ocean breezes, which will affect your shot selection, as will the elevation changes. Keep these factors in mind as you choose your weapon. This is a classic Joe Lee design, with a number of doglegs that ribbon through lagoons, tall pines, and numerous bunkers. In other words, the key to success at St. Simons Island is position, not power.

It's worth noting that St. Simons Island Club is owned by the Cloister, though nonguests enjoy playing privileges. The benefit is private club, Cloister-style service and conditioning, plus public access unlike the Sea Island Club, which requires you to stay at the Cloister to be able to play.

THE REST OF GEORGIA
Callaway Gardens, Garden View Course
U.S. 27, Pine Mountain, GA 31822; phone (800) 225-2929 or (706) 663-2281

Callaway Gardens boasts three 18-hole courses: Garden View, Lake View, and Mountain View. All of them are discussed in this "Major Courses" section.

How to Get On: Guests of the resort can book tee times when they make their reservations. Nonguests can make tee times three days in advance.

Tees:

    Championship: 6,392 yards, par-72, USGA rating 70.7, slope 121

    Regular: 6,108 yards, par-72, USGA rating 69.2, slope 117

    Ladies: 5,848 yards, par-72, USGA rating 72.7, slope 123

Challenge: ★★	Golf Facilities: ★★★
Variety: ★★	14-Club Test: ★★
Terrain: ★★★	Intangibles: ★★★
Beauty/Visual Appeal: ★★★½	Value: ★★½
Pace of Play: ★★★	

Just the Facts Year Opened: 1968; Course Designer: Joe Lee; Walking: Allowed at times; Greens Fee: $70; 9-Hole/Twilight Rate: Yes; Pull Carts: Yes; Practice Range: Yes; Club Rental: Yes.

Description and Comments   As the name implies, the Garden View course plays through lovely vineyards and orchards. Of the three courses at Callaway Gardens, this is the most forgiving, with wider fairways and relatively short yardages. Among the challenges are the many uneven lies you will have on the hilly terrain and multiple greenside bunkers.

Insider Tips   Most of the holes on this course are straight, and thus you can let it rip from the tees. The key to scoring will be your approach shot. Avoid the perils around the greens and you should do just fine. Beginners and intermediates will appreciate the fact that there's only one water hazard on the entire course.

Callaway Gardens, Lake View Course

U.S. 27, Pine Mountain, GA 31822; phone (800) 225-2929 or (706) 663-2281

How to Get On: Guests of the resort can book tee times when they make their reservations. Nonguests can make tee times three days in advance.

Tees:

Championship: 6,006 yards, par-70, USGA rating 69.4, slope 115

Ladies: 5,452 yards, par-71, USGA rating 70.3, slope 122

Challenge: ★★	Golf Facilities: ★★★
Variety: ★★	14-Club Test: ★★
Terrain: ★★★	Intangibles: ★★½
Beauty/Visual Appeal: ★★★½	Value: ★★½
Pace of Play: ★★½	

Just the Facts   Year Opened: 1952; Course Designer: J. B. McGovern; Walking: Allowed at times; Greens Fee: $70; 9-Hole/Twilight Rate: Yes; Pull Carts: Yes; Practice Range: Yes; Club Rental: Yes.

Description and Comments   Lake View, the original course at Callaway Gardens, is a beautifully landscaped layout with azaleas and dogwoods throughout the 18 holes. The shortest and easiest of the three courses at the resort, Lake View has hilly terrain and wide fairways. Water, in the form of Mountain Creek Lake, comes into play on nine holes on this course, which offers scenic views of the area. Most memorable is the waterlogged, 152-yard, par-3 5th, which features an island tee box.

Insider Tips   The course is short and has many trees so it would be advised to leave the driver in the bag for many of the holes if you tend to be even a tad wild off the tee. You can make up the lost yardage on your second shot, and you will end up scoring better in the end run. Because Lake View is so user-friendly, it attracts a lot of beginners. Don't expect play to move very quickly.

Callaway Gardens, Mountain View Course

U.S. 27, Pine Mountain, GA 31822; phone (800) 225-2929 or (706) 663-2281

How to Get On: Guests of the resort can book tee times when they make their reservations. Nonguests can make tee times three days in advance.

Tees:

> Championship: 7,057 yards, par-72, USGA rating 74.1, slope 138
>
> Regular: 6,630 yards, par-72, USGA rating 72.3, slope 129
>
> Ladies: 5,848 yards, par-72, USGA rating 73.2, slope 122

Challenge: ★★★★	Golf Facilities: ★★★
Variety: ★★★	14-Club Test: ★★★★
Terrain: ★★★★	Intangibles: ★★★★
Beauty/Visual Appeal: ★★★½	Value: ★★★★
Pace of Play: ★★★	

Just the Facts   Year Opened: 1963; Course Designer: Joe Lee/Dick Wilson; Walking: No; Greens Fee: $90; 9-Hole/Twilight Rate: Yes; Pull Carts: No; Practice Range: Yes; Club Rental: Yes.

Description and Comments   The Mountain View course, home to the PGA Tour's Buick Challenge, is really the main entree of the resort. It is easily the most challenging of the three courses, with medium-width tree-lined fairways, more than 60 sand bunkers, water on 4 holes, and quick greens with many undulations. Among the PGA Tour notables who have triumphed at Callaway Gardens' Mountain View course are Davis Love III and Fred Funk. Terrain is moderately rolling and covered with tall Georgia pines and magnolias.

The holes on this course tend to be long and challenging, especially the par-3s and 5s. One of the longer ones is the 15th, the course's signature hole, a 530-yard par-5. Water runs up the right-hand side of the hole and then cuts in front of the green. This is a perfect risk/reward hole for big hitters as it is possible to get on in two, but it requires the second shot to clear the water in front. Another great hole is the par-3 fifth, which plays 212 yards from the tips. The tee is on an elevated plateau and the green is also on a plateau. A deep valley separates tee from green. The green slopes from left to right, and many balls end up either in the valley or in one of the two traps on the right.

Though this course is fair and challenging, it isn't particularly memorable due mostly to a lack of dramatic holes or water hazards. It scores high in the "intangibles" department because you know you're walking in the footsteps of the pros (even though carts are mandatory).

Insider Tips   This course is the resort's most demanding, and thus scoring will not be as easy as it will be on the other courses. With this in mind, it is recommended that you bring out that driver, but be cautious with it. The tendency is to put a little more into it on the longer holes, but an errant shot will hurt you much more than a loss of five to ten yards. The greens are fast, so play your putts conservatively, especially during the summer months.

If you want to play Mountain View in the pleasant month of September, call the resort well ahead of time. After Labor Day, the course closes for a bit in order to get it in prime condition for when the PGA Tour pros show up, which usually occurs in late-September or early-October. Obviously, early-to mid-October is a wonderful time to catch Mountain View, because the days are mild, the nights cool, and the golf course is in superior shape, following the visit by the PGA Tour. Greens are firm at this time of year; in summer, like most southern clubs, fairways and greens have to be watered extra amounts to keep them alive during the hot months. As such, they're softer and slower, affording less roll. Call ahead if you want to play here in June or July, as that's when the golf course grasses are in transition, so occasionally you'll get some patchy lies.

As nice as a fall visit to Callaway Gardens is, the best time of year to see this resort is spring. Peak season is mid-March, which is a riot of color when the azaleas burst into view. April and May are also superb times to sample Callaway—by June, the heat and humidity assert themselves, wilting the resort's golfers, if not the flowers.

Try to avoid this course when it's wet, because it turns into an endless slog. The course plays plenty long even when it's dry, for several reasons. First, there is a wagon full of meaty par-4s; from the tips no fewer than eight of them play at 400 yards plus. Second, the course actually plays longer than the scorecard states, thanks to lush fairways, many of which possess upslopes, which seem to catch most drives and inhibit forward roll. Finally, nearly all the greens are elevated from the fairways and often are fronted by sand, making each approach an all-carry proposition. Last but not least, it's not a bad idea to practice sidehill lie shots before teeing it up at Mountain View. You'll find plenty of them here.

Chateau Elan, Chateau Elan Course

6060 Golf Club Dr., Braselton, GA 30517; phone (800) 233-9463 or (770) 271-6050

How to Get On: Guests of the resort can book tee times at the time of their reservations. Nonguests can make tee times seven days in advance.

Tees:

Gold: 7,030 yards, par-71, USGA rating 73.5, slope 136
Green: 6,484 yards, par-71, USGA rating 71.1, slope 125
White: 5,900 yards, par-71, USGA rating 68.9, slope 119
Burgundy: 5,092 yards, par-71, USGA rating 70.8, slope 124

Challenge: ★★★★   Golf Facilities: ★★★★
Variety: ★★★★   14-Club Test: ★★★½
Terrain: ★★★★   Intangibles: ★★★½
Beauty/Visual Appeal: ★★★★   Value: ★★★
Pace of Play: ★★★½

Just the Facts   Year Opened: 1989; Course Designer: Denis Griffiths; Walking: Allowed at certain times; Greens Fee: $70; 9-Hole/Twilight Rate: Yes; Pull Carts: No; Practice Range: Yes; Club Rental: Yes.

Description and Comments   The longest and hardest of the three courses at Chateau Elan, this course presents many challenges for golfers. First off, there is water. Well actually, there is lots of water: Three lakes and two creeks come into play on 10 of the 18 holes. Then there is sand. Well actually, lots of sand: 87 bunkers on the course. In addition, plenty of ball-grabbing bermuda rough awaits the errant shot.

Typical of the challenge of the Chateau Elan course is the 420-yard, par-4 7th, which calls for a long tee shot to the left center of the fairway, short of a creek, followed by a demanding approach to a well-mounded green shaped liked a four-leafed clover.

Insider Tips   At first glance, this course may seem simple. Hit it hard and stay out of trouble, and it is easily manageable. However, venture into one of the many hazards and you will quickly understand why this course is rated so highly. If it has been raining recently, you may find the fairways very soggy, as drainage seems to be a problem. As a result your ball will not roll as much and may plug. Don't assume, however, that the greens will be as soft—play conservatively until you have played the first couple of holes and then go for the flag if they too are soft.

Unique to this course are the hole names. Each hole is named after a type of wine, such as the par-5 9th, called Pinot Noir, or the par-3 12th, called Sauvignon Blanc. Make sure you wait until after your round here to sample the local product. You'll need to tackle this course sober.

Chateau Elan, Legends Course

5473 Legends Dr., Braselton, GA 30517; phone (800) 233-9463 or (770) 932-8653

How to Get On: You must be a guest of Chateau Elan to play this semi-private club.

Tees:

Championship: 6,781 yards, par-72, USGA rating 73.3, slope 133
Men: 6,144 yards, par-72, USGA rating 71.1, slope 123
Ladies: 5,555 yards, par-72, USGA rating 72.1, slope 126

Challenge: ★★★½	Golf Facilities: ★★★★
Variety: ★★★	14-Club Test: ★★★
Terrain: ★★★★	Intangibles: ★★★★
Beauty/Visual Appeal: ★★★★	Value: ★★★
Pace of Play: ★★★½	

Just the Facts Year Opened: 1993; Course Designer: Denis Griffiths; Walking: Mandatory cart; Greens Fee: $125; 9-Hole/Twilight Rate: No; Pull Carts: No; Practice Range: Yes; Club Rental: Yes.

Description and Comments One of the area's premier courses and home for four years to the Gene Sarazen World Open Championship (1994–1997), the Legends Course offers golfers a challenging but fun lay-out. Fairways vary in width and there is water on five of the holes, but the real test lies in the greens. The greens tend to be exceptionally fast and thus require you to be careful not only with chips and putts but also with your approach shots.

One of the intangibles that make Legends a "must-play" is that three Hall of Fame golfers consulted on the design. Sarazen, Sam Snead, and Kathy Whitworth were asked to come up with six of their favorite holes in golf. Architect Denis Griffiths coalesced this all-star line-up into a championship 18.

Insider Tips Given the quick greens, you will want to observe the ground around the green and decide whether it is prudent to go with a lofted approach shot or one that lands short and runs up. On all of your shots, if you are in between clubs, experience on this course says go with the longer one.

As wonderful as the aesthetics are at Chateau Elan's Legends Course, it's not as easy on the ears, mostly due to its proximity to a nearby highway on several holes. *Note:* The Legends course is only accessible to guests of the Chateau Elan resort, whereas the other two courses offer public access.

Chateau Elan, Woodlands Course

6060 Golf Club Dr., Braselton, GA 30517; phone (800) 233-9463 or (770) 271-6050

How to Get On: Guests of the resort can book tee times at the time of their reservations. Nonguests can make tee times seven days in advance.

Tees:

Back: 6,738 yards, par-72, USGA rating 72.6, slope 128

Gold: 6,363 yards, par-72, USGA rating 70.9, slope 124

White: 4,850 yards, par-72, USGA rating 68.5, slope 123

Challenge: ★★★

Variety: ★★★★½

Terrain: ★★★★

Beauty/Visual Appeal: ★★★★

Pace of Play: ★★★

Golf Facilities: ★★★★

14-Club Test: ★★★★

Intangibles: ★★★★

Value: ★★★★

Just the Facts   Year Opened: 1996; Course Designer: Denis Griffiths; Walking: Allowed at certain times; Greens Fee: $70; 9-Hole/Twilight Rate: Yes; Pull Carts: No; Practice Range: Yes; Club Rental: Yes.

Description and Comments   The newest addition at the Chateau Elan, the Woodlands Course offers golfers two diverse looks. The course starts out in a pasture and ends up in dense woodland and has many elevation changes throughout. An extremely tight course that penalizes errant shots, golfers will no doubt find this a challenging but fun course that requires good shotmaking.

If you have to select either the Resort or the Woodlands Course, our nod goes to Woodlands, especially if it has been raining recently—there is better drainage on this course, and it offers more variety and challenge.

Insider Tips   The key to success at the Woodlands Course is to keep it in the fairway, so be smart in your driving and approach to shot decisions—the penalties for venturing off-target are severe. On the par-5 holes that have water, use one less club than you would normally play, as the water is closer than you think. Also, make sure to adjust for the elevation changes—this factor will make a big difference in the yardage. Since this is the newest of the courses, and probably the best, the pace of play, especially on the weekends, tends to be slow (expect a five-hour or longer round).

Reynolds Plantation, Great Waters Course

100 Linger Longer Rd., Greensboro, GA 30642; phone (800) 800-5250 or (706) 467-3151

How to Get On: You must be a guest at the Reynolds Plantation cottages to play this private course.

Tees:

    Gold: 7,048 yards, par-72, USGA rating 73.8, slope 135

    Blue: 6,545 yards, par-72, USGA rating 71.2, slope 130

    White: 6,022 yards, par-72, USGA rating 68.8, slope 124

    Red: 5,057 yards, par-72, USGA rating 69.2, slope 114

Challenge: ★★★★

Variety: ★★★★

Terrain: ★★★★½

Beauty/Visual Appeal: ★★★★½

Pace of Play: ★★★★½

Golf Facilities: ★★★★

14-Club Test: ★★★★

Intangibles: ★★★★

Value: ★★★★

Just the Facts Year Opened: 1992; Course Designer: Jack Nicklaus; Walking: Allowed at certain times; Greens Fee: $95; 9-Hole/Twilight Rate: Yes; Pull Carts: No; Practice Range: Yes; Club Rental: Yes.

Description and Comments Considered by some to be the Pebble Beach of the East, Great Waters isn't quite that, but it's a wonderful track that mixes challenge and beauty into its 18 holes. Former home to the Anderson Consulting World Championship of Golf, Great Waters is a world-class course. As you play the first eight holes you may ask yourself: "Great Waters, so where's the water?" A fair question, as the only water you will find on these starting holes is in the drinking fountains. Instead, you are presented with eight tight holes carved out of magnificent towering pines. Then you reach the ninth green and you begin to realize just how the course earned its name.

The remaining holes all skirt the edge of Lake Oconee, a huge human-made lake that surrounds the Reynolds Plantation. Aside from the obvious hazard value, the lake also produces some of the most spectacular scenery this side of the Monterey Peninsula's 17-Mile Drive.

Though many holes at Great Waters are memorable, there are several that stand out in our minds. The hardest hole on the course is the 5th, an uphill, 422-yard par-4. Number five is a tight, right-to-left dogleg that requires you to drive over a creek to a small landing area. To reach the green, your second shot must then clear another creek. Hole nine is a 392-yard par-4 that provides ample room off the tee, but then challenges you with a healthy carry over an inlet of Lake Oconee to reach the green. Other superb holes are the driveable (for the pros) par-4 11th, which measures 349 yards but plays slightly downhill, with a stunning lake view behind the huge but shallow green, and the all-carry, 170-yard, par-3 14th, which flirts with the same lake.

Insider Tips Errant shots are deadly at Great Waters—you will either be in among deep pines or swimming in Lake Oconee. Course management is the key to success here, so play wisely. For most players, the blue tees offer enough challenge, so unless you are a single-digit handicapper (or a masochist) you should avoid the championship tees. Also, the many uphill/downhill holes as well as the wind will affect your yardage—make sure to adjust for these factors when selecting your club.

All the Reynolds courses, along with Port Armor and Harbor Club, are located an hour's drive from Atlanta and sit at a lower elevation, so you can go visit a little earlier in the year and revisit a little later in the year and the weather and courses will be more favorable than their Atlanta and other northern counterparts.

Reynolds Plantation, National Course

100 Linger Longer Rd., Greensboro, GA 30642; phone (800) 800-5250
or (706) 467-3151

How to Get On: You must be a guest at the Reynolds Plantation cottages
to play this private course.

Tees:

> Blue: 7,015 yards, par-72, USGA rating 72.7, slope 127
>
> White: 6,536 yards, par-72, USGA rating 70.5, slope 123
>
> Red: 5,292 yards, par-72, USGA rating 69.5, slope 116

Challenge: ★★★½	Golf Facilities: ★★★½
Variety: ★★★	14-Club Test: ★★★½
Terrain: ★★★½	Intangibles: ★★★
Beauty/Visual Appeal: ★★★	Value: ★★½
Pace of Play: ★★★½	

Just the Facts   Year Opened: 1997; Course Designer: Tom Fazio; Walking: Allowed at certain times; Greens Fee: $85; 9-Hole/Twilight Rate: Yes;
Pull Carts: No; Practice Range: Yes; Club Rental: Yes.

Description and Comments   The latest addition to the Reynolds arsenal, the
National Course is a fairly wide-open layout featuring a variety of hazards
that challenge the golfer at every turn. First off, there are the large pine trees
that line the fairways. Sand plays a huge role in Fazio's design—more than
80 bunkers guards both fairways and greens. Although this is no "Great
Waters," the National Course does offer ponds and streams that come into
play on every hole. Greens are medium to large in size and have a fair number of undulations, mostly broad contours rather than specific tiers.

As is the case with Great Waters, both nines are spectacular, with sweeping views and many memorable holes. The front nine is a joy to play, but
the back nine is even more striking and challenging. The toughest hole on
the course is number 16, a 216-yard par-3 that plays from an elevated tee
down to a tight green located in the base of an opposing hill. There is a
creek that winds down the fairway on the right, and the green is well
guarded by bunkers on the left.

Insider Tips   As is the case with the other courses at Reynolds, check the
wind that comes off the lake, as it will affect your club selection. In addition, the time of year you are playing will also make a difference—during
the dryer months you will get more roll on the fairways, but the greens will
be a tad faster. The opposite is true during the wetter times of the year.

Our recommendation on number 16 is not to make too much of an
adjustment for the elevation change, as the hazards come into play very
quickly and you will probably need the extra pop. The scale is absolutely
massive at the National, where subtlety takes the back seat to brute force.

The often super-wide fairways don't play quite as wide as they appear because they're mostly hogbacked and slope hard off to one or both sides. Thus, if you hit the fairway, make sure it's in the right spot, or it may kick off a slope and run into the trees or other hazards.

If you're overweight or are otherwise not too limber, you literally may have trouble entering and exiting the course's sand bunkers. Traps this deep, with sand this soft, should have built-in steps to aid in ingress/egress.

Reynolds Plantation, Plantation Course

100 Linger Longer Rd., Greensboro, GA 30642; phone (800) 800-5250 or (706) 467-3151

How to Get On: You must be a guest at the Reynolds Plantation cottages to play this private course.

Tees:

> Blue: 6,656 yards, par-72, USGA rating 71.3, slope 127
> White: 6,017 yards, par-72, USGA rating 68.4, slope 118
> Red: 5,162 yards, par-72, USGA rating 69.1, slope 115

Challenge: ★★½	Golf Facilities: ★★★★
Variety: ★★★	14-Club Test: ★★★½
Terrain: ★★★½	Intangibles: ★★★½
Beauty/Visual Appeal: ★★★	Value: ★★★★
Pace of Play: ★★★★	

Just the Facts   Year Opened: 1987; Course Designer: Bob Cupp; Walking: Allowed at certain times; Greens Fee: $65; 9-Hole/Twilight Rate: Yes; Pull Carts: No; Practice Range: Yes; Club Rental: Yes.

Description and Comments   The original course at Reynolds, Plantation is the shortest and easiest of the three tracts. Though a step below the other two on the "spectacular" scale, Plantation is a fun and challenging course, especially from the tips. The 421-yard, par-4 14th hole typifies the Plantation Course. The number four handicap, this hole is pure Georgia Piedmont foothills: heavily rolling with pines and scrubby oaks lining the fairways, with traces of red clay lining the banks of the lake to the left of the fairway.

Insider Tips   Greens are small, mostly flat, and traditionally shaped (ovals), so the longer you are off the tee, the better your approach shot opportunities to hit it stiff to the flag. Fairways are moderately rolling to hilly, and thus you will need to check your stance and adjust it so that you don't pull or slice. Water seldom comes into play, so you won't have to worry about fishing out your balls as you would on the other two courses at Reynolds. Not only that, but there are only 12 sand bunkers on the entire course, and none of them are fairway bunkers, so skilled sand play techniques aren't crucial here. The scarcity of water hazards, no fairway bunkers, and only 12 traps total? Yep—it's a fun course for any level of golfer, yet somehow good players are still challenged by the hills, trees, and small greens.

A Georgia Sampler

Cobblestone Golf Course

4200 Nance Rd., Acworth, GA 30101; phone (770) 917-5151

Tees: Championship: 6,759 yards, par-71, USGA rating 73.1, slope 140

Greens Fee: $49

Challenge: ★★★★

Variety: ★★★½

Terrain: ★★★

Beauty/Visual Appeal: ★★★

Pace of Play: ★★

Golf Facilities: ★★★

14-Club Test: ★★★★½

Intangibles: ★★★½

Value: ★★★

Description and Comments   A delight for highly skilled players; perhaps a bit too tough for the rest of us, but interesting at every turn. Many greens possess a number of sinister nooks and crannies where they can tuck a flagstick, making it doubly difficult to hold the green on a typical approach shot. This extremely hilly course features several outstanding lake views, but also features heavy, often contrived moundings topped with buffalo grass, which makes recovery shots terribly demanding for the average Joe.

If you don't mind posting more double bogeys than you're used to, you'll find this course an excellent value. If you prefer scoring closer to your regular handicap, you might find Cobblestone a bit severe. If you haven't been to the region for a few years, you may not have heard of this course by this name, but you might know it by its previous name, The Boulders at Lake Acworth.

The Hampton Club

100 Tabbystone, St. Simons Island, GA 31522; phone (912) 634-0255

Tees: Championship: 6,465 yards, par-72, USGA rating 71.4, slope 130

Greens Fee: $58.

Challenge: ★★★

Variety: ★★★

Terrain: ★★★

Beauty/Visual Appeal: ★★★★

Pace of Play: ★★★

Golf Facilities: ★★★

14-Club Test: ★★★½

Intangibles: ★★★

Value: ★★★

Description and Comments   Located on marshland (have that bug spray ready) and carved out of grand oak trees, Hampton Club offers plenty of good golf without beating you up. Water and doglegs will keep you on your toes—if you are a relatively good golfer, make sure to play it from the tips. This is an idyllic, peaceful retreat, with several tees and greens accessible only via long wooden bridges with rope guardrails that traverse dense marshland.

Most memorable are the 570-yard, par-5 3rd hole, which has marsh down the entire left side and a lake on the right side near the green, and the 370-yard, par-4 13th, which hopscotches the marsh via islands of turf. Once in a great while, the afternoon breezes usher in unpleasant odors from a nearby paper mill. In this case, if your game stinks, you can always blame it on the "fresh" air.

Harbor Club

One Club Drive, Greensboro, GA 30642; phone (800) 505-4653 or (706) 453-4414

Tees: Championship: 6,988 yards, par-72, USGA rating 73.7, slope 135

Greens Fee: $52–62

Challenge: ★★★½

Variety: ★★★½

Terrain: ★★★½

Beauty/Visual Appeal: ★★★½

Pace of Play: ★★★½

Golf Facilities: ★★★½

14-Club Test: ★★★½

Intangibles: ★★★½

Value: ★★★½

Description and Comments   A very scenic course that plays alongside Lake Oconee, in the Reynolds Plantation neighborhood. Tight, wooded fairways; hilly terrain; and fast greens produce a fair but challenging test for golfers, though much of the higher, more interesting ground was reserved for houses. A 1991 design from Tom Weiskopf and Jay Morrish, Harbor Club features a sterling example of the duo's architectural trademark, the driveable par-4. In this case, it's the 326-yard 16th, which plays from an elevated tee and calls for a "bite-off-whatever-you-can-chew" drive over Lake Oconee. A bunker cluster to the right and behind the green adds further interest. Designed in classic fashion, with short distances from the green to the next tee and with most of the holes featuring open entrances to the greens, Harbor Club isn't as dramatic as some in the area, but it's remarkably playable for all classes of golfers. There's not much to do in this neighborhood—not even places to eat—but Harbor Club is so much fun to play, it's worth the effort to get here.

Orchard Hills Golf Club

600 E. Highway 16, Newnan, GA 30263; phone (770) 251-5683

Tees:

Logo/Rock Garden: 7,002 yards, par-72, USGA rating 73.4, slope 134

Orchard/Logo: 7,007 yards, par-72, USGA rating 72.9, slope 131

Rock Garden/Orchard: 7,014 yards, par-72, USGA rating 72.8, slope 132

Greens Fee: $39–49

Challenge: ★★★½

Variety: ★★★½

Terrain: ★★★★

Beauty/Visual Appeal: ★★★★

Pace of Play: ★★★½

Golf Facilities: ★★★½

14-Club Test: ★★★½

Intangibles: ★★★½

Value: ★★★★

Description and Comments   Built in a pecan orchard, this is one of Georgia's true hidden gems. The course has a linksy look to it with whispy grasses and open areas. This is a course composed of 3 nines, which can be played in 3 different 18-hole combinations. The Orchard and Logo courses are links-style with very few trees, but knee-high rough and water challenge the golfer. The Rock Garden course also demands accuracy, as the fairways are cut through the woods. Greens on all three nines are fast and tricky. You can see the nines from Interstate 85; this is the perfect stop-off if you're heading to Callaway Gardens from Atlanta.

Osprey Cove Golf Club

123 Osprey Dr., St. Marys, GA 31558; phone (912) 882-5575

Tees: Championship: 6,791 yards, par-72, USGA rating 73.0, slope 130

Greens Fee: $63–89

Challenge: ★★★

Variety: ★★★★

Terrain: ★★★

Beauty/Visual Appeal: ★★★

Pace of Play: ★★★

Golf Facilities: ★★★★

14-Club Test: ★★★½

Intangibles: ★★★

Value: ★★★

Description and Comments   Nestled in a beautiful setting of salt marshes and woodlands, Osprey Cove is a fairly open and flat course that challenges golfers via fast greens, many steep-faced bunkers, water, big mounds, and doglegs. Even though walking is allowed at times, you may want to reconsider hoofing it as greens and tee boxes are quite some distance from each other, which is typical of a real estate development course, even if it is an outstanding example of one. The memorable 9th and 18th holes culminate in a double green that overlooks serene tidal marshes. The signature hole at this Mark McCumber–designed layout is the 426-yard, par-4 15th. Right on the marsh, the magnificently scenic 15th overlooks the Bluffs of Florida. Highlights of the hole include a tree in the middle of the fairway, marsh all along the right side, bunkers to the left, and an elevated, multitiered green fortressed by bunkers.

Port Armor Resort and Country Club

One Port Armor Parkway, Greensboro, GA 30642; phone (706) 453-4564
Tees: Championship: 6,926 yards, par-72, USGA rating 73.6, slope 136
Greens Fee: $50–70

Challenge: ★★★½	Golf Facilities: ★★★½
Variety: ★★★	14-Club Test: ★★★½
Terrain: ★★★½	Intangibles: ★★★
Beauty/Visual Appeal: ★★★½	Value: ★★★
Pace of Play: ★★★½	

Description and Comments   Port Armor is a mostly straightforward course that rewards those who can keep it in the fairway. Challenge comes in the form of water on half of the holes; large, undulating greens; sturdy breezes; and substantial elevation changes of 30 to 40 feet. Architect Bob Cupp has a reputation for dramatic designs, but this is one of his tamer efforts. Perhaps the best hole is the 457-yard, par-4 4th, which features expansive views of Lake Oconee to the left of the fairway and beyond the green.

Renaissance Pinelsle Resort

9000 Holiday Rd., Lake Lanier Islands, GA 30518; phone (770) 945-8921
Tees: Championship: 6,527 yards, par-72, USGA rating 71.2, slope 122
Greens Fee: $54–59

Challenge: ★★½	Golf Facilities: ★★★★
Variety: ★★★	14-Club Test: ★★★
Terrain: ★★★½	Intangibles: ★★★½
Beauty/Visual Appeal: ★★★★	Value: ★★★★
Pace of Play: ★★★	

Description and Comments   Recent renovations have made this modestly challenging course very enjoyable to play, especially the back nine. This is a terrific course for families. Beautiful scenery is provided by lakes that come into play on six of the holes. You may even see a deer or two. Nevertheless, the property is so hilly you could be in trouble if you're prone to car sickness. Site of a fine four-star resort, this Gary Player/Ron Kirby design is a past host to the LPGA Nestle World Championship, from 1985 to 1989. It's a perfect getaway from the congestion of Atlanta, located an hour north of the city.

Typical of the course's beauty and challenge is the horseshoe-shaped 5th hole, a short par-5 of 489 yards that doglegs hard to the left around Lake Lanier. Gamblers can reach it in two, but there's practically more water than grass on this gorgeous hole, so accuracy is paramount.

White Columns

300 White Columns Dr., Alpharetta, GA 30201; phone (770) 343-9025

Tees: Championship: 7,053 yards, par-72, USGA rating 73.6, slope 137

Greens Fee: $60–95

Challenge: ★★★★	Golf Facilities: ★★★★½
Variety: ★★★½	14-Club Test: ★★★★
Terrain: ★★★★	Intangibles: ★★★½
Beauty/Visual Appeal: ★★★★	Value: ★★★★
Pace of Play: ★★★★	

Description and Comments   A public course with a private-course feel, including a sometimes haughty staff. Excellent layout amid pines and oaks with dramatic elevation changes and scenic vistas make this one course you don't want to miss. The enormous, flattish greens aren't particularly memorable in design, but they're renowned for their Tour-quality conditioning. Magnificent shaping of the golf holes into the terrain by master architect Tom Fazio and his crew makes it appear as if this five-year-old course has been around forever. Additional classy touches include old-fashioned rectangular tee boxes and steep-faced vintage bunkers with sand splashed all the way to the top. Several forced carries over a variety of wetland and water hazards make this a good test for the better player.

A truly superior practice facility awaits, with a huge teeing area, practice bunkers, and chipping greens. A word to the wise: White Columns is not the easiest course to find as it's not right off the interstate, unlike many of Atlanta's high-profile courses. Give yourself some extra time to negotiate the many turns and winding roads. The course will be easy by comparison.

Lodging in North Georgia

Expensive

Chateau Elan

100 Rue Charlemagne, Braselton, GA 30517; phone (800) 233-9463 or (770) 932-0900; www.chateauelan.com; Rates: $180–225 (inn); $200–240 (two-bedroom golf villa); $60–90 (lodge)

Chateau Elan is a French-themed resort, located 30 minutes southeast of Atlanta, that opened in 1993 and offers guests a variety of activities, including golf. The resort has more of a hotel feel than a resort feel, so this may not be the place if you want an intimate, cozy destination. Its amenities are also more adult in nature (golf, spa, and winery—although the winery is nothing to write home about), and thus is not our top recommendation for families. It is, however, still recommended if you are looking for a great place to play golf and experience a little taste of France.

The property includes a main hotel modeled after a French chateau that has 227 rooms, including 20 suites, 4 hospitality suites, and a 2,000-square-foot presidential suite. In addition there are The Petite Golf Villas, if you are traveling in a group, and a separate hotel, The Lodge at Chateau Elan, which is located near the main hotel and offers guests a more affordable alternative. The lodge has 80 rooms, as well as its own swimming pool.

Chateau Elan has three 18-hole courses, plus a fun par-3 walking course, a tennis center with seven lit courts, an equestrian center with a 37,500-square-foot covered arena, The Spa at Chateau Elan, and The Chateau Elan Winery (we did not enjoy the wine, however).

Golf Packages   If you are staying at the inn, the package includes breakfast buffet in the Versailles Room and one round of golf each day at either The Chateau or the Woodlands Course.* For the Golf Villas the package includes breakfast in the Clubhouse Grill and one round of golf each day at either The Chateau or the Woodlands course.* If you opt for the lodge, the package includes a continental breakfast at the hotel and one round of golf at the Chateau or the Woodlands Course.

Dining in North Georgia

Chateau Elan offers the following dining options; phone (800) 233-9463 or (770) 932-0900 for information or reservations.

Café Elan   Light entrees; Inexpensive–Moderate; Reservations not required if fewer than six people. Dining in a casual bistro atmosphere in the atrium of the winery.

Clubhouse Grill   American; Inexpensive; No reservations required. Located at the golf course, the grill serves sandwiches and burgers.

Fleur-de-Lis   Health food; Moderate; Reservations requested. Located in the Spa, you may have guessed that this restaurant serves nutritional food, but don't worry—it does have flavor.

Le Clos   American; Very Expensive; Reservations required. This is the resort's formal restaurant, where guests experience a seven- or eight-course meal, which are paired with a selected Chateau Elan wine. Good atmosphere—jacket is required for men.

Versailles Room   French-accented; Inexpensive–Moderate; Reservations requested. The Versailles room is located in the atrium and offers breakfast and lunch buffets as well as an à la carte dinner menu. The food is fine, but because the room is so big this is not the best place for a romantic dinner.

* There is a $10 surcharge during certain times of year on Woodlands.

The 19th Hole in North Georgia

L'Auberge, Chateau Elan Chateau Elan; phone (800) 233-9463 or (770) 932-0900. Lounge overlooking the atrium with big-screen televisions, billiards, darts, and miniature putting.

Paddy's Irish Pub Chateau Elan; phone (800) 233-9463 or (770) 932-0900. Bar featuring live entertainment on Fridays and Saturdays.

Lodging in Central Georgia

EXPENSIVE

Callaway Gardens Resort

U.S. 27, Pine Mountain, GA 31822; phone (800) 225-2929 or (706) 663-2281; www.callawaygardens.com; Rates: $110–150

Callaway Gardens was the brainchild of Carson J. Callaway and his wife, Virginia Hand Callaway, who wanted to create a retreat where visitors could experience the beauty, relaxation, and inspiration of the environment. The result is a 14,000-acre oasis located only 70 miles from Atlanta.

The Gardens offer a variety of activities, including walking, biking, and nature trails; a horticultural center; a chapel; and educational classes, just to name a few. Our favorite activity, though, is the Cecil B. Day Butterfly Center, where guests can walk among 1,000 free-flying butterflies. It is a unique experience and one you will remember for a long time.

When the Callaway Gardens Inn was originally built, it was a Holiday Inn, and the Gardens grew into a resort destination. Since then, the Country Cottages and the Mountain Villas have been added to keep up with the demand for accommodations. The Gardens Inn has 350 rooms and suites, but despite being upgraded, it still possesses a lingering Holiday Inn flavor. There are a few Garden Suites that have one or two bedrooms and a separate parlor. All rooms overlook the pool or the lawn. There are 155 Country Cottages, which have two bedrooms, a living room, dining area, fireplace, screened-in porch, and a deck. The Mountain Creek Villas are very nice with a large living room, dining area, fireplace, fully equipped kitchen, washer/dryer, screened-in porch, and a deck and a separate bathroom for each bedroom.

Golf Packages The Champion Deluxe Golf Package consists of accommodations in the Callaway Gardens Inn; Country Cottages or Mountain Creek Villas; welcome cocktail in the Vineyard Green Lounge; one round of golf daily, cart included; golf souvenir from Lake View or Mountain View pro shops; breakfast at the Plantation Room buffet (if you prefer to dine in one the other restaurants, you will receive a $9 voucher); dinner at the Plantation Room buffet (if you prefer to dine in one the other restaurants, you will receive a $17 voucher); daily use of the Callaway Fitness Center; Gardens and Robin Lake Beach admission, including Sibley Horticultural Center, Pioneer Log Cabin, Day Butterfly Center, Discovery Bicycle Trail, Mr. Carson's Vegetable Garden, Azalea Bowl, Memorial chapel, Meadowlark Gardens area, Florida State University "Flying High" Circus, miniature golf, paddleboats, Ping-Pong, shuffleboard, and a paddlewheeler.

MODERATE

Magnolia Hall Bed & Breakfast

127 Barnes Mill Rd., Hamilton, GA 31811; phone (706) 628-4566; www.bbonline.com/ga/magnoliahall; Rates: $95–115

Only five miles from the Callaway Gardens, this B&B is located in a lovely 1890 Victorian home. There are only five bedrooms, but each is rather roomy and decorated with period pieces.

INEXPENSIVE

Hampton Inn

100 Willis Circle, La Grange, GA 30240; phone (800) 426-7866 or (706) 845-1115; Rates: $58–65; Built: 1996; Renovations: None.

Dining in Central Georgia

The Country Kitchen   Highway 27 near Callaway Gardens; phone (706) 663-2281. Southern; Inexpensive; Reservations not necessary. A great place to have some good old-fashioned Southern cooking. Try the biscuits and gravy or the grits.

The Georgia Room   Callaway Gardens Resort; phone (706) 663-2281. Varied; Moderate; Reservations required. The hotel's main dining room is a formal restaurant that is long on atmosphere—piano and candlelight are nice touches.

The Plantation Room   Callaway Gardens; phone (706) 663-2281. Southern; Inexpensive–Moderate; No reservations needed. All meals are buffet style with lots of food, including fresh vegetables picked from Mr. Carson's vegetable garden. You will love the fresh corn. Sometimes it gets crowded.

The Veranda/The Gardens   Highway 27, near Callaway Gardens; phone (706) 663-2281. Italian; Inexpensive–Moderate; Reservations recommended. This is actually two separate restaurants. The Veranda is less expensive and features pastas and salads. The Gardens is slightly more expensive with steaks and seafood. Request a table that overlooks the golf course.

Activities in Central Georgia

Besides the Callaway Gardens, there are other activities in the area that we suggest you consider:

Andersonville   114 Church St., Andersonville; phone (912) 924-2558. This was the Civil War's most infamous prisoner-of-war camp. At one time there were over 32,000 prisoners living in horrific conditions—more than 13,000 deaths were reported among the inmates. Along with monuments and museums, there is the newly dedicated National Prisoner of War Museum.

The Little White House   401 Little White House Rd., Warm Springs; phone (706) 655-5870. Franklin Roosevelt first came to Warm Springs in 1924 to swim in the healing waters, seeking therapy for his polio. He enjoyed the area so much that he built the "Little White House" in 1932 and visited often during his presidency. Located 17 miles from Callaway Gardens within the Franklin D. Roosevelt State Park.

Lodging on the Golden Isles

Jekyll Island is located nine miles south of Brunswick and is probably the most family-oriented of the Golden Isles, which is ironic given its origins as an exclusive retreat for America's elite, including the Rockefellers, Pulitzers, and Morgans. Though the smallest of the Golden Isles (5,600 acres), it is packed with outdoor activities and, of course, golf.

Sea Island was relatively uninhabited until a causeway was built from Brunswick to St. Simons Island in 1924. Now visitors can make the five-mile drive from Brunswick and escape to this beautiful enclave. There are not many accommodation options on Sea Island—you can either choose from the elegant Cloister Hotel or a variety of cottages and villas scattered throughout the island.

St. Simon's Island is the largest of the Golden Isles (it is the same size as Manhattan) and is the area's most comprehensive destination. There are superb beaches here and more accommodation options than on any of the others.

EXPENSIVE

The Cloister

Sea Island, GA 31561; phone (800) 732-4752 or (912) 638-3611; www.cloister.com; Rates: $340–575

Oaks line both sides of the avenue that leads you to one of America's premier resorts, The Cloister. Built in 1928 this is easily the most elegant development in the Golden Isles and in the top 20 in the country. The hotel's original architect, Addison Mizner, built a resort with a variety of individual buildings designed to reflect an Iberian/Spanish/Mediterranean style. These buildings are complemented by beautiful grounds and landscaping.

Known for its detail and special touches, guests of the Cloister are in for a special treat. You will be pampered from the time you arise to the time your head hits the pillow at night—in between, you will find it hard to fit in all that awaits you beyond your door. Although the Cloister is a year-round resort, its strong children's programs result in an especially busy summer.

A word of caution before we go on—the Cloister doesn't take American Express. Well actually, they don't take Visa or MasterCard either. That's right—no credit cards accepted, so be prepared (they do take personal and traveler's checks).

The Cloister is comprised of 234 rooms and 28 suites, all of which are very spacious and tastefully decorated. The main building boasts the older rooms of the resort, which remain some of the best. These rooms are slightly smaller than others here, but they possess a "traditional" feeling with more antique furniture (try to request one with a private balcony and/or patio). The newer accommodations, both the isolated cottages as well as the ocean-front units, are roomier and have more amenities, such as ironing boards and more modern furniture. Whatever you choose, you will no doubt be happy with your selection.

Top on our recommendation list of activities is a visit to the renowned Golf Learning Center located at Sea Island. Staff members include LPGA Hall of Famer Louise Suggs, and thus it is a great place for a little tune-up or a complete overhaul to your game. Additionally, you will find the following on the island: a beach club, pool, 22 tennis courts (four lit for night play), spa with fitness facilities, archery and skeet shooting, horseback riding, biking, sailing, lawn games, and fishing.

On the culinary side, the Cloister is very impressive. The Beach Club is perfectly situated adjacent to the ocean. At breakfast and lunch there is a buffet, and for dinner there is a buffet as well as an à la carte menu. The food is good, but the menu is on the conservative side, leaning more to traditional tastes rather than contemporary gourmet. Dress for breakfast and lunch is casual, but for dinner, a collared shirt is required (jackets optional). The Main Dining Room is the area's most lavish restaurant, which is reflected in the food and service—the staff wears white gloves. Once again the menu tends to be a tad old-fashioned, offering traditional favorites. Dinner is a five-course meal accompanied by musical entertainment and accentuated by an extensive wine list. When packing your bags take note— collared shirts are required for breakfast and lunch (jackets optional); coats and ties required at dinner, and on Wednesday and Saturday, formal attire is preferred. Finally, there is Sea Island Golf Club, which is actually located on St. Simons; this was once the corn and fodder barn of the Retreat Plantation, but don't worry, it smells much better these days. The food is typical of a golf club, and dress is casual for all meals (collared shirts required; no shorts at dinner).

One of the more charming aspects of this resort is the musical entertainment and dance programs—a signature activity at Sea Island since its inception. Special dance performances are held throughout the year, and guests can dance to the sounds of the Sea Island Orchestra or the Cloister Connection. Both ballroom and contemporary music is played, so get your dancing shoes ready. The Cloister isn't for everybody. It may be a bit stuffy for some tastes. However, if you have an appreciation for Old World relaxed elegance and civility plus outstanding service, you'll do no better than this bastion of southern tradition.

Golf Packages   The resort's golf package includes accommodations, full meal plan (three meals daily), daily greens fees with usually unlimited play (depending on availability), shared golf cart, complimentary range balls, and club cleaning and storage (three-night minimum).

Jekyll Island Club Hotel

371 Riverview Dr., Jekyll Island, GA 31527; phone (800) 535-9547 or (912) 635-2600; www.jekyllclub.com; Rates: $120–170

If the walls could talk . . . . This hotel was built in 1887 as a private resort where the upper crust of America's social register retreated. Today, it is open to everyone, but if you listen very carefully, you may still hear the revelry of the Astors, Morgans, and Macys.

Jekyll Island Club underwent a $17 million renovation in the late 1980s, restoring it to its original splendor. There are 117 guest rooms and 17 suites, each of which is decorated with an amazing attention to detail. Rooms have vaulted ceilings and beautiful furniture, including mahogany beds, armoires, sofa, and chairs. Rooms feature views of the Intracoastal Waterway, Jekyll River, or the hotel's croquet courts.

A word of caution: This hotel does not provide easy access to the Jekyll Island beaches, but it does have a nice swimming pool complex. In addition, there are nine tennis courts, a croquet lawn, a children's program, and bicycle rentals. (For more activities, please refer to the Activities section.)

At the hotel, you will find the Grand Dining Room, one of the Golden Isles' most elegant and formal restaurants (jackets required for dinner). Both the food and surroundings are superb, and the outstanding service may lull you into the sense that you are one of America's elite visiting back in the 1880s. A pianist who plays throughout the dinner hour adds to the elegant atmosphere. Food includes fresh fish of the day, with a tip of the hat to the crab cakes.

Golf Packages The hotel's golf package includes accommodations, greens fees for 18 holes, cart fee, taxes, and daily breakfast.

King and Prince Beach and Golf Resort

201 Arnold Rd., St. Simons Island, GA 31522; phone (800) 342-0212 or (912) 638-3631; www.kingandprince.com; Rates: $145–155

This oceanfront resort was developed in 1932 by a group of individuals who were kicked out of the Jekyll Island Club. The King and Prince is comprised of five buildings, all of which have a Spanish-Colonial architectural theme. This may not be as elegant as other resorts in the area, but it is a warm and inviting destination. For you history buffs, during World War II the resort closed its doors to outside guests and became home to the U.S. Navy, who worked on a radar station located on the island.

Guests can choose from either a room in the hotel or from one of the one- or two-bedroom villas on the property (the villas are privately owned, and thus availability varies). Guest rooms are spacious and nicely furnished; the villas are decorated by the owners, but you can assume all come with fully equipped kitchens and nice living areas.

The resort does boast easy access to the beach, but the beach all but disappears when it's high tide, so you may have to retreat to one of the four outdoor or one indoor pools if you want some water time. The resort also has four tennis courts, a fitness center, and bicycle rentals (for a list of other activities on the island, see the section later in this chapter).

Among the pluses: Its atrium lobby lounge is perhaps the most romantic place in the Golden Isles to share evening cocktails. Also, the dining room is elegant and overlooks the ocean.

Golf Packages The King and Prince package includes accommodations, greens fees, cart rental, breakfast, daily range balls, tennis court time, and a $25 pro shop credit.

Sea Palms Golf and Tennis Resort

5445 Frederica Rd., St. Simons Island, GA 31522; phone (800) 841-6268 or (912) 638-3351; www.seapalms.com; Rates: $120–150

For those who want to vacation where the outside world seems far away, Sea Palms could be for you. Although it is close to golf and tennis, it is very isolated, as it is located in the woodlands of St. Simons Island. Don't expect to be pampered—your first clue will be when you have to carry your own bags to your room.

The resort is comprised of 117 rooms and 27 suites, all of which have a view of either the Marshes of Glynn or Sea Palms. All rooms are conveniently located near the resort's amenities, which include a handsome but narrow 27-hole golf course, which can be fun to play, although none of the three nines are as challenging or as well maintained as many of the region's other courses.

At Sea Palms you will find 12 Rubico clay tennis courts, bicycle rentals, two outdoor pools, and a health club. Beach access is four miles away at the St. Simons Beach Club, where guests have full privileges.

Golf Packages The golf package consists of deluxe accommodations, greens and cart fees (18 holes per day/shared cart), driving range balls, club storage, and a buffet breakfast.

Villas by the Sea

1175 N. Broadway Dr., Jekyll Island, GA 31527; phone (800) 841-6262 or (912) 635-2521; www.jekyllislandga.com; Rates: $134–189

After the Jekyll Island Club Hotel, this is the island's next most upscale development. It is comprised of privately owned individual apartments scattered throughout a 17-acre forest. The apartments have between one and three bedrooms, and each comes with a fully equipped kitchen and a private living room. There is an 1,800-foot beachfront, the longest on the island, accessible via a bridge and a rocky breakwater. It should be noted that there are other villas and condos on the island that may be nicer, but these apartments are spacious and the access to the Crackers Restaurant/Deli puts this place at the top of the list if you are traveling with your family.

Golf Packages The golf package includes accommodations, unlimited greens fees, shared cart for 18 holes, and a full breakfast.

MODERATE
Clarion Resort Buccaneer

85 S. Beachview Dr., Jekyll Island, GA 31527; phone (888) 412-7770 or (912) 635-2261; www.motelproperties.com; Rates: $75–175

A favorite among visitors is the Clarion Resort, which offers nicely furnished rooms and a strong list of amenities. The resort has over 200 rooms, including standard accommodations, efficiencies, large executives, and plush suites. Some of the rooms have private oceanside balconies, so when making reservations, ask about the availability of these units.

The resort also boasts a nice pool complex, hot tub, tennis court, and game room. Like many of the hotels in the area, there is access to the beach, but you will have to travel over a series of raised boardwalks.

Golf Packages Clarion's golf package includes greens fees, shared cart, and daily breakfast.

INEXPENSIVE
Comfort Inn

711 Beachview Dr., Jekyll Island, GA 31527; phone (800) 228-5150 or (912) 635-2211; Rates: $75–179; Built: 1959; Renovated: 1998

Holiday Inn Beachfront

200 S. Beachview Dr., Jekyll Island, GA 31527; phone (800) 753-5955 or (912) 635-3311; Rates: $75–170; Built: 1978; Renovated: 1998

Sea Gate Inn

1014 Ocean Blvd., St. Simons Island, GA 31522; phone (800) 562-8812 or (912) 638-8661; Rates: $50–120; Built: 1984; Renovations: 1998

CONDOS/COTTAGES

For condo/cottage rentals, on Jekyll Island try Jekyll Realty, phone (912) 635-3303 or Parker-Kaufman Realty, phone (912) 635-2190. In addition, there are over 180 privately owned condos and cottages on Sea Island. Tenants of these units have full access to the Cloister and its facilities. Rental of these units is handled by Sea Island Cottage Rentals; phone (800) 732-4752 or (912) 638-5112. On St. Simon's Island, call Golden Isles Realty; phone (800) 337-3106 or (912) 638-8623 or Trupp-Hodnett Enterprises; phone (800) 627-6850 or (912) 638-5450

Dining on the Golden Isles

Blackbeard's   200 N. Beachview Dr., Jekyll Island; phone (912) 635-3522. Seafood; Inexpensive; Reservations not necessary. Tasty fish choices at a very reasonable price.

Blanche's Courtyard   440 Ocean Blvd., St. Simons Island; phone (912) 638-3030. Seafood and Southern; Moderate; Reservations recommended. This is the most popular restaurant on the island, so expect a wait on weekends and during high season. Service tends to be slow, but the food makes up for that—try the blue crab soup and the apple fritters.

Chelsea's   1226 Ocean Blvd., St. Simons Island; phone (912) 634-1022. American; Inexpensive–Moderate; Reservations recommended. Located near King and Prince Hotel, this restaurant offers a simple menu, but you won't be disappointed as all of it is good. If you like lobster, try the unique lobster-tail fingers. Also has excellent prime rib.

Crab Trap   1209 Ocean Blvd., St. Simons Island; phone (912) 638-3552. Seafood; Inexpensive; Reservations not necessary. The restaurant does not have much pizzazz, but the food is tasty and a great value.

Georgia Sea Grill   310-B Mallory St., St. Simons Island; phone (912) 638-1197. Seafood; Inexpensive; Reservations not necessary. Restaurant offers a wide variety of dishes, including local favorite blue crab melt.

The Grand Dining Room   Located in the Jekyll Island Club Hotel, 371 Riverview Dr.; phone (800) 535-9547 or (912) 635-2600. American with seafood emphasis; Expensive; Reservations required. A formal dining experience—great food, wonderful atmosphere. Try the crab cakes.

Latitude 31 Jekyll Wharf, Jekyll Island; phone (912) 635-3800. Seafood; Inexpensive–Moderate; Reservation recommended. Best seafood on the island—great views!

St. Simons Island Golf Club 100 Kings Way, St. Simons Island; phone (912) 638-5132. Low Country; Moderate–Expensive; Reservations recommended. Operated by the Cloister, this is the least formal of their dining options. Atmosphere is nice and even includes an evening pianist. Menu includes a variety of seafood and fowl dishes—this food is fine, but not as exciting as some found in other area restaurants.

Sea Island Golf Club 100 Retreat Ave., St. Simons Island; phone (912) 638-5154. International; Moderate–Expensive; Reservations recommended. Actually located on St. Simons, this was once the corn and fodder barn of the Retreat Plantation, but don't worry, it smells much better these days. The food is typical of a golf club and dress is casual for all meals (collared shirts required; no shorts at dinner).

Activities on the Golden Isles

Bicycle Rentals Jekyll Island Bicycle Rental; phone (912) 635-2648. Bubba's Bike Shop, 210 Skylane Dr., St. Simon's Island; phone (912) 267-0386. Eddie Collins Island Bike Shop, 204 Sylvan Dr., St. Simon's Island; phone (912) 638-0705.

Bird-Watching, Water Expeditions Marsh Hen Boat Tours, 310 Magnolia Ave., St. Simons Island; phone (912) 638-9354. Inland Charter Boat Service, North 1st Street, St. Simons Island; phone (800) 732-4752 or (912) 638-3611.

Carriage Tours Victoria's Carriages, phone (912) 635-9500, take you on tours through the historic district on Jekyll Island.

Fishing and Sightseeing Coastal Expeditions, 1 Harbor Rd., Jekyll Island; phone (912) 265-0392.

Horseback Riding Rides on Driftwood Beach and through the maritime forests on Jekyll Island; phone (912) 635-9500.

Nature Tours Year-round tours given by the University of Georgia Marine Extension Service on Jekyll Island; phone (912) 635-2119. Coastal Encounters, St. Simons Island; phone (912) 638-0221. Beach and marsh walks, marine biology lab.

Turtle Walks   From May through mid-August on Jekyll Island, find out about sea turtles and their habitat and go on shoreline walks in search of turtle tracks and nesting mothers; phone (912) 635-2284..

Water Park   Summer Waves, 210 S. Riverview Dr., Jekyll Island, ; phone (912) 635-2074. Features swimming pool and water slides.

Water Sports   Barry Beach Service, 420 Arnold Rd., St. Simons Island; phone (800) 669-5215 or (912) 638-8053. Southeast Adventure Outfitters, 313 Mallery St., St. Simons Island; phone (912) 638-6732.

The 19th Hole on the Golden Isles

Blackbeard's Restaurant & Lounge   200 N. Beachview Dr., Jekyll Island; phone (912) 635-3522. Outdoor deck overlooking the ocean. Live entertainment, good food, and ales, with an old pirate atmosphere.

Morgan's Grill, Jekyll Island Golf Club House   Captain Willy Rd., Jekyll Island; phone (912) 635-4103. Après-round food and drink in a relaxed, historic setting.

Sea Island Golf Club 100 Retreat Ave., St. Simons Island; phone (800) 732-4752 or (912) 638-5118. The Sea Island Golf Club is the perfect place for a post-round libation, surrounded by plaques, trophies, and old photos of such legends as Bobby Jones, Sam Snead, and Davis Love III.

Part Eight
Mississippi's Gulf Coast

Overview

"Deep in the heart of Dixie . . . is golf?" Although we don't think that is how the song goes, it is nonetheless true. Mississippi is home to several acclaimed private country clubs and public courses scattered throughout the state, but the largest concentration of quality golf is along the Gulf Coast (or perhaps these days, we should say the Golf Coast). The Gulf Coast is an 80-mile stretch of beach located in the southeast section of Mississippi, sandwiched between Alabama and Louisiana. The area has less of a Mississippi feel than a New Orleans feel, which makes sense when you realize that one of the nearest major cities is indeed New Orleans, located 90 miles to the west (Mobile, Alabama, is 35 miles east).

This prime beachfront property, overlooking the Gulf of Mexico, has a colorful past, having been home to the French, English, and Spanish. This diversified heritage is reflected in many aspects of the area, including its people, architecture, and even street names. Today, the three main draws to the area—besides golf—are gambling, more gambling, and beaches. As for the beach scene, it garners somewhat mixed reviews. On the plus side is the brilliant whiteness of the sand; the minus side concerns the water color of the Gulf of Mexico, which usually assumes a dull brown hue.

Those who want to try their hand at lady luck are headed to the Gulf Coast in record numbers, to the permanently docked casinos that are replicas of the grand riverboats that once dominated the Mississippi River. These hotels are basically like barges on the water. It's amazing to contemplate that the casinos have only been around since 1992. Gambling seems such a natural adjunct to the free-and-easy, fun-loving Gulf Coast.

So why go to Mississippi's Gulf Coast for a golf vacation? As an Ohio man who's done this particular trip on three separate occasions says, "The whole area is just a great value. It's still off the beaten path, there's good gambling, reasonable dining and lodging, and the best golf courses cost

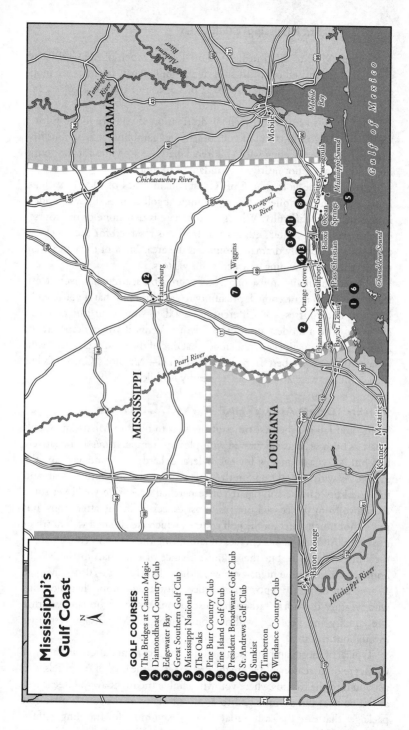

Mississippi's Gulf Coast

N

GOLF COURSES

1. The Bridges at Casino Magic
2. Diamondhead Country Club
3. Edgewater Bay
4. Great Southern Golf Club
5. Mississippi National
6. The Oaks
7. Pine Burr Country Club
8. Pine Island Golf Club
9. President Broadwater Golf Club
10. St. Andrews Golf Club
11. Sunkist
12. Timberton
13. Windance Country Club

$65, versus $150 to $225 in Las Vegas." Even if much of the Gulf Coast clientele is comprised of "third-shift-at-the-mill" types, facilities are modern and clean, and even the snobbiest or savviest of traveling golfers can surely appreciate the bargains to be had.

Though this area is an excellent destination if you are looking for a value-oriented combination of golf, beach, and gambling, it is not our first choice if you are traveling with children. There are activities for the young ones, but they are not nearly as abundant as in other areas.

Now onto the golf. The Gulf Coast's main cities of Ocean Springs, Biloxi, and Gulfport offer a variety of different golf courses that vary widely in maturity and difficulty. What's unfortunate is that none of the courses were routed along water's edge—that land was reserved for the hotels, so there's no single truly dramatic course in the area. Most of the courses are public, though, providing easy access for visitors.

The region's major, must-play courses are a bit scattered. Nevertheless, many are within close enough proximity to each other so that if you're looking to fit two courses—36 different holes a day—into your itinerary, you can do so with a modest amount of driving. Again, if you're desperate for additional high-quality golf, remember that one of the most acclaimed facilities on Alabama's Robert Trent Jones Golf Trail—Magnolia Grove—is less than an hour away, 20 miles east of nearby Mobile.

When to Go and What it Will Cost

Spring and fall are the best times of the year to head to Mississippi's Gulf Coast as both seasons are blessed with pleasant temperatures and relatively low humidity. Summer is for the hale and hardy . . . and perhaps the insane. As with most Deep South locales, summer temperatures soar, and the humidity can be stifling. If you're perched beachside you'll get some assistance from the coastal breezes, most especially in the afternoons, but there's not much relief on the golf courses, which are situated well north of the water. Autumn is our choice. In late spring the area and courses are at their most beautiful, but there's more chance of rain than in the fall. In both seasons, daytime highs average in the delightful mid-70s to low-80s. Winter can be pretty nippy and has been historically unpredictable, with wild weather the norm rather than exception. Visitors who come during late-January and February will no doubt enjoy the Mardi Gras festivities throughout the area.

Typical of most gambling destinations, the accommodations in the Gulf Coast are quite reasonable as are the greens fees—the goal of the hotels is to get you into the casinos where you will gamble the night away. Greens fees at the courses range from $22 to $75, but many of the hotels offer golf packages that ease the cash outlay burden even more for traveling golfers. Spring and fall are the most expensive seasons; during the summer the rates are at their lowest, reflecting diminished occupancy. If you do decide to come during the summer, we recommend that you book an early morning or late tee time and retreat indoors or to the pool during midday.

Given its proximity to the Gulf of Mexico, Mississippi's Gulf Coast is one of the most humid locales in the United States. You might reasonably expect morning fog delays on at least half the days of the year, though the further away the golf course is from the Gulf, the less the possibility of delayed tee times.

As with many locations in the Deep South, tropical storms and the occasional (but rare) hurricane make their appearances from June to November, with the highest likelihood for both from the beginning of August to the middle of September.

WHAT TO BRING

The clothing you pack will depend on when you come to the area. During the fall, spring, and winter, we recommend that you include in your suitcase a sweater, wind clothes, and an umbrella. Spring's major thunderstorms may require an extra-strong umbrella; better yet, don't be foolish. When the big thunderclaps start booming, get off the course quickly. For the summer, the lightest-weight clothes are the ticket. You will also want to have an extra golf glove or two with you. High humidity causes perspiring hands, the end result being a shorter lifespan for your favorite soft leather glove. You might try bringing some synthetic gloves, especially ones suited for wet conditions, in order to ensure keeping a proper grip on things.

Water hazards are everywhere on the Gulf Coast courses, especially on the newer ones, so you will want to bring a couple of extra sleeves of balls. No extra clubs are needed on the courses in the Gulf Coast, but be certain to load up on sunscreen and bug spray.

Pack light. Chances are virtually nil you're going to need fancy, formal clothes. Moreover, the Gulf Coast really is a "long-weekend" type of golf/gambling getaway, as opposed to some of the other destinations in this book, where you'd need a week to experience them properly.

ONCE YOU'RE THERE

The Gulf Coast area is dominated by larger-scale hotels, augmented by the occasional bed-and-breakfast. Many of the new additions to the area offer guests fine accommodations, on-premises gambling, and a variety of other activities, including the newest addition, Steve Wynn's Beau Rivage, which opened in spring 1999. Wynn, of course, is best known for his spectacular Las Vegas properties, such as The Mirage, Golden Nugget, Treasure Island, and the new Bellagio. Beau Rivage isn't nearly as splashy as its Vegas cousins, but it is definitely the most striking property on the Gulf Coast.

There really are only two traditional golf resorts in the area, the President Casino Broadwater Resort in Biloxi and The Bridges at Casino Magic in nearby Bay St. Louis. However, many of the hotels in the area offer golf packages with public and semiprivate courses.

As mentioned earlier, the greens fees here tend to be reasonable, and thus visitors can pretty much afford as much golf as they want to fit into their trip. Biloxi and Gulfport offer three strong courses: Edgewater Bay, Great Southern, and the aforementioned Broadwater Resort. Biloxi and Gulfport are just 15 minutes apart on the same road. Both offer similar aesthetics and attractions, though the prevailing view is that Biloxi offers a bit more action.

In terms of getting around, if you plan on playing several courses, you're going to need a car. Nothing is all that far away, but nothing is all that close, either. Resorts and casino hotels aren't quite enough of the upscale variety to provide consistent, high-quality transportation, unless you're a high roller.

Our recommendations: If you're a serious golfer down for a long weekend, the two must-plays are The Oaks, first and foremost, then The Bridges at Casino Magic. Following very closely are Windance, then either course at Diamondhead. Diamondhead's Cardinal is ever-so-slightly better than its Pine course, but you can't go wrong with either one. Shot-for-shot, Windance is probably the better course than The Bridges, but the novelty of The Bridges' design elevates it just above Windance on the "must-play" scale. If value is your chief concern, try the St. Andrews Golf Club in Ocean Springs and the Sunkist Country Club in Biloxi. On most occasions, these two courses can be played for under $40, and many times for under $30.

Finally, if you're a golf fanatic and have come to the Gulf Coast to pursue your passion, we recommend not only the above-mentioned courses but also two other facilities. Timberton Golf Club is a little more than an hour's drive north from Gulfport/Biloxi, in Hattiesburg. A 27-hole public course, Timberton ranks among the state's top 10 courses of any kind, private, public, or resort. An hour to the east lies Magnolia Grove, near Mobile, Alabama. This complex is one of the most honored of all the facilities on the Robert Trent Jones Golf Trail, with 36 championship holes, plus a marvelous 18-hole par-3 course.

GATHERING INFORMATION

Mississippi Gulf Coast Convention & Visitors Bureau
P.O. Box 6128, Gulfport, MS 39506-6128
Phone (800) 237-9793
www.gulfcoast.org; www.gobiloxi.com
tourism@gulfcoast.com

The Major Courses

The Bridges at Casino Magic

711 Casino Magic Dr., Bay St. Louis, MS 39520; phone (800) 562-4425
or (228) 436-4047

How to Get On: Tee times can be made up to 60 days in advance.

Tees:

Purple: 6,841 yards, par-72, USGA rating 73.5, slope 138

Gold: 6,217 yards, par-72, USGA rating 70.3, slope 132

White: 5,535 yards, par-72, USGA rating 67.3, slope 113

Teal: 5,108 yards, par-72, USGA rating 70.1, slope 126

Challenge: ★★★★	Golf Facilities: ★★★★½
Variety: ★★★	14-Club Test: ★★★
Terrain: ★★★	Intangibles: ★★★½
Beauty/Visual Appeal: ★★★½	Value: ★★★
Pace of Play: ★★	

Just the Facts   Year Opened: 1996; Course Designers: Arnold Palmer and
Ed Seay; Walking: No; Greens Fee: $80; 9-Hole/Twilight Rate: No; Pull
Carts: No; Practice Range: Yes; Club Rental: Yes.

Description and Comments   This is one of the more pricey golf courses in
the area, but it is also one of the more impressive ones, especially as it continues to mature. The course name is derived from the 21 wooden bridges
(nearly a mile's worth) that transport golfers from hole to hole over the
course's many lakes (17) and wetlands (14 acres' worth). The result is a
unique, beautiful, difficult, hazard-filled track. Watch for numerous
wildlife sightings, including a few gators.

The fairways at The Bridges are narrow, but not excessively so. They
just seem tighter than they are because they are so often flanked by intimidating wetlands and bunkers. Designer Arnold Palmer and his team moved
a fair amount of dirt to create some mounds on the course that break up
the monotony of what is otherwise level terrain on the front nine. The
back side is nicer than the front—more memorable with more rolling
topography. Greens are large and are often protected by Scottish-style
bunkers, making your approach shot critical.

When the wind is blowing, the course definitely increases in difficulty,
although even with all the trouble scattered about, it's mostly a playable
course. However, the mid- to high-handicappers will find it more challenging than some of other courses in the area. In fact, if your skills are truly on
the modest side, you might be better off playing one of the less-demanding
courses in the area. On the other hand, if you can handle losing a bunch of

balls and don't mind a higher score than usual, then you'll undoubtedly enjoy what is among the more distinctive courses in the South.

Hole eight, a driveable, risk/reward, 283-yard par-4, is one of the most picturesque holes on the course as it plays to the Bay of St. Louis, providing a beautiful view on the horizon. If you are looking for an opportunity to improve your golf game, The Bridges is home to The Arnold Palmer Golf Academy—one of only five such schools nationwide. The school offers group clinics, video analysis, an 11-acre practice facility, two chipping greens, and a 5,200-square-foot putting green with grass and sand bunkers.

Insider Tips   Leave your driver in the bag or better yet in the trunk of your car, away from temptation. The course is not terribly long, and given the tight fairways and numerous hazards, you may want to use a three wood off the tee for the majority of the holes.

The carts have an electronic yardage system installed—make sure to refer to it, but make adjustments if there is a predominant wind. You will want to have a good supply of backup balls as you may lose a few in the 17 lakes and 14 acres of wetlands located throughout the course. There are some excellent golfers who find The Bridges at Casino Magic both gimmicky and repetitive because of the large number of lay-ups and forced carries and from the actual bridgework, which, while handsome, tends to dominate the landscape, lending a certain sameness to many of the holes. Ultimately, though, these folks are in the minority. The Bridges has been well received by nearly everyone, placing it in the top 10 in the state of Mississippi in several leading polls.

If there is a recurring problem at The Bridges at Casino Magic, it is slow play. This situation is not so much the fault of the club, but simply inherent in the design. For better or worse, when you get a lot of first-time players on a beautiful but difficult, hazard-laden course, especially players whose skills may be overmatched by the nature of the design, you've got the perfect recipe for slow play. To be fair, the computer systems on the carts help alleviate some of the tardiness, but truth be told, if you're in a hurry, play somewhere else. If you don't mind the occasional wait among lovely scenery, you'll be just fine.

What can help in the fight against slow play? Play the proper tee markers. The Bridges is one of those courses that should not be attempted from the back tees unless you are a low-handicap (mid–single digit or less) golfer. There are simply far too many difficult forced carries from the back tees here for a so-so golfer to be able to move around the course comfortably.

Still another tip to avoid slow play: Carry a good sand wedge in your bag, one with ample loft. Many of the sand bunkers, especially around the greens, are of the stacked-sod wall, Scottish variety, which are deeper than they appear at first glance. If you don't swing hard enough or use enough loft on your escape shot, you're likely to leave it in the trap.

Diamondhead Country Club

7600 Country Club Circle, Diamondhead, MS 39525; phone (800) 346-8741 or (228) 255-3910

How to Get On: Tee times can be made two days in advance unless you are part of a golf package.

Cardinal Course Tees:

> Blue: 6,831 yards, par-72, USGA rating 72.7, slope 132
>
> White: 6,163 yards, par-72, USGA rating 71.0, slope 131
>
> Gold: 5,483 yards, par-72, USGA rating 66.1, slope 113
>
> Gold Ladies: 5,483 yards, par-72, USGA rating 72.4, slope 127
>
> Red: 5,065 yards, par-72, USGA rating 69.9, slope 122

Challenge: ★★★	Golf Facilities: ★★★
Variety: ★★★	14-Club Test: ★★★
Terrain: ★★★	Intangibles: ★★★½
Beauty/Visual Appeal: ★★★	Value: ★★★½
Pace of Play: ★★★	

Just the Facts Year Opened: 1972; Course Designer: Bill Atkins; Walking: No; Greens Fee: $60–70; 9-Hole/Twilight Rate: Yes; Pull Carts: No; Practice Range: Yes; Club Rental: Yes.

Pine Course Tees:

> Blue: 6,817 yards, par-72, USGA rating 73.6, slope 133
>
> White: 6,377 yards, par-72, USGA rating 71.1, slope 132
>
> Gold: 5,794 yards, par-72, USGA rating 68.8, slope 118
>
> Gold Ladies: 5,794 yards, par-72, USGA rating 70.0, slope 128
>
> Red: 5,313 yards, par-72, USGA rating 70.0, slope 118

Challenge: ★★★	Golf Facilities: ★★★
Variety: ★★★	14-Club Test: ★★★
Terrain: ★★★	Intangibles: ★★★
Beauty/Visual Appeal: ★★★	Value: ★★★
Pace of Play: ★★★	

Just the Facts Year Opened: 1977; Course Designer: Earl Stone; Walking: No; Greens Fee: $45–58; 9-Hole/Twilight Rate: Yes; Pull Carts: No; Practice Range: Yes; Club Rental: Yes.

Description and Comments   These two 18-hole courses located outside of Biloxi, one hour from New Orleans, lie at the highest elevation on the Gulf Coast. Both courses are cut from a vast wooded area, and thus fairways tend to be tight (oddly enough, however, the Pine course has more generous fairways than the Cardinal course). Neither course is overly long, but both are challenging as reflected in the slopes and ratings for each.

In our opinion, the Cardinal course, once a stop on the Nike Tour, is the stronger of the two. It is a modern design, somewhat compact, yet with extra large bunkers, more water, and no parallel fairways. The Pine course has a more classic look, with wider fairways and doglegs, and tends to play as the slightly harder of the two layouts. The course has recently been upgraded with newly designed greens.

Insider Tips   Flexibility is the strong suit at Diamondhead in that it provides four sets of tees and five ratings. If you are a big-hitting low handicapper, you will probably find the white tees too easy, so if you want a challenge, play from the tips. For women, the same will hold true for the red trees. The gold women's tees will offer a more full, interesting round for the above-average female golfer.

No matter what tee you decide to play, you will find that both courses put a premium on ball placement as there are many hazards awaiting you. Both courses are interesting, enjoyable, and well maintained, but if you're forced to pick between the two, take the Cardinal. Even though Pine is rated as the slightly tougher of the pair, it suffers from easing by one too many condos and lacks the truly memorable hole, as is the case of the 15th on Cardinal.

Of the 36 holes at Diamondhead, the signature hole is the 15th on the Cardinal Course. Fifteen is a long, uphill par-5 that includes an island fairway requiring golfers to cross a double water hazard. Basically, if you don't hit the fairway, you don't play.

Mississippi National

90 Hickory Hill Dr., Gautier, MS 39553; phone (800) 477-4044 or (601) 497-2372

How to Get On: Semiprivate club that allows outside play. Tee times can be made four days in advance.

Tees:

> Blue: 6,983 yards, par-72, USGA rating 73.1, slope 128
>
> White: 6,517 yards, par-72, USGA rating 71.3, slope 123
>
> Red: 5,229 yards, par-72, USGA rating 69.6, slope 113

Challenge: ★★★	Beauty/Visual Appeal: ★★★
Variety: ★★½	Pace of Play: ★★
Terrain: ★★½	Intangibles: ★★★

Golf Facilities: ★★★★   Value: ★★★
14-Club Test: ★★★

Just the Facts   Year Opened: 1965; Course Designer: Earl Stone; Walking: Allowed at certain times; Greens Fee: $42–65; 9-Hole/Twilight Rate: Yes; Pull Carts: No; Practice Range: Yes; Club Rental: Yes.

Description and Comments   Mississippi National is one of the old pillars in the area and offers golfers a solid but not necessarily spectacular layout. The course has excellent playability for golfers of all levels, but the terrain is predominately flat. This means that you won't get a lot of variety in stances and lies, but there is plenty of challenge to be had because of the large profusion of water hazards on many of the holes. More of the challenge comes in the form of trees, bunkers, and elevated greens, making this a fine tournament-caliber track. In fact, it hosted Nike Tour events in 1996 and 1997.

Insider Tips   Formerly known as Hickory Hill Country Club, this course definitely does not live up to its pretentious new name. Though course and facilities are above average for the area, the layout, maintenance, service, and atmosphere don't stack up when measured against newcomers such as The Oaks and The Bridges at Casino Magic. The latter two courses simply have more sizzle, as Mississippi National's terrain is predominantly flat, with few bunkers to define the route and spice up the play. That being said, thanks to its burly 7,000-yard length and honest, straightforward challenge, it's still one of the best courses in the region and one of the better courses in the state open for public play.

Mississippi National's 35-year-old fairways are framed by mature trees, causing the prevailing Gulf winds to swirl considerably, so you will need to think before you make your club selection. Most of the greens are raised, set above the existing fairway grade, so when in doubt, use one extra club on your approach. Check the tops of the trees to get an accurate gauge. Fairways are wide, but don't get greedy and blast away as water menaces more than half the holes. A new clubhouse opened in Fall 1999.

The Oaks

7119 Menge Ave., Pass Christian, MS 39571; phone (228) 452-0909
How to Get On: Tee times can be made five days in advance.
Tees:

   Gold: 6,885 yards, par-72, USGA rating 72.5, slope 131
   Blue: 6,330 yards, par-72, USGA rating 69.6, slope 121
   White: 5,778 yards, par-72, USGA rating 67.3, slope 115
   Red: 4,691 yards, par-72, USGA rating 66.4, slope 107

Challenge: ★★★	Golf Facilities: ★★★★½
Variety: ★★★★	14-Club Test: ★★★½
Terrain: ★★★★	Intangibles: ★★★★
Beauty/Visual Appeal: ★★★★	Value: ★★★★
Pace of Play: ★★★	

Just the Facts   Year Opened: 1998; Course Designer: Christopher Cole; Walking: Yes; Greens Fee: $44–71; 9-Hole/Twilight Rate: Yes; Pull Carts: No; Practice Range: Yes; Club Rental: Yes.

Description and Comments   Host course for the 1999 Nike Tour stop on the Gulf Coast, The Oaks has established itself in short order as the premier course in the region. Although The Oaks opened only in 1998, it is already blessed with a remarkably mature feel, due in part to two factors: the lay of the land and the designers' philosophy.

Situated within a 400-acre residential community some 12 miles west of Gulfport, The Oaks benefits from wonderful rolling topography, extremely unusual for the region. No less than 65 feet of naturally occurring elevation change make the Oaks unique in the area, but what truly separates the course from the pack is the combination of skilled design and a lovely setting. Many of the holes crisscross wetlands and ravines, yet there is a calming Deep South ambience, as multiple holes are dotted with tall pines, magnolias, and, of course, countless live oaks drenched in Spanish moss, from whence the course derives its name. The designers themselves are unabashed fans of classic, 1920s-style golf courses, and they've infused The Oaks with traditional shot values.

What many enjoy about The Oaks is its isolated, "middle-of-nowhere" feel, where each hole is an entity unto itself. The course is difficult but fair, enjoyable, and manageable for nearly all classes of players except virtual beginners. There are many wetlands to navigate throughout the round, but the architects thoughtfully placed at least one tee box per hole clear of most of the trouble, so that nearly every golfer is capable of successfully completing each hole. Others point to the superior quality of the clubhouse, service, and practice facility as factors that set this one apart. As Senior PGA Tour star Dr. Gil Morgan said recently, "The Oaks is a must-play on the Mississippi Gulf Coast." Definitely follow the doctor's orders and give The Oaks your full attention.

Insider Tips   The Oaks is the newest in a family of courses from Landmark National developers, the same folks that gave golf such famous major championship courses as South Carolina's Kiawah Island Resort, Oklahoma's Oak Tree, and California's La Quinta and PGA West. As you would expect, everything about the course and facilities is first rate, especially the service, practice range, and course conditioning.

Because The Oaks is the centerpiece of a residential development, the place retains a touch of a private club feel. If you appreciate this sort of ambience, you'll love The Oaks, but others may find it a bit too "upscale" for their liking.

Do yourself a favor and pick the correct set of tees that matches your game. For instance, if you choose the gold tees, you'll face a brutal but beautiful hole at the 2nd, a 445-yard par-4. From a naturally elevated tee box, golfers must drive over a freshwater wetland and find the fairway 40 feet below. Although the back tee offers spectacular play, it may prove far too difficult for most players, who would be much better off playing the hole from down below, at the more manageable distances of 341 yards and 314 yards from the blue and white tees, respectively.

Mornings tend to be damp here, and afternoons get breezy, so whichever set of conditions you prefer, choose accordingly.

Another plus for traditionalists and health-conscious folks is that The Oaks offers unrestricted walking, unlike most of the Gulf Coast courses, which force you to ride. In summer, riding is the only way to go, but at other times, it's nice to have the option to walk.

Timberton

22 Clubhouse Dr., Hattiesburg, MS 39401 (90 miles north of New Orleans); phone (800) 848-3222 or (601) 584-4670

How to Get On: Tee times can be made two weeks in advance.

Creekside Valley Tees:

> Blue: 7,028 yards, par-72, USGA rating 73.1, slope 131
>
> Green: 6,463 yards, par-72, USGA rating 70.5, slope 128
>
> White: 6,153 yards, par-72, USGA rating 69.7, slope 127
>
> Red: 5,439 yards, par-72, USGA rating 71.4, slope 128

Challenge: ★★★½	Golf Facilities: ★★★
Variety: ★★★★	14-Club Test: ★★★★
Terrain: ★★★★	Intangibles: ★★★½
Beauty/Visual Appeal: ★★★★	Value: ★★★★
Pace of Play: ★★★	

Just the Facts   Year Opened: 1991; Course Designer: Mark McCumber; Walking: Mandatory cart; Greens Fee: $45; 9-Hole/Twilight Rate: Yes; Pull Carts: No; Practice Range: Yes; Club Rental: Yes.

Description and Comments   Twenty-seven challenging holes await the golfer here at Timberton, carved from a densely wooded 4,500-acre tract. You will find every hazard imaginable in abundance. The hilly terrain here produces many challenging lies; there is water on 12 holes; and 54 sand traps on the course, including one hole, the 9th on Creekside, with ten of these bunkers. The 9th also sports a two-level fairway. Finally, copious trees, especially pines and oaks, are everywhere you turn.

Yes, the course is full of peril, but it remains playable for golfers of all skill levels. No doubt golfers will enjoy the beautiful views of the surrounding area. The course is very well maintained and is a great value given its reasonable green fees.

Insider Tips   Timberton is not actually on the Gulf Coast, as it is located an hour to an hour and a half north, in Hattiesburg. However, the course is so good, we feel that it's worth the drive. In one leading poll four years ago, Timberton was ranked the number-one public-access course in Mississippi. Several new courses have edged by it since then, but not by much. Like Windance, it was designed by PGA Tour great Mark McCumber. Fortunately, you don't have to play as well as McCumber does to enjoy the course.

If you're looking to play the "true" Timberton, you need to play the original nines, Creekside and Valley, in that order. The newest nine, which dates to 1998, is called Lakeview. It is lovely in its own right, featuring rolling terrain and offering eye-pleasing views of the property's lakes, but is shorter and not as sound throughout as the original two.

As you have probably assumed, given all the hazards that await you (and certainly given the name of the course), shot placement is the key to scoring well here. Golfers will be required to use all clubs in their bag as they maneuver their way around these three nines. Nevertheless, even if Timberton is one of the best public courses in the state, it is far from the hardest. It's tough, but playable by all, and is generally in marvelous condition.

Two keys to success at Timberton are approach putting and strong course management skills. Putting surfaces here lean toward the large side, with heavy undulations, so you'll have to be skilled with the flatstick in order to avoid numerous three putts. Strategy plays a big role at Timberton. Many holes feature creeks slashing across fairways and in front of greens in diagonal fashion, making the golfer think about how much of the hazard he or she can bite off, or where the proper spot would be to lay up.

Windance Country Club

19385 Champion Circle, Gulfport, MS 39505; phone (601) 832-4871
How to Get On: Tee times can be made six months in advance.
Tees:

> Blue: 6,680 yards, par-72, USGA rating 73.1, slope 129
> White: 6,112 yards, par-72, USGA rating 70.7, slope 124
> Red: 5,208 yards, par-72, USGA rating 70.1, slope 120

Challenge: ★★★	Beauty/Visual Appeal: ★★★
Variety: ★★★½	Pace of Play: ★★★
Terrain: ★★★	Intangibles: ★★★½

Golf Facilities: ★★★   Value: ★★★
14-Club Test: ★★★

Just the Facts   Year Opened: 1986; Course Designer: Mark McCumber; Walking: Mandatory cart; Greens Fee: $55–65; 9-Hole/Twilight Rate: No; Pull Carts: No; Practice Range: Yes; Club Rental: Yes.

Description and Comments   Host to both the Nike and Senior Series Tours, Windance offers golfers a relatively short but still formidable layout. What the course lacks in length it makes up for in terrain and challenge. The fairways are rolling and hilly and tend to be tight, with a moderate number of bunkers and many water hazards. The course is routed around a large reservoir. Some holes are carved from stands of mature pines, and others skirt draws that are edged in cypress. Mostly, architect McCumber has kept the average golfer in mind. The majority of the greens are only bunkered to one side, so there's usually a bail-out option for the less gutsy player. An architectural oddity is the presence of only one par-3 on the front nine.

Insider Tips   The course will require you to strike the ball well to avoid the many hazards. Given its lack of length, you may want to use more three-woods off the tee rather than drivers, especially if you're prone to wildness. The more skilled player will want to play from the tips for more of a challenge. Greens are average in size but are true, virtually always in excellent condition.

Windance is attractive and fun to play, but it may frustrate the first-time player with its multiple hazards and undulating greens, which place a premium on knowing your way around. This is one of those courses where local knowledge is critical. You may need to play Windance twice to fully appreciate its charms, and doing so is well worth it.

A Mississippi Sampler

Edgewater Bay

2674 Pass Rd., Biloxi, MS 39531; phone (228) 388-9670
Tees: Championship: 6,196 yards, par-71, USGA rating 70.0, slope 125
Greens Fee: $25–30

Challenge: ★★   Golf Facilities: ★½
Variety: ★★½   14-Club Test: ★★
Terrain: ★★   Intangibles: ★★★
Beauty/Visual Appeal: ★★★½   Value: ★★★
Pace of Play: ★★½

Description and Comments   Built in 1927, this is one of the oldest courses on the Gulf Coast. Long on scenery, strong on value, with six holes overlooking Biloxi's Back Bay. Short, flat, with small greens, Edgewater Bay won't overwhelm anyone. It's just good, basic golf.

Great Southern Golf Club

2000 East Beach Blvd., Gulfport, MS 39507-1699; phone (800) 221-2816 or (228) 896-3536

Yardages, pars, and greens fees to be determined; ratings not yet available.

Description and Comments This is Mississippi's oldest golf course, dating to 1908, overlooking the Gulf of Mexico. Formerly known as the Sea course of the Broadwater Beach Hotel, it hosted such legends as Byron Nelson, Sam Snead, and Ben Hogan when it was a PGA Tour stop in the 1940s. Currently undergoing complete redesign.

Pine Island Golf Club

2021 Beachview Dr., Ocean Springs, MS 39564; phone (228) 875-1674

Tees: Championship: 6,369 yards, par-71, USGA rating 70.9, slope 129

Greens Fee: $25–30

Challenge: ★★½	Golf Facilities: ★★
Variety: ★★½	14-Club Test: ★★½
Terrain: ★★	Intangibles: ★★½
Beauty/Visual Appeal: ★★★½	Value: ★★½
Pace of Play: ★★	

Description and Comments Don't be misled by the architectural credit: Pete Dye. This is an early Dye design—1973—and not one of his best. It is flat and extremely tight, but is remarkably scenic. If it's pure "back-to-nature" golf you're seeking, this is the place.

President Broadwater Golf Club

200 Beauvoir Rd., Biloxi, MS 39531; phone (800) 647-3964 or (601) 385-4081

Tees: Championship: 7,140 yards, par-72, USGA rating 74.1, slope 134

Greens Fee: $44

Challenge: ★★★½	Golf Facilities: ★★★
Variety: ★★½	14-Club Test: ★★★
Terrain: ★★	Intangibles: ★★
Beauty/Visual Appeal: ★★½	Value: ★★
Pace of Play: ★★★	

Description and Comments Formerly known as the Sun Course at the Broadwater Beach Hotel, this course is now part of the President Broadwater Resort and has split from its neighbor, the Sea Course, which is now known as Great Southern Golf Club. This course offers golfers a playable but not remarkable layout. The terrain tends to be flat, but features a lot of water. Length and water are the primary challenges here, otherwise, the course is quite characterless. Pretty boring, actually. The wind off the bay can play havoc on your shots, so club accordingly.

Pine Burr Country Club

800 Pine Burr Dr., Wiggins, MS 39577; phone (601) 928-4911
Tees: Championship: 6,501 yards, par-72, USGA rating 71.3, slope 130
Greens Fee: $25

Challenge: ★★★	Golf Facilities: ★★
Variety: ★★½	14-Club Test: ★★
Terrain: ★★★	Intangibles: ★★½
Beauty/Visual Appeal: ★★½	Value: ★★★
Pace of Play: ★★★	

Description and Comments   Built among five lakes and a pine, dogwood, and oak forest. Hilly terrain, narrow fairways, and water hazards provide the challenge at Pine Burr.

St. Andrews Golf Club

2 Golfing Green Dr., Ocean Springs, MS 39564; phone (601) 875-7730
Tees: Championship: 6,540 yards, par-72, USGA rating 71.9, slope 117
Greens Fee: $20–24

Challenge: ★★	Golf Facilities: ★★
Variety: ★★½	14-Club Test: ★★
Terrain: ★★	Intangibles: ★★★
Beauty/Visual Appeal: ★★★½	Value: ★★★
Pace of Play: ★★★	

Description and Comments   Another course where you can leave your driver out of your repertoire, as it is very tight and filled with many sand and water hazards. Greens are flat with little break. A scenic course that offers compelling views of the Gulf of Mexico—make sure to take note of the lighthouse from the 13th hole.

Sunkist

2381 Sunkist Country Club Dr., Biloxi, MS 39532; phone (228) 388-3961
Tees: Championship: 6,000 yards, par-72, USGA rating 69.0, slope 117
Greens Fee: $20–45

Challenge: ★★   Golf Facilities: ★★
Variety: ★★½   14-Club Test: ★★
Terrain: ★★½   Intangibles: ★★½
Beauty/Visual Appeal: ★★½   Value: ★★★
Pace of Play: ★★½

Description and Comments   An above-average course built on rolling terrain. Narrow, tree-lined fairways and a few water hazards keep you on your toes. Lacks the amenities of some of the region's more acclaimed courses, but many contend that the course offers better value for the money than some of its more celebrated neighbors.

Lodging

EXPENSIVE

Beau Rivage

875 Beach Blvd., Biloxi, MS 39530; phone (888) 567-6667 or (228) 386-7111; www.beaurivageresort.com; Rates: $99–179

Part of Steve Wynn's Mirage Resorts, Beau Rivage opened in spring 1999 and has already gained quite a reputation. The hotel consists of 1,780 rooms with panoramic views of the Gulf Coast or the bay, including 66 luxurious suites. The guest rooms average 400 square feet and are nicely appointed with custom furnishings and amenities such as an electronic in-room safe, robes, voice mail, and cable television.

Along with an enticing casino, the Beau Rivage offers the following: a pool overlooking beautifully landscaped area (private cabanas available); beach with attendants who can provide you with umbrellas, towels, and lounge chairs; beach volleyball; The Spa, offering massage, steam, sauna, whirlpool, aerobics room, and gym; and access to sport fishing and marina.

Golf Packages   Beau Rivage has access to over 20 courses in the area and can custom-design a package for you based on the type of accommodation you are seeking as well as the number of days you want to hit the links. Here's a sample of what they have to offer: accommodation and taxes, greens and cart fees, daily breakfast buffet, club storage, and spa pass.

The Bridges Golf Resort at Casino Magic

195 Beach Blvd., Biloxi, MS 39530; phone (800) 562-4425 or (228) 386-3035; www.casinomagic.com; Rates: $129–149

Located on the beach in Biloxi, Casino Magic was built in 1998 and offers guests easy access to The Bridges Golf Resort as well as the Arnold Palmer Golf Academy. Hotel guests will find 378 rooms (some with kitchenettes) from which to choose in the 23-floor hotel. The rooms are perfectly adequate but hardly extraordinary. Of course, this is done deliberately as management would much rather have you gambling in their 125,000-square-foot casino than relaxing in their rooms. In addition to the gambling, you will find a pool, whirlpool, health club, spa, and tennis courts.

Golf Packages Package includes: accommodations, 18-hole greens fees per day with cart, Prolink range finder, daily breakfast buffet, $5 match play per person, $5 bonus slot coin with $20 purchase.

MODERATE

Green Oaks

5850 Beach Blvd., Biloxi, MS 39530; phone (888) 436-6257 or (228) 436-6257; www.gcww.com/greenoaks; Rates: $110–135

This bed-and-breakfast, part of the National Registry of Historic Places, was built in 1826 and is the state's oldest remaining beachfront residence. It consists of eight guest rooms in two separate homes, each of which is beautifully decorated with a striking combination of heirlooms and antiques as well as a private bathroom, cable television, and phone. Some of the rooms have fireplaces and grand views of the two acres of beautifully landscaped grounds.

Golf Packages Golf packages can be developed for you, but your best bet is to contact Green Oaks directly.

Isle of Capri Casino, Crowne Plaza Resort

151 Beach Blvd., Biloxi, MS 39530; phone (800) 843-4753 or (228) 435-5300; www.isleofcapricasino.com; Rates: $119–139

The Crowne Plaza Resort was the first gaming hotel to open in Biloxi and thus is well known among those who frequent the area (this results in a lot of weekend business, so make sure to call early for reservations). The hotel features 370 large rooms decorated in Caribbean style; some have balconies that overlook the Gulf of Mexico. The rooms include hair dryer, coffeemaker, wall safe, iron and ironing board, and ceiling fans.

Other amenities include: a pool, whirlpool, and a health spa, as well as a variety of beach activities. The two-level casino features 40 game tables and 1,000 slot machines.

Golf Packages The reservations department at the resort can develop a custom golf package for you with the price depending on the number of nights you stay and what courses you select. For planning purposes, here is a sample package: accommodations, greens and cart fees for one round of golf per night's stay, welcome gift, and daily buffet ticket.

President Casino Broadwater Resort

2110 Beach Blvd., Biloxi, MS 39531; phone (800) 843-7737 or (228) 385-4102; www.presidentbroadwater.com; Rates: $59–79

The President Casino is set among ancient live oak trees and is one of Biloxi's more famous destinations. Many of the hotel's 500 rooms were renovated in 1998, although perhaps its biggest draw is its amenities. First and foremost, you will find easy access to the resort's 18-hole course as well as the learning center. In addition, there are more than 20 courses in the area that can be reached in short order. Beyond golf, the resort has three swimming pools, ten tennis courts, shuffleboard, horseshoes, weight room, gym, jogging trail, 26 miles of beachfront, parasailing, and jet skis. In addition, you can charter a full- or half-day deep-sea fishing boat, which launches from the hotel's Broadwater Marina.

Golf Packages   Package includes: accommodations, one round per day, shared cart, complimentary lunch or dinner buffet, 20% off retail merchandise (excluding sale and sundry items), $5 in Broadwater Bucks per day.

INEXPENSIVE

Comfort Suites

1634 Beach Blvd., Biloxi, MS 39531; phone (800) 228-5150 or (228) 435-1995; Rates: $69–199; Built: 1995; Renovations: 1999

Hampton Inn Ocean Springs

13921 Big Ridge Blvd., Biloxi, MS 39532; phone (800) 426-7866 or (228) 872-6370; Rates: $69–79; Built: 1997; Renovations: None

Dining

All of the major casinos have buffets that offer every imaginable food item—something for everyone, usually at reasonable prices. For more sophisticated tastes, the Gulf Coast offers quite a few quite a few higher-quality culinary options as well. Fresh seafood is obviously the specialty of the region.

Blow Fly Inn   1201 Washington Ave., Gulfport; phone (228) 896-9812. American; Moderate; Reservations suggested on weekends. The best steaks in town.

Coral Restaurant   Beau Rivage Hotel, 875 Beach Blvd., Biloxi, MS 39530; phone (888) 567-6667 or (228) 386-7111. American; Expensive; Reservations suggested. Aquariums filled with fish; a coral reef surrounds the room and creates a memorable setting. Steak and seafood.

Fisherman's Wharf   1409 Bienville Blvd., Ocean Springs; phone (228) 872-6111. Seafood; Moderate; No reservations accepted. As the name implies, this restaurant is located right in the harbor, so along with some tasty seafood, diners will be treated to views of the pier's activities.

Germaine's   1203 Bienville Blvd., Ocean Springs; phone (228) 875-4426. Creole; Expensive; Reservations requested. One of the best restaurants in the area—Germaine's offers a variety of New Orleans–influenced food in a quaint old home.

Jocelyn's Restaurant   U.S. Highway 90 East, Ocean Springs; phone (228) 875-1925. Seafood; Inexpensive–Moderate; No reservations accepted. A wonderful place for you to try out the delicacies of the Gulf Coast region. Specialties include the crabmeat, trout, and snapper. No credit cards accepted.

La Cucine Italina   Beau Rivage Hotel, 875 Beach Blvd., Biloxi; phone (888) 567-6667 or (228) 386-7111. Italian; Expensive; Reservations suggested. Marvelous dishes served here and you can watch your food being cooked in the kitchen, which is located in the center of the room.

Lil Ray's Seafood and Po Boys   500-A Courthouse Rd., Gulfport; phone (228) 896-9601. Seafood; Inexpensive–Moderate; No reservations accepted. Another local favorite that serves a variety of Creole seafood dishes.

McElroy's   695 Beach Blvd., Biloxi; phone (228) 374-0163. Seafood; Inexpensive–Moderate; No reservations accepted. One of the area's best casual dining experiences offering splendid harbor views.

Mary Mahoney's Le Café   110 Rue Magnolia, Biloxi; phone (228) 374-0163. Seafood; Expensive; Reservations accepted. The atmosphere of this 1737 home is a perfect complement to the menu of this local favorite. The entrees are superb, but make sure to leave room for the highly recommended bread pudding for dessert.

Ole Biloxi Schooner   159 E. Howard, Biloxi; phone (228) 374-8071. Southern seafood; Inexpensive; No reservations accepted. Don't expect to be served by a fancy wait staff, but what this place lacks in atmosphere, it more than makes up for in taste, taste, and more taste.

Vrazel's Fine Food Restaurant   3206 West Beach Blvd., Gulfport; phone (228) 863-2229. Seafood; Expensive; Reservations accepted.

Activities

Bicycle Rental   Bikes Ahoy! 702 Beach Dr., Gulfport; phone (338) 896-3469. Daily and weekly rentals are available.

Bayou Tour   Cookie's Bayou Tour, 10774 Highway 603, Bay St. Louis; phone (228) 466-4824. Explore the bayou and wetlands of the Gulf Coast. While in Bay St. Louis, make sure to check out the historic district.

Beauvoir   2244 Beach Blvd., between Biloxi and Gulfport on Highway 90; phone (228) 388-1313. This is the home where Jefferson Davis wrote his memoir, *The Rise and Fall of the Confederate Government.*

Biloxi Lighthouse   U.S. 90 at Porter Avenue, Biloxi; phone (228) 435-6308. A historic landmark that played a key role during the Civil War. Tours by appointment only.

Crosby Arboretum   370 Ridge Rd., Picayune; phone (601) 799-2311. A center dedicated to environmental education, visitors can explore pine forests and grassy areas.

J. L. Scott Marine Education Center and Aquarium   115 Beach Blvd., Biloxi; phone (228) 374-5550. This aquarium includes a 42,000-gallon tank and is a great place for all ages.

Nature Tours   Natural Adventure Touring Kayaks, 21640 Tucker Rd., Long Beach; phone (228) 452-0118. Tours of the salt marshes and backwaters from Ocean Springs to Pass Christian.

Sailboat Charters   Dixie Dreamin' Sailing Cruise, 710 Lewis Ave., Gulfport; phone (228) 863-9355. Biloxi Schooners, P.O. Box 1907, Biloxi; phone (228) 435-6320. Hourly, half-day, and full-day rentals.

Shrimping   Biloxi Shrimping Trip, P.O. Box 1315, Biloxi; phone (800) 289-7908 or (228) 385-1182. Located in Biloxi's Small Craft Harbor, visitors get to learn all about the shrimping process.

Swamp Tours   Gator Swamp Tours, Slidell, Louisiana; phone (504) 484-6100. Located less than an hour from Biloxi, this is a great way to spend two hours seeing nature up close and personal.

The 19th Hole

Each of the hotels in the area have a typical selection of casino- and casual-style bars, so finding somewhere to celebrate your round will be easy.

Part Nine

Northern Florida

Overview

If you ask most seasoned golf travelers for their suggestions of where to take a golf vacation in Florida, no doubt you would hear Tampa/St. Petersburg, Miami, Orlando, and even West Palm Beach as suggestions. If you then asked, "What about Northern Florida?" you probably would hear a resounding "Hmmmm, I can't really say I know much about golfing in that area." Yes, despite having some of the state's best golf resorts as well as spectacular golf, the region remains in relative anonymity. It is, however, this low profile that makes the area so special.

Northern Florida is comprised of two separate regions, the Northeast and the Panhandle. The Northeast area was the site of the state's (as well as the nation's) first settlements, thus earning its nickname "The First Coast." St. Augustine, south of Jacksonville, remains the United States' oldest surviving city, and it was where explorer Ponce de Leon had hoped to stumble on the fountain of youth. Nevertheless, it wasn't until the Union soldiers marched through that it really received any outside recognition. When the soldiers returned home they told of the beautiful area with its oceans and mild temperatures. Lo and behold, Northerners started trickling down south for winter. Soon came the proliferation of the railways and the trickle grew to a steady stream. With the invention of the automobile, this stream became a "Snowbird" flood.

The major city in the Northeast is Jacksonville, but it is really what lies 35 miles east of Jacksonville that attracts most visitors to the area. Today, the prime beachfront area that stretches from the Georgia state line to just south of Daytona Beach is home to Florida's best and most luxurious resorts; this may be surprising given the stiff competition in the rest of the state.

The Panhandle region, or Emerald Coast as it is also called because of its striking water color, is the relatively small stretch of land that separates Georgia and Alabama from the Gulf of Mexico. Long considered Florida's

Northern Florida, The Northeast

N

GOLF COURSES
1. Amelia Island Plantation
2. The Golf Club at Amelia Island
3. LPGA International
4. Matanzas Woods Golf Club
5. Palm Coast Resort, Grand Haven
6. Ponte Vedra Inn & Club
7. Radisson Ponce de Leon Golf & Conference Center
8. Ravines Golf & Country Club
9. Sawgrass Country Club
10. TPC at Sawgrass
11. Windsor Parke Golf Club
12. World Golf Village

best-kept secret, the Panhandle's primary attraction for many years was its pristine beaches—earning it "The Redneck Riviera" tagline. There was the smattering of golf courses, some even notable, and a few resorts, but it wasn't until the golf construction boom that the Panhandle area really hit the golf map. Although you still can find plenty of gun toting and Schaeffer beer drinkers in the area, you now can find a few microbreweries as well.

Although it is part of Florida, the Panhandle oozes more of a Dixie flavor than a Floridian one. The differences can be seen in the geography (rather than palm trees you will find magnolias, live oaks, and pines),

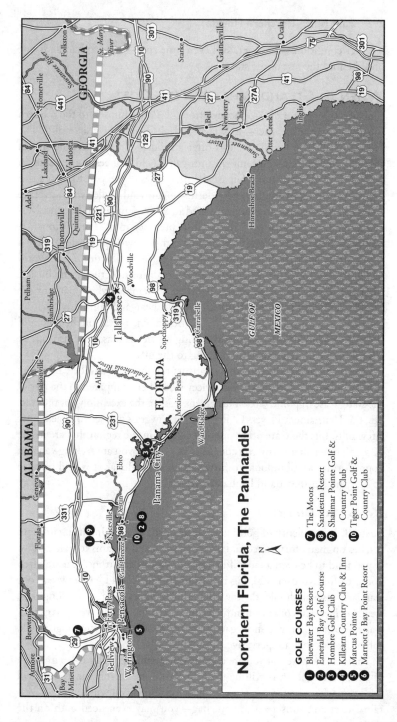

Northern Florida, The Panhandle

GOLF COURSES

1. Bluewater Bay Resort
2. Emerald Bay Golf Course
3. Hombre Golf Club
4. Killearn Country Club & Inn
5. Marcus Pointe
6. Marriott's Bay Point Resort
7. The Moors
8. Sandestin Resort
9. Shalimar Pointe Golf & Country Club
10. Tiger Point Golf & Country Club

weather conditions, character, and even time zone—the Panhandle is one hour behind the rest of the state.

WHEN TO GO AND WHAT IT WILL COST

One of the biggest draws to the area from ol' Ponce himself to the modern vacationers is the weather—it is nearly ideal for golfing year-round. The Northeast and Panhandle regions offer a milder climate than the rest of Florida, and in fact, the temperatures can be 20 degrees cooler than in Miami. Overall, spring and fall are the best times of the year to plan a trip here. October is particularly wonderful in the Panhandle, when average daytime highs are 80 degrees, compared to 87 in September, but the average rainfall drops from 6.75 inches in September to 3.21 in October. A bonus is that, unlike the rest of the state, these two regions don't have a major attraction that draws hordes of tourists (such as Walt Disney World or South Beach), and thus crowds won't be a threat. Actually, the busiest time of the year for these areas is April to September, when many of the Florida residents head north to escape the heat and humidity. Winter weather, as with other southern or Florida areas, is less predictable and there is a chance of rain, especially during hurricane season. It also can be a bit nippy, with daytime lows dipping to the 40s.

Another leading draw to the area is its relative affordability. Both the resorts and courses are on the less pricey side when compared to the rest of the state. Case in point: $100 plus greens fees are the exception not the rule. Yes, the Tournament Players Club (TPC) at Sawgrass will set you back quite a few bills, but there are other premier courses in the region that are in the $25–50 range that many consider hidden gems. If you are seeking value in your Florida vacation, look no further. Dollar for dollar, it would be hard to beat the Northeast and Panhandle regions.

WHAT TO BRING

First off, bring plenty of golf balls. Water is the predominant hazard, and it takes on many forms: ocean, lakes, wetlands, and streams to name a few. If you tend to be even a tad wild with your woods and irons, you are often going to find yourself dipping into your bag to "reload." Clubwise, your standard arsenal should do the trick. The courses tend to be long so a steady driver will come in handy. If you have a lob or gap wedge you may want to bring it, as the short game is a key to success on the tough, slick, rolling greens that are pervasive.

In terms of attire—if you are coming during the spring or fall, a uniform of shorts and golf shirt will be the call. However, during winter you will need to pack a sweater. No matter when you come, you will want to have a rain jacket and sunscreen in your bag—you may even need both on the same day.

ONCE YOU'RE THERE

The crown jewel of the Northeast region, in our opinion, is the Amelia Island Plantation, which is located just south of the Georgia state line, on the southernmost of the Golden Isles. The resort offers both conventional hotel-styled rooms as well as larger villa/condo units. Though the rooms and amenities are superior, it is the golf that makes our hearts race—the resort offers three unique, breathtaking, and demanding courses. But this is only the tip of the iceberg. Nearby are the famed TPC at Sawgrass (Florida's top-ranked course), the Sawgrass Marriott Resort, the World Golf Village, and the new Slammer and Squire course. In culinary terms, the region offers an incredible menu—with a full selection of golf courses and top-notch resorts as your entrees.

For the Panhandle region, you will find the largest concentration of notable golf courses located between Pensacola and Panama City. Leading the way are two premier resorts: Marriott's Bay Point Resort in Panama City, featuring Lagoon Legend (one of Florida's toughest courses), and Sandestin Beach Resort in Destin, home to the Baytowne and Burnt Pines courses.

A word of caution: Perdido Bay Resort may be a resort and course that jumps into your mind when you think of the Panhandle region. Though it was a PGA Tour stop in the 1970s, it ran into recent financial problems and is no longer at the level of the competition in the area. The resort is making strides to regain its once-lofty status, but for now we recommend that you go elsewhere.

If you're looking simply for quality golf at affordable prices, your best bet is to stick with northwest Florida. If you've only got a couple of days and you've come a long way, hit the one "must-play" course in the region, the Stadium course at TPC at Sawgrass, then drop on down and tour golf's Hall of Fame at the World Golf Village. The best hotel that incorporates a golf experience is the Ritz-Carlton at Amelia Island, and the best overall resort/golf/family experience takes place at Amelia Island Plantation.

GATHERING INFORMATION

Northeast

Amelia Island/Fernandina Beach Chamber of Commerce
102 Centre St., Amelia Island, FL 32034
Phone (800) 226-3542 or (904) 261-3248; www.ameliaisland.org

Jacksonville and Its Beaches CVB
201 E. Adams St., Jacksonville, FL 32202
Phone (800) 733-2668 or (904) 798-9111; www.jaxcvb.com

St. Augustine Visitor Information Center
10 Castillo Dr., St. Augustine, FL 32084
Phone (800) 653-2489; www.oldcity.com

The Panhandle

Destin Chamber of Commerce
1021 U.S. 98 E., Destin, FL 32541
Phone (850) 837-6241

Emerald Coast Golf Association
P.O. Box 394, Destin, FL 32540
Phone (850) 654-7086

Panama City Beach CVB
P.O. Box 9473, Panama City Beach, FL 32417
Phone (800) PCBEACH

The Major Courses in Northeast Florida

Amelia Island Plantation, Long Point Golf Club

3000 1st Coast Highway, Amelia Island, FL 32035; phone (800) 874-6878 or (904) 277-5907

How To Get On: You must be a guest of the Amelia Island Plantation to gain access to this course.

Tees:

Championship: 6,775 yards, par-72, USGA rating 72.9, slope 129

Blue: 6,086 yards, par-72, USGA rating 69.8, slope 123

White: 5,539 yards, par-72, USGA rating 67.0, slope 117

Red: 4,927 yards, par-72, USGA rating 69.1, slope 121

Challenge: ★★★	Golf Facilities: ★★★★½
Variety: ★★★½	14-Club Test ★★★★
Terrain: ★★★★	Intangibles: ★★★★
Beauty/Visual Appeal: ★★★★	Value: ★★★
Pace of Play: ★★★	

Just the Facts   Year Opened: 1987; Course Designer: Tom Fazio; Walking: No; Greens Fee: $120; 9 Hole/Twilight Rate: No; Pull Carts: No; Practice Range: Yes; Club Rental: Yes.

Description and Comments   Even without golf, Amelia Island Plantation certainly can rest on its own laurels—it is a magnificent resort offering superior accommodations and a full roster of activities. If you needed another reason to stay there, it would be the access to the golf courses that otherwise are off-limits to outside play. Pete Dye and Tom Fazio are the men behind the magic at Amelia Island with a recent assist from Bobby Weed. In 1973, Dye designed 27 holes, which have undergone recent renovations and are now two separate 18s, the Ocean and Oakmarsh courses, thanks to a 9-hole addition. However, Fazio's 1987 Long Point just may be the best-kept secret in the state.

To be fair, it may not be just Fazio who had an influence on the course—Mother Nature deserves partial credit for the jaw-dropping, awe-inspiring backdrop and terrain inherent to Long Point. What may be more amazing is that this magnificent setting required only minor alterations, and thus the course appeared like a mature, seasoned veteran from day one.

Long Point plays through a variety of topography—dense forests, marsh-land, lakes, ocean knolls—making for quite a scenic fusion. Players will find the front nine to be shorter and narrower with two of the course's most stunning holes (and two of the best par-3s around), holes six and seven, which play dramatically alongside the Atlantic Ocean. Hole six is 166-yarder from the tips, but when the wind is a-howling, as it often is, that yardage can quickly balloon, turning an already tough hole into a real brute. To sum it up: "If you stray, you will pay." The green is nestled between two sand bunkers on the right, the ocean in the back, and a sloping drop-off to the left. Number seven is a tad easier—it measures 158 yards, but still can hurt your score if you miss the elevated, rough-encircled green.

Considered by many as the prettier of the two sides, the back nine tends to be more open—which is both good and bad. Though there is more room for error on your shots, its "unguarded" terrain is more susceptible to the ravages of the wind. The wind will be a huge factor on these final nine holes as many of them call for forced carries over water or salt marshes. For instance, the 424-yard, par-4 11th requires a 224-yard carry from the back tees just to reach the fairway.

Insider Tips   Accuracy versus distance . . . Accuracy wins at Long Point. If you can keep the ball in play and avoid the many hazards, you can ace this scenic test. However, if you are prone to wildness, get the calculator out—you may need it to tally up your score. Often there is a ranger positioned before you reach the tee at the 6th hole. He will provide you with critical information on the wind conditions and on the distance the hole is playing.

The hardest hole on the course is Long Point's signature hole, number two, a 540-yard par-5 that plays to a tight plateau fairway guarded by woods on the right and marshland on the left. If you are a big hitter, you can reach the small green in two, but your second shot is not without peril. The green is set in a marsh and is surrounded by trouble: Traps on both sides; salt marsh in the back. Basically, you need to ask yourself, "Are you feeling lucky?"

Amelia Island Plantation, Oak Marsh Course

3000 First Coast Highway, Amelia Island, FL 32034; phone (888) 261-6161 or (904) 261-6161

How To Get On: You must be a guest of the resort to gain access to this course.

Tees:

> Blue: 6,502 yards, par-72, USGA rating 71.7, slope 130
>
> White: 5,824 yards, par-72, USGA rating 68.6, slope 123
>
> Green: 5,521 yards, par-72, USGA rating 67.1, slope 119
>
> Red: 4,983 yards, par-72, USGA rating 69.9, slope 124

Challenge: ★★★	Golf Facilities: ★★½
Variety: ★★★	14-Club Test ★★★½
Terrain: ★★★	Intangibles: ★★★½
Beauty/Visual Appeal: ★★★★	Value: ★★★½
Pace of Play: ★★★½	

Just the Facts   Year Opened: 1972; Course Designer: Pete Dye; Walking: No; Greens Fee: $85–95; 9 Hole/Twilight Rate: No; Pull Carts: No; Practice Range: Yes; Club Rental: Yes.

Description and Comments   Amelia Island once had three separate 9-hole courses, but recent renovations have resulted in two 18-hole courses, Oak Marsh and Ocean Links. Oak Marsh is comprised of the two nines once known as Oak Marsh and Oyster Bay. The "new" Oak Marsh features typical Dye trademarks: extremely tight fairways guarded by trees and water; small, bulkheaded greens; long and strategically placed bunkers. Additional challenge is provided from the salt marsh creeks that meander through many of the holes. All told, 14 of the 18 holes feature water.

You will get to experience the vigor of Oak Marsh right from the start as the second hole is not only the longest but also the hardest on the course. Number two is a par-5 that plays 540 yards from the tips and requires not only length but precision on each shot. The fairway is carved into a chute of trees and features a looming oak tree on the left that can easily come into play off the tee. The green is guarded by two traps in front as well as a lake, so your approach shot will need to be carefully struck. Another outstanding hole on the front nine is the 7th, a par-3 that plays 184 yards. It is not only the yardage that presents the challenge, it is the many hazards that await your tee shot: a waste bunker and lake guard the entire left-hand side from tee to green; anther bunker lies to the right of the green; trees surround the entire hole.

The back nine is a little more open, but not enough for you to let your guard down. Seventeen and 18 are two terrific finishing holes that really test your game. Seventeen is a long par-4 (441 yards) that requires nearly a 200-yard carry over a waste area off the blue tees, just to reach the fairway. From there you must negotiate your way down the slightly dogleg left fairway to a small green guarded on both sides by bunkers. The final hole is a terrific par-5, known as "Jaws," that plays to one of the wider fairways on the course.

From the tips, the hole measures 502 yards and is ranked as the second hardest hole. This hole requires sound strategy as a waste area cuts directly in front of the well-bunkered green, and thus most golfers will have to lay up.

Insider Tips Oak Marsh demands shotmaking and course management to score well. The tight, sweeping fairways will reward accuracy, but will brutally punish errant shots. Except for the par-5s, the holes here are not overly long, so you may want to consider switching to a three wood off the tee. Your best scoring opportunities will come from the par-3s, which are not overly long and tend to have fewer hazards (number seven is an exception). Also, take note of the prevailing wind, as it will severely affect your yardage, by as much as two clubs on occasion. With gnarled oaks and sea breezes everywhere, our advice is to rein in the power and play lots of three-quarter-swing, low-trajectory shots. The control game rules at Oak Marsh.

Amelia Island Plantation, Ocean Links

3000 First Coast Highway, Amelia Island, FL 32034; phone (888) 261-6161 or (904) 261-6161

How To Get On: You must be a guest of the resort to gain access to this course.

Tees:

Blue: 6,301 yards, par-70, USGA rating and slope not available

White: 5,669 yards, par-70, USGA rating and slope not available

Green: 5,174 yards, par-70, USGA rating and slope not available

Red: 4,550 yards, par-70, USGA rating and slope not available

Note: Star ratings also not available at press time.

Just the Facts Year Opened: 1998; Course Designers: Pete Dye and Bobby Weed; Walking: No; Greens Fee: $85–95; 9 Hole/Twilight Rate: No; Pull Carts: No; Practice Range: Yes; Club Rental: Yes.

Description and Comments Ocean Links is comprised of the nine original holes formerly known as the Oceanside nine, designed by Pete Dye and updated by Bobby Weed, who revamped and lengthened them, as well as nine new holes also created by Bobby Weed. The result: a course boasting five holes that play along the Atlantic Ocean, the most of any of Florida's resorts. Ocean Links travels through sand dunes and along the seashore and features ten holes with lagoons and marshland. Additional challenge comes in the form of small greens, narrow fairways, and prevailing winds.

Three of the final four holes are the most memorable on the course. Fifteen is a par-3 that plays 187 yards straight out to the ocean. It's a beautiful hole that can be severely affected by offshore gusts. Sixteen is a 430-yard par-4 that parallels the ocean and requires a drive that carries part of the adjoining beach. The fairway is located between sand dunes and a large oak hammock. The final hole is a spectacular par-3 that demands only a precise short iron as it plays just 135 yards from the tips. However, the breezes can wreak havoc on even well-struck shots as the green juts out into Red Maple Lake. It's a unique way to end a memorable round.

Insider Tips   At the time of this writing, this course had yet to be officially rated, but it is safe to say that Ocean Links will be the easiest and shortest of the three courses at Amelia Island Plantation, but one fraught with excitement and peril. The course features six par-3s, and thus your short game will be tested on a regular basis. There are four par-5s at the course, but they are not overly long and thus not extremely taxing. This is a course that all levels of players can enjoy and is a true visual treat. If nothing else, its oceanside setting stamps "must-play" status on Ocean Links.

LPGA International, Champions Course

300 Champions Dr., Daytona Beach, FL 32124; phone (904) 274-LPGA

How To Get On: Tee times can be made one week in advance.

Tees:

> Black: 7,088 yards, par-72, USGA rating 74.0, slope 134
>
> Blue: 6,664 yards, par-72, USGA rating 72.0, slope 130
>
> LPGA: 6,435 yards, par-72, USGA rating 70.1, slope 124
>
> Gold: 5,744 yards, par-72, USGA rating 72.4, slope 131
>
> Red: 5,131 yards, par-72, USGA rating 68.9, slope 122

Challenge: ★★★★	Golf Facilities: ★★★★½
Variety: ★★★	14-Club Test ★★★★
Terrain: ★★★½	Intangibles: ★★★★
Beauty/Visual Appeal: ★★★½	Value: ★★★★
Pace of Play: ★★½	

Just the Facts   Year Opened: 1994; Course Designer: Rees Jones; Walking: At certain times; Greens Fee: $25–75; 9 Hole/Twilight Rate: Yes; Pull Carts: No; Practice Range: Yes; Club Rental: Yes.

Description and Comments   The Rees Jones course at the LPGA International headquarters is home to the LPGA's richest tournament, the Sprint Titleholders Championship, and was one of the first courses built in the country specifically for women. But this is not to say that men are not welcome to play—if they dare. Indeed, what awaits you here is a formidable test, no matter what your gender is.

One of the first things you will notice when you arrive at the course is the superior practice facilities, which include three complete practice holes (a par-3, 4, and 5), three putting greens, and an extremely nice driving range. These facilities make practicing almost as fun as playing. We said almost, so make sure you don't get too carried away and miss your tee time.

The course is links-style with only a minimal number of trees. This dearth of trees contributes to the biggest challenge you will find at the course—the wind. There's nothing to deflect it as it blows off the nearby (but unseen) ocean.

Beyond the wind, you will have to negotiate a profusion of wetlands and water hazards that are found on every hole, as well as numerous gaping sand and grass bunkers. Also prominent are the mounds that line both sides of most fairways. The look gets repetitive after a while, but at least they help keep your ball in play. Fairways are fairly wide open and feature undulations that break up the monotonously flat terrain typically found in the area. Greens tend to be enormous and feature broad undulations, with many of them having two or three tiers. They tend to be firm and fast, so be wary.

Insider Tips This course is perennially voted one of America's most "women friendly." However, just because it is friendly doesn't mean it is docile. No, this course has the roar of a lion, or should we say, lioness?

Your best bet is to make sure you arrive early so that you can avail yourself of the excellent practice facilities. You will no doubt need this warm-up to ensure that you can negotiate the first five holes, which require forced carries over water. Once again, the wind is more than likely going to be an imposing factor during your round—take note and club accordingly.

The aforementioned greens are so large that they really could be two or three separate greens. It is therefore critical that your approach shot is on target and near the flag, as wayward shots can result in incredibly long putts—you may walk away thanking the fact that you only had a three putt.

A word of caution: If you want a speedy round at the Jones's LPGA course, make sure to play early in the day, as the course tends to bog down as the day progresses.

Palm Coast Resort, Grand Haven

300 Clubhouse Dr., Palm Coast, FL 32137; phone (904) 445-BEAR

How To Get On: Guests of the resort can book tee times one year in advance. Nonguests can book tee times seven days in advance.

Tees:

    Black: 7,069 yards, par-72, USGA rating 74.9, slope 135

    Gold: 6,695 yards, par-72, USGA rating 72.8, slope 131

    Blue: 6,363 yards, par-72, USGA rating 71.5, slope 126

    White: 5,762 yards, par-72, USGA rating 68.3, slope 120

    Red: 4,985 yards, par-72, USGA rating 70.4, slope 123

Challenge: ★★★½
Variety: ★★★½
Terrain: ★★★½
Beauty/Visual Appeal: ★★★½
Pace of Play: ★★★½

Golf Facilities: ★★★½
14-Club Test ★★★
Intangibles: ★★★½
Value: ★★★½

Just the Facts   Year Opened: 1998; Course Designer: Jack Nicklaus; Walking: No; Greens Fee: $73–88; 9 Hole/Twilight Rate: Yes; Pull Carts: No; Practice Range: Yes; Club Rental: Yes.

Description and Comments   Ten years ago, it was major news when Jack Nicklaus designed a course that offered access to the public. These days, the Golden Bear is much more in touch with the common man, with dozens of resort and daily-fee courses on his ledger. One of his most recent efforts is Grand Haven Golf Club, which opened in October 1998. Grand Haven is the new anchor tenant in the golf mall that is the Palm Coast Resort.

Conveniently located three miles east of Interstate 95 between St. Augustine and Daytona Beach, Palm Coast Resort is worlds away from hustle and bustle. Palm Coast Resort is home to a fine lodge, the Harborside Inn, and is unique in that it's the only resort on earth that features courses designed by golf's big three: Arnold Palmer (Matanzas Woods, Pine Lakes), Gary Player (Cypress Knoll), and Nicklaus. Palm Coast boasts a fifth course as well, called Palm Harbor, crafted by Bill Amick.

Grand Haven features wide fairways, a Nicklaus trademark. Most of the hazard trouble is either to one side or the other, but seldom both, so there's usually a correct side to aim for. Strategy plays a large role at Grand Haven, as the good player will have numerous opportunities throughout the round to test his or her skills against the strategically deployed sand, water, and wetland hazards.

Nicklaus did a fine job of incorporating the site's existing wetlands and wildlife habitats into his design. Mostly the holes ribbon through groves of live oaks and marshy areas as they skirt the Intracoastal Waterway. Contouring on fairways and around greens is surprisingly benign for a Nicklaus design, leading some who play Grand Haven to question its "thrill" factor.

In truth, this is not one of Nicklaus's more memorable or exciting efforts. The greens are on the flat side and are sort of shapeless. On the long par-4s, such as the 464-yard 4th and the 471-yard 15th, the scale of the design is enormous, with 80-yard-wide fairways. These are dull holes, frankly, as is the par-5 11th, while the 400-yard, par-4 10th is just plain bad, with a water hazard that can't be seen from the tee lying in wait on the inside elbow of this dogleg right.

These criticisms aside, Grand Haven is fun and fair. It's definitely one of Nicklaus's most playable designs for all classes of golfers. Grand Haven throws several wonderful holes at you as well. Many people favor the

156-yard, par-3 8th, with its near-island green shored with a bulkhead composed of rock and coquina shells, native to Florida's coast. We like the 434-yard, par-4 13th, which plays up to a rise and finishes at a green bunkered on the left and right that is set nicely in the trees. Another fine par-4 is the 430-yard 16th, which features a slightly uphill approach.

Insider Tips   As is common with a Jack Nicklaus design, the fairways here are amply wide, so expect a workout with your driver. Fairway bunker sand is on the soft side, so practice picking shots clean, rather than digging deep, before you tackle Grand Haven.

Ponte Vedra Inn and Club, Ocean Course

200 Ponte Vedra Inn and Club, Ponte Vedra Beach, FL 32082; phone (800) 234-7842 or (904) 285-1111

How To Get On: You must be a guest of the resort to play this course.

Tees:

> Blue: 6,498 yards, par-72, USGA rating 71.6, slope 134
>
> White: 6,066 yards, par-72, USGA rating 69.2, slope 128
>
> Red: 4,967 yards, par-72, USGA rating 68.3, slope 119

Challenge: ★★★	Golf Facilities: ★★★½
Variety: ★★★½	14-Club Test ★★★½
Terrain: ★★★	Intangibles: ★★★★
Beauty/Visual Appeal: ★★★★	Value: ★★★½
Pace of Play: ★★★½	

Just the Facts   Year Opened: 1928; Course Designer: Herbert Strong; Walking: At certain times; Greens Fee: $90–110; 9 Hole/Twilight Rate: No; Pull Carts: No; Practice Range: Yes; Club Rental: Yes.

Description and Comments   Although the 17th at the TPC at Sawgrass may be the world's most famous island green, it was not the first. That honor goes to the 9th hole at Ponte Vedra's Ocean Course. Ponte Vedra was also the first resort in the area. However, the Ocean Course may be most notorious for what didn't happen rather than what did. The course had been selected to host the 1939 Ryder Cup, but this tournament was cancelled due to World War II, so the course missed out on earning "legendary" status. Although it has hosted its fair share of tournaments, including five U.S. Open qualifiers, it will forever be a postscript in the Ryder Cup annals.

Not content to rest on its past laurels, the Ocean Course recently underwent a seven-month $3.7 million, tee-to-green renovation under the direction of Bobby Weed and reopened in December 1998. The course is a scenic layout that features a plethora of bunkers—65 to be exact. The undulating greens are medium sized—several of them feature classic-style "false-front drop offs—and tend to be relatively quick, except for during the summer months when they slow down considerably. The biggest challenge you will face however, will be the ever-present breezes.

The signature hole at the Ocean Course, as you may have suspected, is the island green, par-3 9th. The hole measures a modest 150 yards, but the almost ever-present wind makes it play a lot tougher than this yardage indicates. The hardest hole is the 4th, a 427-yard par-4 that features a lagoon crossing the fairway.

Insider Tips With many of the surrounding courses having a "modern" feel, it is nice to experience a classic old-timer. Even after Bobby Weed's sprucing up, you still can see the Robert Trent Jones Sr. touch—especially in the bunkering. Jones revised the original Herbert Strong design in the 1950s. His patented deep, yawning traps prevail. The course rewards creative players, especially golfers who can improvise and those who know their own games. For example, you'll have an abundance of approaches to elevated greens when the wind is blowing right into you. Rather than just blasting at it with all your might, how about clubbing down and hitting a low-trajectory shot that just scampers up on the green? Club selection and imagination will be nearly as important as keeping your head down and following through. Angled tee boxes and gently rolling fairways are the products of Weed's recent handiwork; they add variety and challenge at every turn.

A number of greens here feature "false fronts," an old-world design technique whereby the architect gives you a tongue of green as a target in front to shoot for, but it's sloped so that if you hit it, you won't actually stay on the putting surface. Rather, your ball will roll off, back down into the fairway. This deception is clever, but can be frustrating. Make sure you use enough club to get it past these false fronts and onto a safer portion of the green.

Sawgrass Country Club

10034 Golf Club Dr., Ponte Vedra Beach, FL 32082; phone (800) 457-4653 or (904) 273-3720

Sawgrass is comprised of three 9-hole courses that are played in three different 18-hole combinations. The most popular is the East/West combination.

How To Get On: You must be a guest of the Sawgrass Marriott Resort to obtain a tee time at this semiprivate country club.

East/South Tees:

    Green: 6,916 yards, par-72, USGA rating 73.8, slope 136

    Blue: 6,503 yards, par-72, USGA rating 72.0, slope 132

    White: 6,062 yards, par-72, USGA rating 70.0, slope 127

    Red: 5,176 yards, par-72, USGA rating 71.7, slope 120

East/West Tees:

> Green: 6,900 yards, par-72, USGA rating 74.5, slope 140
>
> Blue: 6,438 yards, par-72, USGA rating 72.5, slope 136
>
> White: 6,019 yards, par-72, USGA rating 70.5, slope 131
>
> Red: 5,128 yards, par-72, USGA rating 71.1, slope 119

South/West Tees:

> Green: 6,864 yards, par-72, USGA rating 73.7, slope 139
>
> Blue: 6,451 yards, par-72, USGA rating 71.9, slope 135
>
> White: 6,023 yards, par-72, USGA rating 69.7, slope 130
>
> Red: 5,118 yards, par-72, USGA rating 70.2, slope 117

Challenge: ★★★★	Golf Facilities: ★★★
Variety: ★★★★	14-Club Test ★★★★
Terrain: ★★★★	Intangibles: ★★★★
Beauty/Visual Appeal: ★★★½	Value: ★★★½
Pace of Play: ★★★	

Just the Facts   Year Opened: 1972; Course Designer: Ed Seay; Walking: At certain times; Greens Fee: $80–135; 9 Hole/Twilight Rate: No; Pull Carts: No; Practice Range: No; Club Rental: No.

Description and Comments   The guests of the Marriott have playing privileges at a number of area courses. One of the best on this golfing menu is the Sawgrass Country Club, site of what was known as the Tournament Players Championship before it moved to the Stadium course at the TPC at Sawgrass. Sawgrass is a links-style course in terms of its low-profile nature, but there are too many elevated greens and forced carries across hazards to call this a true links. Its 27 holes travel through forests and marshland and feature a multitude of cavernous bunkers and water hazards. Ed Seay, the lead designer for the Arnold Palmer group, is said to consider this his signature course, to give you some idea of the quality of this layout.

The East and West were the original 18 holes, and was the course used in what is now known as the Players Championship; the South nine was added in 1984. All three nines are formidable, but the East is the most challenging. The fun really begins after a relatively simple opening hole. The 2nd hole is a 394-yard, par-4 dogleg right that features a fairway squeezed by trees on both sides and marshland on the right. You have to smack your tee shot to have any chance of reaching the narrow green in two. The 4th and 5th are considered the best two holes on the course. The 4th is a magnificent short par-5 (501 yards) with an extremely tight landing area guarded by water on both sides of the fairway. The second shot must clear another lake, while your approach is to a minute, elevated green surrounded by trees. As Tour star Raymond Floyd once said of the 4th, "you take your five and you get the hell out." After you have a chance to catch your breath, you head to the 5th, a 419-yard par-4 that plays from an elevated tee to a slightly dogleg right landing strip surrounded by marshes. The green is nestled near a bunker and a lake.

The West offers your best scoring opportunities as it tends to be a tad easier, but it's still a stern challenge in the ever-present wind. Water can be found on five of the holes, most memorably on holes six through nine, where it is on the entire left-hand side of the hole of each hole. These final four holes are the most scenic, spectacular, and deadly on the course. The 6th is a 201-yard par-3 that plays to a narrow green guarded on three sides by bunkers with water cutting in on the left. On the 7th, you have to carry the water not once but twice to an extremely shallow green. The 8th is a pretty straightforward par-4 that plays 439 yards, but, of course, there is still water. Wrapping it up is a tough par-5 that plays 507 yards. The hole bends slightly from right to left and water can be found on both sides. The green is narrow but somewhat receptive as it is the longest on this nine (33 yards), but it is tucked perilously near the lake. Any pulled shot is sure to make a splash.

If you have a chance, you should also play the enjoyable South course. The wind is the most prominent on this nine, and water comes into play on three of the holes. Although not as celebrated as the other two nines, it is well worth your time.

Insider Tips   Accuracy, accuracy, accuracy. This simple eight-letter word is the key to scoring success at Sawgrass Country Club. Though this course doesn't receive the notoriety that the Stadium Course at the TPC at Sawgrass does, it is no less difficult. On the contrary, it poses quite a severe test with its tight fairways and constant blustering wind. If you can keep the ball in play, you've won half the battle.

The other half of the battle comes from good course management. The severe dogleg holes and small greens place a premium on ball position. You need to visualize the best line for your shots and try to leave yourself as-short-as-possible approach shots that can snuggle up to the flag, leaving you with sinkable putts.

Unless you are a near-scratch golfer or a fearsome ball striker, you may want to avoid this course entirely in March. This is when the winds tend to blow strongest, and it can be darned near impossible to keep your shots out of the many hazards on a typical March day. On an average March afternoon, the "challenge" rating jumps to five stars. When the PGA Tour pros played the Players Championship here in March 1977 and 1978, the winners were Mark Hayes and Jack Nicklaus, respectively, both with remarkably high, one-over-par 289 totals.

Tournament Players Club at Sawgrass, Stadium Course

110 TPC Blvd., Ponte Vedra Beach, FL 32082; phone (904) 273-3235

How To Get On: The most conventional way to gain access to TPC Stadium is by staying at the Sawgrass Marriott Resort. There are, however, a couple other lesser-known means. First off, guests of the Ponte Vedra Lodge (though not the Ponte Vedra Inn) have limited access to the course based on availability. If neither of the above sound good, the TPC sells an Associate Membership (cost $150–180), which provides access to the course every day of the week, no matter where you are staying, and allows you to bring up to three guests. In fact, the more guests you bring, the lower your greens fees will be.

Tees:

> TPC: 6,857 yards, par-72, USGA rating 74.0, slope 135
>
> Blue: 6,394 yards, par-72, USGA rating 71.9, slope 130
>
> White: 5,761 yards, par-72, USGA rating 68.7, slope 126
>
> Red: 5,034 yards, par-72, USGA rating 64.7, slope 123

Challenge: ★★★★★ Golf Facilities: ★★★★★
Variety: ★★★★   14-Club Test: ★★★★½
Terrain: ★★★★   Intangibles: ★★★★★
Beauty/Visual Appeal: ★★★★½ Value: ★★★★
Pace of Play: ★★★

Just the Facts   Year Opened: 1980; Course Designer: Pete Dye; Walking: Yes; Greens Fee: $90–160; 9 Hole/Twilight Rate: No; Pull Carts: Yes; Practice Range: Yes; Club Rental: Yes.

Description and Comments   If you ask a group of golfers for their opinion of the TPC Stadium Course, you will no doubt get a variety of responses— the Stadium Course may just be the poster child for "love it/hate it" golf. Some consider it a magnificent layout that is a grand challenge, but others think it is an unfair, tricked-up layout. But one thing that all will agree on is that this is one course that you will not soon forget (of course, that may be because you are still having nightmares). Because of its challenge and its fame, it is the one absolutely "must-play" in Northern Florida.

Pete Dye's Stadium creation quickly gained fame as it became the permanent home to the Tournament Players Championship, but instant acceptance did not quite match the instant notoriety—it was deemed as too sadistically difficult by the majority. Thus, only three years after its opening, Dye oversaw a series of minor adjustments—the fairways were made less severe, the grass lusher, and the extensive waste areas were covered in grass. As you can see from the slope and ratings above, these alterations certainly didn't make this course a walkover—hardly.

The course is the ultimate example of Dye's target style, strategic golf designs where golfers encounter numerous forced carries, tight landing areas, and a variety of hazards throughout the course, including lakes, creeks, bunkers, and robust rough. In fact, water may come into play on every single hole. And then there is the 17th hole—but more on that later. Equally distinctive are the incredibly high "spectator" mounds that frame many of the fairways and greens. These are essentially tall dirt piles, which were then grassed over, providing spots where tournament galleries could congregate and see lots of action when the pros were playing. These "mini-amphitheaters" became a natural part of the course, giving rise to the course's being named the "Stadium" course. Sawgrass had the original. Today, it has spawned a host of imitators.

The Stadium starts out pretty meekly, but gains speed quickly—kind of like a snowball heading down Mt. Everest. The first three holes, a par-4, par-5, and par-3, respectively, are relatively easy and represent the best holes on which to make birdie. You get your first glimpse of what this course is about when you reach the fifth hole. Five is a par-4 that plays 454 yards from the tips and requires your tee shot to carry both water and bunkers. The landing area is extremely narrow and is guarded by a waste bunker running along the right hand side and a pond on the left. The green is medium-sized and is surrounded by both trees and bunkers. You have now arrived at the heart of the Stadium Course.

Though most every hole at this course is memorable, the final three—and more specifically the famed 17th—really give the Stadium Course the "must-play" status. Your tee shot on the 16th hole, a slight dogleg left, par-5, 497-yarder, must clear a lake to a narrow landing strip with a large bunker on the right hand side. For big hitters who strike their shots to the right spot, the green is reachable in two. Of course, it will require yet another perfect shot to a green that has a large body of water on the right, trees on the left, and bunkers all around. If you go for it, you may quickly be muttering those words heard over and over at the Stadium—"Darn that Dye."

And now we finally arrive at the 17th—the most photographed hole anywhere in the world and by far the most famous par-3 island green. It certainly is not the yardage that intimidates players—it's only 132 yards from the tips. This is the tee that the PGA Tour plays from during the Players Championship, so you can experience the exact same hole as the pros do. No, it's not the distance that gets your pulse racing and your palms sweaty, it is the small, apple-shaped landing area, completely encircled by water, that gives you heart palpitations.

Because the tee boxes are not elevated, the mostly round green (which is larger than it looks) is not framed particularly well. The hole is back-dropped by tall pines, but you can't see the water behind the green from the tee. You can make out the mildly undulating putting surface, one lone pot bunker jabbed into the front right of the green, and the narrow dirt-and-grass walkway that transports golfers from the cart path to the green. Other than that, it's just water, water, everywhere. Making your task even tougher are two factors: the remarkable persistent breezes, and the fact that your effort will be watched by both the folks that just got off the 17th green and by the folks playing the adjacent 16th hole. (Not to prolong your misery, there is a limit of two lost balls before you must proceed to the drop area.)

Wrapping it all up is the boomerang-shaped, 440-yard, par-4 18th, which features a lake along the entire left-hand side, sort of a par-4 version of the 18th at Pebble Beach. A well-placed tee shot still leaves you with a challenging second one to an elevated green with five bunkers behind. You will no doubt breathe a sigh of relief once you hear your final putt drop into the cup. You have just survived the TPC Stadium Course! What are you going to do now—go to Disneyland?

Insider Tips Yes, this is one tough course. Yes, you are going to have quite a battle on your hands. Yes, this will more than likely not be a record-breaking round (except for broken clubs) if you're not patient. If you accept all these facts going in, you will undoubtedly enjoy your round more than if you have rose-colored glasses on. Enjoy the task at hand and have some fun.

There are some pointers that we can provide to assist you. First and probably foremost is how to tack the wind. It will more than likely be howling, and it will affect your ball in a way that Dorothy and Toto can relate to. You will need to pick your club, as well as your line, carefully. You will find the greens to be medium-fast, but extremely tricky to putt with lots and lots of undulations—spend some time at the practice putting green before you start.

This course is not necessarily for high handicappers. If you fall into this category you may be lured to the course for notoriety's sake. Our recommendation is to seek an alternative unless you just feel that you can't miss out on the chance to try your luck on the TPC. If you do decide to play here, make sure to pick the suitable tees for your game. You will get a challenge no matter where you play, but give yourself a fighting chance. No matter what level you are or from which tees you play, have some backup balls in your bag. The ever-present water seems to jump out from everywhere to grab quite a few.

When in doubt, play safe. There are numerous humps, hollows, moguls, waste bunkers, and semiblind shots, which can send scores soaring. If you don't care about score, feel free to swing with abandon.

Regarding chipping, this is the course that practically called for the invention of the 60-degree lob wedge. You'll need this club over and over, to loft the ball over greenside trouble and stop it quickly on the putting surface. Another area to avoid is the Bahia grass, which with its broad blades can get so wiry, you could break a wrist trying to extricate a ball from its clutches.

Finally, and we're not kidding, practice some baseball-type swings before you play here. You'll have at least a couple of occasions here where you practically have to stand on your head to hit the shot. One last word to the wise: Dye built most of the spectator mounds to the right side of the fairways so that spectators would be looking into the golfer's faces, so aim left if you wish to avoid these nasty mounds.

Don't forget: This is the home course of the PGA Tour. The locker room, dining facilities, and practice range are second to none on the East Coast for a public-access facility. Don't be surprised to head out to the practice bunkers and see Vijay Singh or Rocco Mediate hitting beside you.

Tournament Players Club at Sawgrass, Valley Course

110 TPC Blvd., Ponte Vedra Beach, FL 32082; phone (904) 273-3235

How To Get On: The most conventional way to gain access to the TPC is by staying at the Sawgrass Marriott Resort. There are, however, a couple of other lesser-known means. First off, guests of the Ponte Vedra Lodge (though not the Ponte Vedra Inn) have limited access to the course based on availability. If neither of the above sound good, the TPC sells an Associate Membership (cost $150–180), which provides access to the course every day of the week, no matter where you are staying, and allows you to bring up to three guests. In fact, the more guests you bring, the lower your greens fees will be.

Tees:

      TPC: 6,864 yards, par-72, USGA rating 72.6, slope 129

      Blue: 6,524 yards, par-72, USGA rating 70.9, slope 125

      White: 6,092 yards, par-72, USGA rating 69.0, slope 122

      Red: 5,126 yards, par-72, USGA rating 63.8, slope 112

Challenge: ★★★½	Golf Facilities: ★★★★★
Variety: ★★★	14-Club Test ★★★★
Terrain: ★★★½	Intangibles: ★★★★
Beauty/Visual Appeal: ★★★½	Value: ★★★½
Pace of Play: ★★★½	

Just the Facts   Year Opened: 1987; Course Designer: Pete Dye; Walking: Yes; Greens Fee: $60–95; 9 Hole/Twilight Rate: Yes; Pull Carts: Yes; Practice Range: Yes; Club Rental: Yes.

Description and Comments With its sister course, the Stadium, receiving the lion's share of attention, the links-style Valley Course is often ignored. This is both an oversight and a blessing, for the Valley is an extremely enjoyable track that is less crowded than the more popular Stadium—making it a favorite among locals.

The Valley is a formidable test, albeit nowhere near the challenge found at the Stadium, but of course, little else is. It too features water on all 18 holes, but unlike the Stadium Course, the location of the water is very predictable—on nearly every hole, water sits on one side of the fairway from tee to green and the other side of the fairway is guarded by trees. You seldom have to carry the water off your tee shots or on your approaches, and when you do, it's of the "bite-off-as-much-as-you-can-chew" variety. So, you just need to avoid either hooking or slicing, depending on where the water is situated on that particular hole, and your ball will remain dry. This predictability in design is the only downfall of the course.

Valley's fairways are nicely contoured and feature more undulations than the Stadium Course. They also tend to be a tad wider, but the aforementioned water and trees nonetheless place a premium on accuracy. The large, often deceptively configured greens are relatively flat and tend to be fast.

Highlights of the course include the second hole, a par-3 227-yarder that has a T-shaped water hazard, with one arm of the lake guarding the entire right side while another protects the back of the green. The putting surface is nestled into the intersection of these two hazards. The 7th hole is a longish par-5 (559 yards from the tips) that bends slightly to the left and features water on the left and trees on the right. The green extends precariously into the lake, and thus going for the green in two is quite a gamble.

The par-4 15th hole is the hardest hole on the course and features a variety of hazards. It's a 462-yard dogleg right that has sand and water on the right and trees lining the fairway to the left. Your tee shot has to be both long and accurate to negotiate this hole.

Insider Tips If you head to the Valley expecting to find a Stadium-like experience with Stadium-like challenge, you will be disappointed. However, if you come to the Valley looking for a fun layout that challenges but doesn't torture, you will thoroughly enjoy the course. Also, if you come to the TPC at Sawgrass complex just to make a pilgrimage and want to sneak in a round, this is the candidate for access and challenge. It's also a pretty good bargain, given the facility, course conditioning, and architectural pedigree.

Pay special attention to where the tee markers are placed. Many times they point you toward a water or sand hazard that you can't carry. Since most of the trouble is on one side or the other (but not both) on most of these holes, you may need to consciously align yourself at an angle and aim well away from the trouble.

Since the course is only one mile from the ocean, the wind will be a definite factor on most days. As with the Stadium, you will need to adjust your club selection and pick your line very carefully—especially with the hazards lurking everywhere. The course is slightly longer than the Stadium, but it plays slightly easier, so this is a great alternative for higher handicappers looking to play at TPC. Also, the course tends to play much faster than its sister course, so this may be your best bet if you are pressed for time.

World Golf Village, Slammer and Squire Course

500 South Legacy Trail, St. Augustine, FL 32092; phone (888) 446-5301 or (904) 940-6100

Ten years in the making, the WGV is a 6,300-acre development that features a variety of accommodations, a 75,000-square-foot Hall of Fame (honoring all three tours), exhibits, and an IMAX theater. Guests to the Hall of Fame can stroll over a replica of the Swilcan Burn Bridge from the famed 18th hole at St. Andrews, putt on an 1880-style green, have your swing analyzed, as well as view the exhibition commemorating the Hall of Fame inductees from all three tours.

All this and we haven't even mentioned the actual golf. The Slammer and Squire is the first of the many courses that are planned for the WGV; next on the docket is the "King and Bear" designed jointly by Arnold Palmer and Jack Nicklaus.

How To Get On: Tee times can be booked one month in advance—longer if you are staying at the resort.

Tees:

Championship: 6,940 yards, par-72, USGA rating 73.8, slope 135

Blue: 6,135 yards, par-72, USGA rating 72.5, slope 128

White: 5,715 yards, par-72, USGA rating 72.5, slope 124

Red: 5,001 yards, par-72, USGA rating 69.1, slope 116

Challenge: ★★★½	Golf Facilities: ★★★½
Variety: ★★★★	14-Club Test: ★★★
Terrain: ★★★★	Intangibles: ★★★★
Beauty/Visual Appeal: ★★★	Value: ★★
Pace of Play: ★★★½	

Just the Facts   Year Opened: 1998; Course Designer: Bobby Weed; Walking: No; Greens Fee: $90–165; 9 Hole/Twilight Rate: Yes; Pull Carts: No; Practice Range: Yes; Club Rental: Yes.

Description and Comments   The powers behind the Slammer and Squire wanted to create a course that would be enjoyable and challenging yet not require six hours for a round or unfairly penalize novice golfers. They turned to Bobby Weed (with consultation assistance from the course's namesakes, Gene Sarazen and Sam Snead) to accomplish these objectives. The course that Weed created has no forced carries or ankle-high rough, but it still manages to offer players an attractive layout that poses a healthy challenge, especially the greens. Though being truly playable for all levels of golfers, it also is the host of the Senior PGA Tour's Liberty Mutual Legends of Golf tournament.

What you will no doubt first notice about the Slammer and Squire is the magnificent surroundings and unique variety of the layout. The front nine plays through peaceful wetlands, pine forests, and lagoons, whereas the back nine has more of a links feel although it winds around lakes. Throughout the course, Weed let nature really speak for itself—the course is a Signature Course in the Audubon International Cooperative Sanctuary Program.

Bobby Weed really shows off his design talents at Slammer and Squire. There are common themes throughout, such as distinctive, closely mown chipping areas around the greens, but his individual touches are what make several holes truly memorable. Architecture students will get a kick out of the 178-yard, par-3 7th, which is a tribute to one of Scotland's greatest holes, the 15th hole (called "Redan") at North Berwick. The huge, elevated green is divided into two sections and falls off sharply on every side.

It is the back nine, however that gets your pulse racing, especially the terrific closing stretch of 14 through 18. The petite 311-yard, par-4 14th is simply a superb option-laden hole. Big hitters can attempt to drive the green, but if they wind up on the wrong side of the putting surface from where the pin is, they'll do well just to three-putt on this wildly sloping green. Huge mounds and bunkers in the landing area for "lay-up" tee shots complicate matters for most players, making this hole a strategic delight.

The only strategy you'll need at the 147-yard, par-3 15th is to stay dry, as the front right portion of the narrow putting surface is flush against a lake. Sixteen is a big par-5 of 576 yards that calls for a huge power fade off the tee, taking care to avoid two Augusta National–looking giant ovals of fairway sand. The hole concludes with a Pinehurst No. 2–style green with severe fall-offs leading to shaved-down chipping areas.

Slammer and Squire finishes with two exceptional par-4s with 17 the longer of the two, but 18 equally demanding, as it curves around a lake to the left and is dotted with a Pandora's box of troublesome bunkers.

You won't be swept away with drama at Slammer and Squire, so at first blush, the greens fee seems excessive, especially in enticing folks to pull off nearby I-95, stop in at the Hall of Fame, and play the course. Still, it only takes one trip around to appreciate the subtlety and variety injected into the design at this course.

Insider Tips   Slammer and Squire was recently ranked one of the top 100 courses in the nation for women, based on criteria that included length of the course, playability, and challenge, as well as the way women are treated by the golf staff.

Like former Ohio State football coach Woody Hayes, Bobby Weed is a proponent of the running game. At Slammer and Squire he has placed emphasis on a bump-and-run–style golf utilizing firm, pronounced slopes around the greens to achieve this aim, which replicates the style of play favored in Scotland. So beware: The greens themselves can be very firm, and à la Pinehurst, many a near-good shot will hit the green, then bound helplessly off the green via contours that funnel the ball away. This can get an average golfer frustrated in a hurry. The Senior Tour pros who played the Legends of Golf held in 1999 hated it—perhaps the greens and their surrounds were too firm on that occasion, because Lee Trevino and Gary Player loved the course when they played it the previous year in Shell's Wonderful World of Golf Match; both men praised its fun factor and playability. When in doubt, hit it slightly short of your usual target and let the ball skip up to its intended destination.

A helpful hint: Missing a green at Slammer and Squire will often leave you with a short recovery shot from a shaved-down chipping area, unlike most courses where your shot will find some rough. The smartest way to play these shots is with a putter. Using a lofted club is risky because it's hard to get the club to sink in to the firm turf, resulting in skulled shots that race across the green.

The Major Courses in The Panhandle

Marriott's Bay Point Resort, Lagoon Legend

4200 Marriott Dr., Panama City, FL 32408; phone (800) 874-7105 or (850) 234-3307

How To Get On: Guests of the resort can book tee times 60 days in advance; nonguests can book tee times 14 days in advance.

Tees:

      Championship: 6,942 yards, par-72, USGA rating 75.3, slope 152

      Pro: 6,469 yards, par-72, USGA rating 73.0, slope 148

      Member: 6,079 yards, par-72, USGA rating 70.7, slope 144

      Seniors: 5,614 yards, par-72, USGA rating 74.0, slope 135

      Ladies: 4,949 yards, par-72, USGA rating 69.8, slope 127

Challenge: ★★★★★	Golf Facilities: ★★★★
Variety: ★★★	14-Club Test ★★★
Terrain: ★★★	Intangibles: ★★★★
Beauty/Visual Appeal: ★★★★	Value: ★★★★
Pace of Play: ★★½	

Just the Facts   Year Opened: 1986; Course Designers: Bruce Devlin and Robert von Hagge; Walking: No; Greens Fee: $50–70; 9 Hole/Twilight Rate: No; Pull Carts: No; Practice Range: Yes; Club Rental: Yes.

Description and Comments   If you look up the word "difficult" in Webster's Golf Dictionary, there may be a picture of Lagoon Legend in the definition. The course's mascot may be the first indication of just how tough a layout this is: It's a fire-breathing dragon. The second indication is the slope, a whopping 152 from the tips. Only a handful of courses in the United States are sloped higher.

So what makes Lagoon Legend so difficult? Let's start with water. Serious water. Water comes into play on no fewer than 16 holes. Then there are the many blind shots that you will encounter throughout your round. Landing areas appear surprisingly small. Adding to the challenge are the numerous bunkers strategically placed throughout the course. To sum up, there is trouble awaiting you at every turn. There are no easy holes on this course, so expect a real fight. The fun factor comes from simply finding out how well you can cope with the course's relentless nature.

Though the front nine is a tad easier than the back, that's not really saying much. You get to cut your teeth early with a longish par-5 (542 yards) that is hard to reach in two. The hole is well bunkered and a lake cuts in front of the green, requiring an all-carry approach shot. The next two holes are long, but less treacherous than others on the course. Water only comes into play at the end of the 2nd hole, whereas hole three is bone-dry. The same cannot be said for the remaining front nine holes, where water seems to be everywhere.

Then comes the back nine. . . . Here you will find lots of islands—island tee boxes, island fairways, and island greens. To start the back nine you must negotiate an inverted L-shaped hole where you drive over a meandering lake to a short fairway. You then have to make an immediate right turn and hit your second shot over the same lake to a green that is surrounded on three sides by, you guessed it, a lake. The green at the 300-yard, par-4 13th is accessible only by walking and is guarded on all sides by the Tai Tai swamp. Holes 14 and 15 are back-breakers as well. Both are long par-4s, guarded by water and sand, requiring precision shots.

The two final holes on the course are spectacular. The 17th is a double dogleg par-5 that plays to a narrow fairway, but it is reachable in two if you hit a pair of perfect shots. The green is well bunkered from behind and guarded by a lake in front and rear. To wrap it all up is the 18th—a V-shaped par-4 where you must drive over a creek to an island fairway and then hit over that same water to a green nearly surrounded by sand.

Insider Tips   If, after reading the above, you are licking your chops rather than shaking in your boots, Lagoon Legend may be just what you are looking for. This is not a course for everyone. If you are a beginner or a high handicapper, you will find this layout to be almost unplayable. Even if you're a middle-handicap golfer, you'll probably find the challenge overwhelming—thrilling, but frustrating.

For those who might try to slay the dragon, there is some ammo that we can give you to make it a fair fight. First off, you need to recognize that you're probably not going to be post your record low score here. In fact, this may be your highest scoring round in a long time. If this is your mindset going in, then you are going to find your round much more enjoyable. Also, if you get the chance to play this course more than once, you will find it less intimidating with each round. Second, make sure to pick the correct tees. The course has developed a guide that describes the tees and the type of player that they are designed for, so make sure to consult it prior to heading out on the course.

A couple of other housekeeping points: The hazards make the landing areas appear to be about as narrow as a single country lane. But in reality they are typically wider than you think—not to say that they are vast, but they are more forgiving than at first glance. That being said, don't go crazy with your driver—errant shots will be severely penalized.

Make sure to get a yardage book as this could be the most important tool in your bag. There are many nuances and tips that can make a direct impact on your game from the word go. Overall, our best recommendation is to play within yourself. You'll have to take a few chances simply because you're forced to, so expect to lose a few balls. By the same token, if you pick the correct set of tees and adopt a mentality of "swing easy, just keep it in play," you should have a good time here.

No matter what you score, you will no doubt remember your visit to Lagoon Legend for years to come.

Sandestin Resort, Burnt Pine

9300 U.S. 98 West, Destin, FL 32541; phone (800) 277-0800 or (850) 267-8000

How To Get On: You must be a guest of the resort to gain access to this semiprivate course.

Tees:

      Championship: 7,046 yards, par-72, USGA rating 74.1, slope 135

      Blue: 6,524 yards, par-72, USGA rating 71.5, slope 130

      White: 6,000 yards, par-72, USGA rating 68.7, slope 124

      Red: 5,096 yards, par-72, USGA rating 69.4, slope 122

Challenge: ★★★½   Golf Facilities: ★★★★

Variety: ★★★★½   14-Club Test ★★★★

Terrain: ★★★★   Intangibles: ★★★★

Beauty/Visual Appeal: ★★★★   Value: ★★★½

Pace of Play: ★★★★

Just the Facts   Year Opened: 1994; Course Designer: Rees Jones; Walking: Yes; Greens Fee: $90–115; 9 Hole/Twilight Rate: Yes; Pull Carts: No; Practice Range: Yes; Club Rental: Yes.

Description and Comments   As legend has it, during the Civil War, a sea captain was trying to sail around a Union blockade and decided to abandon ship when his chances for success looked dim. He took his loot (a chest filled with gold) and buried it under a landmark, a burnt pine. To his dismay, when he returned to retrieve his bounty, he found that there were hundreds of burnt pines. To this day, no one has found the captain's buried treasure—but if you take a really big divot, you might strike gold.

Burnt Pine is arguably the best course in the Panhandle region and in the top 25 for the entire state. It's just that good. But you had better hurry up and play it because as soon as they sell 450 memberships, it will move from a semiprivate course to a private course. Designed by Rees Jones, the "U.S. Open doctor," Burnt Pine is a solid golf course that offers just good ol' golf—no gimmicks to be found here. This is not to say that the course is boring. Hardly! Diverse in its terrain, golfers will be confronted by two separate settings: The front nine plays through a pine forest, and the back nine is bordered by the Choctawhatchee Bay.

On the front nine you will have your best scoring opportunity, which is scary when you consider what awaits you on this side. Not only do huge trees define the fairways, but they also are quick to penalize the wayward shot in the "wooden jail"; there are also lakes that come into play on many of the holes. You will face your first challenge right off the bat. The 1st hole looks innocent on paper (par-4, 404 yards), but in living technicolor however, it is not so easy. You will find a gaping lake along the left-hand side of the hole—not much time for you to warm up before you have to prove your ability to shoot straight.

The back nine is where the "fun" starts. No doubt you will take special notice of holes 13, 14, and 15, a truly awesome stretch of golf. The 13th, a 433-yard par-4, features water, water, and more water. The fairway doglegs around a lake, and the green is nestled in front of Choctawhatchee Bay. The 14th, the signature hole, really shows off Jones's artistry: Where others might have attempted to overdo it and put their stamp on the land,

Jones let the terrain dictate the hole—he let the land speak for itself. Fourteen is a par-3 that plays 212 yards from the tips and requires a tee shot over wetlands to an undulating green. Given its close proximity to the bay, wind will no doubt be a big factor on most days. The final hole of this triumvirate is a long par-4 (489 yards) that tends to be a killer, as you must clear 200 yards of marsh just to reach the fairway.

Jones has created a course that rewards good shotmaking but doesn't penalize you if you don't smash your drives like Tiger Woods. Burnt Pine is on our "must-play" list, but you had better hurry before it goes private.

Insider Tips　As they say, variety is the spice of life, and that adage certainly holds true here at Burnt Pine. Obviously, there is the terrain that changes as soon as you make the turn. But that's not all the variety you will find here. Jones has designed holes that require you to decide how you want to approach them rather than dictating a shot for you. Should you run it up close to the flag with a closed-face iron? How about a lofted sand or lob wedge? Then again, you may want to bump and run with a pitching wedge.

If you are able to keep the ball out of the hazards, you will find this course tamable. However, if you are wild, you are going to take a lot of medicine as you work your way out of the forests or reload after you lose another one in the drink. The wind typically is a major factor on many of the holes so you will need to adjust your club selection accordingly.

One more thing: Make sure to select the tees that best suit your game. One sure-fire test is to check the yardage on the par-3s. If you want a challenge and want to face a 200+ drive, then the championship tees may be for you. However, if don't want to be beaten by the course, move up and enjoy the round.

A Northeast Florida Sampler

The Golf Club at Amelia Island

4700 Amelia Island Parkway, Amelia Island, FL 32034; phone (904) 277-8015 or (904) 245-4224

Tees: Championship: 6,681 yards, par-72, USGA rating 71.7, slope 127

Greens Fee: $67–96

Challenge: ★★★	Golf Facilities: ★★★
Variety: ★★★½	14-Club Test ★★★
Terrain: ★★★½	Intangibles: ★★★
Beauty/Visual Appeal: ★★★½	Value: ★★★½
Pace of Play: ★★★★	

Description and Comments　In this region, perhaps unfairly, the spotlight is concentrated on the star performers, the courses at nearby Amelia Island Plantation. Waiting in the wings, just outside the hoopla and limelight, is a course that is certainly no wallflower understudy—the Golf Club of Amelia Island. Accessible only to the guests of the Ritz-Carlton Hotel, this course is magnificently conditioned with a front nine that plays through towering oaks and pines and a back nine that meanders through marshland and ponds.

Fairways narrowed by trees and water can quickly wreak havoc on your score, as well as your blood pressure, if you stray off target. The greens offer no respite for they are immense—some measure 10,000 square feet!—so make sure to check the pin position or you could be looking at the longest putts of your life. One of the best holes at the course is the 6th, a par-5 where you have to cross the marshland no less than three times. The green is elevated and protected by a mammoth 10-foot-deep bunker.

LPGA International, Legends Course

300 Champions Dr., Daytona Beach, FL 32124; phone (904) 274-LPGA
Tees: Championship: 6,984 yards, par-72, USGA rating 74.5, slope 138
Greens Fee: $45–74

Challenge: ★★★★	Golf Facilities: ★★★★½
Variety: ★★★½	14-Club Test ★★★½
Terrain: ★★★	Intangibles: ★★★★
Beauty/Visual Appeal: ★★★½	Value: ★★★★
Pace of Play: ★★★½	

Description and Comments Set on several hundred acres along the uplands of the Tomoka River, the new Legends Course at LPGA International is a tremendous design from Arthur Hills. In the short time since its 1998 opening, it has climbed right alongside the club's existing Rees Jones course in stature, appearance, and playability.

Before he designed the course, Hills consulted with a number of LPGA Tour players to discuss what their priorities were in a golf course design. The answer from the game's best women players was loud and clear: "Give us a course that tests our shotmaking abilities!" Hill complied.

Hills utilized the site's pines, wetlands, and sandy uplands to create a rare bird: a course fully challenging for all levels of women golfers, as well as all classes of men. Accuracy is paramount, as fairways are narrowed by trees and wetlands and the greens tend to be on the small side.

LPGA Legends Course opens with a gentle 390-yard par-4, though the green is partially blocked by a large mound and a front-right bunker; Hills inflicted an interesting if annoying design gambit that he has perpetrated on other course as well. What follows is one solid hole after another through pines and wetlands.

Tall pines of up to 60 feet in height highlight the play on a very good back nine, which culminates in a strong par-4 finishing hole that doglegs to the left. Towering spectator mounds line the right side of the fairway, and your approach shot must flirt with an oak-studded wetland.

Give this course another year or two to mature and it will easily take its place among the region's "must-plays."

Matanzas Woods Golf Club

398 Lakeview Dr., Palm Coast, FL 32137; phone (904) 446-6330
Tees: Championship: 6,985 yards, par-72, USGA rating 73.3, slope 132
Greens Fee: $40–66

Challenge: ★★★½	Golf Facilities: ★★★
Variety: ★★★½	14-Club Test ★★★½
Terrain: ★★★½	Intangibles: ★★★½
Beauty/Visual Appeal: ★★★½	Value: ★★★
Pace of Play: ★★★	

Description and Comments   Accessible to the public and to guests of the Palm Coast Resort is Matanzas Woods, an Arnold Palmer/Ed Seay layout that, as the name implies, plays through pine trees. Although some of the trees were lost in the devastating 1998 Florida forest fires, the course still lives up to its name. However, it is really water, in the form of the Jefferson Davis Waterway and Lake Success (an ironic name if we do say so), that really poses the challenge for your round. Water plays alongside holes and cuts in front of greens, and there is an abundance of sand bunkers guarding both fairways as well as the greens. Mantanzas Woods has no parallel fairways, so you can enjoy a splendid sense of isolation as you play here.

The par-5 14th (554 yards) is the hardest hole on the course, requiring a tee shot to a tight fairway guarded by Lake Success. It is this lake that you have to carry with your second shot to reach the well-guarded green. It is the final hole that is the most magnificent, however. Also a par-5, the 18th plays 529 yards and features a huge island green backed by sand traps and pine trees. If you hit a strong tee shot, you will be tempted to go for the green in two—it is reachable but requires a nearly perfect stroke. All in all, this course offers quite a challenge, but remains playable no matter what your skill level.

Radisson Ponce de Leon Golf and Conference Center

4000 U.S. Highway 1 N., St. Augustine, FL 32095; phone (888) 829-5314 or (904) 829-5314
Tees: Championship: 6,823 yards, par-72, USGA rating 72.9, slope 131
Greens Fee: $40–80

Challenge: ★★★

Variety: ★★★

Terrain: ★★★★

Beauty/Visual Appeal: ★★★½

Pace of Play: ★★★

Golf Facilities: ★★★

14-Club Test ★★★

Intangibles: ★★★½

Value: ★★★½

Description and Comments   Built in 1916 by the venerable Donald Ross, Ponce de Leon is one of the oldest courses in the area—although you certainly can't tell by the condition or design, as the course has been well maintained and the layout has been seamlessly updated over the years. Water is a common theme on the course, with sweeping views of marshland and the Intracoastal Waterway and water hazards on 14 of the 18 holes. The front nine is an open, links-style course, whereas the back nine plays through a forest of trees, mostly oaks draped with Spanish moss and magnolias. Greens on both sides tend to be very "Ross-like"—small and well-guarded by gaping sand bunkers. The 14th hole is one of the best par-5s in the area. Although it measures a relatively short 498 yards, it is considered by many, including the legendary Sam Snead, to be one of the most difficult par-5s they've ever played. The skinny fairway is edged with trees on the left and a large bunker on the right. Water guards the green, but it's hard to see until you're practically on top of it. Families are sure to enjoy the resort's 9-hole pitch and putt course, which offers yardages from 45 to 100 yards.

Ravines Golf and Country Club

2932 Ravines Rd., Middleburg, FL 32068; phone (904) 282-7888

Tees: Championship: 6,733 yards, par-72, USGA rating 72.4, slope 133

Greens Fee: $33–43

Challenge: ★★★½

Variety: ★★★★

Terrain: ★★★★

Beauty/Visual Appeal: ★★★★

Pace of Play: ★★★

Golf Facilities: ★★★

14-Club Test ★★★½

Intangibles: ★★★½

Value: ★★★★

Description and Comments   Ravines Golf Club may just be the biggest surprise in Florida, for it is located in what passes for a mountainous region, near Jacksonville along Black Creek. Mountains in Florida? Yes, you read correctly, mountains. Offering a nice alternative to the typical flat courses found throughout the state, Ravines challenges golfers with its many elevation changes and forced carries across ravines that plunge to 50 feet deep. In addition, heavily tree-lined fairways (many of which are doglegs), fast greens, and water on eight holes combine to test your game even further. The course's signature hole is the controversial but thrilling par-4 4th that plays 422 yards from the tips and requires you to cross a ravine on both your tee and approach shots.

Windsor Parke Golf Club

4747 Hodges Blvd., Jacksonville, FL 32224; phone (904) 233-4653

Tees: Championship: 6,740 yards, par-72, USGA rating 71.9, slope 133

Greens Fee: $47–55

Challenge: ★★★½   Golf Facilities: ★★★
Variety: ★★★   14-Club Test ★★★
Terrain: ★★★   Intangibles: ★★★½
Beauty/Visual Appeal: ★★★½ Value: ★★★★
Pace of Play: ★★★

Description and Comments   One of the best values in the area is Windsor Parke, an enjoyable Arthur Hills–designed course. The course plays through thick, tall pines and along a succession of lakes (water comes into play on 10 holes), creating a premium on accuracy. If you can keep the ball out of the woods and stay dry, you will likely find this course manageable. The greens tend to be small and mounded with up to four different tiers on the putting surface.

The backdrop of water and towering pines creates quite a few memorable holes. Among the best are the 13th and 16th. The former is a par-4 409-yarder that features water along the entire left-hand side of the fairway. The par-3 16th—one of the prettiest holes on the course—plays 194 yards from the tips and requires a tee shot over water to a boldly bunkered green. It's just one of a quartet of demanding par-3s at Windsor Parke.

A Panhandle Sampler

Bluewater Bay Resort

1950 Bluewater Blvd., Niceville, FL 32578; phone (850) 897-3241

Bluewater Bay is comprised of four nines that can be played in four different 18-hole combinations.

Tees:

Bay/Magnolia: 6,625 yards, par-72, USGA rating 71.8, slope 133

Lake/Marsh: 6,847 yards, par-72, USGA rating 73.4, slope 139

Magnolia/Lake: 6,792 yards, par-72, USGA rating 72.8, slope 136

Marsh/Bay: 6,680 yards, par-72, USGA ratin: 72.4, slope 136

Greens Fee: $30–40

Challenge: ★★★½	Golf Facilities: ★★★½
Variety: ★★★★	14-Club Test ★★★½
Terrain: ★★★½	Intangibles: ★★★½
Beauty/Visual Appeal: ★★★★	Value: ★★★★½
Pace of Play: ★★★	

Description and Comments Though you might consider stopping by Niceville for novelty's sake—"I've been to Niceville"—if you play Bluewater Bay, you will realize that Tom Fazio made sure that the golf here is much more than merely "nice." Fazio designed 27 of the 45 holes (the Bay, Lake, and Marsh nines); Jerry Pate added the Magnolia nine. Each of the courses has its own distinctive personality and character. As they say at Bluewater Bay, variety is the spice of life.

Each nine places a premium on accuracy and shotmaking, as many of the holes travel through thick pine forests and marshland, creating a beautiful but treacherous jail if you stray off the recommended path. On the Lake nine, the signature hole is the 3rd, a par-4, 420-yarder that plays to an elevated, slightly undulating green. A stream guards the entire left-hand side of the hole and then cuts in front of the green. The Bay course features awesome views of Choctawhatchee Bay. Bay and Lake are tighter than the resort's newer nines, Marsh and Magnolia. The Marsh nine also has grand views of the bay, but, as the name implies, has many holes that play through marshland. The hole you'll remember is the 4th, a shortish par-3 that plays to an island green and sports vistas of the bay beyond the green. The newest addition to Bluewater, the Magnolia course may be the prettiest nine, and is the most forgiving, with wider fairways.

Emerald Bay Golf Course

40001 Emerald Coast Parkway, Destin, FL 32541; phone (850) 837-5197
Tees: Championship: 6,802 yards, par-72, USGA rating 73.1, slope 135
Greens Fee: $40–75

Challenge: ★★★½	Golf Facilities: ★★★
Variety: ★★★½	14-Club Test ★★★★
Terrain: ★★★½	Intangibles: ★★★½
Beauty/Visual Appeal: ★★★★	Value: ★★★½
Pace of Play: ★★★	

Description and Comments When Robert Cupp was given the assignment to build Emerald Bay, he took stock of the courses in the area. What he found were many courses that challenged low handicappers, but mid- to higher-handicappers found themselves over their heads. So Cupp set out to build a course designed to entertain the middle-of-the-road golfer. What he created in our opinion is a course that is a fun and enjoyable course for all skill levels. Greens lean toward the small side, but many are rectangularly shaped and deceptively contoured. Notably, missing a green at Emerald Bay will usually mean you're left with a chip shot you can handle, rather than a vicious bunker recovery shot.

Emerald Bay, as the name implies, affords magnificent views of the beautiful green water of Choctaw Bay, but it also plays through an imposing forest. Both nines are appealing, but the back is the most amazing with magnificent postcard views of the bay. Make sure to purchase a yardage book, as it will provide invaluable insight into the hazards that are otherwise invisible off the tee. There are many holes on which you will want to lay up off the tee or you may find your seemingly well-stroked opening shot unplayable.

There are quite a few memorable holes, especially on the back nine. One of the best is the 10th, a relatively long par-4 that plays 455 yards from the tips with water hazards on the left side and forests on the right. And certainly, you'll not soon forget the attractive, 358-yard, par-4 14th hole, which demands a long carry off the tee over a pond laced with lily pads and cattails, followed by a short approach over another pond. Emerald Bay tends to stay in marvelous condition, especially the sugary-white sand bunkers, an added plus in the value department.

Hombre Golf Club

120 Coyote Pass, Panama City Beach, FL 32407; phone (850) 234-3673
Tees: Championship: 6,829 yards, par-72, USGA rating 73.4, slope 136
Greens Fee: $60–65

Challenge: ★★★½
Variety: ★★★½
Terrain: ★★★★
Beauty/Visual Appeal: ★★★½
Pace of Play: ★★

Golf Facilities: ★★★★
14-Club Test ★★★½
Intangibles: ★★★½
Value: ★★★

Description and Comments Hombre was host to Nike's Panama City Beach Classic in 1994 and 1995, helping to build its reputation as one of the better daily-fee courses in the Panhandle. The only problem with this notoriety is that the secret got out, and the course is now often crowded and slow play is the norm, especially during spring and summer. Beyond this pacing problem, Hombre offers golfers a challenging layout, particularly from the tips, and especially in the wind, as the course winds through 145 acres of lakes and dogwoods. Accuracy is paramount here as fairways are slender and water comes into play on 15 of the 18 holes. The 11th hole, a 166-yard par-3, is the signature hole. Your tee shot must carry water, and the smallish green is nearly completely surrounded by water. As if that weren't enough, a series of bunkers provide added protection.

Killearn Country Club and Inn

100 Tyron Circle, Tallahassee, FL 32308; phone (800) 476-4101 or (850) 893-2144

Comprised of three nines that play in three different 18-hole combinations.

Tees:

> East/North: 6,860 yards, par-72, USGA rating 73.1, slope 131
>
> North/South: 6,899 yards, par-72, USGA rating 73.3, slope 132
>
> South/East: 7,025 yards, par-72, USGA rating 73.9, slope 133

Greens Fee: $30–40

Challenge: ★★★½	Golf Facilities: ★★★½
Variety: ★★★	14-Club Test ★★★½
Terrain: ★★★	Intangibles: ★★★★
Beauty/Visual Appeal: ★★★	Value: ★★★½
Pace of Play: ★★★	

Description and Comments Killearn may lack some of the sizzle found on many of the newer courses, but don't disregard it—it still has quite a lot of kick left in it. In fact, the South/East combination was twice the site of the LPGA's Central Classic and the PGA Tour's Tallahassee Open for 18 years. The course has a definite Georgian feel: Moss-draped oaks guard the majority of fairways, creating some very cramped landing areas. Fairways tend to be rolling, with water coming into play on several holes throughout the three nines. From the tips, Killearn can pose a challenge for the low- to mid-handicapper while remaining enjoyable from the middle tees for higher handicappers.

Marcus Pointe

2500 Oak Pointe Dr., Pensacola, FL 32505; phone (800) 362-7287 or (850) 484-9770

Tees: Championship: 6,737 yards, par-72, USGA rating 72.3, slope 129

Greens Fee: $20–40

Challenge: ★★★	Golf Facilities: ★★★
Variety: ★★★	14-Club Test ★★★½
Terrain: ★★★½	Intangibles: ★★★½
Beauty/Visual Appeal: ★★★	Value: ★★★★½
Pace of Play: ★★★	

Description and Comments Located on 600 acres of rolling terrain and cut through oak and pine trees, Marcus Pointe is a beautiful course and one that just may be the best bargain in town. Unlike many of its neighboring courses, Marcus has minimal water that comes into play, although the Bayou Marcus Creek surrounds much of the layout. Not an overwhelming course, Marcus still manages to test the best as those competing in the 1991 and 1992 Ben Hogan Pensacola Opens found out. Especially challenging are the large, hard-to-read greens. The best hole on the course is the par-5 15th, which can be a real bear from the tips, playing 550 yards. The hole plays downhill as it bends slightly to the right. A yawning bunker lies 230 yards away and is often the recipient of many a tee shot. The green is elevated and guarded by a pond located on the right-hand side. If you have limited funds and are looking for a course that will challenge but not break the bank, head to Marcus Pointe.

The Moors

3220 Avalon Blvd., Milton, FL 32583; phone (850) 995-4653
Tees: Championship: 6,828 yards, par-70, USGA rating 72.9, slope 126
Greens Fee: $22–33

Challenge: ★★★
Variety: ★★★½
Terrain: ★★★
Beauty/Visual Appeal: ★★★
Pace of Play: ★★★

Golf Facilities: ★★★½
14-Club Test ★★★½
Intangibles: ★★★½
Value: ★★★★

Description and Comments   If you want to experience a little taste of what golf is like in Scotland, you should put The Moors on your "must-play" list. Just minutes from Pensacola, The Moors is a links-style course designed by John LaFoy, complete with moguls, sand, and exotic grasses, that has its roots in the land of golf's inception. The 10,000-square-foot clubhouse is modeled after Muirfield's, and many of the holes pay homage to classics across the pond, including the 3rd, the signature hole, a par-3 designed after Troon's "Postage Stamp" hole, and the 4th, an imitator of St. Andrews' famed "Road Hole."

Site of the Senior PGA Tour's Emerald Coast Classic and 1994's Nike Pensacola Classic, The Moors' wide-open fairways invite you to really belt it, but the deep pot bunkers ensure that this course is no pushover. While water only comes into play on six holes, there is a definite dearth of trees. Wetlands that are found on a handful of holes remind you that yes, you still are in the Panhandle.

Sandestin Resort, Baytowne Golf Course

9300 Highway 98 W., Destin, FL 32541; phone (850) 267-8155
Baytowne is comprised of three 9-hole courses (Dunes, Harbor, and Troon) that can be played in three different 18-hole combinations.

Tees: Dunes/Harbor: 6,890 yards, par-72, USGA rating 73.4, slope 127
Greens Fee: $65–90

Challenge: ★★★
Variety: ★★★
Terrain: ★★★½
Beauty/Visual Appeal: ★★★½
Pace of Play: ★★★

Golf Facilities: ★★★
14-Club Test ★★★½
Intangibles: ★★★
Value: ★★★

Description and Comments Though Sandestin Resort boasts three courses—Baytowne, Burnt Pines, and Links—Baytowne really is a true "resort course." Baytowne offers a layout that is challenging in its own right with water on many holes, but it is not overly penal, where treachery lurks on every hole. It is truly a course that you can relax and enjoy. Most memorable are its tee boxes perched atop relic dunes.

Until March 1999, Baytowne included a third nine, called "Troon," in addition to the Harbor and Dunes nine. Troon has since been partially abandoned, as it will be incorporated into the new design at Sandestin by Robert Trent Jones Jr., called the Raven at Sandestin, which is set to open sometime in 2000.

The Harbor nine is shorter than Dunes, but it also poses more threats as water comes into play on every hole. The hardest hole on Harbor is the par-5 9th, which plays 529 yards from the tips. The hole is a severe dogleg with water hugging both sides of the fairway and bunkers strategically placed in the prime landing zone. The Dunes nine has a number of memorable, water-infused holes. The par-5 6th is the most difficult hole on this side as it plays extremely long (586 yards), bends slightly to the left, and features an elevated green.

Shalimar Pointe Golf and Country Club

302 Country Club Rd., Shalimar, FL 32579; phone (800) 964-2833 or (850) 651-1416

Tees: Championship: 6,765 yards, par-72, USGA rating 72.9, slope 125
Greens Fee: $21–40

Challenge: ★★★
Variety: ★★★
Terrain: ★★★
Beauty/Visual Appeal: ★★★½
Pace of Play: ★★★

Golf Facilities: ★★★★
14-Club Test ★★★½
Intangibles: ★★★
Value: ★★★½

Description and Comments Shalimar has been around since 1968, but it was really the touch-up job by Pete Dye in 1985 that put it on the map. Dye added a number of waste bunkers and improved the water hazards—The result: a much more enjoyable and challenging layout. The course features rolling, tree-lined fairways and plays with a lovely backdrop of Choctawhatchee Bay—producing many "Kodak-worthy" views. Though the bay doesn't actually come into play, there are plenty of other water hazards to be found on the course. The signature hole is the par-3 11th, which plays 148 yards and requires a tee shot over water to an undulating green.

Tiger Point Golf and Country Club, East Course

1255 Country Club Rd., Gulf Breeze, FL 32561; phone (888) 218-8463 or (850) 932-1333

Tees: Championship: 7,033 yards, par-72, USGA rating 73.8, slope 132

Greens Fee: $38–48

Challenge: ★★★½

Variety: ★★★½

Terrain: ★★★½

Beauty/Visual Appeal: ★★★½

Pace of Play: ★★★½

Golf Facilities: ★★★

14-Club Test ★★★★

Intangibles: ★★★

Value: ★★★½

Description and Comments   Tiger Point has two 18s, but the East Course is the most interesting. Tiger Point East is a Jerry Pate design located on Santa Rosa Sound. Strategically deployed water hazards on 14 holes not only lend character to this links-style course but also add to its difficulty. Additional peril comes in the form of bunkers and breezes. The course's signature hole is the par-4 4th, which plays 390 yards to an island green. One of the more difficult (and at the same time fun) holes to play is the 539-yard, par-5 8th. The hole features two doglegs and requires you to carry a pond on your tee shot as well as a series of white, powdery sand traps. If you decide to cut the angle, the green can be reached in two. However, if you miss, you might be reaching the green in four.

Lodging in Northeast Florida

EXPENSIVE

Amelia Island Plantation

3000 First Coast Highway, Amelia Island, FL 32034; phone (888) 261-6161 or (904) 261-6161; www.aipfl.com; Rates: $245–546

The Plantation offers guests a wide variety of activities and accommodations at this extensive beachfront resort. A 1,300-acre development beautifully set among live-oak forests, marshes, and lagoons, the Plantation features 54 holes of golf and is truly one of America's greatest resort destinations for families.

There are two accommodation options at Amelia Island Plantation: The resort's hotel, called the Amelia Inn and Beach Club, or else condo and home rentals. The Amelia Inn is newly opened and offers 250 rooms. The rooms are nicely appointed and come with a balcony offering glorious ocean views. You will find the majority of housing at the Plantation resort in the many condo and home rentals that are located throughout the resort. These condos and homes range in size from one to three bedrooms and offer a living room, dining area, and fully equipped kitchen, with many having private balconies or patios as well as views of the ocean, marine forests, or tidal marshes.

As we have mentioned a few times already, the activities at this resort are one of the biggest draws for guests. Of course, there is the 54 holes of golf, but that is just the tip of the iceberg. Here's what else is on tap: a fabulous tennis center with 23 Har-Tru clay courts (site each April to the Bausch & Lomb Women's Tennis Championship); 21 pools; health club; racquetball; seven miles of nature trails for biking, walking, and jogging; boating and fishing; horseback riding; bicycle rental; and supervised kids' programs.

Golf Packages   Contact resort for details.

Ponte Vedra Beach Resorts

Ponte Vedra Inn & Club 200 Ponte Vedra Blvd., Ponte Vedra Beach, FL 32082; phone (800) 234-7842 or (904) 285-1111; www.pvresorts .com; Rates: $260–280

Ponte Vedra Lodge & Beach Club 607 Ponte Vedra Blvd., Ponte Vedra Beach, FL 32082; phone (800) 243-4304 or (904) 273-9500; www. pvresorts.com; Rates: $200–280

These resorts operated as separate entities until last year, when the Inn purchased the Lodge. This merger truly benefits the guests, as now they have access to both of the resorts' amenities. Each of the resorts is unique in its own right, but both have high levels of service and hospitality. The accommodations at these properties are superior to those at The Sawgrass Marriott, but there is a hitch. Guests of the Ponte Vedra Resorts have minimal access to the Sawgrass courses, which are really the crown jewels of the area.

Here is how it works: Guests of the Lodge have some reciprocity with Sawgrass, a carryover from when this resort operated independently, based on availability. The Inn has no reciprocity arrangement; however, guests can purchase an Associate Membership card for one year ($150–180) that does provide access to Sawgrass—greens fees are on top of this purchase.

So before you make your decision of where to stay, you must first decide how important the Sawgrass courses are to your itinerary as well as the likelihood of getting on Sawgrass via the reciprocity arrangement.

The Inn is the larger of the two properties with more than 200 rooms and suites located in nine low-rise buildings. Many of the airy rooms overlook the beach and the Atlantic Ocean. Kitchenettes are available based on availability.

The Lodge has 42 rooms and 24 suites, all of which have been recently updated with thoughtful touches, such as window seats and oversized Roman Jacuzzi tubs.

As we already mentioned, the Ponte Vedra Resorts boast a plethora of activities, including a superb children's program, 15 Har-Tru tennis courts (seven of which are lit), four pools (including a lap pool), expansive ocean-front fitness center, daily aerobic and aquacize classes, oceanfront Jacuzzi, steam room and sauna, the largest spa in Northern Florida, bicycling, sailing, fishing (fly casting lessons), lagoon activity (including paddleboat rentals), and riding stables nearby.

Golf Packages   There are a variety of golf packages available, which can be customized by the resorts' concierge. Here is a sample package: 3-night accommodations in oceanfront room; unlimited golf and cart usage; admission to daily 30-minute golf clinic; daily breakfast; range balls; club cleaning and storage; welcome gift; access to fitness center.

The Ritz-Carlton Amelia Island

4570 Amelia Island Parkway, Amelia Island, FL 32034; phone (800) 241-3333 or (904) 277-1100; www.ritzcarlton.com; Rates: $255–$305

This is arguably one of Florida's most elegant hotels and optimizes just what the "Ritz-Carlton experience" is all about. Everywhere you turn you will see the special Ritz-Carlton touches—from the handsomely decorated common rooms with beautiful crystal chandeliers, 18th- and 19th-century antiques, and amazing flower arrangements, to the wonderfully landscaped grounds. Then there is the excellent service—the Ritz is known for pampering, and this site is no exception. In other words, this is a typically wonderful Ritz-Carlton.

The Ritz features 449 guest rooms, including 61 clubrooms, 45 suites, 47 direct oceanfront rooms, and finally 296 coastal view rooms. All of the accommodations are roomy and feature luxurious, English-flavored furnishings. Each room has a private balcony overlooking the beach.

For those who would like a little more pampering, you should request one of the Ritz-Carlton clubrooms. These rooms are located on a special floor, accessible via a separate elevator key, and include such extra touches as an exclusive concierge and valet. There is also food, food, and more food—five servings a day, including a continental breakfast, mid-day snacks, afternoon tea, hors d'oeuvres, and finally, evening chocolates and cordials.

Although not on the level of The Plantation, The Ritz does feature a nice assortment of activities, including the following: nine hard and clay tennis courts (five lit for night play); fitness and recreation center; water aerobics; spa; pool and whirlpool; indoor whirlpool; bicycles; volleyball; and the Ritz Kids, a supervised kids' program.

Golf Packages   Contact resort for details.

Sawgrass Marriott Resort

100 PGA Blvd., Ponte Vedra Beach, FL 32082; phone (800) 457-4653 or (904) 285-7777; www.marriott.com/jaxsw; Rates: $195–245

While we would not call this resort lavish, it is still a superb place for a vacation for both golfers and nongolfers alike, especially conventioneers. As mentioned previously, the main draw of this resort is the access to the great golf courses, including the famed TPC Stadium Course. This is a wonderful resort for a family vacation, as there is something for everyone, including a stunner of a lobby filled with plants and water features.

The resort has a total of 508 guest rooms, including 24 suites and 80 two-bedroom villas. All rooms are spacious and well appointed and have the standard amenities.

Though golf is the main focus, there are a lot of other activities that should keep you busy, including 3 pools and 2 whirlpools; health club with exercise room, massage, facial, and sauna; 17 tennis courts with 4 different surfaces; cabana beach club; jogging and walking trails; miniature golf; horseback riding, fishing, and sailing; bicycle rentals, and children's programs.

Most memorable to the average guest are the unbelievably lush, landscaped grounds. The place practically assumes an "organized jungle" identity, replete with scores of birds and other wildlife, along with all manner of plants, trees, flowers, and shrubs.

Another advantage to staying at the hotel is the access it provides to another marvelous, gorgeous course, which is otherwise private: Marsh Landing Country Club. Even so, access is limited to certain weekdays; we feel more comfortable recommending courses where guests are welcome any day of the week.

Golf Packages Contact resort for details.

Vistana Resort at World Golf Village

100 Front Nine Dr., St. Augustine, FL 32092; phone (904) 940-2000; www.vistanainc.com; Rates: $79–169

The Vistana resort overlooks the 17th and 18th holes of the Slammer and Squire course and is comprised of spacious villas. The majority of these villas are two bedrooms/two baths (some one-bedroom villas are available) and can sleep up to eight people. The units are nicely equipped with a kitchen, spacious living room, dining room, washer/dryer, and a whirlpool in the master bathroom.

At the resort, guests have access to pools, whirlpool, fitness center, tennis, volleyball, and basketball courts.

Golf Packages Packages are available—contact resort for details.

World Golf Village Resort Hotel

500 South Legacy Trail, St. Augustine, FL 32092; phone (904) 940-8000; www.wgv.com; Rates: $99 and up

The World Golf Village is a golfer's dream come true—yes, an amusement park dedicated to golf. While you won't find any roller coasters, you will find the Golf Hall of Fame, a museum dedicated to the game, an 18-hole championship course, and superior accommodations. First off, there is the World Golf Village Resort Hotel, which is a more mainstream lodging option.

The hotel is comprised of 300 rooms and suites in a ten-story building, the focal point of which is a lovely atrium. The rooms are extremely well appointed, with many of them having a balcony with a view of the surrounding village. Located in the atrium is the Cypress Pointe restaurant, which serves breakfast, lunch, and dinner (see Dining for more details).

Besides its obvious proximity to the World Golf Village, the resort has quite a few amenities of its own, including a 24-hour fitness center, massages, outdoor pool, whirlpool, golf swing analyzer, bicycle rentals, access to tennis courts at Vistana Resort, walking and jogging trails, and a children's program.

Golf Packages   The hotel offers a wide variety of golf packages including "The Green": deluxe accommodations, two rounds of golf on the Slammer and Squire course, complimentary club storage, 10% merchandise discount at the PGA Tour Stop and the Slammer and Squire Pro Shop, admission to the World Golf Hall of Fame and IMAX theater, upgrade to a suite for only $50 more, and preferred tee times confirmed 90 days in advance.

MODERATE

Comfort Inn Oceanfront

1515 N. First St., Jacksonville Beach, FL 32250; phone (800) 228-5150 or (904) 241-2311; www.comfortinn.com; Rates: $79–159

As the name implies, this hotel is located on the beach and features 180 rooms, each of which has a private balcony with ocean views. This hotel is a terrific value, with rooms that are more than adequate. In addition, there is a nice pool with a rock grotto, a deli, and a gym.

Elizabeth Pointe Lodge

98 S. Fletcher Ave., Amelia Island, FL 32034; phone (800) 228-5150 or (904) 241-2311; www.ameliaisland.com/pix/netscape/elzbth2.htm; Rates: $110–195

The Elizabeth Pointe Lodge is comprised of three separate buildings with a total of 26 rooms. The Main House has 20 rooms and suites with turn-of-the-century furnishings, including oversized marble tubs. The Harris Lodge has four larger rooms that include a separate sitting room. Finally, there is the Miller Cottage with two bedrooms and two baths. Guests receive a complimentary breakfast, newspaper delivered to each room, beach privileges, and bicycles.

Radisson Ponce de Leon Golf and Conference Resort

4000 U.S. Highway 1 N., St. Augustine, FL 32095; phone (800) 333-3333 or (904) 824-2821; www.radisson.com; Rates: $119–199

St. Augustine's oldest golf resort encompasses 350 acres of lush grounds and marshland. On the lodging side, the resort has 193 rooms and suites, which are tastefully appointed, but the real attraction of this property is what lies outside. First and foremost is the easy access to the Donald Ross–designed golf course, plus six tennis courts, volleyball, croquet, badminton, shuffleboard, horseshoes, pool, and jogging track.

Golf Package The Radisson offers the "Getaway Golf Package," consisting of deluxe accommodations, unlimited greens fees for three days, cart fees, daily range balls, and breakfast.

St. Francis Inn Bed & Breakfast

279 St. George St., St. Augustine, FL 32084; phone (800) 824-6062 or (904) 824-6068; www.francisinn.com; Rates: $75–179 (standard rooms), $149–195 (cottage)

Located in the St. Augustine's historic district, St. Francis Inn has a storied past of its own. Constructed in 1791, St. Francis was a role player in Southern history—the Civil War and slave uprisings just to name a couple of noteworthy events. Today, it is a little more sedate at St. Francis. The inn features rooms, suites, an apartment, and one five-room cottage for its guests to choose from, all of which are decorated in distinctive styles with some having fireplaces, kitchenettes, and whirlpool tubs.

Guests receive complimentary breakfast, use of bicycles, evening social hour with complimentary beverages and treats, and admission to the Oldest House, see Activities in Northeast Florida, below.

INEXPENSIVE

Comfort Suites

475 Commerce Lake Dr., St. Augustine, FL 32095; phone (800) 228-5050 or (904) 940-9500; Rates: $59–129; Built: 1999

Hampton Inn

2549 Sadler Rd., Fernandina Beach, FL 32034; phone (800) 426-7866 or (904) 321-1111; Rates: $89–109; Built: 1997; Renovations: None

Radisson Riverwalk Hotel

1515 Prudential Dr., Jacksonville, FL 33207; phone (800) 333-3333 or (904) 396-5100; Rates: $60–100; Built: 1984; Renovations: 1998

Sea Turtle Inn

1 Ocean Blvd., Jacksonville Beach, FL 32233; phone (800) 874-6000 or (904) 249-7402; Rates: $60–100; Built: 1974; Renovations: 1999

Dining in Northeast Florida

Amelia Inn Dining Room Amelia Island Plantation, 3000 First Coast Hwy., Amelia Island; phone (888) 261-6161 or (904) 261-6161. Continental; Expensive; Reservations recommended. The Plantation's most elegant restaurant serving breakfast, lunch, dinner, and Sunday buffet. Fine regional cuisine choices complemented by striking ocean views.

Augustine Room Sawgrass Marriott Resort, 100 PGA Blvd., Ponte Vedra Beach; phone (800) 457-4653 or (904) 285-7777. American; Expensive; Reservations recommended. A romantic restaurant serving excellent grilled seafood and steaks.

Beech Street Grill 801 Beech St., Fernandina Beach; phone (904) 277-3662. Seafood; Expensive; Reservations recommended. Located in an 1889 building, once a sea captain's home, this restaurant offers memorable atmosphere and an excellent menu. Favorite items include crab-stuffed shrimp and roasted venison—a good wine list, too.

The Café The Ritz-Carlton, 4570 Amelia Island Pkwy., Amelia Island; phone (800) 241-3333 or (904) 277-1100. Varied; Moderate; Reservations suggested. Featuring everything from seafood to Southwest cuisine in a beautiful setting. If you like shrimp you should try the Mayport shrimp with tomato basil sauce. Serving breakfast, lunch, and dinner. Fitness menu is available.

Café on the Green Sawgrass Marriott Resort, 100 PGA Blvd., Ponte Vedra Beach; phone (800) 457-4653 or (904) 285-7777. American; Modest; Reservations accepted. Outstanding views of the 13th hole of the TPC's Stadium Course—serving traditional American favorites for breakfast, lunch, and dinner.

Champs of Aviles 8 Aviles St., St. Augustine; phone (904) 826-8960. Continental; Moderate–Expensive; Reservations required. A local favorite not only for its intimate atmosphere but also for its fine menu. Some of the best items: crab cakes, chicken stuffed with spinach. Bring your own wine or beer.

Conch House   57 Comazes Ave., St. Augustine; phone (904) 829-8646. Caribbean; Moderate; Reservations accepted. Beautiful waterfront spot that features tropical drinks, breezy atmosphere, and a variety of conch-related items. Cracked conch and conch chowder are specialties.

Crawdaddy's   1643 Prudential Dr., Jacksonville; phone (904) 396-3546. American; Inexpensive; Reservations not needed. Mouth-watering Cajun selections at this waterfront restaurant.

Cypress Pointe   World Golf Village Resort Hotel, 500 South Legacy Trail, St. Augustine; phone (888) 446-5301 or (904) 940-8000. Eclectic gourmet; Expensive; Reservations required. Lovely setting in the atrium of the hotel as tall plants surround diners. Our favorite menu item: duck.

Dolphin Depot   704 N. First St., Jacksonville Beach; phone (904) 270-1424. Low Country; Modest; Reservations accepted. Located in a converted gas station, this restaurant is intimate and is decorated in an art deco theme. Try the salmon on a plank.

Florida House Inn   20–22 S. 3rd St., Fernandina Beach; phone (904) 261-3300. American; Inexpensive; Reservations accepted for parties of six or more. This restaurant serves food in boarding house style, including specialties of the house: fried chicken and Southern-style veggies.

The Florida Room   Ponte Vedra Inn & Club, 200 Ponte Vedra Blvd., Ponte Vedra Beach; phone (800) 234-7842 or (904) 285-1111. American; Moderate; Reservations accepted. Casual yet comfortable seaside dining featuring tasty local seafood selections.

The Grill   The Ritz-Carlton, 4570 Amelia Island Pkwy., Amelia Island; phone (800) 241-3333 or (904) 277-1100. Continental; Expensive; Reservations recommended. The Ritz's signature restaurant, The Grill offers guests a wonderful menu in an intimate and charming atmosphere. Arched picture windows provide sweeping views of the ocean, and a piano sets the tone of the meal. As far as dining goes, you will not be disappointed with your selection. Emphasis is on seafood; the pan-roasted prawns are wonderful. Good wine selection. Jackets required.

Gypsy Cab Company   135 Avenida Menendez, St. Augustine; phone (904) 824-8244. Varied American; Inexpensive–Moderate; Reservations accepted for parties of five or more. There's a lot more to this restaurant than just a fun name—it has an extremely varied menu of great selections, too. Everything from pork chops to shrimp with an artichoke sauté to Thai stir fry. Word of warning: This place is very popular, so expect a wait.

Homestead   1712 Beach Blvd., Jacksonville; phone (904) 249-5240. Southern; Inexpensive; Reservations accepted. Serving dinner and Sunday brunches, this restaurant has great down-home cooking—if you like chicken, make sure to order the chicken and dumplings.

La Parisienne 60 Hypolita St., St. Augustine; phone (904) 829-0055. French; Moderate; Reservations essential. A tiny restaurant that has grown in reputation as well as popularity. The menu is straight out of Paris—make sure to leave room for dessert.

Ragtime Tavern and Seafood Grille 207 Atlantic Blvd., Jacksonville; phone (904) 241-7877. American; Moderate; Reservations recommended. A New Orleans–themed restaurant that tends to be busy and noisy, but still worth the hassle. Our favorite menu item: key lime lobster over linguine.

Raintree 102 San Marco Ave., St. Augustine; phone (904) 824-7211. Seafood; Inexpensive; Reservations accepted. Located in the oldest home in the historic district, the atmosphere tends to be more the draw than the food. It is worth the visit just to see the restoration that has taken place.

Salt Water Cowboy 299 Dondanville Rd., St. Augustine; phone (904) 471-2332. Local cuisine; Inexpensive; Reservations not accepted. Located in a former fish camp, this restaurant serves many local specialties, including alligator and jambalaya.

The Seafoam Room Ponte Vedra Inn & Club, 200 Ponte Vedra Blvd., Ponte Vedra Beach; phone (800) 234-7842 or (904) 285-1111. Continental; Expensive; Reservations recommended. Elegant, airy atmosphere with fabulous ocean views. Varied menu and wine list accompanied by romantic piano music.

The Verandah Restaurant Amelia Island Plantation, 3000 First Coast Hwy., Amelia Island; phone (888) 261-6161 or (904) 261-6161. Seafood; Moderate–Expensive; Reservations accepted. A charming setting serving casual dinners with emphasis on local seafood offerings. Nice for a change of pace

West River 1171 S. Englewood Ave., Jacksonville; phone (904) 389-4171. Continental; Expensive; Reservations recommended. A popular Jacksonville restaurant with rotating art displays. Favorite dish: veal chop sautéed with shiitake mushrooms.

The Wine Cellar 1314 Prudential Dr., Jacksonville; phone (904) 398-8989. Continental; Expensive; Reservations recommended. One of Jacksonville's top restaurants, The Wine Cellar is awfully charming and has an acclaimed menu. As you may have guessed, there is an extensive wine list with more than 7,000 choices.

Activities in Northeast Florida

The Amelia Island Historic District An area that contains over 400 structures, many of which are on the National Register of Historic Places and date to the early part of the century. A great way to spend an afternoon as you stroll through history.

Amelia Island Lighthouse   1 Lighthouse Lane; phone (904) 261-3248. Built in 1839, this is one of the more recognizable landmarks of northern Florida. Although not open to the public, it is worth stopping by.

Castillo de San Marcos National Monument   1 Castillo Dr.; phone (904) 829-6506. Originally this was a fort built more than 300 years ago by the Spanish to protect St. Augustine from the British. It then was used as a prison during both the Revolutionary and Civil Wars. Today it has a much more sedate atmosphere, with park rangers giving tours and visitors exploring the moat, turrets, and grounds.

Fort Clinch State Park   North 14th Street; phone (904) 277-7274. The 1,086-acre state park is located on the tip of Amelia Island and is the site of trails, beaches, as well as Fort Clinch, a 19th-century stronghold built to deter further English incursion after the War of 1812. The park rangers wear Civil War uniforms, and on the first full weekend of each month re-create a Civil War encampment. Every Saturday, there are candlelit tours.

Fort Caroline National Memorial   12713 Fort Caroline Rd., Jacksonville; phone (904) 641-7155. A re-creation of an original 16th-century fort is located at this 130-acre park along the St. Johns River (13 miles northeast of downtown Jacksonville). A great place to spend some time, have a picnic, and walk along the hiking trails.

Jacksonville Zoo   8605 Zoo Rd., Jacksonville; phone (904) 757-4462. Located north of the city, this zoo originally opened in 1914, but has recently undergone a huge upgrade. Visitors can now see more than 600 animals in their natural habitat.

Kathryn Abbey Hanna Park   500 Wonderwood Dr., Mayport; phone (904) 249-4700. One of the nicest parks in the area, located just south of Mayport, with a beautiful white-sand beach, fishing in a freshwater lake, hiking along trails, swimming, and picnic areas.

Kingsley Plantation   11676 Palmetto Ave., Fort George; phone (904) 251-3537. Built in 1798, Kingsley, located on the northern end of Fort George, is the oldest plantation house in Florida. Visitors can explore the restored main home as well as the 23 slave cabins near the entrance.

Museum of Science and History   1025 Museum Circle, Jacksonville; phone (904) 396-7061. A great place to take your children for the hands-on Kidspace program as well as a 3-D laser show in the planetarium.

Oldest House   14 St. Francis St.; phone (904) 824-2872. The oldest house in the area dating back more than 300 years.

Oldest Wooden Schoolhouse   14 St. George St.; phone (904) 824-0192. As the name indicates, this is purportedly America's oldest wooden schoolhouse. Whether or not it's true, it is worth your time. The structure was built in the 18th century and is constructed out of cypress and cedar and held together with wooden pins and cast-iron spikes.

Spanish Quarter Museum   33 St. George St.; phone (904) 825-6830. A very informative museum that gives visitors insight into the 18th-century lifestyles. Demonstrations by a blacksmith are a highlight.

Tours of St. Augustine's Historic District   Horse-drawn carriages or miniature tourist trains are a great way to see the main sights in St. Augustine's historic district and learn about the history of the area. Both depart from Avenida Menendez.

World Golf Village   21 World Golf Place; phone (800) 948-4746. Finally, a museum golfers can sink their teeth into. Loaded with exhibits on the game's history and legends as well as the Hall of Fame, the World Golf Village is all golf all the time.

The 19th Hole in Northeast Florida

The 19th Hole   Ponte Vedra Inn & Club, 200 Ponte Vedra Blvd., Ponte Vedra Beach; phone (800) 234-7842 or (904) 285-1111. As the name indicates, this is the place to go after your round at the Ponte Vedra resort courses.

Beach Club Grill   Amelia Island Plantation, 3000 First Coast Hwy., Amelia Island; phone (888) 261-6161 or (904) 261-6161. Nice place for an after-dinner drink or a couple of games of pool.

Café on the Square   1974 San Marco Blvd., Jacksonville; phone (904) 399-4422. Live blues, jazz, and rock, Tuesday through Sunday.

Champs Lounge Green   Sawgrass Marriott Resort, 100 PGA Blvd., Ponte Vedra Beach; phone (800) 457-4653 or (904) 285-7777. Good place to celebrate your Sawgrass experience—nightly entertainment and dancing.

Cypress Pointe Lounge   World Golf Village Resort Hotel, 500 South Legacy Trail; phone (888) 446-5301 or (904) 940-8000. A relaxing atmosphere to unwind and grab a libation.

Grill Lounge   The Ritz-Carlton, 4570 Amelia Island Pkwy., Amelia Island; phone (800) 241-3333 or (904) 277-1100. An elegant site for an after-dinner drink.

Palace Saloon   113 Centre St., Amelia Island; phone (904) 261-6320. Florida's oldest tavern, where the likes of the Vanderbilts, DuPonts, and Carnegies used to hoist a few.

The Seahorse Lounge   Ponte Vedra Inn & Club, 200 Ponte Vedra Blvd., Ponte Vedra Beach; phone (800) 234-7842 or (904) 285-1111. Ponte Vedra's site for live nightly entertainment.

TPC Grill   110 TPC Blvd., Ponte Vedra Beach, FL 32082; phone (904) 273-3235. Superior setting just off the pro shop at one of America's greatest courses. Big screen TV and Players Championship memorabilia add to the ambience.

Lodging in The Panhandle

EXPENSIVE

Marriott's Bay Point Resort

4200 Marriott Dr., Panama City, FL 32408; phone (800) 874-7105 or (850) 234-3307; www.marriotthotels.com; Rates: $139–179

Another distinguished Marriott Resort, Bay Point offers a combination of elegance and user-friendly amenities. The hotel has 355 guest rooms, all of which are nicely decorated with Queen Anne furnishings, whereas the public rooms have more of an English estate feel with wing-back chairs and Oriental rugs. Rooms feature either a Gulf or a golf course view.

Bay Point is never boring. Besides the two golf courses, the resort offers three pools, a whirlpool, 12 tennis courts, a health club, jogging trails, croquet, a dock, boating, jet skiing, fishing, and children's programs. There are four restaurants at the resort: Bayview, serving American cuisine for breakfast, lunch, and dinner in a casual setting overlooking the bay; Stormy's Grille, for lunch; Stormy's Steakhouse, for dinner (both Stormy's restaurants have beautiful views of the bay and golf course); and Teddy Tucker's Beach Club, serving hot dogs, hamburgers, and sandwiches for lunch and dinner.

Golf Packages   Contact the resort for package information.

Sandestin Beach Resort

9300 U.S. 98 W., Destin, FL 32541; phone (800) 277-0800 or (850) 267-8000; www.sandestin.com; Rates: $70–140 (inn); $115–230 (two-bedroom villas)

A jewel along the Panhandle, Sandestin offers its visitors many choices. First off, guests must select the type and location of their accommodation. The resort is comprised of a traditional hotel with 175 well-furnished rooms. There are also 425 villas, which range in size from one to three bedrooms in a variety of different locations: a high-rise tower overlooking the Gulf of Mexico, a mainstream location on the beach or the bay, a secluded location on a golf course, or on a lagoon.

Once you have made your accommodation decision, you must decide how to spend your day. Will it be at one of the three golf courses or at the award-winning tennis facility featuring 16 courts with 3 different surfaces, including some rare grass courts? Also available are a health club, a magnificent beach, bicycles, a marina with boating activities and deep-sea fishing, and children's programs. New for 2000 will be a Robert Trent Jones Jr.–designed course called the Raven Golf Club at Sandestin, which promises to be a sensational addition to the resort's existing tracks.

On the dining side you can choose from two fine restaurants: The Sunset Bay Café, overlooking the bay with a relaxed, tropical setting, and The Elephant Walk, which is located on the beach and features artifacts from around the world (see Dining in the Panhandle, below).

Golf Packages   Contact the resort for details on golf packages.

MODERATE

Bluewater Bay Resort

1950 Bluewater Blvd., Niceville, FL 32578; phone (800) 874-2128 or (850) 897-3613; www.bwbresort.com; Rates: $93–155 (one-bedroom villa)

Located among 1,800 acres of pines and oaks along the shores of Choctawhatchee Bay, Bluewater is a resort that offers guests villa-style accommodations in a multitude of settings. The villas range in size from studios to three bedrooms, many with kitchenettes and patios. Guests can select from "Waterfall," "Golf," "Bayside," or "Garden" locations.

The resort gains its reputation as a fine destination not only for its accommodations but for its activities: 36 holes of golf; 19 tennis courts, a marina with a full menu of boating amenities, four pools, biking and hiking trails, and playground areas.

Golf Packages   The resort offers multiple golf packages, including the Eagle Package—three-night minimum stay, unlimited greens fees, club cleaning/storage, cart for 36 holes, guaranteed second tee time, range balls, and golf gift.

Edgewater Beach Resort

11212 Front Beach Rd., Panama City Beach, FL 32407; phone (800) 874-8686 or (805) 235-4044; www.edgewaterbeachresort.com; Rates: $80–200 (one-bedroom condo); $85–150 (two-bedroom villa); $130–225 (three-bedroom villa)

A Polynesian-themed resort, both inside and out, that offers guests lavish condominiums and villas that are elegantly furnished. The 520 units are spread out around the complex's 110 acres, and guests can choose either a golf course location or a beachside tower.

Speaking of the golf course, Edgewater has a 9-hole executive course, but don't select this resort hoping to get quick access to an 18-hole beauty. The resort does have a lot of other activities in addition to the golf course, such as 12 tennis courts, shuffleboard, beach activities, and a gym, but the big draw is the 11,500-square-foot lagoon pool area.

Perdido Sun

13753 Perdido Key Dr., Pensacola, FL 32507; phone (800) 227-2390 or (805) 492-2390; Rates: $100–200

A high-rise building that offers guests one- to three-bedroom condominiums from which to choose. All units have seaside balconies and feature marvelous ocean views. Activities at the Perdido Sun include indoor and outdoor pool, spa, and health club.

INEXPENSIVE

Village Inn of Destin

215 U.S. 98 E., Destin, FL 32541; phone (850) 837-7413; Rates: $45–80; Built: 1983; Renovations: 1998

Dining in The Panhandle

Bay View Restaurant   Marriott Bay Point Hotel, 4200 Marriott Dr., Panama City; phone (800) 874-7105 or (850) 234-3307. American; Moderate; Reservations accepted. A casual restaurant overlooking the bay serving everything from salads to pasta to hamburgers.

Elephant Walk   Sandestin Resort, 9300 U.S. 98 W., Destin; phone (800) 277-0800 or (850) 267-8000. Continental; Expensive; Reservations recommended. A beachfront location and decorations of treasures from around the world provide the atmosphere. The chef provides a scrumptious menu that concentrates on seafood specialties, including pan-fried jumbo softshell crabs and grouper.

Jubilee   500 Quietwater Beach Rd., Gulf Breeze; phone (850) 934-3108. Seafood; Moderate; Reservations accepted for the upstairs section only. A great site for seafood.

McGuires Irish Pub   600 E. Gregory St., Pensacola; phone (850) 433-6789. Irish/American; Inexpensive–Moderate; Reservations not accepted. Located in an old firehouse, McGuires is a favorite of tourists and locals alike. Steaks and hamburgers are the most popular menu items.

Marina Café   404 U.S. 98 E., Destin; phone (850) 837-7960. Seafood; Moderate–Expensive; Reservations accepted. A superior menu and an extensive wine list complement a beautiful harbor setting. Our recommendations: almond herb-crusted mahi mahi and pepper-crusted yellowfin tuna.

Stormy's Steakhouse   Marriott Bay Point Hotel, 4200 Marriott Dr., Panama City; phone (800) 874-7105 or (850) 234-3307. Steak and Seafood; Expensive; Reservations recommended. The hotel's fine dining restaurant specializing in steaks, though some seafood entrees are also available. Restaurant overlooks the bay and golf course.

Activities in The Panhandle

Bicycle Rentals   Bob's Bike Center, 415 Mary Esther Cutoff, Ft. Walton; phone (850) 243-5856.

Big Kahuna's Lost Paradise   U.S. 98 E., Destin; phone (850) 837-4061. During the summer, the big draw is the water park, but there are also year-round attractions that are great for kids, including miniature golf, go-carts, and a kiddy land.

Boat Charters   East Pass Charters, East Pass Marina, 288 U.S. 98 E., Destin; phone (850) 654-2022. Deep-sea fishing as well as cruising rentals.

Canoe Rentals   Econofina Creek Canoe Livery, Strickland Rd., Panama City; phone (850) 722-9032. Take a trip down Florida's best canoe trail.

Fort Pickens   1400 Fort Pickens Rd., Santa Rosa Island; phone (850) 934-2635. Completed in 1834, this fort was built to defend Pensacola Bay. The most famous resident was Geronimo, who was imprisoned here.

Fountain of Youth Archeological Park   155 Magnolia Ave., St. Augustine; phone (904) 829-3168. A 21-acre park where Ponce de Leon found the natural spring that is alleged to turn back the clocks. Along with the main attraction, you'll find a planetarium as well as a Native American burial ground and an exhibit on Timucuan Indians.

Gulf World   15412 Front Beach Rd., Panama City; phone (850) 234-5271. Home to a variety of sea creatures, such as dolphins, sea lions, and otters.

Indian Temple Mound and Museum   139 Miracle Strip Pkwy., Fort Walton; phone (850) 833-9595. A great site for children who can learn all about the prehistoric people who inhabited the area over 10,000 years ago.

National Museum of Naval Aviation   1750 Radford Blvd., Pensacola; phone (850) 452-2311. Highlights include more than 150 aircraft of varying ages, a 14-seat flight simulator, and an IMAX theater featuring Blue Angels footage.

The 19th Hole in The Panhandle

Governor's Attic Sandestin Resort, 9300 U.S. 98 W., Destin; phone (800) 277-0800 or (850) 267-8000. Second-story location provides great views of the shore below.

Stormy's Marriott Bay Point Hotel, 4200 Marriott Dr., Panama City; phone (800) 874-7105 or (850) 234-3307. Though there is a more conventional 19th hole at the golf course, you should head back here, where the views of the bay and golf course are spectacular.

Part Ten

Central Florida

Overview

If you have kids or are a kid at heart, central Florida means one thing: Walt Disney World. If you're a golfer at heart, central Florida means not only Disney World but also a slew of magnificent public and semiprivate courses. In fact, the central section of Florida has the largest collection of public-access courses in the state and ranks in the top five for the whole country.

For this book we have defined central Florida as the area stretching from greater Orlando in the east to Tampa/St. Petersburg/Sarasota in the west. Orlando is no doubt the state's tourism capital with a mind-boggling array of theme parks, but it was not always the beehive of activity it is today. Orlando basically didn't exist until the 1835 Seminole Indian War, when it served as a campground for soldiers. It then became a trading post until 1857 when the county assumed ownership and since then has been on a steady growth path. When the Kennedy Space Center was built in nearby Cocoa Beach in 1967, Orlando was officially on the map.

Everything changed when Walt Disney moved in. In the 1960s, Disney started purchasing every available parcel of land in and around Orlando without anyone knowing what he was up to. By 1971 everyone knew what he was up to, as a mouse, a sleeping beauty, and seven dwarfs descended on the scene. Fast forward: Today, Disney World is spread out over 28,000 acres, employs more than 35,000 people, and is comprised of four separate theme parks (the Magic Kingdom, Epcot, Disney-MGM Studios, and Disney's Animal Kingdom). It's safe to say that Disney's theory was correct: If you build the right attraction, visitors to Florida will flock to a land-locked destination rather than automatically heading to the beaches.

The unspoken golden golf rule is that golf vacations and family vacations don't mesh. Orlando is the exception to this rule. While you are out enjoying your happiest place on earth—the first tee at one of the area's fine golf

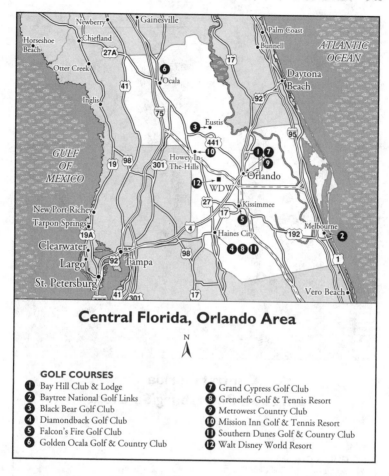

Central Florida, Orlando Area

N

GOLF COURSES

❶ Bay Hill Club & Lodge
❷ Baytree National Golf Links
❸ Black Bear Golf Club
❹ Diamondback Golf Club
❺ Falcon's Fire Golf Club
❻ Golden Ocala Golf & Country Club

❼ Grand Cypress Golf Club
❽ Grenelefe Golf & Tennis Resort
❾ Metrowest Country Club
❿ Mission Inn Golf & Tennis Resort
⓫ Southern Dunes Golf & Country Club
⓬ Walt Disney World Resort

facilities—your offspring can visit the official "Happiest Place on Earth." While you are negotiating your way through a series of water hazards, your kids are at a local water park. As you punch your way out of a sand trap, your kids are building sand castles at the hotel's man-made beaches. The beauty of Orlando as a golf vacation spot is its flexibility: You can fill every minute of every day for a whole week, or you can kick back and do practically nothing. Also, for you night owls, there is as much to do in the evening as there is during the day.

Eighty-four miles southwest of Orlando lies Tampa, Florida's third-largest city and one of the state's premier resort destinations. Tampa, which is a Native American word for "sticks of fire," is the center for western Florida's business and vacation activity. The terrain in the Tampa area varies

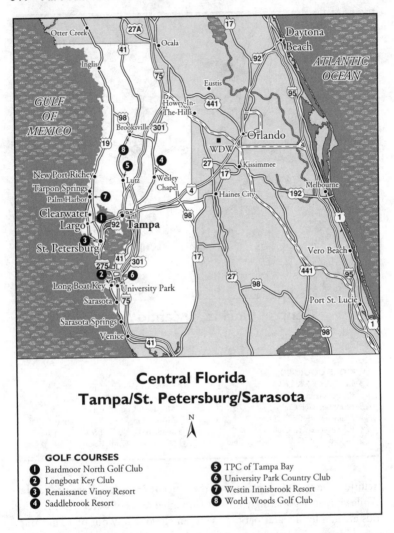

Central Florida
Tampa/St. Petersburg/Sarasota

N

GOLF COURSES

1 Bardmoor North Golf Club
2 Longboat Key Club
3 Renaissance Vinoy Resort
4 Saddlebrook Resort

5 TPC of Tampa Bay
6 University Park Country Club
7 Westin Innisbrook Resort
8 World Woods Golf Club

from hilly pockets that cut through pine forests to cardboard-flat, white sand beaches. Tampa, along with St. Petersburg (21 miles west of Tampa) and Clearwater (12 miles north of St. Petersburg), comprise the Golden Triangle, an area that became famous for its sensational beaches, outstanding sport fishing, and excellent professional baseball spring training games. Today, these attractions continue to entice many visitors, but it is the outstanding golf courses and resorts that have been garnering much of the recent attention.

If you travel some 70 miles south of Tampa, you will arrive at Sarasota, a city that gained fame as being the winter home of John Ringling of Ringling

Brothers Circus fame. Though you will find many fine restaurants and fun activities in Sarasota, it is really Longboat Key, located between Sarasota Bay and the Gulf of Mexico, that is of real importance to us—this is where the best golfing in the area is. Though only 11 miles long, Longboat Key is home to a wonderful resort and some of the area's most scenic golf courses.

Where it comes to gaining access to Orlando's best courses, the city is somewhat unique because almost all of them are open for some sort of public play. However, in many cases access is limited to guests of a particular resort.

In midwinter frost delays are not uncommon early in the morning, but they occur much more frequently near Orlando than they would on the Gulf Coast, where warm waters help to boost nighttime temperatures. Therefore, when in doubt, try to schedule your Orlando tee times for midmorning in winter; that way, even if there is a lengthy frost delay, you'll still be able to complete your round. To that end, because there's minimal daylight in winter, if you and your buddies are fanatical golfers who want to squeeze in 36 holes a day, you're better off being on the coast or to the south.

WHEN TO GO AND WHAT IT WILL COST

Central Florida offers visiting golfers excellent winter weather, as good as nearly anywhere in the country in midwinter except for the southernmost part of the state. Spring and fall tend to be magnificent. Summers can be almost unbearably hot and humid with afternoons often punctuated by severe thunderstorms. However, if you can get out early in the morning before it gets too warm, you will find the golf courses far less crowded than you would at other times of the year.

Along with your golf clubs, we recommend that you pack some serious cash as well. Though this area doesn't compare with Hawaii or California on the high-dollar meter, this region of Florida, especially Orlando, tends to be on the high side of the money scale. Thus, you can find yourself whipping through a number of Ben Franklins in a short amount of time. There are some money-saving scenarios you might want to consider. Most of the resorts offer excellent packages that combine accommodations and golf, but can also include other activities, such as visits to the local theme parks. If you are traveling with your family, you might consider a condo or villa option where you can prepare some of your own meals; you will find that the restaurants here are also rather pricey, though there's more than enough fast food joints to satisfy any craving. Also, if your visit will include a trip to Disney World, purchase a super saver pass. Finally, the summer months offer the best deals at both resorts and the area golf courses. If you can brave the sweltering conditions, you will find the best bargains.

Orlando is the most popular residence for PGA Tour players because of its fine airport, wonderful climate, quality golf facilities, and Florida's lack of a personal income tax. Pros like Tiger Woods, Mark O'Meara, Lee Janzen, Nick Faldo, and Ernie Els hang out mostly at such private enclaves as Isleworth and Lake Nona, but you never know when you'll run into one of these golf celebrities at a restaurant or grocery store. In fact, if you're a guest of the Bay Hill Club & Lodge, you may even get a chance to spy The King himself, Arnold Palmer. It's not hard: Every day Arnie's at home, he puts in at least an appearance at his beloved Bay Hill.

WHAT TO BRING

First and foremost, you will want to have plenty of all-purpose sunscreen and bug spray in your suitcase. Florida surely is the sunshine and bug capital of the United States, so don't be stingy when slathering on protection. Beyond that, we suggest that you pack a rain jacket no matter what time of year (the thunderstorms in summer can be drenching), as well as a light sweater for all seasons but summer. If you are venturing here during the high heat, a uniform of shorts and lightweight golf shirts is recommended. Cotton shirts are preferable, as they tend to breathe better, and colors that reflect the sun (white and yellow) are better than those that absorb it (blues and blacks). Also, make sure that you've got a hat or two in your bag.

On the equipment side, bring plenty of balls—nearly every quality Florida course features multiple water hazards. Also, try to stick a sand wedge in your golf bag that's got a thick flange and plenty of bounce. Most Florida sand is softer than in other areas of the country, and your regular sand wedge might slip too far underneath the ball on a typical Florida sand shot, resulting in a "fat" shot where the ball stays stranded in the bunker.

ONCE YOU'RE THERE

Generally speaking, most folks prefer to stay either in greater Orlando or on the Gulf Coast, but seldom combine both in one trip. Unless you're content to hole up at Disney World for a week, you're going to require a rental car. This way even if you spend the golf portion of your vacation in the greater Tampa area you can still hit Disney's attractions—a couple of hours away—for the day.

If you want beaches right outside your door, you're obviously going to have to stay on the coast. If you're searching for a hill or two during your golf experience, you'll have to head inland. For although central Florida's terrain is predictably flat, there are some notable exceptions near both Orlando and Tampa. Mission Inn, World Woods, and Southern Dunes are central Florida facilities that feature pronounced elevation changes.

On the golf side of the ledger, Orlando has two things going for it: It enjoys beautiful weather for most of the year, and it boasts an extraordinary number of high-quality public-access courses. Orlando is synonymous with

Disney, and the area is dominated by the resort's many accommodations (more than 100,000 rooms are available), theme parks, and golf courses (there are five at Disney). While one of the many Disney offerings may be ideal for you, especially if you are with your children, there is much more to Orlando.

Perhaps the best overall lodging destination for golfers is the pricey but superb in every way Grand Cypress Resort, which encompasses both villas and the marvelous Hyatt Regency Grand Cypress hotel. Its 45 holes of golf, pro shop, and driving and practice facilities are the equal of the lodging. For a more low-key but equally memorable golf experience, try Arnold Palmer's Bay Hill Club & Lodge, which oozes golf from every pore.

As wonderful as Disney, Grand Cypress, and Bay Hill are, they're also pretty pricey. Perfect "next-tier" alternatives include Mission Inn Golf & Tennis Resort and the Grenelefe Golf & Tennis Resort, both just outside of Orlando. Mission Inn's El Campeon course and Grenelefe's West course are two of the region's hidden jewels.

Be that as it may, Orlando is one of the few places where you can stay in modest chain-style digs, yet have dozens of accessible high-quality courses from which to choose. Our advice: If you have extra money but time enough only for a miniscule stay, pick Grand Cypress for its ambience and first-rate golf facility. A close second is Bay Hill, which offers only modest accommodations, but boasts a PGA Tour course and the near-everyday presence of "The King," Arnold Palmer, when he's in town. If wall-to-wall activity is your thing, Disney's the place and it's home to surprisingly good, tour-quality golf.

Being inland, Orlando's courses aren't as affected by wind as those on either coast. At times this is unfortunate as you are forced to play without the benefit of cooling breezes, but at other times it's a blessing because you're not buffeted about by constant, powerful gusts.

In the Tampa area and its environs, the one must-do is the Westin Innisbrook Resort. The golf is truly wonderful, except if you're a near-novice, because all of its courses are also pretty difficult.

A final note: If you're serious about golf, no matter if you're staying in greater Tampa, make the drive to World Woods. Its two courses and practice facility are the finest you'll encounter in Florida, bar none.

GATHERING INFORMATION

Sarasota Convention & Visitors Bureau
655 N. Tamiami Trail, Sarasota, FL 34236
Phone (800) 522-9799 or (941) 957-1877
www.cvb.sarasota.fl.us.com

St. Petersburg/Clearwater Area Convention & Visitors Bureau
Thunderdome, 1 Stadium Dr., Ste. A,

St. Petersburg, FL 33705-1706
Phone (813) 582-7892

St. Petersburg Area Chamber of Commerce
100 2nd Ave. No., P.O. Box 1371, St. Petersburg, FL 33731
Phone (813) 821-4715

Greater Tampa Chamber of Commerce
Box 420, Tampa, FL 33601
Phone (813) 228-7777 or (813) 223-1111 ext. 44

Tampa/Hillsborough Convention & Visitors Association
400 N. Tampa St., Ste. 1010, Tampa, FL 33602
Phone (800) 448-2672 or (813) 223-1111 ext. 44
www.gotampa.com

The Major Courses in Orlando

Bay Hill Club & Lodge

9000 Bay Hill Blvd., Orlando, FL 32819; phone (407) 876-2429

Bay Hill is comprised of three 9s, but it is the Challenger and Champion combination that is the most popular and the one on which the PGA Tour's Bay Hill Invitational is played (it is this course that is described below). The Charger is the third 9 and is a nice addition as a change of pace from the "championship" course if you find yourself wanting to play an additional 9.

How To Get On: You must be a guest of the resort to play here; tee times can be made when you make your reservations.

Tees:

Palmer: 7,114 yards, par-72, USGA rating 74.6, slope 141
Championship: 6,586 yards, par-72, USGA rating 71.8, slope 127
Men's: 6,198 yards, par-72, USGA rating 70.2, slope 124
Ladies: 5,192 yards, par-72, USGA rating 72.3, slope 133

Challenge: ★★★★
Variety: ★★★½
Terrain: ★★★½
Beauty/Visual Appeal: ★★★
Pace of Play: ★★★★

Golf Facilities: ★★★★
14-Club Test: ★★★★
Intangibles: ★★★★★
Value: ★★★

Just the Facts Year Opened: 1961; Course Designer: Dick Wilson; Walking: Allowed at times; Greens Fee: $175; 9-Hole/Twilight Rate: Yes; Pull Carts: No; Practice Range: Yes; Club Rental: Yes.

Description and Comments When you think of Orlando, the words tradition, heritage, and refinement don't readily pop into mind. But all three define Arnold Palmer's Bay Hill—a civilized island in a sea of glitz and glamour.

Palmer first discovered Bay Hill in the mid-1960s when he came to play an exhibition. He quickly fell in love with the course and its surroundings and soon thereafter purchased Bay Hill. It is now his winter home. If you are lucky enough, you might even see him wandering around the grounds or heading to his office, located above the locker room.

Home to the PGA Tour's Bay Hill Invitational, the course presents a fair but challenging layout; the course is pure golf where what you see is what you get. You won't find tricked up holes, surprises, or gimmicks. But you will just find great golf—just what you would expect from Mr. Palmer.

The course starts off with a roar, featuring the toughest opening hole on the PGA Tour. Here's a tip: Visit the driving range before you tackle this 414-yard par-4. Number one is an uphill, dogleg left featuring three bunkers strategically placed where the fairway bends and a small green guarded by four more cavernous bunkers. Get used to seeing sand. If Arnie had added another trap or two in his recent remodeling efforts, he could have changed the course's name to Bunker Hill.

One of the best holes on the front is the par-5 6th. A banana-shaped hole with water along the entire left-hand side, the 6th plays 543 yards from the tips. This hole is reachable in two, but you have to be bold off the tee: You will have to carry quite a bit of the lake to give yourself a chance at gaining the green with your second. Trying to bang it on in two, John Daly, one of golf's longest hitters, plunked six balls in the lake in the final round of the 1998 tournament, on his way to a horrendous 18 on the hole. To his credit, he made a birdie two on the following hole.

The 12th through 15th holes represent the best holes for birdies at Bay Hill. It is, however, the final three holes that really epitomize what this course is all about. The 16th is a reachable par-5 that plays 481 yards downhill, but demands accuracy as the fairway is guarded by trees on both sides, giving it the appearance of a ski run, and there are five traps just waiting for your ball. If you do manage to hit it fairly long and keep it in the fairway, then you've won half the battle. Your second shot will be to a bizarre, horseshoe-shaped green guarded by water in front and to the left and by traps on the right and back. The green has three tiers, and thus accuracy is a key or you could be looking at some nightmarish dogleg putt. The 220-yard 17th is one of golf's most intimidating par-3s (you now know why the pros look a little fearful when they reach this tee box). The hole plays over a lake to an elevated green that is guarded on the front, left, and back by a trio of traps. This is said to be Palmer's favorite hole on the course.

The par-4 18th (441 yards) is the course's signature hole and just may be one of the hardest finishing holes on the PGA tour, unless you are Robert Gamez. In the 1990 Nestle Invitational, Gamez, a then 21-year-old rookie, holed a seven iron from 176 yards out for an eagle, thereby defeating Greg Norman and Larry Mize (a plaque in the fairway commemorates the site of this terrific shot). But if you're not Gamez, this hole will no doubt pose a formidable foe. The hole plays straight off the tee, but then makes a sharp turn to the right before the green. Basically the hole is shaped like the letter "r." Plain and simple, the second shot is a brute. You want to make sure to have enough club because a lake is located along the right-hand side of the fairway and abuts the green, in front and to the right. However, too much club may put you in one of the three bunkers behind the green. Then, the nastiest shot in golf awaits, a downhill shot from a bunker to a slick green that slopes away, toward the water. There's just no safe way to play this hole. If you are lucky (or skillful) enough to make it on in two, you may want to talk to the staff and see if you can get your own plaque.

Insider Tips   Along with being less glitzy than many of its neighbors, Bay Hill also tends to be less visually stunning. It does, however, possess an aura of history and tradition that more than compensate for any aesthetic shortcomings. Bay Hill is kept in near-tournament condition year-round. However, if you want to play it like the pros see it, play it in late February, when the rough is up and the greens are at their firmest, and fastest. Personally, we like it after mid-March, after the pros have departed, when they cut the rough back. The course stays every bit as fun, it just becomes more playable. Summer is a great time to come, if you can stand the heat, because many of the tourists and club members have returned north, so bargains are for the taking and you can buzz around pretty quickly.

Palmer has developed many risk/reward holes, but the underlying theme here is accuracy off the tee. You don't necessarily have to be incredibly long on your tee shots to score well, but you do have to make sure that you are in the fairway. Your best scoring opportunities come on the par-5s, all of which are reachable in two, and the relatively friendly par-3s, with the exception of the 17th. On the other hand, the par-4s are extremely hard to score on.

If you are a higher handicapper, you may find this course to be just too much for you as it has a number of forced carries over seven lakes that come into play on nine of the holes. However, if you manage to negotiate these hazards, we believe that this track is tameable.

Greens here tend to be rather large, which is both good and bad. A generous landing area is nice when you are hitting a long approach shot, but long putts that must negotiate many undulations often result in quite a few three putts.

Granted, the greens fee is awfully expensive, and you're not going to encounter Pebble Beach–type scenery. But there aren't too many PGA Tour courses you can play, and even more significantly for you history buffs, there's nowhere else on earth that you're more likely to run into Arnold Palmer than in the grill room, in the locker room, or on the putting green at Bay Hill.

Grand Cypress Golf Club, New Course

One North Jacaranda, Orlando, FL 32836; phone (800) 835-7377 or (407) 239-1904

How To Get On: You must be a guest of the resort to play here; tee times can be made when you make your reservations.

Tees:

> Black: 6,773 yards, par-72, USGA rating 72.1, slope 126
>
> White: 6,181 yards, par-72, USGA rating 69.4, slope 117
>
> Red: 5,314 yards, par-72, USGA rating 69.8, slope 117

Challenge: ★★★	Golf Facilities: ★★★★★
Variety: ★★★½	14-Club Test: ★★★½
Terrain: ★★★★	Intangibles: ★★★★
Beauty/Visual Appeal: ★★★½	Value: ★★★
Pace of Play: ★★★½	

Just the Facts Year Opened: 1988; Course Designer: Jack Nicklaus; Walking: Yes; Greens Fee: $90–180; 9-Hole/Twilight Rate: Yes; Pull Carts: No; Practice Range: Yes; Club Rental: Yes.

Description and Comments With the New Course, Jack Nicklaus pays homage to St. Andrews, the birthplace of golf. In true links style, this course features no trees, minimal water (in the form of winding burns— "burn" is Scottish for stream), double greens, and a hole that is an exact replica of The Road Hole. It also features more than 140 bunkers, some 12 feet deep, requiring a ladder to gain access, which is where you will find the biggest challenge on the course. You'll even find a trademark Scottish-style starter's shed at the first tee.

You get your first taste of St. Andrews on the opening hole, which shares its fairway with the 18th. There are no trees or rough separating the two holes, a common feature in courses across the pond, but something rarely found here in the United States. There also is a burn directly in front of the green, which makes that first approach shot a tickler.

On the front side, number 6 is one of the best holes. The 6th is a dogleg par-5 that plays 496 yards and provides numerous options for the golfer. The left-hand side of the fairway is a shorter route than the right, but it also features more deceptive mounding, resulting in many an uneven lie. On the other hand, your best line to the green is from the right-hand side, but it will play much longer. Number 8, a par-4, is the hardest hole on the course as it plays 440 yards from the back markers and requires a long drive to give yourself a shot at reaching the green in regulation. Take an extra club on the approach, because that pesky burn meanders directly in front of the green.

The two finishing holes are quite enjoyable and a wonderful way to wrap up your round. Seventeen is a par-5 that plays 485 yards and is modeled after the famed St. Andrews' Road Hole. For those who have not had the honor of playing the original, let us describe the reproduction. The hole veers slightly to the right from tee to green and features a rocky road on the right side of the fairway. The putting surface is a narrow, double green shared by the first hole and is backed by a stone wall. The final hole is a straightforward par-4 that plays 371 yards and takes you back to the shared fairway. You have to negotiate one final burn as you hit your approach shot to a massive green. This is a unique and highly enjoyable golfing experience.

Insider Tips The New Course at Grand Cypress does not suit everybody's tastes. Some folks love it, others hate it, and still others just don't get it. Admittedly, the landscape is pretty bleak, with no tall trees or splashy water hazards to spice things up. Moreover, there are many dips, swales, and mounds, which make for several blind and semiblind shots during the round. This practice is quite common in Scotland and Ireland, where it is considered "sporty," but many American golfers aren't wild about it, preferring a more "fair" experience in which all the fairway landing areas and greens are visible.

Nevertheless, we strongly recommend this course. So many faux Scottish links have been built in the United States in the last 15 years on undesirable sites, where all the character has been manufactured, but this is one of the few that actually succeeds.

Warning: Call ahead for playing conditions. This course is fun and distinctive at any time, but if you're a good golfer, you want to experience it when the turf is firm and the course plays "fast," that is, when your ball hits the turf it runs considerably. This is the Scottish way. Find out if and when the course is being overseeded. The "transition" period usually means that the course will play "slow," because they have to water it frequently and the grass gets too lush to allow for the Scottish "bump-and-run" style to be employed.

As the above yardage illustrates, this course is not overly long. Thus, you can be a medium-length driver and still score well here, provided you are accurate. The pot bunkers that inundate the course can be deadly if you land in one—getting out of a 12-foot trap is no easy task. If you do find yourself in a bunker, our recommendation is to hit a shot that is sure to get you out. Sounds simple enough, but often players will try to do too much with their bunker shots and find themselves humbly hitting another shot out.

As in Scotland, there is nothing to deflect the wind, and so when it is blowing it will play havoc with your shots. You will want to take note of the wind especially with your approach shots. Nicklaus gives you quite a few options on this course, and thus your shots to the green can take on many forms, which may be affected by the wind. You will have to decide whether it is best to fly a shot in or bump and run an iron.

To further enhance your "Scottish" experience here, we recommend that you walk the course and make arrangements ahead of time to reserve a caddie. This is a great way to get some expert local knowledge and at the same time enjoy golf the way it was meant to be, on foot.

Grand Cypress Golf Club, North/East/South Courses

One North Jacaranda, Orlando, FL 32836; phone (800) 835-7377 or (407) 239-1904

This course is comprised of three 9s that can be played in three different 18-hole combinations. The North/South combination is the original course at the resort and is the layout that hosted the LPGA Tournament of Champions from 1994 to 1996, as well as the PGA Tour Skills Challenge and the Shark Shootout.

How To Get On: You must be a guest of the resort to play here; tee times can be made when you make your reservations.

North/South Tees:

    Gold: 6,993 yards, par-72, USGA rating 73.9, slope 130

    Blue: 6,335 yards, par-72, USGA rating 70.7, slope 123

    White: 5,823 yards, par-72, USGA rating 68.5, slope 121

    Red: 5,332 yards, par-72, USGA rating 71.1, slope 119

North/East Tees:

    Gold: 6,955 yards, par-72, USGA rating 73.9, slope 130

    Blue: 6,294 yards, par-72, USGA rating 70.9, slope 124

    White: 5,790 yards, par-72, USGA rating 68.6, slope 121

    Red: 5,056 yards, par-72, USGA rating 69.1, slope 114

South/East Tees:

    Gold: 6,906 yards, par-72, USGA rating 74.4, slope 132

    Blue: 6,363 yards, par-72, USGA rating 71.6, slope 126

    White: 5,789 yards, par-72, USGA rating 69.3, slope 123

    Red: 5,130 yards, par-72, USGA rating 70.2, slope 123

Challenge: ★★★½	Golf Facilities: ★★★★★
Variety: ★★★½	14-Club Test: ★★★½
Terrain: ★★★★	Intangibles: ★★★★
Beauty/Visual Appeal: ★★★★	Value: ★★★
Pace of Play: ★★★	

Just the Facts Year Opened: 1984; Course Designer: Jack Nicklaus; Walking: Yes; Greens Fee: $90–180; 9-Hole/Twilight Rate: Yes; Pull Carts: No; Practice Range: Yes; Club Rental: Yes.

Description and Comments   This course is one of the most beautiful in the area, especially when it is juxtaposed against the relatively dull, flat land surrounding it. The North/South course is the most popular at the resort and is the truest and best test of golf. The Nicklaus-designed layout is a traditional target-style golf course that features mounds that rise dramatically from the flat terrain and are covered with fescue and love grass. Though the terraced fairways offer ample landing areas, the knolls that line them provide many awkward stances if you stray beyond the safe zone. Water is found on 13 of the holes, creating additional peril.

The real challenge on this course comes from the rolling greens that are guarded by pot bunkers and grass depressions. Unlike the New Course, you will have very few opportunities to bump and run the ball onto the green. Instead you will have to use a lofted club and land the ball on the green with your approach, no easy task given the mounding and abundance of hazards.

Two of the best holes on the North are the 7th and 9th. The 7th is a dogleg right par-4 that plays 423 yards. The fairway is guarded on the right by a lake as well as a large bunker strategically located in the prime landing area. For your approach shot you must negotiate this lake and hit a shot to a skinny but deep green. The 9th is also a par-4 (439 yards) guarded by water, this time on the left-hand side, and features two bunkers on the right. Once again, the green is nestled right next to the water, and thus your approach shot is the key.

The most difficult hole on the South course is the 6th, a 570-yard, dogleg par-5 with a series of cavernous bunkers that run from tee to green. The alarmingly small platform green is elevated and guarded by water on the left-hand side and a yawning trap on the right. Overshoot your target and you'll face a scary, scary downhill chip back to the green from a rough-covered hill. The 9th hole on the South is basically a mirror image of the 9th on the North and in fact shares its green.

The East 9 is a worthy addition to your golfing agenda, though not in the class of the North and South 9s. The course has fewer bunkers than the other two 9s and more generous landing areas, but it still poses a challenge in its own right. The best hole is the 5th, a 153-yard par-3 that plays to an island green.

Insider Tips   While the holes aren't extremely long, they are fraught with trouble. This is a course where you might just as well leave your driver in the trunk as Nicklaus has placed emphasis on accuracy rather than distance. However, you want to try and get as much distance off the tee as you safely can as the shorter your approaches, the more lofted the club you can use and thus the more you can work the ball to the flag.

This is a vintage Jack Nicklaus design of the 1980s, when many of his fairways were lined with mounds and he protected his greens as if the hole were housing Britain's crown jewels. Nearly every green at Grand Cypress has multiple tiers, is deceptively configured when eyeballing it from the fairway, and is fiercely guarded by humps, hollows, rough, water, and bunkers. If you're not hitting it just so or putting with a superior touch, the whole experience can get frustrating if you're reverently concerned about your score.

A word to the wise: Spend some time off-course at Grand Cypress. The dining, practice, and pro-shop facilities are without peer in the area, and as a trio, are hard to surpass anywhere in the United States.

Grenelefe Golf & Tennis Resort, West Course

3200 FL 546, Haines City, FL 33844; phone (800) 237-9549 or (941) 422-7511

How To Get On: Registered guests of the resort can make tee times three months in advance. Nonguests can make tee times two weeks in advance.

Tees:

Dark Green: 7,325 yards, par-72, USGA rating 75.0, slope 130

Light Green: 6,898 yards, par-72, USGA rating 73.1, slope 126

White: 6,199 yards, par-72, USGA rating 70.5, slope 122

Yellow: 5,398 yards, par-72, USGA rating 70.9, slope 118

Challenge: ★★★★	Golf Facilities: ★★★½
Variety: ★★★½	14-Club Test: ★★★½
Terrain: ★★★	Intangibles: ★★★
Beauty/Visual Appeal: ★★★½	Value: ★★★½
Pace of Play: ★★★	

Just the Facts Year Opened: 1971; Course Designers: Robert Trent Jones Sr. and David Wallace; Walking: No; Greens Fee: $50–120; 9-Hole/Twilight Rate: Yes; Pull Carts: No; Practice Range: Yes; Club Rental: Yes.

Description and Comments Grenelefe has three courses, but the main attraction is the West course. This course has been the site of many tournaments on the PGA and Senior PGA Tours and was the home of the 1994 PGA Tour Qualifying School Finals. Designed by Robert Trent Jones Sr. and built by David Wallace, the West will no doubt test your game as well as your cart's battery—this course is long, long, long, stretching more than 7,300 yards from the tips. In fact, six of the ten par-4s on the course are over 400 yards and most of the par-3s over 200 yards. But the real beauty of Grenelefe is that it tests your touch as well as your strength. You must be long off the tee, but you also better have some finesse shots in your bag as the greens tend to be small and well bunkered; your approach shots are as important as your drives.

Fairways on the West are lined by tall oak and pine trees that often influence position and strategy. The course features mild elevation changes (up to 20 feet) making for some attractive vistas. If the bad news at Greenelefe West is the extreme length, the good news is there are only two lakes that come into play, so it will be rare that you find yourself wet.

One of the best holes on the course is number 6, one of the only non-400-yard-plus par-4s on the course. Playing 381 yards, the hole doglegs left as the fairway bends around one of the course's two lakes. Your approach shot is uphill to a small green that is well guarded by three bunkers. The hardest hole on the course is the 479-yard par-4 14th. Your tee shot will no doubt benefit from the downhill roll, but you'll still face an arduous approach shot to a narrow, rolling green. Surrounding the green is trouble: traps on the left, in front, and behind; trees lurking not far in the distance.

The final hole epitomizes just what this course is all about. It is a par-5 double dogleg that plays 561 yards from the tips. This hole is not only long, it requires touch and accuracy. The fairway is tight and well guarded by trees, but the green is bunkered both left and right.

Insider Tips You had better have your driver working the minute you step onto the first tee if you want to have a fighting chance at this course. You also better have your approach irons and your putter working for that matter. It is important to get as much yardage as possible on your drives so that you leave yourself a reasonable approach shot to the well-guarded greens. We recommend you play this extra-long course in the afternoon. Morning dew on the fairways tends to linger a while and will rob you of the extra roll you'll need to cope with the rigors of Grenelefe West.

The wind often plays a factor on this course, and some of the holes can play 20 yards longer than the scorecard indicates. One final note: Make sure to play the tees that suit your game. Playing this course from the tips should be reserved for those who have an extremely low handicap or for those who just feel the need for a little torture.

Mission Inn Golf & Tennis Resort, El Campeon Course

10400 CR 48, Howey-in-the-Hills, FL 34737; phone (800) 874-9053 or (352) 324-3885

How To Get On: Contact resort for tee time information.

Tees:

    Blue: 6,860 yards, par-72, USGA rating 73.6, slope 133

    White: 6,283 yards, par-72, USGA rating 70.9, slope 128

    Gold: 5,550 yards, par-72, USGA rating 67.6, slope 119

    Red: 4,765 yards, par-72, USGA rating 67.3, slope 118

Challenge: ★★★	Beauty/Visual Appeal: ★★★½
Variety: ★★★½	Pace of Play: ★★★
Terrain: ★★★★	Intangibles: ★★★

Golf Facilities: ★★★★   Value: ★★★★
14-Club Test: ★★★★

Just the Facts Year Opened: 1926; Course Designer: Charles Clark; Walking: No; Greens Fee: $50–95; 9-Hole/Twilight Rate: Yes; Pull Carts: No; Practice Range: Yes; Club Rental: Yes.

Description and Comments Back in 1916, William J. Howey purchased 60,000 acres in central Florida on which he created a huge citrus farm. To entertain his many visitors from the north, Mr. Howey turned to Captain Charles Clark of Scotland's Royal Troon fame to build a golf course on 225 acres of his land. The Sunset Country Club was completed in 1926 and met with rave reviews and a steady stream of visitors. The tourist flow came to an abrupt stop with the 1929 crash of the stock market. The farm and Mr. Howey's finances fell into ruin, and the course slipped into utter oblivion. And there it stayed until 1964 when the Beucher family recognized the potential that the land held and revived the course and ultimately developed the renowned Mission Inn.

Just like the phoenix rising from the ashes, El Campeon, or the Champion, rose from the overgrown, weed-infested land that had been long neglected and grew into one of Florida's more challenging and revered resort courses. El Campeon plays through 625 acres of isolated, rolling terrain featuring a number of lakes, elevation changes of up to 85 feet, sculpted bunkers, and tight fairways lined with mature oaks.

Your first taste of the "true" El Campeon comes on the 3rd hole as you must negotiate a long par-4 (460 yards) that is a test of both strength and accuracy. The 7th is one of the harder holes on the front. It's a 438-yard par-4 that plays downhill on the tee shot and then back uphill on the approach and features a creek cutting across the fairway. The green is small and is well defined by a series of bunkers.

The back 9 is really where most of the action is. There is a series of difficult and intriguing holes, and the 17th, the course's signature hole, may leave you speechless. Known as the "Devil's Delight," the 17th is a 538-yard par-5 that easily lives up to its moniker. First an overview: The hole plays somewhat downhill and veers gently to the right. Now the play-by-play: Off the tee, you must hit your ball through a tunnel of trees to a blind landing area strategically guarded by a tall oak tree and a gaping bunker. Your second shot offers a true risk/reward decision. If you have hit a perfect tee shot, you can go for the green in two. But what lies between you and the green is the "devil's playground": You must carry a pond and avoid the tree located about 130 yards from the green as well as the many trees and bunkers guarding the green. No matter what you decide to do, if you find yourself in trouble, don't fret. It's not your fault—the devil made you do it.

Insider Tips As you may have gathered from the above description, this course is not for everyone. Good players will love it. However, if you're not up to the rigors of a surprisingly uphill course, where each shot poses significant challenge, you may want to try the resort's second 18, Las Colinas (see "Sampler" section), which embodies the gentler spirit of true resort golf. If the above description makes your mouth water (and at the same time makes your palms sweat), then this is the perfect place for you.

You might have guessed that accuracy is the key here. However, because the course is long and, if you can believe it, actually plays longer than the yardage indicates, especially on the uphill holes, you will need to make sure that you get some good distance off the tees. You will have to be very careful with your club selection since there are so many holes that rise and fall. Finally, the edges of the bunkers tend to be very sharp, so make sure you have enough loft to get out; the sacrifice in yardage will be much less frustrating than finding yourself having to hit yet another shot from the exact same bunker.

You might benefit from a 15th club in your bag: a good fishing rod. The fishing on and around this course is superb, so if you're having trouble reeling in birdies, you might want to try your hand at reeling in fish instead.

WALT DISNEY WORLD RESORTS

The Walt Disney Company has never done anything on a small scale—the massive development in Orlando is evidence to that. Thus, when they set out to develop a world-class golf resort, they built not just one course but five 18-hole courses over a 20-year period, known as "The Magic Linkdom." If you are looking to play one or two of the courses here, we would rank Osprey Ridge at the top of our list followed by Palm, Eagle Pines, and then Magnolia. Osprey Ridge and Eagle Pines are housed as a twosome at something called the Bonnet Creek Golf Club. You'll know you've arrived when you spot the giant spun-metal golf tee sculptures in front of the pro shop. If you're a pretty good to very good player and have to choose between the two courses, pick Osprey Ridge. Eagle Pines is nice, but hardly memorable.

Lake Buena Vista is the weak sister of the five, as it's shoehorned in and among the ever-expanding Disney resort; as are Palm and Magnolia. They're both fine courses, if a bit tired, but Palm is the better of the two. Magnolia is longer and contains Disney's most famous hole, the 190-yard, par-3 6th, with a greenside bunker in the shape of Mickey Mouse's head, ears and all. Still, the rest of the course is a bit dull. Palm is tighter than Magnolia, with more hazards and simply demands better ball striking. Though the still-close-to-wonderful Palm is a bit frayed around the edges these days, its peaceful setting (no houses or roads, an abundance of wildlife) is worth the price of admission in itself.

Walt Disney World Resort, Eagle Pines

3451 Golf View Dr., Orlando, FL 32830; phone (407) 934-7639

How To Get On: Guests of the Disney Resort and its many hotels can make tee times up to 60 days in advance. Nonguests can book tee times up to 30 days in advance.

Tees:

> Talon: 6,772 yards, par-72, USGA rating 72.3, slope 131
>
> Crest: 6,309 yards, par-72, USGA rating 69.9, slope 125
>
> Wings: 5,520 yards, par-72, USGA rating 66.3, slope 115
>
> Feathers: 4,838 yards, par-72, USGA rating 67.6, slope 116

Challenge: ★★★	Golf Facilities: ★★★★½
Variety: ★★★	14-Club Test: ★★★½
Terrain: ★★★	Intangibles: ★★★½
Beauty/Visual Appeal: ★★★	Value: ★★★½
Pace of Play: ★★★½	

Just the Facts   Year Opened: 1992; Course Designer: Pete Dye; Walking: No; Greens Fee: $90–135; 9-Hole/Twilight Rate: Yes; Pull Carts: No; Practice Range: Yes; Club Rental: Yes.

Description and Comments   Eagle Pines and Osprey Ridge are the newest additions to the Disney Resort family. This is the shortest of the five resort courses, but the water on 15 of the holes ensures that it has plenty of challenge. Eagle Pines has a unique look: Each hole is framed by a variety of grasses and dark pine straw that give it a North Carolina feel—something you definitely are not expecting in Orlando.

Remarkably for a Dye course, the fairways are user-friendly as they tend to be forgiving. You won't find that many bunkers here, but you will encounter vast waste areas throughout the layout. The greens can be tricky to putt as they are somewhat rolling and tend to be fairly fast.

As is the case with the majority of courses at Disney, Eagle Pines starts out with some easier holes. You really get the opportunity to warm up and find your swing before you encounter the harder holes, such as the 4th hole. Number four is a long par-5 (570 yards) that bends slightly to the left off the tee, with bunkers on the left, and then curves back to the right with more bunkers in the fairway on the right. This hole is followed by the hardest on the course and one of the more fun to play. The 5th is a big par-4 (463 yards) that doglegs right and employs a slender landing area with water guarding the left side of the green to boost the challenge.

Your best scoring opportunity comes on the 12th hole, a par-3 that plays 150 yards to a large green. Other than a bunker on the left, there are no other hazards on the hole, but because the green is so large, you will need to get the ball close to the pin for a possible birdie. The 414-yard, par-4, dogleg left finishing hole bends around a lake and features a number of bunkers surrounding the banana-shaped green.

Insider Tips This is a true "thinking-person's course," where shotmaking is more critical than distance. The many doglegs require you to select the best line and angle as you negotiate the hole. You want to cut off as much distance as possible on your shots, but at the same time make sure to stay out of the many hazards. If the wind is blowing, think about punching a lower-lofted club since the flat terrain is ideal for just such a shot.

One more note: On the 5th hole (the hardest one on the course) you will want to hit your tee shot to the center of the fairway right where the hole bends. This will leave you with the best angle to the small, undulating green.

Walt Disney World Resort, Magnolia Course

1950 W. Magnolia Dr., Orlando, FL 32830; phone (407) 934-7639

How To Get On: Guests of the Disney Resort and its many hotels can make tee times up to 60 days in advance. Nonguests can book tee times up to 30 days in advance.

Tees:

      Blue: 7,190 yards, par-72, USGA rating 73.9, slope 128

      White: 6,642 yards, par-72, USGA rating 71.6, slope 128

      Gold: 6,198 yards, par-72, USGA rating 69.1, slope 123

      Red: 5,414 yards, par-72, USGA rating 69.1, slope 123

Challenge: ★★★½	Golf Facilities: ★★★
Variety: ★★½	14-Club Test: ★★★½
Terrain: ★★★	Intangibles: ★★★½
Beauty/Visual Appeal: ★★★½	Value: ★★½
Pace of Play: ★★★	

Just the Facts Year Opened: 1971; Course Designer: Joe Lee; Walking: No; Greens Fee: $90–125; 9-Hole/Twilight Rate: Yes; Pull Carts: No; Practice Range: Yes; Club Rental: Yes.

Description and Comments Magnolia is one of the two oldest courses at Disney World, along with the Palm course, and it is also the longest. It is not the length alone that challenges the golfer, but the multitude and variety of hazards that can be found throughout this layout. The course derives its name from the more the 1,500 magnolia trees that are scattered about, but these trees are just the tip of the hazard iceberg. The course includes over 100 bunkers that guard the greens and are strategically placed in the fairways. Speaking of the fairways, they tend to be doglegs and are squeezed by beautiful magnolia trees that come into play with ongoing frequency. Finally, there are ten lakes at Magnolia that are found on 11 of the holes.

The course starts off with a bang. The 1st hole is a 428-yard par-4 that features a lake to the left as you tee off (it really doesn't come into play unless you severely pull the ball), as well as a stream running along the entire right-hand side of the hole. This is ranked as the third-hardest hole on the course and is sure to get your heart racing early. For the next four holes, you don't have to worry about the water, but you will have to negotiate quite a few doglegs, trees, and bunkers. The hardest hole on the course is number 5, a 448-yard, par-4 that doglegs to the right. Trees line the right side of the fairway and two healthy bunkers are strategically placed on the left. The long, narrow, forward-slanting green is trapped both left and right.

When you get to the par-3 6th hole (195 yards), you will want to have your camera ready and take note of the front bunker, which is shaped like Mickey Mouse—if you land in it, you can tell everyone you played out of the mousetrap. On the backside, you will find quite a few challenging holes; numbers 14 and 17 are two of the best. Fourteen is a long par-5 (595 yards) that doglegs abruptly to the right. A lake and four traps patrol the right side of the fairway. Your second shot is mostly straight away, but it is nearly impossible to reach this green in two as there is a lake on the left-hand side that cuts directly in front of the well-bunkered green. The 17th is a 427-yard par-4, the second-hardest hole on the course. This dogleg left is filled with peril as your tee shot must carry a lake that runs parallel to the fairway on the left as well as water on most of the right side of the fairway. The hole affords a nice risk/reward dilemma: The more water you cut off, the less yardage you will have on your second shot, of course. The narrow green is pinched by traps on either side.

Insider Tips   Despite the ominous description above, this course is more forgiving than the Palm and is thus a better choice for the less experienced golfer. The fairways tend to be wider and the trees don't come into play as much as they do on the Palm. However, if you are wild off the tee—or for that matter on pretty much every one of your shots—you will find yourself scrambling to make bogey. The many hazards ensure that this course is still quite a challenge.

One of the best chances for a birdie comes on number 13, the easiest hole on the course. It is a dogleg left par-4 that plays only 375 yards from the tips and features not a drop of water.

One more thing: If your ball does land in the surrounding vegetation, you may want to think twice about searching for it as wildlife abounds not far beyond the fairway. Sightings of a number of birds, alligators, and snakes are not uncommon. Beware: Magnolia is an older course on flattish terrain that doesn't drain particularly well after a good soaking. Early morning rounds and rounds played after a downpour can be soggy, muddy affairs. At these times, we recommend moving to higher ground or to courses that shed water more quickly, such as Disney's Osprey Ridge at Bonnet Creek.

Walt Disney World Resort, Osprey Ridge

3451 Golf View Dr., Orlando, FL 32830; phone (407) 934-7639

How To Get On: Guests of the Disney Resort and its many hotels can make tee times up to 60 days in advance. Nonguests can book tee times up to 30 days in advance.

Tees:

> Talon: 7,101 yards, par-72, USGA rating 73.9, slope 135
>
> Crest: 6,680 yards, par-72, USGA rating 71.8, slope 128
>
> Wings: 6,103 yards, par-72, USGA rating 68.9, slope 121
>
> Feathers: 5,402 yards, par-72, USGA rating 70.5, slope 122

Challenge: ★★★½	Golf Facilities: ★★★★½
Variety: ★★★½	14-Club Test: ★★★★
Terrain: ★★★★	Intangibles: ★★★½
Beauty/Visual Appeal: ★★★★	Value: ★★★½
Pace of Play: ★★★	

Just the Facts　Year Opened: 1992; Course Designer: Tom Fazio; Walking: No; Greens Fee: $90–135; 9-Hole/Twilight Rate: Yes; Pull Carts: No; Practice Range: Yes; Club Rental: Yes.

Description and Comments　Osprey Ridge shares its clubhouse with Eagle Pines as well as the distinction of being the latest addition to the Magic Kingdom golf experience. And what a great addition it is. As you drive into Osprey, take note of the larger-than-life (ten-foot-tall) silver tees that line the driveway.

The clubhouse is just a taste of what is great about Osprey Ridge; what lies beyond is, in short, spectacular. The land the course is built on is a natural wetland preserve. It was Tom Fazio's goal to disturb as little vegetation as possible as he set out to build Osprey. He accomplished this goal quite nicely as the course plays within its surroundings rather than trying to dominate them. Everywhere you look you will find lush vegetation, oak forests, and natural swampland. It is a visual stunner.

Now, on to the actual course. Osprey is a links-style course featuring rolling terrain with undulating mounds scattered throughout the fairways. Elevation changes provide a dramatic appearance and give golfers the chance to see the true layout of the hole and pick the best line to the green. As far as the greens go, they are not as fast as others at the Disney Resort, but they are heavily undulating and tend to range from medium to large to very large to football-field large in size. Thus, you had better be precise with your approaches, or you could find yourself in three-putt land (we think this is right next to Fantasyland). The other looming hazards here are the various lakes on more than half of the holes, and four of the last five holes, as well as the trees that line the fairways.

If we were to compare the course to a horse race it would look like this: The front nine is the warm-up lap where your horse is getting the lay of the land and at the same time looking forward to the start of the race. These holes are relatively straightforward and offer only minimal hazards. On the next three holes, your horse starts to trot, but not too quickly, as the course begins to scratch and claw a little, but it is still quite tameable. Then you reach number seven and your horse is running at full gallop and won't slow down until the final putt on 18.

Seven, a par-5, is the hardest hole on the course as it plays 582 yards with a lake on the left, a smattering of bunkers on the right. and a narrow entrance to a green lined by trees. The other par-5 on the front is the 9th, a 510-yard severe dogleg right that has a lake that hugs the entire right side of the hole. It is the back nine, however, where the course really shines, including three spectacular finishing holes. The 16th is a par-5, 542-yard hole that is a dogleg left with a lake menacing the left side of the hole a little more than 260 yards from the tee. The green is surrounded by bunkers and the lake can come into play depending on far you hit your second shot—it certainly will if you try for the green in two. The 17th is a lovely yet rugged par-3 that measures 216 yards from the tips with water running along the entire left side of the hole. The finishing hole is a sweeping dog-leg right par-4 (454 yards) that plays around still more water on the right with a mounded ridge on the left. The hole finishes with a flurry: One final liquid hazard eats into the green's right side. If you can't control your wicked slice on this hole, you may as well just quit after 17. You have reached the finish line, and no doubt your horse is winded but exhilarated at the same time. Question: Do they allow horses in the 19th hole?

Insider Tips   This course is not overly long, nor is it excessively difficult. On the other hand, if you hit your ball into one of the many hazards with any regularity, you might not agree with this description. For the women: If you are a strong hitter, you may want to consider moving up to the gold tees, or mix and match with the red tees, because your well-struck drive may just find trouble. Because the holes are extremely short from the reds, hazards come into play very quickly.

Sixteen is a very unusually shaped hole—it looks like a question mark—and is best played if you stay on the right side for your first two shots. This will leave you with the best line to the green for your approach shot. On all the holes, try to visualize the best way to get on the green with your approach shots. Many of the holes are receptive to a variety of shots—you can fly a wedge or try a bump-and-run shot—so before you hit, decide what is the best approach for this green.

Pace of play is not the swiftest at Osprey. Conventioneers and "one-round-a-month" vacationers play here in abundance. Seldom do they play courses with so many hazards or on greens that are so large and undulating. Try to beat the crowds and get out early.

Walt Disney World Resort, Palm Course

1950 W. Magnolia Dr., Orlando, FL 32830; phone (407) 934-7639

How To Get On: Guests of the Disney Resort and its many hotels can make tee times up to 60 days in advance. Nonguests can book tee times up to 30 days in advance.

Tees:

> Blue: 6,957 yards, par-72, USGA rating 73.9, slope 133
>
> White: 6,461 yards, par-72, USGA rating 71.6, slope 128
>
> Gold: 6,029 yards, par-72, USGA rating 68.7, slope 124
>
> Red: 5,398 yards, par-72, USGA rating 70.5, slope 123

Challenge: ★★★★	Golf Facilities: ★★★
Variety: ★★★½	14-Club Test: ★★★½
Terrain: ★★★½	Intangibles: ★★★★
Beauty/Visual Appeal: ★★★★	Value: ★★★
Pace of Play: ★★★½	

Just the Facts   Year Opened: 1971; Course Designer: Joe Lee; Walking: No; Greens Fee: $90–125; 9-Hole/Twilight Rate: Yes; Pull Carts: No; Practice Range: Yes; Club Rental: Yes.

Description and Comments   The Palm was one of the original courses, along with the Magnolia course, and is considered to be the most difficult. Palm, one of the sites of Disney World/Oldsmobile Classic, features a multitude of hazards that make this course quite a challenge. There is an abundance of water located on nine holes; tight fairways lined with lovely pine trees (and palms as well); elevated tees and greens; and a load of bunkers (95 to be exact). Despite all of this imposing trouble, there is plenty of room to play on this course, making for a truly enjoyable round.

The first hole lets you cut your teeth and warm up before you encounter any real trouble. It is a slightly bending par-5 that plays 495 yards and features a couple of fairway bunkers and a green surrounded by traps. This hole is a great opportunity to get an early birdie. Then the fun begins. The 2nd hole, a 389-yard, dogleg par-4, features a lake along the entire left side of the hole and is your first taste of just what this course is all about. One of the best holes on the front nine and the number one handicap is the 6th, a 412-yard par-4 where you must negotiate both water (on the right) and trees (on the left) on your tee shot. Now comes the hard part. For your approach, you must carry a large lake that cuts through the fairway and in front of the deep, double-tiered green, guarded by a massive bunker in the back.

The backside is even better than the front and starts out with a magnificent par-4 playing 450 yards from all the way back. Your tee shot must travel some 200 yards to carry a lake that cuts in front of the fairway and at the same time avoid the bunkers on the right and the trees lining both sides of the landing area. The green is encircled by traps and is extremely small. The par-4 final hole is considered one of the hardest finishing holes on the PGA Tour. This 454-yarder requires a tee shot through a tree-lined chute with bunkers on the left. For your second shot you must carry an arm of the lake that wanders through the fairway and then works its way to the left side of the green. The green is well fortified with sand traps. It's quite a finish to an impressive course.

Insider Tips   Although this is part of the Disney Resort, it's certainly not any Mickey Mouse course (sorry, we couldn't resist). The Palm is one of the most difficult at Disney, especially for higher handicappers. If you fit this category, you may want to consider one of the less severe courses at the resort.

For those who decide to play here, be ready. The course has plenty of bite (with all due respect to the *Lion King*), especially when the wind is blowing. You will find that the course is not excessively long and that there are some good scoring opportunities, if you can keep the ball in play. There are more birdie opportunities on the front nine, especially the 4th hole, a 422-yard par-4 that is the second easiest hole on the course.

Although the greens tend to be well bunkered and fast, they are medium to large in size and putt true. Once your ball finally reaches the putting surface, you will find yourself with some makeable putts.

It's easy to find yourself "lost in the woods" at the Palm. Jungle-like forest edges many of the holes, with wildlife to match. A special treat is to get out late in the day here, to take in all the sights and sounds.

The Major Courses in Tampa/ St. Petersburg/Sarasota

Renaissance Vinoy Resort

600 Snell Isle Blvd. N.E., St. Petersburg, FL; phone (727) 896-8000

How To Get On: You must be a guest of the resort to play here; tee times can be made when you make your reservations.

Tees:

    Gold: 6,267 yards, par-70, USGA rating 70.2, slope 118

    Blue: 5,917 yards, par-70, USGA rating 68.6, slope 115

    White: 5,672 yards, par-70, USGA rating 67.4, slope 112

    Red: 4,818 yards, par-70, USGA rating 63.1, slope 101

Challenge: ★★

Variety: ★★★

Terrain: ★★★

Beauty/Visual Appeal: ★★★

Pace of Play: ★★★½

Golf Facilities: ★★★

14-Club Test: ★★★

Intangibles: ★★★

Value: ★★½

Just the Facts   Year Opened: 1992; Course Designer: Ron Garl; Walking: At certain times; Greens Fee: $90–95; 9-Hole/Twilight Rate: Yes; Pull Carts: No; Practice Range: Yes; Club Rental: Yes.

Description and Comments   The Renaissance Vinoy Resort, a member of the National Register of Historic Places, has had quite a roller-coaster existence. When it opened on New Year's Eve 1925, it quickly became the playground for the Hollywood, Wall Street, and Washington rich and famous. Guests included F. Scott Fitzgerald, Jimmy Stewart, Joel McCrae, Herbert Hoover, and Calvin Coolidge, just to name a few. During World War II, the resort was shut down to the public, as were many others in the area, and was taken over by the military, who used it as the site of (among other things) a cook and baker's school. It shifted back to civilian use in 1946, but through the years was unable to keep up with the competition. Lack of amenities that were becoming common at other resorts, such as air conditioning, led to the resort's downfall and ultimate closure in 1974.

The hotel was sold at auction to Stouffer Hotels, who recognized the grand dame's potential and undertook a $93 million revitalization program. Today, the property is run by Renaissance Hotels. One of the main attractions at the resort is the full menu of activities, with the cornerstone being the Renaissance Vinoy Golf Club.

Along with the hotel, the course needed quite a lot of work as well. The powers that be turned to Ron Garl to renovate what was originally known as the Sunset Golf and Country Club. The result of his efforts is the Vinoy Golf Club, a short, fun layout. While the course's underlying theme is playability, the nine water hazards as well as the scattered bunkers combine to make this track relatively challenging.

The course starts out with a great birdie opportunity on the shortest par-4 found at Vinoy. Only 311 yards from the tips, this hole offers you the chance to start in red numbers, that is, if you can stay out of the lake that plays along the entire right-hand side of the hole. The hardest hole on the course is the 9th, a par-4 (421 yards) that plays to a narrow fairway guarded on both sides by trees. Your approach shot will be as important as your drive as the bulkheaded green is guarded on the left by a gaping lake.

Two fine holes on the back side are numbers 16 and 18. The former is a par-5, one of only three on the course. This dogleg left hole measures 562 yards and requires a precise tee shot to avoid the series of bunkers on the right and woods on the left. Once again your approach shot will be key as you will have to be on target to hit the hole's island green. The 18th is a terrific finishing hole with a lake from tee to green. On your approach, you must carry this lake and also avoid the abutting vast sandtrap.

Insider Tips You might be tempted to pull out your driver and blast away, leaving yourself with only a short chip shot to reach the greens in regulation, but we recommend a slightly more conservative approach. It is true that this course is short, but it also has a number of hazards that place a premium on accuracy. Thus, we suggest that you switch to a fairway wood or long-iron off the tee on the narrower holes; you still will be hitting a high-trajectory iron into the green.

This course is ideal for the mid- to high-handicapper. Although so many courses that are designed for players of this caliber tend to be dull tracks that leave little to the player's imagination, Vinoy avoids this pitfall as it features holes that, while being playable, still manage to keep the player on his toes.

Westin Innisbrook Resort, Copperhead Course

36750 Highway 19 N., Palm Harbor, FL 34684; phone (727) 942-2000

How To Get On: You must be a guest of the resort to play here; tee times can be made when you make your reservations.

Tees:

> Tournament: 7,087 yards, par-71, USGA rating 74.4, slope 140
> Championship: 6,536 yards, par-71, USGA rating 71.9, slope 132
> Middle: 6,126 yards, par-71, USGA rating 70.4, slope 125
> Forward: 5,537 yards, par-71, USGA rating 71.8, slope 130

Challenge: ★★★★	Golf Facilities: ★★★★
Variety: ★★★★	14-Club Test: ★★★★½
Terrain: ★★★★	Intangibles: ★★★★
Beauty/Visual Appeal: ★★★★	Value: ★★★
Pace of Play: ★★★	

Just the Facts Year Opened: 1972; Course Designer: Lawrence Packard; Walking: No; Greens Fee: $100–140; 9-Hole/Twilight Rate: Yes; Pull Carts: No; Practice Range: Yes; Club Rental: Yes.

Description and Comments Copperhead. Snakes. As Indiana Jones said in *Raiders of the Lost Ark,* "Snakes—why did it have to be snakes?"

When you play the Copperhead course at Innisbrook, one of Florida's premier courses, you might feel as though you are starring in your own Indiana Jones sequel: The Golfer in Search of the Elusive Par. Although it won't be a life-or-death experience, it will be quite a battle as you, too, will be surrounded by peril at Copperhead. Rather than a sea of snakes, you will find tight fairways lined by Spanish moss–draped trees, numerous bunkers (73 to be exact), a handful of water hazards, and swift greens to contend with. Even Indy would be a tad nervous.

As soon as you step onto the first tee you will see that Copperhead, former site of the JC Penney Classic, is unique in that it doesn't look like a typical Florida course. In fact, you'll probably be astounded that you are in Florida. Elevated terrain, an isolated wooded setting, and exotic foliage give it more of a North Carolina or Georgia feel. You will also see just what we are talking about when we say that this course can be perilous with its many hazards. The opening hole is a 561-yard, par-5 gem that plays from an elevated tee box downhill to a fairway that has three fairway bunkers located smack dab in the middle of the landing area, 310 yards out from the tips. The tree-lined fairway gently doglegs to the right and has a lake off to the right that really shouldn't come into play unless you really slice your shot. The medium-sized green is fronted by two large bunkers.

The hardest hole on the course is number 5, a par-5 that is a real bear as it plays 576 yards uphill. Your tee shot must carry a lake to reach the tight, tree- and bunker-lined fairway. The green, which seems impossibly narrow given its length, is guarded by sand in the front and on both sides and is backed by trees. The following hole is almost as tough. The hardest par-4 on the course and the second longest is number six, a 456-yard downhill dogleg right.

On the back side, holes 14 through 16 are among the best at the course. Fourteen is a double-dogleg par-5 that plays 572 yards from the tips. While the fairway is somewhat forgiving, accuracy is paramount as trees, water, and sand can all be found on this hole. Fifteen, a watery downhill par-3 that plays 212 yards, requires both accuracy and distance. Sixteen is a drastic dogleg right par-4 that plays 458 yards and has water edging the right side of the fairway coming into play on both your first and second shots.

Insider Tips   Copperhead is a course that demands both strength and finesse. You need to be long off the tee to give yourself a manageable approach shot, but at the same time you need to be extremely accurate. Course management is crucial as you negotiate your way around Copperhead. Make sure to get an overview of the hole and select the best line to reach the green and give yourself the best opportunity to avoid the many hazards surrounding the putting surface. Your best scoring opportunities will come at the par-3s, but don't expect to reach too many greens in regulation.

Two more points of note: If you are in the trees, the best bet is simply to take your medicine and punch your way out. Finally, only extremely low handicappers should consider playing the tournament tees and even then, they might want to reconsider. The championship tees present more than enough challenge (even Indy would agree).

This is just sensational Florida golf. The hazard value might prove numbingly repetitive to the so-so golfer, as there are lakes, big bunkers, trees, and elevated greens on so many holes, but good players and course connoisseurs will embrace Copperhead with passion, as it's beautiful, honest, and tough. Come see it in late fall, near PGA tournament time, and you'll get all the golf you'd ever want.

Westin Innisbrook Resort (Island Course)

36750 Highway 19 N., Palm Harbor, FL 34684; phone (727) 942-2000

How To Get On: You must be a guest of the resort to play here; tee times can be made when you make your reservations.

Tees:

> Championship: 6,999 yards, par-72, USGA rating 73.2, slope 133
>
> Middle: 6,557 yards, par-72, USGA rating 71.3, slope 129
>
> Forward: 5,795 yards, par-72, USGA rating 74.1, slope 130

Challenge: ★★★½	Golf Facilities: ★★★★
Variety: ★★★½	14-Club Test: ★★★½
Terrain: ★★★½	Intangibles: ★★★
Beauty/Visual Appeal: ★★★½	Value: ★★★½
Pace of Play: ★★★	

Just the Facts   Year Opened: 1970; Course Designer: Lawrence Packard; Walking: No; Greens Fee: $65–120; 9-Hole/Twilight Rate: Yes; Pull Carts: No; Practice Range: Yes; Club Rental: Yes.

Description and Comments   In comparison to its sister course, Copperhead, the Island Course, the first course at Innisbrook, may seem more like an oasis in a desert of trouble. But the Island Course is hardly a pushover; it can throw a few punches of its own. It held the young and strong at bay when it hosted the 1990 NCAA Men's Championship, won by Phil Mickelson. Island is nearly as long as Copperhead, and it serves up multiple hazards in the form of 74 bunkers and numerous lakes on more than half of the holes.

The first six holes play through flat terrain with fairways that feature water on both sides. The terrain on the next six holes is quite different: Rolling fairways surrounded by cypress and pine trees. The final six holes are a combination of flat and rolling terrain.

The best hole as well as the hardest at Island is the par-5 7th. The hole is a 561-yard dogleg left with a fairway squeezed between a lake on the right and a swamp on the left. The tiny green is protected by bunkers on both the left and right as well as in the rear. Another fine hole is the 18th, a severe, dogleg left par-4 that plays 370 yards from the tips. Your tee shot will need to be right down the middle as there is a lake on the left and trees on your right. Your approach shot is no less perilous as it must carry two lakes and avoid the many bunkers surrounding the small green.

Insider Tips   If you are looking for a "resort course," then you should consider playing Island as it tends to be a more user-friendly layout that Copperhead, though not by much. Island is a fun course to play for all skill levels; however, as is the case with Copperhead, you need to have both your long as well as your short game working to score well here. Once again, course management is key. The numerous hazards and dogleg holes require that you play very strategically.

If you are a serious golfer and can only play one course at Westin Innisbrook, make it Copperhead. However, if you can squeeze two in, don't play twice at Copperhead. Island is worth a go, as a more than worthy companion.

World Woods Golf Club, Pine Barrens Course

17590 Ponce De Leon Blvd., Brooksville, FL 34614; phone (352) 796-5500

How To Get On: Tee times can be made up to a month in advance.

Tees:

>   Tournament: 6,902 yards, par-71, USGA rating 73.7, slope 140
>
>   Back: 6,458 yards, par-71, USGA rating 71.6, slope 134
>
>   Middle: 6,032 yards, par-71, USGA rating 69.6, slope 129
>
>   Forward: 5,301 yards, par-71, USGA rating 70.9, slope 132

Challenge: ★★★★	Golf Facilities: ★★★★★
Variety: ★★★★	14-Club Test: ★★★★
Terrain: ★★★★½	Intangibles: ★★★★½
Beauty/Visual Appeal: ★★★★½	Value: ★★★★½
Pace of Play: ★★★★	

Just the Facts   Year Opened: 1993; Course Designer: Tom Fazio; Walking: Yes; Greens Fee: $50–75; 9-Hole/Twilight Rate: Yes; Pull Carts: No; Practice Range: Yes; Club Rental: Yes.

Description and Comments   World Woods is off the beaten path—way off. It is located over an hour's drive from Tampa in an isolated location. More than likely, the only reason you would head to this area is to play one of the two courses at World Woods. But this is more than enough reason for you to make the drive.

Pine Barrens is the marquee course at World Woods and receives the lion's share of attention. The course is cut through a tall pine forest and features a number of waste areas, earning it comparisons with the venerable Pine Valley, a course that is consistently ranked as the world's best. While that is an impossible legacy to live up to, Pine Barrens succeeds quite well.

Pine Barrens course is good ol' fashioned golf—you won't find any gimmicks or trickery here, though some critics have argued that the greens are too heavily sloped. What you will find here are surprisingly wide fairways, vast waste areas, a myriad of trees, insidious pot bunkers, and lightning-fast greens. Certainly sounds like a descendent of Pine Valley to us.

The course starts out innocently with two par-4s (406 and 453 yards, respectively), the first being easier than the second, but both requiring accurate shot making. It is when you step onto the tee box at number 4 that you start to feel the real heat of Pine Barrens. The 4th, the second hardest hole at the course, is a 494-yard, slight dogleg to the right par-5 that has a waste bunker along the right side from tee to green.

On the back nine, there are quite a few spectacular holes. The hardest hole at the course is number 12, an extremely long (470 yards) par-4 that features two different greens. The right green is the tougher of the two, but both demand accurate shots. Incredible risk/reward options await. The big hitter can attempt a long carry over the waste area to a tiny spit of fairway. If you succeed, you face a ridiculously easy approach. The safer, shorter route off the tee is to the left, but the approach to the green becomes much tougher. Fifteen is the shortest par-4 at Pine Barrens (330 yards from the tips) and also the most beautiful. The hole is encircled by a huge waste area, which you have to carry on both your tee and approach shots. Eighteen is a wonderful finishing hole. The dogleg left par-4 measures 446 yards, but can play shorter if you cut off some of the waste bunker on the left side. The more of the waste bunker you traverse, the shorter the hole will play.

Insider Tips Although this course presents a number of challenges, it is a fair layout that offers you the chance to score well if you can keep your ball out of the many hazards. Your best scoring opportunities will come at the par-5s, as all of them can be reached in two and getting on in regulation should almost be a given if you keep the ball in play. Pine Barrens is a course that demands accuracy. You really don't need to be incredibly long off the tee—especially as there are only a few forced carries—just extremely precise. Make sure that you check the flag positions on the huge greens at Pine Barrens, or you may find yourself having a rough day with the flatstick.

Make sure to arrive early at Pine Barrens so that you can avail yourself of their amazing practice facilities. World Woods might very well claim the finest practice facility on earth, bar none, public or private. The 22-acre driving range is shaped like a square so that you can hit shots into all types of wind directions. The putting green covers two acres; there is a three-hole warmup course and a nine-hole par-3 course.

You should consider making this a doubleheader and play the Rolling Oaks Course as well (the course has a 36-hole rate). While not quite on the same level as Pine Barrens, Rolling Oaks is well worth your time. However, if you only have time to play one course, it should be Pine Barrens. This is simply a great golf course, one of Florida's best and one of the nation's best as well.

World Woods Golf Club, Rolling Oaks Course

17590 Ponce De Leon Blvd., Brooksville, FL 34614; phone (352) 796-5500

How To Get On: Tee times can be made up to a month in advance.

Tees:

>   Tournament: 6,985 yards, par-72, USGA rating 73.5, slope 136
>   Back: 6,520 yards, par-72, USGA rating 71.4, slope 131
>   Middle: 6,069 yards, par-72, USGA rating 69.5, slope 125
>   Forward: 5,245 yards, par-72, USGA rating 70.7, slope 128

Challenge: ★★★½	Golf Facilities: ★★★★★
Variety: ★★★½	14-Club Test: ★★★½
Terrain: ★★★½	Intangibles: ★★★½
Beauty/Visual Appeal: ★★★★	Value: ★★★★
Pace of Play: ★★★½	

Just the Facts   Year Opened: 1993; Course Designer: Tom Fazio; Walking: Yes; Greens Fee: $50–75; 9-Hole/Twilight Rate: Yes; Pull Carts: No; Practice Range: Yes; Club Rental: Yes.

Description and Comments   Tom Fazio went to great lengths to make sure that Rolling Oaks, the sister course to Pine Barrens, had its own identity; he even went so far as to hire separate construction companies to build each course. The result: A course that can stand on its own merits and is a terrific complement to Pine Barrens.

Rolling Oaks is a more traditional design, with rolling fairways lined by a variety of trees, including oaks, dogwoods, and magnolias. While the fairways feature trouble beyond, they are rather wide and are thus much more forgiving than Pine Barrens. The greens also tend to be large and feature multiple tiers, making putting quite treacherous. Although Rolling Oaks has more water on its course as opposed to Pine Barrens, it has much less sand. The signature hole is the 8th, a magnificent par-3 that plays 174 yards from an elevated tee over a creek to a double-tiered green. This hole tests your shotmaking ability and is also a visual stunner.

Insider Tips   As is the case with Pine Barrens, accuracy and course management are the keys to scoring success at Rolling Oaks. Because many of the tees are situated above the fairway, you will have a terrific opportunity to scout the hole before you tee off, identify the hazards, and pick the best line to the green.

The par-3s are all pretty lengthy, but the par-5s are all reachable in two and thus represent your best scoring opportunities. Since the greens are so large and feature numerous tiers, your approach shots will be critical. Make sure to check the pin placements, and snuggle that short iron shot in there close or you will certainly have some terrifying putts.

To reiterate what we said in the Pine Barrens section, make sure to arrive early and make use of the fantastic practice facilities. Also, we suggest that you play both courses in the same day. To this end, it's probably wisest to shoot for spring or fall for your marathon day. For starters, it's too hot in the summer to enjoy 36 holes. Winter can often bring early morning frosts, considerably delaying play. The resulting lack of daylight will probably risk your chances of squeezing it all in. Finally, when booking your tee times, remember that it's tough to arrive "early" in the morning here. It's a good hike from most major resort/vacation destinations, so it's not as if you really want to wake up at 5:30 a.m., then go and do a one- to three-hour drive, then play 36. Give yourself extra time finding the place, as there are lots of back roads, lots of turns, and few signs.

An Orlando Sampler

Baytree National Golf Links

8207 National Dr., Melbourne, FL 32940; phone (800) 955-1234 or (407) 259-9060

Tees: Championship: 7,043 yards, par-72, USGA rating 74.4, slope 138

Greens Fee: $27–85

Challenge: ★★★½	Golf Facilities: ★★★★
Variety: ★★★★	14-Club Test: ★★★★
Terrain: ★★★★	Intangibles: ★★★½
Beauty/Visual Appeal: ★★★½	Value: ★★★★
Pace of Play: ★★★½	

Description and Comments With Baytree, Gary Player created a course with a wide variety of looks and terrain. As you make your way around the course, you will find forests, marshland, a number of lakes, and a series of red shale waste areas that really give the course a unique flavor. All in all this course challenges but doesn't overwhelm—it is a fun layout where you can relax and strike the ball, but you may find yourself in some trouble if you get too wild. The toughest hole on the course is the 447-yard par-4 15th. From the back tees, your tee shot must carry over 200 yards to clear a lake. A red shale waste area plays along the entire left-hand side of the hole. As with many of the newer courses in the area, the practice facility is top notch, as is the clubhouse and pro shop. On a side note, across the street from the course is the Florida Marlins' spring training facility, so you might want to consider doing your own doubleheader: 9 innings of preseason baseball and 18 holes of golf. Sounds like a perfect day to us.

Black Bear Golf Club

24505 Calusa Blvd., Eustis, FL 32736; phone (800) 423-2718 or (352) 357-4732

Tees: Championship: 7,002 yards, par-72, USGA rating 74.7, slope 134

Greens Fee: $35–65.

Challenge: ★★★½	Golf Facilities: ★★★★½
Variety: ★★★½	14-Club Test: ★★★½
Terrain: ★★★½	Intangibles: ★★★
Beauty/Visual Appeal: ★★★	Value: ★★★½
Pace of Play: ★★★½	

Description and Comments   With a name like Black Bear, you would expect this course to be located in some mountainous region, but it is only 40 miles north of Orlando. A links-style layout, the course has some definite Dye touches: P. B. Dye that is, Pete Dye's oldest son. Dye family trademarks, such as undulating greens, vast waste areas, and severe elevation changes, are found throughout the course. The greens are really where the course shows its teeth, or should we say claws. They are extremely hard to hold, and even the most marginal of shot will be punished.

The course features six sets of tees, ensuring that there is something for every level of player—quite a nice touch. Another unique feature is the 19th hole. At this course the 19th hole is not a euphemism for the bar, but rather an extra hole where you can settle those matches tied after regulation. Black Bear has a fantastic practice facility, so make sure to arrive early so you can get warmed up.

Diamondback Golf Club

6501 FL 544 E., Haines City, FL 33844; phone (941) 421-0437

Tees: Championship: 6,805 yards, par-72, USGA rating 73.3, slope 138

Greens Fee: $40–90

Challenge: ★★★½	Golf Facilities: ★★★
Variety: ★★★½	14-Club Test: ★★★★
Terrain: ★★★★	Intangibles: ★★★½
Beauty/Visual Appeal: ★★★★	Value: ★★★★
Pace of Play: ★★★½	

Description and Comments   Diamondback was started by a group of members from Grenelefe who wanted to build their own course. They didn't have to go far to find their location: Diamondback is situated across the street from Grenelefe. This course is a visual stunner as it winds through a gorgeous woodland setting of pine and oak trees, creating a feeling of natural isolation. The course features only a few water holes, but you will have to work hard to avoid the more than 80 bunkers found on the course. The 16th hole is one of the best on the course. It is a dogleg left par-5 (524 yards) that plays to a fairway with a lake on the left featuring a waterfall that flows to down to the 18th hole. Speaking of the 18th, it is a 441-yard, par-4 dogleg right that plays uphill to a tight green guarded by water on the left.

Falcon's Fire Golf Club

3200 Seralago Blvd., Kissimmee, FL 34746; phone (407) 239-5445

Tees: Championship: 6,901 yards, par-72, USGA rating 72.5, slope 125

Greens Fee: $55–105

Challenge: ★★★	Golf Facilities: ★★★★
Variety: ★★★	14-Club Test: ★★★½
Terrain: ★★★	Intangibles: ★★★½
Beauty/Visual Appeal: ★★★½	Value: ★★★
Pace of Play: ★★★★	

Description and Comments   If you are looking for a course where you will receive "country club" treatment as well as a fun but not overly taxing challenge, then Falcon's Fire may be just the course for you. A Rees Jones design, Falcon's Fire features generous landing areas, relatively flat fairways framed by a series of mounds (a Rees Jones trademark for a few years), and large, well-bunkered, undulating greens. The majority of fairways are bordered by tall pine and oak trees. Falcon's Fire's signature hole is the 8th, a 224-yard par-3 that requires a tee shot over water and plays to an undulating green. As part of the "country club" treatment, the carts come with an electronic yardage system, a gadget you will find quite handy. The only drawback to playing Falcon's Fire is on soggy days, when they make you keep the carts on the paths. This is because huge mounds obscure your view of the fairway, so as you advance up the path you have no idea where your ball ended up.

Golden Ocala Golf & Country Club

7300 Highway 27 NW, Ocala, FL 34482; phone (800) 251-7674 or (352) 622-2245

Tees: Championship: 6,735 yards, par-72, USGA rating 72.2, slope 132

Greens Fee: $30–55

Tees:

    Beast: 7,003 yards, par-72, USGA rating 74.3, slope 126

    Gold: 6,306 yards, par-72, USGA rating 70.8, slope 121

    White: 5,700 yards, par-72, USGA rating 68.2, slope 115

    Red: 4,895 yards, par-72, USGA rating 69.3, slope 115

Greens Fee: $27–85

Challenge: ★★★½   Golf Facilities: ★★★

Variety: ★★★★   14-Club Test: ★★★½

Terrain: ★★★   Intangibles: ★★★★

Beauty/Visual Appeal: ★★★½   Value: ★★★★

Pace of Play: ★★★

Description and Comments   Golden Ocala offers you the opportunity to visit courses from around the world without leaving Florida. The course features eight holes that are replicas of some of the best courses worldwide. Here you will get to play Augusta's 6th, 12th, and 13th; St. Andrews' 1st and 17th (the famed Road Hole); Troon's Postage Stamp hole; Baltursol's 4th; and Muirfield's 9th.

The fear whenever you set out to create a course like this is that it will appear contrived. Ron Garl, the course's architect, managed to avoid this and has created a rather interesting and enjoyable track. The setting is lovely, with an abundance of mature pine trees and rolling fairways. On the downside, the course lacks some of the amenities that are the norm at other courses, and the greens tend to be slow. You will want to avoid this course if it has been raining heavily, as the course's drainage is not the best. Despite these problems, Ocala is still well worth your time and is a great value—especially given the fact that you get the opportunity to play many holes that you otherwise might only dream about.

Grenelefe Golf & Tennis Resort, East Course

3200 FL 546, Haines City, FL 33844; phone (800) 237-9549 or (941) 422-7511

Tees: Championship: 6,802 yards, par-72, USGA rating 72.5, slope 124

Greens Fee: $40–100

Challenge: ★★★   Golf Facilities: ★★★½

Variety: ★★★   14-Club Test: ★★★

Terrain: ★★★   Intangibles: ★★★

Beauty/Visual Appeal: ★★★   Value: ★★★

Pace of Play: ★★★

Description and Comments   If you play the West course here at Grenelefe, you will no doubt want a little breather. Although the East is shorter than both the South or West, it still has some bite as it is very tight and has small- to medium-size, well-bunkered greens. Water is scarce and is only on four holes. Rather than saving the best for last, Arnold Palmer and Ed Seay put it right up front. The 1st hole is one of the most scenic on the course, with a bizarre tee box located 50 feet above the fairway. You basically hit from a rooftop locale, from an artificial mat. The par-4 6th is one of the rare water holes on the course, playing 429 yards to a narrow, uphill tree-lined fairway. Your second shot will be downhill to a green encircled by trouble: water on the left and sand on both the left and the right.

Grenelefe Golf & Tennis Resort, South Course

3200 FL 546, Haines City, FL 33844; phone (800) 237-9549 or (941) 422-7511

Tees: Championship: 6,869 yards, par-71, USGA rating 72.6, slope 124

Greens Fee: $40–100

Challenge: ★★★	Golf Facilities: ★★★½
Variety: ★★★½	14-Club Test: ★★★
Terrain: ★★★	Intangibles: ★★★
Beauty/Visual Appeal: ★★★	Value: ★★★½
Pace of Play: ★★★½	

Description and Comments   The South course at Grenelefe is the most forgiving with its wide-open fairways, flat terrain, and huge, receptive greens. There is, however, more water on this course, as well as waste areas that will keep you on your toes. The best hole on the course is the double dogleg, par-5 8th. Measuring 520 yards from the tips, the hole plays over a meandering stream to a tight landing area guarded on the right by a lake and on the left by bunkers. For your second shot you can either go for the green in two (in which case you have to carry a second lake on the left), or lay up on the right, leaving yourself a manageable approach shot.

Metrowest Country Club

2100 S. Hiawassee Rd., Orlando, FL 32835; phone (407) 299-1099

Tees: Championship: 7,051 yards, par-72, USGA rating 73.1, slope 126

Greens Fee: $40–80

Challenge: ★★★½	Golf Facilities: ★★★½
Variety: ★★★½	14-Club Test: ★★★½
Terrain: ★★★½	Intangibles: ★★★
Beauty/Visual Appeal: ★★★	Value: ★★★★
Pace of Play: ★★★½	

Description and Comments   Metrowest, designed by Robert Trent Jones Sr., is a truly fun local favorite that features a variety of hole layouts and offers a good challenge. The holes at Metrowest tend to be pretty forgiving and surprisingly rolling and feature a mix of tight and open fairways, many of which are doglegs and lined by deep rough.

The signature hole is the 568-yard, par-5 4th that doglegs severely to the right and requires an approach shot to an elevated green, surrounded by bunkers. The final hole is where many bets are won and lost. The hole, a par-4 (413 yards), plays straightaway, but water found on both the left and right often comes into play. It is this hole that often separates the men from the boys, as well as from their money.

Mission Inn Golf & Tennis Resort, Las Colinas Course

10400 CR 48, Howey-in-the-Hills, FL 34737; phone (800) 874-9053 or (352) 324-3885

Tees: Championship: 6,879 yards, par-72, USGA rating 73.2, slope 128

Greens Fee: $40–75

Challenge: ★★★	Golf Facilities: ★★★★
Variety: ★★★	14-Club Test: ★★★
Terrain: ★★½	Intangibles: ★★★½
Beauty/Visual Appeal: ★★★½	Value: ★★★★
Pace of Play: ★★★★	

Description and Comments Las Colinas is the sister course to El Campeon, but this may be the only similarity they have in common. The inherent oddity in Las Colinas is that its name is Spanish for "the hills." Strangely, El Campeon, "the champion," is the much hillier of the two. The owners of the Mission Inn recognized that El Campeon, though highly regarded and revered, was extremely hard to play and was just too much course for those looking for a resort golf experience. El Campeon is a pit bull–type course, whereas Las Colinas is more like a friendly beagle—it is enjoyable to play, and you don't have to worry about it biting your hand off. Landing areas are very generous, and the fairway bunkers less severe. The greens feature wide entrances and tend to be flatter, making both your approach shots and your putting strokes much easier.

As soon as you step onto the first tee, you will quickly see the recipe they used to create this course: two tablespoons of enjoyment; one tablespoon of challenge; and three tablespoons of playability. Oh, we forgot the dash of water and sand. The opening hole is a 396-yard par-4 with a large landing area—there is water on this hole, but it doesn't come into play. It does, however, on the 2nd hole, a 181-yard par-3 where your tee shot has to carry a pond. The green, while relatively large, is well protected by five bunkers. The best hole on the course is the finishing hole, a 561-yard par-5 that requires you to hit your second shot over a trench and at the same time avoid the wetlands on your right. You will need to hit these two shots well to leave yourself in a good position to get your ball close to the flag on this deep green.

Southern Dunes Golf & Country Club

2888 Southern Dunes Blvd., Haines City, FL 33844; phone (800) 632-6400 or (941) 421-4653

Tees: Championship: 7,219 yards, par-72, USGA rating 74.7, slope 135
Greens Fee: $21–79

Challenge: ★★★★

Variety: ★★★½

Terrain: ★★★★½

Beauty/Visual Appeal: ★★★★

Pace of Play: ★★★½

Golf Facilities: ★★★★

14-Club Test: ★★★★

Intangibles: ★★★½

Value: ★★★★

Description and Comments Steve Smyers is rapidly earning a reputation as one of America's most talented, innovative golf course architects, and Southern Dunes is a fine example of his work. The course is eye-catching in appearance and provides some diversity from typical Florida terrain. A links-style design that is situated at one of Florida's higher altitudes (though not quite the Rocky Mountains), Southern Dunes features multiple elevation changes, little water, fairly open fairways, and rolling terrain. Smyers is a proponent of bouncy, run-up–style golf, the way it's done in Scotland, so Southern Dunes tends to play firm and fast, with the slopes coming into play as a strategic element. Most memorable is Smyers's bunker design. His expansive sand features are splashed all over the place, etched into hillsides, shoring up greens, as if nature rather than humans put them there.

The pervasive sand traps are filled with very fine sand (think beach sand), making your recovery shot that much more difficult. Greens are average size, fairly easy to read, but at the same time, they are lightning-fast, so make sure to bring your delicate touch with you. The only drawbacks are the condos and homes that line the first few holes, detracting from the pristine beauty of the surroundings.

One of the best things about the course is the staff: You will be treated as though you were playing a private country club, just at a more affordable rate. One example of the amenities available to the player is the GPS system on each cart, which will be of much assistance on this hilly course. Some purists aren't wild about having a screen on your golf cart tell you how far you have to play to the hole and give advice on how to play the hole, but for everybody else, the GPS system is a godsend.

Because of its design, Southern Dunes has exceptional drainage; thus, if you are looking for a course to play after a rainy period, you should consider playing here. We can't guarantee that it won't be a tad soggy, but it will be better than many in the area. Also, if you are looking for a value in the Orlando area, look no further. You will be hard pressed to find a course that offers more dollar for dollar.

Walt Disney World Resort, Lake Buena Vista

One Club Lake Drive, Orlando, FL 32830; phone (407) 934-7639

Tees: Championship: 6,829 yards, par-72, USGA rating 72.7, slope 128
Greens Fee: $90–125

Challenge: ★★★	Golf Facilities: ★★★
Variety: ★★★	14-Club Test: ★★½
Terrain: ★★★	Intangibles: ★★★½
Beauty/Visual Appeal: ★★★	Value: ★★
Pace of Play: ★★★	

Description and Comments   In comparison to the other courses at Walt Disney World, Lake Buena Vista is the least inspiring and most mundane. However, because the course tends to be much more player-friendly—it is shorter, more manageable, and presents less hazards than its sister courses—it may be ideal for beginners or higher handicappers.

The fairways here tend to be narrow as they are lined by pines, oaks, magnolias, and, most recently, by the encroaching Disney resort properties. Although the majority of the holes are pretty straightforward, there are many doglegs to negotiate. The greens are smaller in comparison to the other courses at Disney and are often surrounded by bunkers. The real break for the average or beginner golfer comes from the fact that there is very little water on the course. In fact, only five holes feature any water, and it really isn't a factor on any of them.

One of the best holes is number 16, a 157-yard par-3 bunkered left and back that plays to an island green. The hole was an addition during Lake Buena Vista's extensive 1990 renovations, which made the course more interesting and playable. It's still Disney's weak sister, but it might be the top choice for the occasional, less serious golfer, or a good choice for families, who don't want to get "beat up" by one of Disney's "bigger" courses.

A Tampa/St. Petersburg/Sarasota Sampler

8000 Cumberland Rd., Largo, FL 37777; phone (813) 392-1234
Tees: Championship: 7,000 yards, par-72, USGA rating 74.4, slope 129
Greens Fee: $35–65

Challenge: ★★★	Golf Facilities: ★★★★
Variety: ★★★	14-Club Test: ★★★½
Terrain: ★★★	Intangibles: ★★★
Beauty/Visual Appeal: ★★★	Value: ★★★½
Pace of Play: ★★★	

Description and Comments   Recent renovations and improvements, such as a superior practice facility, have given new life to this former site of the JC Penney Classic on the PGA and LPGA Tours; Bardmoor has again established itself as one of Tampa's better public golf courses. The course has tight fairways with greens that are small, elevated, and undulating, providing a good test for players of all abilities. Water is found on ten holes including the 9th, a 397-yard, dogleg left par-4. One lake is located just off the teeing area on the left while another lies at the elbow of the dogleg on the left-hand side. One of the best holes is the 18th, an extremely long par-5 (573 yards) that plays straight from tee to green and features water on the left from the tee to the fairway. The fairway is lined by trees on both sides with a number of bunkers strategically sprinkled throughout the hole. Given the hazards that fill this hole, par is a good score here.

Saddlebrook Resort, Palmer Course

5700 Saddlebrook Way, Wesley Chapel, FL 33543; phone (800) 729-8383 or (813) 973-1111

Tees: Championship: 6,469 yards, par-71, USGA rating 71.0, slope 126
Greens Fee: $40–130

Challenge: ★★½	Golf Facilities: ★★★
Variety: ★★★½	14-Club Test: ★★★½
Terrain: ★★★½	Intangibles: ★★★½
Beauty/Visual Appeal: ★★★★	Value: ★★★
Pace of Play: ★★½	

Description and Comments   The Palmer Course has quite a different look from its sister course at the resort, the Saddlebrook Course: elevated tees, rolling terrain, and wider fairways. Similar to the other course, you will find many bunkers and lakes guarding fairways and greens. One of the better holes is the par-4 16th. This hole is relatively short—a mere 347 yards—but features three lakes that require near-exact precision. Your tee shot must carry a lake, and the narrow fairway is guarded on both sides by two other lakes. The water can also come into play on your approach shot to the relatively deep green guarded by sand on both the right and left.

Saddlebrook Resort, Saddlebrook Course

5700 Saddlebrook Way, Wesley Chapel, FL 33543; phone (800) 729-8383 or (813) 973-1111

Tees: Championship: 6,564 yards, par-70, USGA rating 72.0, slope 124
Greens Fee: $40–130

Challenge: ★★½	Golf Facilities: ★★★
Variety: ★★★½	14-Club Test: ★★★
Terrain: ★★★	Intangibles: ★★★
Beauty/Visual Appeal: ★★★	Value: ★★½
Pace of Play: ★★★½	

Description and Comments   The resort's original course (locals refer to it as "The Old Course"), the Saddlebrook Course is a tight layout with water on 17 of the 18 holes. This is the better of the two courses at the resort where flat terrain prevails. Many pine and cypress trees line the fairways and surround the greens, placing a premium on accuracy. The signature hole is the slightly dogleg 18th, a 425-yard, par-4 that has a lake guarding the entire right-hand side of the hole. In addition, a narrow fairway that features a number of sand traps and a green that is guarded by both sand and water make this quite a finisher.

Longboat Key Club Islandside Course

361 Gulf of Mexico Dr., Longboat Key, FL 34228; phone (941) 387-1632

Tees: Championship: 6,792 yards, par-72, USGA rating 73.8, slope 138

Greens Fee: $65–95

Challenge: ★★★½	Golf Facilities: ★★★
Variety: ★★★★	14-Club Test: ★★★★
Terrain: ★★★	Intangibles: ★★★½
Beauty/Visual Appeal: ★★★★	Value: ★★★½
Pace of Play: ★★★	

Description and Comments   As the address indicates, this course is located near the Gulf of Mexico and features magnificent views of Sarasota Bay. Situated in a spectacular tropical setting, this course boasts a superb combination of visual appeal and physical challenge. The most pervasive hazards comes in the form of water, or to be more exact, a lot of water. In fact, water comes into play on every single hole. In addition, the fairways are lined by numerous oak and palm trees and the greens are well bunkered. When you throw in the wind that blows off the Gulf, you have quite a test on your hands.

Tournament Players Club of Tampa Bay

5100 Terrain de Golf Dr., Lutz, FL 33549; phone (813) 949-0091

Tees: Championship: 6,898 yards, par-71, USGA rating 73.4, slope 130

Greens Fee: $45–80

Challenge: ★★★½	Golf Facilities: ★★★
Variety: ★★★	14-Club Test: ★★★½
Terrain: ★★★½	Intangibles: ★★★★
Beauty/Visual Appeal: ★★★½	Value: ★★★½
Pace of Play: ★★★½	

Description and Comments   Although nowhere near the challenge of the original TPC Stadium Course, this TPC course has plenty of bite of its own, effectively serving as a challenging host of the Senior PGA Tour, where one of the winners in recent years was Jack Nicklaus. The challenge at this course comes mostly from the extensive lakes and wetlands located on 15 of the holes. Though not excessively long, the course demands accuracy from tee to green. The terrain is mostly flat with an occasional mound thrown in here and there for good measure. The greens are where the course really shines. They are linoleum-fast, tend to be elevated, and feature sharp dropoffs that penalize errant approaches. Since the course is rather wide open, there is nothing to deflect the wind, and thus when it is blowing, it can severely affect your shots. Especially challenging are the watery finishing holes, which can make or break a round in a hurry.

University Park Country Club

7671 Park Blvd., University Park, FL 34201; phone (941) 359-9999

University Park consists of three 9-hole courses that are played in 3 different 18-hole combinations.

Tees:

Course 1 & 19: 7,247 yards, par-72, USGA rating 74.4, slope 132
Course 1 & 10: 7,001 yards, par-72, USGA rating 73.6, slope 138
Course 10 & 19: 7,152 yards, par-72, USGA rating 74.0, slope 134

Greens Fee: $50–75

Challenge: ★★★½	Golf Facilities: ★★★
Variety: ★★★½	14-Club Test: ★★★½
Terrain: ★★★	Intangibles: ★★★
Beauty/Visual Appeal: ★★★½	Value: ★★★½
Pace of Play: ★★★	

Description and Comments   Located 45 miles south of Tampa near Longboat Key, University Park features surprisingly narrow fairways given that it's an awfully long course from the championship tees. Although the fairways tend to be mostly flat, the numerous water hazards that come into play on several holes make it a sound test of your golfing skills, especially from the tips. Greens at University Park are large and undulating. The signature hole is the par-3 5th, which plays 193 yards and requires a tee shot over water to a bulkheaded green.

Westin Innisbrook Resort, Eagle's Watch

36750 Highway 19 N., Palm Harbor, FL 34684; phone (727) 942-2000
Tees: Championship: 6,550 yards, par-71, USGA rating 72.0, slope 127
Greens Fee: $55–100

Challenge: ★★★

Variety: ★★★½

Terrain: ★★★

Beauty/Visual Appeal: ★★★½

Pace of Play: ★★★½

Golf Facilities: ★★★

14-Club Test: ★★★

Intangibles: ★★★½

Value: ★★★½

Description and Comments Eagle's Watch and Hawk's Run are the two newest courses at Westin Innisbrook and were originally part of the 27-hole Sandpiper Course. Eagle's Watch features nine holes from the Sandpiper as well as nine completely new holes. The course, named after an eagle's nest located to the right of the 8th green, is a narrow tract that features an abundance of lakes and greens that are closely guarded by numerous bunkers. One of the best holes is the 7th, a par-3 (210 yards) that plays to an island green. If you are a mid- to high-handicapper and are looking for a course at Innisbrook that is fun to play but that still poses a challenge, you should consider playing either Eagle's Watch or Hawk's Run. Neither course is a cakewalk, but both are easier than the resort's other two courses.

Westin Innisbrook Resort, Hawk's Run

36750 Highway 19 N., Palm Harbor, FL 34684; phone (727) 942-2000

Tees: Championship: 6,260 yards, par-71, USGA rating 70.8, slope 125

Greens Fee: $55–100

Challenge: ★★★

Variety: ★★★

Terrain: ★★★

Beauty/Visual Appeal: ★★★½

Pace of Play: ★★★½

Golf Facilities: ★★★★

14-Club Test: ★★★

Intangibles: ★★★

Value: ★★★½

Description and Comments All the Hawk's Run here were part of the Sandpiper course, but have undergone recent renovations. Although this course is the shortest and easiest at Innisbrook, the new holes play much longer and the added bunkers and waste areas place a premium on accuracy, thereby increasing the challenge. Fairways tend to be quite narrow, and there is no shortage of bunkers surrounding the greens. Keep an eye out for the magnificent red tail hawks and ospreys (as well as the alligators) that can be found throughout the course.

Lodging in Orlando

EXPENSIVE

Grand Cypress Resort

Grand Cypress Resort is Orlando's premier resort destination, offering a variety of first-class accommodations, including the spectacular Hyatt

Regency and the equally impressive Villas of Grand Cypress. No matter what accommodation you select, you have access to the resort's full menu of activities that are available at this 1,500-acre resort.

First and foremost, guests of Grand Cypress have access to the resort's two courses (closed to outside play), the New Course and the three separate 9s (North/South/East). Additionally, guests can enjoy a 45-acre nature preserve; two pools, including an 800,000-gallon one with a grotto, water slide, and 12 waterfalls; hot tubs; health club; gym; lawn games; a dozen tennis courts; beach; lake; water games; equestrian center; miniature golf; and a number of children's programs. The only knock against the resort is that it is big, sprawling, and busy. If you're looking for cozy and charming, head elsewhere. If you want grand and modern with a nearly unrivaled amenities package, the Hyatt Regency Grand Cypress is perfect, even if you have to sidestep a few conventioneers along the way.

Golf Packages   Grand Cypress has a number of golf packages available. The basic package includes 18 holes of golf per day, cart fee, club storage, access to locker room, and full use of the practice facilities and driving range.

Hyatt Regency Grand Cypress Resort   1 Grand Cypress Blvd., Orlando, FL 32836; phone (800) 233-1234 or (407) 239-1234; www.hyatt.com; Rates $255–420

If you are looking for a more traditional hotel experience, you can't go wrong with the Hyatt Regency Grand Cypress. This Hyatt is an elegant 18-story hotel featuring 750 rooms and 75 suites, all of which are superbly appointed. One of the more striking features is the gorgeous atrium around which the hotel is built. It is filled with tropical plants and talking birds. The hotel also features two fine restaurants, La Coquina (see Dining section) for gourmet fare, and the more casual Hemingway's, for seafood.

Villas of Grand Cypress   1 North Jacaranda, Orlando, FL 32836; phone (800) 835-7377 or (407) 239-4700; www.grandcypress.com; Rates: $400 and up.

If you are traveling with a group you may want to consider the Villas of Grand Cypress. The villas, which range from one to four bedrooms, are Mediterranean style and feature patios or verandas overlooking waterways and fairways. The villas are nicely appointed and come with all the standard amenities.

Grand Floridian Resort & Spa (in Walt Disney World)

4401 Floridian Way, Orlando, FL 32830; phone (407) 824-3000; www.disneyworld.com; Rates: $285–530 (double)

Although Disney World offers many lodging options, the Grand Floridian is their shining star. Located on Disney's Seven Seas Lagoon, the Floridian has a rustic, Victorian-era look but is filled with modern conveniences. The resort is comprised of 900 rooms and 90 suites, each decorated in a charming manner.

Along with close proximity to all the offerings at Walt Disney World, including the many golf courses, the Floridian features six restaurants, a pool, whirlpool, two tennis courts, health club, lawn games, beach, boating, water activities, and children's programs. Additionally, there is a fine continental restaurant, Victoria & Albert's (see Dining section).

Golf Packages   Disney World requests that you contact the resort so that they can develop a custom golf package for you.

Grenelefe

3200 FL 546, Haines City, FL 33844-9732; phone (800) 237-9649 or (941) 422-7511; www.grenelefe.com; Rates: $220 (one-bedroom villa); $400 (two-bedroom villa)

If you want to escape the hustle and bustle of Orlando but still be close enough to enjoy some of the many activities the city has to offer, Grenelefe could be just what you are looking for. Located 45 minutes southeast of Orlando, Grenelefe is a 1,000-acre, full-service resort situated on Lake Marion. The resort is comprised of more than 800 suites and villas, but the real attraction here is the full menu of activities available at the resort.

The 54 holes of golf are just the beginning of the recreational feast. In addition, you will find 20 tennis courts (11 lit, 2 grass), an 18-hole miniature golf course, pier, marina, boat cruises, bicycle rentals, jogging and nature trails, fishing, and badminton. Additionally, you will find an exercise facility, pool, whirlpool, and sauna, as well as children's programs. Along with two restaurants, the resort has a grocery store if you prefer to cook in your villa.

Golf Packages   Grenelefe offers the Mulligan's Club Golf Package consisting of a fairway villa suite; 18 holes of golf daily (cart included); guaranteed tee times 90 days in advance; full American plan, including breakfast and dinner in Camelot Restaurant; one bucket of range balls each day; 10% discount on all golf shop purchases; discount on additional rounds; and applicable taxes and gratuities.

Walt Disney World Swan

1200 Epcot Resorts Blvd., Lake Buena Vista, FL 32830; phone (407) 934-3000; www.swandolphin.com or www.disneyworld.com; Rates: $310–430

The Swan is a splashy resort that looks as though it could be part of the Las Vegas strip. The two 45-foot-tall swans situated on the roof of the coral-

and-aqua-colored hotel are just one example of the Vegas influence. Beyond the glitz and color, the hotel offers premium accommodations and amenities, including four restaurants, three lounges, two pools, a grotto, four tennis courts, gym, beach, and water activities.

Golf Packages   Disney World requests that you contact the resort so that they can develop a custom golf package for you.

Walt Disney World Yacht and Beach Club

1700 Epcot Resort Blvd., Lake Buena Vista, FL 32830; phone (407) 934-7000; www.disneyworld.com; Rates: $230–430

You may feel as though you have been transported from Florida to Cape Cod as you arrive at the Yacht and Beach Club. The hotel is modeled after an old New England coastal resort with its gray clapboard exterior and an interior that features hardwood floors and brass accessories. There's even a lighthouse on the hotel's pier. The 1,122 rooms and 112 suites continue this Cape Cod theme and feature nautical appointments, such as a ship's wheel headboard.

On the outside, you will find three pools, two tennis courts, lawn games, a beach, and boating activities.

Golf Packages   Disney World requests that you contact the resort so that they can develop a custom golf package for you.

MODERATE

Bay Hill Club & Lodge

9000 Bay Hill Blvd., Orlando, FL 32819; phone (407) 876-2429; www.bayhill.com; Rates: $80–190

Compared to the flashy and glitzy resorts in the Orlando area, Bay Hill may seem quite staid and conservative. It is, and that is what is so attractive about the resort. Although it is close enough to Orlando's many attractions, it is far enough away to provide a sense of getting away from it all.

Be forewarned: Bay Hill's focus is golf, and though the course is top notch, the accommodations are mired in the 1960s. There is nothing special about the buildings or about the rooms. They are more than acceptable, but don't expect to find modern touches like a phone in the bathroom or a Jacuzzi tub. Also, since Bay Hill offers only minimal activities beyond golf, we suggest that you look elsewhere if you are traveling with your children. All that being said, we highly recommend Bay Hill if you want a true golf experience. Besides having access to the renowned course, the special feeling that you get when you stay at "Arnie's place" just can't be beat.

Golf Packages   Package includes accommodations, advanced reservations for golf, cart fees, and access to spa, salon, and pool.

Caribe Royale

14300 International Dr., Orlando, FL 32821; phone (800) 823-8300 or (407) 238-8000; www.cariberoyale.com; Rates: $179–209

Caribe Royale's big appeal is its location—near the many Walt Disney World attractions. The 1,218 all-suite rooms at Caribe are more than acceptable and include a complimentary full breakfast buffet (a great money saver if you are with your family). The hotel also features tennis courts, pools, a whirlpool, a gym, and children's programs.

Grosvenor Resort

1850 Hotel Plaza Blvd., Lake Buena Vista, FL 32830; phone (800) 624-4109 or (407) 828-4444; www.grosvenorresort.com; Rates: $160–215

Located in Walt Disney World Village, Grosvenor is not the most visually stunning building in the area by any means—it looks more like an office building than a resort. Once you get inside, you will find that the rooms and the facilities more than compensate for the building's drabness. Rooms are well furnished and are decorated with brilliant colors. For activities, you will find two pools, a whirlpool, two tennis courts, basketball and volleyball courts, lawn games, and a children's playground. The resort also features a Sherlock Holmes Museum and hosts a murder mystery dinner show each Saturday.

Mission Inn Golf & Tennis Resort

10400 CR 48, Howey-in-the-Hills, FL 34737; phone (800) 874-9053 or (352) 324-3101; www.missioninnresort.com; Rates: $175–195 rooms; $320–380 villas

A handsome, family-owned resort located on beautifully manicured grounds just outside Orlando. The resort features 176 rooms and suites and 15 separate villas, all of which are nicely appointed. The big draw here is the access to the two golf courses and the many other amenities, including a private lake with boating, marina, bicycle rental, lawn games, eight tennis courts, and a gym. The elegant El Conquistador restaurant (see Dining section) offers wonderful menu items.

Golf Packages   Mission Inn offers a number of golf packages including the "Golf Classic": accommodations, 18 holes of golf daily (including cart fee), dinner, breakfast, Lake Harris Cruise, yardage book and bag tag, range, and golf clinic.

INEXPENSIVE

Courtyard by Marriott

1805 Hotel Plaza Blvd., Lake Buena Vista, FL 32830; phone (407) 828-8888; Rates: $89–175; Built: 1989; Renovations: 1999

Hampton Inn

7110 S. Kirkman, Orlando, FL 32819; phone (800) 426-7866 or (407) 345-1112; Rates: $69–89; Built: 1991; Renovations: 1997

Riu Orlando

8688 Palm Pkwy., Lake Buena Vista, FL 32836; phone (888) 222-9963 or (407) 239-8500; Rates: $90–125; Built: 1989; Renovations: 1996

Dining in Orlando

Arthurs 27   Buena Vista Palace Resort, 1900 Buena Vista Dr., Lake Buena Vista; phone (407) 827-3450. Continental; Expensive; Reservations essential. Arthurs is Orlando's premier fine dining restaurant where meals last two to three hours. Breathtaking views from the 27th floor of the hotel complement the mouthwatering food. You should consider ordering the prix-fixe menu as it is a better bargain than the à la carte option.

El Conquistador   Mission Inn Golf & Tennis Resort, 10400 CR 48, Howey-in-the-Hills; phone (800) 874-9053 or (352) 324-3101. Continental; Moderate–Expensive; Reservations accepted. Scenic views of the golf course complement a varied menu of tasty dishes, including many seafood specialties.

Enzo's on the Lake   1130 S. U.S. Highway 17-92, Longwood; phone (407) 834-9872. Italian; Inexpensive–Moderate; Reservations accepted. The best Italian food in Orlando can be found at this local favorite. It's well worth the half-hour drive from Orlando.

La Coquina   Hyatt Regency Grand Cypress Resort, 1 Grand Cypress Blvd., Orlando; phone (800) 233-1234 or (407) 239-1234. French; Expensive; Reservations required. Renowned for their Sunday brunch as well as many French specialties. Seating in the kitchen is available and is quite entertaining.

Le Coq au Vin   4800 S. Orange, Orlando; phone (407) 851-6980. French; Inexpensive–Moderate; Reservations accepted. One of Orlando's best French restaurants and a local favorite. Favorite menu items include the liver pâté and the crème brûlée.

Pebbles   12551 FL 535, Lake Buena Vista; phone (407) 827-1111. Continental; Inexpensive; Reservations not required. A terrific casual restaurant offering a variety of dishes. The atmosphere is enhanced by views of the lake. One of the best menu items is the Mediterranean chicken salad.

Siam Orchid   7575 Republic Dr., Orlando; phone (407) 351-0821. Thai; Moderate–Expensive; Reservations accepted. Wonderful Thai dishes served in an authentic setting. Warning: When they say spicy, they mean spicy.

Spoodles   Boardwalk Inn, 2101 N. Epcot Resort Blvd., Lake Buena Vista; phone (407) 939-2380. Mediterranean; Inexpensive–Moderate; Reservations accepted. Tapas-style menu items let you sample a wide variety of selections. Among the best are the Moroccan beef skewers and the duck sausage pizza; the $21 sampler allows you to try a little bit of everything.

Victoria & Albert's   Grand Floridian Hotel, 4401 Floridian Way, Orlando; phone (407) 824-3000. Continental; Expensive; Reservations essential. Lovely Victorian-themed decor complements the tasty seven-course, prix-fixe menu that changes daily. There is one seating nightly (7–7:45 p.m.) which costs $80.

Activities in Orlando

Disney Theme Parks

Disney's Animal Kingdom   Interstate 4, Epcot/Downtown Disney Exit (Exit 26); phone (407) 824-4321. The newest addition to the Disney World family, the Animal Kingdom is part wildlife and part entertainment park. The Tree of Life is dramatic.

Disney–MGM Studios Theme Park   I-4, Epcot/Downtown Disney Exit (Exit 26); phone (407) 824-4321. Visitors can go behind the scenes at this studio and enjoy some of the many thrill rides.

Disney Water Parks   To escape the heat, you might want to head to one of Disney's three water parks: Blizzard Beach, River Country, or Typhoon Lagoon; phone (407) 824-4321.

Epcot   I-4, Epcot/Downtown Disney Exit (Exit 26); phone (407) 824-4321. It was Walt Disney's dream to build the "Experimental Prototype Community of Tomorrow" where nations existed in peace and could share technologies. Epcot, built 16 years after Disney's death, offers exhibits on various countries, their traditions, and their people.

Magic Kingdom   I-4, U.S. 192 (Exit 25); phone (407) 824-4321. Mickey, Minnie, Donald, Goofy, and the rest of the gang await you at this world-famous amusement park.

Non-Disney Attractions

Flying Tigers Warbird Air Museum   231 Hoagland Blvd., Kissimmee; phone (407) 933-1942. Museum has a collection of 30 vintage aircraft.

Gatorland   14501 S. Orange Blossom Trail; phone (800) 393-5297 or (407) 855-5496. If you want to see some alligators, this is the place for you.

Harry P. Leu Gardens   1920 N. Forest Ave.; phone (407) 246-2620. Over 50 acres of spectacular flowers and trees.

Orlando Museum of Art 2416 Mills Ave.; phone (407) 896-4231. Craving a dose of non-Disney culture? You might want to head here. Lots of hands-on exhibits that kids love.

SeaWorld Orlando 7007 Sea Harbor Dr., Orlando; phone (800) 327-2424 or (407) 351-3600. A chance to see mammals, fish, birds, and reptiles as they live in re-creations of their natural habitats.

Universal Studios Florida 1000 Universal Studios Plaza; phone (407) 363-8000. Another opportunity to go behind the scenes of a working movie studio.

The 19th Hole in Orlando

Grand Cypress Lounge 1 North Jacaranda, Orlando; phone (800) 835-7377 or (407) 239-1904. Excellent, two-level friendly room that celebrates good times and great golf.

Members Lounge Bay Hill, 9000 Bay Hill Blvd., Orlando; phone (407) 876-2429. Cozy and comfortable with the feel of a private club, all you really need to know is that this is where Arnie hangs out.

Lodging in Tampa/St. Petersburg/Sarasota

EXPENSIVE

Renaissance Vinoy Resort

501 5th Ave. NE, St. Petersburg, FL 33701; phone (800) 228-9290 or (727) 894-1000; www.renaissancehotels.com; Rates: $260–325

Although a recent $100 million renovation provided modern amenities and some much-needed touch-ups, the historic essence of this 1925 landmark hotel remains in full force. Listed on the National Register of Historic Places, the Vinoy has a colorful history. The resort features 360 spacious rooms, which are decorated in stylish patterns and feature all the modern conveniences. Among the five restaurants is Marchand's Grill, a lovely, romantic gastronomic haven (see Dining section).

The only drawback on the activity side is the beach access. The resort overlooks Tampa Bay, but the hotel's beach is not vast, and thus transportation is provided to nearby beaches. Beyond the beach and, of course, the golf, there is much to choose from: 12 clay tennis courts, gym, sauna, steam room, and lawn games.

Golf Packages Package includes accommodations, 18 holes of golf per day, range balls, nightly bag storage.

Resort at Longboat Key

301 Gulf of Mexico Dr., Longboat Key, FL 34228; phone (800) 237-8821 or (941) 383-8821; www.longboatkey.com; Rates: $215–345

Located on 1,000 acres of beautifully landscaped grounds, Longboat Key is one of Tampa's premier resort destinations. Situated along the ocean, the resort features 233 units, most of which (220) are suites, all decorated in a tropical theme. Each room sports a balcony overlooking either the golf course, beach, or lagoon. Although golf is the focus here, the resort offers countless amenities, including 38 tennis courts, a private beach with water activities, a gym, sauna, bicycles, and lawn games.

The resort features four different restaurants, offering everything from fine to casual dining. Orchids is the most elegant restaurant, whereas Spike 'n' Tees has the more relaxed atmosphere.

Golf Packages   Longboat's basic package includes accommodations, unlimited golf (including cart), use of the driving range, and nightly bag storage.

Saddlebrook Resort

5700 Saddlebrook Way, Wesley Chapel, FL 33543; phone (800) 729-8383 or (813) 973-1111; www.saddlebrookresort.com; Rates: $225–375

Saddlebrook is located on 480 isolated acres and is renowned for both its golf and tennis facilities. The accommodations vary from single units to one- to three-bedroom condos with their own kitchens. The rooms are tastefully decorated, each with its own patio or balcony. You will find three restaurants at the resort, including the Cypress Restaurant (see Dining section).

Along with the 36 holes of golf, Saddlebrook features 45 tennis courts as well as the Harry Hopman Tennis Academy, pools, health club, sauna, steam room, nature trails, fishing, bicycle rental, and children's programs.

Golf Packages   Saddlebrook offers an extensive golf package, including accommodations, daily breakfast, one dinner per three-night stay, 18 holes of golf daily (including cart), a second round of golf at cart-fee-only rate, club cleaning and storage, 60 days in advance tee times, golf gift set, access to S'Kids club, daily fitness center and spa admittance, 1-hour bike use daily, half-day use of lake tackle per day, and a welcome cocktail.

Westin Innisbrook Resort

36750 N. U.S. 19, Palm Harbor, FL 34684; phone (800) 456-2000 or (727) 942-2000; www.westin-innisbrook.com; Rates: $170–485

A spectacular, 600-acre resort that features 1,000 spacious units, all of which have their own kitchens (some have private balconies or patios as well). Along with access to the 90 holes of golf at the resort, Innisbrook features a number of other activities, including six pools, saunas, a miniature golf course, 13 tennis courts, a health club, jogging trails, racquetball, a wildlife sanctuary, a freshwater lake, bicycle rentals, and lawn games.

Golf Packages Innisbrook's golf package consists of deluxe accommodations, 18 holes of golf per day (including cart), advance starting times, club storage, locker room access, and unlimited use of fitness center.

MODERATE

Hyatt Regency

2 Tampa City Center, Tampa, FL 33602; phone (813) 225-1234; www.hyatt.com; Rates: $180–200

Centrally located in downtown Tampa, this Hyatt offers easy access to the surrounding area as well as all the city's restaurants and activities. The 17-story hotel features 520 rooms as well as a gym, pool, and whirlpool.

Radisson Lido Beach Resort

700 Benjamin Franklin Dr., Sarasota, FL 34236; phone (941) 388-2161; www.radisson.com; Rates: $219–295

An intimate, beautiful beachfront resort with only 116 units, all of which have a refrigerator; some come with a full kitchen. Request a room on the west wing as they feature balconies. Resort also has a pool, sauna, gym, dock, and boating activities.

Wyndham Harbour Island

725 S. Harbour Island Blvd., Tampa, FL 33602; phone (813) 229-5000; www.wyndham.com; Rates: $199–245

Located on a 177-acre island, just a stone's throw away from the mainland, this Wyndham provides a unique setting for a vacation. All of the 300 rooms in the 12-story hotel feature spectacular views, and the hotel is known for its superior service. In addition to an impressive beach and a full-service marina, including a variety of water sports, the hotel has an on-premises pool as well as access to the next-door Harbour Island Athletic Club and its health club and 20 tennis courts.

INEXPENSIVE

Best Western Golden Host Resort

4675 N. Tamiami Trail, Sarasota, FL 34234; phone (800) 722-4895 or (941) 355-5141; Rates: $89–109; Built: 1959; Renovations: 1999.

La Quinta Inn

4999 34th St. N, St. Petersburg, FL 33714; phone (727) 527-8421; Rates: $82–92; Built: unknown; Renovations: 1999.

Quality Suites

3001 University Center Dr., Tampa, FL 33612; phone (800) 228-5151 or (813) 971-8930; Rates: $99–159; Built: 1989; Renovations: 1997.

Dining in Tampa/St. Petersburg/Sarasota

Armani's   Hyatt Regency Westshore, 6200 Courtney Campbell Causeway, Tampa; phone (813) 281-9165. Italian; Expensive; Reservations required. One of Tampa's most romantic spots, with sweeping views of Tampa and its environs. The menu features tempting Italian favorites, including outstanding seafood. The signature dish is the veal Armani. Jackets and ties required.

Bijou Café   1287 1st St. S, Sarasota; phone (941) 366-8111. Continental; Moderate–Expensive; Reservations accepted. Famous for its extensive seafood selections, Bijou is one of Tampa's best continental restaurants. Take note, this restaurant is housed in what once was a 1920s gas station.

Café L'Europe   431 St. Armands Circle, Lido Key; phone (941) 388-4415. Continental; Moderate–Expensive; Reservations accepted. This restaurant offers a varied menu with special nods going to the veal and seafood selections. Terrific atmosphere provided by the surrounding art exhibits.

Cactus Club   1601 Snow Ave., Tampa; phone (813) 251-4089. Southwestern; Inexpensive; Reservations not needed. For a little Tex-Mex treat, head to the Cactus Club, Tampa's best Southwestern restaurant. The fajitas and a tasty Ultimate Margarita are hard to beat.

Colonnade   3401 Bayshore Blvd., Tampa; phone (813) 838-7558. Seafood; Inexpensive–Moderate; Reservations not needed. Family-owned since 1935, Colonnade is renowned for their seafood selections and is one of the best overall values in town. Memorable menu items include the lobster. Nautical decor and views of the Tampa Bay are bonuses.

Columbia   2117 E. 7th Ave., Tampa; phone (813) 248-4961. Spanish; Moderate; Reservations accepted. Since 1905, Columbia has been serving some of the best Spanish food in Tampa. The meal is complemented by an entertaining flamenco dancing show.

Cypress Restaurant and Terrace on the Green   Saddlebrook Resort, 5700 Saddlebrook Way, Wesley Chapel, FL 33543; phone (800) 729-8383 or (813) 973-1111. Continental; Expensive; Reservations accepted. Diners can choose to either eat inside at the Cypress Restaurant or on the adjoining Terrace on the Green at Saddlebrook's golf course. Whichever setting you choose, you will no doubt enjoy the extensive menu, with specialties including steak and veal.

Kojak's House of Ribs 2808 Gandy Blvd., Tampa; phone (813) 837-3774. American; Inexpensive–Moderate; Reservations not accepted. A local favorite, this family-run, casual restaurant serves some of the tastiest ribs around. The restaurant tends to be crowded, but the ribs are worth the wait.

Marchand's Renaissance Vinoy Resort, 501 5th Ave. NE, St. Petersburg; phone (800) 228-9290 or (727) 894-1000. Mediterranean; Moderate–Expensive; Reservations accepted. This is one of Tampa's most romantic dining spots. Menu favorites include shrimp and scallop ravioli and pan-seared bass. Contemporary jazz band provides evening entertainment Thursday through Sunday.

Marina Jack 2 Marina Plaza, Sarasota; phone (941) 365-4232. Seafood; Inexpensive–Moderate; Reservations accepted. For the best views of Sarasota Bay, head to Marina Jack or better yet, take the paddle wheeler dinner cruise on the *Marina Jack II* Wednesday through Sunday.

Michael's on East 1212 East Ave. S., Sarasota; phone (941) 366-0007. Continental; Moderate–Expensive; Reservations accepted. Located in downtown Sarasota, Michael's is an elegant restaurant that features a wide range of contemporary menu items, including grilled filet and pastas. An intimate bar with entertainment is a perfect place to start or end your evening.

Ophelia's on the Bay 9105 Midnight Pass Rd., Siesta Key; phone (941) 349-2212. American; Moderate; Reservations suggested. A wonderful waterfront setting complements a strong menu. Our recommendation: the cioppino.

Patrick's 1400 Main St., Sarasota; phone (941) 952-1170. American; Inexpensive; Reservations not accepted. Serving some of Tampa's best American favorites, such as steaks and cheeseburgers, Patrick's is always busy. If you want good ol' fashioned cooking then you will want to head here.

Activities in Tampa/St. Petersburg/Sarasota

Adventure Island 10001 Malcolm McKinley Dr., Tampa; phone (813) 987-5660. An offshoot of Busch Gardens (located less than a mile away), Adventure Island is a water park with slides, pools, and games to entertain kids of all ages and is an ideal escape from the heat.

Busch Gardens 3000 E. Busch Blvd., Tampa; phone (813) 987-5082. The 335-acre park is divided into eight different settings, each depicting a different African region. Visitors can see the various animals and birds that inhabit these regions as well as enjoy the many thrill rides throughout the park. For the adults, there is a beer-tasting class. Although this park has a petting zoo, it is best for the older kids.

Florida Aquarium   701 Channelside Dr., Tampa; phone (813) 273-4000. A terrific place to take the kids to see the many exhibits at this expansive aquarium. The 500,000-gallon tank with viewing windows is a highlight.

Great Explorations!   1120 4th St. S.; phone (813) 821-8885. A wonderful hands-on museum that is ideal for kids. Exhibits include the Touch Tunnel, a 90-foot-long maze where you can't see two inches in front of you.

Lowry Park   7530 North Blvd., Tampa; phone (813) 932-0245. Focal point of the park is the 24-acre zoo featuring a number of exotic animals. Additionally, the park has a section with statues of fable and nursery rhyme characters, an amusement park, and a lake with boat rides.

Marie Selby Botanical Gardens   811 S. Palm Ave., Sarasota; phone (941) 366-5730. A wide variety of beautiful flora are on display at this 11-acre garden. A highlight is the numerous orchids.

Ringling Museum of Art   U.S. Hwy. 41; phone (941) 355-5101. John Ringling, of Ringling Bros. fame, left his 66-acre estate to the people of Florida in 1936, and it has since been turned into a local attraction where visitors can tour the Ringling Residence, an art gallery, and see Ringling's extensive collection of circus memorabilia.

Salvador Dali Museum   1000 3rd St. S., St. Petersburg; phone (813) 823-3767. This museum houses the world's most extensive collection of surrealist Dali's work. If you are into Dali, you will love this place.

Spongeorama Exhibit Center   510 Dodecanese Blvd., Tarpon Springs; phone (813) 943-9509. An offbeat but interesting exhibition where you can learn about sponge diving and the sponge production industry.

Sunken Gardens   1825 4th St. N., St. Petersburg; phone (813) 896-3186. These gardens are visually stunning and feature a wide variety of exotic birds and flowers.

Part Eleven

Southern Florida

Overview

Southern Florida's motto could well be "Diversity Is Us," as the region has an astounding mix of ethnic, economic, social, and geographic personas. Nowhere else in the state will you find such a melting pot. For our purposes we have divided southern Florida into two regions: the southeast, stretching from Miami to Palm Beach, and the southwest, running from Marco Island up to Fort Myers.

The southeast region is dominated by two major but rather distinct cities, Miami and Palm Beach. Miami was once a retirement mecca with a median age nearly as high as the sultry summer temperatures. Recently, Miami has changed drastically, moving from the *Golden Girls* image to more of a *Miami Vice* look (and now even their clothes are back in style). The city has a distinct Latin flavor as it has become a modern-day Ellis Island for numerous immigrants from such areas as Cuba, Colombia, Panama, and Nicaragua. As in any major city with such a disparate ethnic and economic mix, there is a dark side. Miami has more than its fair share of violence and crime, and thus you should be on your toes when venturing out.

Palm Beach and its surroundings have a personality quite the opposite of Miami. From the beginning, Palm Beach was where the old money folks, such as the Rockefellers, Vanderbilts, and Kennedys, called home. Or more correctly, called their winter home. Palm Beach is the richest city in Florida and is dominated by stylish single-family residences and glorious estates.

The southwest of Florida has almost a mundane history in comparison to its more famous neighbors to the east. However, this is probably just how the residents of this area prefer it. Southwest Florida is a vacation hot spot for nonresidents and Florida locals alike. They come here to experience the outstanding beaches and participate in the numerous activities the area has to offer. Fort Myers, situated 140 miles west of Palm Beach, is one of the area's more prominent cities, despite the fact that it is not located on the

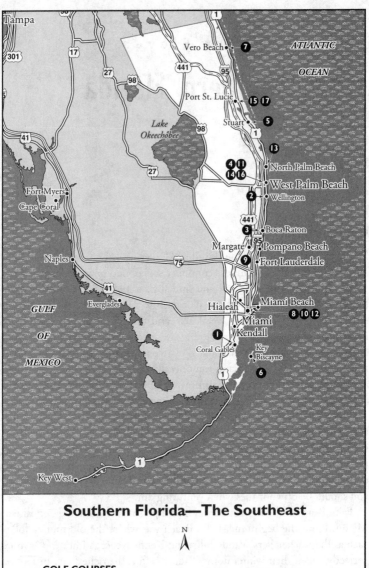

Southern Florida—The Southeast

N

GOLF COURSES

1. The Biltmore Golf Course
2. Binks Forest Golf Course
3. Boca Raton
4. Breakers West
5. Champions Club at Summerfield
6. Crandon Park at Key Biscayne
7. Dodger Pines
8. Doral Golf Resort & Spa
9. Colony West Country Club
10. Doral Golf Resort & Spa
11. Emerald Dunes Golf Course
12. Golf Club of Miami
13. North Palm Beach Country Club
14. Palm Beach Polo & Country Club
15. PGA Golf Club at The Reserve
16. PGA National Golf Club
17. St. Lucie West Country Club
18. Turnberry Isle Resort & Club

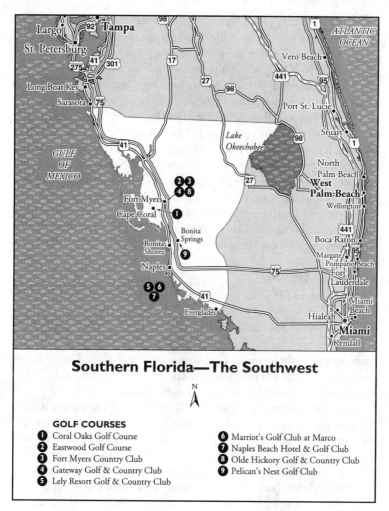

Southern Florida—The Southwest

N
↑

GOLF COURSES

1. Coral Oaks Golf Course
2. Eastwood Golf Course
3. Fort Myers Country Club
4. Gateway Golf & Country Club
5. Lely Resort Golf & Country Club
6. Marriot's Golf Club at Marco
7. Naples Beach Hotel & Golf Club
8. Olde Hickory Golf & Country Club
9. Pelican's Nest Golf Club

ocean. It is known as "the city of palms," a nickname resulting from the numerous palm trees planted by Thomas Edison on McGregor Boulevard. The other major city is Naples, 45 miles south of Fort Myers. Naples is quickly growing in reputation and per capita income and is fast becoming the southwest's answer to Palm Beach.

WHEN TO GO AND WHAT IT WILL COST

There is just no getting around it: during the summer, southern Florida is miserable. It is hot and humid—think steam room with a sauna thrown in. Highs during the summer reach into the 90s with a humidity factor just as high. It takes some getting used to, and only the truly brave or the deranged can be found playing golf at high noon. On the other hand, winter is unbelievably pleasant with highs in the mid- to upper-80s and lows in the 70s. Adding further intrigue to the area is the hurricane season that lasts from mid-summer to November. During this period, there is a real risk of heavy rain and strong winds. In fact, locals swear they can set their watches to summer afternoon thunderstorms, which usually roll in around 4 p.m.

There is also no getting around the fact that southern Florida is expensive. The rates at the golf courses and at the resorts tend to be the highest in the state. However, there are still some bargains out there, both in terms of when you travel as well as at the courses you play. Naturally, the best bargains can be found during the summer; if you book your tee times either very early in the morning or later in the day, and then retreat to a cool place during the high heat, this may be an ideal time for you. If you are looking for some rock-bottom golf bargains, the southwest area has more public-access courses and some grand values.

WHAT TO BRING

As with the rest of Florida, you will want to make sure you have plenty of sunscreen with you when you venture to the southern tip of the state. Even during the winter, the sun is quite strong and can burn your skin quickly. A sunscreen/bug repellant might be even more useful. South Florida is unchallenged as the flying and crawling bug capital of the United States. We also advise that you pack a rain jacket, especially during hurricane season, when the weather can be wet and unpredictable.

Along with your trusty clubs, you will need an ample arsenal of balls, as the common theme at southern Florida's golf courses is water. It comes in many forms and is the recipient of many a Titleist and Top Flite. As for your clubs, your standard 14 should do the trick. Remember, though, steady wind is a predominant factor on both coasts. You may want to work on your knock-down shots and three-quarter swings before you come down. Dust off your long irons; they'll get a workout in the windy conditions. Sure, you might be tempted to try and swat your fairway woods over all the sand and water hazards, but too often your high-flying woods will balloon in the wind and finish way offline—sometimes embarrassingly so.

Speaking of sand, remember also that most of the bunkers in southern Florida are filled with soft, thick, white sand. Stick a sand wedge in your bag with plenty of bounce; your normal sand wedge might slip underneath the ball, leaving you stuck in the bunker.

ONCE YOU'RE THERE

Southern Florida is dominated by a few premier resorts and a large number of public-access courses, more than anywhere else in the state. In the

Miami area, the Doral Resort and its Blue Monster receives the most attention, and deservedly so. This resort tends to be rather pricey, but it does offer a terrific array of activities as well as access to the five courses, most notably the Blue Course. Another spectacular resort in the Miami area is Turnberry, which has a comprehensive golf package.

In the Palm Beach area, there are three major golf resorts: Boca Raton and PGA National, along with the aforementioned Breakers hotel, which is worth stopping by just to take in the historic aura even if you can't spend the night. The Breakers boasts a 6,000-yard, on-property course that is one of the state's oldest. It is flat and short and has lots of similar holes. Only play it if you need a "museum piece" course for your collection. The setting is remarkable, and the course is fun in the wind, but it's not the kind of course you build your vacation around. The hotel, however, is absolutely fabulous.

Over in the southwest, the golf resorts are concentrated in the Marco Island area, where you can find two nationally run chains, Marriott Marco Island and Hilton Marco Island. In and around Naples, there is a large selection of public access golf courses, but only a handful of good resorts, most notable being the Naples Beach Hotel & Golf Club. For luxurious lodging try the Ritz-Carlton Naples, which has access to several local courses.

One of the best things about this area is the large number of high-quality courses open to the public. The downside is that they are almost always crowded. Among the best are Champions Club near Boca Raton; Crandon Park, site of the Royal Caribbean Classic in Key Biscayne; Emerald Dunes in West Palm Beach; PGA Golf Course at The Reserve located near Palm Beach; and Pelican's Nest outside of Fort Myers.

Gathering Information

Southeast Florida

Greater Miami Convention & Visitors Bureau
701 Brickell Ave., Suite 2700, Miami, FL 33131
Phone (800) 464-2643 or (305) 539-3000

Key Biscayne Chamber of Commerce
Key Biscayne Bank Building, 95 W. McIntyre St.,
Key Biscayne, FL 33149
Phone (305) 361-5207

Palm Beach County Convention & Visitors Bureau
1555 Palm Beach Lakes Blvd., Suite 204,
Palm Beach, FL 33401
Phone (800) 833-5733 or (561) 575-4636
www.palmbeachfl.com

Southwest Florida

Lee County Visitor and Convention Bureau
2180 W. 1st St., Fort Myers, FL 33901
Phone (800) 533-4753 or (941) 338-3500

Naples Area Chamber of Commerce & Visitors Center
895 5th Ave. S, Naples, FL 34102
Phone (941) 262-6141; www.naples-online.com

The Major Courses in Southeast Florida

Boca Raton

501 E. Camino Real, P.O. Box 5025, Boca Raton, FL 33431-0825; phone
(800) 327-0101 or (561) 395-3000

How To Get On: You must be a guest of the hotel to play at this golf
course.

Tees:

> Gold: 6,253 yards, par-71, USGA rating 69.3, slope 128
>
> Blue: 5,902 yards, par-71, USGA rating 67.6, slope 124
>
> White: 5,602 yards, par-71, USGA rating 66.4, slope 119
>
> Green: 5,160 yards, par-71, USGA rating 64.3, slope 107
>
> Red: 4,577 yards, par-71, USGA rating 65.5, slope 112

Challenge: ★★½	Golf Facilities: ★★★½
Variety: ★★★	14-Club Test: ★★½
Terrain: ★★★	Intangibles: ★★★½
Beauty/Visual Appeal: ★★★★	Value: ★★★½
Pace of Play: ★★★½	

Just the Facts   Year Opened: 1997; Course Designers: Gene Bates and
Fred Couples; Walking: No; Greens Fee: $125; 9-Hole/Twilight Rate: Yes;
Pull Carts: No; Practice Range: Yes; Club Rental: Yes.

Description and Comments   Boca Raton features a brand-new course in
the shadows of one of the nation's most honored, historic hotels. Previously, there was an ancient (for Florida) course on this site designed by
William Flynn in 1928, which was then redesigned by Robert Trent Jones
Sr. and Joe Lee. The Boca Raton hosted many celebrities in its heyday and
was even home to two celebrity staff professionals—the great Tommy
Armour in the 1930s and 1940s, followed by the even greater Sam Snead
in the 1950s and 1960s. But all along, the flat 18-hole championship
course wasn't that interesting. Enter Gene Bates and his design consultant,

Fred Couples. In 1997, they literally transformed the landscape. Spending more than $6 million, the resort and its architects created a shorter but far more exciting test of golf that was much more eye-pleasing as well.

Today, the Boca Raton Resort course is tightly packed with many parallel fairways, but all of them are gently rolling instead of pancake flat as in the old days, and nearly all of them are framed by mounds on both sides. Many of the holes contain spectacular water features, including tropical rock gardens and waterfalls. The greens tend to be large, firm, and medium-fast, with lots of interesting chipping areas around the greens for those who fail to find the putting surfaces with their approach shots. Despite its extremely short yardage, the course can be demanding in its own right because it tends to be fairly narrow. Most of the holes are fun to play—even the short ones—but several in particular are quite memorable. Topping the list is the petite 132-yard par-3 13th hole, which is especially lucky for those who get to play it. Just left and short of the green is an island with incredible plantings, water cascades, banyan trees, and a large bunker in the back right portion of the putting surface. Equally memorable and even more challenging is the 380-yard par-4 18th, which features a hugely elevated back tee, a serpentine bunker down the right-hand side, and an island green, all with a backdrop of palm trees and the lovely hotel.

Insider Tips This is not a particular easy course despite its miniscule yardage. A good player can truly get around with no more than a three wood off the tee the entire round. For the weaker golfer, it is highly advisable to simply put the ball in play, sacrificing distance for accuracy, because of the many narrow fairways and water hazards. A wild hitter is especially punished here because both sides of nearly every fairway are heavily mounded, so that if you get on the wrong side of the mound you have a totally blind shot to get it back in play.

Sharpen your sand wedge before you come to the Boca Raton Resort course: The bunkers are quite handsome, and surprisingly deep for a resort course. This can be a fun course for every class of player, especially intermediates; however, if you're not comfortable carrying the ball over water off the tee, it's going to be a long day. No less than 15 holes feature beautiful but pesky water hazards. March is when the wind tends to blow the strongest: Work on your low-trajectory shots if you want to conquer this course at that time of year.

Champions Club at Summerfield

3400 S.E. Summerfield Way, Stuart, FL 34997; phone (561) 283-1500
How To Get On: Tee times can be booked up to seven days in advance.
Tees:

   Gold: 6,809 yards, par-72, USGA rating 72.8, slope 131

Blue: 6,335 yards, par-72, USGA rating 70.5, slope 125

White : 5,614 yards, par-72, USGA rating 68.7, slope 117

Green: 4,941 yards, par-72, USGA rating 69.4, slope 116

Challenge: ★★★	Golf Facilities: ★★★½
Variety: ★★★½	14-Club Test: ★★★½
Terrain: ★★★½	Intangibles: ★★★
Beauty/Visual Appeal: ★★★½	Value: ★★★★
Pace of Play: ★★★	

Just the Facts   Year Opened: 1994; Course Designer: Tom Fazio; Walking: No; Greens Fee: $20–58; 9-Hole/Twilight Rate: Yes; Pull Carts: No; Practice Range: Yes; Club Rental: Yes.

Description and Comments   Located a half-hour north of North Palm Beach, Champions is one of the more open Fazio courses that you will find in the country, featuring fairly wide fairways and only scattered thickets of trees. However, this is not an easy course—it also features more than 90 sand traps and is situated among surrounding wetlands, which create multiple hazards both literally and figuratively. The wetlands are filled with wildlife (the Discovery Channel could film here for weeks), so if you hit your ball into them, wave goodbye and move on—you don't want to search for it here. This area is also known for its bald eagle nesting grounds, so keep your eyes peeled.

The course is very Florida-like, with flat terrain and wetlands that come into play on 12 of the holes. The course reflects the architectural move toward creating courses that might not offer stunning drama everywhere you look but do provide enough scenery to please the senses and at the same time offer a sound challenge. All of the tee boxes are elevated, providing scenic views of the surrounding areas as well as a great vantage point to scope out the hole.

The fairways here tend to be receptive to tee shots and provide options on your approaches. On nearly every hole you can opt to bump-and-run your shot, or you can hit a more traditional aerial approach. Champions is known for its par-3s, all of which are picturesque and at the same time pose a good challenge. The 2nd hole is a 197-yard par-3 that plays over wetlands and requires a precise shot. Another dandy is the watery, 178-yard 6th. It is the 17th, however, that is the course's signature hole. This par-3 plays 210 yards and features water to the right and bunkers all around. You need both length and accuracy to birdie here, just as you would have needed at the rugged, 434-yard, par-4 16th.

Insider Tips   The key to scoring well at Champions is a combination of accuracy as well as the ability to work the ball. You will often need to fade or draw the ball to reach a green as you must negotiate your way over the nearby wetland. Due to the profusion of wetlands and water hazards that jut into play, this course can discourage power players until they've played here a few times. Champions is a very good value, especially in comparison to the courses in the area, and is a terrific opportunity to play a Fazio creation. The only drawback is that most of the holes look just like the one before. Still, Champions has a modest but handsome pro shop/clubhouse and a first-rate driving range and putting green, underscoring what a bargain this place is. Don't let the "rat-tat-tats" disturb your concentration. It's not gang activity, it's the numerous woodpeckers that frequent the course.

Crandon Park at Key Biscayne

6700 Crandon Blvd., Key Biscayne, FL 33149; phone (305) 361-9129
How To Get On: Tee times can be made up to five days in advance.
Tees:

> Blue: 7,099 yards, par-72, USGA rating 74.0, slope 139
> White: 6,457 yards, par-72, USGA rating 71.0, slope 125
> Forward: 5,662 yards, par-72, USGA rating 72.7, slope 129

Challenge: ★★★★	Golf Facilities: ★★
Variety: ★★½	14-Club Test: ★★★
Terrain: ★★★	Intangibles: ★★★½
Beauty/Visual Appeal: ★★★★	Value: ★★★★
Pace of Play: ★★	

Just the Facts   Year Opened: 1972; Course Designers: Robert von Hagge and Bruce Devlin; Walking: At times; Greens Fee: $45–90; 9-Hole/Twilight Rate: Yes; Pull Carts: No; Practice Range: Yes; Club Rental: Yes.

Description and Comments   Crandon Park recently changed its name from Links at Key Biscayne. Though its identity may have been altered, its reputation remains intact: This is one of Florida's best public courses, and may well be the best value around. It is not often that we recommend a municipal course, but Crandon Park is the exception to the rule (how many times is a municipal course the site of a major stop on a tour, as Crandon is for the Royal Caribbean Classic on the Senior PGA Tour?). Crandon owes much of its success to Hurricane Andrew. Andrew caused massive destruction all around Miami in 1992, and the nearby communities and these areas received federal disaster relief. Dade County decided that rather than just repairing the course, they would use the funds to rebuild and improve. They turned to Robert von Hagge, the original architect for this task.

Although von Hagge made it a tougher and much more demanding layout, much of the credit still goes to Mother Nature for Crandon's awe-inspiring setting. The course is surrounded by palm and mangrove trees, but you might not even notice them as the spectacular views of Biscayne Bay and the Miami skyline beyond are mesmerizing. Water really is the prevalent theme here, with 13 holes featuring some form of the liquid substance and five holes playing right along the Biscayne Bay. Another noteworthy point is that you won't find any housing on this course . . . and you never will. The land the course was built on was donated to the county under the condition that its use would be solely for golf. The result is a pristine, sensational setting for a terrific round of golf.

As you make your way through the first few holes, you will quickly realize that this is no typical "muni" course. The 3rd hole is a demanding par-3 that plays 187 yards through tunnel of mangroves, over a small lake, to a well-bunkered green. But it is really number four, the hardest hole on the course, where Crandon shows its teeth. The par-5 hole is incredibly long, 642 yards, and is a slight dogleg left that plays to an immense green guarded on the left by a trap. Many argue, however, the toughest hole is really the par-4 7th. Another dogleg, this time to the right, plays to a tight fairway. Your approach shot is over water, and the green is protected like an armored car, with water on both sides.

The back nine kicks off with two tough holes. The 10th is a 561-yard par-5 that demands accuracy from tee to green. The double dogleg hole requires a tee shot to a well-guarded landing area protected by a pond as well as traps. Your second shot must avoid more water located on both sides of the fairway, and then your approach shot is to a massive green surrounded by sand traps. The 11th is a par-4, 427-yard dogleg right with a fairway flanked by bunkers on the left and a lake on the right. The approach shot must carry water, and the green has bookend sand traps as well as water behind.

If some of the holes start to look alike, it is because nearly every green appears to be adrift in a sea of traps. Things actually get a bit monotonous, because you can seldom run a ball onto these greens, an obvious advantage in the wind, because traps block the entrances. Thus, you wind up having to hit a numbing array of sand shots during your round, which can get a bit frustrating.

Insider Tips   To score well at Crandon, course management is paramount. There are many hazards and doglegs on the course; thus, picking your line and playing the shortest angle will help you negotiate your way around in the fewest strokes possible. Also, as with most of the courses situated near the water, the yardages at Crandon will be severely influenced if the wind is blowing, so make sure to take note and club correspondingly.

A word of caution: Though the course itself is top notch, the pro shop, clubhouse, and practice facilities are not much to write home about. They are very municipal-like; don't expect a "country club" experience here.

This course is popular with the locals and, because tee times can only be booked five days in advance, it is often hard to get on. Once you do get on, play can be awfully slow, as golfers can't help but watching their wind-blown shots drift into bunkers and water hazards. Too much time is wasted with rakes and ball retrievers. Nevertheless, we suggest that you either give the telephone booking service a chance or try to walk on and fill a foursome. No doubt you will find your efforts to be well worth it to play a tour-quality course.

Doral Golf Resort and Spa, Blue Course

4400 N.W. 87th Ave., Miami, FL 33178; phone (800) 713-6725 or (305) 592-2000

How To Get On: Guests of the resort can make tee times when they make their reservations. Nonguests can make tee times 30 days in advance.

Tees:

>   Blue: 6,939 yards, par-72, USGA rating 72.0, slope 127

>   White: 6,597 yards, par-72, USGA rating 70.4, slope 122

>   Forward: 5,786 yards, par-72, USGA rating 71.8, slope 124

Challenge: ★★★★	Golf Facilities: ★★★★½
Variety: ★★★½	14-Club Test: ★★★★
Terrain: ★★★½	Intangibles: ★★★★½
Beauty/Visual Appeal: ★★★★	Value: ★★★½
Pace of Play: ★★★½	

Just the Facts   Year Opened: 1961; Course Designer: Dick Wilson; Walking: At times; Greens Fee: $90–220; 9-Hole/Twilight Rate: Yes; Pull Carts: No; Practice Range: Yes; Club Rental: Yes

Description and Comments   If you ask the average person to name some famous monsters they probably will mention the elusive Loch Ness Monster, the unenviable "Green-Eyed" Monster, or even Cookie Monster. If you ask the average golfer to name a famous monster, the Blue Monster will probably top the list. Other monsters may have scared more people, but the Blue Monster, more formally known as Doral's marquee Blue Course, truly makes golfers shake in their Foot-Joys.

When the Blue Course opened in 1961, it quickly earned the reputation of being one of the most difficult tracks in the nation for amateurs and pros alike. Raymond Floyd even went so far as to call it "the hardest course I'd ever seen." It was a relentless combination of green grass, white sand, blue water, and fierce wind. Thus, the moniker of "Monster" was born—

just like a monster, the course had fangs, claws, and even some fire shooting from its mouth. It was just plain tough. Over the years however, the course has mellowed in its old age and lost much of its fury. When KSL Recreation purchased the resort from the founding Kaskel family, they undertook a multimillion-dollar renovation of the entire resort and each of its courses. Ray Floyd, ironically enough, was hired to put some fire back into the Monster, a task he enthusiastically embraced—a little too enthusiastically, many argued, after they played his updated version. The new Monster was considered overly penal, and thus not long after its 1997 reopening, the course underwent some minor adjustments, including the removal of seven of Floyd's 18 new bunkers (don't worry, there still are more than 120 left) and the addition of landing/bail-out areas. The final result: The Monster has returned, and it has its bite back. But at the same time, the golfer, like the story of David and Goliath, has a fighting chance to slay it (though you might consider using a sand wedge rather than a sling shot).

If you're a television golf viewer, you no doubt have spent many a March day watching the pros enjoy the beautiful sun of southern Florida during the Doral Ryder Open while you made excuses as to why that snowy driveway has not been shoveled. Nearly every great modern pro has competed at Doral and among past champions are Jack Nicklaus, Greg Norman, and Floyd himself. Although TV provides a pleasant, all too brief escape, you cannot really appreciate the true essence of Doral until you play the Blue Course in person. Some of the best holes at the course are the par-3s, a collection of visually stunning and physically demanding gems. The first you will encounter is the 4th, a 237-yard par-3 that is considered one of the toughest in the country. The yardage is long enough on its own, but the hole tends to play even longer as your tee shot must carry one of the eight lakes found on the course guarding the entire right side of the hole. The green is immense, slopes severely, and is well protected by bunkers.

The final hole on the front side is also a par-3 and is nearly as demanding. The hole measures 163 yards and is completely encircled by water. When the wind is blowing, this hole can be a true bear. Number 13 is bone dry, but is a fearsome challenge at 246 yards; luckily it typically plays downwind, but still requires quite a poke.

Although the par-3s garner much attention, it is number 18 that is the headlining star on the Blue Course. Considered to be one of the hardest holes on the PGA Tour (it is actually the hole known as the Blue Monster), 18 is a par-4, slight dogleg left that plays 425 yards from the back tees. Your tee shot must avoid the lake that runs the entire length of the hole on the left as well as the trees and bunkers that skirt the narrow landing area. Water will come into play again on your approach shot as you hit to the long and narrow green.

Insider Tips Some folks honestly wonder what all the fuss is about at Doral's Blue Monster. It sits on flattish land, has no ocean views, and costs more than $200 to play in high season. Well, it's partly a fair question. We'll concede that there are probably two dozen courses in Florida alone that are more dramatic.

Nevertheless, we feel that the Blue is "sneaky great." For starters, access is superb. The 1st hole is right outside the pro shop door, which is not far from whichever room you're staying in. Second, the course just oozes a mature feel, with huge palms and pines, unusual banyan trees, and a surprising amount of lush vegetation on many holes. Third, there's simply an aura about the place. The PGA Tour has stopped here every year since 1962, making it the longest-running act on the Tour except for Augusta National and Pebble Beach. There's just a palpable sense of history here, especially as you arrive at the 18th hole and picture all the incredible duels and great stars that have been influenced by this demanding course.

Finally, nothing is terribly fancy here, but you'll be asked to play one solid shot after the next in order to avoid the sand and water. Each hole boasts subtle differences from the one before it; when the wind gets up, especially as it does in the spring, it can make the course's 127 slope seem like a joke. During these times, the slope should check in at 172. The Blue Monster isn't as flashy as it would have been touted in the 1960s. It's simply an old-fashioned, excellent test of golf soaked in lore. If you're looking for sizzle, you may find Doral's Blue Monster a disappointment. If it's steak you seek, you've come to the right place.

It is safe to say that this course will present a challenge, but it is also safe to say that the Monster can be tamed if you heed some warnings. First and foremost is course management. Ball positioning is key at the Blue Course, as water and sand are so prevalent and can turn a par or birdie possibility into double bogey in a heartbeat. As you stand on the tee, visualize the best line to the green, not only for your tee shot but also for the succeeding shots. Also, make sure to practice your bunker shots before you hit the course. Traps proliferate the course, and the sand tends to be of the fine variety, so you will want to have your sand game up and running.

The predominant wind can have a stunning effect on the ball, so make sure to make adjustments in regard to yardages and direction. Finally, the greens tend to be large, so try to nuzzle your approaches as close to the pin as possible though you'd rather have a 20-foot uphill putt than a 10-foot downhiller. The good news is that the greens do putt very true and are not overly fast. The bad news is that the combination of wind and grass grain can turn seemingly easy putts into brutes. It's best to factor in both, before striking any putt.

A great way to experience the Blue Monster is on foot. It's an easy, pleasant walking course, and caddies are available. To play the Blue in its finest form, try it in mid-February, just before tournament time, when the rough is up and the greens are quick, but before the March winds get testy.

Emerald Dunes Golf Course

2100 Emerald Dunes Dr., West Palm Beach, FL 33411; phone (561) 684-4653

How To Get On: Tee times can be made 30 days in advance.

Tees:

> Gold: 7,006 yards, par-72, USGA rating 73.8, slope 133
>
> Blue: 6,558 yards, par-72, USGA rating 71.7, slope 129
>
> White: 6,120 yards, par-72, USGA rating 69.7, slope 125
>
> Green: 5,593 yards, par-72, USGA rating 72.2, slope 126
>
> Red: 4,676 yards, par-72, USGA rating 67.1, slope 115

Challenge: ★★★½	Golf Facilities: ★★★★
Variety: ★★★½	14-Club Test: ★★★★
Terrain: ★★★★	Intangibles: ★★★★
Beauty/Visual Appeal: ★★★★	Value: ★★★½
Pace of Play: ★★★	

Just the Facts Year Opened: 1990; Course Designer: Tom Fazio; Walking: Yes; Greens Fee: $45–140; 9-Hole/Twilight Rate: Yes; Pull Carts: Yes; Practice Range: Yes; Club Rental: Yes.

Description and Comments Emerald Dunes gained near-immediate notoriety for its outstanding golf experience and for the fact that its "SuperDune" was the highest elevation in Palm Beach (except for the local landfill site). Don't worry if you're afraid of heights, however—SuperDune only rises 50 feet above sea level.

Though the course's setting may be down to earth, its reputation as one of Florida's best high-end daily-fee courses continues to soar. As soon as you set foot inside the $2.5 million clubhouse, you start to think that this is no average public golf facility. Once you reach the first tee, you know that this is no average golf facility. The course itself is a blend of Scottish-style links and a rolling, mounded, Carolina-like layout. These two disparate styles were blended seamlessly by golf's most honored designer, Tom Fazio. As you make your way around the course, you will see that the challenges lie in the form of numerous bunkers and lateral water hazards. The fairways tend to be relatively open with only a minimal number of trees, but the course still has quite a bite.

So what is SuperDune? SuperDune is a manmade creation of piled-up dirt and sand, grassed over. It rises five stories above the course, not exactly nosebleed territory, but substantial for south Florida. It is quite memorable, as it is comprised of three greens and three tee boxes and provides panoramic views of the surrounding 60 acres. SuperDune also features a lovely waterfall behind the 5th green.

One of the best holes on the front side is the par-5 5th, which plays 555 yards from the tips. This is a true "three shotter" featuring all kinds of hazards, including water all along the left side and a number of strategically placed bunkers. You will want to stay to the right side of the fairway on both your tee and second shots to leave yourself in the best position for your approach shot. Number nine is known as the "Green Monster," a par-4 that plays a whopping 474 yards and features water along the right side of the hole running from tee to green, as well as several fairway bunkers. If you land in one of the bunkers, you can kiss getting on in two goodbye.

The 18th is a wonderful finishing hole. The tee box is situated atop SuperDune, and between the waterfall behind, the nearby creek and the stunning view, you may not want to ever leave the teeing ground. But we promise it will be worth it. The hole, a par-4 that measures 436 yards, plays left to right and is guarded by a series of bunkers and water on the right, while the left is not much easier as the fairway narrows and there is another bunker as well as a handful of bushes.

Insider Tips   If you are on a budget, you may consider Emerald Dunes well out of your price range, especially since it is a public course. Though we agree it tends to be a tad pricey, we want to assure you that it is no typical public course—in fact it is one of Florida's best public golf courses. From the minute you step out of your car, you will be treated as though you are a member, rather than just a visitor to a public course. If you can stomach the entry fee, you can't go wrong here.

The key to scoring at Emerald Dunes is a happy marriage between length and accuracy, but as with many marital unions, it's one that is hard to achieve. Unlike many courses these days, Emerald Dunes lets the golfer determine his or her own destiny; this is not a course that is tricked up, but one that allows the golfer to make aggressive swings. However, it is also a course that can penalize if the shots are errant.

You won't find many forced carries, making this a contender for higher handicappers, but what you will find are a number of strategic bunkers and even a few lakes that place a premium on accuracy. Greens are vast and can sport tricky pin positions, so you will need to have your short game working to avoid those dreaded three putts.

PGA Golf Club at The Reserve, North and South Courses

1916 Perfect Dr., Port St. Lucie, FL 34986; phone (800) 800-GOLF

How To Get On: The Reserve features three 18-hole courses. Tee times can be made up to three days in advance.

North Course Tees:

> Championship: 7,026 yards, par-72, USGA rating 73.8, slope 133
>
> Blue: 6,649 yards, par-72, USGA rating 72.1, slope 129
>
> White: 6,254 yards, par-72, USGA rating 70.1, slope 124
>
> Red: 4,993 yards, par-72, USGA rating 67.5, slope 118

South Course Tees:

> Championship: 7,087 yards, par-72, USGA rating 74.5, slope 141
>
> Blue: 6,606 yards, par-72, USGA rating 72.3, slope 137
>
> White: 6,147 yards, par-72, USGA rating 70.1, slope 129
>
> Red: 5,590 yards, par-72, USGA rating 67.6, slope 123

Challenge: ★★★★	Golf Facilities: ★★★★
Variety: ★★★★	14-Club Test: ★★★★
Terrain: ★★★½	Intangibles: ★★★★
Beauty/Visual Appeal: ★★★★	Value: ★★★★½
Pace of Play: ★★★	

Just the Facts   Year Opened: 1996; Course Designer: Tom Fazio; Walking: Yes; Greens Fee: $7–60; 9-Hole/Twilight Rate: Yes; Pull Carts: No; Practice Range: Yes; Club Rental: Yes.

Description and Comments   Though the PGA of America is entrusted to oversee all levels of golfers, its courses tended to cater to the affluent as well as the professional player. The PGA Golf Club at The Reserve changed all that. As the course's tagline says: "Home to the pros, open to the public." The Reserve is Tom Fazio's creation, but golf almost takes a back seat to the environment here. This course has earned the highly coveted "signature" status from the Audubon Society, an honor that has only been given to a handful of courses nationwide. As you can imagine, this course is visually stunning with its lovely, lush flora and fauna, which includes an array of birds that live in the manmade birdhouses built out of recycled materials.

Both courses at The Reserve have unique and distinct personalities. The South course is the most impressive of the two as it winds its way through the tropical surroundings. It will no doubt intimidate the average golfer even though its fairways feature huge landing areas, as there are numerous, multi-tiered bunkers and lakes that hug the fairways and nestle up to the greens. The North course resembles a North Carolina track. The layout tends to be less demanding than the South, but you will find more sand traps as well as fairways that have more mounding. The greens on the North are massive and can be very tricky to putt, since they are undulating. There are also a number of blind shots that you will encounter since many of the holes feature elevation changes. Note: A third public course recently opened at PGA Golf Club in December 1999, designed by Pete Dye.

Insider Tips The North and South Courses are designed to challenge but not overpower; golfers who can keep the ball in play will no doubt find these courses to be honest and conquerable. The biggest problem you will encounter is keeping your mind on your golf game as the surroundings and setting of both courses are overwhelming and can be pleasantly distracting.

We suggest that you try to fit both courses into your day, as each offers very distinct golfing experiences. If you do have to choose between the two courses, we recommend the South since it offers more of a "true" golf experience. Another wonderful feature is that walking is encouraged at The Reserve. The courses are walker-friendly, and hoofing it is a delightful way to play them. Finally, take note of the greens fees. You will be hard pressed to beat the rate that is charged at The Reserve (sometimes as low as $7 for twilight play). This truly is a course for every golfer, and no doubt everyone will enjoy it.

PGA National Golf Club, Champion Course

1000 Avenue of the Champions, Palm Beach Gardens, FL 33418; phone (800) 633-9150 or (561) 627-1800

How To Get On: You must be a guest of the resort to play this course; guests can make tee times up to a year in advance.

Tees:

    Black: 7,022 yards, par-72, USGA rating 74.7, slope 142

    Gold: 6,742 yards, par-72, USGA rating 73.2, slope 134

    Blue: 6,373 yards, par-72, USGA rating 71.1, slope 129

    White: 6,023 yards, par-72, USGA rating 69.1, slope 124

    Red: 5,377 yards, par-72, USGA rating 71.1, slope 123

Challenge: ★★★★½	Golf Facilities: ★★★
Variety: ★★★½	14-Club Test: ★★★★
Terrain: ★★★	Intangibles: ★★★★
Beauty/Visual Appeal: ★★★½	Value: ★★★
Pace of Play: ★★½	

Just the Facts Year Opened: 1981; Course Designers: Tom Fazio and Jack Nicklaus; Walking: No; Greens Fee: $150–170; 9-Hole/Twilight Rate: Yes; Pull Carts: No; Practice Range: Yes; Club Rental: Yes.

Description and Comments PGA National is the headquarters of the PGA of America, the club professionals' governing body, which is responsible for promoting the game of golf and maintaining its integrity. It is thus fitting that the Champions Course is dedicated to Jack Nicklaus, a man who personifies all that is good about golf. As it says on the scorecard: "The Champion Golf Course is dedicated to Jack Nicklaus in honor of those whose commitment to golf has been an inspiration to the game." But this is not Nicklaus's only connection to the course; in 1990 he redesigned the Fazio creation, making it more playable and spectator-friendly. Fairways were made concave and very receptive to shots, and mounds were added throughout to accommodate galleries during professional tournaments.

The Champions Course has hosted quite a few champions of its own during the 1983 Ryder Cup, 1987 PGA Championship, and multiple PGA Seniors Championships, all held here. Yet, despite this outstanding tournament history and architectural pedigree, the course is really about relentless challenge rather than outstanding design.

The course features a variety of hazards, which eventually wreak havoc on nearly every golfer. Although there are more than 50 bunkers strategically placed throughout the course, the water, found on no less than 16 holes, poses the biggest challenge. The greens here will keep you on your toes as they vary in size, from 20 to 43 yards deep, and tend to be fairly fast with a number of undulations.

Holes six and eight are two of the best holes on the front side. The former is a par-5 that plays 484 yards from the black tees. Though the yardage is not all that intimidating, the hazards will no doubt get your heart racing. The hole features a fairway as slender as a supermodel that is surrounded by trouble: On the left is a lake that extends from tee to green, and on the right is a series of sand traps. Your tee shot must also carry a portion of this lake from all teeing grounds except the reds. The 8th is a long par-4 (422 yards) that is the first and really only hole where you can "grip and rip" your tee shot. The fairway is extremely wide (in comparison with the rest of the course), and there is nary a hazard off the tee. But this hole didn't earn its ranking as the second hardest on the course for nothing. Trouble is brewing with your approach shot, which must carry a lake that bisects the fairway to an elevated green pinched by bunkers on each side.

The backside of the course is really where Champions bears its fangs. The hardest hole on the course is number 11, a 444-yard par-4 with a green that hugs a lake on the right and has bunkers and water to the left. You really need to strike your tee shot perfectly to have any chance of getting on in two. Your best club may just be that trusty extension-rod ball retriever (or a snorkel and mask). Holes 15 through 17 comprise something called "the bear trap." All three are demanding and visually stunning. The 15th is a par-3 that plays 179 yards and has water running from tee to green on the right and a bunker guarding the green on the left. It was here that Raymond Floyd plunked two balls into the drink in the final round of the 1994 Senior PGA Championship, losing his lead and the tournament to Lee Trevino. So if you find yourself following suit, you can be consoled that it even happens to the best of them.

Sixteen is a brutal, watery par-4, and the 17th another insidious par-3 with more water. The final hole is a double dogleg par-5 with a fairway snaking between a multitude of bunkers on the left and a long strip of water on the right. The medium-sized green is no less perilous as it is encircled by even more gaping sand traps and has water awaiting any wayward shots to the right. At least if you play 18 smart, you can have a good shot at par or birdie. Playing the bear trap you need more than smarts—you need raw courage.

Insider Tips This is one course where you really need all aspects of your game to be in sync to score well. Precise and long tee shots are critical, as are well-struck approaches. Unless you are having the round of your life, you also need to have your sand wedge warmed up as it will no doubt get quite a workout. We haven't even talked about the wind yet—it can add even more treachery to an already demanding course.

Honestly, this course is a handful for most folks, even if they pick the most appropriate set of tees. If you're a golfer who pays close attention to the scorecard, you're going to have a round full of headaches. It's just too hard—too many forced carries over awkwardly placed water hazards to slender fairways and oddly shaped greens. If, on the other hand, you're comfortable with making a few double bogies and want the satisfaction of doing battle with a true championship course, you'll love the Champions.

The black tees should be reserved for those low, low handicappers who enjoy a good challenge. One major drawback to the course is its popularity. Since it is head and shoulders above the other courses at the resort, it tends to get a lot of play. Add this to the fact that the layout is not all that conducive to quick play, and what you get is a long day on the links. You will want to check with the starter to see if there are big groups of conventioneers that are going off and try to avoid playing after them. Early morning and off-season often afford speedier rounds.

Turnberry Isle Resort and Club, South Course

19999 W. Country Club Dr., Aventura, FL 33180; phone (305) 933-6929

How To Get On: You must be a guest of the resort to play this course; guests can make tee times when they make their reservations.

Tees:

   Blue: 7,003 yards, par-72, USGA rating 73.7, slope 136
   Green: 6,458 yards, par-72, USGA rating 71.0, slope 118
   White: 6,078 yards, par-72, USGA rating 68.7, slope 111
   Red: 5,581 yards, par-72, USGA rating 71.3, slope 116

Challenge: ★★★½   Golf Facilities: ★★★★
Variety: ★★★½   14-Club Test: ★★★½
Terrain: ★★★   Intangibles: ★★★
Beauty/Visual Appeal: ★★★½   Value: ★★★½
Pace of Play: ★★★★

Just the Facts Year Opened: 1971; Course Designer: Robert Trent Jones Sr.; Walking: No; Greens Fee: $45–90; 9-Hole/Twilight Rate: Yes; Pull Carts: No; Practice Range: Yes; Club Rental: Yes.

Description and Comments Turnberry is one of South Florida's most revered resorts, having built a reputation for quality accommodations, a full menu of activities, and superb service. The resort boasts two golf courses, but the South Course basks in the limelight. A traditionally designed layout, built by Robert Trent Jones Sr., the South is impeccably maintained and conditioned and has established its own reputation for a high level of service.

The course itself is a very playable "resort" course featuring healthy challenges, but it is not intended to break one's spirit. Water is the prevailing theme here. It can be found on 14 of the holes and on all the par-3s and par-5s, you will be required to carry some form of the liquid hazard. The other big challenge can be found in the many elevated greens, targets that are shrunken even further by the wind that blows off the nearby Atlantic Ocean. Trees are plentiful on the South, though not as thick or as troublesome as they were pre–Hurricane Andrew in 1992.

Your first taste of Turnberry's hazards comes at the 2nd hole, a 526-yard par-5. The hole's main trouble comes in the form of a lake that stretches the second half of the hole before it cuts in front of the elevated green. The next hole is the first par-3, and it plays 208 yards with more of that pesky watery stuff in front. Another front-nine favorite is the 539-yard, par-5 6th, which features the lovely, Mediterranean-style hotel in the background and an equally lovely, flower- and rock-lined pond in the foreground.

The biggest challenge comes on the backside, especially the final six holes, all of which feature water that can quickly come into play if you aren't careful. The final hole, however, receives the most attention, and deservedly so. The 18th is a narrow, 545-yard par-5 guarded on the right by a lake that begins 250 yards off the tee and then proceeds to run down the entire length of the hole. Avoiding the water along the fairways is tough. Avoiding the water around the green is even more difficult, for the green is located smack dab in the middle of the lake. Your approach to this island green is demanding given the psychological intimidation and the wind. It is a fine way to wrap up a delightful course.

Insider Tips   This course is demanding, especially on the short game, but it is not overwhelming. The holes are not overly long, and you won't find any tricks or gimmicks. What you will find is just solid Trent Jones Sr. golf. If you can keep your ball dry, you've won half the battle. Though on many courses that means being cautious off the tee, here you have to be careful on every shot. Your second shot approaches are equally critical, as many of them will need to fly over water. The difficulty factor of the course rises sharply when the wind blows, as it often does, this being southern Florida. Couple this with the elevated greens (though not as elevated as typical Robert Trent Jones greens) and you have a good challenge on your hands.

And now, some helpful hints when you play the signature hole, number 18. There is little room for error here. Not only must you avoid the water on the right as well as the trees on the left, but you also need to stay on the right side of the fairway with your second shot to ensure that you have the best approach to the green. You must be as close to the hazard as possible so that you can use a well-lofted club on your approach. The green tends to be slick and if the ball doesn't come in high, it won't hold and you will, sadly enough, see your ball skid into the lake.

If you enjoy walking in famous footsteps, it is worth noting that Arnold Palmer won the prestigious PGA Seniors Championship over the South course in 1980. Amy Alcott, Nancy Lopez, and Patty Sheehan are among the greats who triumphed here when the LPGA's Elizabeth Arden Classic was contested at Turnberry from 1979 to 1986.

The Major Courses in Southwest Florida

Marriott's Golf Club at Marco

3433 Marriott Club Dr., Naples, FL 33937; phone (941) 793-6060

How To Get On: Guests of the resort can book tee times up to 30 days in advance. Nonguests can book tee times two days in advance.

Tees:

> Blue: 6,898 yards, par-72, USGA rating 73.4, slope 137
>
> White: 6,471 yards, par-72, USGA rating 71.4, slope 126
>
> Forward: 5,416 yards, par-72, USGA rating 70.9, slope 122

Challenge: ★★★½	Golf Facilities: ★★★★
Variety: ★★★½	14-Club Test: ★★★½
Terrain: ★★★½	Intangibles: ★★★
Beauty/Visual Appeal: ★★★½	Value: ★★★½
Pace of Play: ★★★	

Just the Facts Year Opened: 1991; Course Designer: Joe Lee; Walking: No; Greens Fee: $35–115; 9-Hole/Twilight Rate: Yes; Pull Carts: No; Practice Range: Yes; Club Rental: Yes.

Description and Comments The Golf Club at Marco Island is a prime example of Joe Lee's architectural philosophy: the simpler, the better. Lee has the knack of creating courses where "what you see is what you get;" there won't be any hidden hazards, gimmicks, or tricks. You can stand on the tee box and see all that awaits you—and that often is quite a bit, especially at the Golf Club at Marco Island.

This course slices its way through 240 acres of cypress, palm, and pine trees. These wooden hazards are complemented by 45 acres of lakes, which come into play on 15 holes. Throw in a number of doglegs and some sand and you have all the elements required for good golf. On the positive side is the fact that the fairways tend to be very generous. The greens, although well protected by both sand and water, are large in size and very puttable.

On the front side, the 9th hole is one of the best. This par-5 (547 yards) is horseshoe-shaped and requires three precise shots to find the green in regulation. Your first shot must avoid the sand on the left and water on the right, and your second needs to be struck to the right of center of the fairway to leave you with the best approach to the green.

The 16th is the course's signature hole. It is a par-3 that measures 165 yards, but typically you will be playing directly into the wind, and thus the hole will play 15 yards longer when it's blowing. The hole is all carry as you must fly over one of the many lakes to a bulkheaded, elevated green. The final hole is a par-4 (398 yards) that has been a watery graveyard for many a ball. Your tee shot must carry a lake, there is water along the entire right side, and your approach must also traverse more water. "What you see is what you get"—and what you get is a solid, challenging course.

Insider Tips At this course, you decide your own fate. If you mess up, there is no one else to blame, as The Golf Club at Marco is just plain, good golf. There are no tricks, no gimmicks. If you hit it into the water, it was because you stroked it poorly, not because the fairway unjustly sloped into a hidden pond. So put away all your patented excuses, bring out your A game, and have some fun.

You will do well here if your A game includes strong course management. You need to stand on the tee and pick the path of least resistance—the best route to avoid the hazards. Another key factor will be club selection. With so many of your shots carrying some sort of hazard and the usual presence of a prevailing wind, selecting your weapon will be vital to keeping your ball in play. Finally, almost all of the greens are forward sloping and are thus very conducive to the bump-and-run shot. This often-forgotten approach shot is also a perfect way to take the wind factor out of play.

Pelican's Nest Golf Club

4450 Pelican's Nest Dr., Bonita Springs, FL 34134; phone (800) 952-6378
or (941) 947-4600

How To Get On: Tee times can be made up to 30 days in advance.

Gator/Hurricane Tees:

> Champions: 7,016 yards, par-72, USGA rating 74.8, slope 139
>
> Blue: 6,579 yards, par-72, USGA rating 72.0, slope 131
>
> White: 6,010 yards, par-72, USGA rating 68.8, slope 122
>
> Forward: 5,201 yards, par-72, USGA rating 68.2, slope 119

Panther/Seminole Tees:

> Champions: 6,975 yards, par-72, USGA rating 74.2   , slope 133
>
> Blue: 6,528 yards, par-72, USGA rating 72.1, slope 127
>
> White: 5,949 yards, par-72, USGA rating 69.5, slope 120
>
> Forward: 5,149 yards, par-72, USGA rating 70.0, slope 120

Challenge: ★★★★	Golf Facilities: ★★★★½
Variety: ★★★★	14-Club Test: ★★★★
Terrain: ★★★★	Intangibles: ★★★★
Beauty/Visual Appeal: ★★★★	Value: ★★★★
Pace of Play: ★★★★	

Just the Facts   Year Opened: 1985; Course Designer: Tom Fazio; Walking: No; Greens Fee: $45–135; 9-Hole/Twilight Rate: Yes; Pull Carts: No; Practice Range: Yes; Club Rental: Yes.

Description and Comments   If you play Pelican's Nest, you should be warned: You probably won't look at other public golf facilities the same once you've experienced this one. Pelican's Nest was one of the first daily-fee courses to offer the "country club for a day" feel to its guests, and it remains one of the best in the nation. Nice touches, such as ice chests on the cart, free yardage books, complimentary range balls, and unbeatable service, are just a few of the elements that earn this facility the reputation as first class.

Equally as superb is the golf course, or should we say golf courses. Pelican's Nest boasts four separate nine-hole courses, all of which embody the distinctive Tom Fazio artistic touch. Admittedly, Fazio was given quite a spectacular canvas on which to create his masterpiece: The courses are cut through a striking landscape of mangroves and wetlands. Nature was thus a big influence on the courses' designs. Fazio worked with the natural surroundings, letting Mother Nature lend a helping hand.

As stunning as these surroundings are, they can also be deadly if you stray off the beaten path, for these courses are as tight as those newly washed blue jeans you tried to squeeze into after Thanksgiving dinner last year. There is little room—one could argue, no room—for error here. Even the slightest slice or hook and your par is a thing of the past. Also contributing to the difficulty factor are the numerous sand and water hazards strewn throughout the course placing even more of a premium on accuracy. There is one piece of good news (we thought you could use some at this point): There are no long, forced carries over any hazards, except from the back tees (even more reason to play the middle teeing ground).

Number nine is Gator's hardest hole, and it may well be one of the most challenging par-4s in the country. The hole, a dogleg left, plays 434 yards and requires both accuracy and length. You need to be right down the middle to have any shot at getting on the green in regulation. If you are to the left, you can't even see the green; if you're too far right you will have to negotiate your way through a mine field of mangroves, water, and bunkers. On the Hurricane, it is also the 9th hole that caught our fancy: a double-dogleg par-5 that plays 517 yards and features water and trees on the entire left side as well as a gaping lake on the right. You can be a daredevil and fly your ball over the lake on your second shot, thereby cutting off yardage, or you can play it more conservatively and avoid the lake. One of the best holes on the Panther course is number eight, a 526-yard par-5 that has sand aplenty. On the Seminole, the opening hole requires both strategy and accuracy. This hole is a dogleg left par-4 (390 yards) with trees strategically placed so you can't cut the corner, water along the entire right side, and a massive sand trap that cuts through the entire fairway.

Insider Tips　As you probably have figured out, accuracy, accuracy, and accuracy are the three key elements here—oh, did we mention accuracy? We're sure you get the point, but the treacherous hazards (trees, water, and marshland) all come into play much quicker than you may think. We barely mentioned the greens, but they, too, are challenging—fast and true.

These courses offer plenty of bite from the blue and white tees, and thus only those who can hit their drives with extreme precision should consider playing from the championship tees (you may want to get your head examined at the same time). If you have the time, we recommend that you play all 36 holes. Each nine has its own personality, and you will be hard pressed to find another course, at these relatively low greens fees, that provides you with this level of service.

A Southeast Florida Sampler

The Biltmore Golf Course

1210 Anastasia Ave., Coral Gables, FL 33134; phone (305) 460-5364
Tees: Championship: 6,642 yards, par-71, USGA rating 71.5, slope 119
Greens Fee: $12–44

Challenge: ★★
Variety: ★★★
Terrain: ★★½
Beauty/Visual Appeal: ★★★
Pace of Play: ★★★

Golf Facilities: ★★★
14-Club Test: ★★★
Intangibles: ★★★½
Value: ★★★½

Description and Comments   Oh, if these greens could talk. The Biltmore Golf Course opened in 1925 as part of the historic and famed Biltmore Hotel and quickly became the place to be. The course has thus witnessed dozens of notable characters and celebrities and surely was privy to some interesting conversations. The original Donald Ross design underwent a needed renovation in 1992 with the result being an updated, well-conditioned, and fun course to play.

The fairways are wide open, so you can swing away—be careful not to hit one of the million-dollar homes that line the fairways or you may find this to be an extremely expensive round. Along with your driver, you will need to use your brain quite a bit as the Biltmore does require good course management skills to score well.

The hardest hole at the Biltmore is the 6th, a 391-yard par-4 that requires a long and accurate tee shot setting up your approach to a bulk-headed green guarded by a stream in the front.

Binks Forest Golf Course

400 Binks Forest Dr., Wellington, FL 33414; phone (561) 795-0595
Tees: Championship: 7,065 yards, par-72, USGA rating 75.0, slope 138
Greens Fee: $27–65

Challenge: ★★★★
Variety: ★★★½
Terrain: ★★★½
Beauty/Visual Appeal: ★★★★
Pace of Play: ★★★

Golf Facilities: ★★★★
14-Club Test: ★★★½
Intangibles: ★★★½
Value: ★★★★

Description and Comments   Binks Forest, a Johnny Miller design, opened in 1990 and was originally a private facility. In 1994, it was sold to the American Golf Corporation, which quickly pumped $200,000 into it and opened it to public play. Today, the course is quite a test of your golfing skills. In describing it, a slew of adjectives pop into mind: long, narrow, tough, challenging, beautiful, and scenic. There are others as well, but you get the picture.

The course is located in a pine forest, a setting that you just don't find often in southern Florida. The course itself places a premium on accuracy for all your shots. The greens are magnificent, with most of them set at angles to the fairway requiring precise approach shots.

Breakers West

1550 Flagler Pkwy., West Palm Beach, FL 33411; phone (561) 653-6320

Tees: Championship: 6,905 yards, par-71, USGA rating 73.9, slope 135

Greens Fee: $60–110

Challenge: ★★★½	Golf Facilities: ★★★½
Variety: ★★★½	14-Club Test: ★★★
Terrain: ★★★	Intangibles: ★★★½
Beauty/Visual Appeal: ★★★	Value: ★★★
Pace of Play: ★★★★	

Description and Comments   Breakers West was recently renovated, elevating the course to "you really don't want to miss this one" status. The only catch is that you have to be a guest of the Breakers hotel, ten miles to the east, to gain access to the course. So if you are a guest, don't miss this one. The course is relatively long and poses a good challenge, especially from the back tees. Water can be found on a number of holes, and thus you need to be accurate to score well here. Although the fairway landing areas are generous, they are bordered by pines, palms, and oaks.

The signature hole is number nine, a par-4 435-yarder that plays straight off the tee and then veers to the left just beyond a lake. You need to be long off the tee to have a shot at the elevated green, as there is a pocket of trees on the left that stand in your way if your tee shot is short.

Colony West Country Club

6800 N.W. 88th Ave., Tamarac, FL 33321; phone (954) 726-8430

Tees: Championship: 7,271 yards, par-71, USGA rating 75.8, slope 138

Greens Fee: $35–70

Challenge: ★★★★	Golf Facilities: ★★★½
Variety: ★★★½	14-Club Test: ★★★★
Terrain: ★★★½	Intangibles: ★★★½
Beauty/Visual Appeal: ★★★½	Value: ★★★★
Pace of Play: ★★★	

Description and Comments   You better have your driver working before you get to Colony West—this is one of the longest courses in the area. In fact, 4 of the par-4s are over 400 yards—from the white tees. For crying out loud, the course opens with a 621-yard par-5, 580 yards from the whites! The course was originally constructed to host the Jackie Gleason Tournament. Though length is critical, you also must avoid the surrounding cypress trees and the water that comes into play on the majority of holes.

The signature hole, and the second hardest on the course, is the 12th, a par-4 that plays 452 yards. The hole doglegs to the left and features a relatively open fairway. All the trouble can be found near the large green, which is guarded on both sides by sand as well as water in the front. Another fine hole is the 18th, a par-4 that also plays 452 yards. The fairway is lined by trees on the left and bunkers on the right. Water cuts through the fairway approximately 75 yards out from a deep green encircled by bunkers.

Dodger Pines

4600 26th St., Vero Beach, FL 32966; phone (561) 569-4400
Tees: Championship: 6,692 yards, par-73, USGA rating 71.2, slope 122
Greens Fee: $25–45

Challenge: ★★½	Golf Facilities: ★★★½
Variety: ★★★	14-Club Test: ★★½
Terrain: ★★½	Intangibles: ★★★
Beauty/Visual Appeal: ★★★	Value: ★★★
Pace of Play: ★★★	

Description and Comments For Los Angelenos, Vero Beach means one thing: home of the LA Dodgers spring training. Well, as you might have inferred from the name, this course is owned by the Dodgers, so don't be surprised if you see Vin Scully or Tommy LaSorda hanging out in the spring. The course itself is not as spectacular as many in the area; however, for novelty's sake, it is hard to beat. Dodger Pines is ideal if you are looking for a course that is fun to play and at the same time provides somewhat of a challenge. The challenge here comes in the form of surrounding pine forests and water, which can be found on seven holes. The 3rd hole is the best one here: a 670-yard par-6 (in honor of Steve Garvey) that doglegs left with an out-of-bounds area along the entire left-hand side. The home run–caliber finishing hole is a 421-yard par-4 that is the toughest two-shotter on the course.

Doral Golf Resort and Spa, Gold Course

4400 N.W. 87th Ave., Miami, FL 33178; phone (800) 713-6725 or (305) 592-2000
Tees: Championship: 6,602 yards, par-70, USGA rating 73.3, slope 129
Greens Fee: $75–185

Challenge: ★★★	Golf Facilities: ★★★★½
Variety: ★★★½	14-Club Test: ★★★½
Terrain: ★★★	Intangibles: ★★★½
Beauty/Visual Appeal: ★★★	Value: ★★★
Pace of Play: ★★★	

Description and Comments The Gold course is the second hardest at Doral behind the Blue Monster, earning this reputation from its numerous hazards that seem to be just about everywhere. Length is nowhere near as important as accuracy here, where you will find water on every hole, narrow fairways that feature difficult bunkers, and half of the holes doglegging. The original course was difficult, but Ray Floyd made it even more of a challenge when he remodeled it in 1994.

You certainly don't get any time to warm up before you encounter the Gold's first real test. The 2nd hole, a dogleg left par-5 that plays 502 yards, is the hardest hole on the course and features water on the left and a series of bunkers on the right. The green runs at an angle to the fairway and is well bunkered. The front nine is the tougher of the two, and it plays nearly 300 yards longer. Number 18 is one of the more memorable holes at all of Doral. A 380-yard par-4, it is relatively tame off the tee, but the green is an island and thus your second shot is sink or swim.

Doral Golf Resort and Spa, Red Course

4400 N.W. 87th Ave., Miami, FL 33178; phone (800) 713-6725 or (305) 592-2000

Tees: Championship: 6,214 yards, par-70, USGA rating 69.9, slope 118

Greens Fee: $70–160

Challenge: ★★½	Golf Facilities: ★★★★½
Variety: ★★½	14-Club Test: ★★½
Terrain: ★★½	Intangibles: ★★★
Beauty/Visual Appeal: ★★★	Value: ★★½
Pace of Play: ★★★	

Description and Comments The Red course is the second shortest at Doral (behind the White) and offers more of a resort layout for those who want a little less bite from their golf course. This is not to say that you won't find a challenge here. On the contrary, the Red course features a plethora of bunkers and water on 16 holes. The holes are much more manageable yardage-wise, with the longest par-4 coming in at 383 yards.

One of the best holes on the Red is the par-3 15th. Measuring a mere 141 yards, it is menaced by a wild green complex. First off, the green is encircled by water. Then throw in the fact that the putting surface has three tiers and is severely sloped from front to back and you will certainly understand why this hole is ranked so highly.

Golf Club of Miami, West Course

6801 Miami Gardens Dr., Miami, FL 33015; phone (305) 829-4700

Tees: Championship: 7,017 yards, par-72, USGA rating 73.5, slope 130

Greens Fee: $20–65

Challenge: ★★★½	Golf Facilities: ★★★
Variety: ★★★½	14-Club Test: ★★★½
Terrain: ★★★	Intangibles: ★★★½
Beauty/Visual Appeal: ★★★½	Value: ★★★★
Pace of Play: ★★★	

Description and Comments   While you play this course, you may hear the phrase "Straight to the moon, Alice!" echoing from nowhere. Don't be alarmed—Jackie Gleason used to make this his home, and his spirit may just be lurking nearby. The aura of history can also be felt here: Arnold Palmer was the club's first pro, Lee Trevino had his first win, and a young lad named Jack Nicklaus made his professional debut here. The course also hit the national radar as it was once managed by the PGA Tour. Dade County recently took it over, hired an outside management company, and hosted a number of Tour events. Okay, enough waltzing down memory lane. What have you done for me lately?

To keep the course fresh and modern, the original Robert Trent Jones Sr. design was updated in 1989 by Bobby Weed, who added his own special touches to the Jones layout. The resulting course features water on a number of holes, although most are lateral, with treacherous bunkering and lush fairways. The greens are some of the best in all of southern Florida.

The course really has two signature holes, both on the front side. The 6th is a long and tight 461-yard par-4 that plays to a skinny green guarded by three yawning bunkers. Number nine is also a par-4 that plays 425 yards, slightly downhill, and doglegs to the left. The green is protected by water on the right, and thus a precise approach is critical.

North Palm Beach Country Club

951 U.S. Hwy. 1, North Palm Beach, FL 33408; phone (561) 626-4344
Tees: Championship: 6,275 yards, par-72, USGA rating 70.0, slope 117
Greens Fee: $20–50

Challenge: ★★½	Golf Facilities: ★★★
Variety: ★★½	14-Club Test: ★★½
Terrain: ★★½	Intangibles: ★★
Beauty/Visual Appeal: ★★½	Value: ★★★
Pace of Play: ★★	

Description and Comments   Although there are some scenic holes here, specifically number two, which borders the Intracoastal Waterway, this course is not one of the superstars of the region. We include it because it's good, basic, affordable golf with fine facilities in a very ritzy neighborhood. The course tends to be very crowded with play often in fivesomes.

Palm Beach Polo and Country Club, Cypress and Dunes Courses

11830 Polo Club Rd., West Palm Beach, FL 33414; phone (561) 798-7401

Tees:

    Cypress Course: 7,116 yards, par-72, USGA rating 74.4, slope 138

    Dunes Course: 7,050 yards, par-72, USGA rating 73.6, slope 132

Greens Fee: $75–100

Challenge: ★★★½	Golf Facilities: ★★★★
Variety: ★★★½	14-Club Test: ★★★½
Terrain: ★★★½	Intangibles: ★★★½
Beauty/Visual Appeal: ★★★★	Value: ★★★
Pace of Play: ★★★★	

Description and Comments Palm Beach Polo and Country Club features two separate 18-hole courses, each with its own character. The Cypress Course, a Pete and P. B. Dye design, is the better of the two, since it is a long and demanding course that features six par-4s measuring more than 420 yards from the tips. It also features some unusually rolling topography for southern Florida. Dunes, though nearly as long as Cypress, tends to be a little more forgiving and features visually stunning par-3s. It is more open than Cypress, with a linksy feel. The only downside to getting on these hidden gems is that you must be either a guest of the resort or a member of a private country club and have your pro arrange play here.

St. Lucie West Country Club

951 S.W. Country Club Dr., Port St. Lucie, FL 34986; phone (800) 800-4653 or (561) 341-1911

Tees: Championship: 6,905 yards, par-72, USGA rating 74.0, slope 134

Greens Fee: $15–59

Challenge: ★★★½	Golf Facilities: ★★★★
Variety: ★★★½	14-Club Test: ★★★½
Terrain: ★★★	Intangibles: ★★★
Beauty/Visual Appeal: ★★★	Value: ★★★½
Pace of Play: ★★★	

Description and Comments This course is not overly long, but it demands accuracy since there is a boatload of water that comes into play on most holes. Additional challenge comes in the form of gaping bunkers, numerous trees, rolling fairways, and a number of holes that dogleg. The greens are elevated and tend to be flat, but they are also fast and don't hold approaches very well. One of the best features at this course is its staff. The service rivals many of the high-end daily-fee courses in the area.

A Southwest Florida Sampler

Coral Oaks Golf Course

1800 N.W. 28th Ave., Cape Coral, FL 33993; phone (941) 283-4100
Tees: Championship: 6,623 yards, par-72, USGA rating 71.7, slope 123
Greens Fee: $22–27

Challenge: ★★½	Golf Facilities: ★★★
Variety: ★★½	14-Club Test: ★★★
Terrain: ★★★	Intangibles: ★★½
Beauty/Visual Appeal: ★★★	Value: ★★★½
Pace of Play: ★★★	

Description and Comments   When you arrive at Coral Oaks you may be surprised at what you find: a terrific Arthur Hills layout that plays through towering trees and features rolling fairways that vary in width. Coral Oaks's greens range in size from small to large with some having undulations and others being flat. This course is not all that challenging, but the price is hard to beat—it is hard to imagine that you can experience an Arthur Hills creation for under $30. If you are on a budget and are looking for a solid course, Coral Oaks may just be the ticket.

Eastwood Golf Course

4600 Bruce Herd Lane, Fort Myers, FL 33994; phone (813) 275-4848
Tees: Championship: 6,772 yards, par-72, USGA rating 73.3, slope 130
Greens Fee: $27–50

Challenge: ★★★	Golf Facilities: ★★★
Variety: ★★★½	14-Club Test: ★★★½
Terrain: ★★★½	Intangibles: ★★★
Beauty/Visual Appeal: ★★★½	Value: ★★★★
Pace of Play: ★★★	

Description and Comments   Eastwood has been a favorite among locals for many years, but it is gaining national recognition. Always in terrific shape, Eastwood is a tremendous value because it offers golfers a strong challenge and demands good course management. Adding to the difficulty factor are the fairly hilly fairways and water, found on all but two of the holes. Its woodsy setting makes this a haven for wildlife.

The best hole on the course is the 10th, an extremely long (628 yards) par-5 that veers sharply to the left halfway down the fairway. Golfers can either go for broke and aim over the trees on the left or play it safe down the right. Either way, you will need to be precise since the fairway is narrow and bordered by trees. Better to start on hole one, rather than 10, which is a rough-and-tumble 414-yard par-4 smothered in sand and water.

Fort Myers Country Club

3591 McGregor Blvd., Fort Myers, FL 33901; phone (941) 936-2457
Tees: Championship: 6,414 yards, par-71, USGA rating 70.5, slope 118
Greens Fee: $12–32

Challenge: ★★½	Golf Facilities: ★★★
Variety: ★★½	14-Club Test: ★★★
Terrain: ★★★	Intangibles: ★★★
Beauty/Visual Appeal: ★★½	Value: ★★★
Pace of Play: ★★★	

Description and Comments   This is the oldest course is southwest Florida and is a prime example of architect Donald Ross's design techniques. The terrain tends to be flat, and fairways are relatively wide open with a smattering of trees here and there. There is also some water on the course, in the form of two ponds and a meandering canal, which can be found on eight holes and adds a definite bite to the course. But it is really the greens where Ross's true flavor comes alive and where the course snaps like an alligator. The putting surfaces are small but domed, similar to Pinehurst No. 2, site of the 1999 U.S. Open. Thus, approaches need to be struck delicately and perfectly, or you will find your ball running down to areas surrounding the green. You will be hard pressed to find another opportunity to play a Donald Ross design at the low greens fees you pay here.

Gateway Golf and Country Club

11360 Championship Dr., Fort Myers, FL 33913; phone (941) 561-1010
Tees: Championship 6,974 yards, par-72, USGA rating 73.7, slope 130
Greens Fee: $35–102

Challenge: ★★★½	Golf Facilities: ★★★★
Variety: ★★★½	14-Club Test: ★★★★
Terrain: ★★★½	Intangibles: ★★★
Beauty/Visual Appeal: ★★★½	Value: ★★★★
Pace of Play: ★★★½	

Description and Comments   Gateway and its sister course, Pelican's Nest, were designed by Tom Fazio and developed by Westinghouse. So it should come as no huge surprise that like Pelican's Nest, Gateway has superior service and top-notch amenities. That is where the similarities end, however, as Gateway is a much different course. Gateway's fairways are more open and tend to be more forgiving, but they also feature greater mounding, so level stances can be hard to find. Unusual are Fazio's mounded bunkers, which he calls "Cape Cod–style."

The front side is a links-style layout with only a few trees, but a beachful of sand. Conversely, the back nine features an abundance of trees, mostly cypress. The 3rd hole is one of the best at the course. It is a 408-yard par-4 featuring 4 pot bunkers on the left of the green and a slender bunker running over 100 yards on the right.

Lely Resort Golf and Country Club (Lely Flamingo Island Club)

8004 Lely Resort Blvd., Naples, FL 34113; phone (800) 388-4653 or (941) 793-2223

Tees: Championship: 7,171 yards, par-72, USGA rating 73.9, slope 135

Greens Fee: $35–135

Challenge: ★★★½	Golf Facilities: ★★★★
Variety: ★★★½	14-Club Test: ★★★★
Terrain: ★★★½	Intangibles: ★★★
Beauty/Visual Appeal: ★★★★	Value: ★★★
Pace of Play: ★★★★	

Description and Comments   Lely Flamingo is not your typical public golf course. Your first indication of this are the five bronze horses that grace the entrance to the course. Your second sign comes when you reach the expansive practice facilities. When you finally get to the first tee, you may be double-checking your greens fee receipt to see if there wasn't a mistake. This is Naples's premier course and is truly one of southern Florida's hidden gems. If you have any doubts, check with Robert Trent Jones Sr., the architect, who considers this course to be the best public access facility he has ever built.

From the tips, this course is a true challenge, but from the other tees, it is very playable. As you make your way around, you will encounter tree-lined, hourglass-shaped fairways, as well as numerous hazards in the form of water found on 11 holes and deadly bunkers—some with trees growing in them. The course's signature hole, and the most photogenic, is the 5th, a 200-yard par-3 that plays to a peninsula green.

Naples Beach Hotel and Golf Club

851 Gulf Shore Blvd. N., Naples, FL 34102; phone (800) 237-7600 or (941) 435-2475

Tees: Championship: 6,500 yards, par-72, USGA rating 71.2, slope 129

Greens Fee: $39–100

Challenge: ★★★	Golf Facilities: ★★★
Variety: ★★★	14-Club Test: ★★★
Terrain: ★★★	Intangibles: ★★½
Beauty/Visual Appeal: ★★★	Value: ★★★
Pace of Play: ★★½	

Description and Comments   This is one of the oldest courses in the area, built in 1920 and updated in 1979 by Ron Garl, and offers a traditional layout and good, old-fashioned golf. The tree-lined fairways are very generous and tend to be rolling. Though only one-third of the holes feature water, it is an imposing hazard and requires you to strike your shots with precision. Two prime examples are the 3rd and 18th holes. The 3rd is a par-3 that plays 173 yards and requires you to carry a large portion of a lake. The 18th is the course's signature hole. It is a dogleg-right, 398-yard par-4 with water on both sides of the fairway and requires an approach over more water to a well-bunkered green.

Olde Hickory Golf and Country Club

14670 Olde Hickory Blvd., Fort Myers, FL 33912; phone (941) 768-3335

Tees: Championship: 6,601 yards, par-72, USGA rating 71.9, slope 127

Greens Fee: $20–30

Challenge: ★★½	Golf Facilities: ★★★½
Variety: ★★½	14-Club Test: ★★★
Terrain: ★★★	Intangibles: ★★★
Beauty/Visual Appeal: ★★★	Value: ★★★★
Pace of Play: ★★★	

Description and Comments   Olde Hickory is another Ron Garl design that is a fine course at a great value. Although not overly long, it is filled with hazards in the form of nearly 30 bunkers and water, mostly swampland, that can be found on each and every hole. The greens are large and undulating and tend to be medium to fast speed-wise. One of the best holes is number 17, a par-3 that measures 185 yards and features an island green.

Lodging in Southeast Florida

EXPENSIVE

Boca Raton Resort & Club

501 E. Camino Real, Boca Raton, FL 33431-0825; phone (800) 327-0101 or (561) 395-3000; www.bocaresort.com; Rates: $230–430

In 1926, famed architect Addison Mizner's The Cloister Hotel at Boca Raton Resort opened and quickly became an instant success. Soon the likes of the Vanderbilts and Ziegfelds were flocking to Boca Raton to soak up the sun and all that the resort has to offer. Although the resort has expanded and grown over the years, the essence of Boca Raton Resort still remains.

The resort now features a total of 963 rooms, including 39 suites, 76 junior suites, and 60 one-bedroom villas. Guests can choose from four different accommodation options. The Cloister, a Spanish-Mediterranean-themed building, has 328 rooms, which tend to be small and traditionally decorated. Within the Cloister are 49 rooms that have their own concierge and receive special treatment, such as wine and champagne in the lounge. The 27-story Tower offers guests a more contemporary option with rooms that are larger and feature sweeping views of the surrounding area. Finally, there is the Boca Raton Resort & Club, which is less formal and offers 214 rooms, including nine suites, that overlook the Intracoastal Waterway.

You certainly won't get bored here, as there are 36 holes of golf, 34 tennis courts, five pools, water sports, three fitness centers, bicycling, lawn games, and a children's program. The resort features seven restaurants, among the best being Top of the Tower, offering Italian delicacies and grand views.

Golf Packages The resort requests that you contact them directly regarding golf packages as they tend to vary based on accommodations.

The Breakers

1 S. County Rd., Palm Beach, FL 33480; phone (800) 833-3141 or (561) 655-6611; www.thebreakers.com; Rates: $340–600

Nothing epitomizes the essence of Palm Beach and its reputation of Old World wealth and elegance like The Breakers. After fire destroyed the original structure in 1903, and again in 1925, Flagler's heirs commissioned Leonard Schultze, of Waldorf-Astoria fame, to rebuild The Breakers in 1926. Schultze created an Italian Renaissance–style resort spread out over 140 acres right next to the Atlantic Ocean. Listed on the National Register of Historic Places, The Breakers recently underwent a $75 million renovation during which the 572 rooms were updated, further improving an already spectacular resort.

The resort features two 18-hole golf courses, but there is a number of other activities available here including tennis, lawn games, a beach with water sports, sauna, steam rooms, gym, and children's programs. Make sure to include a stop at The Florentine Room, the best of the resort's five restaurants, a fine dining experience that offers a sensational menu and an equally good wine list (see Dining section). If you get a chance to stay here, you won't regret it, for this is truly one of the world's finest resorts.

Golf Packages   The Breakers offers "The Golfer's Delight Package," which includes: three days/two nights accommodation, a welcome gift, two days of golf at the Ocean and/or Breakers West golf course, range balls and cart fee, unlimited use of practice facilities, weekly golf clinic, 50-minute sports massage, and unlimited use of the Spa at Breakers.

Doral Golf Resort & Spa

4400 N.W. 87th Ave., Miami, FL 33178; phone (800) 71-DORAL or (305) 592-2000; www.doralgolf.com; Rates: $385–745

Doral is one of southern Florida's premier resorts, offering a terrific combination of world-class golf and other fine activities and amenities. Golf enthusiasts will no doubt be foaming at the mouth in anticipation of playing the five championship golf courses at the resort, including the famed Blue Monster. But Doral offers much more than just golf. There is a sensational full-service spa, four pools, 15 tennis courts, fishing, and biking, just to name some of the other activities you can find here.

The resort recently underwent a $30 million renovation during which all the rooms, located in eight separate, cozy lodges, were updated and redecorated in lighter, more Florida-like tones. Each room has its own balcony or terrace, affording views of the surrounding resort. You certainly won't starve at Doral—the resort has four restaurants with varying menus. The Provare Italian Restaurant offers a classic menu and an extensive wine list. The Sandpiper Steak & Seafood Restaurant and Champions Restaurant & Bar features more traditional items and tend to be a tad less pricey.

Golf Packages   Doral's golf package includes Garden room accommodations, 18 holes of golf per day (surcharge for play at the Blue Monster), full American breakfast, introductory golf clinic, unlimited use of the driving range, bag storage, and advanced tee times.

The Four Seasons

2800 S. Ocean Blvd., Palm Beach, FL 33480; phone (800) 432-2335 or (561) 582-2800; www.fourseasons.com; Rates: $350–625

This Four Seasons is an intimate hotel with a mere 210 rooms. All of them are tastefully decorated in understated elegance, with many having a balcony overlooking the spectacular surroundings. The beachfront resort encompasses six acres and features access to nearby Emerald Dunes golf course, a pool, a sauna, three tennis courts, a gym, and beach activities. For dining, make sure to try The Restaurant at Four Seasons (see Dining in Southeast Florida), one of the area's best restaurants. A great way to wrap up your evening is in the Living Room lounge, where you can grab a nightcap and on weekend evenings hear some piano music.

Golf Packages   The Four Seasons offers the "Sport & Surf Package," which includes 18 holes of golf, a one-hour spa treatment, one hour of water sports, and one hour of tennis instruction.

PGA National Resort & Spa

400 Avenue of the Champions, Palm Beach Gardens, FL 33418; phone (800) 633-9150 or (561) 627-2000; www.pga-resorts.com; Rates: $309–369

This is one of the area's newer and most complete golf resorts. PGA National sprawls over 2,340 acres and features five highly regarded golf courses, a spa, tennis courts, a gym, nine pools, a 26-acre sailing lake, and the largest croquet complex in the Western Hemisphere. Accommodations at PGA National include 275 rooms, 60 suites, and 85 cottages. All of the rooms are modern and decorated in a rich, floral style. The resort features four restaurants, with Arezzo and the Crab Catcher (see Dining in Southeast Florida for more details on both of these) being at the top of our list.

Golf Packages   PGA National's golf package includes accommodations, one round of golf each day (including cart), one range ball token daily, second round (excluding cart) to be confirmed on day of play and based on availability.

Turnberry Isle Resort and Club

19999 W. Country Club Dr., Aventura, FL 33180; phone (800) 327-7028 or (305) 932-6200; www.turnberryisle.com; Rates: $395–495

You may not want to stay at Turnberry, for it just may spoil you for all other golf resorts. Turnberry is a spectacular resort where the attention to detail almost boggles the mind. Guests at the resort can choose to stay either in the Marina Hotel, located logically enough near the 117-slip marina, or the Country Club, near the golf course. All rooms are large and elegantly appointed in a Mediterranean theme with marble floors, Oriental rugs, and oversized furniture. The resort features a staggering 13 restaurants, which will no doubt satisfy all types of palates.

Outside, you will find a full menu of activities, including two golf courses, 24 tennis courts (18 lit for night play), a spa, marina with boating rentals, three pools, a whirlpool, private beach, dive shop, jogging trail, and racquetball. There's even a helipad if you prefer to arrive by helicopter.

Golf Packages   Turnberry offers a comprehensive golf package that includes: accommodations, welcome drink, complimentary fruit basket in your room, daily American breakfast, unlimited golf, golf cart for one round each day, golf visor, club storage, weekly golf clinic, one bucket of range balls daily, golf bag tag, chaises longues and towel at poolside and Ocean Club, free shuttle service, room tax, service charge, and other taxes.

MODERATE
Chesterfield Hotel
363 Cocoanut Row, Palm Beach, FL 33480; phone (561) 659-5800; Rates: $185–299

This is an elegant and stately hotel that resembles an English country estate. The hotel has a very intimate feeling with only 55 rooms and 11 suites, all of which are nicely decorated, in a three-story building. The hotel features a pool, whirlpool, health club, cigar room, library room, as well as a top-notch restaurant, The Leopard Room (see Dining section).

Fontainebleau Hilton Resort and Towers
4441 Collins Ave., Miami, FL 33140; phone (800) 548-8886 or (305) 538-2000; www.hilton.com; Rates: $260–390

You no doubt have seen the Fontainebleau—it is one of Miami's legendary landmarks. It embodies the architectural mindset that was rampant in the 1950s in Miami: the bigger and more brash, the better. In fact, this is the city's largest and most ornate hotel and is a big attraction for vacationers, conventioneers, and sight-seers alike (Fontainebleau has convention facilities that are second in size only to Miami's official convention center).

The resort could not have lasted as long as it did without offering guests superior accommodations and service as well as great recreational options. The 1,146 rooms are elegantly decorated in a decor ranging from 1950s style to more contemporary. Fontainebleau offers 12 restaurants, four lounges, two pools, saunas, a 30,000-square-foot beachside spa, seven lit tennis courts, a gym, volleyball, water activities, and a fine children's program.

Radisson Bridge Resort
999 E. Camino Real, Boca Raton, FL 33432; phone (561) 368-9500; www.radisson.com; Rates: $295–375

This resort features 121 rooms in the 11-story building, many of which have balconies overlooking the Intracoastal Waterway. Activities at the resort include tennis and golf privileges, pool, gym, and sauna. Guests receive a complimentary breakfast, but a real treat is the hotel's restaurant, Carmen's (see Dining section), where guests are treated to spectacular views of nearby surroundings.

Sonesta Beach Resort
350 Ocean Dr., Key Biscayne, FL 33149; phone (800) 766-3782 or (305) 361-2021; www.sonesta.com; Rates: $255–395

This beachside resort offers guests quality accommodations in a spectacular setting with more recreational options than you will know what to do with. Sonestra has 284 rooms, 14 suites, and 2 villas, all of which are tastefully decorated. The resort itself is situated on a 750-foot beach, one of Florida's best, and thus a bounty of beach, water sports, and boating activities await guests. In addition, there are nine tennis courts (three lit), a pool, massage and steam rooms, a gym with aerobics, and a good children's program. The resort also has a fine restaurant, the Purple Dolphin (see Dining section). Also, don't miss the drawings by Andy Warhol and Mick Jagger located in the hotel's disco.

Westin Resort Miami Beach

4833 Collins Ave., Miami, FL 33140; phone (800) 996-3426 or (305) 532-3600; www.westin.com; Rates: $275–395

Recent and extensive renovations ($30 million) have revamped this Westin and put it back on the recommended map. The new rooms are decorated in colorful tones and feature nice touches such as mini-refrigerators, large closets, and phones in the bathroom. The resort boasts three restaurants, three lounges, a pool, tennis courts, a gym, and beach. Free transportation to the Doral Resort is available.

INEXPENSIVE

Beacharbour Resort

18925 Collins Ave., Miami, FL 33160; phone (800) 643-0807 or (305) 931-8900; Rates: $85–115; Built: 1955; Renovations: 1999

Comfort Inn

1901 Palm Beach Lakes Blvd., West Palm Beach, FL 33409; phone (800) 228-5150 or (561) 689-6100; Rates: $66–180; Built: 1976; Renovations: 1996

Doubletree Hotels in the Gardens

4431 PGA Blvd., Palm Beach Gardens, FL 33410; phone (800) 222-TREE or (561) 622-2260; Rates: $69–$99; Built: 1974; Renovations: 1999

Fairfield Inn by Marriott—South

1201 N.W. LeJeune Rd., Miami, FL 33126; phone (800) 228-2800 or (305) 643-0055; www.marriott.com; Rates: $99–125; Built: 1992; Renovations: 1999

Dining in Southeast Florida

Amici 228 S. County Road, West Palm Beach; phone (561) 832-0201. Italian; Expensive; Reservations essential. This is one of West Palm Beach's most trendy restaurants, but unlike many that come and go, Amici has a menu that backs up its in-style status. Serving some of the best Italian items around, you should put this one on your list. Be prepared for a large crowd at dinner and a noisy atmosphere.

Arrezo PGA National Resort, 400 Avenue of the Champions, Palm Beach Gardens; phone (800) 633-9150 or (561) 627-2000. Italian; Moderate; Reservations accepted. A relaxed and casual atmosphere where guests can choose from an extensive and varied menu of Italian selections.

Carmen's Radisson Bridge Resort Hotel, 999 E. Camino Real, Boca Raton; phone (561) 368-9500. Continental; Moderate; Reservations accepted. Stunning views of the Intracoastal Waterway and the Atlantic Ocean provide a perfect atmosphere. The menu at Carmen's is varied from veal to seafood to pasta—something for everyone's taste.

Casa Juancho 2436 S.W. 8th St., Little Havana, Miami; phone (305) 642-2452. Spanish; Moderate; Reservations accepted. Strolling musicians provide atmosphere at this Spanish-themed restaurant. Some of the best items on the menu include the hake, which is flown in from Spain, or the jumbo red shrimp.

Chef Allen's 19088 N.E. 29th Ave., North Miami Beach; phone (305) 935-2900. American; Expensive; Reservations accepted. A 25-foot-wide window provides a view directly to the kitchen, where you can watch Chef Allen Susser create his unique masterpieces. Specialties of the house include local seafood delicacies.

China Grill 404 Washington Ave., Miami Beach; phone (305) 534-2211. Chinese; Expensive; Reservations suggested. One of *the* places to dine in Miami—don't be surprised if you see a celebrity sitting next to you. The atmosphere is not all that warm, but the food more than makes up for that.

Crab Catcher PGA National Resort, 400 Avenue of the Champions, Palm Beach Gardens; phone (800) 633-9150 or (561) 627-2000. Seafood; Moderate; Reservations accepted. Decorated in a nautical theme, the Crab Catcher features a menu that specializes in Florida seafood. An adjacent piano bar is a perfect place to grab a before- or after-dinner drink.

The Florentine Room Dining Room The Breakers Hotel, 1 S. County Rd., Palm Beach; phone (800) 833-3141 or (561) 655-6611. Mediterranean; Expensive; Reservation required. The atmosphere of The Breakers Hotel is reason enough to come to the Florentine room, but the sensational menu makes your trip even more worthwhile. Florentine offers a full menu with a number of terrific seafood specialties, such as Mediterranean swordfish.

Islas Canarias 285 N.W. 27th Ave., Little Havana, Miami; phone (305) 649-0440. Cuban; Inexpensive; Reservations not needed. Make sure to come here if you want to sample some native Cuban dishes. This is a favorite restaurant among Cuban locals.

Joe's Stone Crab Restaurant 227 Biscayne St., Miami; phone (305) 673-0365. Seafood; Inexpensive–Moderate; Reservations accepted. An ideal place to take a load off, do some serious people-watching, and chow down some of the best stone crabs in the area. Operated by the same family for four generations, it is hard not to enjoy this always crowded local favorite.

La Vieille Maison 770 E. Palmetto Park Rd., Boca Raton; phone (561) 391-6701. French; Expensive; Reservations suggested. Located in a 1920s-era building, this restaurant has the taste and feel of good ol' Paris. Rich and sinful are two adjectives that pop to mind to describe the menu. Make sure to leave room for the "L'Indulgence de Chocolate" dessert.

Le Festival 2120 Salzedo St., Coral Gables; phone (305) 442-8545. French; Moderate–Expensive; Reservations accepted. This is one of Miami's best French restaurants, serving a variety of dishes in a pleasant atmosphere. Among the best on the menu were the stuffed quail and the fresh salmon. There is also an extensive wine list.

The Leopard Room Chesterfield Hotel, 363 Cocoanut Row, Palm Beach; phone (561) 659-5800. Continental; Moderate–Expensive; Reservations accepted. Guests can either dine indoors or outside and can choose from an extensive menu including rack of lamb. A pianist provides delightful atmosphere.

Purple Dolphin Sonesta Beach Resort Hotel, 350 Ocean Dr., Key Biscayne; phone (800) 766-3782 or (305) 361-2021. Continental; Moderate; Reservations suggested. Scenic view overlooking the Atlantic is a great complement to a varied menu specializing in seafood.

The Restaurant at the Four Seasons Four Seasons Hotel, 2800 S. Ocean Blvd., Palm Beach; phone (800) 432-2335 or (561) 582-2800. Continental; Expensive; Reservations required. An extensive wine list and beautiful surroundings are perfect companions to an extensive menu featuring Southeastern delicacies, including blue crab and yellowtail snapper.

Ristorante La Finestra 171 E. Palmetto Rd., Boca Raton; phone (561) 392-1838. Continental; Expensive; Reservations required. Serving some of the best continental cuisine around, La Finestra has a wide and expansive menu offering unique items, such as scaloppini of veal stuffed with crabmeat and lobster.

Shorty's Bar-B-Q 9200 S. Dixie Hwy., Kendall; phone (305) 670-7732. Barbecue; Inexpensive; Reservations not accepted. This restaurant has been operating since 1951 and serves some of the best ribs and barbecue specialties around. The atmosphere is pure "down-home," and the food is purely mouth-watering.

Tropical Chinese Restaurant 7991 S.W. 40th St., Miami; phone (305) 262-7576. Chinese; Inexpensive–Moderate; Reservations accepted. Serving some of the best Chinese food in Miami, you will find tasty delicacies such as Peking duck and prawns. The dim sum lunch is a terrific way to try a little bit of everything.

Two Sisters Hyatt Regency, 50 Alhambra Plaza, Coral Gables; phone (305) 441-1234. Contemporary; Moderate; Reservations accepted. You can't go wrong at this restaurant, which serves amazing Pacific Rim entrees, including curry shrimp and marinated snapper.

Activities in Southeast Florida

Besides a plethora of beach activities, professional sports teams, and the nearby Everglades, Southeast Florida has quite a lot to offer its visitors.

American Police Hall of Fame and Museum 3801 Biscayne Blvd.; phone (305) 573-0070. Exhibits here include more than 11,000 law enforcement items, including displays of weapons and other paraphernalia.

Bethesda-by-the-Sea 141 S. County Rd., Palm Beach; phone (561) 655-4554. This church is a prime example of Spanish Gothic architecture.

The Breakers 1 S. County Rd., Palm Beach; phone (561) 655-6611. If you don't get a chance to stay here, you should at least take time to visit this historic structure. The current Breakers, built by the heirs of Henry Flagler (the man most associated with southwest Florida's Golden Age) in 1926, this hotel is one of the finest in the world and has almost a museum-like feel.

Henry Morrison Flagler Museum 1 Whitehall Way, Palm Beach; phone (561) 655-2833. Originally Flagler's home but now a 55-room museum with exhibits on the local as well as Flagler family history.

Gumbo Limbo Nature Center 1801 N. Ocean Blvd., Boca Raton; phone (561) 338-1473. A favorite with the kids who enjoy checking out the four massive saltwater tanks. In the spring, plan your visit at night so that you can participate in the turtle walks to see females come ashore to lay their eggs.

International Museum of Cartoon Art 201 Plaza Real, Boca Raton; phone (561) 931-2200. If you have a kid or are a kid at heart, you will no doubt enjoy a visit to this museum, where you will find more than 160,000 cartoons.

Lion Country Safari Southern Blvd. W, West Palm Beach; phone (561) 793-1084. Drive through a 500-acre zoo where animals roam free as they would in their natural habitat—just make sure your windows are rolled up.

Lummus Park 404 N.W. N. River Dr. and N.W. 3rd St.; phone (305)

673-7730. Located at this park is one of the oldest remaining pioneer structures left in Dade County, Wagner House, as well as stone barracks built in 1835.

Mar-a-Lago 1100 S. Ocean Blvd., Palm Beach. Make sure to drive by this magnificent home, which was originally the home of Marjorie Meriweather Post, of Post cereal fame, and is now owned by Donald Trump.

Miami Seaquarium 4400 Rickenbacker Causeway; phone (305) 361-5705. A terrific place to take the kids with its many sea critters. A shark pool, 235,000-gallon tropical reef aquarium, and daily shows are among visitors' favorites.

Miami's South Beach Make sure to spend some time hoofing around South Beach, Miami's famous art-deco neighborhood. The sightseeing will be matched only by the people-watching. On your tour of the area make sure to check out:

- **Welcome Center** 1001 Ocean Dr.; phone (305) 531-3484. Stop by to get details on the many sights of South Beach. Visitors can rent audio cassettes or purchase maps for a self-guided tour.
- **Espanola Way** This street is filled with Mediterranean Revival buildings, constructed in the 1920s. A hot spot for artists, musicians, and writers alike.
- **Fontainebleau Hilton Resort and Towers** 4441 Collins Ave.; phone (305) 538-2000. Even if you decide not to stay here, it is well worth your time to see this grand hotel with its 1950s-style architecture.

Museum of Science & Space Transit Planetarium 3280 S. Miami Ave. (in Coconut Grove area); phone (305) 854-4247. Kids will have a field day with the more than 150 hands-on exhibits on light, chemistry, physics, and the human body.

Norton Gallery of Art 1451 S. Olive Ave., West Palm Beach; phone (561) 832-5194. Home to an expansive collection of 19th- and 20th-century artists, including a large exhibit on French Impressionists.

Old Northwood Historic District West of Flagler Drive, between 26th and 35th Streets, West Palm Beach. This section of the city is listed on the National Register of Historic Places since it features many magnificent 1920s-era buildings. A great place to take a walk.

Parrot Jungle & Gardens 11000 S.W. 57th Ave. S. (off U.S. 1); phone (305) 666-7834. This is a perfect place for you to ask that proverbial question: "Polly want a cracker?" A petting zoo and baby bird training area are two "must-sees" for kids.

Worth Avenue Between Cocoanut Row and S. Ocean Boulevard. This is the Rodeo Drive of Palm Beach with posh shops, such as Cartier and Armani.

The 19th Hole in Southeast Florida

Champions Doral Golf Resort and Spa, 4400 N.W. 87th Ave., Miami; phone (800) 713-6725 or (305) 592-2000. Indoor and outdoor seating available overlooking the famed 18th hole at the Blue Monster.

The Signature Lounge or **Chris'** Turnberry Isle Resort & Club, 19999 W. Country Club Dr., Aventura; phone (305) 933-6929. Two different lounges, both with unique atmosphere and both overlooking the golf courses.

Lodging in Southwest Florida

EXPENSIVE

Marriott's Marco Island Resort

400 S. Collier Blvd., Marco Island, FL 33937; phone (800) 438-4373 or (941) 394-2511; www.marriott.com; Rates: $250–350

Marriott's Marco Island is one of the few resorts in the area that offers golf on the premises. This Marriott is a more traditional hotel, but has a spectacular setting and a tremendous array of activities. The resort is located adjacent to one of Florida's best and most pristine beaches, with water so clear you can see 100 feet down at times.

The resort features 735 rooms and six suites, all of which are large and decorated with oversized furniture. Each room has its own private balcony with good views of the Gulf beyond. Along with access to the golf course, the resort has a number of other recreational options: three pools, 16 tennis courts, a gym, private beach with a full array of water activities, miniature golf, bicycles, and children's programs.

Golf Packages   Marriott's package includes: pool-view room accommodations, 18 holes of golf per day (including cart), bag storage, bag tag, range balls, golf gift, and transportation to the course.

Marco Island Hilton Beach Resort

560 S. Collier Blvd., Marco Island, FL 34147; phone (800) 443-4550 or (941) 394-5000; www.hilton.com; Rates: $219–329

If you want a more intimate hotel and don't care about being right on the golf course, and also want to avoid shelling out too much money, then you should consider this Marco Island Hilton. Each of the 298 rooms has a private balcony with sweeping views, and all are well appointed with such special touches as a sitting area, wet bar, and refrigerator. The resort is conveniently located near the area golf courses, but guests can certainly keep busy at the hotel as there is a pool, three tennis courts, a gym, beach, windsurfing, parasailing, and water-skiing. The resort also has Sandcastles Restaurant (see Dining section), which features sweeping views of the Gulf.

The Ritz-Carlton, Naples

280 Vanderbilt Beach Rd., Naples, FL 34108; phone (800) 241-3333 or (941) 598-3300; www.ritzcarlton.com; Rates: $425–770

If you have a few extra Ben Franklins lying around, you might want to consider this Ritz-Carlton, which offers a terrific combination of elegance and recreation in a spectacular setting. Spread out among the hotel's 23 acres, guests can choose from a full array of activities, including a white-sand beach, pool, saunas, six tennis courts, a gym, water programs, bicycles, children's programs, as well as access to nearby golf courses.

As you may expect, the rooms here are exquisite, but it really is the public rooms that garner the most attention. Lavishly decorated, these rooms feel almost like a museum—the fine collection of art helps add to the ambience. The hotel also boasts two fine restaurants (see Dining section), The Dining Room and The Grill Room, which offer terrific menus to satisfy every taste.

MODERATE

Inn by the Sea

287 11th Ave. S, Naples, FL 34102-7022; phone (800) 584-1268 or (941) 649-4124; Rates: $149–169

Built in 1937, this is a cozy inn that offers only five rooms and is a great alternative to the typical large-scale, chain hotels that dominate the area. Complimentary breakfast is included with your stay, and the hotel is within walking distance to many local restaurants.

Naples Beach Hotel & Golf Club

851 Gulf Shore Blvd., Naples, FL 34102; phone (800) 237-7600 or (941) 261-2222; www.naplesbeachhotel.com; Rates: $205–355

This beachfront resort is a family hotel—that is, it has been owned and operated by the same family since 1946. Sprawling along the beach, this resort features rooms decorated in a tropical motif, floral prints, and wicker furniture, with many having views. Along with the 18-hole golf course, guests are treated to six tennis courts, a beach, health club privileges, lawn games, boating, and bicycles.

Golf Packages   The Naples golf package includes: accommodations, buffet breakfast, golf clinic, greens fees, cart privileges, confirmed tee times, and bag storage.

Radisson Suite Beach Resort

600 S. Collier Blvd., Marco Island, FL 34145; phone (941) 394-4100; www.marcobeachresort.com; Rates: $260–370

A terrific beachfront family resort, this Radisson offers 55 standard rooms as well as 214 one- to two-bedroom suites, all of which have private balconies. If you are traveling with your family, you should consider the suites since they tend to be a little roomier and have fully equipped kitchens. The grounds are packed with fun activities, including a pool, a gym, parasailing, bicycles, a game room, tennis, and children's programs. The hotel's concierge can assist you in setting up tee times at local courses, including the Marriott Marco Island.

INEXPENSIVE

The Boat House

1180 Edington Place, Marco Island, FL 34145; phone (800) 528-6345 or (941) 642-2400; www.theboathousemotel.com; Rates: $83–138; Built: 1981; Renovations: 1999

Hampton Inn

3210 Tamiani Trail (U.S. 41), Naples, FL 34103; phone (800) 426-7866 or (941) 261-8000; www.hampton-inn.com; Rates: $129–139; Built: 1989; Renovations: 1998

Dining in Southwest Florida

Café de Marco 244 Royal Palm Dr., Marco Island; phone (941) 394-6262. Continental; Moderate; Reservations accepted. Beautiful stained-glass windows set the tone at this European-themed restaurant. Seafood is the specialty of the house, but save room for one of the sensational desserts.

The Dining Room The Ritz-Carlton, Naples, 280 Vanderbilt Beach Rd., Naples; phone (800) 241-3333 or (941) 598-3300. Continental; Expensive; Reservations required. A top-notch restaurant where the elegant atmosphere is almost as good as the menu . . . almost. The mouth-watering menu and extensive wine list will leave you breathless.

The Grill Room The Ritz-Carlton, Naples, 280 Vanderbilt Beach Rd., Naples; phone (800) 241-3333 or (941) 598-3300. Continental; Expensive; Reservations accepted. The atmosphere is Old World England and the menu is Old World Florida. The restaurant specializes in seafood; atmosphere is provided by a pianist and vocalist.

Ristorante Ciao 835 4th Ave. S., Naples; phone (941) 263-3889. Italian;

Moderate; Reservations accepted. This restaurant is very elegant and features terrific Italian dishes. Our recommendations: calamari and a nice Chianti.

Sandcastles 560 S. Collier Blvd., Marco Island; phone (800) 443-4550 or (941) 394-5000. Continental; Moderate; Reservations accepted. Spectacular views of the pool area and the Gulf set the tone at Sandcastles. The menu here is varied, with specialties ranging from steak to seafood.

Terra 1300 3rd St. S., Naples; phone (941) 262-5500. Continental; Inexpensive; Reservations accepted. A casual restaurant where diners can choose from a varied menu. Entertainment is provided Thursday through Saturday, and guests can choose to sit on the patio.

Activities in Southwest Florida

Babcock Wilderness Adventures 8000 Route 31, Punta Gorda; phone (941) 489-3911. A 90-minute tour will take you through portions of this 90,000-acre development where you can see just what the ecosystem of south Florida looked like before humans and machines arrived.

Caribbean Gardens & Zoological Park 1590 Goodlette Rd., Naples; phone (941) 262-5409. This 52-acre park is home to a variety of wildlife, including lions, tigers, and monkeys. A highlight is the Primate Expedition Cruise, where visitors can see monkeys and apes living in a natural habitat.

Collier County Museum Airport Road at U.S. Highway 41, Naples; phone (941) 774-8476. A museum devoted to the history of the area.

Corkscrew Swamp Sanctuary CR 846 (20 miles northeast of Naples); phone (941) 657-3771. Take a self-guided tour of the two miles of swampland at this Audubon Society preserve.

Teddy Bear Museum 2511 Pine Ridge Rd., Naples; phone (941) 598-2711. If you are a teddy bear lover, this is the place for you, with over 3,000 bears and a library filled with books on—what else?—teddy bears.

Thomas Edison's Winter Home 2350 McGregor Blvd., Fort Myers; phone (941) 334-3614. This 14-acre estate was not only Edison's home but also where he worked on many inventions, including the phonograph and teletype machine. His laboratory is just how he left it when he passed away.

The 19th Hole in Southwest Florida

The Grill Marriott's Golf Club at Marco Island, 3433 Marriott Club Dr., Naples, FL 33937; phone (941) 793-6060. A terrific location overlooking the golf course with both indoor and outdoor seating.

Part Twelve

The Mid-Atlantic

Overview

The Mid-Atlantic region is a diverse area that offers visitors a chance to relive history, get back to nature, and enjoy a beachfront vacation. The region includes states stretching from the District of Columbia in the north to West Virginia in the south, but we have chosen to select three distinct areas to recommend for golfing excursions. That's not to say there aren't other wonderful courses and resorts in the region, just that these three destinations offer the most variety and bang for your buck. In future years, look for the quickly growing Virginia Beach area to jump into the realm of first-rate golf vacation spots. For now, the Mid-Atlantic has a "Big Three."

First, we have Ocean City, located on the eastern tip of Maryland. Ocean City is a mini–Myrtle Beach and resembles what the mega-golf resort looked like some 25 years ago. The big draw to Ocean City is its prime beachfront location and its fun downtown filled with restaurants, shopping, and quaint beachy hotels. This is a strong family vacation destination as it has a little something for everyone, including golf, but more on that later.

The second region is Williamsburg, Virginia, an area that combines golf, natural beauty, and history in a seamless quilt. Colonial Williamsburg was the site of much of Virginia's history, but fell into disarray when the capitol moved to Richmond. Thanks to the efforts of John D. Rockefeller Jr. the area has been totally revitalized and now provides a glimpse into American colonial life. Although we appreciate a chance to enjoy a taste of antique Americana, we dearly enjoy the area because of its world-class resorts and scenic golf courses.

For our final area, we have selected West Virginia. The state is a nature lover's paradise with recreation revolving around camping, fishing, and boating. There is, however, a handful of golf courses and one stunning resort that make it worthy of a golf trip.

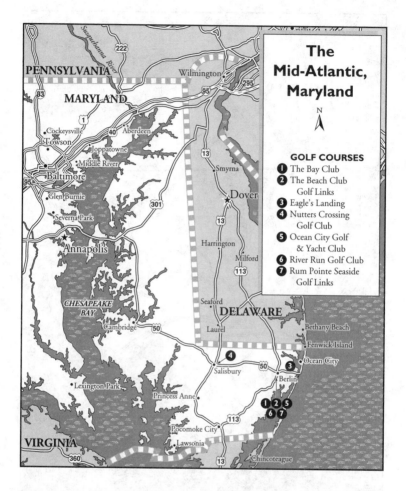

The Mid-Atlantic, Maryland

N

GOLF COURSES
1. The Bay Club
2. The Beach Club Golf Links
3. Eagle's Landing
4. Nutters Crossing Golf Club
5. Ocean City Golf & Yacht Club
6. River Run Golf Club
7. Rum Pointe Seaside Golf Links

WHEN TO GO AND WHAT IT WILL COST

Deciding when to take a golf vacation will depend on where you go. Conversely, where you decide to go depends on when you decide to go. Ocean City is a year-round golfing destination, although the best times to head here to golf are spring and fall, when the weather is seasonable and the scenery is at its peak. Summertime is packed with tourists, many with children, who are heading to the shore for a beach vacation. Winter in Maryland is unpredictable, with rain and cold temperatures making frequent appearances.

On paper, Williamsburg is a year-round golf destination. However, like Ocean City, the weather here is unpredictable at best. It would be hard to

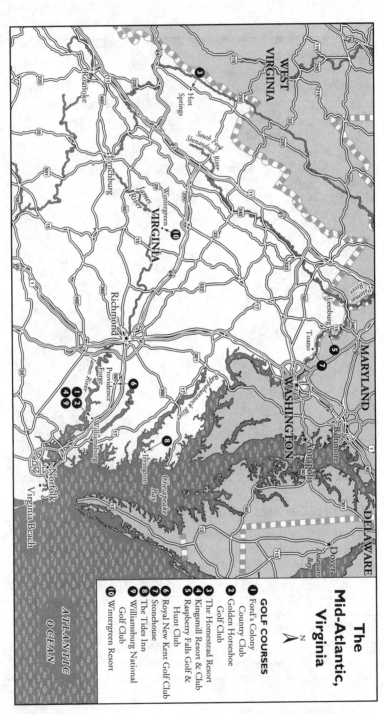

The Mid-Atlantic, Virginia

N

GOLF COURSES

1. Ford's Colony Country Club
2. Golden Horseshoe Golf Club
3. The Homestead Resort
4. Kingsmill Resort & Club
5. Raspberry Falls Golf & Hunt Club
6. Royal New Kent Golf Club
7. Stonehouse
8. The Tides Inn
9. Williamsburg National Golf Club
10. Wintergreen Resort

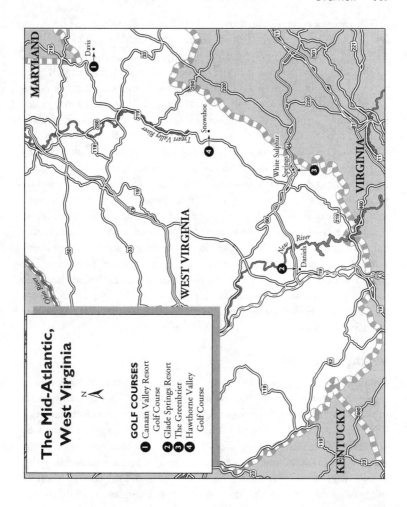

The Mid-Atlantic,
West Virginia

N

GOLF COURSES
1. Canaan Valley Resort
   Golf Course
2. Glade Springs Resort
3. The Greenbrier
4. Hawthorne Valley
   Golf Course

find your ball at the nearby mountain courses during the winter, as they are transformed into icy wonderland. The best time to head to Williamsburg is the spring and fall. Keep in mind, though, that the mountain courses will still be waking up from their winter nap in early spring, so you may want to wait until mid-spring to experience the true essence of the track. Summertime in Williamsburg can be stifling—be prepared to melt if you're golfing in July—but the mountains provide a nice escape from the heat.

For your West Virginia excursion, we recommend spring, summer, or fall. Most of the courses we have identified are located in the mountains, so the summer is pleasant and the spring and fall magnificent. In particular, fall foliage is superb at West Virginia's Greenbrier in late October, just as it is for Virginia's Homestead, some 50 miles away.

On the cost scale, Ocean City is where you will find the best bargains, but less so in the summer when the tourist glut hits. The first two or three weeks of June offer a wonderful window for golfers, as it's just prior to when all the schools let out and families arrive in droves. Hotel and golf rates mesh perfectly in this period. Ocean City is also home to a variety of value-priced daily-fee courses, so golf bargains abound. Virginia is more pricey than Ocean City, but in comparison to Florida and other major golf destinations, it is still quite affordable. Virginia has several premier resorts that will set you back some serious Franklins. A bit isolated but absolutely wonderful are the Tides Inn and Tides Lodge in Irvington, which offer a pair of equally admirable golf courses. Another off-the-beaten-path Virginia favorite is the Wintergreen Resort in Wintergreen, with two superb mountain courses of its own. But if you aren't looking for a full-service resort experience, you can find value-priced accommodations and reasonable daily-fee courses. West Virginia boasts the expensive but superior Greenbrier, the nation's top-ranked resort, and then there's everything else. The Lakeview Resort in Morgantown has two courses, one ranked in the state's top 10, plus easy access to the University of West Virginia. If you're into modest accommodations but sensational value, the resorts of the West Virginia State Parks system are among the best in the nation.

What to Bring

If you are heading here in the spring and fall, make sure to have a good jacket and a warm sweater. For the summer, if you are going to one of the mountain resorts or courses, you will still want those warm clothes in your suitcase. If you are heading to Williamsburg, you will want to make sure you have some good walking shoes to explore the many environs of the town. For those mountain excursions, make sure to have some bug spray in your bag, or you may be itching your way around the course. Many of the courses feature a combination of marshland and water, and thus you will need to have some extra balls in your bag. If you're fortunate enough to be headed to the Homestead, the Greenbrier, or the Williamsburg Inn, bring a blazer and a tie.

Once You're There

Ocean City is a typical beach destination that offers tourists a terrific place to play in the water, make sand castles, and catch a few rays. What it does not offer are any courses along the ocean with stunning views. The majority of Ocean City's courses are actually located a short drive inland, set among the beautiful surroundings of Maryland. Both the accommodations as well as the golf ranges from fair to good. There are no world-class resorts or renowned "must-play" golf courses, but both the lodging and golfing options are reasonably priced. Within the Ocean City area, Eagle's Landing is the best course and should go to the top of your list. Ocean City is a true family destination because it has a little something for everyone.

Williamsburg is the exact opposite of Ocean City. First, golf courses can be found in the heart of the city as well as on the outskirts. The region is dominated by top-notch resorts, including the spectacular Anheuser-Busch–operated Kingsmill and the historic Williamsburg Inn. Elsewhere in Virginia is the one-of-a-kind Homestead, which is definitely worth a side trip. The price tag for both the golf and the accommodations can be pretty steep. Tipping the dollar scale are the courses at the premier resorts, which can cost up to $200 or more; there are, however, more affordable daily-fee courses nearby. Part of Williamsburg's appeal is that it's an ideal place to combine golfing with sightseeing and an interesting history lesson. Fitting in all that the city and its surroundings has to offer will require quite a balancing act.

It is hard to think of West Virginia without hearing the late John Denver crooning those immortal words: "Blue Ridge Mountains, Shenandoah River. Life is old here, older than the trees. . . ." You get the point. If you have the opportunity to visit West Virginia, you will see just why this region had such an impact on Denver. It is a gorgeous state with breathtaking vistas and unlimited outdoor recreational options. The best resort in the country, the Greenbrier, can be found in White Sulphur Springs. If you have the chance and the means to stay here, we highly recommend it. The resort offers a combination of accommodations, amenities, and recreational activities that is unrivaled.

GATHERING INFORMATION
Maryland

Maryland Tourism Development
217 E. Redwood St., Baltimore, MD 21202
Phone (800) 543-1036

Ocean City Chamber of Commerce
12320 Ocean Gateway, Ocean City, MD 21842
Phone (410) 213-0552

Ocean City Department of Tourism
4001 Coastal Hwy., Ocean City, MD 21842
Phone (410) 289-7787; www.mdisfun.org

Virginia

Colonial National Historic Park
Box 210, Yorktown, VA 23690
Phone (757) 898-3400

Colonial Williamsburg Visitor Center
Box 1776, Williamsburg, VA 23187-1776
Phone (800) 447-8679

Virginia Tourism Corporation
901 E. Byrd St., Richmond, VA 23219
Phone (800) 932-5827 or (804) 786-4484

Williamsburg Chamber of Commerce
201 Penniman Rd., P.O. Box 3620, Williamsburg, VA 23187
Phone (757) 229-6511

Williamsburg Attraction Center
5715-62A US 60, Berkeley Commons Outlet Center,
Williamsburg, VA 23187
Phone (757) 253-1058
www.virginia.org; www.williamsburgcc.com

West Virginia

Potomac Highland Travel Council
1200 Harrison Ave., Lower Level, Suite A, Elkins, WV 26241
Phone (304) 636-8400

West Virginia Division of Tourism
State Capitol Complex, 2101 Washington St. E,
Charleston, WV 25305
Phone (800) 225-5982

West Virginia Scenic Trails Association
633 West Virginia Ave., Morgantown, WV 26505
www.state.wv.us/tourism

The Major Courses in Maryland

Eagle's Landing

12367 Eagle's Nest Rd., Berlin, MD 21811; phone (410) 213-7277
How To Get On: Tee times can be made up to one year in advance.
Tees:

Beast: 7,003 yards, par-72, USGA rating 74.3, slope 126
Gold: 6,306 yards, par-72, USGA rating 70.8, slope 121
White: 5,700 yards, par-72, USGA rating 68.2, slope 115
Red: 4,895 yards, par-72, USGA rating 69.3, slope 115

Challenge: ★★★½   Golf Facilities: ★★½
Variety: ★★★½   14-Club Test: ★★★½
Terrain: ★★★½   Intangibles: ★★★½
Beauty/Visual Appeal: ★★★★   Value: ★★★★
Pace of Play: ★★½

Just the Facts   Year Opened: 1991; Course Designer: Michael Hurdzan; Walking: Yes; Greens Fee: $20–32; 9 Hole/Twilight Rate: Yes; Pull Carts: Yes; Practice Range: No; Club Rental: Yes.

Description and Comments   Houston, the Eagle has landed . . . smack dab in the middle of a spectacular setting just outside of Ocean City, Maryland. Eagle's Landing is a publicly owned course where the environment was at the forefront of architect Michael Hurdzan's design, earning it Audubon Sanctuary certification. Not only is the course surrounded by spectacular salt marshes of the Sinepuxent Bay but within its confines are numerous environmentally sensitive areas where wildlife abounds. The old television show *Wild Kingdom* would really have a field day here.

The layout is a blend of a links-style course and a Myrtle Beach–like course where playing among salt marshes is a common feature. In fact, Eagle's Landing has water on 16 holes, including 6 that meander through the salt marshes of Sinepuxent Bay. The fairways here are lush, rolling, and well maintained. But don't let the stunning location and pristine environment fool you—this course has some true bite to it, especially when the wind kicks off the bay.

The hardest hole on the course is the par-4 6th (435 yards). Nicknamed "The Hole From Down Under," this is a slight dogleg left that is a great risk/reward hole. Your tee shot must carry a lake on the left that runs from tee to green; the more water you carry, the less yardage you have on your second shot. The two-tiered green abuts the lake on the left and features a grass hollow directly in front. The two final holes at Eagle's Landing are arguably two of the best finishing holes in the mid-Atlantic region. The former is a delightful par-3 that plays 207 yards from the Beast tees. The green is the largest on the course, which is both good news and bad news: Though you have a lot area to work with, three putts are not uncommon here. Adding to the challenge on this hole is the salt marsh that separates the tee from the green, the grass bunker directly in front of the putting surface, the sand bunker to the left, and the trees beyond.

Seventeen, however, is just a warm-up for the final hole, known as the "Beast of the East." The course's signature hole (par-4, 393 yards) is as challenging as it is scenic. Even a good drive leaves you with a second shot of 160 yards or so, where you have to carry a large section of the salt marsh to reach the green that has no bailout area. The beast has a lot of teeth and isn't afraid to bite you.

Insider Tips This is one of Maryland's best values, but it is no hidden gem—locals are very aware of just what they have available to them, and thus the course is more crowded than not and play can be slow. Tee times can be difficult to get if you wait until the last minute, so book early.

Once you get here, you can quickly discern the course's quality with its eagle-head tee markers. You will find out early that you better have your whole game working. You need to have your driver grooved, since the course is long and demands accuracy off the tee as well as length. Eagle's Landing is a terrific blend of golf and nature, and as with most courses where the environment plays such a vital role, course management is critical. Your best bet is to survey the hole before you put your tee in the ground, identify where the trouble is, and plan a route of least resistance to the hole. Unlike courses where sand or trees are the prevailing hazard, there is no recovering from water and salt marshes, there is just a penalty. So many holes demand forced carries over marshy wetlands that this course is a no-no for mediocre players who have trouble getting it airborne.

Eagle's Landing encourages walking, and this is a very walker-friendly course. Both pull carts and caddies are available at certain times, so you may want to consider hoofing it. Take note that there is no range here, so you might want to hit balls elsewhere and then come to Eagle's Landing. Finally, the salt marshes produce awesome views, but they also produce awesome bugs—bring some bug spray to ward off the little pests.

The Major Courses in Virginia
Golden Horseshoe Golf Club, Gold Course

401 S. England St., Williamsburg, VA 23185; phone (800) 447-8679 or (757) 220-7696

How To Get On: Guests can book tee times when they make their reservations; nonguests can make tee times up to two weeks in advance.

Tees:

Gold: 6,817 yards, par-71, USGA rating 73.6, slope 138

Blue: 6,522 yards, par-71, USGA rating 72.4, slope 135

White: 6,248 yards, par-71, USGA rating 70.7, slope 129

Red: 5,168 yards, par-71, USGA rating 70.6, slope 127

Challenge: ★★★½

Variety: ★★★★

Terrain: ★★★★

Beauty/Visual Appeal: ★★★★

Pace of Play: ★★½

Golf Facilities: ★★★½

14-Club Test: ★★★½

Intangibles: ★★★★

Value: ★★★½

Just the Facts   Year Opened: 1963; Course Designer: Robert Trent Jones Sr.; Walking: Yes; Greens Fee: $85–100; 9 Hole/Twilight Rate: Yes; Pull Carts: No; Practice Range: Yes; Club Rental: Yes.

Description and Comments   As the legend goes, Golden Horseshoe's name comes from an expedition led by Governor Alexander Spotswood over the Blue Ridge Mountains to the Shenandoah Valley. When he returned from his trip, he gave each member of his expedition team a golden horseshoe to commemorate the adventure. Golf at the Golden Horseshoe won't be quite as demanding as Spotswood's trip, but it will be an adventure.

Leading the way at the Golden Horseshoe resort is the Gold course, a delightful layout from Robert Trent Jones Sr. Although he might be prejudiced, Jones Sr. once said that "the Golden Horseshoe is the equal of Augusta National and one that will not take second place to any in the world." If that alone doesn't pique your interest about this course, maybe you need to check your pulse.

The Gold course personifies the design style pioneered by Jones where he combines elements from two schools of golf architecture: penal and strategic. Although Jones's son Rees completed a major renovation project at the course in 1998, much of his father's design philosophy remains. As Rees said, "The restoration maintains my father's architectural intent and improves the course with today's technology and standards." Most of the $4.5 million renovation was spent rebuilding the tees and greens that showed years of wear and tear, as well as the bunkers to improve drainage. Additionally, the second hole was redesigned and now plays 497 yards and has a more level fairway, though there's still that pesky pond to clear 50 yards short of the green.

The Jones boys' course plays over 125 acres of stunningly beautiful, rolling land that includes a 5-acre lake found on seven holes, ravines, and vast wooded valleys. The fairways are extremely tight, guarded by trees that have been around long before even the *Nina*, the *Pinta*, and the *Santa Maria* set sail across the Atlantic. In true Jones Sr. fashion, the hazards found throughout are as integral to the course as are the tees, fairways, and greens. In no way do the hazards feel contrived, and soon you can't imagine the course without them.

Your first real taste of the course comes at the par-5 2nd. The hole plays through a tree-lined fairway that slopes to a large pond nestled in front of the elevated green. If you are long off the tee, you can try for the green in two, but you will more than likely have a downhill lie to hit from. But no matter when you decide to go for the green, it will certainly require accuracy—the putting surface is minute, only 14 yards deep. The hardest hole at the course is the 411-yard, par-4 4th featuring another tree-lined fairway, as well as a deep green pinched by traps on both sides.

The Gold course is known for its par-3s, a collection that might just rival any other course in the nation. You first encounter one at the 3rd hole. Not only does this hole require a good smack off the tee—it measures 190 yards—but demands accuracy as trees line and back the hole and a lake cuts diagonally across the fairway near the green. The 206-yard 7th is a visually stunning hole where you must carry a large lake and play to a green guarded by a trio of bunkers. On the back, the 12th (188 yards) has water in front and to the right of the green that is bisected by a ridge down the center. The final par-3 is the Gold's most memorable—and it's one of the most memorable you'll ever play. Number 16 plays 169 yards from a highly elevated tee in the woods to a pear-shaped island green set on a diagonal encircled by sand traps. A view of the uphill 17th hole lies just beyond the 16th green, but be careful not to get ahead of yourself.

Insider Tips The Gold course is a rigorous test of golf—you will be challenged at every turn. It demands your attention from start to finish and requires that you have all aspects of your game working to score well. A true shotmakers course, the Gold rewards accuracy and penalizes wayward shots as they did criminals in colonial days—severely and swiftly. Your score on the Gold will be a factor of two things: your ability to stay out of hazards and your ability to recover if you do land in these danger zones. Our advice is that if you manage to land in the trees, take your medicine and punch out. An attempted heroic shot more often than not will quickly turn a bad predicament into an even worse one.

On the plus side, the Gold course features holes that for the most part are wide open in front of the green. This design allows golfers to play a variety of approach shots. The shot you select will be influenced by a number of factors: pin placement, your lie, wind conditions, and the time of year. If it has been raining recently, you will find it much more difficult to bump- and run, whereas in the drier months, this shot may be just the ticket. Nevertheless, a number of uphill approaches await, foiling any bump-and-run attempts. The Gold is hilly and narrow, which means several things. First, it would help if you're adept at working the ball, curving it with the shape of the hole and with the tree lines. Second, you'd better practice your shots from uneven lies and stances before you come here—you're going to see a lot of them. Finally, be patient with club selection. Don't rely just on the distance you have left, as so many approaches are either uphill or downhill (mostly uphill), thanks to a number of elevated greens. Sometimes, it can be a two club difference.

The Homestead Resort, Cascades Course

U.S. Highway 220, P.O. Box 2000, Hot Springs, VA 24445; phone (800) 838-1766 or (540) 839-3083

How To Get On: You must be a guest to play at this resort. If you are on a golf package, you can book tee times up to 60 days in advance. If you not on a golf package, you can make tee times 30 days in advance.

Tees:

> Blue: 6,566 yards, par-70, USGA rating 72.9, slope 136
>
> White: 6,282 yards, par-70, USGA rating 71.6, slope 134
>
> Forward: 5,448 yards, par-71, USGA rating 72.9, slope 137

Challenge: ★★★½	Golf Facilities: ★★★½
Variety: ★★★★½	14-Club Test: ★★★★½
Terrain: ★★★★½	Intangibles: ★★★★½
Beauty/Visual Appeal: ★★★★½	Value: ★★★★½
Pace of Play: ★★★	

Just the Facts   Year Opened: 1923; Course Designer: William Flynn; Walking: At times; Greens Fee: $75–125; 9 Hole/Twilight Rate: Yes; Pull Carts: No; Practice Range: Yes; Club Rental: Yes.

Description and Comments   Since the late 1700s, visitors have come to The Homestead Resort for the opportunity to dip into the waters and feel the medicinal healing powers of the local hot springs. These days, visitors still frequent The Homestead Resort, but their goal has changed: They want to stay out of the water, at least on the golf course. The Homestead is one of America's most storied landmark hotels. Thomas Jefferson slept here, but golf at the resort has an illustrious reputation of its own: This is where Sam Snead learned the game, and it has been the site of many professional and amateur tournaments. Its first major tournament was held in 1928, when it hosted the U.S. Women's Amateur, where Glenna Collett Vare defeated Virginia Van Wie 11 and 10. Since then it has been the site of the Curtis Cup, State Amateurs (including one won by Lanny Wadkins), U.S. Senior Amateur, Men's U.S. Amateur, and the 1967 U.S. Women's Open.

The Cascades, located a few minutes down the road, is the resort's premier course and is considered by many to be one of the best mountain courses in the country. Quite simply, Cascades is a unique, quirky, wonderful course that will severely test every golfer. Ranked by many as one of America's top 25 courses, Cascades is among the hilliest of the top championship courses anywhere. The variety of lies, stances, and imaginative shots you will need to play is outstanding. As Sam Snead said, "There isn't any kind of hill you don't have to play from, or any kind of shot you won't hit here."

Cascades' routing is superb, with holes doglegging this way and that, climbing uphill and then plummeting down, then playing across a slope. The terrain is magnificent with thousand-year-old trees everywhere, rushing cascades, and eye-popping scenery making it extremely difficult to concentrate on your game. All this amid one of the most peaceful settings this side of your local library branch.

The front nine certainly puts golfers to the test as the holes are hemmed in by thick woods, requiring accurate shotmaking. The hardest hole on the course is the 576-yard 5th, where the tight fairway has two sand bunkers dangerously located in the landing area on the left. If your tee shot lands too far to the left, you will have a blind uphill shot out of some nasty rough to a slender, well-guarded green. The 9th is a par-4 (450 yards) that is both visually inspiring and physically demanding. Off the elevated tee, you must carry a ravine and valley to a plateau landing area. If you make it across, that is only half the battle: Your second shot is to a small green situated in a valley encircled by trees and sand traps.

If asked to pick one hole on this course as being the best, it would be a difficult choice. Our nomination is the gargantuan par-4 12th, which plays nearly 480 yards. An elevated tee overlooks a narrow fairway hemmed in by trees on both sides. A curling brook crawls up the left side and the hole swings gently to the left, guarded at its elbow by some small trees. Mountains thick with greenery rise in the distance behind the green, but make sure to keep your eye on the ball, for your long iron or fairway wood approach is played to an extremely long and narrow green with a ridge that splits the middle. Cross bunkers well in front of the green will punish the topped shot, while the sand on either side of the green makes things interesting for those who aren't arrow-straight.

The final four holes pose a quirky finish: pars of 3, 5, 5, and 3 that could be a terrific opportunity to make a few birdies. The first par-3 is a 213-yarder that requires a tee shot through a tunnel of trees to a well-bunkered, multitiered green; the final hole is a stunning par-3 that measures 192 yards and plays to an elevated green.

Insider Tips   If you were to look solely at Cascades' yardage, you may think that this is a pushover course, a Bloody Mary without any spices. You couldn't be more wrong. The spice here is provided from the numerous trees that line the fairways as well as the many bunkers and inevitable uneven lies. Throw in punishing rough and a sinister stream that snakes its way throughout the layout and you have one tough "short" course. The prudent thing would be to put your driver in the trunk when you get to the course, lock it up, and throw away the key. You need to be accurate here, but you don't need to be long off the tee. If you have your fairway woods and short irons working you have a good chance of scoring well here. Also, this is an old-fashioned course where it would be helpful to know how to "work" the ball with your woods and irons, and it would be helpful to be patient, as there are a number of semiblind shots.

Cascades is a prime example of a risk/reward course where the architect lets you decide your own fate. You can knock some strokes off your score if you are willing to take some risks, but should you fail, well, that is where the risk factor comes in. One false step and what once was a terrific birdie or eagle opportunity is quickly reduced to a scrambling par or worse.

As you make your way around the course, keep in mind both the elevation changes as well as the position of the ball in relation to your feet. Balls below your feet will to fade, and the opposite is true for those located above. Also, the mountains provide a spectacular backdrop, but they also can play havoc with your mind, distorting your depth perception and making you rethink your club selection. Our recommendation: Check your yardage and club accordingly, keeping all the other factors mentioned previously in mind. As you approach the ball, take a look at your target line, but try to avoid staring too long at the mountains behind.

If you are a long but wild hitter, play the course early in the morning. The heavily sloping fairways shed side-spinning shots when they're dry, but you can hold them pretty well in the early morning dew, or after a mountain shower. Likewise, short hitters should avoid Cascades when it's wet. The normally challenging rough becomes impenetrable and the fairways with upslopes in the landing areas will catch drives in the soft turf and plug, or else propel them backward.

Cascades is a mountain course in a ski area, so in early spring the thawing course can play wet and muddy. Better to wait until the course dries out and firms up (late June and beyond) to guarantee the full measure of the course's playing value.

Kingsmill Resort and Club, River Course

1010 Kingsmill Rd., Williamsburg, VA 23185; phone (800) 832-5665 or (757) 253-5960

How To Get On: Guests of the resort can book tee times when they make their reservations. Nonguests can make tee times one day in advance.

Tees:

   Blue: 6,797 yards, par-71, USGA rating 73.3, slope 137

   White: 6,022 yards, par-71, USGA rating 69.7, slope 129

   Forward: 4,646 yards, par-71, USGA rating 65.7, slope 116

Challenge: ★★★★	Golf Facilities: ★★★
Variety: ★★★★	14-Club Test: ★★★★
Terrain: ★★★★	Intangibles: ★★★★
Beauty/Visual Appeal: ★★★★	Value: ★★★★
Pace of Play: ★★½	

Just the Facts Year Opened: 1975; Course Designer: Pete Dye; Walking: No; Greens Fee: $60–125; 9 Hole/Twilight Rate: Yes; Pull Carts: No; Practice Range: Yes; Club Rental: Yes.

Description and Comments The River Course is home to Kingsmill's signature layout and is recognized as one of the best in the Mid-Atlantic region. Spectacularly located along the James River, this course is also home to a couple of great classics: the PGA Tour's Michelob Championship (formerly known as the Anheuser-Busch Classic) and Curtis Strange. Strange moved to Kingsmill in 1977 and quickly earned favorite son status after his two consecutive U.S. Open wins. Although he spends much of his time on the road, he is still the unofficial spokesman for Kingsmill and its spectacular golf courses (he may be prejudiced, as he had a hand in building the Woods course).

The River course is the most demanding at the resort, since golfers must negotiate their way through tight, tree-lined fairways and over deep ravines, taking care to avoid the more than 90 bunkers and water that comes into play on 9 holes. Renowned for its small elevated greens and plateaued landing areas, the River Course is a true shotmakers course where accuracy and pure ball striking is rewarded. As proof, consider two golfers who have won consecutive events at Kingsmill's River course in the past 20 years: Calvin Peete and David Duval, two of the most accurate drivers in history. The course recently underwent minor renovations overseen by original architect Pete Dye, who lengthened a number of holes and added a new irrigation system.

Picking the best holes on the course is no easy task because there are so many. On the front side, we nominate the 4th and 8th holes for this honor. The former is a slightly dogleg left par-4 that plays 437 yards from the back tees. This hole has a rather simple recipe for hazards: A stream that runs directly in front of the tee boxes (and really shouldn't come into play, unless you dribble one off the tee) and then runs down the entire left side, and a series of four bunkers that guard the green almost as intently as the Secret Service does the president. The 8th is also a par-4, and it plays 413 yards and doglegs right. This is a perfect example of a hole where position far outweighs brawn. If your tee shot travels too far and doesn't follow the contour of the hole, it runs the danger of running into the lake. The green is equally as demanding as it is undulating and deep with a narrow entrance way, and is also nearly encircled by sand traps.

On the back side our nominations (and remember, it is just an honor to be nominated) for the best holes goes to the final two. Seventeen, the course's signature hole, is a delightful par-3 that plays 179 yards and looks pretty simple on paper. But throw in an often present swirling wind and a deep and narrow green with a large bunker on the right and two smaller ones on the left and you have quite a challenge. The hole sits high above and affords a marvelous view of the James River, to the right. The final hole is a dogleg-left, 438-yard par-4 where you must clear Moody's Pond off the tee and then try to avoid taking a dip in the pond on each of your subsequent shots. Adding further difficulty to the hole are the numerous trees that seem to be everywhere (although rumored to be 90% air, we recommend avoiding them) and the occasional bunker thrown in for good measure.

Insider Tips Our first word of advice here is don't even think about ordering a Coors Light or one of those imported brews. As for the golf, we recommend that you think. This is truly a course that rewards smart play but on the other hand severely penalizes errant shots. You in no way need to be a distance monster off the tee; rather, you need to focus on accuracy and ball position. Placement is the key to success on the River Course, as many of the holes dogleg one way or the other and feature hazards that can quickly jump up and grab your ball and at the same time, cast your par down the river. Women should note that this course was voted as one of the top courses in the nation for female golfers.

Pay special attention when you arrive at the 17th tee. The hilltop tee abuts fortifications to the left that date back to the Revolutionary War. Then, check the usually gusty breezes. If the wind is strong, your smartest play may be to land the ball on the hillside left of the green and hope it trickles down onto the putting surface.

Royal New Kent Golf Club

5300 Bailey Rd., Providence Forge, VA 23140; phone (888) 253-4363 or (804) 966-7023

How To Get On: Tee times can be made nine months in advance.

Tees:

Invicta: 7,291 yards, par-72, USGA rating 76.0, slope 147

Gold: 6,985 yards, par-72, USGA rating 74.9, slope 144

Black: 6,581 yards, par-72, USGA rating 73.1, slope 141

White: 6,179 yards, par-72, USGA rating 70.8, slope 135

Green: 5,231 yards, par-72, USGA rating 72.0, slope 130

Challenge: ★★★★½	Golf Facilities: ★★★½
Variety: ★★★½	14-Club Test: ★★★★
Terrain: ★★★★	Intangibles: ★★★★
Beauty/Visual Appeal: ★★★★	Value: ★★★★
Pace of Play: ★★★	

Just the Facts Year Opened: 1996; Course Designer: Mike Stranz; Walking: Yes; Greens Fee: $60–85; 9 Hole/Twilight Rate: No; Pull Carts: No; Practice Range: Yes; Club Rental: Yes.

Description and Comments   Royal New Kent and Stonehouse (see the Sampler section) are sister courses—twins that were separated at birth. There is no doubt that Stonehouse is a Virginia course, but her sister's roots lie thousands of miles east in Ireland. Royal New Kent is a tribute by up-and-coming architect Mike Stranz (formerly a protégé of Tom Fazio) to the famed courses across the pond. Stranz turned to Royal County Down and Ballybunion, among others, for inspiration, and was so successful that you may find yourself ordering a Guinness at the turn and looking for the Blarney Stone to kiss.

The course's links-style fairways are relatively open, but are surrounded by deep fescues that play a mean game of hide and seek with golfers looking for their wayward shots. Although you won't have any trouble finding your ball in one of the 140 or so pot bunkers scattered about, extricating yourself is another matter entirely. If you land in a trap, along with your sand wedge, you might want to bring a ladder, a flare gun, and some survival gear—these are some tricky bunkers to get out of. Another Irish-like feature at Royal Kent, though not necessarily a favorite among American golfers, are the occasional blind shots where you must follow a position rock to find the fairway. The greens here are also very challenging as they are lightning-fast and feature prominent swales and mounds; to practice, you might want to putt on the warped linoleum in your kitchen. The Irish sure know how to put a golf course together.

Royal New Kent greets you with both guns blazing. The 1st hole is a stunning 418-yard par-4 (from the Invicta tees, meaning "unconquerable") with a narrow, banana-shaped fairway that is an island in a sea of fescue grass. The 2nd hole is a long par-5 (557 yards) that is basically a 90-degree dogleg left and is one of the best holes on the course. A well-struck drive will leave you with the option of cutting off yardage and carrying the waste area or playing it more conservatively and following the fairway to the green. You really don't encounter any traps until the 4th hole, but from here on in sand tends to dictate your play. The hardest hole on the course is number six (427 yards), which plays straightaway to a tight fairway pinched on both sides by sand traps. Trees guard the entire left side of the hole, and grass runs from tee to green on the left. The green is multitiered and deep.

On the back nine, you will find that the bunkers are slightly less severe than on the front and that the elevation changes are not as severe. Nonetheless, the back side still manages to challenge. The 12th is Royal New Kent's best par-3, demanding both length and accuracy. The hole plays 221 yards from the tips and requires a tee shot that traverses grassland, avoids the seven bunkers, and finds the pin on this hourglass-shaped green that measures 86 yards deep. This has three putt written all over it. The finishing hole provides no letdown. Your tee shot on this 418-yard par-4 must traverse a lake and come to rest on a rather wide landing area. Your next shot, however, is truly fraught with peril. The narrow green is surrounded on three sides by a lake, thus club selection and accuracy are critical to your success. This is one hole that can make or break a round.

Insider Tips As with its Irish cousins, Royal New Kent offers golfers options and requires that they think their way around, as the majority of holes can be played in a variety of ways. Is it best to fade a ball in or bump and run? Should you cut off distance and play over the fescue or play it safe and stick to the fairway? To answer these questions, you must survey the hole and take into account factors such as wind, turf conditions (e.g., wet or dry), elevation, pin placement, and ball flight trajectory.

With its five sets of tees, the course advertises playability and challenge for all levels of players. However, be forewarned: If you decide to play the Invicta tees, you will have the test of your life on your hand. These tees are appropriately named, for they are unconquerable for mere mortals. We recommend that you avoid these tees unless you just can't resist. (It's kind of like a wet paint sign: You still want to touch even though you know it will result in a mess.) The many hazards found throughout the course are more than enough to keep any golfer on their toes. In all candor, Royal New Kent is simply too hard for most intermediate golfers from any set of tees. It's so spectacular, you must play it once—or even twice, such is the value of course knowledge here. But for so-so golfers, this can be a frustrating, difficult day.

Finally, a few words of advice on getting out of those pesky traps. Pot bunkers differ from other sand traps as they are shaped almost like a coffee cup sunk into the ground. You need to make sure that you have selected a club that is lofted enough to clear the side of the trap, or you may find yourself hitting from the same spot again. These are not bunkers where you can gain a lot of yardage getting out. Rather, you need to take your medicine and make up for it on your next shot.

The Major Courses in West Virginia

The Greenbrier, Greenbrier Course

300 W. Main St., White Sulphur Springs, WV 24986; phone (800) 624-6070 or (304) 536-1110

How To Get On: Resort guests can make tee times up to four months in advance; nonguests can book tee times three days in advance.

Tees:

Blue: 6,681 yards, par-72, USGA rating 73.7, slope 136

White: 6,311 yards, par-72, USGA rating 71.7, slope 133

Red: 5,280 yards, par-72, USGA rating 71.5, slope 123

Challenge: ★★★½	Golf Facilities: ★★★★½
Variety: ★★★★	14-Club Test: ★★★★
Terrain: ★★★★	Intangibles: ★★★★½
Beauty/Visual Appeal: ★★★★	Value: ★★★½
Pace of Play: ★★★	

Just the Facts   Year Opened: 1925; Course Designers: Seth Raynor and Jack Nicklaus; Walking: Yes; Greens Fee: $72–225; 9 Hole/Twilight; Rate: Yes; Pull Carts: No; Practice Range: Yes; Club Rental: Yes.

Description and Comments   The premier course at this five-star resort is the Greenbrier, a fine test of golf in a spectacular setting. Although the course has murky architectural origins, what is certain is that this wasn't a particularly distinguished course until 1977, when Jack Nicklaus was tapped to remodel the old layout in preparation for the 1979 Ryder Cup (won by the United States 17-11). Since then, the Greenbrier course also hosted the 1994 Solheim Cup. Nicklaus's remodeling efforts were extensive, and the Greenbrier was transformed from a ho-hum course to a "hang on until the ride comes to a complete stop" course.

Unlike many of Nicklaus's other courses, the Greenbrier is not overly long, playing less than 6,700 yards from the tips. Like many of his other courses, the Greenbrier is filled with diverse risk/reward opportunities that demand accuracy and precision and at the same time reward creativity. Holes play along the Allegheny Mountain valley through stands of maple, oak, and pine trees. These wooden hazards combine with just enough sand and water to produce a course that keeps golfers on their toes and birdies just out of reach. Getting to the green is half the battle, while putting is the other half. The greens tend to be small to medium in size and are very tricky to putt as they are severely undulating.

Your first true Greenbrier challenge comes at the par-4 2nd, known as "The Cape." The hole plays a sturdy 403 yards from the tips, and there is a lake that cuts into the fairway, further narrowing an already tight entryway to the green. The hardest hole on the course is the par-4 6th (456 yards), an uphill test where the fairway is guarded on both sides by dense trees. The green is guarded by a lone bunker, but it is amazing just how drastically this single hazard affects play. Par on this hole is a solid score. Perhaps the most fun, scenic hole on the Greenbrier course is the 10th, a 339-yard par-4 that calls for a forced carry second to a narrow green over a wide, deep creek. A bridge links golfers to the green.

The final hole, a par-5 of 560 yards, is a perfect risk/reward layout where golfers have to work hard to find the fairway off the tee. Trees surround the hole from tee to green. The deep green is very receptive to the bump-and-run shot, but the surrounding sand will quickly punish any off-target shots.

Insider Tips   Typically when you play a Nicklaus course, you have to be very long off the tee as well as very accurate. At Greenbrier, Nicklaus has cut us a break and created a course where length is not all that critical. Accuracy, however, is still paramount. If you can keep your drives in the fairway, you have an opportunity to score well. If, however, you find yourself off the beaten path, it's going to be a long day filled with a bevy of recovery shots. Because accuracy is so important, higher handicappers who spray the ball may find this course out of their league. It just won't be all that fun for you if you can't keep the ball in play.

Big hitters will find that the par-5s here offer the biggest risk/reward opportunities as well as the best scoring chances—the score will depend on how the risk pays off. The best holes to test your fate are numbers three and eight, where the greens are relatively open in front and thus highly receptive to run-up shots.

An important note about scheduling: Because the course is set in the mountains, the sun tends to disappear earlier as it sneaks behind its surrounding backdrop. Thus, you will want to avoid having too late of a start if you want to finish without the aid of a flashlight. The course opens in April, but don't expect pristine playing conditions on opening day. Even a resort of this stature needs the opportunity to let the courses wake up from their winter hibernation. You will see the real Greenbrier if you wait until later in the spring. Also, frost delays are a common occurrence all season long, and thus you may want to avoid the first or last tee times of the day.

The Greenbrier, Old White Course

300 W. Main St., White Sulphur Springs, WV 24986; phone (800) 624-6070 or (304) 536-1110

How To Get On: Resort guests can make tee times up to four months in advance; nonguests can book tee times three days in advance.

Tees:

     Blue: 6,640 yards, par-70, USGA rating 72.1, slope 130

     White: 6,353 yards, par-70, USGA rating 70.6, slope 127

     Red: 5,216 yards, par-70, USGA rating 69.9, slope 119

Challenge: ★★★½	Golf Facilities: ★★★★½
Variety: ★★★★	14-Club Test: ★★★½
Terrain: ★★★★	Intangibles: ★★★★
Beauty/Visual Appeal: ★★★★	Value: ★★★½
Pace of Play: ★★★½	

Just the Facts   Year Opened: 1913; Course Designers: Seth Raynor and C. B. Macdonald; Walking: Yes; Greens Fee: $72–225; 9 Hole/Twilight Rate: Yes; Pull Carts: No; Practice Range: Yes; Club Rental: Yes.

Description and Comments   You might not want to mention that the Greenbrier is the premiere course at the resort to Sam Snead, the professional emeritus at the resort, as he has had a lifelong love affair with the Old White course. As he says, "I like every hole on the Old White." If you get a chance to play Old White, you no doubt will agree with slamming Sammy. Although the Greenbrier went through a complete makeover, Old White has pretty much stayed the same over the years. Charles Blair Macdonald, with assistance from his associate, Seth Raynor, is the man behind the course. Macdonald is also the man behind such venerable tracks as the Chicago Golf Club, National Golf Links, and Yale. But as most of these courses are exclusively private, Old White may be your one and only opportunity to experience the Macdonald touch.

Old White is gentler than the Greenbrier course, but it's not without its share of drama—beginning with the 1st hole, which sports a terrifying elevated tee, in full view of the assembled crowds. Many a topped shot has found the creek below. A hillside forest full of oaks, with a few pines, frames the fairway and forms a gorgeous backdrop in late October. The 2nd hole is another sound test of your skills. Named "Creekside," this superb hole is a 405-yard par-4 featuring a crowned fairway that skirts a creek, which lines the hole's right side. The hardest hole on the course is number six, called "Lookout." This par-4 hole plays a stern 444 yards and demands an approach shot off a wildly sloping fairway. Another standout is the 16th, or "Narrows," a 417-yard par-4 that has tree, creek, and pond trouble throughout. The final "Home" hole is a par-3 (162 yards) and finishes in the shadows of the striped awnings of the clubhouse and has settled many a wager.

Insider Tips   This course is more forgiving than the Greenbrier, but you don't want to let your guard down too much. The terrain is flatter there, but greens are more bunkered and smaller. Adding to the furor is the fact that the greens slope severely back to front, a true Old World touch, and thus staying below the hole is the best recommendation. As with the Greenbrier, accuracy is much more critical than distance. Those who have a solid game including course management and strategy will be the ones who score well here. Another Old World touch is the old-fashioned quirky par of 34–36–70. Big hitters, don't expect to get off to a fast start on the par-5s, because there are only two of them and the first doesn't appear until the 12th hole!

If you are a higher handicapper, you will enjoy this course much more than you would the Greenbrier. You still will have the same five-star service and get the opportunity to soak up the spectacular surroundings, but you won't find yourself hitting your head against the wall as you probably would at the more demanding Greenbrier. One of the easier holes is the 340-yard, par-4 5th, but it's not exactly driveable, unless you are a young

Sam Snead, who did just that in the 1930s. Don't let the 10th hole fool you. It's called "Pond" on the score card, but there's no longer a drop of water on it. The pond was removed years ago.

Old White is also open from April through October, so the same warnings we discussed in the Greenbrier section regarding frost, daylight, and course conditions hold true for this course as well.

A Maryland Sampler

The Bay Club

9122 Libertytown Rd., Berlin, MD 21811; phone (800) 229-2582 or (410) 641-4081

Tees: Championship: 6,958 yards, par-72, USGA rating 73.1, slope 126

Green Fees: $20–55

Challenge: ★★★	Golf Facilities: ★★★½
Variety: ★★★	14-Club Test: ★★★½
Terrain: ★★★	Intangibles: ★★★
Beauty/Visual Appeal: ★★★	Value: ★★★
Pace of Play: ★★★	

Description and Comments   The Bay Club is the only course in the area built and owned by PGA golf professionals. Located in a beautiful wooded setting, predominantly scrubby oaks and pines, Bay Club is a traditional test of golf with many classic risk/reward holes. Not only do the stands of trees affect your play but the numerous lakes often wreak havoc. The Bay Club is renowned for its par-3s, especially the lovely 143-yard 12th and the rugged 14th hole (187 yards), which plays to the area's only island green. The course's signature hole is the 18th, a 578-yard par-5 that shares a double green with the 542-yard, par-5 9th. A solid drive will leave you with two options to reach the green. You can play it safe and lay up with a long iron, leaving you a short approach over a lake to the double green shared with the 9th hole, or you can go for broke and hit a fairway wood. The clubhouse overlooks the 9th and 18th greens, so there's nowhere to hide if you can't cope with the water hazards at both holes.

The Beach Club Golf Links

9715 Deer Park Dr., Berlin, MD 21811; phone (410) 641-4653

Tees:

>Inner Links Course: 7,020 yards, par-72, USGA rating 73.0, slope 128

>Outer Links Course: 6,548 yards, par-72, USGA rating 71.7, slope 134

Greens Fee: $25–60

Challenge: ★★★	Golf Facilities: ★★★½
Variety: ★★★	14-Club Test: ★★★
Terrain: ★★★	Intangibles: ★★★
Beauty/Visual Appeal: ★★★½	Value: ★★★
Pace of Play: ★★★	

Description and Comments   Beach Club features two distinct 18-hole courses, the Inner and Outer Links courses. The Inner Links, the original and longer course at the Beach Club, winds through a forest of hardwood and pine trees. Adding to the difficulty factor are the many forced carries and an infusion of water, found on 12 holes. The Inner Links course possesses a strong set of par-5s, especially the 3rd hole, where the approach calls for a "field goal" between two trees. The Outer Links is shorter but requires solid mid-iron play, shotmaking ability, and sound course management to score well. This course also has a plethora of water, found on 15 of the holes. Given its prime location near the ocean, the wind can also be a factor. Fine finishing holes on each nine characterize the new course, designed by Brian Ault, who co-designed the original course with his late father, Ed. Also, the Beach Club offers a nice range and practice area, so come early and get warmed up.

Ocean City Golf and Yacht Club

11401 Country Club Dr., Berlin, MD 21811; phone (800) 442-3570 or (410) 641-1779

Tees:

Newport Bay: 6,526 yards, par-72, USGA rating 71.7, slope 121

Seaside Course: 6,520 yards, par-72, USGA rating 70.9, slope 115,

Greens Fee: $45–79 (Newport Bay); $30–65 (Seaside Course)

Challenge: ★★★	Golf Facilities: ★★★
Variety: ★★★	14-Club Test: ★★★
Terrain: ★★★	Intangibles: ★★★
Beauty/Visual Appeal: ★★★½	Value: ★★★★
Pace of Play: ★★★	

Description and Comments   This course, or more specifically the Seaside course, is the birthplace of golf in the Ocean City area. Seaside may have been the first, but Newport Bay is the best at Ocean City Golf Club. Originally known as Bayside, this course recently underwent a complete makeover where it was redone, reformatted, and renamed. Newport Bay is a pure blend of nature and golf: There are no homes or traffic infringing on your experience. What you'll find, however, are eight holes located directly on the marsh or on the water with nearly half the holes requiring a forced carry over one or the other.

The Seaside course is much less challenging and thus may be ideal if you are a higher handicapper. Also located in an appealing setting, Seaside features wider fairways and is thus more forgiving, though the back nine is well wooded. There are two keys to scoring well here: course management, as there are wetlands and maritime forests throughout, and sound approach shots to the small and fast greens. Both courses are a terrific value.

Nutters Crossing Golf Club

30287 S. Hampton Bridge Rd., Salisbury, MD 21801; phone (410) 860-4653

Tees: Championship: 6,033 yards, par-70, USGA rating 67.1, slope 115

Greens Fee: $30–40

Challenge: ★★	Golf Facilities: ★★★
Variety: ★★★	14-Club Test: ★★
Terrain: ★★★	Intangibles: ★★½
Beauty/Visual Appeal: ★★★	Value: ★★★
Pace of Play: ★★★	

Description and Comments   Nutters Crossing is owned and operated by the same group that developed Rum Pointe and has earned a reputation as being one of the area's best public golf courses. Located 25 miles inland, Nutters is unlike many of the Ocean City courses in that it features elevation changes. The rolling fairways and gently sloping hills often afford uneven lies and interesting stances. The course is quite short overall, but it is always interesting. It's really a placement course, where fairway woods or long-irons are the ticket off most tees. The front nine is wide open, but the back nine flirts with the woods. Water can be found on eight holes, but the real test comes from the more than 50 bunkers scattered about. Solid approaches are required as the greens are good sized and feature a number of undulations. Nutters is always in terrific condition and is an ideal course for the high handicapper. An excellent colonial brick clubhouse awaits after the round.

River Run Golf Club

11605 Masters Lane, Berlin, MD 21811; phone (800) 733-7786 or (410) 641-7200

Tees: Championship: 6,705 yards, par-71, USGA rating 70.4, slope 128

Greens Fee: $10–40

Challenge: ★★★	Golf Facilities: ★★★
Variety: ★★★	14-Club Test: ★★★
Terrain: ★★★	Intangibles: ★★★
Beauty/Visual Appeal: ★★★	Value: ★★★
Pace of Play: ★★★	

Description and Comments   River Run takes its name from its location, as it's perched on the banks of the historic St. Martins River. Designed by the legendary Gary Player, River Run blends challenge and scenery in equal doses. The landscape is speckled with numerous pot bunkers, which contrast nicely with the huge "beach" bunkers that also await errant shots. This course isn't terribly long, but the back nine is a tight ride through the trees, and the well-defended greens often have two and three tiers. When they're cut low, they can offer a supreme putting challenge. Most memorable is the 13th hole, which sits astride Little Sound Creek with a green menaced by marsh.

Rum Pointe Seaside Golf Links

7000 Rum Pointe Lane, Berlin, MD 21811; phone (888) 809-4653 or (410) 629-1414

Tees: Championship: 7,020 yards, par-72, USGA rating 72.6, slope 122

Greens Fee: $25–57

Challenge: ★★★
Variety: ★★★½
Terrain: ★★★★
Beauty/Visual Appeal: ★★★★
Pace of Play: ★★★

Golf Facilities: ★★★
14-Club Test: ★★★½
Intangibles: ★★★
Value: ★★★½

Description and Comments   Rum Pointe is one of Ocean City's most spectacular golf courses. Designed by the team of P. B. and Pete Dye, Rum Pointe is located adjacent to the Sinepuxent Bay. Seventeen of its holes have a view of the bay, and several of them play directly alongside. Rum Pointe is a true Scottish links–style course where you will be hard pressed to find any trees on the course except for holes 10, 11, and 12. What you will find are risk/reward-style holes that feature tough bunkering, elevated tees, and big greens. The par-4 18th is a perfect example, with a huge lake down the right side and a wild mix of bunker shapes at the green, including a hook-shaped trap on the right that wraps behind the green. The other challenging component is the wind, which whips off the bay and might make you think you're in Scotland. Rum Pointe may be the only course in the region with bentgrass fairways. They'll offer a superior playing surface, but will be the first to burn out in hot, hot weather.

A Virginia Sampler

Ford's Colony Country Club

240 Ford's Colony Dr., Williamsburg, VA 23188; phone (757) 258-4130

Tees:

> Blue Course: Yardage, par, USGA rating rating, and slope not yet available
>
> Blackheath: 6,621 yards, par-71, USGA rating 71.8, slope 133
>
> Red/White (Marsh Hawk): 6,738 yards, par-72, USGA rating 72.3, slope 126

Greens Fee: $45–95

Challenge: ★★★	Golf Facilities: ★★★
Variety: ★★★½	14-Club Test: ★★★½
Terrain: ★★★½	Intangibles: ★★★
Beauty/Visual Appeal: ★★★½	Value: ★★★½
Pace of Play: ★★★	

Description and Comments Ford's Colony is a highly-acclaimed semiprivate club located on 2,400 wooded acres just outside downtown Williamsburg. For those who aren't members, you can gain access to the club through one of two ways: You can book a stay at the on-site Manor House and tee times can be made when you book your reservation, or nonguests can make tee times one week in advance.

Ford's Colony is currently undergoing a major makeover with the addition of two new 9s, bringing the total number of holes at the club to 54; at the same time, the original 9s are being realigned and renamed. What is now known as the Red/White course will next May be renamed the Marsh Hawk course (once the new nine on the Blue Course has been added). This layout features rolling fairways that cut through tall trees, water on 9 holes, 21 fairway bunkers, and greens that are well protected by another 37 bunkers. The signature hole on this course, as well as the number one handicap, is the 4th, a par-4 that plays 402 yards from the back tees. A lake separates the tee box from the landing area and then runs along the entire left-hand side of the hole. After carrying the water off the tee, you must then play a long shot to a small green protected by water on three sides and a series of bunkers.

Blackheath is comprised of the nine formerly known as the Gold course and an entirely new nine. Like its sister, Blackheath is stocked with hazards in the form of 28 fairway bunkers, 30 greenside bunkers, and 13 holes that feature water. A fun but potentially deadly hole is the 187-yard, par-3 3rd. The tee is located on an island, and you must carry a large lake to reach the smallish green that is guarded by three bunkers. The finishing hole, a 356-yard par-4, also is dominated by water. Water can be found directly in front of the tee and along the entire left side of the hole. On your drive, you must select a line where you can comfortably cut off as much of this lake as possible, leaving you with a prime angle and minimal yardage on your approach to an island green guarded by two bunkers. All of the golf holes at Ford's Colony were designed by Dan Maples, a native of Pinehurst, North Carolina, renowned for his attractive, challenging, but funto-play layouts.

At the time of writing, the Blue course was still under construction, and thus ratings or a description could not be included.

Golden Horseshoe Golf Club, Green Course

401 S. England St., Williamsburg, VA 23185; phone (800) 447-8679 or (757) 220-7696

Tees: Championship: 7,120 yards, par-72, USGA rating 73.4, slope 134
Greens Fee: $85–100

Challenge: ★★★½	Golf Facilities: ★★★
Variety: ★★★½	14-Club Test: ★★★½
Terrain: ★★★★	Intangibles: ★★★
Beauty/Visual Appeal: ★★★★	Value: ★★★½
Pace of Play: ★★★½	

Description and Comments   Rees Jones's connection to the Golden Horseshoe goes beyond the renovations he made to his father's Gold Course. In 1992, the younger Jones was given the task of building his own course. The result is the visually stunning and challenging Green Course, located on 250 acres of rolling terrain that once was part of the Bassett Hall Plantation. In fact, remnants of the plantation can be seen throughout the course.

The Green Course plays through beautifully wooded, rolling terrain as well as over and around a number of ravines. The fairways at Green are links-style and feature a multitude of mounds, a Rees Jones architectural trait, that are very user-friendly as they funnel the ball into the landing area. Not so user-friendly are the more than 110 bunkers and the water found on six holes.

The hardest hole on the course is the 6th, a 450-yard par-4 that features a mounded fairway lined by trees with a landing area protected on both sides by sand. For your second shot you have to play uphill to a green that drops off severely to the right and is guarded on both sides by yawning sand traps. The back side plays longer and tougher than the front. One of the best holes on this nine is the finishing hole, a par-5 that plays 531 yards from the tips. From the elevated green you are treated to an eye-catching view of the surroundings. The fairway is relatively wide open, but your tee shot must carry a stream. The hole then plays uphill to a green that is cut out of the hill and slopes both to the right and forward. Adding a significant degree of difficulty are the series of traps that start a little over 135 yards out and guard both sides of the fairway.

The Homestead Resort, Lower Cascades

U.S. Highway 220, P.O. Box 2000, Hot Springs, VA 24445; phone (800) 838-1766 or (540) 839-3083

Tees: Championship: 6,619 yards, par-72, USGA rating 72.2, slope 127

Greens Fee: $45–90

Challenge: ★★★	Golf Facilities: ★★★
Variety: ★★★½	14-Club Test: ★★★
Terrain: ★★★★	Intangibles: ★★★½
Beauty/Visual Appeal: ★★★★	Value: ★★★½
Pace of Play: ★★★★	

Descriptions and Comments   Located five miles from the Cascades Course is Lower Cascades, a relatively wide-open course that served as co-host to the 1988 U.S. Amateur. This is one of Trent Jones's gentler efforts, but is the perfect choice for many players who want a stiffer test than the Old Course but aren't up to the rigors of Cascades. The best holes on Lower Cascades feature the attractive but pesky Cascades Stream, which affects play on 9 holes. Providing added difficulty are the more than 70 gaping, Jones-like bunkers that place a premium on accuracy.

The hardest hole on the course is the 450-yard, par-4 3rd. The dogleg hole, already a long hole, plays uphill and features trees guarding the right side. Another fine hole is the 18th, a 379-yard par-4 that doglegs over a clear, rushing mountain brook and plays to a green guarded on the left by a bunker and on the right by walnut trees. One final word of advice: Try to keep your ball below the hole. The greens are often forward sloping and are very slick. Some folks feel the Lower is a bit overrated because it's short on dramatics, especially compared to its neighbor, the Cascades. Others disagree, citing its solitude and "ease-of-play" factor in that it's not particularly difficult and it's easy to get around. We lean toward the latter evaluation.

The Homestead Resort, The Old Course

U.S. Highway 220, P.O. Box 2000, Hot Springs, VA 24445; phone (800) 838-1766 or (540) 839-3083

Tees: Championship: 6,200 yards, par-71, USGA rating 70.1, slope 121

Greens Fee: $45–90

Challenge: ★★½	Golf Facilities: ★★★
Variety: ★★★	14-Club Test: ★★★
Terrain: ★★★★	Intangibles: ★★★★
Beauty/Visual Appeal: ★★★★	Value: ★★★½
Pace of Play: ★★★	

Description and Comments   As Johnny Carson and Ed McMahon used to say, "The Old Course is so old." "How old is it?" "The Old Course is so old that golfers had to keep score on an abacus." Well, maybe not, but it is still old. Golf has been played at The Old Course, once known as the Homestead Course, since 1892. Nearly all of the original Donald Ross layout has vanished, but the first tee is still in use and for all you golf trivia buffs this is the oldest first tee in continuous use in the country. This was also the first course in Virginia, and it played host to William Howard Taft, America's first golf-playing president.

The Old Course is the shortest and easiest of the three courses at the Homestead Resort. It is a traditional layout that has been redesigned numerous times over the years, most recently by Rees Jones. The course winds through the Allegheny Mountains, placing a premium on even-level stances and creating a stunning backdrop for your round (the back 9 is especially filled with Kodak moments). One of the more fun holes on the course is the extremely short, par-4 3rd, which plays a mere 298 yards. The hole plays completely downhill to a tiny, Ross-like green. Several holes throughout the round boast appetizing views of the Homestead's famous Kentucky red brick clock tower that rises up through the trees. If you play here and are an above-average golfer, you probably won't find this to be a very challenging course. But no matter what level golfer you are, you will undoubtedly find this a delightful and historically significant course.

Kingsmill Resort and Club, Plantation Course

1010 Kingsmill Rd., Williamsburg, VA 23185; phone (800) 832-5665 or (757) 253-5960

Tees: Championship: 6,605 yards, par-72, USGA rating 72.1, slope 126
Greens Fee: $68–100

Challenge: ★★★	Golf Facilities: ★★★
Variety: ★★★	14-Club Test: ★★★
Terrain: ★★★½	Intangibles: ★★★
Beauty/Visual Appeal: ★★★½	Value: ★★★
Pace of Play: ★★★	

Description and Comments   The Plantation course, an Arnold Palmer/Ed Seay design, is located on the site of a former working plantation that dates back to 1736. It is the easiest of the triumvirate at Kingsmill as it is the most playable but still requires accurate iron play. The real challenge however, comes from the greens, which are highly contoured and feature many undulations. Though they aren't all that fast, they can be hard to read and thus often result in many three-putts.

The signature hole is the 503-yard, par-5 2nd, a severe dogleg right that features a variety of hazards. Off the tee, you must carry a grassy area and both sides of the fairway are lined by trees. Halfway down the fairway is a looming lake on the left. Near the green it looks more like a beach than a golf course since there is so much sand surrounding the circular green.

Kingsmill Resort and Club, Woods Course

1010 Kingsmill Rd., Williamsburg, VA 23185; phone (800) 832-5665 or (757) 253-5960

Tees: Championship: 6,784 yards, par-72, USGA rating 72.7, slope 125

Greens Fee: $60–100

Challenge: ★★★	Golf Facilities: ★★★
Variety: ★★★½	14-Club Test: ★★★½
Terrain: ★★★½	Intangibles: ★★★
Beauty/Visual Appeal: ★★★★	Value: ★★★
Pace of Play: ★★★½	

Description and Comments   The Woods Course is the newest addition to the Kingsmill golfing menu. Designed in part by local hero Curtis Strange, the course is a traditional golf experience—there are no homesites, no condos, just good old-fashioned golf over a series of hills and gullies. Head designer Tom Clark had Augusta National in mind when he and Strange created the course, so rough is minimal. As the name implies, the course is located in and among Virginia's hardwoods. Surprisingly though, the course features fairly wide fairways. Oh sure, there are enough trees to get Paul Bunyan smacking his lips, but you have a fair shot at hitting the fairway. Other challenge comes from the five man-made lakes that come into play on seven holes as well as the strategically located bunkers. The signature hole on this course is the 12th, a 195-yard par-3 where your tee shot must carry a lake in front of the double green, shared with the 15th hole. A word of caution: The front nine is relatively flat, but the back nine is hilly. If you enjoy walking we suggest you walk the front and then ride the back nine.

Raspberry Falls Golf and Hunt Club

41601 Raspberry Dr., Leesburg, VA 20176; phone (703) 779-2555

Tees: Championship: 7,191 yards, par-72, USGA rating 74.3, slope 134

Greens Fee: $40–55

Challenge: ★★★½	Golf Facilities: ★★★
Variety: ★★★	14-Club Test: ★★★½
Terrain: ★★★½	Intangibles: ★★★
Beauty/Visual Appeal: ★★★½	Value: ★★★★
Pace of Play: ★★★	

Description and Comments   Raspberry Falls, the first Gary Player course in the area, is located on 400 acres of land that was once one of Virginia's most productive plantations, dating back to the 18th century. Nowadays, the land doesn't yield raspberries but rather pars, birdies, and bogies. The course is a links-style layout that resembles Scotland's Carnoustie, site of 1999's British Open and of Jean Van de Velde's almost unfathomable collapse on the 18th hole. The challenge here comes in the form of excessive mounding that produces uneven lies throughout. The bunkers here are also quite remarkable as they are deep and feature stacked sod walls, a common feature at Scottish courses.

Stonehouse

9540 Old State Rd., Toano, VA 23168; phone (757) 566-1138

Tees: Championship: 6,963 yards, par-72, USGA rating 75.0, slope 140

Greens Fee: $85

Challenge: ★★★★	Golf Facilities: ★★★
Variety: ★★★½	14-Club Test: ★★★★
Terrain: ★★★★	Intangibles: ★★★½
Beauty/Visual Appeal: ★★★★	Value: ★★★
Pace of Play: ★★½	

Description and Comments   This sister course to Royal New Kent embodies the elements of a true Virginia course. As are most of the surrounding courses, it is carved from magnificent forests of hardwood, holly, and mountain laurel. The course features drastic elevation changes—some up to 70 feet—fairways that cut through valleys, and plateau greens that are draped atop cliffs. Even the history of the name is quintessential Virginia. Stonehouse refers to "the old stone house" that once stood where the development now exists and was believed to be the meeting place for Pocahontas and Captain John Smith. Others believe that Smith built the structure as a fort.

One of the best holes on the course is the 17th, a par-3 that plays 172 yards from the back tees. The hole plays from elevated tees to an elevated green with a mess of trouble in between and a green that is surrounded by a combination of sand traps and trees. Due to the hilly nature of this course, walking is not recommended. Again, this course is not for everybody. Some folks, especially good players, place Stonehouse among the five best courses they've ever played. Others decry its trickery and raw difficulty. We feel it fits somewhere in between.

The Tides Inn, Golden Eagle Course

Golden Eagle Drive, Irvington, VA 22480; phone (800) 843-3746 or (804) 438-5501

Tees: Championship: 6,963 yards, par-72, USGA rating 74.3, slope 134
Greens Fee: $40–70

Challenge: ★★★½

Variety: ★★★½

Terrain: ★★★★

Beauty/Visual Appeal: ★★★★

Pace of Play: ★★★

Golf Facilities: ★★★

14-Club Test: ★★★★

Intangibles: ★★★½

Value: ★★★½

Description and Comments The Tides Inn and Tides Lodge, friendly competitors for 30 years, recently merged, making it the largest family-owned resort in the mid-Atlantic. This partnership may change the unofficial tag line earned by the resorts and their golf courses: "the best kept secrets in Virginia." Golden Eagle, the premier course at the resort, may just well be the hidden gem on Virginia's golf menu. The course winds its way around forests of pine, oak, and cedar that line the already narrow, rolling fairways, making them just that much harder. Other challenge comes in the form of over 120 bunkers that dot the landscape and water, specifically Lake Irvington, which affects play on seven holes. The greens at Golden Eagle are also difficult as the majority are medium-sized, undulating, and lean to the fast side of the scale.

The signature hole, and the number one handicap, is the par-4 5th. The hole plays a long 463 yards and requires both length and precision as it doglegs to the left and features a lake on the left running from tee to green. On your drive, you want to carry as much of the lake as you safely can to leave yourself an approach shot of a reasonable distance. No matter how far you hit it, though, you still will have a demanding second shot that must travel through a narrow opening to the green guarded on the left by bunkers and on the right by the aforementioned lake. The fine finishing par-4s on each nine traverse Lake Irvington as well.

Tides Lodge, Tartan Course

1 St. Andrews Lane, Irvington, VA 22480; phone (800) 248-4337 or (804) 438-6200

Tees: Championship: 6,586 yards, par-72, USGA rating 71.5, slope 124

Greens Fee: $25–53

Challenge: ★★★

Variety: ★★★½

Terrain: ★★★½

Beauty/Visual Appeal: ★★★½

Pace of Play: ★★★

Golf Facilities: ★★★

14-Club Test: ★★★

Intangibles: ★★★

Value: ★★★

Description and Comments The resort's Tartan Course is not nearly as demanding as the Golden Eagle Course, but if you relax too much, it can surprise you with a bite of its own. This course is ideal for higher handicappers or for golfers looking for a fun layout that challenges but doesn't overwhelm. The course features lush fairways that are cut through trees and the ever-present Carter's Creek, which can be found on ten holes. The greens here are large and very receptive to lofted approaches.

One of the best holes on the course is the 15th, a 371-yard par-4 where you will be hard pressed to find a level lie. The fairway slopes steeply to the left where a watery grave, in the form of a pond, is the final resting place for many a ball. Adding more difficulty are the trees on the right. For your approach, you will have a steep uphill shot to a small well-bunkered green.

Williamsburg National Golf Club

3700 Centerville Rd., Williamsburg, VA 23188; phone (757) 258-9642
Tees: Championship: 6,950 yards, par-72, USGA rating 72.9, slope 130
Greens Fee: $30–50

Challenge: ★★★
Variety: ★★★
Terrain: ★★★½
Beauty/Visual Appeal: ★★★½
Pace of Play: ★★★

Golf Facilities: ★★★
14-Club Test: ★★★½
Intangibles: ★★★½
Value: ★★★½

Description and Comments   Located a few miles north of Williamsburg among the area's farmland is Williamsburg National, a handsome course that winds through a series of pine, oak, maple, cedar, and dogwood trees, as well as surrounding wetlands. The course was designed by Jim Lipe, a strong player himself who worked at Nicklaus's design firm for many years, so you know this course will be both scenic and challenging. The first 6 holes won't exactly linger in memory, but the final 12 are exceptional for they feature dramatic elevation changes as the course plays over, down, and around a series of ravines. Water, in the form of wetlands and ponds, can be found on seven of the holes, adding to the difficulty that the elevation changes provide. The most scenic as well as most difficult hole on the course is number 16, a 202-yard par-3 that plays sharply downhill. Not only do you need the correct club off the tee to have any shot at a birdie, but you must be accurate as well since your drive must carry a wetland and nestle near the pin on this large green. This isn't the toughest course in the region, but it truly appeals to all levels of players. After getting beat up by Stonehouse, Golden Horseshoe, and Royal New Kent, Williamsburg National is the perfect respite.

Wintergreen Resort, Devil's Knob Golf Club

Route 664 W., P.O. Box 706, Wintergreen, VA 22958; phone (800) 325-2200 or (804) 325-8240 or (804) 325-8250

Tees: Championship: 6,576 yards, par-70, USGA rating 72.4, slope 126

Greens Fee: $48–72

Challenge: ★★★	Golf Facilities: ★★★
Variety: ★★★½	14-Club Test: ★★★½
Terrain: ★★★★	Intangibles: ★★★½
Beauty/Visual Appeal: ★★★★	Value: ★★★½
Pace of Play: ★★★	

Description and Comments   Wintergreen is renown for its skiing and its golf—two sports that at first glance have little in common. Upon closer look, however, there are some similarities. Both sports require adroitness, balance, and weight transference. When skiing, you select the best route to the bottom; when golfing, you select the best route to the hole. In both sports it is wise to stay out of the trees.

Whether you are schussing down or playing through Devil's Knob, you will no doubt be awed by your surroundings. Devil's Knob is the highest course in Virginia at 3,850 feet and is cut through towering forests and the fairways look too tight to execute a parallel turn on your skis, much less execute a 250-yard drive. Surprisingly, the course features fairways that are relatively flat, and thus level lies are common. Devil's Knob does feature dramatic elevation changes that can wreak havoc with your club selection. The course is typically open from mid-April to mid-November for golf.

One of the best holes at the resort, as well as the hardest at Devil's Knob, is the par-5 7th. The hole plays a demanding 600 yards and is a double dogleg where you must carry water not once but twice. The green is relatively small with bunkers on both sides. It slopes from back to front, so the wise play is to keep the ball below the hole.

Wintergreen Resort, Stoney Creek at Wintergreen

Route 664 W., P.O. Box 706, Wintergreen, VA 22958; phone (800) 325-2200 or (804) 325-8240 or (804) 325-8250

Tees:

Monocan/Shamokin: 7,005 yards, par-72, USGA rating 74.0, slope 132

Monocan/Tuckahoe: 6,951 yards, par-72, USGA rating 74.0, slope 130

Shamokin/Tuckahoe: 6,998 yards, par-72, USGA rating 73.8, slope 130

Greens Fee: $45–95(Monocan/Shamokin and Monocan/Tuckahoe);
   $45–65(Shamokin/Tuckahoe)

Challenge: ★★★½	Golf Facilities: ★★★
Variety: ★★★½	14-Club Test: ★★★½
Terrain: ★★★½	Intangibles: ★★★½
Beauty/Visual Appeal: ★★★½	Value: ★★★½
Pace of Play: ★★★	

Description and Comments   Stoney Creek offers sensational scenery like its sister course Devil's Knob, but it is quite a different course. Stoney Creek plays along the valley floor, some 3,000 feet below Devil's Knob, and cuts through natural wetlands, lakes, and forests.

Rees Jones recently added 9 holes, bringing the total to 27 at Stoney Creek. All of the nines have their own character, but the common denominator is a plethora of sand, trees, and water. The Monocan 9 (all 9s have Native American–related names) is a more open layout and features mounding reminiscent of a Scottish course. Water is the prevailing hazard, as it can be found on eight of the holes. The Shamokin 9 features narrow fairways that are surrounded by trees, a large number of bunkers, and elevated tees. The final nine, the Tuckahoe, is the newest addition to the resort and is a more traditional layout with water and sand coming into play on nearly every hole.

A West Virginia Sampler

Canaan Valley Resort Golf Course

Route 1, P.O. Box 330, Davis, WV 26260; phone (800) 622-4121 or (304) 866-4121 x2632

Tees: Championship: 6,982 yards, par-72, USGA rating 73.4, slope 125

Greens Fee: $24–30

Challenge: ★★★	Golf Facilities: ★★★
Variety: ★★★	14-Club Test: ★★★
Terrain: ★★★	Intangibles: ★★★
Beauty/Visual Appeal: ★★★	Value: ★★★½
Pace of Play: ★★★	

Description and Comments   Canaan is way off the beaten path, but it is worth the extra effort it takes to get there. Located adjacent to the Monongahela National Forest, 3,200 feet above sea level, the course is surrounded by jaw-dropping scenery. The course winds through a portion of 6,000 acres filled with woodlands, meadows, hills, and streams, and is framed by the spectacular Allegheny Mountains and the West Virginia countryside. If this isn't enough to make you want to come here, the golf course will. Canaan is a terrific value and a solid layout. The course is a links-style track where the front nine is narrower than the back. Admittedly, the fairways themselves are flat and wide and the trapping is kind of monotonous, mostly large ovals. The greens are enormous, with little slope. However, the 65 bunkers and water that is found on nearly half the holes ensure that you better keep your ball in play or you will find your score quickly soaring. The par-3s are especially beefy here. From the back markers, they measure 214, 194, 256, and 233 yards, respectively. Also, watch out for deer and other wildlife—you may not want to wander too far into the woods looking for wayward shots. In fact, even on the course you'll run into it—the 18th hole is renowned for its endless parade of ducks and geese.

Glade Springs Resort

200 Lake Dr., Daniels, WV 25832; phone (800) 634-5233 or (304) 763-2050

Tees: Championship: 6,941 yards, par-72, USGA rating 73.5, slope 135

Greens Fee: $40–65

Challenge: ★★★½	Golf Facilities: ★★★
Variety: ★★★½	14-Club Test: ★★★½
Terrain: ★★★½	Intangibles: ★★★
Beauty/Visual Appeal: ★★★½	Value: ★★★½
Pace of Play: ★★★	

Description and Comments   West Virginia is renowned for its state parks and state resorts. Glade Springs is the premier resort, and its golf course is one of the hidden gems and best values in the state. Glade Springs is a traditional layout where gently rolling fairways surrounded by trees is the name of the game. The course is long and tough, but the relatively open fairways allow golfers to swing away. Greens tend to be large in size, but are well guarded by bunkers and an occasional water hazard. The course is framed against the Appalachian Mountains; elevation changes of more than 200 feet are common on many holes. The course's signature hole is number 16, a 419-yard par-4 that requires a 200-yard carry over a lake to reach the landing area. For the second shot you must carry more water to reach the undulating green.

The Greenbrier, Meadows Course

300 W. Main St., White Sulphur Springs, WV 24986; phone (800) 624-6070 or (304) 536-1110

Tees: Championship: 6,807 yards, par-71, USGA rating 73.3, slope 130

Greens Fee: $72–225

Course Ratings not yet available

Description and Comments   Formerly known as the Lakeside course, Meadows is a Robert Cupp layout that is the resort's newest course.

Hawthorne Valley Golf Course

10 Snowshoe Dr., Snowshoe, WV 26209; phone (304) 572-1000

Tees: Championship: 7,045 yards, par-72, USGA rating 72.1, slope 130

Greens Fee: $43–58

Challenge: ★★★½	Golf Facilities: ★★★
Variety: ★★★½	14-Club Test: ★★★
Terrain: ★★★½	Intangibles: ★★★½
Beauty/Visual Appeal: ★★★★	Value: ★★★★
Pace of Play: ★★★	

Description and Comments   When Snowshoe Resort, a ski playground, decided to take the plunge and add a golf course and become a year-round resort, they wanted to make sure they did things right. So they turned to Gary Player. Now Player is a fine architect, but we give half the credit for the fine course he created to Mother Nature. The course is located in the foothills of the spectacular Allegheny Mountains of West Virginia and features dramatic elevation changes, sweeping views, and a rather playable but still demanding course. The front nine plays through and around hardwood trees and several lakes; the back nine is really where the elevation changes come into play. The 13th hole drops 200 feet from tee to green. You could get dizzy just looking down from the back tee to the fairway. We mentioned the lakes already, but water comes in many forms at Hawthorne: lakes, ponds, and creeks. Player was very creative in his use of water. For instance, the green on the 2nd hole is completely surrounded by a creek, while another creek winds its way down the middle of the fairway on both the 14th and 18th holes. Try to get here once in your life at the peak of fall foliage—the scenery is simply spectacular.

Lodging in Maryland

EXPENSIVE

Coconut Malorie Resort

200 59th St., Ocean City, MD 21842; phone (800) 767-6060 or (410) 723-6100; www.coconutmalorie.com; Rates: $164–290

In a sea of beachfront hotels, this English-themed resort certainly stands out. Each guest room is a suite and is decorated with a Caribbean flavor with a bedroom and separate sitting and dining areas. Each room has a private balcony, kitchen, bar, refrigerator, microwave, and coffee service. The resort boasts a pool and sundeck.

Lighthouse Club Hotel

Fager's Island, 56th St., Ocean City, MD 21842; phone (410) 723-6100; Rates: $199–269

This hotel is located on the Isle of Wright Bay and has an exterior resembling that of a lighthouse. As soon as you walk through the door, you will bask in the cozy atmosphere that exudes from every nook and cranny. All of the units are decorated with homey furnishings, some with fireplaces, Jacuzzis, and balconies. All of the rooms feature a wet bar, microwave, ice maker, and coffee service.

MODERATE

Comfort Inn Boardwalk

507 Atlantic Ave., P.O. Box 1030, Ocean City, MD 21842; phone (800) 228-5155 or (410) 289-5155; www.comfortinnboardwalk.com; Rates: $164–209

Comfort Inn is one of the newest additions along the boardwalk. All rooms are decorated in a light nautical theme with each having a separate sleeping area, kitchenette, and sitting area, as well as a private balcony.

Phillips Beach Plaza Hotel

1301 Atlantic Ave., Ocean City, MD 21842; phone (800) 492-5834 or (410) 289-9121; Rates: $119–174

Also located on the boardwalk, Phillips Beach is a Victorian-themed hotel that has old world charm. The hotel is comprised of both standard rooms as well as apartments. The apartments come with separate dining and/or living areas as well as full kitchens. For dinner you might try Phillips Crab House (see Dining section).

INEXPENSIVE

Atlantic Hotel

2 N. Main St., Berlin, MD 21811; phone (401) 641-3589; Rates: $85–150; Built: 1895; Renovations: 1988

Comfort Inn Gold Coast

11201 Coastal Hwy., Ocean City, MD 21842; phone (800) 228-5150 or (410) 524-3000; www.comfortinn.com; Rates: $30–165; Built: 1988; Renovations: 1999

Dining in Maryland

Bonfire 71st and Coastal Hwy., Ocean City; phone (410) 524-7171. Continental; Moderate–Expensive; Reservations recommended. Attractive views of the bay accompany a menu that is highly diverse with everything from jumbo shrimp to 25 different Chinese offerings.

Fager's Island 201 60th St., Ocean City; phone (410) 524-5500. Continental; Moderate; Reservations recommended for dinner. An ideal place to watch the sunset and enjoy a fine array of seafood and steak entrees. Outdoor seating is available, but you may want to bring a jacket to ward off the chill.

Harrison's Harbor Watch 806 S. Boardwalk, Ocean City; phone (410) 289-5121. Seafood; Moderate; Reservations recommended. The restaurant is located on the southernmost point of the boardwalk, and diners are treated to striking views of the bay and nearby Assateague Island. Picking a seafood entree may be one of the tougher decisions you've had all day, as there are so many mouth-watering items.

Hobbit 101 81st St., Ocean City; phone (410) 524-8100. Seafood; Inexpensive–Moderate; Reservations recommended for dinner. This is one of Ocean City's hidden gems with the most impressive views of the ocean—the food is terrific, too.

Phillips Crab House Phillips Beach Plaza Resort. 1301 Atlantic Ave., Ocean City; phone (800) 492-5834 or (410) 289-9121. Seafood; Inexpensive; Reservations not accepted. A trip to Ocean City wouldn't be complete without a stop by Shirley and Brice Phillips' original crab house. Nothing fancy, just good, old-fashioned delicious crabs.

Activities in Maryland

Assateague Island National Seashore Mother Nature is the best attraction in the area since she has created a magnificent 37-mile barrier strand with an extensive ecosystem. For even more adventure, try the nearby Assateague State Park, where you will find 755 acres, including 2 miles of oceanfront land with swimming, fishing, and boating. Phone (410) 641-1441.

City Factory Outlets Phone (800) 625-6696. More than 40 stores can be found at this outlet mall.

Jolly Roger 30th St. and Coastal Hwy.; phone (410) 289-3477. Home to SpeedWorld, the country's largest go-cart racing complex.

Trimper's Amusement Park Located at the south end of the boardwalk; phone (410) 289-8617. Trimper's is a terrific place for kids. The focal point of the park is the century-old Hirschell Spellman Carousel.

Wheels of Yesterday 12708 Ocean Gateway; phone (410) 213-7329. A car enthusiast's dream museum filled with more than 30 classic cars.

Lodging in Virginia

EXPENSIVE

The Homestead

U.S. Highway 220, Hot Springs, VA 24445; phone (800) 838-1766 or (540) 839-1766; www.thehomestead.com; Rates: $212–306

Tucked away in a gorgeous, sleepy pocket in the Allegheny Mountains, The Homestead has been welcoming visitors to its Hot Springs location since 1766. Thomas Jefferson, the first of eight presidents to visit, was among guests who came to the resort to experience the healing powers found in the natural hot and warm springs that bubbled up nearby. Today, The Homestead is still attracting visitors from all over, but now they are coming to experience the healing powers of a little rest and relaxation.

You can tell The Homestead is special just by looking at the hotel from a distance. The enormous Georgian-style edifice is constructed of Kentucky red brick and is topped by a white clock tower that rises up through the trees. Once you enter the hotel, you really begin to appreciate the full extent of The Homestead's grandeur. The lobby is a magnificent spot that exudes warmth and comfort. Rooms in the older section of the hotel are decorated in a Victorian theme with Chippendale reproductions. The rooms in the newer section of the resort are nicely appointed duplexes complete with fireplaces and private bars.

Your biggest decision here may well be what to do first. Not only are there the three spectacular golf courses, which limit access to resort guests, but you will also find one indoor pool, two outdoor pools, a spa, eight tennis courts, an eight-lane bowling alley, a movie theater, horseback riding, bicycles, and a sports bar with billiards and darts. After all of this activity, you no doubt will build up quite an appetite. No worries, for The Homestead has a dazzling array of 10 restaurants to choose from.

Golf Package The Homestead offers a golf package that includes accommodations, breakfast and dinner, unlimited golf, golf cart for all your rounds, and driving range usage.

Kingsmill Resort

1010 Kingsmill Rd., Williamsburg, VA 23185; phone (800) 832-5665 or (757) 253-1703; www.kingsmill.com; Rates: $189–269

Located near historic downtown Williamsburg, Kingsmill Resort is beautifully set on the banks of the James River and is owned and operated by Busch Properties, a subsidiary of Anheuser-Busch, the king of beers (in fact you can sample one of the 51 family brands at Moody's Tavern). Along with access to the three 18-hole and par-3 courses, Kingsmill offers a full menu of activities at this 3,000-acre resort, including indoor/outdoor pools, whirlpool, tennis and racquetball courts, gym, sauna, spa, marina privileges, and children's programs.

Accommodations at Kingsmill come in the form of 400 privately owned guest rooms and suites (one to three bedrooms). All of the rooms are nicely decorated, with suites having fully equipped kitchens and washers and dryers. For dining, you can head to the pricey Bray Dining Room (see Dining section). Free shuttle service is provided to nearby Colonial Williamsburg, Busch Gardens, and Water Country USA.

Golf Packages   Golf packages are available, but you are requested to contact the resort for more details.

Williamsburg Inn

136 E. Francis St., P.O. Box 1776, Williamsburg, VA 23187-1776; phone (800) 447-8679 or (757) 229-1000; www.history.org; Rates: $245–345

The Williamsburg Inn was built in 1937 as part of John D. Rockefeller Jr.'s restoration of Colonial Williamsburg. Although just steps away from the heart of town, Rockefeller envisioned that the inn would have its own character and would stand out from the surrounding Georgian-style architecture. Thus, it was built in a neoclassical style with tall portico columns, wide arches, and white-washed bricks. Listed on the National Register of Historic Places, the inn features 92 rooms in the main hotel, all of which are pleasantly decorated with fine colonial reproductions. If you are looking for something a little less formal, you may want to consider one of the 43 rooms in the Providence Hall Wings.

One of the benefits to staying at the inn is its quick access to Colonial Williamsburg and all of its sights. Back at the inn, however, you will find more than enough to entertain you. First and foremost in our books are the Gold and Green Courses at the Golden Horseshoe Golf Club, but the fun doesn't stop there. The inn also has tennis facilities, a gym, sauna, steam room, lawn games, and children's programs. Make sure to make time to dine at the Regency Room (see Dining section), a restaurant where the menu is nearly rivaled by the marvelous atmosphere.

Golf Package   The golf package at The Williamsburg Inn consists of accommodations, breakfast, and 18 holes of golf per day.

MODERATE

Colonial Houses

302 E. Francis St., Williamsburg, VA 23185; phone (800) 447-8679 or (757) 565-8440; www.history.org; Rates: $215–225

If you are traveling with your family, you may want to consider renting one of the 25 colonial homes located in the heart of Williamsburg. All of the homes are furnished with antiques and period pieces, but also include modern amenities, such as hair dryers. Guests of the Colonial Houses have full access to all of the facilities of both the Williamsburg Inn and Lodge (including room service from the inn).

Liberty Rose

1022 Jamestown Rd., Williamsburg, VA 23185; phone (800) 545-1825 or (757) 253-1260; www.libertyrose.com; Rates: $135–205

This inn dates back to the early 1920s and is located on an acre of land on a hill above Williamsburg. A spectacular forest surrounds this quaint inn, filled with European antiques. Daily breakfast is included in your room rate.

Williamsburg Lodge

310 S. England St., Williamsburg, VA 23187-1776; phone (800) 447-8679 or (757) 229-1000; www.history.org; Rates: $175–$235

The Williamsburg Lodge opened in 1939 and is a tad less formal than the Williamsburg Inn, its sister hotel across the street. However, it is as attractive in both location and furnishings. The lobby is decorated with reproductions from the Abby Aldrich Rockefeller Folk Art collection. Rooms are nicely appointed and come with all the modern touches such as ironing boards and hair dryers. Guests of the lodge have full access to all the facilities at the inn, including the two Golden Horseshoe courses.

INEXPENSIVE

Holiday Inn—Downtown

814 Capitol Landing Rd., Williamsburg, VA 23185; phone (757) 229-0200; www.holidayinn.com; Rates: $89–109; Built: 1968; Renovations: 1999

Quality Inn Lord Paget

901 Capitol Landing Rd., Williamsburg, VA 23185; phone (800) 537-2438 or (757) 229-4444; www.qualityinn.com; Rates: $59–89; Built: 1954; Renovations: 1997

Dining in Virginia

Aberdeen Barn 1601 Richmond Rd., Williamsburg; phone (757) 229-6661. American; Expensive; Reservations accepted. A traditional steak-and-potatoes restaurant located in a converted barn decorated in true barn-like fashion with saws and pitchforks hanging on the walls.

Berret's Restaurant and Raw Bar 1999 S. Boundary St., Williamsburg; phone (757) 253-1847 Seafood; Moderate–Expensive; Reservations are accepted. Known for its delightful selection of seafood and for its equally delightful outside bar. The soft-shell crabs are a specialty of the house.

Bray Dining Room Kingsmill Resort, 1010 Kingsmill Rd., Williamsburg; phone (800) 832-5665 or (757) 253-1703. Continental; Expensive; Reservations recommended. The resort's premier restaurant affords sweeping views of the James River. The restaurant's specialties include contemporary items and specialties of Chesapeake Bay.

Christiana Campbell's Tavern Waller Street, Williamsburg; (757) 229-2141. American; Moderate–Expensive; Reservations accepted. One of the area's most historic restaurants—George Washington ate here. Seafood is the specialty of the house, but the food almost takes a back seat to the old-fashioned atmosphere.

Dynasty 1621 Richmond Rd., Williamsburg; phone (757) 220-8888. Chinese; Moderate–Expensive; Reservations accepted. For a change of pace, you may want to try Dynasty, serving up some of the best Chinese food in the mid-Atlantic. Specialties of the house include General Zuo's chicken and Peking duck.

La Yaca 1915 Pocohantas Trail, Williamsburg; phone (757) 220-3616. French; Moderate–Expensive; Reservations accepted. Located in the Village Shops at Kingsmill, near Busch Gardens, La Yaca is a cozy restaurant offering fine delicacies from Southern France. The menu is also very French-like with 4 prix-fixe meals as well as 10 entree selections. A fine wine selection complements every meal.

Regency Room Williamsburg Inn, 136 E. Francis St., Williamsburg; phone (800) 447-8679 or (757) 229-1000. Continental; Expensive; Reservations recommended. The Regency is the premier restaurant at the Williamsburg Inn and Lodge and offers a splendid setting to enjoy your meal. Specialties of the house include veal and rack of lamb.

The Trellis 403 Duke of Gloucester St., Williamsburg; phone (757) 229-8610. American; Moderate; Reservations accepted. Though the menu is filled with a variety of items, the seafood selections are the most popular. Guests can dine either in the colonial-style building or outdoors, under the trees.

Whaling Company 494 McLaw Circle, Williamsburg; phone (757) 229-0275. Seafood; Moderate; Reservations accepted. As you can guess from the name, seafood is the main attraction to this restaurant, which looks like it has been transplanted from a New England fishing town.

Activities in Virginia

You will have to look far and wide to find a town with more historic sightseeing within walking distance than Colonial Williamsburg. Williamsburg was the focal point for much of Virginia's history, both politically and culturally. When the capitol was shifted to Richmond in 1780 for safety and convenience during the American Revolution, Williamsburg faded into the background. There it rested, its glory fading as quickly as the paint on the many dilapidated buildings. In 1926, John D. Rockefeller Jr. and Dr. W. A. R. Goodwin, rector of Bruton Parish Church, recognized the potential of the town and began a mission to restore Williamsburg to its original grandeur. The result is a mile-long by half-mile-wide section known as Colonial Williamsburg. To date, 88 of the original buildings have been restored, and 50 buildings, houses, and shops have been reconstructed on the original sites. There is so much to do in Colonial Williamsburg that you could spend a fair amount of time just exploring the city's confines. Detailed below are some highlights of Williamsburg, as well as some other sites, but our recommendation is to purchase a guide of the area to get the full picture.

Busch Gardens Williamsburg U.S. 60 (3 miles east of Williamsburg); phone (800) 343-7943 or (757) 253-3350. A 360-acre amusement park that features over 30 rides as well as recreations of 17th-century German, English, French, Italian, Scottish, and Canadian villages.

College of William and Mary West end of Duke of Gloucester Street; phone (757) 221-4000. A walk through America's second oldest college (after Harvard) offers the chance to view impressive architecture. Make sure to see the Wren Building, America's oldest academic building.

Abby Aldrich Rockefeller Folk Art Center York St., half a block southeast of the Capitol. Extensive collection of American folk art.

The Capitol East End of Duke of Gloucester Street. The site where the House of Burgesses met and where Patrick Henry gave his speech opposing the Stamp Act.

Carriage and Wagon Rides Delightful means of touring this historic area. Purchase tickets at Lumber House.

Courthouse Duke of Gloucester Street, east of Palace Green. Site of both county and city government from 1770 to 1932.

Governor's Palace and Gardens North end of Palace Green. Former residence of the royal governor; one of the most elegant mansions in America (situated on ten acres of land). Elaborate hedge labyrinth in the gardens a unique family attraction.

Visitor Center Colonial Parkway and VA 132; phone (757) 220-7645. A perfect place to kick off your tour.

Water Country USA Route 199 (3 miles off Interstate 64), Exit 242B; phone (757) 253-3350. An amusement park filled with 30 water rides, live entertainment, and restaurants. Highlights include the Nitro Racer, a 382-foot slide, and a 4,500-square-foot pool.

The 19th Hole in Virginia

Sam Snead's Tavern The Homestead, U.S. 220, Hot Springs, VA 24445; phone (800) 838-1766 or (540) 839-1766. Good food and drink and outstanding golf memorabilia in the town where Slammin' Sammy grew up.

Lodging in West Virginia

EXPENSIVE

The Greenbrier

300 W. Main St., White Sulphur Springs, WV 24986; phone (800) 624-6070 or (304) 536-1110; www.greenbrier.com; Rates: $210–292

Take the service and amenities of Manhattan's finest hotels, blend them with equal parts of historic West Virginia and rural mountain charm, then toss in a remarkable golf complex, and you have The Greenbrier. Few resorts can match The Greenbrier's rich tradition. Visitors have been drawn to the site since 1778, when its healing sulfur springs were first discovered. Since then, there's been little letup in the rich and famous brigade on the guest registers.

From the moment you drive up the long Greenbrier driveway and see the magnificent hotel unveiled in front of you, you know you've arrived at a special place—this is America's best resort. The Greenbrier is an enormous Georgian structure with tall white columns, yet somehow it manages to fit comfortably into a landscape of trees and flowers at this 7,000-acre resort. The interiors are equally impressive, including the memorable Georgian lobby. All of this may sound stuffy, but it really isn't. In fact, it is downright comfortable, although jackets are required in some rooms at some times. Each of the 596 rooms in the main lodge as well as the 103 guest houses are handsomely decorated; no two rooms are exactly alike.

At the Greenbrier, the staff has made an art form out of pampering its guests. Many employees have more than ten years of service, with some boasting up to 25 years. The resort also has made an art form out of keeping its guests busy. Along with access to the three renowned golf courses, The Greenbrier also has two pools, a whirlpool, five indoor tennis courts and 15 outdoor courts, a platform tennis court, canoeing, rafting, stables, jogging/walking trails, bicycling, lawn games, trap and skeet shooting, a gym, a sauna, a spa, a steam room, and a children's playground.

On the dining side, both the Greenbrier Main Dining Room and the Tavern Room (see Dining section) will satisfy all your culinary cravings.

Golf Package The Deluxe Golf Package includes unlimited golf, preferred starting times, daily club cleaning and storage, unlimited use of the practice range, a golf memento, golf clinic, golf cart, personalized bag tag, locker accommodations, and breakfast and dinner in the Main Dining Room.

MODERATE

Canaan Valley Resort

HC 70, Box 330, Davis, WV 26260; phone (800) 622-4121 or (304) 866-4121; www.canaanresort.com; Rates: $74–86

Canaan Valley Resort offers an affordable alternative for those looking for a full-service golf resort in West Virginia. Canaan's 250 rooms are all adequately appointed, but the real appeal is all the amenities that lie outside. Besides easy access to the Canaan Valley golf club, the resort also has two pools, a whirlpool, tennis courts, bicycles, lawn games, a gym, a sauna, fishing privileges, and children's programs.

Golf Package The resort has a variety of golf packages, including the "Swing into Spring" package, which includes three days' and two nights' accommodations, greens fees, shared cart, two breakfasts, and two dinners.

INEXPENSIVE

Blackwater Lodge

Box 490 (3 miles southwest of Highway 32 in Blackwater Falls State Park), Davis, WV; phone (304) 259-5216; Rates: $55–63; Built: 1957; Renovations: 1999

Old White

865 E. Main St., White Sulphur Springs, WV 24986; phone (800) 867-2441 or (304) 536-2441; Rates: $36–44; Built: 1951; Renovations: 1998

Dining in West Virginia

The Greenbrier Main Dining Room Greenbrier Resort, 300 W. Main St., White Sulphur Springs; phone (800) 624-6070 or (304) 536-1110. Continental; Expensive; Reservations required. A spectacular restaurant in a spectacular resort. Specialties of the house include seafood and veal dishes. Jacket required at dinner.

The Tavern Room Greenbrier Resort, 300 W. Main St., White Sulphur Springs; phone (800) 624-6070 or (304) 536-1110. Continental; Expensive; Reservations required. Another fine restaurant at The Greenbrier. Menu is prix fixe with a variety of seafood, veal, and beef. Jacket required for all meals.

Activities in West Virginia

West Virginia is dominated by state parks, and thus the majority of the activities are of the outdoor kind. Whether it is fishing, hiking, boating, walking, or camping, there is a state park right around the corner, including the following.

Blackwater Falls State Park Two miles west of Highway 32, Davis; phone (304) 259-5216. A 1,688-acre park featuring swimming, boating, nature trails, and horseback riding.

Cathedral State Park One mile east on U.S. Highway 50, Aurora; phone (304) 735-3771. This park features 132 acres replete with hiking trails.

Canaan Valley Resort State Park Nine miles south on Highway 32, Davis; phone (304) 866-4121. This park sprawls over 6,000 acres, located 3,200 feet above sea level. Spectacular views of the surrounding mountain areas, a pool, fishing, boating, and hiking trails can all be found here.

Greenbrier State Forest Three miles west on U.S. Highway 60, White Sulphur Springs; phone (304) 536-1944. Greenbrier's park encompasses more than 5,000 acres and has a swimming pool, hiking trails, and fishing.

The 19th Hole in West Virginia

Greenbrier Ryder Cup Lounge The Greenbrier Resort, 300 W. Main St., White Sulphur Springs; phone (800) 624-6070 or (304) 536-1110. Regal yet comfortable spot adorned with memorabilia from the 1979 Ryder Cup played at the Greenbrier.

Part Thirteen

New England

Overview

New England offers golfers superior diversity because it is a region of three well-defined geographic areas. It sweeps from the low coastlines of Connecticut, Rhode Island, and southeastern Massachusetts up through a central plain to some pretty impressive mountains in Vermont and the northern reaches of New Hampshire and Maine. Consequently, this landscape offers a wonderful variety of courses on which to play golf.

The sandy spit of Cape Cod has relatively flat terrain and an abundance of short scrub pine, which line nearly every fairway. An explosion of well-designed municipally operated courses in the 1980s and 1990s has made the Cape an exceptional golf destination. The mountains of Vermont, New Hampshire, and Maine have long been the destination of holiday travelers looking to beat the summer heat by climbing to cooler heights. It's little wonder that the valleys there are home to some of the country's finest golf resorts and public-access courses. The central plain that runs diagonally north from New Hampshire through Maine is a district known for its beautiful lakes and sleepy country lanes. It's not unusual to catch glimpses of sailboats from a tee set on a bluff. Alternately, the rocky coast of Maine has a "down East" flavor all its own: fairways punctuated by glacial boulders, roadsides dotted with antiques shops, and plenty of restaurants serving red lobster, fried clams, and native corn.

For our purposes, we've broken the golfing experiences into two distinct areas, using colloquial terms to define each: the North Country and the Flatlanders. Use those terms and everyone will think you're an aficionado of golf in New England.

Getting to New England is simple enough by car, and it has become even more convenient by plane. At one time nearly everyone ventured in and out via Logan International Airport in Boston. Air travelers are still apt to save a little money by doing so, but they will find suitable jet service to

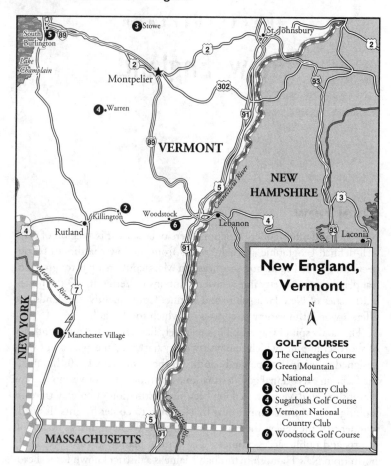

New England, Vermont

N

GOLF COURSES
1. The Gleneagles Course
2. Green Mountain National
3. Stowe Country Club
4. Sugarbush Golf Course
5. Vermont National Country Club
6. Woodstock Golf Course

and from the smaller airports in the region: Burlington, Vermont; Manchester, New Hampshire; Portland, Maine; Providence, Rhode Island; and Hartford, Connecticut. Be sure to look into the so-called discount airlines, such as Southwest Airlines, which offers terrific bargains in and out of Manchester and Providence.

Even so, Boston still deserves its nickname of "The Hub." Nearly every major interstate in the region runs like a spoke out of New England's unofficial capital. But step back from a road map of New England and you'll discover an annoying fact about driving in the region that every local knows all too well: Nearly every major highway runs north–south with only one exception, the Massachusetts Turnpike (Interstate 90). This is important to bear in mind if you're considering a grand tour of the area. A road trip from Vermont to Maine can be tedious on a hot summer day at 45 mph behind a large, smelly truck. Note that Saturday is known as "moving day," the day

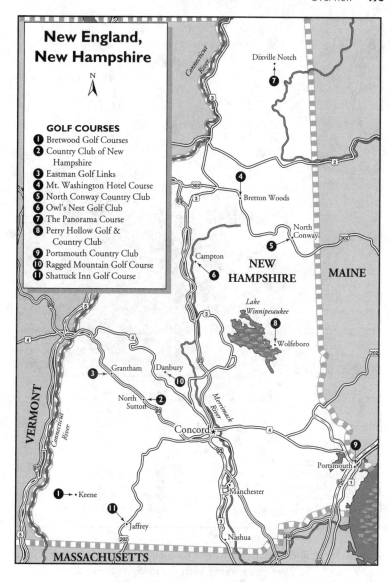

**New England,
New Hampshire**

N

GOLF COURSES
1. Bretwood Golf Courses
2. Country Club of New Hampshire
3. Eastman Golf Links
4. Mt. Washington Hotel Course
5. North Conway Country Club
6. Owl's Nest Golf Club
7. The Panorama Course
8. Perry Hollow Golf & Country Club
9. Portsmouth Country Club
10. Ragged Mountain Golf Course
11. Shattuck Inn Golf Course

Dixville Notch

Bretton Woods

North Conway

NEW HAMPSHIRE

MAINE

Campton

Lake Winnipesaukee

Wolfeboro

Grantham   Danbury

North Sutton

VERMONT

Connecticut River

Merrimack River

Concord

Portsmouth

Keene

Manchester

Jaffrey

Nashua

MASSACHUSETTS

when campers and cottage renters either check in or check out. The traffic on all the northbound highways (I-89, I-91, I-93, and I-95) can be horrendous in July and August. The worst of these is I-95, which turns into a parking lot at the toll booth in Hampton, New Hampshire, between 10 a.m. and 3 p.m. every Saturday during the summer. The other most loathsome stretch of highway in New England is the Maine (alleged) Turnpike, which becomes a tedious two-lane affair north of York. Parrying a comment

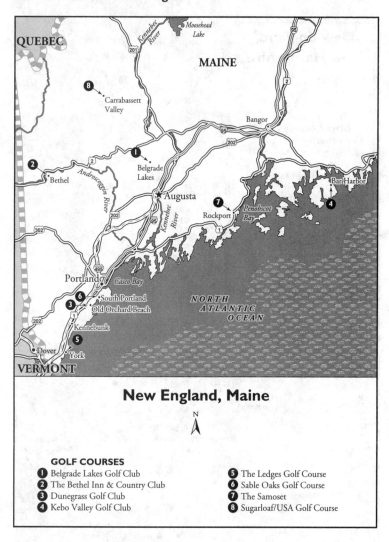

New England, Maine

N

GOLF COURSES

1. Belgrade Lakes Golf Club
2. The Bethel Inn & Country Club
3. Dunegrass Golf Club
4. Kebo Valley Golf Club
5. The Ledges Golf Course
6. Sable Oaks Golf Course
7. The Samoset
8. Sugarloaf/USA Golf Course

that no one should be charged to drive on such a terrible road, a toll keeper responded, "There's nothing wrong with the road; it's the cars."

Cape Cod has its own traffic problems, which we'll discuss later. As you already know, no matter where you live, traffic everywhere is worse during the middle of the day. Get where you're going early, and, if possible, leave either very early or very late.

And there's one more disturbing fact about New England, although you won't discover it by looking at a map: Connecticut and Rhode Island have no exceptional public-access courses or resort courses worth traveling to play. Good courses? Sure. Historic courses? No doubt. Courses good

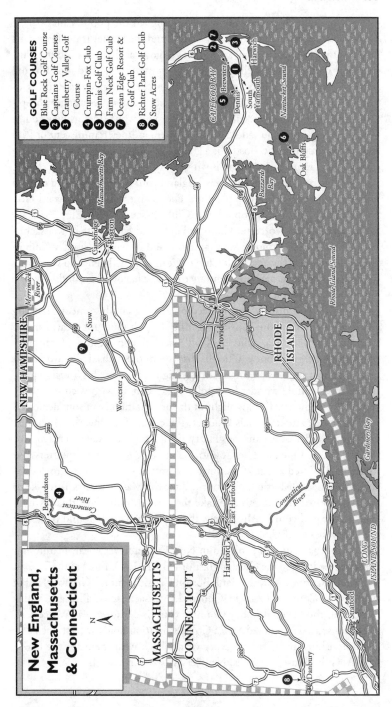

New England, Massachusetts & Connecticut

N

GOLF COURSES

1. Blue Rock Golf Course
2. Captains Golf Courses
3. Cranberry Valley Golf Course
4. Crumpin-Fox Club
5. Dennis Golf Club
6. Farm Neck Golf Club
7. Ocean Edge Resort & Golf Club
8. Richter Park Golf Club
9. Stow Acres

enough to make the politically correct ratings in the popular magazines? Only Alaska doesn't. But between you, me, and the lobster trap, if you can't find a course in your own backyard that's as good as those in both the Nutmeg and Ocean states, well, you must be living in Baghdad—or Boston! That's right, Boston is also a golfing wasteland. Sensational museums, symphonies, pro sports teams, universities, medical centers, restaurants, hospitals—sounds a bit like ancient Athens—but you won't find a single course worth playing until you saddle up and make a journey reminiscent of Paul Revere's midnight jaunt. Boston is a golfing desert dotted with walled sheikdoms, each a tempting green oasis with an exceptional, historic golf course. The notable private courses in New England you've probably heard of (and will need a personal favor to play) are The Country Club, Eastward Ho!, Salem Country Club, Myopia Hunt Club, Essex County Club, Sankaty Head, Brae Burn, Worcester Country Club, and Kittansett in Massachusetts; Ekwanok in Vermont; Wannamoisett and Newport Country Club in Rhode Island; and the Yale Golf Club in Connecticut. There's no secret way or backdoor method of gaining entrance to these hallowed grounds—you've got to be invited by a member.

If you're a golf history buff in need of a fix, or simply someone looking to kill a rainy afternoon, consider visiting the golf museum located in the headquarters of the Massachusetts Golf Association in Weston. Hardly anyone knows it exists—but you do! Its displays of old clubs, balls, attire, and tournament programs are interesting in light of today's high-tech equipment. You'll simply wonder how golfers played at all with such seemingly "crude" implements. The highlight of the presentation is a room dedicated to the great amateur Francis Ouimet, the caddie from nearby Brookline who defeated British champions Harry Vardon and Ted Ray in a playoff for the 1913 U.S. Open at The Country Club. The MGA headquarters and museum is located about 20 minutes due west of downtown Boston, adjacent to the Leo J. Martin Golf Course. Take the Massachusetts Turnpike to the Weston exit (Route 30) and take the first left onto Park Road, which leads to the golf course. Alternately, the museum is easily found by taking the U.S. 20 exit off U.S. 128/I-95.

Top tournament golf is played in New England every year. Fixtures on the schedule include the Greater Hartford Open (PGA Tour) at the TPC in Cromwell, Connecticut; the Bank Boston Classic (Senior PGA Tour) at the Nashawtuc Country Club in Concord, Massachusetts; Pleasant Valley (LPGA) at the Pleasant Valley Country Club in Sutton (near Worcester), Massachusetts. The United States Golf Association holds at least one of its championships in the region every year. Check with them for the latest: USGA, Golf House, Far Hills, New Jersey (www.usga.org).

WHEN TO GO AND WHAT IT WILL COST

New England has all four seasons and temperatures that range from well below zero in January right up to the 100-degree mark in July. The best season for golf is, obviously, summer. Yet the "summer months" differ throughout the region. In the mountainous North Country of Vermont, New Hampshire, and Maine they are June through August, which are celebrated as the "100 days of summer." Along the southern tier "summer" arrives a month earlier and stays a month longer. The entire region experiences days of "Indian summer," those delightful days in October when the sun is warm, the wind is calm, and the forecast is for an overnight frost! Cape Cod's summer season is greatly affected by ocean temperatures: Cooler days in the spring and warmer ones in the fall than on the mainland. The truly hardy look to play golf year-round on the Cape.

Oddly enough, the summer weather in New England can be every bit as hazy, hot, and humid as that in the Deep South. It is not unusual for a large high-pressure system over the Carolinas to pump muggy weather up from the Caribbean, across the Ohio Plain, and into the northeast. It can last up to two weeks. If you're expressly looking to travel north to escape such weather, be sure to head for the mountains, where the overnight conditions are always mild. If New England has a predictable rainy season it is typically April into early May. With great folly, and fully understanding why old-timers in New England are fond of saying "If you don't like the weather, wait an hour, it'll change," we present the following guide:

- Spring is usually cool and wet with warmer temperatures inland.
- June tends to be dry and hot.
- July and the first half of August are hot and humid.
- The second half of August and all of September are warm and less humid (that is, sensational).
- October is cooler still, but visually spectacular.
- November is very cool to downright cold with the exceptional day in the mid-60s (always a Tuesday, while you're at work). Post-Thanksgiving is out of the question in the northern mountains, very iffy in the central plain, and hit or miss along the southern coast and on Cape Cod.

Summer everywhere has its perils of nature. Thunderstorms are common throughout the area in the late afternoon, especially during July and August. A morning tee time is by far your best bet to avoid one. Lyme disease, which first came to prominence in Lyme, Connecticut, is also a serious concern. Educate yourself on both its prevention and its symptoms. Wild animals in the northeast, such as raccoons and foxes, have been victimized by rabies in much greater numbers lately. These animals are not by nature friendly and docile; beware of those that remain in the open and unfazed by your presence. And while driving your car, please take the "Moose Crossing" signs seriously! Moose are most active at dawn and around dusk, the times of day when it's most difficult to see! Although moose are not aggressive creatures, they are very dangerous because they lack any conception of vehicular traffic. Without any warning whatsoever, these tall (7 feet and taller) gangly beasts might lumber out of the woods onto a highway, where their spindly legs can be clipped by a low bumper of a car and their immense torsos (around 1,200 pounds) tossed through its windshield. Driving in moose country is a bit like flying, "An accident is highly unlikely, but in the case of an emergency . . ."

On the other hand, nearly everyone will be hounded and probably bitten by the dreaded black fly. These pesky varmints are too small to show up in the promotional brochures, but they're in every picture! Fairly small and thankfully slow, they have an innate sense of knowing just when you need to hit a straight drive or make a ten-footer to save par. Their buzz is annoying, but more important, their bite can be quite nasty. The black fly is a menace primarily in May, although small numbers of them can be seen on dive-bombing missions during June in the North Country. Your strategy is to wear a hat and long-sleeved shirt whenever possible, forgo wearing aftershave or perfume, and procure a product specifically designed to discourage them. The black fly is particularly fond of nibbling behind the ears, on the neck, and along the hairline. If you don't want to put these chemicals directly on your skin, wear a hat or visor and douse it.

One more warning: Although spring can be a glorious time to golf New England, natives often refer to this time of year as "mud season." As one local put it, "We have winter, then when all the snow melts, it's mud season. Then, finally, summer comes." If you're willing to put up with some occasionally sloppy conditions, you'll find outstanding scenery, temperatures, and bargains to be had in a New England spring.

The various costs of your sojourn to New England can vary greatly with the calendar. As a rule, greens fees stay constant throughout the golf season. Few courses lower their rates in the spring and fall, although it is possible to see coupons in the local newspaper advertising a lower rate for four golfers. Golf courses are less crowded in the fall, especially during the afternoon hours on weekends when football is on television.

Golf resorts are much more savvy with their pricing in their attempts to lure customers. All of them charge top rates during the peak months of July and August. They lower them slightly during May and early June when the kiddies are still in school. They play with them considerably in September and early October, trying to snag good rates during the foliage season and hoping to get anyone to show up once the leaves have littered the ground.

During the spring and fall you are certain to find discounts at resorts if you are willing to stay Sunday through Thursday.

Speaking of foliage season, it is a major attraction. Visitors arrive from all over the world to watch the glorious red, orange, and yellow tide sweep down from the mountains to the sea. And when exactly is that? Answer: Only Mother Nature knows exactly when in September and October. The best places to see the foliage are along the high country roads of the North Country, where the views across the valleys are simply spectacular. The roads do get congested, yet most of the "leaf peepers" are native New Englanders out on a day trip, so hotel rooms are usually available. You might not get the room you want in your preferred hostelry, but you can usually find a room.

Fall is also a great time to go whale-watching. Migrating humpbacks and finbacks headline a show on display primarily in the mid-region waters between the Isles of Shoals off Portsmouth, New Hampshire, and Chatham on Cape Cod.

The single most important question to ask when reserving a tee time in the fall season is, "When are you aerating your greens?" Typically, greens superintendents in New England perform deep-time aeration in October, although courses in the North Country may do so earlier. Such greens are never as enjoyable, so be sure to ask about the condition of the greens beforehand.

WHAT TO BRING

We told you that New England has four seasons; understand that you might experience all four of them during the same round of golf! This is because New England sits right where the Gulf Stream brings warm, humid air from the south to meet its cool, dry cousin from Canada. It's not an amicable get-together. Lightening can flash. Hail can fall. The shorts you wore under a blazing sun on Friday can be replaced by rain gear on Saturday and long pants topped by a sweater on a cool, breezy Sunday. Bring a large suitcase and fill it.

ONCE YOU'RE THERE

Perhaps we should call this section "How to Do New England." Because New England "plays longer than its actual yardage," you really must decide beforehand just how much driving you want to do during your visit. Obviously, you'll do the least amount if you stay in one of the resorts. Most of them are found in the mountains of northern New England, although the Samoset by the Sea and Ocean Edge offer ready access to the sea. The single greatest drawback to staying at any resort is the lack of variety in golf courses. Most resorts have a single noteworthy course. That's not all bad because players attain "local" knowledge with each round and tend to play better. Unfortunately, the pace of play at resorts tends to be quite a bit slower. "A chain is only as strong as its weakest link, and a golf course plays only as quickly as its slowest group." The best strategy for playing something close to a four-hour round of golf is to play either early in the morning, or late in the day. Be prepared to play at a leisurely pace if you tee it up after 9 a.m.

If you're not keen on staying at a resort, New England offers one—and only one—locale that provides a large number of exceptional courses: the central part of Cape Cod. Specifically, you can drop anchor somewhere in the towns of Brewster, Harwich, Dennis, Chatham, or Yarmouth and have 20-minute access to a half dozen well-designed, well-maintained, and reasonably priced municipal courses. And these aren't your average municipal courses; for example, the original course at The Captains won a much-admired "Best New Course" award from a leading golf publication. You will find all manner of accommodation in the area, from resort to the most modest motel.

If you have the time, you can take the Grand Tour of New England. We've developed one for you that's designed to take you through all the top venues over two weeks. It can easily be adapted to shorter stays and shorter drives.

Day One: Arrive at Albany County Airport in upstate New York, rent a car, and drive a little less than two hours to The Equinox Hotel for a two-night stay. Play the course as often as possible.

Day Three: Drive another two hours south along I-91 into north-central Massachusetts and play Crumpin-Fox in Bernardston.

Day Four: Drive east to Cape Cod along the Massachusetts Turnpike (I-90) and stay two nights at the Ocean Edge Resort in Brewster. Play the course, and then nip out to play one of the fine public courses in the area. We suggest the original Captains Course or Cranberry Valley.

Day Six: Depart the Cape before 9 a.m. and slip up U.S. 3 into Boston for one of the following: a baseball game at venerable Fenway Park (while it's still there); a tour of the Freedom Trail; a night on the Charles River Esplanade with the Boston Pops; a journey to Camelot (the Kennedy Presidential Library); or a shopping binge at Quincy Market (lunch at Ye Olde Oyster House).

Day Seven: Drive north along I-95 toward Maine with a stop in New Hampshire at the Portsmouth Country Club for 18 holes. Get directions to Strawberry Banke, a collection of furnished colonial homes in downtown Portsmouth. Dine in one of the city's exceptional restaurants, preferably the casual Ferry Landing owned by the family of former LPGA star Jane Blalock.

Day Eight: Arrive at the Samoset Resort along the rocky Maine coast. Awake and play one of the region's most spectacular courses. Stay another day so that you can play golf in the morning and then tour scenic Camden, which is particularly famous for its masted schooners.

Day Ten: Drive through the woodlands of western Maine, dodge all the moose, and arrive safely at the northern wonderland known as The Balsams Grand Resort. Play the Panoramic Course. Stay overnight and play the course again.

Day Twelve: Fly home from the international airport at Burlington, Vermont.

If you are looking for either a three- or four-night getaway, and you want to play a variety of courses rather than the one offered at most resorts, you have two excellent options if you're looking for some great value. The first is to head to Cape Cod and play the sensational municipal courses in the Dennis-Harwich-Brewster area. This part of the Cape offers the full range of accommodations, so you can have exactly the experience you want. The other option is to head toward Portland, Maine, for some down East fare and fairways. Portland itself provides Sable Oaks Golf Course, but you will have to drive a bit to play our other recommendations: 20 minutes south to Dunegrass Golf Club in Old Orchard Beach, and about 50 minutes north to play the much-admired Belgrade Lakes Golf Course. Portland is one of those "most livable" cities you hear about: low crime rates, good schools, lots of entertainment and sports, a historic district, and plenty of shopping.

GATHERING INFORMATION

Vermont

Manchester and the Mountains Regional
Chamber of Commerce
3451 Manchester Center, Manchester, VT 05254
Phone (802) 362-2100

Stowe Area Association
P.O. Box 1320, Stowe, VT 05672
Phone (800) 24-STOWE or (802) 253-7321

Sugarbush Chamber of Commerce
P.O. Box 173, Waitsfield, VT 05673
Phone (802) 496-3409

Vermont Chamber of Commerce
Box 37, Montpelier, VT 05602
Phone (802) 223-3443

New Hampshire

Mt. Washington Valley Visitors Bureau
Box 2300, North Conway, NH 03860
Phone (800) 367-3364 or (603) 356-5701

New Hampshire Office of Travel and Tourism Department
Box 1856, Concord, NH 03301
Phone (800) 386-4664 or (603) 271-2343

Maine

Maine Publicity Bureau
P.O. Box 2300, 325-B Water St., Hallowell, ME 04347
Phone (888) 624-6345 or (207) 623-0363

Rockland-Thomaston Area Chamber of Commerce
Harbor Park, Box 508, Rockland, ME 04841
Phone (800) 562-2529 or (207) 596-0376

Rockport-Camden-Lincolnville Chamber of Commerce
Public Landing, Box 919, Camden, ME 04843
Phone (800) 223-5459 or (207) 236-4404

Massachusetts

Cape Cod Chamber of Commerce
Routes 6 and 132, Hyannis, MA 02601
Phone (800) 332-2732 or (508) 362-3225

Massachusetts Office of Travel and Tourism
100 Cambridge St., Boston, MA 02202
Phone (800) 447-6277 or (617) 727-3201

The Major Courses in Vermont

The Gleneagles Course

The Equinox Hotel, Historic Route 7A, Manchester Village, VT 05254;
phone (800) 362-4747 or (802) 362-4700

How To Get On   Tee times can be made up to a week in advance.

Tees:

Blue: 6,423 yards, par-71, USGA rating 71.3, slope 129

White: 6,069 yards, par-71, USGA rating 69.1, slope 125

Red: 5,082 yards, par-71, USGA rating 65.2, slope 117

Challenge: ★★★½

Variety: ★★★½

Terrain: ★★★★

Beauty/Visual Appeal: ★★★★

Pace of Play: ★★★

Golf Facilities: ★★★

14-Club Test: ★★★½

Intangibles: ★★★★

Value: ★★★

Just the Facts   Year Opened: 1926; Course Designers: Walter Travis and Rees Jones; Walking: Yes; Greens Fee: $85; 9 Hole/Twilight Rate: Yes; Pull Carts: Yes; Practice Range: Yes; Club Rental: Yes

Description and Comments   It seems that whenever the USGA rating needs one of America's classic courses revised for a national championship it turns to Rees Jones, the son of world-renowned course designer Robert Trent Jones. As a result, the younger Jones has had the enviable task of updating a fair number of this country's more treasured courses: Congressional, Hazeltine National, and The Country Club.

It seemed natural, therefore, that The Equinox Hotel in Manchester Village, Vermont, would turn to Jones in 1991 to revise their run-down Walter Travis/John Duncan Dunn design of the 1920s. It would be yet another intriguing challenge for Jones, one made even more appealing by the $3.5 million budget. One could build an entirely new course for much less, but deciding not to do so is one of those decisions that makes human beings so darn interesting. So here in the lovely Green Mountains above the trout-filled Battenkill River is your opportunity to experience the Jones style on an abbreviated scale (6,423 yards off the tips).

Jones' revisions are quite noticeable. They're downright startling to anyone who knew the old course because Jones didn't change the routing one iota. It's as if Charlie Brown took Pig Pen to the La Costa Spa for a complete makeover. The Gleneagles Course at The Equinox, as the course is now known, no longer has the look, feel, or playability of an old New England track. Gone are the greens that had shrunk to the size of a picnic blanket. Passed on are the haggard-looking bunkers. Soon forgotten are the small—and consequently scruffy—tee boxes. In their places are the well-manicured bits and pieces of a modern golf course. Mounds, fairway bunkers, and contour mowing lead the eye from one pretty hole to the next while making the challenge new and fresh.

Insider Tips   If you're at all fit, walk the course. (Wouldn't caddies bring back the feeling of days gone past in a big way?!) This is an old course with each tee set right beside the preceding green, so you really will enjoy the stroll. And if you're a big hitter, you can lighten your bag by leaving out a mid-iron or two. The best advice for playing the course is an old adage:

Turn every par-4 into a 150-yard par-3 by hitting something less than a driver whenever possible. (Hit nothing more than a five-iron at the 5th under any circumstances.)

The practice putting green has more tilt than the tower in Pisa—with good reason! You'll face plenty of awkward putts out on the course, so do yourself a favor and practice, practice, practice.

You do not need to stay in the hotel in order to play the course. The greens fee was $85 for all-day play in 1999. Golf clubs may be rented, but the golf course has no practice range.

You do need to stay in the hotel if you want to encounter the full flavor of the experience. It's a wonderful old white-washed building that has undergone 17 major architectural changes since it first opened as a hostelry in 1769 as Marsh's Tavern. Visits by Mary Todd Lincoln cemented the hotel's reputation as a premier summer resort back in 1864. Four U.S. presidents have stayed in the hotel, which in 1972 was added to the National Register of Historic Places. Today, The Equinox is a proud member of the Historic Hotels of America.

We can tell you that The Equinox Hotel is a sensational destination during foliage season, but expect to pay a premium. Reserve well in advance; your best bet is one of the last two weeks in September.

We can't give you any insider information on how to play the historic course of the hyper-exclusive Ekwanok Club, which is out of bounds to the right of the fourth hole. We're also useless when it comes to accessing the nearby Dorset Field Club, where golf is believed to have been played in 1886, two years before the Apple Tree Gang formed the "first" golf club in America at Yonkers, New York. But alas, we can strongly suggest that while you're in the neighborhood you take an hour's drive south through Brattleboro into northern Massachusetts and play the much-ballyhooed Crumpin-Fox Golf Course (see page 509).

The Major Courses in New Hampshire

The Panorama Course

The Balsams Grand Resort, Route 26, Dixville Notch, NH 03576; phone (800) 255-0600 or (603) 255-4961

Ask anyone mildly interested in presidential politics where Dixville Notch is and you will likely hear a spontaneous "New Hampshire." The reason is simple: The town's 20 or so voters gather in the Ballot Room of The Balsams Grand Resort at promptly midnight in order to vote in the nation's first primary. Politically speaking, Dixville Notch attains Warholian fame every four years. Recreationally speaking, the tiny hamlet achieves great distinction every winter and summer as the home of one of the finest golf/ski resorts in the world.

The resort might well attract countless visitors even without those two sports, for it rests in a snug river valley surrounded by inspiring mountains, waterfalls, and all creatures great and small. The addition of a Donald Ross golf course makes it irresistible to golfers. Their journey into the rugged North Country is rewarded by a modern resort that astoundingly has retained its style, grace, and indeed pace, of nearly a century ago. Guests arrived in plush railway cars back then, but today they zip along I-93, perhaps stopping to gaze skyward at the stately granite profile of the famed Old Man on the Mountain. Others come up through North Conway, driving for miles along the shore of the Androscoggin River with its fly-fishers thigh-deep in churning water. The lull of those last few country miles adds to the dramatic impact of first seeing The Balsams. The mountain road dips suddenly, and in the green valley below is the sprawling white hotel with its red roof set before the cold blue water of Lake Gloriette.

How To Get On   Guests of the Balsams can make tee times one week in advance; nonguests three days in advance.

Tees:

> Blue: 6,804 yards, par-72, USGA rating 73.9, slope 136
>
> White: 6,097 yards, par-72, USGA rating 70.5, slope 130
>
> Red: 5,069 yards, par-72, USGA rating 69.9, slope 124

Challenge: ★★★★	Golf Facilities: ★★★★
Variety: ★★★★	14-Club Test: ★★★★½
Terrain: ★★★★½	Intangibles: ★★★★½
Beauty/Visual Appeal: ★★★★½	Value: ★★★★
Pace of Play: ★★★	

Just the Facts   Year Opened: 1912; Course Designer: Donald Ross; Walking: Yes; Greens Fee: $50–60; 9 Hole/Twilight Rate: Yes; Pull Carts: Yes; Practice Range: Yes; Club Rental: Yes.

Description and Comments   Donald Ross laid out the Panorama Course on the westward slope of nearby Mount Keazer between 1912 and 1915. Most wouldn't consider it walkable, but it must have been great exercise in the company of a caddie. It's a Ross thoroughbred with broad fairways, greens perched slightly—but significantly—above the fairway, and flat-bottomed greenside bunkers positioned to the side so that players can run the ball on if necessary. It has 18 perfectly sound holes, yet not one is captivating enough to compete with the glorious panoramic views.

Its only startling aspect is the distance of the back markers, a whopping 6,804 yards. That would be a challenging distance in flat ol' Florida, but on this hilly terrain you wind up with holes like the 18th: 560 yards to a green 142 feet above the tee. Hit *that* in two, Tiger. The slope rating off the back is an imposing 136, which suggests that perhaps the course would benefit from a fourth set of tee markers that split the distance between the tips and the regular tees (6,097 yards). As it stands, you must choose between tee markers that average nearly 40 yards in difference.

Insider Tips   The course is 2.3 miles from the hotel, so many golfers bring a box lunch from the dining room. The better alternative is to get a chit from the maitre d' in the hotel so that you can eat in the clubhouse at the course, which has a dining terrace overlooking the Connecticut River Valley, the farms of neighboring Vermont, and even the foothills of distant Quebec, Canada.

The Panorama Course is open to the public. We'd love to recommend another course in the area, but there simply isn't one. The Balsams actually has another course, a 9-hole "Coashaukee" track, which is great for beginners, but not to be considered by any golfer who takes him- or herself seriously.

Country Club of New Hampshire

Kearsarge Valley Road, North Sutton, NH 03260; phone (603) 927-4246

Ranked as one of America's best public courses by a major magazine, this one deserves the distinction. It's a gem laid out through a wooded countryside with absolutely nothing around it. No houses on the fairways, no traffic beyond the rough, no airplanes in the sky. Uncomplicated, straightforward golf of the highest (and fairest) order in a natural setting.

How To Get On   Tee times can be made a week in advance; nearby hotels can make them longer in advance.

Tees:

>   Gold: 6,727 yards, par-72, USGA rating 71.6, slope 125
>
>   White: 6,226 yards, par-72, USGA rating 69.6, slope 122
>
>   Red: 5,446 yards, par-72, USGA rating 71.7, slope 127

Challenge: ★★★½	Golf Facilities: ★★★★
Variety: ★★★★	14-Club Test: ★★★★
Terrain: ★★★★	Intangibles: ★★★½
Beauty/Visual Appeal: ★★★★½	Value: ★★★★½
Pace of Play: ★★★★	

Just the Facts   Year Opened: 1957; Course Designer: William Mitchell; Walking: Yes; Greens Fee: $25–32; 9 Hole/Twilight Rate: Yes; Pull Carts: Yes; Practice Range: Yes; Club Rental: Yes.

Description and Comments   Architect William Mitchell deserves credit for the present design of Country Club of New Hampshire. His enormous talent is on full display here in the quiet foothills of Mount Kearsarge. Unlike many of the courses in the region, this one has few dramatic changes in elevation. The front 9 is virtually level, but the back takes on a rolling aspect that helps earn the layout its high reputation. Especially good back there are the par-3s. The 11th is 145 yards over water and the 15th is a mighty 217 yards to a green set above three deep bunkers. The 16th is ranked toughest of all. It's a 445-yard dogleg to another well-bunkered green. This is the sort of challenge that this fine course presents.

Insider Tips   It's a brave player indeed who takes on this course at its full 6,727 yards (slope 125). Walking is permitted, and this is a good track to walk. Greens fees are always some of the most reasonable in the state. A modest condo-complex/motel beside the course offers stay-and-play packages. Lauren's Dining Room and Lounge can accommodate groups of up to 120. Do yourself a favor, stay overnight and play it again in the morning. Just don't expect an exciting nightlife.

The Major Courses in Maine
The Samoset

220 Warrenton St., Rockport, ME 04856; phone (800) 341-1650 or (207) 594-2511

The Samoset commands a magnificent view of the islands of Penobscot Bay that has been likened to that seen from another clifftop course along the Monterey Peninsula south of San Francisco. Others would compare the courses, but what would be the point? It's enough to know that visitors to the Samoset will find an outstanding layout that has been consistently rated among the top American resort courses.

One of the more difficult tasks for a golf resort is to provide a single course that challenges both the modest and the accomplished player. The Samoset Resort does so superbly. This incredibly scenic layout has a wonderful rhythm that keeps players on their toes. Seven holes skirt Penobscot Bay, while no less than 14 holes boast views of the Atlantic Ocean.

How To Get On   Hotel guest may book tee times with room confirmation. Nonguests can book tee times two days in advance.

Tees:

> Blue: 6,515 yards, par-70, USGA rating 70.3, slope 128
>
> White: 6,021 yards, par-70, USGA rating 68.4, slope 127
>
> Red: 5,432 yards, par-70, USGA rating 70.1, slope 120

Challenge: ★★★

Variety: ★★★★

Terrain: ★★★★

Beauty/Visual Appeal: ★★★★½

Pace of Play: ★★★

Golf Facilities: ★★★★½

14-Club Test: ★★★½

Intangibles: ★★★★

Value: ★★★★

Just the Facts   Year Opened: 1978; Course Designer: Robert Elder; Walking: Yes; Greens Fee: $55–100; 9 Hole/Twilight Rate: Yes; Pull Carts: Yes; Practice Range: Yes; Club Rental: Yes

Description and Comments   Among the greatest holes at Samoset—and among some of the most memorable holes you will ever play—are the 4th, 6th, and 12th. If you haven't been to Samoset in a couple of years, the course has been reconfigured, so that the famous old par-5 7th is now the famous new 4th. As a matter of fact, the open, links-like front 9 is sprinkled with outstanding holes, with the 4th being the most notable. Four stretches more than 500 yards from the tips, but most folks play it at a more sensible 481 yards. Whichever tee you select, you'll encounter a slender, fiercely bunkered fairway that curves in a crescent to the left along the ocean's shoreline, culminating in a well-bunkered green perched at water's edge. Another distinctive element to the hole is the lovely Rockland Breakwater, which extends a full mile into the bay that backdrops the green.

Nearly as spectacular as the 4th—and probably a tougher one to par—is the 6th, a 406-yard par-4. Six is a wide-open hole, buffeted by breezes, that turns gently to the right at the green. The putting surface is oddly -shaped, like a hammer, with bunkers crammed into every greenside nook and cranny. Putts of more than 100 feet are not uncommon, because in reality this is a double green, serving not only the 6th hole but also the 3rd.

Perhaps the finest hole on Samoset's back 9 is the 12th, a monstrous par-5 of 565 yards. A narrow green and no fewer than eight bunkers make the 12th a formidable challenge. Oh yes, the greens. Did we mention the greens? They are thoroughbreds, beautiful and fast. Not quick, fast, routinely kept at 12 on the Stimpmeter. Down East linoleum. And so it goes at The Samoset.

Insider Tips   Perched on the coast, as Samoset is, it is very susceptible to wind. Samoset is splendid fun in a good breeze, but can be a brute in a stiff wind. The wind tends to blow year-round at Samoset, so if you're not particularly adept at coping with breezy conditions, we suggest you play Samoset in the morning when it's a bit calmer.

Sugarloaf/USA Golf Course

R.R. No. 1, P.O. Box 5000, Carrabassett Valley, ME 04947; phone (800) 843-5623 or (207) 237-2000

How To Get On   Guests may book tee times with their reservations. Nonguests can book up to two weeks in advance.

Tees:

> Blue: 6,956 yards, par-72, USGA rating 74.4, slope 151
>
> White (back): 6,456 yards, par-72, USGA rating 72.3, slope 146
>
> White (front): 5,946 yards, par-72, USGA rating 70.0, slope 141
>
> Red: 5,365 yards, par-72, USGA rating 73.7, slope 136

Challenge: ★★★★½   Golf Facilities: ★★★
Variety: ★★★★½   14-Club Test: ★★★½
Terrain: ★★★★½   Intangibles: ★★★★½
Beauty/Visual Appeal: ★★★★★   Value: ★★★★
Pace of Play: ★★★½

Just the Facts   Year Opened: 1986; Course Designer: Robert Trent Jones Jr.; Walking: Yes; Greens Fee: $45–69; 9 Hole/Twilight Rate: Yes; Pull Carts: No; Practice Range: Yes; Club Rental: Yes

Description and Comments   Unquestionably, this is one of the prettiest and most challenging golf courses in the entire country. Unquestionably, too, this is one of America's most remote "great" courses, located in the mountains of western Maine. Other than the course, some pretty good lodging, and countless moose, there's nothing else around. It's pretty because its heaving terrain affords great views of the mountainous countryside—especially during foliage season—and testing because you can go back to the tips and bite off 151 units of USGA rating-approved slope. You will be bitten back, so move up to an appropriate tee. Strangely enough, one of the most difficult holes at Sugarloaf is the 355-yard, par-4 10th—and it plays downhill! Even so, the fairway is only wide enough for two moose to exchange a hello, so hit a mid-iron. It is immediately followed by the signature hole, the one shown in all the magazines, a 216-yard par-3 that plays downhill—about 125 feet downhill. Beyond is the entire expanse of the Carrabassett Valley, which is aflame with reds and oranges in the fall. The tee shot is undeniably one of the great ones in golf for its combination of natural beauty and testing golf. Oh yes, the golf. The Carrabassett River flows along the left side of the green, which is pinched on the right by a pair of bunkers. The task is simply to pick the right club after calculating the effects of the drop and the wind—and then hit a good shot to the tiny green, which is backdropped by tall white birch trees. Good luck.

Insider Tips   The golf here is unquestionably outstanding but . . . this is a mountain course and it takes a while to get the grass woken up in the spring. Sometimes it falls prey to "winter kill" and doesn't come back at all. Don't expect it to look like Augusta National. Also, the black fly is a full-time summer resident at Sugarloaf, so be prepared.

If you haven't seen a moose yet, the resort offers a Moose Cruise, which is actually more like a safari. It's great fun as well as informative.

The Major Courses in Massachusetts

Crumpin-Fox Club

Parmenter Road, Bernardston, MA 01337; phone (413) 648-9101

For years, rugged, beautiful Crumpin-Fox was regarded as one of the nation's five finest 9-hole courses. A tiny minority feels the mystique was ruined when they finally added another 9 in 1991, but an overwhelming majority happily disagrees.

How To Get On Tee times can be made three days in advance (they can be made longer in advance with certain packages).

Tees:

> Blue: 7,007 yards, par-72, USGA rating 73.8, slope 141
>
> White: 6,532 yards, par-72, USGA rating 71.3, slope 137
>
> Member: 6,095 yards, par-72, USGA rating 70.1, slope 133
>
> Red: 5,432 yards, par-72, USGA rating 71.5, slope 131

Challenge: ★★★★½	Golf Facilities: ★★★★
Variety: ★★★★	14-Club Test: ★★★½
Terrain: ★★★★★	Intangibles: ★★★★½
Beauty/Visual Appeal: ★★★★½	Value: ★★★★½
Pace of Play: ★★★★	

Just the Facts Year Opened: 1978; Course Designer: Roger Rulewich; Walking: Yes; Greens Fee: $59; 9 Hole/Twilight Rate: Yes; Pull Carts: No; Practice Range: Yes; Club Rental: Yes.

Description and Comments This sensational course is consistently rated among the best courses in America by the popular press. It's a wooded and hilly track—it sits in the foothills of the Berkshire Mountains—designed by Roger Rulewich. It's as Yankee as (dare we say) Ted Williams! The layout is pure New England, weaving through a hilly forest of splendid isolation. You'll find picturesque brooks, ponds, and plenty of trees, but more important, you'll encounter plenty of sand around the greens and more than enough undulation in the putting surfaces. This is a second-shot golf course that rewards excellent iron play. It has two of the better par-5s in the region: The 8th hole is indexed number one, and the 14th is a downhill affair to a fairway alongside a lake. If you go out of your way to play one course in New England, this should be it.

Insider Tips Be careful, you could encounter a well-deserved slope rating of 141 if you march back to the tips. The 7,007 yards fully tested those who tried to qualify for the U.S. Open on this course in 1991 and 1994. Three other sets of tees make this course enjoyable by all. In fact, our advice is to move up one set of tees because shots that leave the fairway are dealt with harshly. The management can arrange a stay-and-play package. Understand that the wonderful isolation you enjoyed out on the course means you won't find a large, upscale hotel nearby.

Stow Acres

58 Randall Rd., Stow, MA 01775; phone (978) 568-1100

Northwest of Boston you'll find a pair of fine golf courses laid out in a rural setting amid towering fir trees, the North and the South of the Stow Acres Country Club. Long recognized by leading golf periodicals as one of the better public courses in the United States, the North received the ultimate recognition when the USGA rating named it as the host of the 1995 U.S. Amateur Public Links Championship, won by Chris Wollmann.

How To Get On Tee times can be made six days in advance.

North Course Tees:

>   Blue: 6,939 yards, par-72, USGA rating 72.8, slope 130
>   White: 6,310 yards, par-72, USGA rating 69.8, slope 127
>   Red: 6,011 yards, par-72, USGA rating 73.6, slope 130

Challenge: ★★★½	Golf Facilities: ★★★★
Variety: ★★★★	14-Club Test: ★★★★
Terrain: ★★★	Intangibles: ★★★½
Beauty/Visual Appeal: ★★★	Value: ★★★★
Pace of Play: ★★	

South Course Tees:

>   Blue: 6,520 yards, par-72, USGA rating 71.8, slope 120
>   White: 6,105 yards, par-72, USGA rating 70.5, slope 118
>   Red: 5,042 yards, par-72, USGA rating 72.5, slope 120

Challenge: ★★½	Golf Facilities: ★★★★
Variety: ★★★★	14-Club Test: ★★★½
Terrain: ★★★	Intangibles: ★★★½
Beauty/Visual Appeal: ★★★	Value: ★★★½
Pace of Play: ★★	

Just the Facts Year Opened: 1965; Course Designer: Geoffrey S. Cornish; Walking: Yes; Greens Fee: $30–40; 9 Hole/Twilight Rate: Yes; Pull Carts: No; Practice Range: Yes; Club Rental: Yes

Description and Comments Stow Acres North is a tough, sandy course dotted with ponds, but from the appropriate tee boxes it is a sensible challenge you'll certainly enjoy. You will undoubtedly come away impressed by the 460-yard 9th hole, a two-shotter you'll be happy to reach in three. The South Course is worth a serious look, although it occupies hillier terrain and consequently has a few too many blind shots for the purist.

Insider Tips There's not a lot of quality public-access golf in and around Boston, with Stow Acres a notable exception. Consequently, these courses tend to be quite crowded, with heavy play and outings the norm rather than the exception. Our advice is to play early in the week, avoiding the weekend if possible. Beginners might be intimidated by the big crowds combined with challenging courses.

The Major Courses on Cape Cod

The best concentration of public-access courses in New England is located on Cape Cod, that stretch of sand and scrub pine jutting out into the cold Atlantic like a defiant arm and fist telling King George III and Parliament just exactly how the colonists felt. We won that war, stole their game, and learned to play it better, so come to Cape Cod and celebrate. Ideally, your destination is the mid-Cape area near the towns of Brewster, Harwich, and Dennis, all of which have developed outstanding municipal courses.

You have undoubtedly heard of the Country Club of New Seabury. It has two courses, the Blue Course being one of the best in the entire country, the Green being a well-conceived "executive course." Unfortunately, only residents of the New Seabury resort can play the Blue Course, and only members have access during the height of the summer. The Green Course is terrific, really, but you won't be happy sitting in the clubhouse and just staring at the magnificent Blue Course a few steps away outside.

Cape Cod is no golfer's Shangri-La, however. The Cape is burdened by too many people in too many automobiles, and that is a big problem indeed. Only three strands of road bear all the traffic flowing from the mainland to the "elbow" of Chatham. The major road is a two-lane divided highway—the infamous Route 6. In fact, it's only two lanes and divided up through Exit 9, which is, fortunately enough, just where any sensible golfer should get off. Also note that while you are driving east into the rising sun along Route 6 the road sign indicates that you are traveling "north." This will all make sense when the road bends 90 degrees at Chatham, and you actually are headed north toward Provincetown.

Here's a tip on choosing your accommodations on Cape Cod. The better beaches and warmer temperatures are located along the southern shore between Woods Hole and Harwich. The water temperatures are significantly cooler from the Cape's "elbow," Chatham, north to Provincetown. The "inside" of the Cape has warm water but enormous changes in the tide, which means lots of walking on some days.

One other bit of insider info: You will hear that the Truro Golf Club is a 9-hole affair of true linksland, the only true linksland in America. Think about it: If that were true the course would be on everyone's top 25. The layout is on hilly, rocky terrain, and the grass is unwatered and has that burned-out look of a links without actually being one. That's not to say it doesn't play a lot like a links, but you're better off spending your time in

Truro at the adjacent lighthouse watching the whales frolic in the surf below the high cliff.

Ocean Edge Resort and Golf Club

Route 6A, Brewster, MA 02631; phone (800) 343-6074 or (508) 896-5911

On the inside of the elbow, at Brewster, is the Cape's only resort with a "championship" golf course fully opened to guests and greens-fee players alike.

How To Get On: Guests can make tee times with their with reservations. Nonguests, call for policy.

Tees:

> Blue: 6,665 yards, par-72, USGA rating 71.9, slope 129
> White: 6,127 yards, par-72, USGA rating 68.7, slope 125
> Red: 5,098 yards, par-72, USGA rating 73.2, slope 129

Challenge: ★★★	Golf Facilities: ★★★½
Variety: ★★★½	14-Club Test: ★★★½
Terrain: ★★★★	Intangibles: ★★★
Beauty/Visual Appeal: ★★★	Value: ★★★
Pace of Play: ★★½	

Just the Facts   Year Opened: 1986; Course Designer: Geoffrey Cornish/Brian Silva; Walking: At times; Greens Fee: $36–54; 9 Hole/Twilight Rate: Yes; Pull Carts: No; Practice Range: Yes; Club Rental: Yes.

Description and Comments   The course at Ocean Edge, which has hosted the New England PGA championship many times since its opening in 1986, takes full advantage of the rising and falling land. No where is this more evident than at the 8th, a true three-shotter played down out of a chute, up to a plateau, and then a hard left across a deep depression to the green. It's little wonder no one has ever hit the darn thing in two off either the blue markers (601 yards) or the championship tee.

Yet Ocean Edge is no trail of torture. It is a remarkably well-conditioned course that's pleasant and testing—no small feat—largely because it emphasizes the need for accuracy over length. Long-ball knockers who abhor drive-and-pitch courses raise their eyebrows over such descriptions, but they will find that the blue markers (6,665 yards) bring a lot of trouble into play.

Everyone will find the greens "interesting," a compliment in every sense, for they are imaginatively shaped and sensibly contoured. The real task at Ocean Edge is avoiding the 64 sand traps, many of which are tiny, sunken pot bunkers reminiscent of their more terrifying sod-faced cousins in the British Isles.

Although the course meanders throughout the resort, the villas are positioned well out of play or behind thick natural borders. That diminishes the annoying sense of playing in someone else's backyard prevalent at so many resorts. Still, you can't ignore them, so if you're not wild about condo golf, you may not be enamored with Ocean Edge.

Insider Tips   The only real drawback at Ocean Edge is the large distances between greens and tees that essentially rules out walking. In addition, you won't be riding too quickly either. This is a remarkably popular course, so summer crowds make this an awfully slow-playing course. If you can play this one in the fall, you'll buzz around a lot quicker. Finally, big, wild hitters may want to try another course if they want to play to their handicap.

This is a course that rewards thinking, imagination, and above all, accuracy. Oh, one more thing: It's the resort itself that is set "Ocean Edge." The golf course itself is located in the trees, on the other side of Route 6A, so don't expect quality ocean vistas until after your round when you go back to the resort. Ocean Edge accepts greens-fee players, so stop in if you're in the area enjoying one of the outstanding local municipal courses designed by either Cornish, Silva, or both.

The Major Courses in Connecticut

As we mentioned earlier, the otherwise lovely state of Connecticut isn't a great place to go for a vacation. That might change in the near future as the new golf course at the Foxwoods Casino on the Native American reservation in eastern Connecticut matures. But as for now we feel your odds are better at the blackjack table and keeping your golf on the old standby, Richter Park.

Richter Park Golf Club

100 Aunt Hack, Danbury, CT 06811; phone (203) 792-2552

This public course is consistently ranked among the best public courses in New England and no one in western Connecticut knows why. Talk to locals and you hear, "Yeah, it's nice . . . not bad . . . but it's not great either." That's a pretty good indication that Richter Park rates high because the surrounding courses are rather poor. Maybe not. There's certainly no harm in playing it yourself, plenty of others do, for it's one of the busiest courses in the northeast.

How To Get On   Nonresidents can call Thursday prior for weekend play.

Tees:

      Blue: 6,740 yards, par-72, USGA rating 73.0, slope 130

      White: 6,325 yards, par-72, USGA rating 71.1, slope 126

      Gold: 5,626 yards, par-72, USGA rating 72.8, slope 122

      Red: 5,202 yards, par-72, USGA rating 70.3, slope 117

Challenge: ★★★★

Variety: ★★★½

Terrain: ★★★

Beauty/Visual Appeal: ★★½

Pace of Play: ★★½

Golf Facilities: ★★★

14-Club Test: ★★★½

Intangibles: ★★½

Value: ★★★

Just the Facts Year Opened: 1971; Course Designer: Edward Ryder; Walking: Yes; Greens Fee: $27–44; 9 Hole/Twilight Rate: Yes; Pull Carts: Yes; Practice Range: No; Club Rental: Yes

Description and Comments In all fairness, this nearly 30-year-old layout does possess some classic virtues: attractive, multiple water hazards and one all-world hole, the 529-yard, par-5 12th. Number 12 calls for a blind tee shot, followed by a gradual downhill approach to a peninsula green that is nearly encircled by water. Richter Park features a highly attractive, challenging back nine, replete with lakes, trees, and bunkers. Unequivocally it's a fine test of your golf skills.

Insider Tips If you're not a resident, it's nearly impossible to obtain a prime tee time in prime season. You're better off showing up Monday through Thursday fairly early in the morning. If you're a single or twosome, you've got an excellent chance of getting out for a slow but enjoyable round.

A Vermont Sampler

Green Mountain National

Barrows-Towne Rd., Killington, VT 05751; phone (800) 635-6343 or (802) 422-4653

Tees: Championship: 6,589 yards, par-71, USGA rating 72.6, slope 139

Greens Fee: $38–42

Challenge: ★★★★

Variety: ★★★★

Terrain: ★★★½

Beauty/Visual Appeal: ★★★½

Pace of Play: ★★★★

Golf Facilities: ★★★★

14-Club Test: ★★★½

Intangibles: ★★★★

Value: ★★★

Description and Comments Another terrific new course in the area is Green Mountain National, which is west of Woodstock in Killington. It has received little national press, but all the locals recognize it as one of the more memorable public courses in the state. Opened in 1996, it has quickly overtaken the more highly publicized Killington Golf Course, which occupies a more vulnerable site in town near the top of a mountain. Green Mountain National is already noted for its excellent service, its isolated fairways, and the abundance of wildlife wandering about. Seriously consider staying overnight at The Summit, it's only a few minutes away, caters to golfers, and has an outdoor heated pool, Jacuzzi, and two excellent restaurants.

Stowe Country Club

5781 Mountain Rd., Stowe, VT 05672; phone (800) 253-4754 or (802) 253-4893

Tees: Championship: 6,206 yards, par-72, USGA rating 70.4, slope 122

Greens Fee: $35–65.

Challenge: ★★★	Golf Facilities: ★★★
Variety: ★★★½	14-Club Test: ★★★★
Terrain: ★★★½	Intangibles: ★★★★
Beauty/Visual Appeal: ★★★½	Value: ★★★
Pace of Play: ★★★½	

Description and Comments   Have you played enough new-fangled courses lately? Here's a design with little length, few bunkers, and hardly any water hazards that will still give you a run for your money. Its challenge comes from the clever, old-fashioned way the fairways and greens are positioned so that the natural fall of the land punishes mediocre shots. That's the essence of old-time New England golf. So, too, is the clubhouse, which has altogether too many friendly people! The Stowe area has lots of accommodations, including the hotel run by the Von Trapp family featured in the film The Sound of Music. The course itself is located beside the Stoweflake Mountain Resort & Spa (phone (800) 253-2232), which offers a golf academy.

Sugarbush Golf Course

Access Road, Warren, VT 05674; phone (800) 537-8427 or (802) 583-6725

Tees: Championship: 6,524 yards, par-72, USGA rating 71.7, slope 128

Greens Fee: $38–49

Challenge: ★★★	Golf Facilities: ★★★
Variety: ★★★★	14-Club Test: ★★★★½
Terrain: ★★★★	Intangibles: ★★★
Beauty/Visual Appeal: ★★★★½	Value: ★★★★
Pace of Play: ★★★	

Just the Facts   Opened in 1962, this design by Robert Trent Jones Sr. is really what "mountain golf" is all about. This very hilly layout rises and falls spectacularly. It also twists and turns with no fewer than 11 doglegs setting the challenge. The trick to scoring well here is to make yourself take a longer club on the uphill holes and play conservatively on the downhill holes. A word to the wise: Don't attempt to walk this course. Take a cart and enjoy the spectacular scenery. If you only take one golf photograph on your vacation, do so at the panoramic 7th hole. If you forget, you can get a fine shot at the 11th. Also, play the course more than once. If you haven't used every club in your bag at least once during the two rounds, we'd be surprised!

Vermont National Country Club

1227 Dorset St., South Burlington, VT 05401; phone (802) 864-7770
Tees: Championship: 7,035 yards, par-72, USGA rating 74.2, slope 133
Greens Fee: $35–60

Challenge: ★★★★	Golf Facilities: ★★★★½
Variety: ★★★★	14-Club Test: ★★★★
Terrain: ★★★½	Intangibles: ★★★★
Beauty/Visual Appeal: ★★★½	Value: ★★★
Pace of Play: ★★★½	

Description and Comments Perhaps you're looking for a new-fangled course? Here is one of the latest from the man considered the greatest. Jack Nicklaus and his son, Jackie, laid out this 18-hole, semiprivate course in the late 1990s. Each of the 9s has its own personality: The first half is very open, and the second 9 is closed in a bit more by trees. Be forewarned, courses take a good while to mature in these northern climes, so don't expect pristine conditions. Even so, the layout is very sensible and should develop into one of the North Country's better tracks. The small and friendly city of Burlington is an entertaining place with plenty of music, art fairs, and sports activities on the social calendar. Wander about and you'll discover that it's really just an overgrown college town.

Woodstock Golf Course (Woodstock Inn & Resort)

Fourteen the Green, Woodstock, VT 05091; phone (800) 448-7900 or (802) 457-6674
Tees: Championship: 6,001 yards, par-69, USGA rating 69.0, slope 121
Greens Fee: $49–63

Challenge: ★★★	Golf Facilities: ★★★½
Variety: ★★★½	14-Club Test: ★★★★½
Terrain: ★★★★	Intangibles: ★★★
Beauty/Visual Appeal: ★★★★	Value: ★★★★
Pace of Play: ★★½	

Description and Comments The ultimate movie about life in a New England town would surely be set in picturesque Woodstock, Vermont. And why not? Michael J. Fox already lives there, probably lured by the 17th-century brick architecture and the village green with its wrought-iron fence and ancient statuary. Across the street rises the white-columned facade of the Woodstock Inn, which astonishes by being equally stately and rustic. Guests have access to the Woodstock Country Club, a 100-year-old semiprivate club with a 35-year-old course by Robert Trent Jones Sr. Long it ain't, but if you're looking to feather short irons onto tiny greens perched just beyond a rushing stream, you're gonna love it. Practice your short-iron game before playing, and if you don't have the time, bring along that retractable ball retriever. Be sure to bring your putter and a golf ball back to the hotel. You can savor a beverage and roll a few putts in the central garden behind the hotel while the sun sets.

Please note, however, that the Woodstock Country Club is not the best course around. That accolade belongs to the Quechee Club, which sports a pair of sensational courses. Officially, these are private courses, but we know better. You can play these exclusive (and expensive) courses if you book a stay at the Kedron Valley Inn. This lovely 27-room hostelry is located on Route 106 in South Woodstock (phone (802) 457-1473). Another option is to contact Quechee Lakes Rentals (phone (802) 295-1970). The Highlands Course is preferred ever so slightly over the Lakeland Course, both of which were designed by Canadian-born and New England–adopted Geoffrey Cornish.

Purists be warned: Woodstock presents itself as quintessential Vermont, although the natives don't spend a lot of time there buying bagels, mugs of chocolate-strawberry coffee, pints of microbrew ales, or bowls of venison chili. Old Vermont is ten miles east in White River Junction, where you can grab a barstool in the VFW, talk snow tires with Clayton and Woody (not Ben & Jerry), and sink a few cold Buds. You can savor a truly Rockwellian moment at the close of business when the colors are presented, all the John Deere hats cover hearts, and today's Green Mountain Boys sing "God Bless America." Yep, there's Vermont, and then there's nouveau Vermont, which brings to mind the immortal words of Lee Trevino, "Is this a great country, or what?"

A New Hampshire Sampler

Bretwood Golf Courses

East Surry Road, Keene, NH 03431; phone (603) 352-7626

North Course
Tees: Championship: 6,974 yards, par-72, USGA rating 73.3, slope 139
Greens Fee: $28–35

South Course
Tees: Championship: 6,952 yards, par-72, USGA rating 73.7, slope 136
Greens Fee: $28–35

Challenge: ★★★★
Variety: ★★★★
Terrain: ★★★½
Beauty/Visual Appeal: ★★★½
Pace of Play: ★★★★

Golf Facilities: ★★★★
14-Club Test: ★★★★
Intangibles: ★★★★
Value: ★★★★½

Description and Comments   A real gem in western New Hampshire, Bretwood's North Course has long been rated among New Hampshire's top five public courses by the leading consumer golf magazine. A pair of opening par-5s indicate that long hitting might be of considerable value. Indeed, the course reaches 6,974 yards from the tips, but four sets of tees let the visitor select an appropriate length. The Ashuelot River comes into play on a half dozen holes. It flows along the left of the 11th, one of the longest holes in New Hampshire at 629 yards. The next hole is somewhat unusual as it shares a green with the 14th.

The North Course has been joined by the equally beautiful and challenging South Course, which, like its older sibling, is well known for its outstanding par-3s. It is the work of Hugh Barrett, a former associate of Geoffrey Cornish. There are many other great reasons to play the courses at Bretwood: unlimited walking at all times, grass driving range, large practice area, and a ranger that ensures a well-paced game.

Eastman Golf Links

Clubhouse Lane, Grantham, NH 03753; phone (603) 863-4500
Tees: Championship: 6,731 yards, par-71, USGA rating 73.5, slope 137
Greens Fee: $38

Challenge: ★★★★
Variety: ★★★★½
Terrain: ★★★½
Beauty/Visual Appeal: ★★★½
Pace of Play: ★★★★

Golf Facilities: ★★★½
14-Club Test: ★★★★½
Intangibles: ★★★½
Value: ★★★★½

Description and Comments   Located just up I-89 from the Country Club of New Hampshire, this course is a favorite of many New Englanders. It occupies a hilly site, and the distances between some greens and the next tee are formidable, so don't plan on walking here. If you've heard the term "strategic design school" and never been quite sure what it is, play this course and see it in full bloom. Designer Geoffrey Cornish has short holes with tiny greens; medium holes with landing areas pinched by bunkers that make long hitters decide whether or not to squeeze a driver onto the narrow part of the fairway; and long holes that consistently reward long, accurate drives and those who plod along with great trust in their wedge and putter. You'll enjoy this course immensely because it's attractive and fair.

Mt. Washington Hotel Course

Route 302, Bretton Woods, NH 03575; phone (800) 258-0330 or (603) 278-4653

Tees: Championship: 6,638 yards, par-71, USGA rating 70.1, slope 123

Greens Fee: $20–30

Challenge: ★★★	Golf Facilities: ★★★
Variety: ★★★½	14-Club Test: ★★★½
Terrain: ★★★	Intangibles: ★★★★
Beauty/Visual Appeal: ★★★½	Value: ★★★
Pace of Play: ★★★	

Description and Comments This grand resort has a checkered past filled with heydays as well as days when its Donald Ross golf course seemed likely to be turned into a hay field. Prosperity came, went, and hopefully has returned to this old-style property that rekindles memories of horse-drawn carriages; golfers in white, starched shirts; and ladies in hoop skirts. Vacationers have been trekking here for nearly a century. In those days many arrived through cavernous Franconia Notch, a wonderland of streams, waterfalls, and sheer cliffs. Now you can toot up I-93, turn right at Twin Mountains, and find this elegant white-washed, red-roofed resort set in a valley directly beneath Mt. Washington, the highest peak in the northeast. It's hard to say why this resort never garners the laurels of The Balsams or The Equinox, but the shortcomings are real—if only slight.

Nevertheless, the opportunity to play a Donald Ross course (1915) is reason enough to visit. The course was restored in 1991 by New England architects Geoffrey Cornish and Brian Silva. Set on a river plain, its sandy soil encourages the long fescue grass that gives it a distinctly links feel. It's well worth playing, especially if you walk back to the championship tee markers. So, too, is the resort's 18-hole putting course, which winds around glacial rocks and flower beds.

North Conway Country Club

Main Street, North Conway, NH 03860; phone (603) 356-9391

Tees: Championship: 6,659 yards, par-71, USGA rating 71.9, slope 126

Greens Fee: $28–35

Challenge: ★★★½	Golf Facilities: ★★½
Variety: ★★★★	14-Club Test: ★★★★
Terrain: ★★★½	Intangibles: ★★★★
Beauty/Visual Appeal: ★★★★	Value: ★★★★½
Pace of Play: ★★★	

Description and Comments A semiprivate club, the NCCC is right in the middle of town. In fact, the opening drive is across the local railway tracks down onto an old flood plain of the Saco River. There's nothing truly outstanding about the course—it sports minimalist architecture in the extreme, if you'll pardon the oxymoron—but the golf is consistently rewarding. Off in the distance is the scarred face of Cathedral Ledge, where the gen-X kids do some pretty nifty—and harrowing—rock climbing. Keep an eye on the clouds above the ledge because a thunderstorm can roll in unseen from that direction. Get back in the clubhouse and watch the show from safety. Always in good shape with fast greens, and always spiffed up with plenty of colorful flower beds, this course is a definite must-try for visiting golfers.

Owl's Nest Golf Club

1 Clubhouse Dr., Campton, NH 03223; phone (888) OWL-NEST or (603) 726-3076

Tees: Championship: 7,012 yards, par-72, USGA rating 74.0, slope 133

Greens Fee: $22–58

Challenge: ★★★★	Golf Facilities: ★★★
Variety: ★★★★	14-Club Test: ★★★★
Terrain: ★★★★	Intangibles: ★★★★
Beauty/Visual Appeal: ★★★★	Value: ★★★★
Pace of Play: ★★★½	

Description and Comments A newcomer to the North Country, this design by Mark Mungeam is getting a great deal of praise. As with any young course in the north, it will take a while to fully mature. Even so, this course is a beauty from both a playing and a viewing point of view. And you can quote us, this is the best course in the North Country to play and view the foliage. If you're an admirer of short, testing par-4s you'll find the 15th a delight: Only 308 yards, it doglegs up a slope to a two-level green you'll feel proud about two-putting. Owl's Nest is located in the Waterville Valley recreational area about 20 minutes north of the college town of Plymouth.

Perry Hollow Golf & Country Club

250 Perry Hollow Rd., Wolfeboro, NH 03899; phone (603) 569-3055

Tees: Championship: 6,338 yards, par-71, USGA rating 71.0, slope 132

Greens Fee: $28

Challenge: ★★★½	Golf Facilities: ★★★½
Variety: ★★★★	14-Club Test: ★★★½
Terrain: ★★★★	Intangibles: ★★★½
Beauty/Visual Appeal: ★★★★½	Value: ★★★★½
Pace of Play: ★★★	

Description and Comments   Anyone spending time in the Lakes Region of New Hampshire will certainly want to tee it up at this fine course. It didn't burst on the scene with much fanfare back in 1989. That's because it had horrific luck with the off-season weather killing its fairways. Nevertheless, the hilly routing has been sound from the outset, and the course is maturing nicely. The elevated clubhouse has sensational views, decent food, and plenty of cold beverages. This public course is located at the southern end of Lake Winnipesaukee in the town of Wolfeboro.

Portsmouth Country Club

1 Country Club Lane, Portsmouth, NH 03840; phone (603) 436-9719
Tees: Championship: 7,050 yards, par-72, USGA rating 74.1, slope 127
Greens Fee: $40–50

Challenge: ★★★★	Golf Facilities: ★★★★½
Variety: ★★★★	14-Club Test: ★★★
Terrain: ★★★½	Intangibles: ★★★★
Beauty/Visual Appeal: ★★★★	Value: ★★★★
Pace of Play: ★★★★	

Description and Comments   Long considered one of the finest courses in the state, this design by Robert Trent Jones Sr. and Frank Duane favors big hitters. Low rough and large greens soften the long trek, which can be as much as 7,068 yards. Opened in 1957, this par-72 layout is also one of the prettiest golf courses anywhere because a stretch of holes on the back nine wanders along the shore of beautiful Great Bay. The 12th is a long par-4 out to Pierce's Point with the prevailing wind smack in one's face. A deceptive par-3 follows—it's a full club longer than you'd expect—and then a shortish par-5 wraps around the bay. Understandably, this club has hosted many top state events and helped produce one of the LPGA's all-time greats, Jane Blalock. Other amenities include a driving range, putting green, and a brand-new restaurant/lounge facility. Greens-fee players must call in advance to reserve a tee time, but they expect few openings on the weekend. Portsmouth CC just might have the finest pro shop in New England. After golf, consider heading into Portsmouth for some seafood at the Ferry Landing on the Ceres Street Wharf, which is run by the Blalock family.

Ragged Mountain Golf Course

R.R. 1, Box 106E, Ragged Mountain Road, Danbury, NH 03230; phone (603) 768-3300
Tees: Championship: 7,059 yards, par-72, USGA rating 75.0, slope 151
Greens Fee: $29–49

Challenge: ★★★★★ Golf Facilities: ★★★

Variety: ★★★½ 14-Club Test: ★★★½

Terrain: ★★★½ Intangibles: ★★★

Beauty/Visual Appeal: ★★★ Value: ★★★½

Pace of Play: ★★★

Description and Comments Remember the craze to build longer and hideously difficult courses? This course should remind you. A whopping 7,059 yards off the two-diamond tees, this creation by New England pro golfer Jeff Julian "boasts" the highest slope rating in New Hampshire: 151. Like the Bacardi 151 you barely survived in college, this one should be approached with severe caution. We recommend one of the sets of tees, the one-diamond, a very reasonable challenge for the proficient golfer at 6,482 yards, and the blue tees suitable to those short but straight hitters. The high challenge is due primarily to forced carries over wetlands. Equally influential is the terrain, which includes flat stretches with deceiving distances and hilly areas requiring adjustments in club selection. A new course of the granite landscape, it is destined to become a must-play for those who dare.

Shattuck Inn Golf Course

28 Jaffrey Rd., Jaffrey, NH 03452; phone (603) 532-4300

Tees: Championship: 6,701 yards, par-71, USGA rating 74.1, slope 145

Greens Fee: $35

Challenge: ★★★★★ Golf Facilities: ★★★

Variety: ★★★★ 14-Club Test: ★★★★

Terrain: ★★★★ Intangibles: ★★

Beauty/Visual Appeal: ★★★★½ Value: ★★★½

Pace of Play: ★★★

Description and Comments So you think you're pretty good, eh? Well, be prepared to leave your crushed ego on these fairways along with all the others. The Shattuck Inn Golf Course came along back in the 1980s when it was fashionable—who knows why?—to build "target" golf courses where any misplay was severely punished. This is New Hampshire's edition courtesy of architect Brian Silva. It's not all bad news, however. The course is well known for its superb conditioning and technically sound architecture. But one cannot dispel the thought that if every course had the severity of this one, no one would play the game. Yep, the slope rating off the back is an overbearing 145 and it "tumbles" only to 140 off the middle tees. This 6,701-yard brute passes through rugged forest and past boulders, bunkers, and wetlands. No fewer than 16 holes have water in play. Even so, this monster at the base of Mount Monadnock is worth playing if only to confirm one's antipathy for nouveau course architecture, which has, thankfully, already become passé. Then again, if you're a low-handicapper looking for an outstanding challenge, you've come to the right place. Walking is permitted. The slope of 145 was the highest in the state until upstart Ragged Mountain came along, but we think someone's math is off. This is still the sternest test of golf in the Granite State.

A Maine Sampler

Belgrade Lakes Golf Club

West Road, Belgrade Lakes, ME 04918; phone (207) 495-4653
Tees: Championship: 6,629 yards, par-71, USGA rating 71.6, slope 142
Greens Fee: $38–75

Challenge: ★★★★
Variety: ★★★★½
Terrain: ★★★★
Beauty/Visual Appeal: ★★★★½
Pace of Play: ★★★★★

Golf Facilities: ★★★½
14-Club Test: ★★★½
Intangibles: ★★★★½
Value: ★★★★★

Description and Comments   Wow, is Sugarloaf in for a run as the best course in Maine now that Belgrade Lakes has opened. Designed by Clive Clark, a former Ryder Cup player and BBC golf commentator, this course takes full advantage of a number of dramatic elevations to provide both an excellent test of golf and stunning views of Long and Great Ponds as well as the distant mountains. Despite its youth, the course has fully matured fairways because the local owner had them fully sodded. In true British style, the layout has a double green, this one shared by the 9th and 18th holes. Atypically, the architect stretched huge piles of glistening granite rocks to form "island" fairways; the effect is similar to the dark lava fields at Mauna Lani in Hawaii, but this being Maine, the rough resembles a crowd of pine trees packed together as tightly as commuters on a New York City subway platform.

That metaphor is appropriate, for Belgrade Lakes is something of a "commuter" golf course. The accommodations in this area are primarily summer camps and the odd bed-and-breakfast. The nearby state capital, Augusta, is a snooze, so stay down in the Portland area if you must and commute to play a course where walking is actually encouraged, caddies are available, and the tee times are 15 minutes apart. They call the experience at Belgrade Lakes "pure golf," and it's hard to argue with them.

The Bethel Inn & Country Club

Broad Street, Bethel, ME 04217; phone (800) 654-0125 or (207) 824-2175

Tees: Championship: 6,663 yards, par-72, USGA rating 72.3, slope 133
Greens Fee: $26–33

Challenge: ★★★	Golf Facilities: ★★½
Variety: ★★★	14-Club Test: ★★★½
Terrain: ★★★½	Intangibles: ★★★★
Beauty/Visual Appeal: ★★★½	Value: ★★★★
Pace of Play: ★★	

Description and Comments   This golf resort has none of the pretension or beehive ambience that plagues so many golf destinations. The inn itself is the picture of elegant country lodging where a hearty breakfast prepares you for a tour of the truly old-fashioned golf course. The essence of old New England is found right away at the third, where the tee shot is over the 150-year-old mill pond to a small green. Quite a few of the greens are small, but remember, this isn't a long course. Big hitters aren't entirely frustrated, however. The 5th is a fine par-5 that will reward anyone who assumes the risk of missing the fairway left into the woods. If you're looking for a nice laid-back vacation with a little golf, some tennis, and a moment or two in the gym, this place is perfect. If your golf vacation is more about tackling and subduing some "name course," go someplace else.

Dunegrass Golf Club

P.O. Box 325, Wild Dunes Way, Old Orchard Beach, ME 04064; phone (800) 521-1029 or (207) 934-4513

Tees: Championship: 6,515 yards, par-71, USGA rating 69.5, slope 126
Greens Fee: $45–65

Challenge: ★★★	Golf Facilities: ★★★★½
Variety: ★★★★	14-Club Test: ★★★★
Terrain: ★★★½	Intangibles: ★★★★
Beauty/Visual Appeal: ★★★★	Value: ★★★★
Pace of Play: ★★★	

Description and Comments   Previously, New Englanders had to travel to the Carolinas to play a Dan Maples design, but now they can head just down the coast from Portland to the beach town of Old Orchard Beach to play what is quickly becoming regarded as one of the best courses in southern Maine. Six sets of tees let you wander through this woodland—you didn't really expect the sandhills of Ballybunion here, did you?—at any distance from 4,846 to 6,515 yards. The young course opened in 1998, but has already earned a reputation for having superb greens. This is a spikeless facility. Well-conditioned and with plenty of tilt, they require you to stay below the pins if you're to have any chance of a good score. Five par-3s contribute to an overall par of 71. The last of these one-shotters is the 17th, which features an island green. It is followed by a terrific par-5 where you will need three shots to get home. These last two holes will convince you that Dunegrass is one of the few tracks that truly deserves the compliment, "It's a shot maker's course." The club has plenty of nice touches, including bentgrass fairways and greens as well as sprinkler heads with yardages to the front, middle and back of each green. The practice facility is the best in southern Maine. Tee reservations can be made up to seven days in advance. Golf packages can be arranged with the help of the Pro Shop, which is run by Ann McClure, Maine's only female head professional. Her pro shop is well stocked and located in one of the best yet most unpretentious clubhouses in the northeast.

Kebo Valley Golf Club

Eagle Lake Road, Bar Harbor, ME 04609; phone (207) 288-5000
Tees: Championship: 6,131 yards, par-70, USGA rating 69.0, slope 130
Greens Fee: $25–50

Challenge: ★★★	Golf Facilities: ★★★
Variety: ★★★½	14-Club Test: ★★★½
Terrain: ★★★★	Intangibles: ★★★★½
Beauty/Visual Appeal: ★★★★½	Value: ★★★½
Pace of Play: ★★★½	

Description and Comments Vacationing golfers have been journeying to Kebo Valley since 1888; that's right, well over a hundred years! Golf history buffs know that it was originally laid out by H. C. Leeds and it is now the eighth-oldest course in America. It's hardly outdated, however. The 6,131-yard layout has been sloped at a hefty 130 and played host to the Maine Amateur Championship as recently as 1998. Nevertheless, the course has its share of old-time characteristics: A grass bunker surrounds the 3rd green, and a blind shot third-shot awaits anyone more than 150 yards from the par-5 5th's green. The 13th fairway has "chocolate drops," small grass-covered mounds under which the architect had unwanted stones buried; you've been on a real New England track when you've been in the chocolate drops. You've played better golf than President William H. Taft if you score better than a 27 on the uphill, par-4 17th, too.

Located on Mount Desert Island, the course has terrific views of the area's peaks, all of which appear much taller than inland mountains because they rise virtually from sea level. The course has ready access to one of the east coast's greatest natural treasures, Acadia National Park, a wonderland of hiking trails, mountain streams, and wildlife managed by the National

Park Service. The area's "capital," Bar Harbor, is the quintessential Maine seaport. And by the way, it's pronounced "Baa Haabaa," no Rs.

The Ledges Golf Course

One Ledges Drive, York, ME 03909; phone (207) 351-3000
Tees: Championship: 6,981 yards, par-72, USGA rating 74.3, slope 144
Greens Fee: $35–65

Challenge: ★★★½	Golf Facilities: ★★½
Variety: ★★★★	14-Club Test: ★★★
Terrain: ★★★★	Intangibles: ★★★
Beauty/Visual Appeal: ★★★★	Value: ★★★★
Pace of Play: ★★★	

Description and Comments The lovely colonial town of York has long been a frustration to golfers: The local private club has a wonderful Donald Ross course. Ah, but now vacationers have a sensational new course to play designed by a genuine Mainer—no, they're not called Maniacs—the talented W. Bradley Booth. His creation here is new, so don't expect pristine conditions, but you can expect a clever layout through some rolling, granite-dotted woodlands that is pure Maine. You'll find four sets of tees that stretch the challenge from 4,988 to 6,981 yards. Some of the yardage is murky because the holes frequently rely on elevation changes. Your ability to take an extra club and subtract one is key here. This is extremely important at the 8th where the tee sits nearly 60 feet above and 200 yards from a green virtually surrounded by water. What sets this course apart from many others is that Booth has left ample driving areas, so hit your driver as often as you like. He also provided fairly large greens, but you must be on the proper level to score well. That's sound golf, and given the beauty of this course, it's just a matter of time until its reputation extends far beyond New England.

You cannot leave town without seeing Nubble Lighthouse, one of the most photographed coastal facilities in the world. It's picture-postcard pretty. And if you love to body surf, visit the beach immediately south of it, known as Long Sands. The water's a bit cool, but the visitors from Quebec don't seem to mind.

Sable Oaks Golf Course

505 Country Club Dr., South Portland, ME 04106; phone (207) 775-6257
Tees: Championship: 6,359 yards, par-70, USGA rating 71.8, slope 134

Greens Fee: $23–29

Challenge: ★★★½	Golf Facilities: ★★★★
Variety: ★★★★	14-Club Test: ★★★
Terrain: ★★★★	Intangibles: ★★★
Beauty/Visual Appeal: ★★★½	Value: ★★★½
Pace of Play: ★★★	

Just the Facts   Okay, this is the best course in Maine that no one talks about. We know why: It's a public course that presents a bit more challenge than the average golfer is up to. By challenge we mean course management. Most of us aren't very good at that, are we (be honest)? So, more than a few golfers walk away from Sable Oaks without a lot of good things to say. More likely than not, that's their own fault. This narrow, tree-lined, and often hilly course by Geoffrey Cornish and Brian Silva is no place to bang your driver off every tee, shoot at every pin, and charge every putt. Calm yourself and you'll discover that this is a very fair course that's well worth playing. Most memorable is the long par-4 12th, which fortunately plays steeply downhill and enjoys spectacular views of both the White Mountains of New Hampshire and the surrounding Maine landscape.

This public course hosts lots of outings, so try to get out early. Bring an extra sleeve of balls, too. After playing, be sure to head into the Olde Port section of downtown Portland for some great bars and restaurants. Consider a night out at Hadlock Field for some low-cost, entertaining, AA baseball played by the Portland Sea Dogs (Florida Marlins affiliate). If you're absolutely starving, you can gorge yourself at the Old Country Buffet in the Maine Mall for a low fixed price.

The course sits atop the Marriott and AmeriSuites hotels and is a two iron's toss away from the Sheraton Tara and the local Days Inn, yet no local hotel offers golf packages. Go figure.

A Cape Cod Sampler

Blue Rock Golf Course

48 Todd Rd., South Yarmouth, MA 02664; phone (504) 398-9295

Tees: Championship: 1,962 yards, par-54, USGA rating 56.4, slope 83

Greens Fee: $24–29

Challenge: ★★★	Golf Facilities: ★★★★
Variety: ★★★	14-Club Test: ★★½
Terrain: ★★	Intangibles: ★★★½
Beauty/Visual Appeal: ★★★	Value: ★★★½
Pace of Play: ★★★	

Description and Comments It's a mystery, really, why the world doesn't have more par-3 courses. Think about it, you should be able to hit all the greens in regulation (usually with an iron), you get to chip and putt just as often as on a regulation course, the walk is shorter, and the time to play is shorter. Sounds great, doesn't it? Well, it does if every par-3 course were as imaginative and well maintained as this one. The holes are as short as 103 yards and as long as 247 yards, and they reveal one of golf's truisms: The greens are the heart of any layout. These come in all shapes and sizes. Unfortunately, they are always slow, so rap the ball into the back of the cup or you'll be very, very frustrated at the end. If you're still unconvinced about this course consider that Francis Ouimet, Patty Berg, Dave Marr, Betsy King, Beth Daniel, and Pat Bradley are just a few of golf's luminaries who have taken on its challenge. (The course record is only five under par!) Give it a chance and you'll be impressed while at the same time watching the junior golfer in the family have a much better time than on a longer course where the greens are out of reach.

Captains Golf Courses

1000 Freeman's Way, Brewster, MA 02631; phone (508) 896-5100
Tees: Championship: 1,985 yards, par-72, USGA rating 72.7, slope 130
Greens Fee: $25–40

Challenge: ★★★½	Golf Facilities: ★★★★½
Variety: ★★★★	14-Club Test: ★★★★
Terrain: ★★★★½	Intangibles: ★★★★
Beauty/Visual Appeal: ★★★½	Value: ★★★★
Pace of Play: ★★★	

Description and Comments Opened in 1985 to much acclaim, America's leading golf publication called Captains the nation's "Best New Course" that year. It is well worth a visit, if only to learn about the legendary sea captains for whom each hole is named. It sports the quintessential look, feel, and design of what has become known as nouveau Cape Cod architecture. It's a delightful melding of sandy terrain, scrub pine, and modest elevation changes with multiple tee boxes and raised and (artificially) humped greens. The layout bears the strong imprint of its architects, Canadian-born and New England stalwart Geoffrey Cornish and his clever partner, Brian Silva, both of whom deserve enormous credit for elevating the state of golf in the region. You'll especially love the contrast of the downhill par-3 11th with the back-breaking 13th, a 426-yard two-shotter, and the 14th, the toughest par-5. A second 18-hole course has recently opened, although it's too new to have been reviewed for this edition. Both courses are virtual next-door neighbors to the Ocean Edge Resort.

Cranberry Valley Golf Course

183 Oak St., Harwich, MA 02645; phone (508) 430-7560

Tees: Championship: 6,745 yards, par-72, USGA rating 71.9, slope 129

Greens Fee: $35–45

Challenge: ★★★	Golf Facilities: ★★★½
Variety: ★★★½	14-Club Test: ★★★½
Terrain: ★★★½	Intangibles: ★★★
Beauty/Visual Appeal: ★★★½	Value: ★★★½
Pace of Play: ★★★	

Description and Comments   Of all the fine municipal courses to have emerged on Cape Cod over the past 25 years, Cranberry Valley is consistently regarded as the number one or two pick by visitors. Its holes blend naturally with the terrain, and that's a tribute to its designer, Geoffrey Cornish. It is perhaps best known for its fine doglegs: some long, some short, but all adorned with clever fairway bunkering to challenge appropriately. Cornish is a minimalist, choosing common sense over flamboyance. For example, short par-4s have small greens, not horrific hazards; long holes have wide fairways and play downwind, not the opposite. If the course has a quirk, it's the double-dogleg, par-5 18th that frustrates long hitters by a stand of trees to shut out the second shot. You can always count on Cranberry Valley being in top condition. The driving range is both ample in size and stocked with clean, relatively new balls. If only every range served its customers with such basic essentials. Alas, if only the town fathers would put in a 19th hole to better serve the public! Head professional Dennis Hoye deserves credit for maintaining a staff with a high level of friendly service, something out-of-town golfers will surely appreciate.

Dennis Golf Club

Dennis Highlands

825 Old Bass River Rd., Dennis, MA 02638; phone (508) 385-8698

Tees: Championship: 6,464 yards, par-71, USGA rating 70.4, slope 118

Greens Fee: $35–40

Challenge: ★★½	Golf Facilities: ★★★★
Variety: ★★★★	14-Club Test: ★★★
Terrain: ★★★½	Intangibles: ★★★½
Beauty/Visual Appeal: ★★★	Value: ★★★½
Pace of Play: ★★½	

Dennis Pines

Golf Course Road, Dennis, MA 02641; phone (508) 395-9826

Tees: Championship: 7,029 yards, par-72, USGA rating 71.9, slope 127

Greens Fee: $20–40

Challenge: ★★★½	Golf Facilities: ★★★★½
Variety: ★★★★	14-Club Test: ★★★½
Terrain: ★★★	Intangibles: ★★★½
Beauty/Visual Appeal: ★★★	Value: ★★★★
Pace of Play: ★★½	

Description and Comments The town of Dennis sports a pair of fine courses, each providing its own challenges and own appeal. The elder, Dennis Pines (1965), is a 7,029-yard track routed through a thick forest of pine trees. That means tight fairways throughout and a premium on well-placed shots. Water is in play on four holes, and the 12th, a 518-yarder, is one of the most difficult anywhere.

Dennis Highlands gets its name from the high ground it occupies. It's not the sort of high ground that's going to impress someone from the Green Mountain state (Vermont), but it provides plenty of uneven lies. Those difficulties are tempered somewhat by the course's par (71) and reasonable length (6,464 yards). Designed by Jack Kidwell and Mike Hurdzan, it has received rave reviews since its opening in 1984. Its practice range is one of the best on the Cape.

The administrators of these two fine courses should be applauded for adopting the sensible R&A rule that stones in bunkers may be removed without penalty. If you give it a moment's thought, you'll realize that the USGA rating cares less about your expensive clubs (and perhaps the health of your wrists) than their British cousins, who could hardly be accused of thumbing their collective noses at the game's traditions.

Farm Neck Golf Club

Farm Neck Way, Martha's Vineyard, Oak Bluffs, MA 02557; phone (508) 693-3057

Tees: Championship: 6,777 yards, par-72, USGA rating 72.1, slope 129

Greens Fee: $35–75

Challenge: ★★★	Golf Facilities: ★★★
Variety: ★★★½	14-Club Test: ★★★½
Terrain: ★★★½	Intangibles: ★★★★
Beauty/Visual Appeal: ★★★★½	Value: ★★★
Pace of Play: ★★½	

Description and Comments Technically not on Cape Cod at all, Farm Neck is the golf course on Martha's Vineyard, which has long been a summer haven for wealthy New Englanders and New Yorkers. The Vineyard is a treasure trove of elegantly rustic architecture: white clapboard homes, all-black shutters, and porches adorned with rockers and pots of bright red geraniums. The island is a must-see for anyone looking to find the pace of a prewar America. That lazy summer feel carries over to the golf course where, believe it or not, they'll actually let you walk and carry your bag. Recreation and exercise—what a concept! While the publicity of a presidential visit in 1993 has made tee times a bit more scarce, recent changes by architect Brian Silva have made the course more playable. What it lacks in length (6,777 yards) it makes up in treacherous rough and challenging greens (slope 129). Every hole, or so it seems, is a beautiful picture postcard.

The front 9 is relatively tight, whereas the back side is more open but longer. Saltwater ponds, meadows dotted with wild flowers, and a vast array of birds are all components of the Farm Neck experience. Farm Neck is a treat for mid- to high-handicappers not only visually but from a playability standpoint, as landing areas are reasonably wide and there are few forced carries off the tees or into the greens. A humorous local rule allows you to replace your ball "if moved or stolen by a seagull."

Lodging in Vermont

EXPENSIVE

The Equinox

Route 7A, Manchester Village, VT 05254; phone (800) 362-4747 or (802) 362-4700; www.equinoxresort.com; Rates: $170–270 (hotel rooms), $390 (townhomes)

Dating back to 1769, the Equinox is a grand resort located on 1,000 acres of beautiful surroundings filled with a variety of activities. The rooms in the main hotel tend to be small, but the newer townhomes offer a larger, more modern alternative. Oddly enough, its decor reflects the resort's enormously rich fishing heritage. Some of the best trout fishing in the world is done below the golf course in the Battenkill River. Guests can learn the finer points of fly fishing at the world-famous Orvis Fly Fishing School and also visit the nearby American Museum of Fly Fishing.

Besides access to The Gleneagle Course, other sporting activities include the British School of Falconery and the Land Rover Driving School. In addition, the resort features pools, sauna, steam room, tennis courts, croquet, health club, horseback riding, fishing, hiking, biking, and easy access to nearby outlet shopping. A half mile away, the village of Manchester is overrun with upscale factory outlets (Armani, Brooks Bros., London Fog, etc.).

Golf Packages   Package includes two nights accommodation, unlimited golf, sleeve of golf balls, club storage, Equinox golf shirt, use of spa.

1811 House

Box 39, Route 7A, Manchester, VT 05254; phone (800) 432-1811 or (802) 362-1811; Rates: $110–210

An English country home surrounded by three acres of beautifully land-scaped grounds. Rooms feature antiques, and many have fireplaces. Worth noting is The Robinson's Room, which has a marvelous bathroom. Full breakfast and access to tennis included.

Inn at Ormsby Hill

Box 3264, Route 7A, Manchester, VT 05255; phone (800) 670-2841 or (802) 362-1163; Rates: $140–230

Once a place of refuge for Ethan Allen and a stop on the Underground Railroad, this inn today is filled with antiques with many of the public and private rooms having fireplaces. Request a room that has a view of the Green or Taconic Mountains.

Kedron Valley Inn

Route 106, South Woodstock, VT 05071; (800) 836-1193 or (802) 457-1473; www.bbonline.com/vt/kedronvalley; Rates: $120–230

Kedron is one of the state's oldest inns and has been operating nearly 170 years. It has 26 rooms, which are all very quaint; many have either a fireplace or a Franklin stove. The back motel is more rustic than the front with its log cabin walls, but both are decorated in a similar manner.

One big appeal of Kedron for the golfing set is that it provides access to the nearby Quechee Club—an otherwise private course. Additionally, the inn has a pond and a beach on its 15 acres. (See Dining for details.)

Quechee Lakes Rentals

Route 4, P.O. Box 385, Quechee, VT 05059; phone (888) 654-9560 or (802) 295-7225; www.pbpub.com/quecheelakes/index.html; Rates: $315–375

A private resort community where guests can rent condos and homes at the 5,500-acre development. Besides access to the coveted Quechee Club, Quechee Lakes offers tennis (15 courts), horseback riding, a polo field, pools, a pond, a 50-acre lake with boating, racquetball, a health club, and hiking along the Appalachian Trail, which cuts through the development.

Topnotch at Stowe

4000 Mountain Rd., Stowe, VT 05672; phone (800) 451-8686 or (802) 253-8585; www.topnotch-resort.com/spa; Rates: $210–280 (hotel), $300–625 (townhomes)

A 120-acre resort located in the Stowe Mountains with 92 rooms and 15 kitchen townhomes. An impressive lobby with floor-to-ceiling windows, a circular stone fireplace, and a cathedral ceiling that set the tone for the whole resort. Amenities include: pools, tennis courts, health club, horseback riding, as well as a complimentary full breakfast.

Trapp Family Lodge

42 Trapp Hill Dr., Stowe, VT 05672; phone (800) 826-7000 or (802) 253-8511; www.trappfamily.com; Rates: $145–220

Owned and operated by the Von Trapp family made famous in The Sound of Music, who decided to settle in Stowe after fleeing Austria. The lodge features 73 rooms in the main lodge and 20 rooms in the lower lodge as well as 100 guest houses. Beyond the buildings lies some beautiful scenery with acres of pastures and panoramic views of the local mountains. In the summer, the lodge hosts a series of outdoor music performances. The only drawback to the resort is that it does attract a number of tourists who visit for novelty's sake. Gym, sauna, lawn games, and hiking trails also located at the resort.

Woodstock Inn & Resort

14 The Green, Warren, VT 05091; phone (800) 448-7900 or (802) 457-1100; www.woodstockinn.com; Rates: $160–300

Woodstock Inn was originally constructed by Laurance Rockefeller, grandson of John D. Rockefeller, and features 144 rooms all decorated with specially designed furniture and homemade quilts. Guests have access to the Woodstock Country Club and other activities at the resort include a 40,000-square-foot fitness center, indoor tennis courts, racquetball courts, pools, saunas, squash, croquet, and children's programs. Also, there is nearby hiking, biking, horseback riding, canoeing, and fishing. See Dining in Vermont for information on the restaurant. It's one of the top-rated hotels in the country and justly so.

Golf Package   The Green Mountain Weekend Golf Plan: Two nights accommodations, three days of unlimited golf (cart extra), breakfast and dinner daily, club storage, one bucket of range balls, and a gift from the pro shop.

MODERATE

Manchester Highlands

Highland Avenue, Manchester, VT 05255; phone (800) 743-4565 or (802) 362-4565; www.highlandsinn.com; Rates: $85–105

An 1898 inn that offers guests very nice attention to details—most rooms have a rocking chair and a featherbed. Turret and Tower Rooms are the most romantic.

Battenkill Inn

Route 7A, Sunderland, VT 05254; phone (800) 441-1628 or (802) 362-4213; Rates: $75–135

A quaint inn located in an 1840 Victorian home filled with antiques.

Some rooms have fireplaces and balconies. Complimentary breakfast and afternoon refreshments.

Edson Hill Manor

1500 Edson Hill Rd., Stowe, VT 05672; phone (800) 621-0284 or (802) 253-7371; Rates: $95–130

Situated atop 225 acres of rolling terrain, Edson Hill was built in 1940 and features a French-Canadian architectural style. Small in size with only 25 rooms, Edson offers guests handsome rooms including fireplaces and canopy beds. Additionally, the resort has a pool, hiking, and horseback riding.

Stowe/Snowdrift

2043 Mountain Rd., Stowe, VT 05672; phone (800) 829-7629 or (802) 253-7629; www.stoweinfo.com/saa/stowe/hotel; Rates: $85–115

Located on 16 acres, this is a well-priced lodging option for the area. There are 58 units, 28 with kitchens. There also is tennis, lawn games, bicycles, pools, whirlpool, as well as impressive views of the nearby mountains.

Sugarbush Resort

Sugarbush Access Road, Warren VT 05674; phone (800) 537-8427 or (802) 583-2301; www.sugarbush.com; Rates: $90–400

A condo complex that varies in size from singles to much larger units. Amenities, such as fireplaces and balconies, vary between condos. Access to tennis courts, exercise equipment, and sauna.

Golf Packages   Available—contact resort for details.

Quechee Bed and Breakfast

753 Woodstock Rd., Quechee, VT 05059; phone (802) 295-1776; Rates: $95–140

An eight-room B&B located in a building dating back to 1795. Try to request one of the four rooms that overlook the Ottauquechee River.

Sugarbush Village

Sugarbush Access Road, Warren, VT 05674; phone (800) 451-4326 or (802) 583-3000; www.madriver.com; Rates: $90–$330

A condo complex that offers lodges with one to five bedrooms. Units come with refrigerators and some have microwaves, fireplaces, patios and balconies.

INEXPENSIVE

Brittany Inn

Route 7A, Manchester Center, VT 05255; phone (802) 362-1033; Rates: $59–64; Built: 1958; Renovated: 1997

Eyrie

U.S. 7 and Bowen Hill Road, East Dorset, VT 05253; phone (888) 397-4388 or (802) 362-1208; Rates: $65–85; Built: 1969; Renovated: 1998

Buccaneer Country Lodge

3214 Mountain Rd., Stowe, VT 05672; phone (800) 543-1293 or (802) 253-4772; www.stoweinfo.com/buccaneer; Rates: $75–100; Built: 1958; Renovated: 1991

Innsbruck Inn

Mt. Mansfield Road, Stowe, VT 05672; phone (800) 225-8582 or (802) 253-8582; Rates: $65–80; Built: 1974; Renovated: 1998

Golden Lion Riverside Inn

Route 100, Warren, VT 05674; phone (802) 496-3084; Rates: $55–85; Built: 1976; Renovated: 1998

Braeside

P.O. Box 411, Woodstock, VT 05091; phone (802) 457-1366; Rates: $50–90; Built: 1979; Renovated: 1999

Dining in Vermont

Barrows House Box 98, Route 30, Dorset; phone (800) 639-1620 or (802) 867-4455. Continental; Expensive; Reservations suggested. Located in a historic building dating to 1796. Specialties include rack of lamb and crab cakes.

Bistro Henry's Route 11 and 30, Manchester; phone (802) 362-4982. Mediterranean; Inexpensive–Moderate; Reservations accepted. A menu that features a variety of Mediterranean dishes, including lamb shank and sweetbreads.

Chantecleer Route 7A, East Dorset; phone (802) 362-1616. Continental & Swiss; Expensive; Reservations suggested. Menu reflects the Swiss-born chef.

The Colonnade (located in The Equinox), Route 7A, Manchester Village; phone (800) 362-4747 or (802) 362-4700. American; Moderate–Expensive; Reservations recommended. A more relaxed alternative to Marsh.

Marsh Tavern (located in The Equinox), Route 7A, Manchester Village; phone (800) 362-4747 or (802) 362-4700. American; Expensive; Reservations required. "Very Vermont"—country setting with a variety of down-home dishes.

Quality Restaurant Main Street, Manchester; phone (802) 362-9839. American; Inexpensive; Reservations accepted. Building was the inspiration for Norman Rockwell's War News painting. Everything here from meatloaf to salmon.

Edson Hill Manor 1500 Edson Hill Rd., Stowe; phone (800) 621-0284 or (802) 253-7371. Continental; Expensive; Reservations recommended. Terrific atmosphere and an eclectic menu combine to make this a top dining spot—pan-seared salmon caught our eye.

Foxfire Inn Route 100, Stowe; phone (802) 253-4887. Italian; Inexpensive; Reservations accepted. Located in an old farmhouse, this restaurant features mouth-watering dishes, including veal rollatini.

Isle de France Mountain Road, Stowe; phone (802) 253-7751. French; Expensive; Reservations accepted. Elegant dining in a formal setting with a variety of French dishes. Specialties of the house include lobster Newberg and Dover sole.

Whisker Mountain Road, Stowe; phone (802) 253-8996. Seafood; Moderate; Reservations accepted. Tasty seafood entrees are the specialty at this restaurant located in an old farmhouse—outdoor and greenhouse seating available.

Bass Sugarbush Access Road, Warren; phone (802) 583-3100. Continental; Moderate; Reservations accepted. Beautiful views of the mountains add a lot of spice at this three-tiered restaurant. Specialties include fresh seafood and steak.

Bentley's 3 Elm St., Woodstock; phone (802) 457-3232. American; Inexpensive; Reservations accepted. Popular with locals and visitors alike, featuring everything from hamburgers to pasta.

The Common Man German Flats Road, Warren; phone (802) 583-2800. International; Moderate–Expensive; Reservations accepted. Located in a mid-1800s barn with a menu that features some unique items, including rabbit and escargots.

Eagle Café Woodstock Inn, 14 The Green, Warren; phone (800) 448-7900 or (802) 457-1100. American; Moderate; Reservations suggested. A more casual alternative at the resort serving breakfast, lunch, and dinner.

Kedron Valley Inn Route 106, South Woodstock; phone (800) 836-1193 or (802) 457-1473. Continental; Expensive; Reservations accepted. Candlelight and a fireplace set the mood in this romantic, cozy dining room. Many of the ingredients come from the inn's own or nearby gardens. Specialties include confit of duck and seafood in puff pastry.

Woodstock Inn Dining Room 14 The Green, Warren; phone (800) 448-7900 or (802) 457-1100. Continental; Expensive; Reservations recommended. An elegant setting, jackets are strongly suggested for men; includes expansive menu and wine list. Known for their Sunday brunch.

Activities in Vermont

American Museum of Fly Fishing   Corner of Route 7A and Seminary Avenue, Manchester; phone (802) 362-3300. If you are a fly fishing fan, this is the place for you. Includes collection of memorabilia and a look at famous participants.

Bennington Battle Monument   15 Monument Ave., Bennington; phone (802) 477-0550. A 306-foot-tall obelisk commemorating General Stark's victory over the British, who were trying to capture Bennington's supplies. Elevator to top of monument provides memorable view.

Emerald Lake State Park   Six miles north on U.S. 7, North Dorset; phone (802) 362-1655. 430-acre park with swimming, hiking, fishing, and boating.

Factory outlet stores   Located along Vermont Highways 11, 30, and 7A.

Historic Hildene   Two miles south on Route 7A, Manchester Village; phone (802) 362-1788. Home of Robert Todd Lincoln (Abraham Lincoln's son). Visitors can tour the 24-room Georgian mansion, the carriage barn, and the formal gardens via nature trails.

Southern Vermont Art Center   One mile north off West Road, Manchester; phone (802) 362-1405. Painting and sculptures.

Mt. Mansfield Gondola   Vermont 108, North of Stowe Village. An eight-passenger gondola that takes riders to the top of Vermont's highest peak.

Mt. Mansfield State Forest   A 38,000-acre forest with a variety of activity options including hiking, swimming, fishing, and boating. There are three recreation areas including Smugglers Notch (phone (802) 253-4014) and Underhill (phone (802) 899-3022).

Trapp Family Concerts   42 Trapp Hill Dr., Stowe; phone (800) 826-7000 or (802) 253-8511. Summer concert series held at lodge (see section above) featuring classical performances (June through mid-August).

The Billings Farm and Museum   Route 12 and River Road, P.O. Box 489, Woodstock; phone (802) 457-2355. A working dairy that dates back to 1860. Included on the tour: Queen Anne farmhouse, general store, and school.

Marsh-Billings Rockefeller National Historic Park   P.O. Box 178, 54 Elm St., Woodstock; phone (802) 457-2355 or (802) 457-3368. Site includes one of America's oldest planned and managed woodlands, as well as the Billings-Rockefeller mansion featuring an extensive art collection.

Plymouth Notch Historic District Route 100-A, Plymouth Notch. A step back in time—the hometown of Calvin Coolidge is considered one of the best preserved presidential birthplaces in the country.

Sugarbush Sports Center Sugarbush Village; phone (802) 583-2391. Center features pools, whirlpools, steam rooms, saunas, massage, gym, tennis courts, racquetball, and squash.

The 19th Hole in Vermont

Dormie Grill Located at the Equinox golf course. Perfect place to unwind after your round; bar overlooks the golf course.

Richardson's Tavern Located at Woodstock Inn. Relaxing old-fashioned bar featuring porch with rocking chairs.

Lodging in New Hampshire

EXPENSIVE

The Balsams Grand Resort Hotel

Route 26, Dixville Notch, NH 03576-9710; phone (800) 255-0600 or (603) 255-3400; www.thebalsams.com; Rates $230–245

The Balsams takes some effort to get to—it is located only 12 miles south of the Canadian border —but is well worth the effort. Built in 1866, The Balsams is a 15,000-acre resort that features sensational scenery and wonderful amenities and is a premiere site for a family vacation. Rooms tend to be small but well appointed—the best rooms are the Tower Suites if you can afford the price tag (if you are coming in the summer make sure to book early, as the resort fills up quickly).

For all its apparent opulence, The Balsams is elegant without being pretentious. The staff is genuinely friendly, and not the least interested in rushing anyone. This is no golf factory. Quite to the contrary, The Balsams would exist just fine without golf, thank you, having been selected a Historic Hotel of America for maintaining its historical character and architectural integrity. An example is the lack of air conditioning, something rather impractical at its altitude and latitude. Each room has a fan, and this being New Hampshire, guests sleep with the windows open and wake to the chirping of robins, blue jays, and mourning doves.

The Balsams is home to the Panorama Course, but the resort is about much more than golf. The activities board in the lobby is filled with everything from arts-and-crafts lessons by local artisans to three-on-three basketball games. Only the comatose miss the other ongoing activities: badminton, bocce, tennis (all-weather and clay), shuffle board, sand volleyball, and a swim in the heated pool. Some go on short excursions to The Flume or The

Cascade. Others merely cross the road and climb to Table Rock, a flat precipice from which golfers have been known to hit balls into Lake Gloriette, some 700 feet below. Rainy weather? Go on inside and work on a jigsaw puzzle, play billiards, enter an impromptu bridge game, zap video villains, or perhaps curl up with a paperback mystery in your spacious room.

There is also an abundance of live entertainment at the Balsams, not to mention a variety of attractions, events, and movies. In the main ballroom there is a six-piece orchestra with a singer. The resort also features a variety of other acts, including a nightclub performer, a musical combo in the lounge, and a piano for evening enjoyment. Beyond the confines of The Balsams, there is mostly wilderness and parks including Beaver Brook Falls, Coleman State Park, and the Columbia Covered Bridge.

The Balsams has one other eccentricity: Guests must book the all-inclusive American plan. For golfers, this means that the price of their room includes three meals a day, unlimited use of all the recreational facilities, loads of in-house entertainment, and all the golf they want on both the 18-hole "Panorama" course and the 9-hole "Coashaukee" track, which is great for beginners but not to be considered by any golfer who takes him- or herself seriously.

Unusual in this day and age, on arriving at the resort you are assigned a table in the elegant dining room, and this is where you have all your meals. You quickly get to know your server, and vice versa, as well as those dining near you. For breakfast it is pretty standard fare, but for lunch during the summer, guests get to pick and choose from a sumptuous 100-foot long buffet. Dinner is a formal affair (jackets for men are required) with a variety of menu items that feature locally grown fresh fruits and vegetables. Reservations are essential.

When evening comes there's always time for a drink or a stroll around the beautifully landscaped grounds. And then with men nattily attired in a jacket, and women in their informal evening wear, it's off to sample a magnificent choice of American or continental cuisine prepared by chef/part-owner Phil Learned and his award-winning staff. The menu is always imaginative, and the buffet table is always near breaking.

Mount Washington Hotel & Resort

Route 302, Bretton Woods, NH 03575; phone (800) 258-0330 or (603) 278-1000; www.mtwashington.com; Rates: $210–290 (classic), $290–390 (Renaissance), $370–510 (family chamber).

After making the turn off Route 302, it is another mile up the driveway until you actually arrive at the Mount Washington Hotel. Constructed in 1902, the resort took two years and 250 people to build and is now a National Historic Landmark. The Victorian-style hotel consists of 200 tastefully decorated rooms; a 900-foot-long veranda wraps around the outside of the inn.

A day's leisure here can be as varied as the moods of the cloud-dappled mountains. Play a few sets of tennis on one of the 12 red-clay courts. The resort is one of the top 100 tennis facilities in America, so you just might want to sign up for a private lesson or clinic. Take a bracing dip in a crystal stream, or either the indoor or outdoor pool. Saddle a mount and explore the scenic bridle paths throughout the National Forest. Go mountain biking, or hiking along a wooded trail in Crawford Notch. Ride the world-famous Cog Railway to the summit of Mount Washington. But whatever you do, be sure to bring your camera!

Dinner is a formal affair—men are required to wear a jacket and tie—and patrons are served a four-course meal while being serenaded by an orchestra. There is also Stickney's restaurant for lunch on the patio level with indoor and outdoor seating and panoramic views. After dinner, the hotel offers a variety of entertainment options from which to choose: dancing and floor shows in the main dining room, jazz in the Cave Lounge, as well as other special performances throughout the season.

Golf Packages Package includes Renaissance accommodations, dinner, breakfast, unlimited golf and cart, unlimited access to tennis courts, and a private one-hour lesson daily.

MODERATE

Bretton Arms Country Inn

Route 302, Bretton Woods, NH 03575; phone (800) 258-0330 or (603) 278-1000; Rates: $90–170

The appeal of this inn, which dates back to the 1890s, is not only its quaint atmosphere but also its access to the facilities at the Mount Washington Hotel, located across the way, during the summer and the nearby Bretton Woods Motor Inn year-round. The inn consists of 31 rooms, and there is an intimate dining room (expensive) which is very popular—be sure to make your reservations as soon as you arrive.

INEXPENSIVE

Northern Comfort Inn

R.R. 1 Box 520, Colebrook, NH 03576; phone (603) 237-4440; Rates: $55–70; Built: 1950s; Renovated: 1998

Dining in New Hampshire

As most visitors to the area stay at one of the resorts, there are few additional dining options beyond the confines of the resorts. Here are two near Mount Washington.

Darby's Restaurant (located in Bretton Woods Motor Inn), Route 302, Bretton Woods; phone (603) 278-8838. Continental; Moderate–Expensive; Reservations accepted. A rustic, cozy restaurant where diners are served around a circular fireplace. Beautiful views of Presidential Range.

Fabyan's Station Route 302 at Mount Washington Hotel, Bretton Woods; phone (603) 278-2222. American; Inexpensive; No reservations needed. A hamburger and hot dog joint in a renovated railway station.

See The Balsams and Mount Washington sections under Lodging in New Hampshire for more dining information.

The 19th Hole in New Hampshire

The Cave Lounge Mount Washington Hotel. Entertainment nightly, such as jazz.

The Clubhouse Balsams Hotel. Located at the golf course; features a panoramic view.

The Conservatory Mount Washington Hotel. Great place for an after-round or a before-dinner cocktail.

Lodging in Maine

EXPENSIVE

Samoset Resort

220 Warrenton St., Rockport, ME 04856; phone (800) 341-1650 or (207) 594-0722; www.samoset.com; Rates: $100–260 (hotel), $185–380 (time-share condo)

Samoset opened in 1889 and quickly earned its reputation as Maine's premiere coastal resort. Located on Penobscot Bay, Samoset is a 230-acre resort offering guests an amazing seaside location as well as top-notch accommodations. Visitors can choose from 150 nicely appointed rooms, each with a private balcony or patio and many with a spectacular view of the environs beyond.

The hotel itself is a beautiful haven with public areas constructed almost entirely from the tawny old timbers of a deserted Portland granary. It's home to Marcel's Restaurant, the culinary center that earns high marks indeed. It's open throughout the morning and afternoon for casual dining, but it sparkles in the evening when the starched white linen is presided over by a tuxedo-clad waitstaff. Seafood is supreme with a variety of Maine lobster specialties heading the list. The wine steward is a popular person with an outstanding selection at his disposal that is staggering in number (250 or more labels) and choice (Wine Spectator has given it an award). Less elegant service is available next door in the newly refurbished Breakwater Lounge, where beer drinkers will delight at the prospect of 17 taps spewing draft beer, ale, and stout from around the world.

Activities are plentiful at Samoset with an indoor golf center, swimming, four tennis courts, fitness center, racquetball, hot tubs, massage, basketball, croquet, badminton, fishing, volleyball, bicycling, and children's activities. The rocky coast of Maine is well known for its many picturesque lighthouses and fishing villages. Nearby is the quaint town of Camden, whose sheltered bay is home to a historic schooner fleet. Lots of small shops dot the main street, and many take time to visit both the Farnsworth Art Museum and The Maine Coast Artists Gallery. In the evening one can head off to the Camden Shakespeare Theater. And here's the best tip of all: Visit during August, when Rockland hosts the Maine Lobster Festival.

Sugarloaf Inn Resort

R.R. 1, Box 5000, Carrabassett, ME 04947; phone (800) 843-5623 or (207) 237-6814; www.sugarloaf.com; Rates $95–315

Situated on the slope of Sugarloaf Mountain, this resort offers a variety of lodging options from standard rooms to deluxe rooms to condominiums. Spectacular panoramic views are what most remember about this resort, but it also has a lot of activities to offer: swimming pools, racquetball, volleyball, tennis, health spa, sauna, steam room, massage, fishing, hiking, whitewater rafting, bicycles, and lawn games.

MODERATE

Capt. Lindsey House Inn

5 Lindsey St., Rockland, ME 04841; phone (800) 523-2145 or (207) 596-7950; Rates: $95–160

Located in a home dating back to 1837, Capt. Lindsey's is a small inn that offers nine "cozy" rooms that are nicely appointed with down comforters and antiques. Breakfast served daily.

Grand Summit Resort Hotel

Route 27, R.R. 1, Box 5000, Carrabassett, ME; phone (800) 527-9879 or 202) 237-2222; www.sugarloaf.com; Rates: $100–289

Built in 1984, this resort is located at the base of the Sugarloaf Mountain and has 119 rooms, which are adequately but modestly appointed. Activities at the resort include: gym, health spa, hiking trails, fishing, racquetball, swimming, and children's activities.

INEXPENSIVE

Herbert Inn

Main Street, Kingfield, MN 04947; phone (800) 843-4372 or (207) 265-2000; www.byme.com/theherbert; Rates: $38–65; Built: 1917; Renovated: 1998

Navigator Motor Inn

520 Main St., Rockland, ME 04841; phone (800) 545-8026 or (207) 594-2131; Rates: $70–100; Built: 1979; Renovated: 1990

Dining in Maine

Double Diamond (located in Grand Summit Resort Hotel), Route 27, R.R. 1, Box 5000, Carrabassett; phone (800) 527-9879 or (202) 237-2222. Continental; Moderate; Reservations not needed. A casual dining experience in the heart of Sugarloaf Mountain featuring native Maine cuisine—of course, lobster is a specialty.

Seasons Restaurant (located in Sugarloaf Inn), R.R. 1, Box 5000, Carrabassett; phone (800) 843-5623 or (207) 237-6814. Continental; Expensive; Reservations required. A fine but relaxed restaurant offering a varied, appealing menu, and spectacular panoramic views.

Breakwater Café (located in Samoset Resort), 220 Warrenton St., Rockport; phone (800) 341-1650 or (207) 594-0722. New England; Inexpensive–Moderate; Reservations accepted. Diners can choose from complete dinners to lighter fare. Good stop for an after-dinner drink.

Clubhouse Grille (located in Samoset Resort), 220 Warrenton St., Rockport; phone (800) 341-1650 or (207) 594-0722. American; Inexpensive; Reservations not needed. A great place to grab a quick bite; serving breakfast, lunch and dinner.

Jessica's, 2 South Main St./Route 73, Rockland; phone (207) 596-0770. Continental; Moderate; Reservations accepted. Serving a variety of European dishes in four comfortable rooms in a renovated Victorian home. Chef specialties include pork Portofino and veal Zurich.

Marcels (located in Samoset Resort), 220 Warrenton St., Rockport; phone (800) 341-1650 or (207) 594-0722. Continental; Expensive; Reservations required. A classical and elegant restaurant serving a fine selection of New England cuisine (e.g., lobster!). An extensive wine list is available as is tableside service such as rack of lamb for two.

Water Works Pub and Restaurant, Lindsey Street, Rockland; phone (207) 596-7950. American; Moderate; Reservations accepted. Microbrewery beer flows freely here and is complemented with typical pub fare, including everything from hamburgers to soups.

Activities in Maine

Bay Island Yacht Charters 117 Tillson Ave., Rockland; phone (800) 421-2492 or (207) 596-7550. Boat charters and sailing lessons.

Farnsworth Art Museum and Wyeth Center 356 Main St., Cushing (14 miles south of Rockland); phone (207) 596-6457. Strong collection of American art.

Owls Head Transportation Museum Route 73, Owls Head (2 miles south of Rockland); phone (207) 594-4418. Displays of antique cars, aircraft, and steam engines.

Shore Village Museum 104 Limerock St., Rockland; phone (207) 596-0376. Unique collection of artifacts and lenses from lighthouses.

The 19th Hole in Maine

Clubhouse Grille (located in Samoset Resort), 220 Warrenton St., Rockport; phone (800) 341-1650 or (207) 594-0722. Great way to celebrate your round on the veranda of the Clubhouse which overlooks the 10th tee and the 18th fairway.

Double Diamond (located in Grand Summit Resort Hotel), Route 27, R.R. 1, Box 5000, Carrabassett; phone (800) 527-9879 or (202) 237-2222. Great views and musical entertainment on select weekends.

Lodging on Cape Cod

EXPENSIVE

Ocean Edge

2907 Main St./Route 6A, Brewster, MA 02631; phone (800) 343-6074 or (508) 896-9000; www.oceanedge.com; Rates: $140–350 (rooms), $280–630 (two-bedroom villa), $95–$140 (one-bedroom golf course villa)

Once you arrive at Ocean Edge, you may never have to leave the grounds: The resort offers guests superb accommodations, a wide variety of activities, and a full menu of entertainment. The resort is comprised of a 19th-century mansion and a separate carriage house and is really the premier upscale resort in an area that is dominated by the quaint and the "beach-like." Spacious guest rooms in the hotel have either garden or ocean views. These are located adjacent to the Mansion, which houses reception, the Ocean Grille Restaurant, and part of the conference facilities. Ocean Edge has the usual array of dining experiences from après-golf casual at Mulligan's in the golf clubhouse to "resort elegant" in the Mansion. The Mansion and its adjacent Carriage House are excellent examples of the "summer cottages" erected by well-to-do families in 1912.

Between the hotel and the beach are the multi-bedroom Bay Pines Villas. Golfers might consider one on the golf course, which is across Route 6A, a pleasant two-laner with miles of antique shops, art galleries, restaurants, and old New England homes, white with black shutters, all seemingly with porches bearing pots of geraniums and caned rocking chairs.

On the activity side, let's just say you won't be bored. There's a total of six pools (two indoor and four outdoor), ponds, saunas, 11 tennis courts, basketball, gym, private beach, walking/jogging trails, fishing, sailing, horseback riding, and children's programs. Many guests rent a bike and pedal along the popular Cape Cod Rail Trail, a 19.6-mile track that runs through the resort with one terminus at the National Seashore. The seashore itself is 40 miles of natural seascape that stretches from nearby Chatham north to Provincetown. The shoreline is pristine is every sense, and one can even see finback and humpback whales frolicking below the cliffs at Truro. Then of course, there's the golf.

There are a couple of restaurant options at the resort. The Ocean Grille is the most formal and features panoramic views of the Atlantic Ocean. On the less formal side is the Reef Café, which overlooks the fifth green and fairway and has a Caribbean flavor. For a drink after the round you can either head to Mulligan's, overlooking the ninth green or to the pub where you can try your hand at billiards and listen to the piano. Throughout the summer, there are myriad special activities held at the resort, including concerts and clambakes.

Golf Packages Package includes deluxe accommodations, daily golf with cart, and breakfast.

MODERATE

High Brewster Inn

964 Satucket Rd., Brewster, MA 02631; phone (508) 896-3636; (800) 203-2634 Rates: $90–110

Situated on three acres of land, High Brewster is a restored Colonial farmhouse that quickly will evoke images of days gone by with its low, wooden beamed ceilings. Filled with antiques, the inn offers guests a beautiful setting as well as easy access to the recommended High Brewster restaurant.

INEXPENSIVE

Bay Motor Inn

223 Main St., Buzzards Bay, MA 02532; phone (508) 759-3989; Rates: $72–99; Built: 1950s; Renovated: 1999

Dining on Cape Cod

Captain Linnell House 137 Skaket Beach Rd., Orleans; phone (508) 255-3400. Continental; Expensive; Reservations required. One of the area's most romantic restaurants with indoor and outdoor seating in an 1840 mansion. Menu is heavy on seafood, but the rack of lamb is scrumptious.

Chillingsworth 2449 Main St., Route 6A, Brewster; phone (508) 896-3640. French; Very Expensive; Reservations essential. The Cape's most formal and most expensive restaurant offers a classical French menu and a vast wine cellar. A seven-course meal is served to diners either inside or on the patio, with specialties including roast lobster, veal, and pheasant.

High Brewster 964 Satucket Rd., Brewster; phone (508) 896-3636. Continental; Expensive; Reservations required. Located in High Brewster Inn, this is an intimate restaurant with great atmosphere. Diners can select the five-course prix-fixe meal, which changes often—highlights include fresh local seafood and grilled duck.

Kadee's Lobster & Clam Bar Main Street, Orleans; phone (508) 255-6184. Seafood; Inexpensive–Moderate; Reservations not accepted. A Cape Cod favorite serving great clams from its take-out window. Great outdoor dining experience.

Activities on Cape Cod

Cahoon Museum of Art 4676 Route 28, Cotuit; phone (508) 428-7581. A renovated 1775 farmhouse with displays of Ralph and Martha Cahoon as well as other 19th- and 20th-century artists.

Cape Cod National Seashore 99 Marconi Site Rd., Wellfleet; phone (508) 349-3785. A 40-mile/44,000-acre stretch of land with unsurpassed beaches.

Cape Cod Museum of Natural History 869 Main St., Route 6A, Brewster; phone (800) 479-3867 or (508) 896-3867. A wonderful museum with nature and marine exhibits and trails through its 80 acres of forest and marshland.

Cape Cod Sailing 17 Eventide Lane, Hyannis; phone (508) 771-7918. Lessons and boat rentals.

Heritage Plantation Grove and Pine Streets, Sandwich; phone (508) 888-3300. A variety of exhibits can be found at this 76-acre complex, including displays of historic cars, firearms, miniature soldiers, a Currier & Ives collection, as well as beautiful flowers.

John F. Kennedy Hyannis Museum 397 Main St., Hyannis; phone (508) 790-3077. The museum has 80 photos that depict Kennedy's time in Hyannis from 1936 to 1963. Old Town Hall,

Pilgrim Monument and Museum High Pole Hill Road, P.O. Box 1125, Provincetown; phone (800) 247-1620 or (508) 487-1310. Monument commemorating the landing of the Pilgrims on North American soil. Panoramic view of the cape from the top of the structure.

Index